D1599662

Opera and Sovereignty

Opera and Sovereignty

Transforming Myths in Eighteenth-Century Italy

MARTHA FELDMAN

The University of Chicago Press CHICAGO AND LONDON

MARTHA FELDMAN is professor of music at the University of Chicago and the author of *City Culture and the Madrigal at Venice.*

The University of Chicago Press, Chicago 60637
The University of Chicago Press, Ltd., London

Printed in the United States of America

16 15 14 13 12 11 10 09 08 07   5 4 3 2 1

ISBN-13 (cloth): 978-0-226-24112-8
ISBN-13 (paper): 978-0-226-24113-5
ISBN-10 (cloth): 0-226-24112-2
ISBN-10 (paper): 0-226-24113-0

This book has received a Gladys Krieble Delmas Foundation publication grant, given in recognition of its contribution to Venetian history and culture and the study of the performing arts, and a grant from the Lloyd Hibberd Publication Endowment Fund of the American Musicological Society.

Library of Congress Cataloging-in-Publication Data

Feldman, Martha.
Opera and sovereignty : transforming myths in eighteenth-century Italy / Martha Feldman.
p. cm.
Includes bibliographical references and index.
ISBN-13: 978-0-226-24112-8 (cloth : alk. paper)
ISBN-13: 978-0-226-24113-5 (pbk. : alk. paper)
ISBN-10: 0-226-24112-2 (cloth : alk. paper)
ISBN-10: 0-226-24113-0 (pbk. : alk. paper)
1. Opera—Italy—18th century. 2. Mythology, Classical, in opera. 3. Opera—Social aspects—Italy—18th century. I. Title.
ML1733.3.F45 2007
782.10945′09033—dc22

2006026243

This book is printed on acid-free paper.

FOR PATRICIA

Sovereignty

1. (a) supreme power, especially over a politically organized body.
   (b) freedom from external influence or control; autonomy.
   (c) controlling influence.
2. an autonomous state.

The Penguin English Dictionary, 2000

Contents

Illustrations

MUSICAL EXAMPLES

PLATES *(following page 116)*

FIGURES

TABLES

Acknowledgments

I wish to extend my warmest thanks to the following institutions, which supported this work with grants and fellowships: in particular to the University of Chicago, for ongoing support that began with a Junior Faculty Fellowship and a two-quarter fellowship at the Franke Institute for the Humanities, both in 1994–95; the Gladys Krieble Delmas Foundation for Research in Venice for a grant in 1994–95; the Getty Research Institute of the Getty Center in Los Angeles for a nine-month residency as a Getty Scholar in 1998–99, and especially its director emeritus Salvatore Settis and associate director emeritus Michael Roth; and the National Endowment for the Humanities for a Fellowship for University Teachers in 2002–2003. I am grateful to the Music Department at the University of Chicago, Anne Walters Robertson, Richard Cohn, and Thomas Christensen, past chairs, and Robert L. Kendrick, present chair, as well as to the Humanities Division, Philip Gossett and Janel Mueller, dean emeriti, and Danielle Allen, present dean, for their research support. For their generous support of publication, I thank the American Musicological Society and its Lloyd Hibberd Publication Endowment Fund, and similarly the Gladys Krieble Delmas Foundation for Research in Venice.

A book so long in the making incurs too many debts to repay, but I must thank very specially several people who went well beyond the call of duty. Bruce Alan Brown did detailed, erudite readings of chapters 1 through 4 on the very busy eve of his editorship of the *Journal of the American Musicological Society.* Catherine Cole read the entire manuscript and gave me an astute appraisal that I have borne in mind at each step since. Elisabeth Le Guin's reading of the manuscript was filled with her enviable imagination and perspicacity. Other readers were engaged by my department or by the University of Chicago Press, and their comments too were extremely helpful, including Ellen Harris, Ellen Rosand, Reinhard Strohm, and several anonymous readers. The three readers for the Press, Sergio Durante, Marita McClymonds, and Downing Thomas, were all generous with their time and support and highly instructive in their criticisms.

Daniel Heartz, a great mentor, model, and friend, is the person most responsible for my fascination with the eighteenth century. His many accounts of opera seria, now concentrated in *Music in European Capitals* (2003) and scattered throughout his many essays, some collected in *From Garrick to Gluck* (2004), are incomparable for their breadth and depth of knowledge and passion for the subject. I am also grateful for the dialogues I have had with Lorenzo Bianconi, always a formidable and stimulating interlocutor, and Judith Zeitlin, a specialist in seventeenth-century Chinese theater. My dear friend Tullia Magrini did not live to see the completion of this book, but our conversations about music, ritual, spectacle, and festivity in the Mediterranean continue to be deeply important to my thinking.

I am thankful to the staffs of many libraries in Italy, in particular, in Naples, those at the Conservatorio di Musica di San Pietro e Majella, the Biblioteca Nazionale Vittorio Emmanuelle III, the Archivio di Stato, especially Dottoressa Azzinari, and most especially to Sergio Ragni for facilitating entry to libraries in Naples and giving me access to his extraordinary private collection; in Rome, staff members at the Archivio di Stato, the Biblioteca Casanatense, the library of the Conservatorio di Santa Cecilia, the Biblioteca Nazionale Centrale, and the Biblioteca Apostolica Vaticana; at Venice, Maria Teresa Muraro, Gilberto Pizzamiglio, and Franco Novello of the Fondazione Giorgio Cini, Cristiano Chiarot, Franco Rossi, and Marina Dorigo of the Archivio Storico della Fondazione di Teatro La Fenice (formerly at the Fondazione Ugo e Olga Levi); Alessandra Samba, Alessandra Schiavon, and others now or formerly at the Archivio di Stato, and all the staff members at the Museo Civico Correr and the Biblioteca Nazionale Marciana; at Parma, Luigi Allegri of the Instituto di Musicologia, Leonardo Farinelli, Giustina Scarola, and Nicoletta Agazzi of the Biblioteca Palatina, and the very helpful personnel at the Archivio di Stato, especially Marzio dall'Acqua; at Perugia, the generous staff of the Biblioteca Augusta Comunale, including Anna Maria Clementi, Francesca Grauso, Angela Iannotti, Rosanna Valigi, and Gabriele de Veris; Dom Paolo of the Basilica Benedettina di San Pietro, Archivio e Museo della Badia; and Clara Cutini Zazzerini at the Archivio di Stato. I am very grateful to innumerable individuals at theaters, in particular to Mauro Gatti of the Teatro Pavone and Giorgio Pangarò of the Teatro Morlacchi, and to Pasquale Valerio, formerly in the orchestra of the Teatro di San Carlo at Naples, and his wife, Frances Ellerbe. I have been helped too by staff at the Biblioteca Municipal Almeida Garrett, Porto, Portugal, the Bibliothèque Nationale de France (Louvois, Richelieu, and Tolbiac), the Conservatoire Royal de Musique, Brussels, the Preussischer Kulturbesitz, Berlin, and many others.

Kind assistance has come from staff members at the following North American libraries: at the University of Chicago Regenstein Library, Deborah Davies, Deborah Gillaspie, and Scott Landvatter, Music Library, Alice Schreyer, Special Collections, and Sem Sutter, assistant director, Humanities and Social Sciences, as well as the staff at Interlibrary Loan; Paul Gehl, Paul Saenger, and Mary Springfels at the Newberry Library, Chicago; Annette Fern of the Harvard Theatre Collection; the staffs of Harvard's Houghton and Fine Arts Libraries; staff members at the Library of Congress, Music Division, and the New York Public Library, Rare Books and Manuscripts and Performing Arts; John Roberts of the Music Library at the University of California at Berkeley, and the staff of Berkeley's Bancroft Library; Special Collections of the Music Library at the University of California, Los Angeles; and the Walter Havighurst Special Collections Department of Miami University, Ohio. Special thanks are due to Charles Salas and Marcia Reed of the Getty Research Institute and Kevin Salatino, formerly of the Getty Research Institute and now at the Los Angeles County Museum of Art.

My research in Parma was much helped by Luigi Allegri and Renato di Benedetto, who in 1994 gave me direct access to the handwritten files on archival documentation of eighteenth-century Parmesan spectacle created by a research team that they convened in 1980–82 at the Instituto di Musicologia, University of Parma.

I owe a very special thank you to my mother, Gabrielle Feldman, an artist of classical training who also has a considerable background in fabric and fashion design. Together we fell in love with the eccentric brilliance of Petitot in Parma and sat mesmerized by the performances of Daniel Oren at the San Carlo in Naples. When I tried to persuade her to recreate the costume designs for *Ippolito ed Aricia*, she protested that it was contrary to the nature of an imaginative artist to work under such constraints. In the end she capitulated, and gave life, soul, and beauty to some of the lost treasures of the famed Parmesan reform. Permission was kindly granted by her to reproduce selections from her watercolor sketches in chapter 3.

Permission to print revisions of two previously published articles was granted by the Berliner Wissenschafts-Verlag for "Nature Personified: Remaking Stage and Spectator in 18th-Century Parma," with costume reconstructions by Gabrielle Feldman, from *The Faces of Nature* (2003), edited by Lorraine Daston and Gianna Pomata (here chapter 3); and "Abandonments in a 'Theater State': Opera and the Undoing of Sovereignty during the Great Famine of 1764," from *Italian Opera in Central Europe*, vol. 1, *Institutions and Ceremonies* (2006), edited by Melania Bucciarelli, Norbert Dubowy, and Reinhard Strohm (here chapter 5). Permission was granted by the Johns Hopkins University Press for chapter 9, a revision of "Opera, Festivity, and Spectacle in 'Revolutionary' Venice: Phantasms of Time and History," from *Venice Reconsidered: History and Civilization of an Italian City-State, 1297–1797* (2000), edited by John Martin and Dennis Romano. Brief sections of chapters 1, 2, 6, and 8 have evolved from "Magic

Mirrors and the Seria Stage: Thoughts toward a Ritual View," published in the *Journal of the American Musicological Society* 48 (1995): 423–84, which served as a kind of prolegomenon to this book, and of chapter 8 from "The Absent Mother in Opera Seria," a meditation on gender issues in opera seria, published by Princeton University Press in *Siren Songs: Representations of Gender and Sexuality in Opera* (2000), edited by Mary Ann Smart.

Translations throughout the book are generally mine unless otherwise stated. Courtney Quaintance volunteered translations of some untranslated material in chapter 9 while reviewing my Italian translations and proposed various emendations as to the latter. Lucia Marchi was very helpful in doing final edits on recalcitrant passages from the Padre Martini letters and on selected archival documents in chapter 7. Shawn Deeley kindly helped render a couple of troublesome passages in Latin.

Between 2002 and 2005, I worked intensively with Drew Edward Davies, who served as my research assistant. My gratitude to him for his great energy, intellect, and skill is truly bottomless. His work included research tasks, correspondence in several languages concerning permissions and images, editing bibliography, inputting, editing, and typesetting all musical examples in Finale, and preparing final camera-ready copy. Our collaboration has improved this book in ways that go beyond words.

Patricia Firca, Shawn Marie Keener, and Courtney Quaintance came on board for research assistance in the last year of work on this book. I am especially indebted to Shawn Keener for final formatting of the manuscript and for countless hours spent persistently collecting all images and permissions, including in Venice and Milan, and to Courtney Quaintance for help with the last and for checking some documents in Venice. Their generosity in all things has been prodigious and their intelligence indispensable.

My genial research assistant at the Getty Research Institute was Nasser Taee of UCLA, to whom I offer sincere thanks. Melissa Reilly is responsible for intelligent indexing. Kathleen Hansell, my acquisitions editor at Chicago, made thoughtful recourse to outside reviewers and offered expert help in matters of philology and music editing. Others at the Press, especially designer Matt Avery, were consistently helpful. My copyeditor, Carlisle Knowlton Rex-Waller, has become my second hand. She has managed that intimate relationship of unwonted delicacy with care, sensitivity, and a canny intelligence, to my everlasting thanks.

Beyond those named above, I have many too many Virgils, Boswells, and Micawbers to thank them all properly. They include Michael Anderson, Arjun Appadurai, Franca Barricelli, Thomas Bauman, Lorenzo Bianconi, Roberto Bizzocchi, Mark Blackbird, Raffaella Bonaca, Valerie Booth, Horst Bredekamp, Elspeth Brown, Norman Bryson, Biancamaria Brumana, Melania Buccarelli, Geoffrey Burgess, Giulia Calvi, Emanuela Zanotti Carney, Stefano Castelvecchi, Giulio Cattin, Marta Cavazza, Donald Chae, Thomas Christensen, Jean Comaroff, John Comaroff, Chris Cuevas, Luigi Cuoco, Lorraine Daston, Luisa del Giudice, Renato di Benedetto, Mare Earley, Paula Findlen, Betty Fonseca and Dick Cornuelle, Philip Fisher, Roger Freitas, Maria Fusaro, Philip Gossett, Andy Greenwood, Errol Gaston Hill and Grace Hill, Berthold Hoeckner, Christopher Johns, Robert Kendrick, Marianna Kohl, Juliet Koss, Richard Kramer, David J. Levin, Cecilio Lo, John Marino, John Martin, Susan McClary, Yossi Maurey, Richard Meyer, Reinhart Meyer-Kalkus, Ingrid Monson, Robert Morgan and Ewa Gorniàk, Diego Lanza, Nancy Munn, Jud Newborn, Ottavia Niccoli, Daniela Pastina, Lynda Paul, Sergio Perini, Pierluigi Petrobelli, Adrian Piper, Martha Pollak, Rumya Putcha, Regula Burckhardt Qureshi, Alberto Rizzuti, Hans Peter Reill, Dennis Romano, Susan Rosa, Mark Sandman, Marija Šarač, Carolyn Sargentson, Nicola Savarese, Elaine Scarry, William H. Sewell, Jr., Mary Ann Smart, Ruth A. Solie, Lesley Stern, Martin Stokes, David Summers, Geoffrey Symcox, Stanley Tambiah, Ferdinando Taviani, Jay ten Hove, James Grantham Turner, Billy Vaughn, Bill Viola, and Meng Yue—a list much too arid to speak to all the good deeds, sage caveats, and lively conversations it truly represents.

* * *

My family and friends put up with the writing of this book and made the difference in finishing it. I am especially grateful to my stepdaughters, Emily Bauman and Rebecca Bauman; my siblings, Rebekah Boyer, Fred Feldman, Amy Tecosky-Feldman, and Rachel Nazareth; my mother, Gabrielle Feldman; my uncle and aunt, Thornton Hagert and Annie Stanfield-Hagert, and my great friends Anne Brody, Sara Danius and Stefan Jonsson, Linda Kroning, Dominique Moody, Marian Alessandroni Parrott, Shulamit Ran, and Kate van Orden—guardian angels all.

Above all I thank my partner, Patricia Barber. As I write this I hear an exquisite "Moon River" floating from the piano in the next room. For that, for her encouragement, wisdom, genius, help, inspiration, companionship, humor, and tough criticism, I dedicate this book to her with love.

Abbreviations

ARCHIVES AND LIBRARIES

A-Sm	Salzburg, Internationale Stiftung Mozarteum, Bibliotheca Mozartiana
ASTF	Venice, Fondazione Teatro La Fenice, Archivio Storico del Teatro La Fenice (available online on the Web site of the Archivio Storico Gran Teatro La Fenice, http://81.75.233.46:8080/fenice/GladReq/index.jsp)
A-Wn	Vienna, Österreichische Nationalbibliothek, Musiksammlung
A-Wgm	Vienna, Gesellschaft der Musikfreunde
B-Bc	Brussels, Conservatoire Royal, Bibliothèque / Koninklijk Conservatorium, Bibliotheek
D-B	Berlin, Staatsbibliothek zu Berlin Preußischer Kulturbesitz
D-Mb	Munich, Bayerische Staatsbibliothek
F-Pn	Paris, Bibliothèque Nationale de France
HR-Dsmb	Croatia (Republika Hrvatska), Dubrovnik, Samostan Male Brace (Franciscan Minor Monastery), Glazbeni arhiv
I-Bc	Bologna, Civico Museo Bibliografico Musicale
I-Gl	Genoa, Biblioteca del Conservatorio Statale di Musica "N. Paganini"
I-Mc	Milan, Biblioteca del Conservatorio Giuseppe Verdi
I-Mn	Milan, Biblioteca Nazionale Braidense
I-Mr	Milan, Biblioteca della Casa Ricordi, Archivio Storico, housed at I-Mn
I-Na	Naples, Archivio di Stato
I-Nb	Naples, Biblioteca Nazionale, Vittorio Emanuele III

I-Nbs	Naples, Biblioteca della Società Napoletana per la Storia Patria
I-Nc	Naples, Conservatorio di Musica San Pietro e Majella, Biblioteca
I-PAas	Parma, Archivio di Stato
PAas.AdT88	*Vestiario,* Archivio Du Tillot, b. 88, no. 3
PAas.Cfb932.4	Payment receipts, Computisteria farnesiana e borbonica—Teatro, 1758–59, b. 932, fasc. 4
I-PAim	Parma, Istituto di Musicologia, Università di Parma
I-PAp	Parma, Biblioteca Nazionale Palatina
I-PEas	Perugia, Archivio di Stato
I-PEc	Perugia, Biblioteca Augusta Comunale
Atti	Archivio Morlacchi, *Atti amministrativi,* libro 1, 1778–1783
Carteggi	Archivio Morlacchi, *Carteggi privati*
Verbali	Archivio Morlacchi, *Verbali delle adunanze,* libro 1, 21 dic. 1777–18 dic. 1786
I-PEsp	Perugia, Basilica Benedettina di San Pietro, Archivio e Museo della Badia
I-Ras	Rome, Archivio di Stato
I-Rc	Rome, Biblioteca Casanatense
I-Rn	Rome, Biblioteca Nazionale Centrale Vittorio Emanuele II
I-Rsc	Rome, Conservatorio di Musica Santa Cecilia, Biblioteca Musicale Governativa; musical holdings now at the Bibliomediateca dell'Accademia Nazionale di Santa Cecilia, Rome
I-Rvat	Vatican City, Biblioteca Apostolica Vaticana
I-Tf	Turin, Accademia Filarmonica, Archivio
I-Vas	Venice, Archivio di Stato
I-Vcg	Venice, Casa di Goldoni, Biblioteca
I-Vgc	Venice, Fondazione Giorgio Cini, Istituto per le Lettere, il Teatro ed il Melodramma, Biblioteca
I-Vlevi	Venice, Fondazione Ugo e Olga Levi, Biblioteca
I-Vmc	Venice, Museo Civico Correr, Biblioteca d'Arte e Storia Veneziana
I-Vnm	Venice, Biblioteca Nazionale Marciana
P-La	Lisbon, Biblioteca do Palácio Nacional da Ajuda
RISM B.II.1	*Recueils imprimés XVIIIe siècle,* ed. François Lesure, ser. B, vol. 2, part 1 (Munich: Henle, 1964)
Sgavetti	Sgavetti—Cronaca, MS 27, vols. 5–7, in I-PAas
US-BEm	Berkeley, University of California, Music Library
US-CAh	Cambridge, Massachusetts, Harvard University, Houghton Library
US-CAt	Cambridge, Massachusetts, Harvard University Library, Theatre Collection
US-Cn	Chicago, Newberry Library

US-Cu	Chicago, University of Chicago, Joseph Regenstein Library, Special Collections
US-LAur	Los Angeles, University of California at Los Angeles, Music Library
US-NYn	New York, New York Public Library
US-Nyp	New York, New York Public Library at Lincoln Center, Music Division
US-OXs	Oxford, Ohio, Miami University, Walter Havighurst Special Collections
US-Wc	Washington, D.C., Library of Congress, Music Division
US-Wcg	Washington, D.C., General Collections, Library of Congress
US-Wf	Washington, D.C., Founder's Library, Harvard University

Editorial Principles

In editing eighteenth-century Italian texts, I follow different sets of principles depending upon whether the text in question is archival or not.

For archival and manuscript texts, I generally leave orthography as is, except for making tacit modifications of punctuation to clarify textual meaning and turning *v*'s into *u*'s and *j*'s into *i*'s. I follow the same principle for transcriptions of printed broadsides in the appendices to chapters 3 and 4.

For all other eighteenth-century texts, I mostly hew to current-day principles of Italian philology as summarized in Giuseppina la Face Bianconi, "Filologia dei testi poetici nella musica vocale italiana," *Acta musicologica* 66 (1994): 1–21 (for an example, see Francesco Algarotti, *Saggi* [1963]). These principles include modernizing accents, deleting capitalizations, and rendering punctuation silently in modern style for the sake of clarity. For eighteenth-century French and German published prose, I retain original orthography. In all instances, I indicate any expansion of abbreviations by means of italics.

Character names are usually given in the language of their dramatic source, but I often use common English name forms when speaking of characters as broadly historical or mythical types (e.g., Phaedra and Alexander).

Musical examples are made from original sources except in the case of Mozart, where editions are adapted from Mozart, *Neue Ausgabe sämtlicher Werke* (1986).

CHAPTER 1

Evenings at the Opera

"The late king of Poland would pay 100,000 ecus for the performance of each new opera. Spain has displayed a luxury in music whose like cannot be found in all of history. . . . Russia, which had not sounded a note at the beginning of the century, has acquired such a taste for opera that it pays more for an opera singer than a military general." ANGE GOUDAR, *Le brigandage de la musique italienne,* 1777[1]

"Here [opera] is for conversation, or for visiting box to box: people don't listen and they go into ecstasy only for arias." ABBÉ COYER, *Voyages d'Italie et de Holande,* letter of January 22, 1764[2]

At the Teatro San Carlo in Naples, Gilda and her father sing the duet from the end of act 2 of Verdi's *Rigoletto.* The uproar during curtain calls is deafening, and the Israeli conductor Daniel Oren—a brilliant ham and a great favorite with Neapolitan and Roman operagoers—encores the whole number with little delay. If that were not rare enough nowadays, he then repeats the encore a second time.

Oren's theatrics are unprecedented in my experience of opera conductors. On this evening, they combine with his quicksilver timing to cause even more commotion than usual, and the Neapolitans match him blow by blow. Not everyone is glad about it. At one point, after the crowd erupts in yet another volcano of *bravi,* things become too much for one of the highbrows in a lower tier, and after the noise dies down he cries out in spite of himself, "Aspettate almeno che finisca la musica!" (At least wait until the music is over!). His well-heeled Florentine accent sounds a decorous note in a raucous ensemble of cheering, clapping, and stomping—disarmingly so, since these days class in the opera house is more often signaled by the cut of a suit than the tone of the voice. The outburst is one among many that marks the evening as an event. Two days later an incredulous reviewer from the Roman daily *La repubblica* writes that the eve-

1. "Le feu roi de Pologne payait cent mille écus de la représentation de chaque opéra nouveau. L'Espagne a étalé un luxe à musique dont on ne trouve aucun exemple dans l'histoire. . . . La Russie qui n'étonnait pas une note au commencement du siècle, a pris un tel goût pour les ariettes, qu'elle paye plus un chanteur d'opéra qu'un général d'armée" (Goudar, *Le brigandage,* 2–3).

2. "[I]ci, [l'opéra] c'est pour la conversation, ou pour se visiter de loge en loge: on n'écoute, on ne s'éxtasie qu'à l'Ariette" (Coyer, *Voyages d'Italie* 1:192).

ning had a "clima da stadio" (atmosphere of a sports arena), adding that the act 2 duet was encored twice "a furor del popolo."[3]

Small wonder he was amazed. Even in Naples, where audiences are reputed to be among the most demonstrative in Italy—certainly more than in northern Europe or America—ambient noise is usually limited to the seating of latecomers, the sound of elderly spectators humming along with their favorite numbers, or fans covering the ends of arias with shouting and applause. On this night the public's behavior put it in dialogue with the performers in a way redolent of reports from the eighteenth century. But there was an ironic difference. Public excitement was ignited from the orchestra pit, through the mediation of a conductor, whose very existence was still relatively novel in Verdi's time and unknown fifty to a hundred years earlier. That the drama at hand was emanating from the pit was obvious from my box near the proscenium in the sixth tier at the top of the house, the so-called *piccionaia* (pigeon gallery), which gave an almost perfect view onto the pit. From that vantage point, Oren's histrionics outdid even those of the famous Leo Nucci, who sang the title role, or the new starlit soprano, Maureen O'Flynn, as Gilda.

All the same, once activities in the house heated up into the double encore and continued through the last act, it was not just Oren's conducting but the dynamics of the whole house that played on the audience's attentions. This reality of collective and reciprocal participation—and the voyeuristic amusement that my bird's-eye view gave onto it—would have been far less possible in an opera house built to modern specifications, in which most of the seating points directly to the stage. The commercial theaters of the eighteenth century are another matter. Built for large public spectacles utilizing a horseshoe arrangement, most of their seating is disposed in separate boxes, each of which recedes from its front rail to form a deep well, often with an antechamber, leading in turn to the broad inner corridor of the hall. The Teatro San Carlo, erected in 1737, is a classic, if particularly large, exemplar of this type, with boxes stacked up and circling round in curvilinear ribbons, stretching from either side of the proscenium around toward the back of the hall (see figs. 1.1 and 1.2).

Given such an arrangement, any view of the stage is forever fragmented. Good sightlines are hard to come by, and many boxes yield no real view of the stage unless the spectator pulls a chair up to the rail or cranes her neck. From many boxes, viewing the stage continuously requires an ongoing, strenuous effort no matter where one is seated, and nothing is easier than eyeing others across the hall or turning inward to fidget with garments, whisper to friends, stretch out in the back, or fondle a lover.[4] A spectator strongly resistant to distractions might yield to them rarely and reluctantly, but will have trouble

3. *La repubblica,* March 26, 1996.

4. See di Robilant, *A Venetian Affair,* 110–11 and 134–45, with references from the early 1750s to lovemaking in a Venetian theater box, quoted from a privately owned cache of letters exchanged between Giustiniana Wynne and Andrea Memmo.

FIG. 1.1. Teatro San Carlo, Naples, audience awaiting start of performance, ca. 1960s. Photograph from *Il Teatro di San Carlo, 1737–1987*, ed. Franco Mancini, Bruno Cagli, and Agostino Ziino (Naples: Electa Napoli, 1987), 2:193. Reproduced by kind permission of the publisher.

avoiding them altogether, and a less resistant one can happily succumb. Even people in the parterre who can see the stage head on from seating affixed to the floor are not immune to distractions imposed by the majority inhabiting boxes throughout the periphery.

Events in the San Carlo on that night can help us think about how space mediates feelings and practices in the theater and works to accommodate them. The multiplicity of spaces and sightlines in an eighteenth-century opera house runs counter to modern demands—demands on spectators to view the stage in a

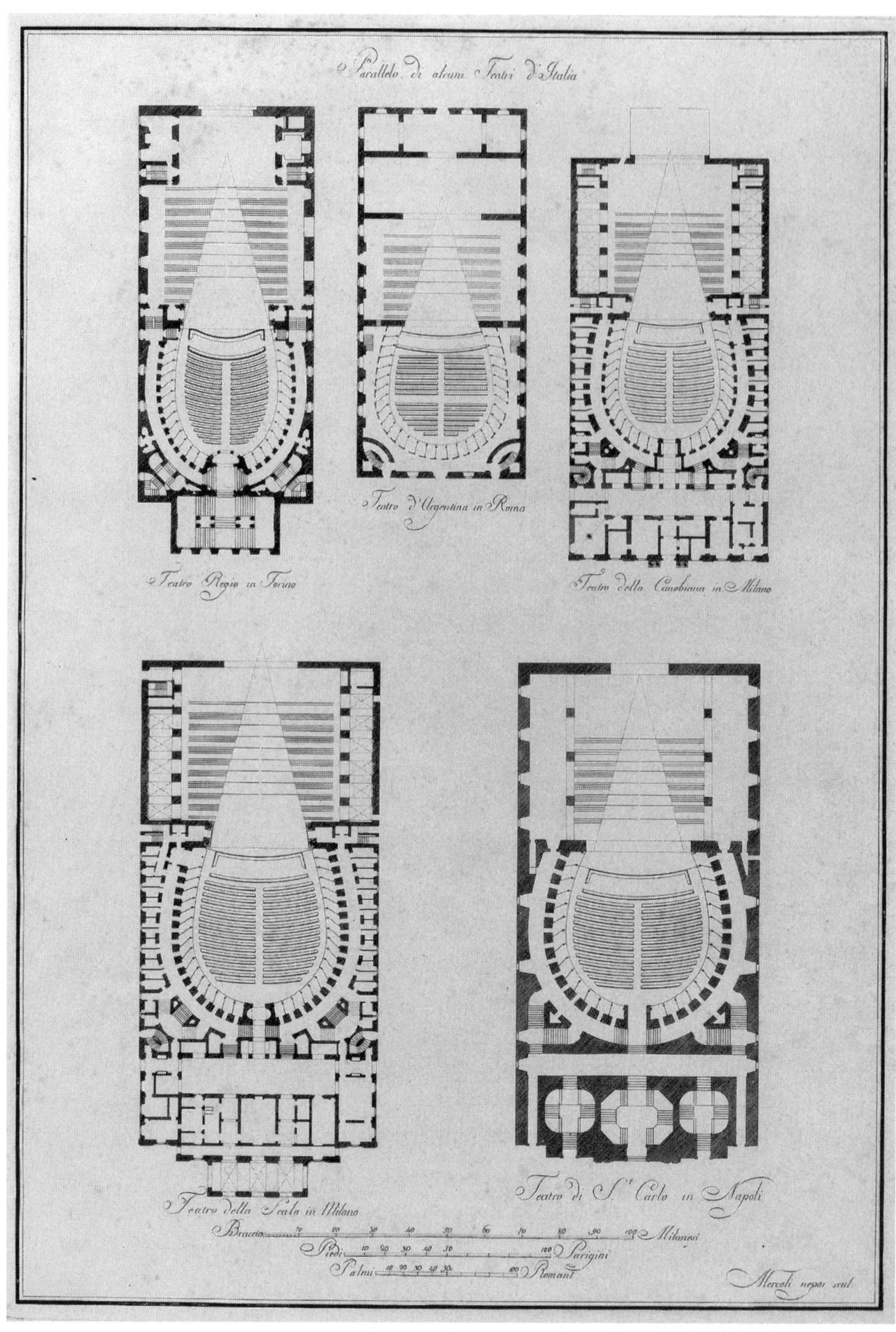

FIG. 1.2. "Parallelo di alcuni teatri d'Italia." Engraving showing the varied horseshoe shapes of five eighteenth-century theaters. From Giuseppe Piermarini, *Teatro della Scala in Milano* (Milan, 1789). By permission of the Avery Architectural and Fine Arts Library, Columbia University.

state of absorbed silence and demands on musicians to adhere to the dictates of the score. The special way that Oren exploited such a theater made a virtue of this multiplicity, getting the audience to clamor for a command performance.

But Oren's exploits assumed a form that also underscores the gulf between the realities of our time and those of the eighteenth century. None of his encores was done during the opera proper, much less in the middles of acts. Instead, they were initiated after the end of an act, in the forestage in front of the opera curtain while singers were taking their curtain calls. In that time and space the two darlings of the stage—one many years beloved by the public, the other vaunted as its new star—could be relocated to a theatrical borderland at a climactic moment. Facing their admirers in direct address, they had dropped character and become performers, not figures in a drama. Their encores became more like a concert—with Oren as one of its stars—delivered with an alleged spontaneity at the special urging of an adoring public. And the encores were in turn efficacious in consolidating the growing affections between the performers and their fans.

OPERA SERIA, SOVEREIGNTY, PERFORMANCE

This book explores the relationship between "dramma per musica"—known more colloquially, especially in its twilight years, as "opera seria," as I call it here—and various crises of social and political transformation in eighteenth-century Italy.[5] It is not about opera seria per se, but about its reflexive relationship with those transformations, especially as they concern sovereignty in the latter half of the century, when the principal trope of opera seria, elaborating the motif of the magnanimous prince, was colliding with a growing bourgeois public sphere.

Most of today's opera lovers still know of opera seria from only a few works by Handel (*Poro, Giulio Cesare, Rodelinda, Xerxes*) and Mozart (*Idomeneo* and *La clemenza di Tito*). Names from the 1720s and 1730s like Leo, Vinci, Porpora, Pergolesi, and Hasse, or Traetta, Jommelli, and Galuppi from midcentury, may slip off the tongues of musicologists or connoisseurs but not average music fans.[6] Even Cimarosa, Zingarelli, Paisiello, and Mayr, so popular in the late eighteenth century, are far from household names. Scholars of the past knew the genre well, but many found it unintelligible. Yet opera seria reigned supreme among all musical and theatrical genres across most of eighteenth-

5. See Strohm, *Dramma per musica*, 1–4; and McClymonds with Heartz, "Opera Seria."

6. The situation may be changing, thanks especially to the artistry of Cecilia Bartoli and her big-selling adventures through Antonio Caldara, Alessandro Scarlatti, and others. See the review of her Chicago recital at Orchestra Hall, October 16, 2005, by von Rhein, in the *Chicago Tribune*, October 18, 2005.

century Europe.[7] Getting to write the music or, even more prestigiously, the poetry for an opera seria was like getting to write a feature for Dreamworks. And as a dramatic form that allegorized sovereignties throughout Europe—from the elector Palatinate to the tsar of Russia, the kings of England, Spain, Prussia, and Sweden (indeed everywhere, save France, which had its own high lyric genre of *tragédie lyrique*)—it was the genre par excellence of highbrow lyric theaters.[8]

In Italy, few of those theaters had as direct an association with kingship as the San Carlo, built to celebrate the advent of a new king (indeed a new kingship); yet the San Carlo typified the great commercial opera houses that produced opera seria. Everywhere, whatever forms of rule prevailed, opera seria thrived in the glow of old-regime sovereignty. In this sense, it thrived in a world endlessly marked by the reiteration of social hierarchies whose implications were nothing short of cosmological—implicit assertions of a world order in which ranks cascaded downward in the great chain of being from God to sovereign or ruling class to the various classes and orders below. All the concrete spaces and operations of such theaters were rooted in this fundamental political model, even as some practices put it in doubt. When elite public theaters were not direct outcroppings of a court, as was the San Carlo—attached in 1737 to the royal palace complex, though with its own public entrance (figs. 5.1 and 5.4)—they were invariably overseen by ruling persons or groups: the prince's superintendent, an aristocratic family, a society of oligarchs, or members of a theater academy. In this respect, opera seria invariably reproduced, as narrative and social/symbolic practice, the prevailing social structure, broadly supporting the absolutist trope of sovereignty despite inflections indigenous to different forms of political organization across Italy: kingships at Naples or Turin, dukedoms at Parma, Modena, and Mantua, oligarchic republics at Venice, Lucca, and Genoa, the papal monarchy in Rome and the Papal States.

Of the fifty or so new serious operas being produced around midcentury every Carnival season (the number including comic genres is much higher), only a fraction used entirely new libretti. Until the early 1780s but even beyond, from one city to another, there was an amazing persistence in the reuse of libretti (usually revised on site), and hence in the presentation and representation of sovereignty. Individual city-states, with their own political forms and civic ideologies, did produce distinct local physiognomies of the genre, but a limited set of narrative archetypes circulated, which were repeatedly set and reset anew and stocked by an absolutist panoply of symbolic tropes and classical references.

Yet politically, opera seria was a paradoxical beast. In one sense it was a

7. This was often noted by European intellectuals of the time (e.g., d'Alembert's *On the Liberty of Music*, 87; *De la liberté de la musique*, in Launay, *La querelle des bouffons* 3:2201–82).

8. For opera seria generally, see Heartz, *Music in European Capitals;* Strohm, *Dramma per musica;* Chegai, *L'esilio di Metastasio;* Robinson, *Naples and Neapolitan Opera;* Weimer, *Opera Seria;* and Moindrot, *L'opéra seria.* Good short introductions are Libby, "Italy: Two Opera Centres," 15–60; Bauman, "The Eighteenth Century," 47–83; and Bianconi, *Il teatro d'opera*, 54–65 and passim.

FIG. 1.3. Engraved illustration on the opening page of act 3 from Goldoni's comedy *La putta onorata*, showing masked theatergoers purchasing tickets at a *botteghino* (or *biglietteria*) at the entrance to a theater in Venice. From Carlo Goldoni, *Opere teatrali* (Venice: Antonio Zatta, 1791), vol. 11. By permission of the Casa Goldoni, Biblioteca, Venice.

protocapitalist bourgeois form, attended by a mixed populace, including paying customers—some of them social climbing—and managed through various combinations of state, court, and private persons and funds. Among its patrons was a middle class of moderate means consisting of doctors, lawyers, teachers, civil servants, and the like, many of whom bought tickets on a nightly basis because they could not afford the stiff annual costs of seasonal subscriptions or box ownership even when it was permitted to them. (See the frontispiece to a play by Carlo Goldoni in fig. 1.3.) But opera was kept afloat by wealthy patrons, many, but by no means all, aristocrats, who owned their boxes like little landed estates on which they nevertheless paid annual levies. Only if forced by necessity did they pay annually to rent them.[9] Along with these wealthy audience members came servants, both liveried servants and servants of a lower order (valets and chambermaids indoors, footmen and coachmen outdoors), who would populate hallways and were sometimes given official admission to the upper-

9. Sometimes nobles also were forced by diminished circumstances to rent their boxes out, and sometimes they too had to have tickets to enter. A fine account of boxes in the seicento can be found in Glixon and Glixon, *Inventing the Business of Opera*, chap. 2.

most gallery. Theater workers, including members of the military guard, staffed the corridors, atriums, and passageways of the opera house, and the stalls were populated by military men, students, professors, and other bourgeois intellectuals, some of whom entered on free lists.

Unlike theaters tightly enclosed within a court, commercial opera houses, even when dominated by the aristocracy, thus housed a broad and fluctuating assemblage of competing social positions, which could variously combine to reflect, embellish, substitute for, or undermine a prevailing sovereign person or group. For the upper classes, opera seria was to, for, and about the sovereign(s), but it was also to, for, and about themselves. Who implicitly it addressed was prone to slippage and probably tempered by many factors. How did Prince Artaserse's dilemma over divided loyalty speak to the Venetian patrician? To the nobleman in Modena in the presence of his duke (or in his absence)? To the Roman abbot who prattled in the shadows of the Teatro Argentina, safe from the governor's gaze? These kinds of questions have no ready answers. Opera seria rested on new modes of production and new forms of social and political organization that were beginning to eclipse the old quasi-feudal ones. No one person or group could claim its symbolic capital in toto, and the mechanisms of identification were many, varied, and complexly mediated. If opera seria was at root the king's opera, its relations of production and its sociabilities also tested the king, manifesting the very crisis it denied.

* * *

The period up through the 1780s was one of glory days for opera seria. Despite substantial reforms and shifts in musical and poetic style, especially from the late 1750s onward, opera seria endured in a more or less "classic" form codified during the 1720s, telling tales of heroes, young and old, who make their way through a labyrinth of passions, from jealous desire to filial love, rage, joy, pity, sorrow, remorse, and piety, and through various vicissitudes—bitter loss, divided loyalty, sacrifice, and redemption—serving up a banquet of opportunities for audience identification. Dispersed throughout the operas with classical regularity, these various passions emerged over the course of three acts, played by six to seven characters ordered both horizontally and vertically: a young prima donna and primo uomo, a seconda donna and secondo uomo, and a ruler, plus one or two additional characters. Typically the primo and secondo uomo (at minimum) were played by castrati and the ruler by a tenor, but departures from these norms were numerous, including across gender. In off seasons, when theaters in secondary cities created casts from the best available singers, voice parts were often distributed in a less orthodox way, a ruler being played by a castrato or even a bass, for instance, a prima donna by a castrato, or a primo or secondo uomo by a female soprano or alto. The one general desideratum was for high, piercing, flexible, and intensely moving bel canto. Only occasionally in this classic form was there a chorus, save the very last number in act 3, and rarely an ensemble, unless a duet at the end of either act 1 or act 2, or both. Numerous short scenes followed upon one another, with action and dialogue given out in rapid recitative, repeatedly sending one character into the lyrical effusion of an aria and thus guaranteeing audiences recurrent, often flamboyant or passionate, solo displays and exits (at least until the 1790s).[10]

In a preface to the eleventh volume of Carlo Goldoni's comedies, edited by Giovanni Battista Pasquali (1761–78), the great playwright and comic librettist pictured this dissociated dramaturgy, speaking through the mouth of a host with whom as a young man he had just shared his only stab at writing an opera seria libretto. Goldoni began reading his libretto aloud to his hosts, later joined by two castrati, including the famous Neapolitan Caffarelli (Gaetano Majorano). Before long the castrati were mocking his mistakes, and Goldoni, humiliated, was led from the room as his host explained that although he had observed the Aristotelian principles of tragedy, which demanded unity of place and time, he had not followed the rules of opera seria.

> The first soprano [i.e., castrato], the prima donna, and the tenor (the opera's three principals) must sing five arias each, a pathetic, a bravura, a parlante, a mezzo carattere, and a brillante. The second man and second lady must have four each, and the sixth and seventh characters three . . . ; parenthetically there must be no more than six or seven characters in the opera and you have nine. The seconds aspire to have pathetic arias too, but the lead singers forbid it, so if the scene is pathetic the aria can't be more than of mezzo carattere. The fifteen arias of the leads must be distributed in such a way that two of the same color don't follow one another, and the arias of the other actors help create the chiaroscuro. You make a character remain on stage and this is against the rules. To the contrary, you make a lead singer exit without an aria, after a *scena di forza*, and this too is against the rules. You have in your opera only three scene changes and six or seven are needed. The third act of your opera is the best, but this is against the rules.[11]

10. On March 18, 1771, the librettist Gaetano Martinelli still wrote to composer Niccolò Jommelli about an "indispensable requirement that the first soprano not exit without singing an aria" (obligo indispensabile per non far' entrar dentro il primo soprano senza cantar l'aria) even though the two had participated centrally in early reform initiatives of opera seria in the 1760s; see McClymonds, *Niccolò Jommelli*, 636.

11. The libretto was *Amalasunta*, the year allegedly 1732: "Il *primo Soprano*, la *prima Donna* e il *tenore*, che sono i tre principali Attori del Dramma, devono cantare cinque arie per ciascheduno, una *patetica*, una di *bravura*, una *parlante*, una di *mezzo carattere* ed una *brillante*. Il secondo Uomo e la seconda Donna devono averne quattro per uno, e l'ultima parte tre, ed altrettante un *settimo* personaggio . . . ; poiché (per parentesi) i personaggi non devono essere più di sei o sette, e voi ne avete nove nel vostro Dramma. Le seconde parti pretendono che anch'esse le arie *patetiche*, ma le prime non lo permettono, e se la Scena è *patetica*, l'aria non può essere che al più di *mezzo carattere*. Le quindici arie dei primi Attori devono essere distribuite in maniera, che due non si succedano dello *stesso colore*, e le arie degli altri Attori servono per formare il *chiaro scuro*. Voi fatte cantare un personaggio che resta in Scena, e questo è contro le *regole*. Voi all'incontro fate partire un Attor principale senz'aria, dopo una *Scena di forza*, e questo ancora è contro le *regole*. Voi non avete nel vostro

In sum, the genre was dominated by arias and powerfully mediated by a cast hierarchy, one that bore little relation to the drama's hierarchy of social and political relationships. Through the totality of arias, a gallery of psychological portraits evolved kaleidoscopically for each character/singer across an evening, but its makeup was not predetermined purely by considerations of musical dramaturgy, much less literary or dramatic principles. To the contrary, portrayal of character was deeply implicated in the star system.

Goldoni's version of things was brought to a satiric crescendo by Joseph Baretti in his "Opere drammatiche dell'abate Pietro Metastasio poeta cesareo," published in his literary rag *La frusta letteraria* in 1763.

> It's essential that the poet . . . attend to the music and its limited faculties . . . . It's essential that every drama not exceed a certain number of verses, and that it be divided only into three acts and not five, as Aristotelian rules would require. It's essential that every scene end with an aria. It's essential that one aria not issue after another from the same character. It's essential that all recitatives be brief, and broken up by the alternating speech of whoever else appears on stage. It's essential that two arias of the same character not follow one another immediately, even if sung by two different voices, and that the allegro aria, for instance, not come on the heels of the allegro, or the pathetic on the pathetic. It's essential that the first and second acts finish with an aria that is more impressive than those strewn about elsewhere in them. It's essential that in the second and third acts two good niches be found, one for a noisy recitative followed by a bustling aria, the other for a duet or trio, without forgetting that the duet must always be sung by two principal heroes, one male and one female. These and other laws of drama look ridiculous according to the logic shared by all poetry: but anyone who wants to conform to the distinctive logic of drama for singing has to utilize all these laws, as harsh as they are strange, and mind them even more than the intrinsic beauties of poetry.[12]

Dramma che tre *cambiamenti di Scena*, e ve ne vogliono sei o sette. Il terzo Atto del vostro Dramma è il migliore dell'Opera, ma questo ancora è contro le *regole*" (Goldoni, "Prefazioni," 688–89; and cf. Goldoni, *Mémoires*, part 1, chaps. 28–29). Writing in 1789, the Scotsman John Brown categorized arias as cantabile (tender and singing), di portamento (dignified), di mezzo carattere (pleasing, middling style), parlante (for agitated passions), and bravura (virtuosic)—a fivefold scheme like Goldoni's, but less grounded in real Italian practice (Brown, *Letters upon Poetry and Music*, 36–40). Compare Daines Barrington's 1771 report to the Royal Society (*Philosophical Transactions* 60:54–64) on a test given Mozart in London 1765 for which the young composer had to invent extempore opera seria arias of three types: a "Love Song," a "Song of Rage," and a "Song of Anger" (excerpt quoted in Eisen and Sadie, "Mozart"). On such classification schemes, see Robinson, *Naples and Neapolitan Opera*, 88–91.

12. "[È] forza che il poeta . . . abbia riguardo alla musica e alle ristrette facoltà di quella . . . . [È] forza che ogni dramma non oltrepassi un certo numero di versi, e che sia diviso in tre soli atti, e non in cinque, come le aristoteliche regole richiederebbono. È forza che ogni scena sia terminata con un'aria. È forza che un'aria non esca dietro un'altra dalla bocca dello stesso personaggio. È forza che tutti i recitativi sieno brevi, e rotti assai dall'alterno parlare di chi appare in iscena. È forza che due arie dello stesso carattere non si sieguano immediatemente, anchorché cantate da due diverse voci, e che l'allegra, verbigrazia, non dia ne' calcagni all'allegra, o la patetica alla patetica. È forza che

Baretti's account, like Goldoni's, reflects a growing discontent among literati at midcentury that opera seria was too rigid and too starstruck. But both also inhabit the same festive spirit about which they write, a spirit manifest in the laughter and fearsomeness of the castrati, the mocking allusion to Aristotelian principles, the whims and demands of stars, the inane servility of composers, the disdain for common sense, and above all the flagrant appeal to showbiz. At play too is a spectacular, indeed specular, view of opera seria as a practice that thrives in the space-time of the lived event.[13]

RITUAL AND EVENT

It is these rules that have often prompted modern observers to criticize opera seria as a rigid set of conventions. But understanding these conventions as part of a ritual and spectacular process, compounded from formal elements, social practices, sensory media, and performative acts, enacted and reenacted over time, elucidates their premodern status, with its wider political and artistic implications.[14] Not all viewers shared the same relationship to the opera, of course. For some, like Giustiniana Wynne, who boasted that she and her sisters "were the real show" at the opera at Turin, the opera was a place to be seen.[15] Others lived and died by favorite singers, and still others fancied themselves *eruditi* who attended fiercely to every verse, note, and sight.[16] With food, drinks, gambling, visiting, reading, cards, lotteries, games—sometimes even brawls—on top of listening, watching, and people watching (see fig. 1.4), Italy's commercial theaters were not just the most splendid but the maddest in Europe. The English historian Charles Burney captured the contradiction in 1773 when he described the Regio Ducal Teatro in Milan.

> The theatre here is very large and splendid; it has five rows of boxes on each side . . . ; each box will contain six persons, who sit at the sides, facing each other; some of the front-boxes will conveniently contain ten. Across the

---

il primo e second'atto finiscano con un'aria di maggior impegno che non l'altre sparse qua e là per quegli atti. È forza che nel secondo e nel terzo atto si trovino due belle nicchie, una per collocarvi un recitativo romoroso seguito da un'aria di trambusto, e l'altra per collocarvi un duetto o un terzetto, senza scordarsi che il duetto dev'essere sempre cantato dai due principali eroi, uno maschio e l'altro femmina. Queste ed alcune altre leggi de' drammi appaiono ridicole alla ragion comune d'ogni poesia; ma chi vuole conformarsi alla privata ragione de' drammi destinati al canto è duopo si pieghi a tutte queste leggi non meno dure che strane, e che badi ad esse anche più che non alle stesse intrinseche bellezze della poesia" (Baretti, *Opere*, 311–12).

13. On space and time as indivisible, see Munn, "The Cultural Anthropology of Time," 93–94.

14. See Feldman, "Magic Mirrors." Many studies have criticized the conventionality and stereotypy of opera seria, but paradigms of ritual have not been invoked to explain it. For ritual in French opera, see Burgess's excellent "Ritual in the *Tragédie en Musique*."

15. Quoted in di Robilant, *A Venetian Affair*, 142.

16. Stefano Arteaga writes about five "classes of spectators" at the theater, "l'uomo di mondo, il politico, l'erudito, l'uomo di gusto e il filosofo" (*Le rivoluzioni del teatro musicale* 1:10).

FIG. 1.4. Scene inside a box at the opera, where occupants read, receive visitors, and watch other occupants with binoculars, while spectators from across the hall gaze back at them. From *Strenna italiana* (Milan, 1844). Biblioteca Nazionale Braidense, Milan. By permission of the Ministero per i Beni Culturali e Ambientali. Any further reproduction or duplication by any means is expressly forbidden.

> gallery of communication is a complete room to every box, with a fire-place in it, and all the conveniences of refreshments and cards. In the fourth row is a *pharo* table, on each side the house, which is used during the performance of the opera. There is in the front a very large box, as big as a common London dining-room, set apart for the Duke of Modena, governor of Milan, and the *Principessa Ereditaria*, his daughter . . . . The noise here during the performance was abominable, except while two or three airs and a duet were singing, with which every one was in raptures: at the end of the duet, the applause continued with unremitting violence till the performers returned to sing it again, which is here the way of encoring a favourite air.[17]

Similar vignettes about Venice, Rome, Naples, and elsewhere appeared often.[18] They portrayed the Italian opera house as a space dense with expressive media, dynamic and disjointed, a place to be scrutinized and inspected, and to scrutinize and inspect at will. In their natural habitat, Burney's viewers are perched in their boxes not in direct address to performers but to one another, as apt to watch the spectacle of the duke's box or another spectator as they are to gaze at the stage. Far from dancing attendance on all the singers, they seem mostly to ignore them. But once roused to pivot stageward, they may quickly coalesce into a single "rapturous" body and display a level of will and passion little known among modern spectators. They are actors in a kind of ritual that, like many religious and civic rituals, requires an intuitive sensory familiarity with formal and semantic cues, allowing participants to tune in and out without missing the prime vertices of the event.

Some decades ago, Victor Turner made a notable attempt to conceive theater as ritual in ways that still have something to reveal—if improbably so—about the horizon of expectations modern understandings have brought to opera seria.[19] The preeminent theorist of ritual in the later twentieth century, Turner

17. Burney, *An Eighteenth-Century Musical Tour in France and Italy*, 66–67. Unlike what happened with Oren's *Rigoletto*, it was the singers who decided whether or not to grant encores, though encores were sometimes prohibited (and indeed were often sung anyway). Innumerable accounts discuss noise in Italian theaters, e.g., Anton Raaff's letter to Padre Martini, which sighed relief over the silence at Mannheim (I-Bc, I.4.101); cf. Schnoebelen's catalog, *Padre Martini's Letters*, no. 4254 (see also chaps. 2–4 below). Lest we think eighteenth-century theaters the only raucous ones, however, note the following (thanks to Bruce Alan Brown) from the *Daily Telegraph*, February 2, 2003: "Stressed patrons of Vienna's State Opera . . . are resorting to violence. . . . Police have had to step in after arguments over stolen seats exploded into fisticuffs. Other causes of conflict include bouffant hair styles that block people's views and ringing mobile phones. . . . 'It is becoming increasingly brutal.'"

18. Italian theaters were targeted by many parodies circa 1800 and after, notably Donizetti's opera *Le convenienze e inconvenienze teatrali* (Naples, 1827; revised and expanded Milan, 1831), based on two plays by late-eighteenth-century librettist Antonio Simeone Sografi, *Le convenienze teatrali* (1794) and *Le inconvenienze teatrali* (1800). As I discuss further in chapter 4, the eighteenth-century produced such parodies mostly in the literary forms of satires and comedies. See Savoia, *La cantante e l'impresario*.

19. For my fuller critique of Turner's ritual/theater linkages, see Feldman, "Magic Mirrors," 433–40.

initially combined his interest in Arnold van Gennep's concept of liminality and "rites of passage" with a lifelong love of theater to develop an anthropological model of the "social drama."[20] Social dramas were periods of heightened intensity in group emotions, theorized in four classic phases: the social breach, crisis, self-reflection by a group along with redressive measures, and reintegration of persons and principles back into norms of living.[21] Claiming that staged dramas ritually resemble social dramas, Turner developed the idea of "cultural performances" as theatrically styled events that operate in a mood in which place, time, and genre are altered to allow explorations of an if-it-were-thus and if-I-were-you kind. Theater was thus not ritual per se but a metalanguage for talking about intense ritualized aspects of social drama. It was a reenactment framed as a performance, a staged performance about a social performance—or "acting about life" rather than "life as acting."

Here Turner was hoist by his own petard. His effort to link theater to ritual was founded in the romantic conception of an aestheticized and fundamentally textualized artwork, produced by a transcendent author. Bound off from an invisible crowd of onlookers who gaze on the work to gain purchase on their inner selves, the authorial theater Turner envisioned could not account for what goes on at a theatrical event where life is indeed in action and the imaginary wall does not exist—and where theater, no matter how make-believe, is always understood as part of life. Turner's assumptions could never apply to a pre-nineteenth-century theatrical form, since they reproduced the ideological claims of a European work-centered tradition.[22]

The modes of spectatorship and production of opera seria—the former highly fractured and the latter baldly collaborative—produced a different kind of art form than what Turner had in mind. A singer who disliked an aria, failed to learn it in time, or wanted to succeed with a different one might substitute an aria di baule, a favorite "suitcase" aria carried around as a moveable part of the show, much as costumes were. Notoriously arrogant singers, like Caffarelli and Luigi Marchesi, were known to insist on doing so, often using them as entrance arias where they functioned as "signature tunes."[23] But new music was

20. Turner, *Schism and Continuity*, 92. Turner's later explanation appears in "Social Dramas," 137–64. On "rites of passage," see van Gennep, *The Rites of Passage*, inspired by Hertz's "Contribution à l'étude sur la représentation collective de la mort." Turner schematizes relationships between social drama and ritual process in "Are There Universals of Performance?" 8–18, esp. 10. His dramatic metaphor became prevalent in studies of social forms, e.g., Duvignaud, *Spectacle et société*.

21. For Turner, social dramas occur at all levels of social organization, familial, civic, national, etc. His mirror image is meant to convey the reflexivity of theater as a device for scrutinizing life problems (*From Ritual to Theatre*, 16 and passim).

22. Turner's stress on multiplicity, process, and experience contradicts his romantic aesthetics, walling in actors as if there were no one to be performed *for* ("Liminality and the Performative Genres," 19). His performer is a limpid medium of authorial intention, while authors are veritable prophets, whose "metastatements" performers allow to "flow" (*Dramas, Fields, and Metaphors*, 28). Compare Jean and John Comaroff's critique in *Modernity and Its Malcontents*, xxi.

23. For similar accounts, see Heriot, *The Castrati*, 76 (amusing though unreliable); Freeman, "Farinello and His Repertory," 301–30; Price, "Pasticcio," 213–16; Strohm, "Handel's Pasticci," 164–

FIG. 1.5. Marco Ricci, *Rehearsal of an opera.* Oil on canvas, ca. 1709. Yale Center for British Art, Paul Mellon Collection. Reproduced by permission.

always in demand because arias were usually made fresh to order for productions, being tailored for specific singers, who learned them in brief rehearsal times (fig. 1.5). While some singers were very literate, others did not read music well, and therefore did not use reading for learning and mastering arias for performances.[24] Antonio Salieri recounted that in 1785 he played his new hal-

211; and Freeman, "An 18th-Century Singer's Commission," 427–33. On nineteenth-century aria substitution, see Poriss, "Artistic License" and "A Madwoman's Choice," 1–28. For the seventeenth century, see Brown, "Con nuove arie aggiunte" and "On the Road with the 'Suitcase Aria,'" 4–23.

24. The quasi-satirical *Lettre sur le méchanisme de l'opéra italien* (1756) alleged that Italian singers generally first saw their new arias just weeks before an opera opened. On recitative the *Lettre* (44) alleged: "They content themselves with repeating what the prompter utters in a louder voice and the harpsichord keeps them on key" (ils se contentent de répéter ce que le Souffleur pronounce plus haut qu'eux, e le clavecin les tient dans le ton). Formerly attributed to Josse de Villeneuve or Giacomo Durazzo (the latter deftly refuted by Brown, *Gluck and the French Theatre*, 53–57), the *Lettre* has been convincingly assigned to Calzabigi by Heartz, *Haydn, Mozart, and the Viennese School*, 158–64. Evidence of how extensively singers practiced recitatives and adhered to their notation is mixed.

lelujah, 132 bars long, three times for soprano Brigida Banti, whereupon she sang it back note-perfect. Salieri's account pictures singers learning new music through coachings by the composer that took place shortly before first performances—often on texts that were already well known.[25] Leopold Mozart wrote on July 30, 1768, that some of the singers slated to perform Wolfgang's *La finta semplice* in Vienna (ultimately never mounted) could only learn the music from him, since they learned everything by ear.[26] Even late in the century, tenor Gioacchino Caribaldi (Garibaldi) had to be cured of thinking he could only succeed in arias in E flat by being given one in B flat in which a third flat had secretly been written into the signature.[27] Since composers seem typically to have set libretti to music in the space of about six to eight weeks—with the poet and scenographer often beginning their work only a short time earlier if text and sets were new, and singers arriving just three to four weeks before opening night—adherence to conventions was a necessity. In this heyday of opera seria, stage sets were reused in much the same way as arias and costumes, except by the most prestigious productions and theaters. Thus, even as a stagework, an opera seria emerged not merely, or even principally, from dramaturgical ideals but from a motley agglomeration of social facts.

Once sweeping attempts at reform were made beginning in the 1750s, critics battled two main features of these rituals: the predictability of scenic and aria form and singers' alleged abuses of their virtuosic rights. The second included singers hogging the stage for lengthy passagework, improvising long cadenzas, neglecting recitative, and interacting with audience members during the opera. Reformers charged that normal practice gave too little authority to poets and composers and too much liberty to performers. Gluck, probably with his libret-

---

The German student Ignazio Wierl worked on recitative in lessons with Anton Raaff (see chap. 2, n. 8, below), and singing teacher Pierfrancesco Tosi paid much attention in his 1723 treatise to the three "types of recitative": *da chiesa, da camera,* and *da teatro (Opinioni de' cantori,* 41–49). Probably some singers learned simple recitatives conscientiously, while others fudged them.

25. Rice, *Antonio Salieri,* 122–24.

26. Mozart, *Briefe* 1:270.

27. Thayer, *Salieri,* 49–51. On singers' training, see Rosselli, *Singers of Italian Opera,* chap. 5, esp. 93; and Durante, "The Opera Singer," 272–82. By the time of Algarotti's treatise, Metastasio had already been complaining about singers' "caprice and ambition," their "extravagance" and "vocal symphonies," and specifically the aria di bravura. See letters of January 28 and August 1, 1750, to Farinelli; July 15, 1765, and January 14, 1766, to the Chevalier de Chastellux; May 30 and September 18, 1771, to Saverio Mattei; and September 8, 1776, to a Roman abbot (Metastasio, *Opere,* vols. 3–5; the letters appeared in translation in 1796 in Burney, *Memoirs of . . . Metastasio*). Similar charges became widespread after midcentury in works like Johann Joachim Quantz's *Versuch einer Flötetraversiere zu spielen,* 330, first published in 1752 (translated as *On Playing the Flute,* see esp. 334), which was already in its third edition by 1789. At the same time, there were cries to prevent singers from dropping character by the likes of Francesco Milizia in his *Trattato completo* (Prefazione, 3), first issued as *Il teatro* in Rome on December 25, 1771 (although by January 11, 1772, all copies had disappeared both because it was sold out and because it was suppressed by the Maestro del Sacro Palazzo Pontificio).

tist Calzabigi as ghost- or cowriter, delineated the contradiction in his 1769 preface to an edition of *Alceste* addressed to the Grand Duke of Tuscany. Music was to work no charms on the senses that might lessen an actor's ability to portray accurately the travails of human nature. The new role of music was to be the virtually "diegetic" one of enhancing the narrative flow on stage.[28] Poetry was to mediate between the willful singer and the obliging actor to ensure that both would serve the poet's ends. As protector of the submissive actor, the author(s) had to fend off the vainglory of singers, whose double identity splits, Jekyll-and-Hyde-like, as the preface draws to a close.[29]

The invective of the Gluck/Calzabigi preface merely codified the authorial politics that had chafed at the surface of nostalgic polemics like the *Saggio sopra l'opera in musica* of Francesco Algarotti, first published fourteen years earlier.[30] Algarotti described the symptoms of the opera seria disease in various forms of audience inattention. Its cause he diagnosed in opera's loss of the court, with its quasi-feudal patronage system, and the consequent advent of public theater and the open market—a complaint that tacitly took aim at the hybridity of opera seria (and one to which we will return).[31] Having sapped opera of its ancient dignity to pay pricey singers, he lamented, audiences now relied on singers for spectacle. Opera had become singer-take-all, especially in cantabile and bravura arias.[32] Composers were urged to intervene by composing their own cadenzas and ornaments, instead of leaving them in the tyrannical hands of singers.

Diatribes launched at singers, especially castrati, sought to remove their authorial powers and move the institution of opera seria closer to the work concept that led Turner to oppose theater-as-make-believe (life as acting) to ritual-as-real-life (acting as life). For Turner, theater pieces were essentially authorial creations whose purpose was to draw audiences into states of absorption. Theater, he claimed, took place in a subjunctive mood, in which normal time and action were culturally suspended. Theater was ritual only insofar as it repro-

28. Mulvey, "Visual Pleasure and Narrative Cinema," 6–18, originally articulated the concept. Cf. Elsaesser, *Early Cinema*.

29. The Gluck/Calzabigi preface is translated in Treitler, *Strunk's Source Readings*, 932–34; facsimile in *The New Grove Dictionary of Music* 7:466.

30. The *Saggio* appeared anonymously in 1755 and attributed in 1763, with several editions following. See Algarotti, *Saggio*, ed. Bini, and *Saggi*, ed. da Pozzo, 145–223; excerpts in Treitler, *Strunk's Source Readings*, 902–22, which quotes from the 1768 English translation, published as *An Essay on the Opera* in Burgess's 2005 edition. Algarotti's polemics circulated widely throughout Europe, engendering many offshoots. *The Lyric Muse Revived* (1768), for instance, juxtaposed translated extracts with extracts from travelers' accounts, including Samuel Sharp's *Letters from Italy* (1767) and Vincenzo Martinelli's *Lettere familiari* (1758).

31. Useful on the distinction between feudal versus bourgeois musical patronage, albeit relative to twentieth-century India, is Qureshi's "Mode of Production," 81–105, and her forthcoming *Master Musicians of India*, where the issues are grounded in the experience of living musicians who have thrived in a feudal, quasi-feudal, or post-feudal world of courtly patronage.

32. Heriot, *The Castrati*, 75–83; but see Alexandr Belosel'skii-Belozerskii, who in 1778 still vaunted castrati over female sopranos (*De la musique en Italie*, 38).

duced real life in a stylized, framed, and symbolically charged form. Hence its ritual status could have no practical relation to the transcendent state that was theater's most characteristic feature: the state of cultural subjunctivity.

But put to a use Turner did not intend, his "cultural subjunctivity" describes opera seria both as an artwork and as an event that exceeds it. The metaphor of subjunctivity underscores the way operatic events functioned to bracket space-time, allowing well-worn propositions to be tried on by listeners without requiring that those propositions be affirmed or negated. They might be expressed in narratives that advocate the virtue of the monarchical subject, stress the importance of social hierarchy, propose the monarch as divinely ordained, or dictate the proper resolution of conflicts. They could teach viewers how to treat fathers, brothers, sisters, enemies, and friends, how to stay the tide of amorous feeling or channel it into virtuous action, how to balance love against duty to state, and how to honor the king. None of these functions is characteristic of opera seria alone, but opera seria made them explicit, symbolic, and overriding. Recognizing the axiomatic and didactic function of the institution is thus crucial to any analysis that hopes to explain how it both fit into and affected the changing sociopolitical climate of eighteenth-century Europe. For it was through such propositions that conventional knowledge was reiterated and reaffirmed, but also recast and reinterpreted. This fact made intermittent attention not just acceptable but essential within an institution in which operas were heard repeatedly by the same listeners. The behavior of spectators resembled the noise at a synagogue or a Baptist service where the congregation knows its cues by heart (when to rise, kneel, sit, sing, recite), intuits them over its own commotion, and marks what it must at least enough to participate in crucial moments of ritual action. Appealing to such a paradigm makes it possible to apprehend these formal and performative elements, and clarifies what was at stake in them.

Although polemicists in the second half century were pushing opera seria in a more authorial direction, no amount of agitation could get production mechanisms to change very fast, much less change the wishes of many spectators and entrepreneurs (indeed, in Italy they never entirely did). Italian political geography made any rehabilitation of staging and spectatorship especially difficult, as production was highly decentralized and almost always depended for financing and management on multiple parties: a court superintendent appealing directly to a monarch (as at midcentury Parma); more commonly, an impresario hired by and answering to a court bureaucracy—usually the court superintendent—but also to box owners (as at Bourbon Naples); an academy of nobles or the head of a noble family (as in eighteenth-century Rome and Florence).

Most critical to these conditions was the hard fact that the solo singers who performed in opera seria generally had more pull and prestige than any of the other figures involved in an opera's preparation, certainly before about 1770–80, and considerably more than its authors. Better paid than anyone else because (ideally) they could draw crowds and steal the show, singers ruled over the performative event—a condition satirized in Anton Maria Zanetti's caricature, ostensibly of the famous Neapolitan Caffarelli, carrying a theater away on his back (fig. 1.6).[33] Listeners in turn wielded power by applauding, whistling, shouting, beating their canes, singing, booing, and not least ignoring the goings-on onstage, all of which eighteenth-century observers report at levels unimaginable in the theaters of present-day Western elites. Vulnerable to these expressions of pleasure and displeasure, singers could be undone at any given performance. Their arias could be replaced after opening night, and whole scenes altered or cut. Indeed, an entire opera might quickly be dropped and replaced to suit the pleasure of a disgruntled crowd.

Susceptible to the unexpected, an opera seria occasionally even took on the character of an "event" in the historian's sense of an occurrence that called into question fundamental premises of the cultural order. Yet that very susceptibility was indivisible from the flux inherent to opera seria performances tout court—between fixed and conventional elements on the one hand and aleatory ones on the other—a flux that indeed marks ritual processes more widely.[34] Among the fixed aspects were the dramaturgical elements enumerated by Goldoni and Baretti, but also the performative processes of singers and viewers—acting in stylized gestures, clapping when the king clapped, or erupting at expected musical cues, orchestral fanfares, or cadenzas. Among the aleatory elements for performers were improvisations, substitutions, altered recitatives, sudden droppings of character, and mugging at viewers; for spectators disrupting a show by booing or misplacing applause, demanding proscribed encores, exiting unexpectedly en masse, or cheering for a secondary or unknown singer, or even no singer at all, as Burney described in the royal theater at Milan:

> I went to the opera-house, where the audience was very much disappointed; [Garibaldi], the first tenor, and only good singer in it, being ill. All his part was cut out, and the *Baritono*, in the character of a blustering old father, who was to abuse his son [actually his daughter's lover] violently in the first scene and song, finding he had no son there, gave a turn to his misfortune, which diverted the audience very much, and made them submit to their disappointment with a better grace than they would have done in England; for, instead of his son, he fell foul on the prompter, who here . . . pops his head out of a little trap-door on the stage. The audience were so delighted with this attack upon the prompter, who is ever regarded as an enemy to their pleasures, that they encored the song in which it was made.[35]

First and foremost, such contrasts require a performative model that stresses communication and interaction through lived experience and even artistic pro-

33. On fees paid to singers, composers, and scenographers, as well as various production expenses, see Rosselli, *The Opera Industry*, chap. 3, and *Singers of Italian Opera*, chap. 6. Heriot notes that Senesino was once paid eighteen times what the composer got for an operatic run (*The Castrati*, 66–68). For the identity of the singer, see fig. 1.6, caption.

34. Strohm points to something similar but in terms of system rather than performance (*Dramma per musica*, 12).

35. The opera was Goldoni and Gassmann's opera buffa *L'amore artigiano*, July 21, 1770 (Burney, *The Present State of Music in France and Italy*, 102).

FIG. 1.6. Antonio Zanetti. "The celebrated Caffarelli, who sang at the Teatro San Giovanni Grisostomo, and carried away the theater, since his aria, once finished, completely emptied the theater out." Pen and sepia ink with trace of black pencil on paper, probably 1730s. By permission of the Fondazione Giorgio Cini, Venice, Raccolta bibliografica e artistica, no. 310. The text, not in the artist's hand, was apparently added later. The figure represented in the image is believed by Alessandro Bettagno to be Farinelli, not Caffarelli as claimed by the anonymous author of the text (*Caricature di Anton Maria Zanetti*, 103).

duction over text, narrative archetypes, and symbolic functions.[36] The foundational sketch of a performative model for ritual was ventured in the 1970s by Stanley Tambiah, who looks at how different media combine in ritual action, stressing the visceral effects those media produce via particular formal patterns.[37] In this respect, Tambiah's approach, though not oriented to theater, is helpful in reconceptualizing eighteenth-century opera. Not unlike music theorists of the eighteenth century, Tambiah highlights the performative role of formal patterns in contributing to quasi-magical ritual effects, returning to the famous case of Trobriand magic spells in order to integrate cultural content with formal analysis.[38] *In nuce*, Trobriand garden magicians execute spells by repeating key words "'with inventory expressions' in such a way as to produce the effect of 'rubbing' verbs into action in a succession of dazzling metaphors," taking them from a range of different sensory domains, or using them to enumerate parts of an object and assembling it as a whole by "step-by-step metonymic recitation." This kind of "redundant rhetoric 'generates' a 'magical missile,'" using various metaphorical expressions or metonymic parts of objects invoked, reciting words at different tempos and dynamics and in different rhythms, and combining them with various physical manipulations to the objects the magician hopes to conjure up.[39]

Of course Tambiah's Trobriand example has nothing like a direct parallel with the case at hand. Rather, it underscores the tripartite conjunction of the formal, sensory, and performative that figures in my exploration of elite eighteenth-century opera houses in Italy. Relatedly, a magical discourse resonates with metaphors often invoked by bedazzled eighteenth-century listeners responding to aria performances that were highly formalized and repetitive but also subject to extensions, and sometimes improvisations, and that generated increasing levels of surface activity and harmonic tension. I return to these matters

36. For reviews of "performance studies" focused on cultural metaphor, creativity anthropology, interaction rituals, and speech acts, see Bell, *Ritual Theory*, 37–46, and for performed arts as special cases of daily life, Beeman, "The Anthropology of Theater," 369–93. Both consider studies that emphasize performer/spectator interactions, shifting from the stability of works, texts, and authors to the instability of communicative acts (one-on-one speech interactions, communal interactions, theatrical interactions, etc.). During the 1980s, ritual-oriented performative studies explored dramatic/expressive media and poetics, stressing semantic surplus over predetermined order (see Kelly and Kaplan, "History, Structure, and Ritual," 137). Such views touched musicology little before the 1990s, but recent musicological studies such as Small, *Musicking*, and especially Le Guin, *Boccherini's Body*, have taken on performance issues directly. See too Abbate's skeptical plea, "Music—Drastic or Gnostic?" 505–36, her translation of Jankélévitch, *Music and the Ineffable*, and Berger's response to the former, "Musicology according to *Don Giovanni*," 490–501, which advocates treading a line between text and performance. Older musicological work (e.g., Cone's *Musical Form*) on the whole remained firmly text-centered.

37. Tambiah, "A Performative Approach," 123–66. Compare older ethnographies, for example, Radcliffe-Brown's *The Andaman Islanders* and Lévi-Strauss's *The Raw and the Cooked*.

38. See Malinowski, *Coral Gardens and Their Magic*.

39. Tambiah, "A Performative Approach," 142, 143. Cf. Rappaport, "Ritual," 249–60.

in chapter 2. For now, what is important to note apropos ritual process in opera seria is that this doubleness accords with the main idea in Tambiah's performative approach, namely, that ritual action, in creating visceral effects through charged sensory devices carried in fixed formal containers, always involves a "dual aspect": it simultaneously utilizes stereotyped invariant sequences and variant features that are generally aleatory. Changes in practice and slippages in meaning take place as rituals circulate among different practitioners in different social situations and groups, since their particular forms "are always linked to the status claims and interests of the participants, and therefore are always open to contextual meanings."[40]

Given the pervasive tension in opera seria between fixity and license, both on stage and in listening practices in the house, the utility of this approach is twofold. First, it adapts well to the ritualized nature of opera seria, an institution that was widespread, conventional, and highly reproductive in its morphology, but at the same time subject to variations in individuals' performances and in the performative conditions of different locales. Second, as I noted above, it highlights the simultaneous inclusion of fixed forms and unfixed elements and sequences—both the "variant" and the "invariant."

MAGIC AND MYTH

Understanding how this communicative tension operated depends on understanding how eighteenth-century public theaters were managed and laid out, and what spectators expected to find in them. The impresario who typically managed a theater depended on the mixture of privilege and responsibility attendant on upper-class audience members in order to make up losses incurred in running an opera house.[41] This held true for virtually all opera houses, no matter what system of ownership and management prevailed. Impresarios were normally awarded concessions and endowments by noble box owners, whose satisfaction with the operas was important to maintaining their goodwill and some modicum of financial solvency. Only when a monarchical or civic agenda called for a lavish production might a theater grossly ignore financial constraints, as happened in midcentury Parma under the minister of entertainments, Guillaume du Tillot.[42] Disregarding the level of expenditures over a sustained period to the extent that Du Tillot did in the 1750s and 1760s was rare, though it was normal to have ongoing losses.

When Italian theaters were in season during the festive periods of Carnival

40. Tambiah, "A Performative Approach," 125.

41. I am indebted here to Rosselli, *The Opera Industry*, esp. chap. 3; Piperno, "Opera Production to 1780," 1–79; Rosselli, "Opera Production, 1780–1880," 81–164; and Pastura Ruggiero, "Per una storia del teatro pubblico in Roma," 453–86. See too Heriot, *The Castrati*, chap. 4, and Lee, *Studies of the Eighteenth Century.*

42. See Feldman, "L'opera seria," 127–51, and chap. 3 below.

and Ascension, and sometimes during the autumn celebrations of the church year, nobles could pass in them nearly half their waking hours. A typical night of opera seria included not just the opera but two to three separate ballets, and gala nights might have special additions as well: an encomiastic cantata to a local monarch or a visiting dignitary, a special lottery run by the impresario, and often a ball with masking and dancing after the show (see figs. 4.2 and 4.3). Set up to accommodate a wide-ranging sociability, theater was the hub of an upper-class Italian's social life at a time of year when no other public institutions of entertainment were usual, and no dinner parties were generally given. In such circumstances, listening to the opera was not prescribed but selected, except when royalty or dignitaries were present. Chroniclers usually noted that in the presence of a sovereign Italians listened with respect, "through the king's ear," as it were.[43] There were deviations, of course. While "listening through the king's ear" meant reproducing the sovereign's social-political body by reproducing his actions and habits, not all sovereigns listened attentively. Those who did not, like King Carlo III of Naples, might render listening optional for their subjects, even when they were present at the theater.[44] When no single sovereign existed, as in the republics of Venice and Genoa, or when none kept court, listeners might attend keenly if a work was fresh or hardly at all if it was well-known.

The dialectic between fixity and freedom that shaped the dramaturgical structure, aria forms, performance, and listening practices of opera seria manifested a larger dialectic between constraint and license in the sociopolitical domain. Chapter 4 shows how, during Carnival and other festive times, a certain freedom of action was rewarded in return for constraints imposed in more sober seasons, principally Lent. Such fluxes clarify the dynamic that marked the institution of opera seria in its classic form: its abundance of closed forms, its communicative exchanges between singers and spectators, and its many disjunctions of narrative, sense, and sight: the high sounds that issued from male bodies, the fetching sight of females in trousers, the stylistic jolts from recitative to arias, and the ballets that sprang up between acts, often unrelated (at least until later in the century) to what preceded and followed them.

These disjunctions cannot be separated analytically from the underlying premises of opera seria stories, which presume a set of absolutist claims about a cosmic order wherein the benign sovereign stands in for God, the heroic youth for the ideal enlightened subject or the sovereign whom he sometimes succeeds as heir, and the dramatis personae as a whole for the hierarchy of the sociopolitical order. Reworked many times over, characters in the opera achieved

43. On "listening through the king's ear," see, for example, Beckford, *The Travel Diaries* 1:252. Sommer-Mathis situates the phenomenon within the theatrical habitus of eighteenth-century Habsburg wedding operas in *Tu felix Austria Nube*.

44. On the idea that imitating the sovereign's actions reproduces the sovereign's social-political body, see famously Elias, *The Court Society*. An early but very limited musicological attempt in this direction was Dunning, "Official Court Music," 17–21.

their status by passing through harsh tests posed by political struggles, personal passions, family conflicts, and the winds of fate. Whether they were sovereigns or unproven youths, their odysseys had to be undertaken in order to eradicate whatever shadows and strife beset events. As elaborated in chapters 5 and 6, the passions in these odysseys are challenged by different kinds of political battles: contests of state (as in *Didone abbandonata*), the perils of tyrannicide (*Siroe*), intrigues at court (*Ezio*), or the demands of loyalty to one's country (*Attilio Regolo*). Whatever the case, personal conflicts between duty and desire have to be resolved. Only thus can negative feelings be conquered, negative social elements be expunged, and the social order be set aright. To that extent, the progress of an opera seria is a Turneresque rite of passage.

I have argued elsewhere that since this narrative telos was largely preordained, it lay fundamentally beyond human probity. The social order was—by ideology, not in reality—meant to exist naturally, inevitably, and endlessly. The opera that represents it merely turns the pages of eternal time, its messages and denouements hardly susceptible to validation through inspections by earthly mortals. Viewed as deep structure, its characters therefore did not need to be situated in purportedly "real" histories of family, place, or time, as they were in opera buffa, the dramma giocoso, and late-century opera seria. They function instead as abstract actors of a transcendental truth, divine messengers of absolutist metaphysics. Like Athena, they spring fully formed from the head of Zeus—almost literally, for the father is so engendering that in most opera seria, especially in that produced during its classic phase when the libretti of Pietro Metastasio (1698–1782) were repeatedly set, mothers are dispensed with altogether.[45]

The claims of an opera seria thus exceeded the possibility of representation in the material world. Discontinuous listening, as I have also argued, was possible precisely because endless, insuperable patriarchy was a foregone conclusion, one that excused spectators from affirming narratives by hearing them through.[46] The taken-for-granted nature of these narratives depended on mechanisms that circulated ideas, acts, and objects in highly saturated signs—the divine king, noblesse oblige, the magnanimous prince, the royal crown, the divine sword, altar and sun, the sacred cup. Usable for many different purposes, such signs might be constituents of rituals and ceremonies carried out onstage, but invariably they were also pliable symbols of the viewer's world writ large. They could in effect pretend to a certain significance without contributing signification because they were unencumbered with such burdens.

For all these reasons, operas could more easily articulate messages at a generalized structural level by *dis*articulating the process by which viewers might test

45. See Feldman, "The Absent Mother," 29–46 and 254–59, where I characterized this in a less qualified way than now.

46. Ibid.

them. Promoters and producers had no need to "prove" to listeners by means of tangible evidence or realistic circumstance such propositions as "the king is omnipotent and magnanimous," "princes are valiant lovers," or "subjects must imitate codes of honor of royal superiors." They had no need to deploy the modalities of showing and telling—of narrative—in ways deemed proper to drama in the modern sense, since their propositions could be ratified only through the persuasive force of transcendent qualities that exceeded logic. Indeed, viewers could arguably accept the meanings of timeless symbols and axioms sooner if the physical and discursive guarantees of their existence were displaced.

Opera seria, then, was not fundamentally animated by narrative but by the sensuality of the voice and the euphony of the Italian language. Charles de Brosses claimed that on meeting the Italianized Saxon Johann Adolph Hasse, the composer exclaimed, "[T]here is no singing language but Italian and one can have no music but Italian!"[47] De Brosses climbed onto the Italian bandwagon by insisting that arias were the heart and soul of opera seria and the reason it was superior to French *tragédie en musique,* adding that it mattered little that Italian arias made only rough correspondences between words and sounds (as Hasse acknowledged).[48]

Much of the explanation given by de Brosses and others for disjunctions between words and sounds, opera acts and ballet entr'actes, singers and genders, recitatives and arias, and much of their justification for the predictable scenic forms that went with them, lay in the magical power of arias. Sensory stimuli to the ear (and in ballets, also to the eye) were the touchstones of Italian opera, and arias were its locus and primum mobile. Only the great scenic spectacles and ballets could begin to compete. Hence, among travelers and gazetteers who reported on Italian theaters, arias were perpetually troped as magic. For these commentators, lyric singing could weave magic spells on distracted audiences, reflexively intertwining the arts of *cantare* and *incantare,* singing and enchanting.[49] Even an avowed reformer of singers' abuses from midcentury, Vincenzio Martinelli, gushed of Regina Mingotti that what she sang were "not arias but enchantments," soothing drinks "to make one forget the most irremediable ills from the first beat."[50] Martinelli wanted a lady friend to share this experience,

47. "Lettre a M. Malateste," in Bézard, *Lettres familières* 2:325–70; excerpt in Fubini, *Music and Culture,* 199–208.

48. See Tomlinson, *Metaphysical Song,* 54–61.

49. Likewise note the affinities of *cantante* or *cantatrice* and *incantatore/incantatrice* (singer and enchanter).

50. "Le arie poi che questa musa soprannumeraria canta in questa opera non sono arie, sono incantesimi, sono nepenti da fare scordare i mali più irrimediabili alla prima battuta" (Martinelli, *Lettere familiari,* "A Milady Newdigate a Arbury, invitandola a venire a Londra per veder l'opera del *Siroe,*" 135). Infatuated with Mingotti's androgynous feint, Martinelli told his female correspondent that she mustn't miss Mingotti's fetching performance. The opera was *Siroe, re di Persia* as set by Giovanni Lampugnani for the royal theater at the Haymarket in 1755. Mingotti was famous for trou-

for enchantments were not just personal but communal, collectivizing at their best what was otherwise a splintered crowd.

In the atmosphere of the first half of the century, singing was especially prized for its ability to move the spirit, to affect it "magically" and thus draw auditors forth from the dispersion of their separate boxes. Efficacious singing was a form of rhetorical prowess, not unrelated to the power of oratorical speech. Sometimes the power of oratory was asserted directly by operatic characters. But it was not so much rhetorical persuasion that was sought in arias as a kind of nonverbal meaning: the ineffable power of the human voice, whether virtuosic like an instrument, with rapid trills, roulades, and diminutions, or lyrical and touching, with prolonged sostenuti, *messe di voce*, delicate turns, Lombard sighs, chromatic inflections, and appoggiaturas.

Among many issues fiercely debated through much of the era was whether the utterance of the voice should be legible as a kind of hyperspeech or should devote itself to stirring the listener to heights of ecstasy. Did words really matter and if so how? The question intensified from the mid- to late eighteenth century, but the importance of poetic meaning had early advocates in writers like the Arcadian Lodovico Antonio Muratori (1672–1750).[51] Not surprisingly, agitators for reform identified the magic of arias with the dangers of artifice, especially with the artifices of the great virtuosi, in keeping with a wider and more pointed discourse against magical arts during the 1740s.[52] If some singers appeared to have beguiled composers into writing them awe-inspiring passaggi, others could conjure up astonishing cadenzas and ornaments *all'improvviso*. None could deny the power of particular virtuosi over listeners, yet virtuosic arias ran *contra naturam*. Antonio Planelli, advocating the pathetic in opera seria, warned in his reform treatise of 1772 that listeners, being wooed by the stunning instrumental feats of the virtuosi, were being deprived of the chance to follow the meanings and moods of characters, and thus to experience verisimilitude through singing.[53] They were deprived of the referential. One diva pro-

---

ser roles (especially her portrayal of Publio in *Attilio Regolo* at Dresden in 1750), but Martinelli's memory must have played him false because in *Siroe* she sang the role of Emira, whereas Rosa Curioni played the male role of Medarse. On Martinelli's comment, see di Benedetto, "Poetics and Polemics," 35–36 ("Poetiche e polemiche," 39).

51. A good general introduction to Muratori is Diaz, "Politici e ideologici," 105–36, with bibliography on 277–79. Among discussions related to music, see Durante, "The Opera Singer," 367–69, and Freeman, *Opera without Drama*.

52. Notably in the Venetian Giuseppe Gorini Corio's book denying the magical arts, *Politica, diritto, e religione* (1742); see Venturi, *Settecento riformatore*, vol. 1, *Da Muratori a Beccaria*, 355–89, translated as "Enlightenment versus the Powers of Darkness," in Venturi, *Italy and the Enlightenment*, 103–33, citation on 104.

53. Arguments in favor of verisimilitude were long-standing in polemics over Italian opera. They emerged in the early eighteenth century with the Roman Arcadians, who were instrumental in turning opera seria from an eclectic dramaturgical form made up of multiple plots, mixed genres, frequent mythological themes and characters, and marvelous machinery to a tightly knit historical one; see, for example, Muratori's moralist diatribes in *Della perfetta poesia italiana*.

ficient in the "marvelous," he charged, speaking tacitly of the famous Caterina Gabrielli,

> has made our composers euphoric. Since she began to appear in European theaters . . . everything in them has turned into a trill. Bewitched by this novel musical spell, the public was convinced it was hearing for the first time the only style worthy of opera, and the *maestro di cappella*, similarly touched by such sorcery, imagined that he was entering a new musical world. Setting foot in that enchanted land . . . he blessed the heavens.[54]

Planelli's elision between dazzling virtuosity and the charms it worked on composers and audiences made the singer out as a conjurer who enraptured and transported others to a false Elysium.[55]

* * *

Among rare attempts to reflect seriously on the relationship between magicality and art is anthropologist Alfred Gell's "The Technology of Enchantment and the Enchantment of Technology." Gell's essay starts from the assumption that much cultural production cannot be understood within the framework of "fine art" or the Western concept of the "aesthetic," since aesthetics relies on the acceptance of certain "initial articles of faith": namely, that "in the aesthetically valued object there resides the principle of the True and the Good, and that the study of aesthetically valued objects constitutes a path toward transcendence."[56] But Gell only rejects aestheticism as a moral discourse, continuing to insist that imperative to any anthropology of art is the aestheticist's investment in close examination of "the objects themselves." His central and most salient point is that arts of various kinds are "components of a vast . . . technical system, essential to the reproduction of human societies." Hence his coinage "the technology of enchantment" to underscore the means by which extraordinary skill can charm and persuade individuals in the interests of some larger collective.

Focused as they are on "primitive" and visual art, Gell's concepts are variously freighted from the start: by his traditionalizing insistence on the function of art in reproducing and reinforcing the status quo over and above a willingness to see how art may question it; by his notion that art always serves a collectivity

54. "La maravigliosa gorga d'una celebre odierna cantatrice ha ingerito su questo particolare uno spirito di vertigine nei nostri compositori. Da che ella cominciò a comparire sui teatri d'Europa . . . tutto divenne gorgheggio sopra i teatri. Il popolo ammaliato da quel nuovo incanto, credé di sentire allora per la prima volta il solo stile degno dell'opera in musica; e 'l maestro di cappella, tocco anch'egli da quella malia, s'immaginò d'entrare in un nuovo mondo musicale. Mettendo il piede in quell'incantato paese . . . benediceva il cielo" (Planelli, *Dell'opera in musica*, 70; excerpts translated in Fubini, *Music and Culture*, 240–51).

55. See also Metastasio, *Opere* 3:555, and other passages from his letters cited in n. 27 above.

56. Gell, "The Technology of Enchantment," 41. My thanks to Donald Chae for the reference. See further on magical relationships in chapter 2 below.

rather than (or as well as) subverting it; and by his focus on the concreteness of graphic and decorative arts to the exclusion of performed ones, not least music. These objections might seem to cast too dark a shadow over Gell's theories to recuperate what remains of them. But his central insight is suggestive for studies of opera seria, especially the idea that the power of art stems in large part from its embodiment of technical processes—and hence, in Gell's words, the idea that "the *technology of enchantment* is founded on the *enchantment of technology*."[57] The dialectic has been suppressed in aestheticist analyses, which downplay the physical skill demanded in artistic production and disdain the power of "art" to trade in cheap thrills that might root it in mere physical labor or spectacle and militate against higher spiritual planes. Bucking this tendency, Gell sees technical processes as having the power to cast spells over us, to make enchantment seem like the way of the world. "Magic haunts technical activity like a shadow," Gell writes. Especially in "prescientific" societies, he argues, magic represents a kind of ideal technology.[58]

Wherever hard-core persuasion is needed, such magic also takes strategic forms of what Gell calls "psychological warfare," epitomized for him by Kula practices of exchange conducted island-to-island in elaborately carved canoes with which the Kula hope to inspire offers of better valuables by dazzling their beholders and thereby causing them to interpret Kula canoes as magically empowered. The complex carving of the great canoe-board serves both as a "physical token of magical prowess on the part of the owner" and a sign that "he has access to the services of a carver whose artistic prowess is also the result of his access to superior carving magic."[59] The example is provocative. Considered against the phenomenon of opera seria, it brings to mind the great contests among singers who made bold, competitive displays of technical prowess in solo arias, angling to surpass the glories of their peers, win the attentions and hearts of listeners, and command extraordinary fees in international markets. Vocal performances betrayed the agonism of combat, enlisting the mercenary voice to deploy its virtuosic weaponry against that of its opponent. But voices could also draw around the listening subject a kind of magical harmony, an aura that enabled the magicalized agent-singer to overcome the fragmentation of attentions to which the hall lent itself, enticing and transforming viewers, and putting them into states of collective trance and effervescence. Indeed, in an eighteenth-century theater, this mood is still necessary to collectivize modern viewers, as seen at the climax of a recent show in Perugia's Teatro Pavone (see fig. 1.7).

Here is Burney's famous tale of how Carlo Broschi, "Il Farinelli," the most dazzling of all eighteenth-century castrati, was first catapulted to stardom. Based on Burney's interview with Farinelli himself, the tale stresses the dimensions of competition, extraordinary virtuosity, and the strife and bravura

57. Ibid., 44.
58. Ibid., 59.
59. Ibid., 46.

FIG. 1.7. A moment of collective effervescence during the festival Umbria Jazz, concert by Patricia Barber, Teatro Pavone (1723; rebuilt 1773), Perugia, July 14, 2003. Photograph by author.

of physical labor, all of which probably accrued greater and greater value from the time it had actually occurred up until the time of Farinelli's retelling and Burney's retelling in turn.

> [Farinelli] was seventeen when . . . during the run of an opera, there was a struggle every night between him and a famous player on the trumpet, in a song accompanied by that instrument: this, at first seemed amicable and merely sportive, till the audience began to interest themselves in the contest, and to take different sides: after severally swelling out a note, in which each manifested the power of his lungs, and tried to rival the other in brilliancy and force, they had both a swell and a shake together, by thirds, which was continued so long, while the audience eagerly waited the event, that both seemed to be exhausted; and, in fact, the trumpeter, wholly spent gave it up, thinking, however, his antagonist as much tired as himself, and that it would be a drawn battle; when Farinelli with a smile on his countenance, shewing he had only been sporting with him all this time, broke out all at once in the same breath, with fresh vigour, and not only swelled and shook the note, but ran the most rapid and difficult divisions, and was at last silenced only by the acclamation of the audience. From this period may be dated that superiority which he ever maintained over all his cotemporaries [*sic*].[60]

60. Burney, *An Eighteenth-Century Musical Tour in France and Italy*, 153. See also Sacchi, *Vita del cavaliere Don Carlo Broschi*, 35; and Celletti, *A History of Bel Canto*, 81–82, on Handel's treatment of the relationship between trumpet and voice in Rinaldo's arias with trumpet obbligato.

Accounts like this one suggest how technical bravura could be staged as competition for the benefit of fascinated spectators, bedazzling them in ways that they already longed for ("the audience eagerly waited the event"). In this sense, enchantments depended on mechanisms of desire—the desire for the royals and heroes represented to transcend earthly realms, the viewers' desire to identify with royal and heroic impersonations by singers, the desire to displace veneration from religious and political objects onto performers.

Gell glossed this phenomenon through a theoretical premise whose source he must have recognized as apt but also ironic, namely, the classic theory of money put forward by philosopher Georg Simmel, which maintains that objects are valued to the extent that they resist our desire. Recast for the purpose of a theory of art, art objects "present themselves to us surrounded by a kind of halo-effect of resistance,"[61] crucial to which is the spectator's perception of the artist's special agency and elusiveness to normal human possibility. The artist seems powerful in *representing* power and in thus seeming almost to *ascribe* it, though ultimately this power will tend to be reascribed back to whoever controls the artist: "What Bernini can do to marble . . . Louis XIV can do to you. . . . The man who controls such a power as is embodied in the technical mastery of Bernini's bust of Louis XIV is powerful indeed."[62] By these lights, the production of art, far from being socially disembodied, constitutes itself through a special kind of technology that flows directly into the production of social relations. Nor is the perceived relationship between art and magic that it entails a random or irrational one. On the contrary, while the magical attitude of the beholder may be a "by-product of uncertainty," of processes that are not well understood, it is also a by-product of objectives pursued through technical means that are founded in reason, calculation, and foresight.[63]

The nexus here among technical virtuosity, art, magicality, and social relations is provocative in trying to tease out the "magical" status of opera seria performances, and it will figure in my analysis of opera seria arias in chapter 2. Yet ironically, it is precisely this performative dimension, and thus the relations among patrons, makers, performers, and spectators crucial to our concerns here, that Gell's essay leaves largely untheorized.[64] Nor does it take into account the specific sorts of claims made in artistic production of different kinds, or the messages proposed by any of these agents or their expressive objects. Efficacy in Gell's argument—effectively the *product* of attempts by makers and doers—is nearly all that counts, and specifically the technical mechanism that makes artistic virtuosity instrumental in attaining objective ends.

61. Gell, "The Technology of Enchantment," 48.

62. Ibid., 52.

63. Ibid., 57.

64. Of course, there is a performed dimension to Kula exchange: the boatmen who display the canoes and engage in exchange are "performers" by contrast with the carvers, who do primary artistic creation beforehand (somewhat as opera singers are to composers)—a distinction Gell fails to make.

* * *

What, then, to make of the magical views of opera seria called up repeatedly by eighteenth-century observers? In calling the effects of seria singers "magical," observers had in mind nothing like the secret rites usually linked with the arts of magic. Yet they were certainly thinking of an arcane, intangible congeries of skills and powers—something more like the ensemble of techniques and effects that Marcel Mauss maintained in his general theory of magic were typical of many different magical rites historically the world over and of the magicians who conducted them. Among these in opera would figure the efficacy with which singers could call upon their extraordinary skills, the sense of mystery they could evoke, the states of ecstasy they aroused, the perceived primacy of their souls in influencing their auditors, and the passions that singers transmitted to them.[65]

Whether praised or damned, magic in eighteenth-century theatrical accounts always had as its primary referent the singer's art—the sonic counterpart to the visual spectacle supplied by ballet entr'actes. "Magic" here always refers to effects of performance, and never to magical events, magicians, enchantresses, magical rites, spells, or physical transformations within the opera.[66] Indeed, by direct contrast with French *tragédie en musique*, magical motifs and characters were typically excluded from eighteenth-century opera seria plots (or at least muted, as for example, in Armida operas or other operas based on the Renaissance epics of Ariosto or Tasso).[67] Ideologically at least, they were disqualified from the narratives of opera seria by Arcadian reformist thinking.

In the optic of this book, magic is a trope best viewed through its ancient coupling with myth—myth understood not as a specific corpus of stories but as a particular work that stories do. Opera seria could charm audiences because it mediated through sensory means propositions, feelings, and possible solutions about a variety of social and political phenomena and presented them in mythical forms. Even though most libretti were outwardly historical in content, they looked to ancient histories for their explanatory political value toward the work of legitimating a traditional world. In delivering their parts, singers stood in as royal figures, heroes, counselors, generals, and confidantes. The singing master Giambattista Mancini declared, "When a singer performs well, investing strongly in the character he is playing, and projects him naturally, with actions, voice, and proper gestures, and brings him to life with clarity, the listener will say that he is truly, for example, Caesar; or that another one is Alexander."[68]

65. Mauss, *A General Theory of Magic*, esp. chaps. 2 and 3.

66. Burgess's critique of my "Magic Mirrors" misconstrues this point ("Ritual in the *Tragédie en Musique*," 124–28).

67. Cagiano de Azevedo, "I viaggiatori francesi," 89–99.

68. Mancini went on to advise that singers listen to the discourse of a great orator and note the "diverse passions he intends to arouse in listeners" (le diverse passioni, che intende muovere nell'uditore); see *Pensieri, e riflessioni practiche* [1774], 150, art. 13; *Practical Reflections*, 65.

In this way singers served as representational instruments of a hierarchically ordered world, making the inner turmoil of their characters palpable through a plastic if conventional repertory of mimetic devices.

As arias grew in size (and audiences listened increasingly little to recitative), the absolute semantic content of operas counted less. Or rather, semantic value resided instead in metaphor ("I am a ship rocked by a stormy sea"; "My tender plant that withers in the shade"), or in simile ("like the fearless lion that stalks its prey"), or sometimes in direct address ("Tell him that I am faithful"); but semantic value was small compared with, say, Mozart's comic operas or Verdi's psychological tragedies. Especially once text repetitions and their accompanying music increased sharply in the 1750s to 1770s, with no concomitant expansion of poetic texts, the rational material assurances of word/sound correspondences were radically attenuated. In their place, arias worked to dissolve the narrative of recitative into mesmerizing lyric magic—those outbursts of unfathomable, mystically empowered song.

Song was given particular definition through spatial location. Before various reforms of opera seria initiated in Parma, Vienna, and Stuttgart became influential across Italy, singers typically struck a pose during an opening instrumental ritornello and then delivered the words of the aria proper while facing the audience in direct address. Situated in the liminal space of the proscenium, arias served to transcend the more everyday operations of plot and action, particularly as the proscenium was flanked by boxes that caused stage space and audience space to overlap and suggested that singers were neither wholly within the drama nor without. Not until late in the century did aria performances begin to occur more deeply within the space of the stage and thus to inhabit something analogous to Turner's liminal space where normal time and action were suspended, feeling temporarily annihilated reason, and passion collected in the recitative could be unleashed in the lyricism at the scene's end.[69]

* * *

Ritual recitations of various kinds have accompanied the telling of myths in many different contexts worldwide. In Mircea Eliade's words, a myth traditionally forces its receiver to return magically "*to its origins*, to repeat its exemplary creation, whether the object of narration is rice, rain, fire, or the sovereign and his realm."

> Knowing the myth of origin is often not enough; it must be recited; knowledge of it is proclaimed; it is *shown*. By reciting myths, one reintegrates the fabulous time of origins, becomes in a certain way "contemporary" with the events that are evoked, shares in the presence of the Gods or Heroes.[70]

69. For a Lacanian interpretation, see Poizat, *The Angel's Cry.*

70. Eliade, "Toward a Definition of Myth," 4–5.

Understood as a story that provides an exemplum from the past concerning what *should be* in the present, Eliade's formulation strikes close to the heart of the tales told in Metastasian libretti and others of similar time and ilk.[71] In its widest interpretation, myth here suggests how things in the present first came into existence and showed themselves: codes of behavior, forms of power, the social order, and the institutions that sustain it. The stories of opera seria present models of what those who know the tale in the present can hope to "master" and "manipulate" as a result of that knowledge. And yet (and here is the critical point) the tales of opera seria, like other myths, were not learned primarily as content but as feeling, feeling internalized through the expressive power of a ceremonial recitation, itself justified by the myth. Hence the sovereign body delineated in opera seria—affirmed, at least in principle, through the narration of its ideal origination and existence at an earlier time, a time when it was fully meaningful and manifest—is reactualized as a force that is primordial, timeless, and sacred. At its moment of occurring, opera seria was already a lament for a lost past, reproducing itself as a desire to recapture that past in all its present glory. More specifically, in opera seria the telling heralds a crisis, since the very context of the bourgeois commercial theaters in which it was given constitutes from the outset a negation of its absolutist claims.

* * *

For Stendhal in the early nineteenth century, a magical state differentiated Italian listeners from French. The souls of Italians could be "transplanted into some seventh heaven of delight" to show moments of

> entrancement, when singers and audience alike forget themselves so as to be sensible to nothing but the beauty of a finale by Cimarosa. It's not enough in Paris to give 30,000 francs to Crivelli; one would still have to buy an audience fit to listen to him, and nurture the love he has for his art. . . . An Italian surrenders unreservedly to the sheer pleasure of admiring a beautiful aria that he hears for the first time; a Frenchman will applaud only with a sort of anxiety, for he is afraid of approving of something mediocre.[72]

71. Mladen Dolar says as much, albeit without fixing on opera seria, when he writes that foundational to opera was the turn to a mythical, "fabulous past transcending time . . . raised to the temporality of the fantasy" and that crucial at the same time were "new forms by means of which the myth can find a dramatic realization and a corresponding new social function and hence, in its very above-time nature, introduce new temporality" (Žižek and Dolar, *Opera's Second Death*, 6).

72. "Vous verrez de ces moments d'entraînement où, chanteurs et spectateurs, tous s'oublient pour n'être sensibles qu' à la beauté d'un *finale* de Cimarosa. Ce n'est pas assez de donner, à Paris, trente mille francs à Crivelli; il faudrait encore achêter un public fait pour l'entendre et pour nourrir l'amour qu'il a pour son art. . . . Un Italien se livre franchement à la jouissance d'admirer un bel air qu'il entend pour la première fois; un Français n'applaudit qu'avec une sorte d'inquiétude, il craint d'approuver une chose médiocre" (Stendhal, *Vies de Haydn, de Mozart et de Métastase*, 379; for Coe's translation, see Stendhal, *Lives of Haydn, Mozart, and Metastasio*, 242).

Stendhal's gloss gave voice to a standard nationalist distinction, recapitulating the words of critics, theorists, and connoisseurs throughout the eighteenth century. The distinction resonates, for example, with observations by the flutist and theorist Johann Joachim Quantz, teacher of Frederick the Great at Berlin, who in 1752 commended the Italians in composition for originality, independence, vivacity, and expressivity, all at the expense of the French:

> In *composition* the *Italians* are unrestrained, sublime, lively, expressive, profound, and majestic in their manner of thinking; they are rather bizarre, free, daring, bold, extravagant, and sometimes negligent in metrics; they are also singing, flattering, tender, moving, and rich in invention . . . . In *composition* the *French* are indeed lively, expressive, natural, pleasing and comprehensible to the public, and more correct in metrics than the Italians, but they are neither profound nor venturesome. They are very limited and slavish, always imitating themselves, stingy in their manner of thinking, and dry in invention. They always warm up the ideas of their predecessors.[73]

PUBLIC OPINION

Champions at debate, eighteenth-century operagoers squabbled continually over the relative virtues of French versus Italian opera. Italy in particular was a factory of public opinion, utterly distinct from France or elsewhere. Although it was bound by a common literary language and broad cultural identity, it was radically splintered politically. Its cultural and physical geography were uniquely decentralized, and changes in the political landscape of various cities were a relatively common fact of life. Italy never did suffer from any one totalizing revolutionary rupture on anything like the order of France, yet it heaved with smaller ones throughout the century. Consider that in the few decades between 1713 and 1748, northern and southern Italy were redistributed and split as the south came to be dominated by Habsburg rule and the north by a Bourbon bloc. The Italian states were long since used to being territorialized by foreign conquerors, but the extent of Habsburg domination in the north and Bourbon domination in the south brought with it tectonic shifts of social organization. Too, while Italy had for some centuries been the single most ur-

73. "Die Italiäner sind in der Composition uneingeschränket, prächtig, lebhaft, ausdrückend, tiefsinnig, erhaben in der Denkart, etwas bizarr, frey, verwegen, frech, ausschweisend, im Metrum zuweilen nachläßig; sie sind aber auch singend, schmeichelnd, zärtlich, rührend, und reich an Erfindung. . . . Die Franzosen sind in der Composition zwar lebhaft, ausdrückend, natürlich, dem Publikum gefällig und begreiflich, und richtiger im Metrum, als jene; sie sind aber weder tiefsinnig noch kühn; sondern sehr eingeschränket, sklavisch, sich selbst immer ähnlich, niedrig in der Denkart, trocken an Erfindung; sie wärmen die Gedanken ihrer Vorfahren immer wieder auf" (*Versuch einer Flötetraversiere zu spielen*, chap. 18, §76, p. 323, translation adapted from Quantz, *On Playing the Flute*).

banized region in all of early modern Europe, now the balance between urban social populations was quickly changing as rural dwellers came crushing into cities, sometimes by tens of thousands. With manufacturing on the wane and service industries on a steep rise, all manner of social forms that had depended on the feudal structures of the countryside were being reorganized through new urban institutions and rituals.

It should come as no surprise, then, that the Italian public sphere differed significantly from the one famously described by Jürgen Habermas.[74] Most pointedly, with the mid-eighteenth-century advent of newspapers, variety magazines, literary periodicals, and various new oral forums, Italian publics were processing knowledge and experience on a large scale in numerous different city-states and at unprecedented speed, extending traditions that had deep roots in Italian soil.[75] From at least the mid-seventeenth century, Italy's many cities had formed veritable citadels of public opinion about matters ranging from politics and family to arts and music. Cities and city spaces were places to argue, judge, and pronounce.[76] In the eyes of many, public opinion was a hedge against outright tyranny by the country's many foreign rulers. Moreover, because there were so many schools, salons, academies, and bookshops, Italy's reading publics were, and had long been, considerable. The Arcadian Academy alone, which tried to codify opera seria starting in 1690, had major branches in Rome and Venice. By 1710 it counted 1,163 members, half of them laymen, and 2,619 members by 1723, with outcroppings spread all throughout the peninsula. Eventually, from the 1760s onward, there were also numerous coffee shops that hosted legions of intellectuals.

Italy's roaring public sphere made it an utterly operatic place—not just a place that had birthed opera and loved it like a child but one where opera and its personnel could reseed themselves almost without end and where public opinion was continually vented. After the opening of the first public opera house in Venice in 1637, opera shortly began to undergo an enormous boom. Already around 1700 over forty Italian towns had public opera houses (mostly of the tiered sort). By the mid-1780s the number of towns and cities with opera houses was nearly one hundred, and by 1823 about two hundred.[77] Historians

74. Habermas, *Structural Transformation of the Public Sphere.*

75. See Dooley, *Science, Politics, and Society,* and "The Public Sphere," 209–28, esp. 214 and 220–27; Dooley and Baron, *The Politics of Information;* and Pasta, "The History of the Book," 200–17.

76. I avoid "despot/ism" here in favor of "absolutism" and its variants. On the former, see Venturi, "Contributi ad un dizionario storico," 119–28, translated without notes as "Toward an Historical Dictionary," in *Italy and the Enlightenment,* 33–62, esp. 41–47. Roberts, "Enlightened Despotisms," 25–44, explains diverse Italian polities through the lens of "enlightened despotism," with examples related to "sovereignty" (esp. 26–29), but whereas his approach reproduces the jargon of historians, Venturi's historicizes the terms.

77. For early public opera, see Rosand, *Opera in Seventeenth Century Venice.* An incisive account of the entire period appears in Bianconi, *Il teatro d'opera,* esp. chap. 1 and table 1 on p. 13, related to Bianconi, "Italy," tables 1 and 2, in *Grove Music Online.*

nowadays may still largely ignore the opera house, but no cultural institution indexed public sentiment more widely or vividly.

To the extent that opera seria thrived in a wild diversity of polities and arrangements of ownership, financing, and management—parallel to Italy's larger diversity of absolutist forms of governance—and was continually pumping a vast diaspora of performers, composers, and institutions into Europe, my geographic purview is somewhat wider than Italy, but overwhelmingly the main data are drawn from Italian cities.[78] "Absolutist" here refers above all to the idioms and narratives of rule borrowed from Louis XIV and his imitators. Effectively all of the polities in eighteenth-century Italy were marked by those idioms, even the republics.[79]

Notwithstanding continuities in the sociopolitical premises that marked the Italian peninsula over the course of the eighteenth century, there were also striking shifts: from governance by sovereigns and sovereign groups little questioned by everyday subjects to governance in a climate that often doubted the legitimacy of sovereign rule; from forms of social organization purportedly ordained by God to ones that challenged the divine rank and file; from festive rituals that littered the yearly calendar to festivities that were fewer and sobered by new, French-influenced notions about the virtues of labor and the rights and duties of sovereign citizens, and attended by new ideas of natural law and individual equality; and from a collection of city-states dominated by the church to a place that pried itself apart from the church bit by bit by removing many of its landed estates and tax privileges. Like France, but much less dramatically, Italy in the end saw the ideological machine of patriarchal state monarchies challenged by new tests of truth, increasing insistence on moral rectitude, new paradigms of personal feeling, and new family mores. And so did its operas.

EVOLUTIONS

An important claim of this book is that communicative action was the essence of Italian theater and its relationship with the outside world. Without such a

78. Hence the stunningly beautiful opera seria by Handel, much written about, falls outside the purview of this book because it was all produced in London and had little circulation in Italy or even elsewhere.

79. See Marino, *Early Modern Italy;* Symcox, *Victor Amadeus II;* and the indispensable writings on intellectual and political history of Venturi, esp. *Italy and the Enlightenment;* the five-volume *Settecento riformatore* (vol. 3 translated as as *The End of the Old Regime in Europe, 1766–1776,* and vol. 4 as *The End of the Old Regime in Europe, 1776–1789*); *Utopia and Reform;* and *Illuministi italiani,* coedited with Giarrizzo and Torcellan. On how "absolutist Italy" accords with Europe at large, see also Anderson, *Lineages of the Absolutist State;* Doyle, *The Old European Order;* and Mandrou, *L'Europe "absolutiste."* Beyond France and Italy absolutist idioms proliferated in Habsburg Spain and Austria, Frederick the Great's Prussia, Catherine the Great's Russia, and most other European rulerships, east and west, all predicated on some feudal structure, often (but not always) in a state of decline or obsolescence. On problems of usage, see Bonney, "Absolutism," 93–117.

view, opera seria has struck many latter-day observers as fundamentally opaque. Indeed, in older Anglo-Saxon histories, which contributed much in the way of documentary data, source studies, and compositional histories, its alterity looms like the elephant in a room. Using modern criteria that value linear musical drama motivated by a synthesis of feeling and action, critics tended to dismiss opera seria as failed drama. Others scrambled to rehabilitate it by forgiving its dramatic peccadillos as socially unavoidable in their time,[80] invoking a drama-versus-spectacle argument reminiscent of the Arcadian Academy and Jacopo Martello's *Della tragedia antica e moderna* (Rome, 1715), which had long since implied that opera seria was a kind of ungainly variety show.[81]

Here I try to understand those spectacular elements, inseparable from the characteristic forms of attention and inattention that mark the institution, as part of a ritual process. But I also conceive that process in relation to structures of feeling, practices of festivity, and their place in a wider political world vested in myth. Doing so has posed a considerable formal challenge to this book as I have wrestled with how to illuminate the dynamic inner workings of the institution and its world while stepping back far enough to visualize a larger landscape.

The solution I offer tries to balance the close ethnography of the hedgehog with the comparatism of the fox, oscillating between individual case studies of events—bounded temporally as operatic evenings, openings, or seasons—and programmatic essays on broader issues. The first of the case studies (chap. 3) shows how in 1759 the Francophilic Spanish Bourbons of Parma utilized a series of official edicts to gain dominion over their subjects' listening experience, controlling modes of production and dramaturgy along reformist lines but ironically securing opera as an absolutist tool in the process. The result was the significant, if tentative, reform project, Carlo Frugoni and Tommaso Traetta's *Ippolito ed Aricia.* The second case study (chap. 5) explores how the Bourbon kingship of Naples—archetype of absolutist sovereignty in Italy for much of the eighteenth century—managed a crisis of famine when rioting and looting broke out around the royal theater in 1764. It asks how events in and around the San Carlo upset claims of royal munificence that were narrativized in the opera house and enacted symbolically in related Carnival rituals immediately outside it; and it contemplates disruptions in the power claims of opera seria that threatened when popular pleas for salvation subsequently forced the upper classes to renounce opera during Carnival. The third case study (chap. 7) shows how a large group of middle-class men in the papal state of Perugia as-

80. One can count in the first category Dent, *Mozart's Operas;* Kerman, *Opera as Drama;* and Freeman, *Opera without Drama;* in the second, Strohm, *Dramma per musica,* whose view is highly sympathetic and informed by an extraordinary knowledge of the institution and musical exemplars, especially from the early layer of the genre. For a good counterbalance, albeit focused on the late 1700s and beyond, see Chegai, *L'esilio di Metastasio,* chap. 1, who glosses my work in calling the genre a "drammaturgia dello spettacolo" (p. 34 and chap. 1, n. 117).

81. See Weiss, "Pier Jacopo Martello on Opera," 378–403; Durante, "Vizi private e virtù pubbliche"; Freeman, *Opera without Drama,* 35–51; Binni, *L'Arcadia e il Metastasio.*

serted the sovereignty of their rank in fall 1781 by opening their own theater to emulate that of the nobles, thus co-opting the symbolic prerogatives of the aristocracy while trumping them in size and grandeur. Finally, the fourth case study (chap. 9) traces the fate of opera seria in 1797 as the institution was appropriated and reworked in Venice in the days following the fall of the five-hundred-year-old oligarchy.

Although these studies are arranged chronologically, they in no way trace a history of opera seria, much less its artistic high points. Nor do they deal with very apposite issues surrounding opera buffa and very little with ballets, issues I hope others will take up in relation to various questions raised in this book. Rather, the operas I discuss, as often conservative as progressive, function as a particularly revealing set of sites that put pressure on the underlying premises of absolutist politics—premises of princely beneficence, heroic virtue, social hierarchy, class status, and passion as political and moral cure. They also explore those pressures through a range of theatrical and paratheatrical media that go beyond words and sounds, from lighting, masking, dancing, pantomiming, and costuming to managing, financing, building, decorating, contracting, propagandizing, judging, satirizing. Far from proving that opera seria was a mirror of particular political situations, they show that in the politically heterogeneous landscape of Italy, opera seria was a floating signifier. Only sometimes was it enlisted to project local political forms or events (republicanism at Rome or Venice; wedding operas with added *licenze*). At least as often, places drew their own meanings from the highly generalizable signs that were the institution's stock-in-trade. It is difficult to imagine how such a prolific institution could have functioned otherwise on a peninsula where idioms of government and idioms of reform were so varied.[82]

Working inductively, each case study leads into chapters that explore thematically wider aspects of opera's changing relationship to notions of sovereignty. Chapter 2 reexamines the aria in its archetypal form from about the 1720s up through the 1770s as a dynamic vehicle of rhetorical exchange. Chapter 4, following on the study of Parma, shows how Carnival festivities, analyzed through government edicts, travelers accounts, satires, broadsides, archival documents, and periodicals, encompassed the equivocal ways that cities under absolutist governments orchestrated the practices of theatergoing and masking, how theatergoing articulated festive time, and how festivities were gradually attenuated by both state controls and bourgeois ideologies. From the cataclysmic events at Naples in 1764, chapter 6 takes up the tales of enlightened monarchy produced in the archetypal opera seria narratives—indebted to the French classical dramas of Corneille and Racine and epitomized by the leading librettist of dramma per musica Pietro Metastasio—to show how they functioned as myths. Characteristic of myths, it argues, they were not merely idealized portraits of absolutist sovereigns and subjects, as often claimed, but telling avowals of its fragil-

82. Symcox, "The Political World of the Absolutist State," 199ff.

ity; not just stable or transparent messages, but also tales of insoluble paradox, susceptible to continual contemplation and reinterpretation. Chapter 8 goes on to show that the inherently contradictory nature of the absolutist myth is consistent with the hybrid nature of opera seria, an institution that was at once monarchical and bourgeois and that increasingly gave the lie to the shaky status of the patriarchal order. Long seen as the symbolic father, the monarch had come to represent a highly ambivalent figure. By slow, subtle, but sure degrees, his absolutist regime was displaced ideologically by the regime of the "natural" and allegedly sovereign "subject," who resides in the sensible spectator, a real person by turns touched, tearful, or horror-struck. Socially the subject/spectator came to dwell most especially in the regime of the conjugal family, which began to replace the patriarchal (and virtually motherless) family onstage, and late in the century even to replace the radically patriotic character who found himself at odds with a traitorous foe or a tyrannical ruler.

Over the course of this historical juncture, running roughly through the latter half of the eighteenth century, "sovereignty" points in different ways: initially toward the monarch who reigns supreme among all his subjects, or at least toward the ruling class that occupies his structural place, but increasingly toward self-determining groups and their ideals, or the ideals of the citizen who is no longer subject but sovereign himself. The evolution is never total. Yet opera seria figures all of these motions and helps give them expression.

CRISIS AND INVOLUTION

It should come as no surprise that opera seria was rarely a complete success either as the expression of myth or as a communicative act. Least of all was this so later in the century when confidence in the old regime was at a low ebb throughout much of Europe. Sovereign regimes had long since become hybridized with state bureaucratic machinery, all the more so by the late eighteenth century, and ideas about sovereignty were under pressure. As the status of the old order came into question, so did the experiences, beliefs, and sentiments it perpetuated, which fell into a growing state of disunity and ambivalence. For opera seria, the result was a fraught relationship between the function of the story and the mode of its telling—between a mythical function and the ritual recitation that gave it magical force. The mythical function depended on a mystified view of the world order narrated in the story, while what I have called here the "ritual recitation" (the reiteration of plots and arias, but also the repetitive rhythm of scenes and scenic liaisons) made recourse to a segmentary and hence inherently nonnarrative mode of delivery, compatible with the genre's overall stylization and lack of realism.

That nonnarrative means of delivery was what the brilliant Milanese intellectual and sensist Pietro Verri described on August 19, 1778, as "spectacle," drawing much the same distinction between spectacle and drama that I have signaled above. Specifically, Verri argued that because Italian audiences went to their operas in enormous halls, night after night, it was

> necessary that the spectacle divert, like a musical concert, interrupted by some lovely pantomime and, disregarding the dramatic side, intersperse within that sterile representation a lovely scene, a superbly performed aria, a beautiful duet, an interesting ballet; in short, to have it go on, it is necessary to proceed along the hitherto beaten track, a detestable thing compared with the dramatic art, but the only way to suit a very large gathering, which forms as many conversational groups as there are boxes and seeks to pass the evening with novels or gambling, enjoying the interruption of these with a brief and restricted attention to some musical piece that interests it. A fine singer brings some novelty to his aria every evening. In my opinion, northerners are wrong to criticize our opera with the laws of the theater. The theater can never be too large a hall; ours are spectacle of another sort.[83]

Verri's was a theater of attractions, a curiosity cabinet filled with novelties, from pantomimes and ballets to astonishing vocal decorations to combats, sieges, cavalry, chariots, and grand princely rites.[84] The articulation of the whole was sectional rather than smooth, paratactic rather than syntagmatic. Verri's incisiveness in differentiating Italian spectacle from drama is unique among *eruditi* of the time mainly in its tolerance. By 1778, there had been a number of experiments in a more Gluckian or otherwise "dramatic" form of opera, and every erudite cosmopolitan in Italy and northern Europe could cite the efficacy of more rational principles of theater of the kind argued by Algarotti and Calzabigi in Italy and Diderot and Marmontel in France.

To this extent Verri's comment underscores aspects of Italian opera seria that stand outside a modern theatrical practice. Only one commercial theater of the mid-settecento even tried to make a substantial incursion on that practice, namely, the Ducal Theater at Parma. Otherwise the fixity and variability theorized by Tambiah—here, roughly written text and performative power—formed twin members of a covalent bond that endured substantially on the peninsula until reform experiments were ventured in the 1760s.

By later decades of the century, opera seria had changed considerably. Re-

83. Verri and Verri, *Carteggio* 10:54–55; translation from Hansell, "Opera and Ballet" 1:27–28.

84. Here I gloss Gunning's "The Cinema of Attractions," 56–62. Strohm's take is intriguing: "The *dramma per musica* survived by transforming itself beyond recognition: the tightrope-walk between anti-naturalist artificiality and idealist simplicity had been successful. The elasticity of the genre was its lifeline; had it conformed to a rigid formula such as the separation of drama and music (claimed by Freeman), it would have ended with Mozart, of course. But it seems that the *dramma per musica* reached the nineteenth century because it had always been a reform genre striving for an ever-increasing identification of music and drama. Admittedly, its fate was also linked to the social framework of a retrospective court culture, and for that reason opera seria in the narrow sense of the word was, after about 1789, gradually pushed back by bourgeois realities. But opera seria in the wider sense of the word did survive, perhaps even into the age of Hollywood cinema" (*Dramma per musica*, 29).

forms began to displace the spectacular nature of the genre's formal frames by pulling its set numbers into a more continuous, quasi-narrative flow through less sectional arias and more obbligato recitatives, in time through ensembles and scenic tableaux, and ultimately through the radical reduction or elimination of the exit aria.[85] As formal continuities began to break through the old closed number, attempts were made to smooth out representational incongruities. Many stage designs began to lose their purely referential function in favor of an illusionistic stage, founded in ideals of verisimilitude and naturalism; stylized acting was gradually superseded by more naturalistic acting; side spaces and backdrops were increasingly activated by staging and lighting effects; and costumes and props began to call up purportedly more authentic worlds.[86] Over many years, the net force of such changes undoubtedly worked against audiences' demonstrative interactions with onstage action, even in Italy. At the same time, in late-eighteenth-century Italy, representations of sovereigns became more ambivalent. Many sovereigns who had renounced their tyrannical ways onstage in earlier decades became irredeemable by the 1790s, and some were brutally killed off. The music and dramaturgy of opera seria in its earlier forms became a less reliable medium of collective renewal, and the magical ritual of the *lieto fine* was abolished along with the magic of sovereign invincibility.

This is not to say that collective catharsis was no longer to be had, but that the requirements necessary to achieve it were changing along with changes in the wider world. In the 1780s, sentimentality was more likely to achieve collective catharsis than virtuosity and pomp. The pathetic, always central to opera seria, was now advocated in place of virtuosity, and in simpler musical forms. Meanwhile, the greater attentiveness demanded of viewers and the pervasiveness of dramaturgical forms that worked to inhibit their demonstrations was encroaching on the carnivalesque. In the great metropoles, even the more conservative ones, modern modes of viewing and listening could no longer be ignored.

85. See especially the following works by McClymonds: "The Role of Innovation and Reform," 281–300; "Transforming Opera Seria," 119–32; "La clemenza di Tito," 766–72; "The Evolution of Jommelli's Operatic Style," 326–55.

86. Praise of acting, such as Quantz's of Faustina Bordoni (quoted in Dean, "Bordoni"), was not as common before about 1760 as afterward, but neither was it unheard of. By 1773 the kind of scorn Leopold Mozart showed for the acting of an inexperienced tenor given the title role of *Lucio Silla* at the last minute had become common. On acting in opera seria generally, see Hansell, "Stage Deportment," 415–24; and Robinson, *Naples and Neapolitan Opera*, 60–63.

CHAPTER 2

Arias: Form, Feeling, Exchange

"The singers you find mediocre will be electrified here [in Italy] by a sensitive audience capable of real enthusiasm; the flame shoots back and forth from audience to stage, from stage to audience." STENDHAL, *Lives of Haydn, Mozart, and Metastasio*, 1814[1]

"Ladies and Gentlemen, what you are about to witness is America's finest form of live entertainment. Unlike TV and movies, our performers can hear your applause. So if you see something you like, put your hands together and let them hear how much you appreciate what they're doing. And they'll work that much harder just for you." KELLY RAWLS, ringmaster, Kelly Miller Circus, Warren, Pennsylvania, July 4, 2003

A common truism in music histories holds that the art music of nineteenth-century Europe tried to escape convention while that of the eighteenth century was beset by it.[2] Yet conventions in opera seria not only made possible the continual production of new operas, they also helped shape interaction rituals between performers and listeners, and in ways that transcended the form and letter of the scripted note.[3] When reimagined this way, eighteenth-century arias, with the stock formal plans and tonal strategies that we know from surviving scores, must be radically rethought. Conceived as templates for interaction rituals, scores will no longer be static textual artifacts but artifactual traces of dynamic phenomena in lived time. They will be intention-laden objects, events in potentia (and not only performing scores). Nor will scores transmit "merely" conventional evidence (read repetitive, predictable) as older histories often had it, but rather evidence that can be taken to point from the artifact to the phenomenon. While the phenomenon was without a doubt convention-bound, it also rested crucially on tensions between the expected and the unexpected, the invariant and the variant, indeed thrived on them. Whether or not the "unex-

1. "[L]es chanteurs que vous trouvez médiocres ici seront életrisés par un public sensible et capable d'enthousiasme; et le feu circulant du théâtre aux loges, et des loges au théâtre" (Stendhal, *Vies de Haydn, de Mozart et de Métastase*, 378–79).

2. Among attempts to look critically at questions of convention are Allanbrook, Levy, and Mahrt, *Convention in Eighteenth- and Nineteenth-century Music*, and McClary, *Conventional Wisdom*.

3. Some recent musical studies theorize genre in relation to convention and audience, e.g., Wheelock, *Haydn's "Ingenious Jesting with Art"*; Kallberg, *Chopin at the Boundaries;* Castelvecchi, "Sentimental Opera"; Head, "Like Beauty Spots on the Face of a Man."

pected" in a given instance was spontaneous or calculated, more or less conventional, arias in such an optic will start to betray a less static and orthodox set of historical realities than the written surface of scores might suggest. Furthermore, those realities will be less saddled with compositional stereotypes than generally imagined, moving beyond the sheer distinction of written versus sounded notes in a performance to include what is mutually produced by performers and spectators: the flame that shoots back and forth, the grain of the singer's voice, the urging of the fans (or their ignoring or disdaining), the circulation of nervous impulses.[4]

This chapter draws on evidence from travelers' anecdotes, letters, diaries, teaching manuals, treatises, and scores to argue that the execution of arias, and the experiences audiences had of them, especially though not only in Italy, both motivated and relied on these realities. The keenest of such accounts were left by teachers, singers, composers, and other well-trained musicians. In general they confirm that different performances of a given aria, whether by the same singer or different ones, could vary substantially from one occasion to another. Most obvious, of course, and sanctioned through convention, were the ornaments and cadenzas applied to arias, sometimes improvised, sometimes not (though expected to sound improvised). In 1774 and again in 1777, the singing teacher Mancini still advocated extemporized embellishments as an ideal, as did Johann Adam Hiller in 1780, in chapter 8 of his *Anweisung zum musikalischer-zierlichen Gesange* (*Treatise on Vocal Performance and Ornamentation*).[5] The fact that Italian arias (unlike French ones) commonly duplicated the melodies of singers with accompanying violins—whether to underscore the voice, support intonation, or facilitate learning new arias[6]—might mean that singers rarely altered structural pitches. But as Quantz commented in his *Versuch einer Flötetraversiere zu spie-*

4. Variant elements are not necessarily coextensive with spontaneous, improvised, or unconventional ones. All such categories require their own conceptual apparatus. "Improvisation," in particular, typically refers to a practice that is more oriented to performance than text, but relies on convention as much as, if differently than, textually oriented traditions do. "Improvisation" also signals a style in which only the performer, a fellow performer, or repeat listener can know what is actually changed in performance. Whatever the case, there is nothing inherently unexpected about the content of improvisation; rather, a strongly improvisatory approach leaves itself open to the unexpected, and in some traditions (e.g., bebop) the radically unexpected.

5. Mancini, *Pensieri, e riflessioni pratiche* (1774), 123ff.; *Riflessioni pratiche* (1777), 179ff., art. 11, "Delle cadenze." The latter edition is much revised, acknowledging indirectly then ongoing debates about whether cadenzas had become overly ostentatious and how they were managed by singers (whether by advance preparation or spontaneous invention and what the role of the cadences); but it retains the assertion that the cadence requires an "inventive mind." Glossed in the 1777 edition, this reads: "[E] questi sono quei tratti dell'estro inaspettati ed improvvisi, parti della mente creatrice, che fanno in un punto distinguer l'uomo, o portarlo coll'evviva alle stelle." Hiller's treatise has been translated by Suzanne Beicken as *Treatise on Vocal Performance and Ornamentation*.

6. For a different explanation, however, see Freeman, "Farinello," esp. 314 n. 45. On learning methods and schedules see John Rosselli, *Singers of Italian Opera*, chap. 5, and Durante, "The Opera Singer."

len (Study of Playing the Transverse Flute) of 1752, Italian works (again, unlike French) gave performers much discretion. Singers of Italian music had to know rules of harmony, basso continuo, and composition because passages were often written very simply (for example, vocal lines as "canto spianato") to allow changes according to singers' capabilities and judgment and in order to surprise listeners.[7] Multiple sources for a given aria do show variants, even at times in structural pitches, while other phenomena subject to variation were less tangible in performance—phrasing, passion, and articulation, not to mention numerous aspects of breathing and vocal emission: chest versus head, covering breaks, *messe di voce,* sharp versus slow inhale or exhale of breath, placement relative to palate, teeth, and so on. Minimally held notes were decorated in reprises, especially in arias or sections in pathetic or cantabile styles, both of which were on the slow side and used portamento singing much graced with gruppetti, acciacciature, appoggiature, and little runs between notes.[8] Therefore, when Mozart embellished Italian arias (his own or others') with written-out divisions, he was supplying solutions to singers who were not ready to write or improvise their own, and he did alter pitches.[9] Between circa 1780 and 1810, Domenico Corri published volumes of instruction for singers on embellishing songs and arias, anthologizing numerous arias with written-out divisions and graces by way of example.[10] Frederick the Great's favorite prima donna, Madame Mara, in encoring Handel's "Consider Fond Shepherd" for soprano and oboe obbligato (English but in Italian style) from *Acis and Galatea,* sang seemingly prepared embellishments while her oboist had to invent new passaggi on the spot to match hers, akin to trading in jazz but with the singer taking a decisive lead. As John Spitzer stresses, the embellishments she varied were themselves already written out, and the ones she "extemporized" must have been written out too, or else memorized aurally, to judge from her confession about how she bested her rival Brigida Banti in a bravura aria from Gazzaniga's *Gli argonauti* (Venice, 1790).[11]

7. Quantz, *Versuch einer Flötetraversiere zu spielen,* chap. 10, §13. Candida Felici treats oral-to-written transmission of eighteenth-century ornamentation in "Dall'oralità alla scrittura," 369–97, albeit largely on instrumental music, because, as she notes (387), vocal music left so much freedom to performers and thus few written examples of how arias were actually sung.

8. See Crutchfield, "Voices," 301–10. On possible improvisation of simple recitatives, see my discussion above (chap. 1, n. 24) and Strohm, *Dramma per musica,* 10. Some did take simple recitative quite seriously, e.g., Anton Raaff, as his student Ignazio Wierl wrote to Padre Martini: "Egli favorisce di darmi scuola ogni matina con sommo mio piacere, mi fa studiar a pronuntiar ben i recitativi con una infinita patienza" (letter from Naples, May 13, 1766, in I-Bc, I.1.166 = Schnoebelen, *Padre Martini's Letters,* no. 5636).

9. Mozart's letter of February 14 and Leopold's answer of February 25/26, 1778 (Mozart, *Briefe* 1:280–82, 298–303; Anderson, *Letters of Mozart,* 482, 494); cf. Crutchfield, "Voices," 305 (point 7).

10. See especially Corri's extended embellishments for Paisiello's "Ah, che nel petto io sento," published in Corri's *A Select Collection of the Most Admired Songs* 4: 36–38, facsimile in *Domenico Corri's Treatises,* vol. 3.

11. Spitzer, "Improvized Ornamentation," 514–22. Quantz recommended such matched embellishments in his *Versuch einer Flötetraversiere zu spielen,* chap. 16, §30. For Mara's confession, see Riesemann, "Ein Selbstbiographie der Gertrud Mara," cols. 11–12.

"Variant" possibilities were thus highly divergent as to type, but variability of some definite kind was the norm throughout the century.

Less obvious is a point I argue below: namely, that the formal process of the standard da capo aria and its variants thrived on stage because it furnished a "script" for performative exchange that optimized the physical, pragmatic, and experiential conditions of the opera house.[12] Embellishments aside, the aria was far from a pure transitive phenomenon, much less an autonomous one. Rather it was a reciprocal exchange that utilized a variety of formal cues, playing on the expectations of listeners. In opera seria, arias manipulated responses through musical stimuli to the nervous energy of the crowd as they attempted to draw out its collective emotions by maximizing the ineffable power of song, especially (though by no means only) in arias for lead singers. Exchange was foundational to the entire syntax and style of the da capo aria, which in turn underpinned, and to a lesser extent drew on, the rhetorical language of many other eighteenth-century genres. And it remained foundational even as formal norms of arias gave way to less sectionalized types: the dal segno aria in the 1760s, the sonata-like aria around 1770, and increasingly thereafter to various binary forms, cavatinas, two-tempo arias, and rondòs, often preceded by obbligato recitative.[13]

It was precisely the conventional nature of opera seria arias that made it possible to vary performances of the same numbers night after night, animating listeners in the opera house and transforming the identity of arias as sounding objects. My claim is not just that opera seria arias played on conventions that enabled exchange, but that the very possibility of exchange depended on a strong use of convention.

Moreover, in its classic form, the dramaturgical rhythm of an entire opera seria was plotted to capitalize on arias. In most scenes recitative spilled into lyrical song, or a succession of several scenes in recitative culminated in one of recitative → aria. Much as ballets (discontinuous from the opera) could excite spectators' visual sense, arias (discontinuous from the recitative) were what excited

12. I use the term "script" by analogy to film scripts or scripts of spoken plays. Both prescribe far less than a typical common-practice musical score: words, some blocking and other stage directions or filmic effects, but not the whole range of actions and nuances. In general, to approximate norms of art music scores—even eighteenth-century not to mention later ones—scripts would have to notate the twitch of every eyebrow or tightening of shoulders, thus rendering them virtually unusable.

13. Especially important was of course the relationship of the aria to the concerto, as noted by, for example, Scheibe, *Critischer Musikus*, 631–32, and Koch, *Versuch einer Einleitung zur Composition*, esp. vol. 3, part 3, §156–58 (in English as *Introductory Essay on Composition*, 244–48). Koch's *Musikalisches Lexikon* called the concerto "an imitation of the solo song with full accompaniment, or in other words, an imitation of the aria" (col. 351). [So wie die Instrumentalmusik überhaupt Nachahmung des Gesanges ist, so ist insbesondere das Concert eine Nachahmung des Sologesanges mit vollstimmiger Begleitung, oder mit andern Worten, eine Nachahmung der Arie.] Among modern writings see in particular Tovey, *Concertos*, 6–14 and 176; Strohm, "Merkmale italienischer Versvertonung," 219–36; Flothuis, "Bühne und Konzert," 45–58; and Feldman, "Staging the Virtuoso," 149–86 (= "Il virtuoso in scena," 255–98), and the literature cited therein.

spectators' sense of hearing.[14] De Brosses wrote that that Italian recitative was monotonous but allowed him to play an uninterrupted game of chess in his box, which arias made it harder to do. At another order of disjunction, he praised the ballets as welcome diversions from the opera.[15] There are some few accounts of recitatives, even simple ones, moving audiences too. In 1754, the violin virtuoso Giuseppe Tartini probably was thinking of recitative when he recounted a series of performances in Ancona from forty years before that had "stirred such intense feeling, both in us orchestra players and in the listeners" at the beginning of act 3 "that we all watched each other's faces to observe the change of color it caused in each of us. The affect was not one of sorrow (I remember very well that the words were angry) but a certain coldblooded grimness which really shook one's feelings."[16] Still, arias, operating at different moments and levels of temporal hierarchy, were the usual highpoints in a spectacle that was parceled into chunks of sensory gratification and segmented by different media, genres, and styles. Before the advent of ensembles, which did not become standard elements until the 1780s, arias were the great thrill for listeners, the glue that bound them to one another and to the stage. Much as they waited for ballets to retire each act, they waited for arias to burst forth from recitative.

Chapter 4 explores how opera seria, as spectacle, was bound up with festive forms of social exchange characteristic of the old order. Here instead we will see that lyrical aspects of opera seria (not just narrative ones) operated on more organic and formally *nonsegmentary* principles too, contrary to common representation. Typically recitatives would move from blank verse in heptasyllables and hendecasyllables to a final rhymed couplet (still in recitative) just prior to the aria, smoothing the transition to the latter's rhymed verse and metered music. Nonsegmentary too was the linkage of scenes in concatenations from one to the next. Over the course of an act, the number of characters onstage would increase or decrease incrementally, as singers exited one by one when their arias ended and were later brought back incrementally through vicissitudes of the plot. A Metastasian opera would often bring the full or nearly full cast onto the stage midway through each of the first two acts, and shrink them down to a sin-

14. Like many French and other viewers, Montesquieu claimed that the dances were terrible but the audiences entranced with them (*Voyages*, 70). Until about 1760, ballets were often internally discontinuous too, formed from court dances comprising entr'actes (Hansell, "Theatrical Ballet," 198–203).

15. De Brosses, *Lettres familières* 2:337–38 and 360.

16. Tartini, *Tratado di musica*, 135 (translated and discussed in Downes, "*Secco* Recitative in Early Classical Opera Seria," 53). Algarotti quoted Tartini, claiming the opera was by Gasparini and sung by the castrato Senesino's brother, also called Senesino (see Petrobelli, *Giuseppe Tartini*, 55–56 n. 3.) On relevant issues and sources, see Cyr, "Declamation and Expressive Singing," 233–34, which cites d'Alembert, Tosi, Rousseau, and others as praising the possibilities of unaccompanied recitative, contra many others who inveighed against it. Bergeret de Grancourt said in 1774 that audiences did not listen to it, but were silent when a beautiful aria started, though they could lose half the aria with frenzied applause. See Fubini, "L'orecchio del viaggiatore," 79–87.

gle character by the time each of the first two acts ended. The third act—usually shorter than the previous two, and increasingly so as the century progressed—would repeat half of this process, swelling to the full cast at the opera's end. The result was a series of stage pictures, shifting in density by graduated degrees before peaking at resolution.[17]

The structural crescendos formed by these scenic liaisons had their counterpart—less obvious but nonetheless striking—in the aria performances idealized by pedagogues and critics. By convention, singers were expected to make each of an aria's parts increasingly ornate. The phenomenon is generally tacit in earlier eighteenth-century scores, but singing teachers made a point of it in their manuals. The most famous teacher from the early part of the century, Pierfrancesco Tosi, in his *Opinioni de' cantori antichi e moderni* of 1723, criticized those singers in his day who overdid the practice by making three final cadenzas, each elaborately ornamented.[18] Tosi was master in a hierarchical relationship with his pupils and, in urging modern notions of good taste, wanted them and other singers to stop showing off. But as musical scores became more and more ornate in the middle of the century and on into the 1770s, this tendency to thicken the surface of vocal melodies over the course of arias was prescribed. At text repetitions, composers themselves often fleshed out the vocal lines of the initial stanza and, increasingly by the 1760s or 1770s, wrote out varied repeats—particularly once the da capo aria yielded to the shortened form of the dal segno aria: hence A, B, A′, or A, A′, B, A″, A‴, with A indicating the first stanza, B the second, and prime signs indicating varied repeats, typically with increased levels of decoration.[19] The vocal repetitions of the first stanza in the entrance

17. Examples among many include Metastasio's *Attilio Regolo, Artaserse,* and *Demetrio.* On this dramaturgy see Heartz, "The Poet as Stage Director," 89–105, esp. table 6, 92–93.

18. Tosi, *Opinioni de' cantori,* 101. Johann Friedrich Agricola published a German paraphrase of Tosi in 1757 with updatings and revisions, but nevertheless repeated this point (*Anleitung zur Singkunst;* translated as *Introduction to the Art of Singing,* 205).

19. Reinhard Strohm notes that, at least in the earlier period he considers, the first poetic unit was understood through long-standing poetic tradition as a refrain and only the second unit as a stanza (*Italienische Opernarien* 1:111–18). Elsewhere, Strohm summarizes the da capo as "a poetic refrain form . . . derived from the traditional *canzonetta* and [consisting] of a single stanza (middle section) and a refrain (*intercalare,* da capo section) sung before and after" (*Dramma per musica,* 14). Here I use the term "stanza" exclusively for both poetic units because the second half century on which I focus saw an attenuated relationship to the earlier refrain structure. On the later musico-poetic history of the da capo, Strohm notes that despite midcentury criticisms circa 1740–60, often inspired by naturalism or verisimilitude, the da capo repetition nevertheless "remained in use for longer than the musical da capo form itself, until c. 1780, when modified or climactic musical repetitions had become the norm" (ibid.). In later arias, dal segnos might or might not use written-out repeats, but increasingly they did, and the "segno" could appear almost anywhere in the A section (e.g., after the opening ritornello, at the middle ritornello in the secondary key, or at the last iteration of the first stanza). See summaries in McClymonds, "Aria." See too Rosen, *Sonata Forms,* 71 and passim; and Brown, "Music, Poetry, and Drama," 263–88. McClymonds, *Niccolò Jommelli,* 229–39 and passim, gives similar examples.

aria "Il tenero momento" from Mozart's *Lucio Silla* of 1772, discussed below at example 2.4, is a case in point.

Singing teachers universally approved such filling out of surfaces in the repeat of A; it was the degree and kind of density and who decided on it that was at issue. As arias used progressively longer and more ostentatious fioritura, cadenzas at the endings of A, B, and A′ sections also seem to have grown in size, sometimes with multiple cadenzas in each section, requiring in turn greater and greater flexibility and breath control and aiming to instill greater and greater awe in listeners.[20] Such cadenzas were not for the fainthearted would-be diva, but singers who could carry them off helped mitigate the stop/restart effect caused by the aria's division into formally distinct sections. According to reports and written musical evidence, this increasing floridity was most pronounced in pathetic arias (where it was intended to be expressive) and bravura arias, the two showiest, most keenly anticipated aria types and the ones also reserved for lead singers, whose claims over heightened expressivity and virtuosity were virtually exclusive.[21] Not least, in yet another gesture toward syntagmatic and climactic effects, singers themselves typically upped the ante on ornamentation and cadenzas when called to encore arias.

In addition, as Reinhard Strohm points out, "An ideal place for arias was . . . the moment when one of the dialogue partners [in the recitative] has 'hit the nail on the head,' making further discussion unnecessary" and producing what he calls a "threshold aria."[22] Plentiful in operas, such arias alleviated discontinuities in texture, performing forces, metrical flow, and melodic style by using a narrative and rhetorical pivot to link recitative to aria. This is not the only instance of continuities in content between recitative and aria, the break between which was often less sharp than imagined. Recitative was not solely about action and deliberation but traded in emotion, and a given aria was not restricted to emotion but, as Metastasio explained, could include "caratteri, situazioni, affetti, senso, ragione."[23] The divide between the two lay far more in style and

20. Quantz, who taught flute to Frederick the Great, thought one cadenza enough, and more than one in the A section plus an additional one later an abuse. He was scandalized that singers in his day were inclined to insert five (*Versuch einer Flötetraversiere zu spielen*, chap. 15, art. 5; *On Playing the Flute*, 180–81), though he sanctioned the cadenza over an opening sostenuto, thus implicitly allowing for at least four cadenzas in a binary or rounded binary form. Leopold Mozart simply mentions one cadenza at the end of "a solo" (*Versuch einer gründlichen Violinschule*, chap. 11, §7; translated as *A Treatise on the Fundamental Principles of Violin Playing*, 205). Cf. Brown, "Embellishing Eighteenth-Century Arias," 258–76.

21. See my discussion below on Farinelli's arias. I have argued previously that "if-then" rhetorical structures built into standard seria verse smoothed the segmentary quality of the big da capos and dal segnos by making the second stanza a consequent of the first ("Staging the Virtuoso," 176–78), but of course many aria texts do not use such structures. Often the first stanza is rhetorically self-contained—partly a vestige of the old refrain function (cf. n. 19 above).

22. Strohm, *Dramma per musica*, 13.

23. Quoted in Gallarati, *Musica e maschera*, 60.

delivery than in content, and was further allayed once dramatic, orchestrally accompanied recitative became more plentiful in the 1760s and beyond.[24]

RITORNELLO FORM AS RHETORICAL EXCHANGE

Listeners were drawn to this lyric world not just because it moved them and spotlighted singers in a context where other distractions were legion, but because they had an active role in trading tuttis and solos. To say so is to make a strong claim about both listeners and arias, and I will flesh out its bases as I go. The first of these, formally speaking, is rhetorical, but ultimately pragmatic: in the eyes of eighteenth-century writers, the gestalt of the aria was rhetorical through and through. In fact, many writers—from Johann Mattheson, Johann Adolph Scheibe, Joseph Riepel, Johann Philipp Kirnberger, and Heinrich Christoph Koch in the north to Pierfrancesco Tosi, Giambattista Mancini, and Francesco Galeazzi in the south—conceived the aria as a dynamic form of oratory, articulated in linear time and three-dimensional space and describable through the formal nomenclature of paragraphs, sentences, periods, semicolons, and commas. From composition teachers, theorists, and singing masters, we also read about arias as oratory. Oratory meant idealized affects and gestures, words delivered strategically to a percipient body, an interlocutor or auditor, but in any case an audience with its own space and sensory technology.[25] In this sense, eighteenth-century rhetorical models accommodate the poststructural view of "the work" as the sum total of a text, an enactment, and a reception better than twentieth-century analytic models do,[26] especially when it comes to theatrical song. Such earlier models suggest that arias, generated from the energy of social space, are practically meaningless when studied from scores as if scores were works.

Reenvisaging arias within the sociabilities of the opera house leads to an understanding of aria scores as the phenomenal traces of a hypothetical event. These "traces" are obviously not records of any single, real performance. They are the footprints of performances past, the dust of old intentions. They can tell us how composers helped choreograph singer/listener interactions by imagining them in some future occurrence, and occasionally they may even suggest what actually happened when singers took those choreographies into the footlights.

24. Accompanied recitative, as I discuss below (chap. 7), was a unique dramatic vehicle without equal elsewhere in opera seria. There were early exemplars, perhaps most famously in Dido's final suicide in Metastasio and Vinci's *Didone abbandonata,* written for Maria Bulgarelli Benti in Naples 1724, and imitated in numerous resettings of the scene.

25. For further on the relationship between form and rhetorical gesture in Mozart's arias, see Feldman, "Staging the Virtuoso."

26. See Kapferer, "Performance and the Structuring of Meaning," 188–203; Ricoeur's *Interpretation Theory* and his *Hermeneutics and the Human Sciences,* esp. chaps. 4 and 7; and Roman Ingarden's classic *The Work of Music.*

Table 2.1. Aria plans: (a) five-part da capo aria; (b) dal segno aria; (c) bithematic ternary (or sonata-like) aria

a.											
Form		A1		A2		B		A1		A2	
Section	Introductory ritornello	Solo	Ritornello	Solo	Ritornello	Solo	Introductory ritornello	Solo	Ritornello	Solo	Ritornello
Stanza		1				2		1			
Harmonic plan:											
Major	I	V		I		more remote key(s)	I	V		I	
Minor	i	III		i (placement of return variable)			i	III		i	

b.									
Form		A1		A2		B		A2*	
Section	Introductory ritornello	Solo	Ritornello	Solo	Ritornello	Solo	(Ritornello)	Solo	Ritornello
Stanza		1				2		1	
Harmonic plan:									
Major	I	V		I		more remote key(s)		I	
Minor	i	III		i (placement of return variable)				i (placement of return variable)	

c.												
Form			A				B		A′			
Section	Introductory ritornello		Solo (exposition)			Middle ritornello	Solo (development?)	(Ritornello)	Solo (reprise)			Ritornello
Stanza			1				2		1			
Themes	theme 1	theme 2	theme 1	modulatory theme	theme 2			retransition	theme 1	modulatory theme	theme 2	
Harmonic plan:												
Major	I			V			more remote keys		I			
Minor	i			III					i			

*Placement of dal segno is variable: sometimes the return of A2 is written out in order to allow for variation.

In this sense, eighteenth-century aria scores are more fully "intentional" objects than any genre of nineteenth-century scores. This is particularly evident when we recall that in creating arias, composers and singers worked in the face of constant attempts, by other composers and singers and by disgruntled or distracted audiences, to usurp or undercut them. They were always looking from the edge of imminent failure for a route to triumph.

* * *

For many decades, opera seria arias of the da capo or dal segno type were poured into a fairly set mold. Braced by declarative but tonally static ritornellos, they separated the more finely wrought surface activity and modulations of the soloist from the coarser rhythms and textures of the band, opposing the solidity of many to the dynamism of one.

This division of labor has been pressed by traditional musicology into highly normative, schematic charts, like the one in table 2.1a, which represents a so-called five-part da capo. About 1760, when aria lengths had often grown to outsize proportions, the dal segno aria, with a shortened and sometimes varied return of A (table 2.1b), began to overtake the da capo, and not long afterward arias with a sonata-like plan (nowadays sometimes called ternary arias, compressed da capos, or concerto-like arias), with no internal return to the tonic and main theme until the repetition of the initial stanza, became common (table 2.1.c), though historically there was considerable overlap between the three.[27]

If schemes like these have heuristic value, they nonetheless tend to imply that ritornello arias exist as fixed entities, stubborn in their loyalty to norms and existent outside the presentness of historical time and place, and above all, outside an etiology of performance.[28] They do not contradict notational or tonal-thematic facts in gross formal terms, but emphasize blunt alternations of forces and musical structures rather than exchange in any lived social or bodily sense. As mere normative descriptions, they cannot begin to address how differentiations between orchestral ritornellos and vocal solos made by composers carried sensory cues for listening and responding, and how composers used them to manipulate the involvement of listeners. For this, anecdotal evidence complements scores.

* * *

We can picture an instance of such stimulus-response exchange between music-makers and listeners through a single solo-to-ritornello joint, the passage

27. In 1769, Jommelli was told to make his new arias for *Nitteti* "like those of *Vologeso*, with the sign in the middle of the aria so that they will not become too long" (McClymonds, *Niccolò Jommelli*, 606). For a fuller explanation of these variations, see Feldman "Staging the Virtuoso," esp. 151–59.

28. See Döhring, "Die Arienformen," 66–76; Solie, "Aria Structure," 31–47; Stevens, "The 'Piano Climax,'" 245–76, and "Patterns of Recapitulation," 397–418.

that runs from the end of the first main solo section (A) through the ritornello that follows it. In the expansive da capo or dal segno aria that was typical of the mid-eighteenth century, in which the first stanza gave way to many text repetitions, solo sections usually deferred the most eclipsing moments of vocal display or the most literally breathtaking cantabile until shortly before the return of the orchestra. Attendant on this deferral, especially in the case of bravura or allegro arias, was a typical decrease of orchestral activity and a prolongation of harmonic rhythm (see example 2.3 below, mm. 124–27), which enhanced the tension accompanying the listener's expectation of the final (and most pronounced) tonic cadence. Once a singer had unburdened him- or herself of the final stretch of vocal work—whether winding out a passage of graceful cantilena, pulling off some demanding fioritura, or executing a battery of martellato figures—the orchestra would reenter, landing directly on the singer's cadential downbeat with a straightforward passage on the prevailing tonic, often using one or two motives from the opening ritornello or previous orchestral interjection. The simultaneity of the singer's cadential chord with the orchestra's entrance chord in middle and final ritornellos was crucial to aria rhetoric, as the pivot chord kept motion driving (sometimes hurtling) forward.[29]

The ritornello would then normally progress with relative efficiency. In the case of an important ritornello like the one at the end of the entire A section, a decisive one- to two-measure cadential extension on the tonic chord would provide closure of all statements of the main stanza as the singer waited before returning in the succeeding solo section and second stanza, B. And the same device would again provide closure of a da capo (or modified da capo–type) aria when it ended completely at A′. Whether called "flourishes" (as by Robert D. Levin) or "appendices" (by Karol Berger), these short extensions of the tonic cadence are squarely root-position emphases and are section-ending.[30] By suspending the soloist's work they distinguish the singer's relationship to the orchestra from the orchestra's relationship to the singer: the singer waited imposingly until the air was cleared to begin anew after the orchestral commotion ended, whereas the orchestra adopted the servant role of enhancing the singer's endings by leaping in immediately to add weight and emphasis to what the singer had uttered.

Thus, in addition to grounding the relatively free display of the singer, the ritornello following the first big solo was an invitation, but importantly also an

29. Feil, "Satztechnische Fragen," esp. chap. 6; and Strohm, *Italienische Opernarien* 1:181–221. Hell, *Die neapolitanische Opernsinfonie* remains important on periodic and cadential structures in opera *sinfonie*.

30. For a model incorporating postcadential "flourishes," see Levin, "Das Konzert für Klavier und Violine," 304–26, esp. 310ff; refined in Leeson and Levin, "On the Authenticity of K. Anh. C 14.01 (297b)," 70–96, and Levin, *Who Wrote the Mozart Four-Wind Concertante?* chap. 5. Karol Berger considers "flourishes" under the rubric "appendices," which fall under his broader category of "punctuation form" (following Koch). See Berger, "The First-Movement Punctuation Form," 239–59, and on the distinction, 244–46; see too Broyles, "The Two Instrumental Styles," 210–42, who argues that "symphonic style" stresses pivot cadences whereas "sonata style" tends to avoid them.

accompaniment, I would argue, to the inhalations and exhalations, cries and clamor of the audience, which often added its own considerable ongoing noise as well. The orchestra's ritornello prompted the crowd to demonstrate. We will see in chapter 3 how hard this kind of exchange was fought in midcentury Parma by a newly installed dynasty that fancied itself an enlightened monarchy—hence socially moral and decorous—but also how resistant the practice was to efforts at reform. When Charles Burney voiced his exasperation at trying to listen to arias in the San Carlo at Naples in 1773, he inadvertently underscored this resistance in a way that also helps explain it. Claiming that the pandemonium drowned out everything but the ritornellos, he dismissed the result as a babel of instruments, without delicacy or distinction:

> [M]uch of the *clairobscure* was lost, and nothing could be heard distinctly but those noisy and furious parts which were meant merely to give relief to the rest; the mezzotints and back-ground were generally lost, and indeed little was left but the bold and coarse strokes of the composer's pencil.[31]

Burney's account implies that noise at the San Carlo produced a music that ranged between relatively audible and practically inaudible while confirming that orchestral ritornellos could push their way through a roar of ambient sounds. A peak volume was reached when all the racket of the theater, the audience's voices, and the instruments of the orchestra conspired together.

Further on, he suggests that in addition to the "bold and coarse strokes of the composer's pencil," the articulation of noise was also affected by orchestral staffing. The first violinist, Fabio of the "great opera orchestra" at Naples, told him that the orchestra there included "18 first, and 18 second violins, 5 double bases [*sic*], and but two violoncellos." To that Burney snorted that all those double basses had a "bad effect, the double base being played so coarsely throughout Italy, that it produces a sound no more musical than the stroke of a hammer."[32]

What Burney failed to concede was that the hammer stroke of the basses supplied a noise that could hold its own amid the general din. It gave the initial call to attention and supplied resting cues after singers' solos. When the basses entered, the audience could boo, cheer, or sigh—if it had decided to care at all. A bass plays behind the composer Nicola Logroscino in a caricature that shows him aptly pounding on the keyboard to keep time (fig. 2.1).

Functionally, the various ritornellos that did this work fell into three groups: opening, medial, and final. Of these the final ritornello, which ended the A section on both its occurrences in a standard da capo or dal segno aria, had a special function, whether or not theorists spelled it out.[33] It crowned the entire aria and

31. Burney, *An Eighteenth-century Musical Tour in France and Italy,* 279. Mozart wrote to his sister on January 7, 1770 (Mozart, *Briefe* 1:301), that Italian theaters always had such audible murmuring "che non si sente niente" (you can't hear anything).

32. Burney, *An Eighteenth-Century Musical Tour in France and Italy,* 283–84.

33. Koch wrote, "After this period also [i.e., the second main solo in A] the instruments play a short ritornello which cadences in the main key, because with the repetition of the first section, the entire aria ends with it" (*Introductory Essay on Composition,* 171, part 4, §84). [Auch nach diesem

FIG. 2.1. Pier Leone Ghezzi, caricature of the composer Nicola Logroscino accompanying his own opera at the Teatro Argentina, Rome, 1753. He pounds in time on the side of the keyboard cabinet as a bass saws away behind him. Pen and ink on paper, 1753. The British Museum. Reproduced by permission.

scene, and accompanied the singer's exit from the stage. In the best of cases, it prompted cries for an encore. In this respect, its role was analogous to the sonic markers often used in spoken drama of the time. In her study of civic life and spoken theater in late-eighteenth-century Venice, Franca Barricelli points out that actors sometimes asked for special lines at the end of a scene to help garner public plaudits, since their success or failure was "measured vocally, at the time of performance. Audience response developed into the very *praxis* of theatre in the Settecento. Actors began requesting . . . that playwrights intentionally end scenes with emphatic statements, which the players recited with the requisite intensity to excite public response."[34]

Medial ritornellos had a function similar to final ones, except that they might be more lyrical or less emphatic, relative to the expressive character of their aria. Only the opening ritornello functioned on a different principle. There the orchestra typically made a display of the various motives to come, or, in a monothematic section, at least that of the main melody, announcing to the audience the mood of the aria and the spirit in which it was to be heard, as well as announcing that the aria had begun. As Koch put it, the purpose of the opening ritornello was to allow the singer, following the recitative, "to recover and prepare himself for the performance of the aria"; but principally "to prepare the listener for the enjoyment of the feeling which the aria [was] . . . to arouse."[35] It conjured up a metaphorical stage and provided a metaphorical and pragmatic frame for the audience's engagement with the singer.

Earlier eighteenth-century arias by Leo, Vinci, and Pergolesi made less of this structural process than arias of the mid-eighteenth century, because the number and kinds of motives laid out in the opening ritornello tended to be far fewer—the soloist's opening theme and a closing gesture or two; or sometimes just a short passage unrelated to the soloistic material followed by modest soloistic extensions. By midcentury, on the other hand, showy arias often had opening ritornellos that had swelled to include two principal themes, each one of which might be extended by several closing ideas and finished off with one

---

Perioden machen die Instrumente wieder ein kurzes Ritornell mit einer Cadenz im Haupttone, weil alsdenn bey der Wiederholung des ersten Theils die ganze Arie damit schließt. (*Versuch einer Einleitung zur Composition* 3:246).]

34. Barricelli, "Civic Representations," 58, and the reference there (n. 46) to Piazza's 1778 work *Il teatro* 2:91.

35. Koch, *Introductory Essay on Composition*, 169–70, part 4, §84. "Zweytens aber, und hauptsächlich dient es dazu, die Zuhörer zu dem Genusse der Empfindung vorzubereiten, welche die Arie erwecken soll" (*Versuch einer Einleitung zur Composition* 3:242). Koch ends, "It consists mainly of such phrases which belong to the plan of the aria, performed without special fragmentation and in the main key, in which this ritornello always closes with a formal cadence" (*Introductory Essay*, 170, part 4, §84). [Es bestehet hauptsächlich aus solchen Sätzen, die zu der Anlage der Arie gehören, die aber ohne besondere Zergliederung, und zwar in der Haupttonart vorgetragen werden, in welcher auch jederzeit dieses Ritornell mit einem förmlichen Tonschlusse schließt" (*Versuch einer Einleitung zur Composition* 3:242–43).]

or more cadential flourishes following the perfect tonic cadence. The articulation of the audience's role vis-à-vis the singer was then radically broadened. Each musical idea conjured up by the band helped predispose the crowd to a particular listening state of mind and articulated *avant la scène* their attentions and energies: some announced impending themes, others extended cadences with flourishes, and still others reinforced them. The exposition of ideas was typically concise, since the point of the opening ritornello was to establish a given affect and a listening attitude, without usurping the soloist's prerogative to expand on it (as set forth, at least in large part, by the composer).

As the length of the opening ritornello grew in proportion to the level of discursive expansion arrogated by the soloist, treatment of periodicity became increasingly hierarchical—a tendency that led to each distinct function of the ritornello being articulated that much more clearly.

* * *

Mozart was one of many composers who were bred on the expansive seria arias that developed at midcentury. By 1765, he was well acquainted with the Italianate opera seria composer Johann Christian Bach, whom he encountered as a boy in London, and by 1770 he had already written a number of concert arias on texts from opera seria. Between 1770 and 1773, during his midteen years, he conquered the stage of the Regio Ducal Teatro in the Habsburg-occupied archduchy of Milan. Milan in the early 1770s was still relatively traditional in its operatic habits compared with experimental cities like Parma, Stuttgart, or Vienna, so it made sense for Mozart, working under the abiding gaze of his father, to ignore the protestations over aria length and excessive virtuosity that by then had been voiced by many reform-minded intelligentsia across Europe. Fashioning immense dal segno arias, along with some sonata-like ones, he was able to campaign for the favor of leading singers and the mainstream Milanese public.[36] The arias for his setting of Vittorio Amedeo Cigna-Santi's *Mitridate, re di Ponto* of 1770 were multisectional ritornello numbers like those for the *festa teatrale Ascanio in Alba* the following year and the opera seria *Lucio Silla* of 1772.[37] A repository of huge dal segno and sonata-like arias, *Lucio Silla* includes many that outstrip in size anything in Mozart's previous two Milanese operas, not least because the leading man, soprano castrato Venanzio Rauzzini, and the leading lady, soprano Anna de Amicis, were among the most agile virtuosi of the day.

36. The Mozarts cultivated intensively the friendship of the great diva Anna de Amicis, for example (Mozart, *Briefe* 1:463–77, letters 268–81). Mozart also did off-season work writing the *Exsultate jubilate* (K. 165/158*a*) for Venanzio Rauzzini, who sang the role of Cecilio in *Lucio Silla* in 1772–73.

37. *Mitridate, re di Ponto* (Mozart, *Neue Ausgabe sämtlicher Werke* II.5.4 [series, workgroup, part]) was a dramma per musica on Vittorio Amedeo Cigna-Santi's libretto after Giuseppe Parini's translation of Racine's *Mithridate*, which opened on December 26, 1770; *Ascanio in Alba*, a *festa teatrale* on text by Parini (ibid., II.5.5) that opened on October 17, 1771; and *Lucio Silla*, a dramma per musica on text by Giovanni de Gamerra (ibid., II.5.7) that opened on December 26, 1772.

The opera's arias provide an object lesson in how hierarchically deployed tonal-thematic-cadential strategies could be coordinated with instrumental/solo interchange, and stand as an example of Mozart's phenomenal instinct for masterminding the dynamic interchange to take place between singers and spectators.

Imagine the following scene on the stage of the ducal theater in Milan. The opera has progressed to its second number in act 1, scene 2, in which the primo uomo, Cecilio—declared dead by the Roman dictator Lucio Silla and arrived in secret—will deliver his entrance aria, "Il tenero momento." Anxiously anticipated by obbligato recitative, the aria allows Cecilio to express his tender expectancy at seeing once again his beloved Giunia, who is being betrothed to Lucio in Cecilio's absence (stanza 1).

Il tenero momento,	[The tender moment,
Premio di tanto amore,	Reward for such love,
Già mi dipinge il core	Already colors my heart
Fra i dolci suoi pensier.	Amid such sweet thoughts.]

As the orchestra brandishes the themes and flourishes of its opening ritornello, Rauzzini strikes his pose downstage. The ritornello is a full bithematic type, so a considerable time elapses before his vocal entrance: two thematic groups, the first moving to a half cadence, the second to a full cadence, both in the home key and both ending with noisy cadential extensions. At last the final flourish is elided into Rauzzini's entering leap to a sostenuto high f′, hushing the audience as the violins retire into sighing third figures and allowing him an ostentatious *messa di voce* that crescendos and decrescendos—something for which castrati, with their great lung capacity and breath control, were famous, even a very good but not spectacular one like Rauzzini (example 2.1).

This is the first confrontation of tutti and solo, and already it points up a division of labor that spatializes the house and the stage. The tutti-solo split corresponds to a division between audience and vocalist in which even the most fleeting punctuations of the orchestra will henceforth continually call forth and shadow the audience's response, accompanying the listeners' riposte to the vocal phrases with which Rauzzini angles to win their acclaim. Held in the balance of this exchange are changing levels of repose and tension, drawing the nervous energies of performers and spectators into a collective neurosystem that courses throughout the entire house. In punctuating Rauzzini's phrase endings (mm. 26 and 29), the winds mark a release of tonal, poetic, and vocal tensions—a release at once performed and perceived. The written exchange between soloist and orchestra echoes a vanished, unwritten one between soloist and listener, with an accumulation and release of tensions that propels the dialogue being vocalized from each side of the house.

Once Rauzzini has secured the stage in the guise of the hero Cecilio, the orchestra makes its interjections fleetingly, staying out of the way until a strong bravura cadence ushers it back in. Only after he has navigated the vaulting leap of a twelfth, covered a double octave, and landed on the tonic at measure 34

EXAMPLE 2.1. Wolfgang Amadeus Mozart, aria for Cecilio, "Il tenero momento," mm. 22–70

From *Lucio Silla* (Milan, 1772), 1.2. Text by Giovanni da Gamerra, short score adapted from Mozart, *Neue Ausgabe sämtlicher Werke*, 5.7.1.

EXAMPLE 2.1. *(continued)*

(continued)

EXAMPLE 2.1. *(continued)*

does the orchestra prompt the audience with a more prominent and extended interjection—namely, the same tonic flourish that had cued in the audience to the end of the ritornello and announced Cecilio's initial entrance. Thereafter, the balance of power tips increasingly toward the singer, putting orchestra and audience at bay as Cecilio seizes more and more of the musical ground by modulating and expanding on verses 3 and 4. Rhetorically discursive, these expansions spill finally into an extended fioritura that subdues the orchestra almost completely. The grander Cecilio becomes in spinning out virtuosic extensions and skirting the big dominant cadence, the more restrained his interlocutors. The most the orchestra does is to reinforce his final cadential bars (mm. 49–54), leading to his triumphant cadence in the dominant when at last the band is allowed to begin the delicate second theme. Cecilio is now temporarily spent, and the orchestra's thematic music marks his release with a new serenity of key, theme, and meter and a somewhat blander surface. If Rauzzini managed to keep the Milanese hushed and spellbound through all his pyrotechnics, here they might have murmured or cried out a bit before his sojourn through another stanza.

* * *

To this point, Cecilio has delivered only a small slice of the aria, a single statement of the first quatrain out of no less than four that set the first stanza its first time round. But it is these *local* tutti-solo interactions that suggest with particular clarity how opera seria scores carry imprints of social practices in the opera house. My description intentionally overdetermines suggestions immanent in the score in order to point up the possibilities of a performative reading—a reading that foregrounds the interactions of singer and listener, not with the hope of recuperating how singer-audience interactions actually went, but of learning what aria scores can tell us about how they could have gone. An anecdote in the Mozart family letters affirms, at least generically, that "Il tenero momento" was rooted in rhetorical exchange. Rauzzini, it seems, was crafty enough to get applause even on opening night by means of what Leopold Mozart called a "castrato's ruse" pulled on the archduchess, who was told that without great applause he would be too nervous to sing. Whereas premieres typically played to a primly undemonstrative royal box and a house that dutifully followed suit, the castrato in this case had ensured that "the court would encourage and applaud him," to the detriment of the leading lady (de Amicis), who was thrown off and sang badly as a result.

In fact, Rauzzini succeeded in manipulating a situation that was already tense. According to Leopold, the archduke did not see fit to finish his midday meal until just before the Ave Maria rang, even though the new opera was to start an hour later, at which time he had to pen "with his own hand five letters of New Years greetings to Their Majesties the Emperor and Empress," writing them, as Leopold grumbled, "very slowly." This meant that the opera began three hours late.

> Picture to yourself the whole theatre which by half past five was so full that not another soul could get in. On the first evening the singers are always very nervous at having to perform before such a distinguished audience. But for three hours singer, orchestra and audience (many of the latter standing) had to wait impatiently in the overheated atmosphere until the opera should begin. Next, the tenor, who was engaged as a stop-gap, is a church singer from Lodi who has never before acted on such a big stage, who has only taken the part of a primo tenore a couple of times, and who moreover was only engaged a week before the performance. At the point where in her first aria the prima donna expected from him an angry gesture, he exaggerated his anger so much that he looked as if he was about to box her ears and strike her on the nose with his fist. This made the audience laugh. Signora De Amicis, carried along by her own enthusiasm, did not realise why they were laughing, and, being thus

> taken aback, did not sing well for the rest of the evening. Further, she was jealous because as soon as the primo uomo came on the stage, the Archduchess clapped her hands. This was a ruse on the part of that castrato [Rauzzini], who had arranged that the Archduchess should be told that he would not be able to sing for nervousness in order that he might thus ensure that the court would encourage and applaud him.[38]

Leopold's account may not explain the specific interventions made by spectators in the course of Rauzzini's aria, but it shows in the baldest terms that social reactions and interactions made pointed contributions to the composer's score—and that, in the event in which the aria unfolded, the audience functioned as a kind of coauthor of the work.[39] The composer Quirino Gasparini told Padre Martini in 1776 about another performance involving de Amicis that was affected midcourse by the sudden arrival of the monarchs.

> Monday the dress rehearsal of Ottani took place in the Real Teatro della Musica. The great crowd began to applaud the composer by clapping their hands right after the sinfonia and thenceforth until by chance and quite exceptionally there appeared in a loge near the stage the Prince of Piedmont and the Duke of Chiablay, who heard the whole second act. Out of respect for the royal princes the public could no longer make such acclamations, but Signora de Amicis, having sung her huge, wonderfully composed aria, the prince of Piedmont clapped his hands and with all his gestures showed the audience his pleasure, which was echoed by them.[40]

38. Letter from Milan, January 2, 1773 (Anderson, *Letters of Mozart,* 223). "Stelle dir nun vor, das ganze theater war um halbe 6 uhr so voll, daß niemand mehr hineinkonnte. die Sänger und Sängerinnen sind den ersten abend in einer grossen Angst sich das erste mahl einem so ansehnlichen Publico zu zeigen. Die beängstigten Singenden Personen musten in ihrer Angst, das Orchester und ganze Publicum in ungedult und auch Hitze viele stehenden fusses 3 stunde auf den Anfang der opera warten. *zweytens.* ist zu wissen, daß der Tenor, den wir aus Noth nehmen müssen ein KirchenSänger aus Lodi ist der niemals auf einem so ansehnlichen theater agiert hat, der nur etwa zwey mahl in Lodi einen primo Tenore vorgestellt, endlich erst 8 täg vor der opera ist verschrieben worden. dieser, da die prima Donna in ihrer ersten Aria von ihm eine action des zorns erwarten muß, machte diese zornige action so übertrieben, daß es schiene als wolte er ihr Ohrfeigen geben, und ihr die Nase mit der faust wegstossen, bewog das Publicum zum lachen. die Sig[a]: de amicis beobachtete nicht so gleich im Eyfer ihres Singens, warum das Publicum lachte, und sie war betroffen, und wuste anfangs nicht wer ausgelacht wurde und sang den ganzen ersten Abend nicht gut, weil noch die Eyfersucht dazu kam, daß dem Primo Uomo, so bald auf das theater tratt die Hände von der Erzherzogin geklatschet wurde. dieß war ein Castratenstreich, dann er machte, daß der Erzherzogin gesagt wurde, daß er für forcht nicht werde singen können, um dadurch zu erhalten, daß ihm der Hof gleich Courage und applauso machen sollte" (Mozart, *Briefe* 1:472).

39. The coinage comes from sociolinguist Alessandro Duranti, "The Audience as Co-Author," 239–47.

40. "Lunedì si fece la prova generale nel Real Teatro della Musica del Sig*nor* M*aestro* Ottani. Il concorso fù grande, che cominciò ad applaudire il Compositore con sbattimento de mani subito dopo la sinfonia indi nel resto sino a quando accidentalmente e straordinariamente comparvero le

Leopold continued his account of the *Lucio Silla* debacle by telling his wife about the aftermath, when de Amicis managed to get compensation from the court and the audience for the ill that had been done her, and also managed to influence subsequent performances to her own benefit:

> To console Signora de Amicis the court summoned her about noon on the following day and she had an audience with their Royal Highnesses which lasted a whole hour. Only then did the opera begin to go well; and . . . on the first six evenings (today is the seventh) the hall was so full that it was hardly possible to slip in. Further, the prima donna is still having it all her own way and her arias have to be repeated.[41]

* * *

With all this in mind, let us return to the instrumental interventions that I take to articulate the interventions of auditors, and fasten them onto the background of Kochian rhetorical analysis. We can start by extending analytically the function of local interjections to the weightier ritornellos that tie off entire sections. Internal and final ritornellos provided the sort of emphatic definition that Koch called "punctuation" on the scale of larger grammatical structures, or *Perioden*. At both functional levels, foreground and background, small and large, the joints between solos and ritornellos marked the joints in social exchange. Whether or not these joints were signaled audibly from the hall, as happened more readily when royalty were absent than present, they enabled listeners to mobilize collective feelings of anticipation and repose, longing and release. This is what is implied by Koch's description of the aria as a genre that "portrays in

---

loro *Altezzi Reali* il Sig*nor* Principe di Piemonte ed il Duca di Chiablay in una loggia vicina al Teatro, che sentirono tutto il secondo atto. Il Pubblico non potè più far tal ecelatto [French, *éclat*] per il rispetto di questi Reali Prencipi, ma la Signora De Amicis, avendo cantato la sua aria grandiosa eccelsamente composta, il Sig*nor* Prencipe di Piemonte battè esso le mani, e con tutti i suoi gesti dimostrò al pubblico il suo aggradimento, che fù eccheggiato dell'istesso Pubblico." Gasparini continued, "Il signor Aprile piace assai, piace qual sempre, piacerà quantunque sii la sestavolta che su queste scene appare. La decisione addonque del Pubblico è che la Musica vale e piace, sperando grandemente che dimani sera nascerà maggior approvazione, e ciò in onor del Sig*nor* Scolaro che rende preggio al gran Maestro ed alla Patria. Mi riserbo l'ordinario venture adonque darle le notizie che molto le spero felici con mia piena consolazione" (Turin, December 25, 1776, in I-Bc I.21.75 = Schnoebelen, *Padre Martini's Letters*, no. 2225). The opera was Bernardino Ottani's *Calipso* staged at the Regio Teatro "alla presenza delle maestà loro" for Carnival, with de Amicis in the title role and Giuseppe Aprile as Telemaco.

41. "Um nun die de amicis wieder zu trösten, wurde sie gleich den tag darauf gegen Mittag nach Hofe beruffen, und hatte eine ganze Stunde bey beyden Königl Hoheiten audienz, dann fieng die opera erst an gut zu gehen, und da sonst bey der ersten opera das theater sehr lehr ist, so waren nun die ersten 6 abend |: heut wird der Siebende:| so voll daß man kaum hineinschliefen kann, und hat nich meistens die prima Donna die Oberhand deren Arien wiederhollt worden" (Mozart, *Briefe* VI:472).

Table 2.2. Koch's *Perioden:* A generative scheme of the dal segno aria and its variants

	First *Periode* [first ritornello]		First *Hauptperiode* [first solo]		[instrumental "interlude"]	Second *Hauptperiode**		[ritornello]
	Satz 1	Satz 2	Satz 1	Satz 2		Satz 1	Satz 2	
			Stanza 1 (without textual repetition and fragmentation)	Stanza 1 (with textual repetition and fragmentation)		Stanza 2 (modulatory, with new melodies, meter and tempi, or original ones)	Stanza 1 (material of first Hauptperiode; Sätze 1-2 rewritten or Satz 2 only)	
Harmonic progress of arias in major keys	I or			←V→ or	V or	V or modulatory or I	I	I or
Harmonic progress of arias in minor keys	i			iii (position variable)	iii	iii or modulatory or i	i return to main key may take place later	i

*This has either a variably positioned dal segno repeat or everything written out in the main key (à la sonatas).

various modifications that feeling [that is] *induced [in listeners] by the subject of the vocal work.*"[42]

At this higher level of definition, "Il tenero momento" is laid out as a large, through-composed dal segno aria, with the first stanza tracing a full modulation to the dominant and return to the tonic, the second stanza making a couple of fleeting bows toward more distant keys, and the first returning for an abbreviated written-out reprise in the tonic. Overall, the aria endows these textual expositions with a crystalline rhetorical clarity typical of Mozart from a young age, with keys, themes, performing forces, and text all coordinated in tight synchronicity and given classical balance. The tonal-thematic development of the first stanza (A) is harnessed to a highly symmetrical fourfold exposition of the text (later returning in a twofold reprise in A′). At each of its iterations, the stanza corresponds to a particular stretch of tonal color and tonal movement and to a set of motivic gestures.[43]

Arguably all these stanzaic repetitions are adumbrated motivically by the twenty-one-measure bithematic ritornello that opens the aria and sets the stage for Cecilio's outpouring. The ritornello's two halves are rolled out before us like shimmering lengths of silk, the first moving from the tonic to the V chord (a half cadence), the second moving back to the tonic and up onto the singer's entering sostenuto. Koch named each half a *Satz*, a "phrase" (or literally, and aptly, a "movement"), and he viewed the whole of the ritornello as combining *Sätze* into a single *Periode* (literally, grammatical "period" or "sentence").[44]

Once prepared by the ritornello, the audience went on hearing these motivic ideas elaborated in the *Perioden* of the vocal sections. Koch recognized the latter as grammatically similar to the opening instrumental *Periode* in that they combine *Sätze*—tantamount to verbal clauses—which together create larger, more complex "sentences."[45] (See Koch's *Perioden* indicated in table 2.2.) The sentences of the solo sections obviously differ from those of the opening instrumental *Periode* in the dynamism given them by modulations. And Koch also noted the increasing repetition and fragmentation of text that characterized the vocal *Perioden* as they move along—particularly in the second *Hauptperiode*. He

42. Koch, *Introductory Essay on Composition*, 169, part 4, §83. (emphasis mine). "Die Arie, so wie sie in der Cantate und im Drama erscheint, bestehet aus einem ausgeführten, sehr ausgebildeten, und von Instrumenten begleiteten Gesange, wodurch eine Person diejenige Empfindung in verschiedenen Modificationen schildert, in die sie durch Veranlassung des Gegenstandes versezt worden ist, welchen das Singstück behandelt" (*Versuch einer Einleitung zur Composition* 3:240–41).

43. This was more characteristic of the teenage Mozart than of his contemporaries; see Feldman, "Staging the Virtuoso" and "Mozart and His Elders," 564–75.

44. Again, not all arias had opening ritornellos, even before around 1770, and opening ritornellos of early arias from the 1720s–40s often had only one thematic group or phrase—hence in Koch's terms one *Satz* or *Periode*.

45. I draw here on Koch's comments on *modified* da capo arias—dal segno and sonata-like arias (art. 84)—though Koch also treats the more modern rondò and two-tempo types (§§85–87) and duets (§88). See *Introductory Essay on Composition*, 169–79; *Versuch einer Einleitung zur Composition* 3:248–66.

was less clear about the status of the internal ritornellos than about the solo sections, though essentially he took them to be extensions of those same *Hauptperioden* that begin as solo sections, which they follow and finish off.[46]

* * *

The kind of rhetorical paradigm sketched above, encompassing audience and actor in the eighteenth-century aria score, has been surprisingly absent from modern accounts, even though most agree that rhetoric, with all its performative and communicative corollaries, underpinned views of eighteenth-century music and performance tout court.[47] In fact, eighteenth-century modes of aria production affirm that in lay consciousness, the very concept of "music" as a physical object, as distinct from musical performance, hardly existed, except as a part of compositional or theoretical study or a mode of transmission and preservation. Least of all could a notion of music as physical, written object have applied to Italian arias, whose modes of production and circulation made them rhetorical through and through. Arias meant fast composition, circulation overwhelmingly in manuscripts rather than printed scores, or else in albums of "favourite songs," and easy substitution and insertion into given performances or productions. They involved theatrical contexts and contests for attention, adulation, suasion, and commemoration.

To the extent that this rhetorical framework was pervasive, it calls for a pervasively rhetorical analytic. Mark Evan Bonds's *Wordless Rhetoric* takes up the gauntlet by considering rhetoric as the foundation for all eighteenth-century musical analysis, even as it focuses on instrumental music. Bonds contrasts the eighteenth century's "pragmatic" approach to musical form to the "expressivism" of later full-blown romanticism, following the dichotomy sketched by M. H. Abrahms, for whom the "pragmatic" signaled works of an *intentional* nature that aim to elicit a particular emotional response in the listener and carry out their formal work to that end.[48]

46. "After the first main period makes a full cadence in this most closely related key, the instruments play a short interlude which, according to whether it is longer or shorter, closes either with a cadence or only with a V-phrase in this key" (*Introductory Essay on Composition*, 171, part 4, §84). [Nachdem dieser erste Hauptperiode mit einer vollkommenen Cadenz in dieser nächstverwandten Tonart geschlossen hat, machen die Instrumente in dieser Tonart noch ein kurzes Zwischenspiel, welches, je nachdem es länger oder kürzer ist, entweder mit einer Cadenz, oder nur mit dem Quintabsatze in dieser Tonart schließt (*Versuch einer Einleitung zur Composition* 3:245).]

47. Major recent interlocutors include Dahlhaus, "Das rhetorische Formbegriff," 155–76; Sisman, *Mozart: The Jupiter Symphony*, part of the theoretical foundation for which comes from Sisman's earlier work on Koch, "Small and Expanded Forms,"; Bonds, *Wordless Rhetoric;* and Beghin, "Haydn as Orator," 201–54. Interest in eighteenth-century music as rhetoric continues apace (witness the session of the 2003 meeting of the American Musicological Society, "Perception and Rhetoric in Classical Music").

48. Compare Mozart's comments regarding his 1778 "Paris Symphony" on appealing to his publics (Mozart, *Briefe* 2:377–79; Anderson, *The Letters of Mozart*, 352), and on his early Viennese piano

On this view, music is arbitrated by listeners for whose consumption passions are continually harnessed and directed.[49] As we have begun to see, eighteenth-century evidence for such a modus is rampant. Composers and performers were compared with and conceived as orators. Composition and its attendant skills (notation, figured bass, harmony, and counterpoint) figured as equivalents to grammar or grammatical knowledge.[50] Form and genre were construed through analogies to large-scale rhetorical processes. More generally, music was persistently metaphorized as language, as an intelligible instrument that could signify and persuade. It could present "propositions" through central musical ideas, unfolded and elaborated in a series of "proofs" (at least by analogy).[51] In specific analytic terms, as Bonds points out, the link of music to rhetoric was secured through a focus in treatises of the second half century on periodicity, which worked to refine a long tradition dating back to the Renaissance (and to chant theory long before that) of grounding music concretely in strategies of musical grammar.[52] It is precisely this that Koch elaborates with respect to arias, and in a way that expands on analytical ideas that had already been broached by Riepel and, earlier, Scheibe.

* * *

The same rhetorical superstructure that housed German thought had currency among Italians well into the second half century. In the 1770s, Mancini was still emphatically rhetorical. His 1774 *Pensieri e riflessioni pratiche sopra il canto figurato* (republished in revised and expanded version in 1777 as *Riflessioni pratiche sul canto figurato*) exhorted the pupil to "Listen to the discourse of a good orator,

---

concertos of 1782 (K. 413–15) (Mozart, *Briefe* 3:245–46; Anderson, *Letters of Mozart,* 833); and see my discussion in Feldman, "Music and the Order of the Passions," 37–67.

49. What is least clear in Bonds's approach is the status of the listener—more an abstraction than a flesh-and-blood creature.

50. See Bonds, *Wordless Rhetoric,* 68ff.

51. Among Italians on this last, see the 1791 treatise by Francesco Galeazzi, *Elementi teorico-pratici di musica,* who compares the structure of an oration with a musical work on the grounds that both elaborate a central idea (for an annotated translation, see Frascarelli, "Elementi teorico-pratici di musica"). Cf. Bonds, *Wordless Rhetoric,* 94. Bonds also notes (94 n. 134) that Salvatore Bertezen, Italian singing teacher and author of the *Principi di musica teorico-prattica* (Rome, 1780), stresses the primacy of theme both in the compositional process and final product. For Bonds's other examples of how music was thought to persuade and explicate, see 96ff.

52. Bonds develops the idea that periodicity is the link to grammar and rhetoric (*Wordless Rhetoric,* 71ff.), demonstrating how writers like Kirnberger, and later Riepel and Koch, stress grammatical-cum-rhetorical intelligibility as key to form (74–75), and noting further that once rhetorically oriented theorists have dealt with periodicity, they invariably turn to individual genres—as do manuals on performance like Leopold Mozart's *Versuch einer gründlichen Violinschule* and manuals on rhetoric (84–85). He also observes (78–79) the same is true of the historical/theoretical treatise by Antonio Eximeno y Pujades, *Dell'origine e delle regole della musica,* which had a wide readership in Italy where it was published in 1774.

and hear what pauses, what variety of voice, what diverse strength he adopts to express his ideas; now he raises the voice, now drops it, now he quickens the voice, now harshens, now makes it sweet, according to the diverse passions which he intends to arouse in listeners."[53] His proposed education for vocal students was intended to cultivate their rhetorical intelligence by having them read "Tuscan books" (shorthand for books in an elevated vernacular), acquire knowledge of history, and study grammar—the last because "[g]rammar teaches the regulated way of reading and speaking," where the pauses and emphases should be made, and how meanings are thus shaped for the listener through expression. Mancini relied on the old Ciceronian idea that meanings of words were not immanent and immutable but related to their sounds and indeed produced in living sound: "The virtue and strength of a word are not always perceived through its nature alone, but often in the manner with which words are pronounced, whence they gain strength."[54] Even at a moment when theatrical illusion was growing in importance, Mancini advanced these precepts as the very foundation of a convincing portrayal on the stage: "A singer performs well when, investing strongly in his character, he projects him naturally with his actions, his voice, and his own affects [figuratively, gestures], and brings him to life with such clarity that the listener will say that this one is truly Caesar, for example, or that one Alexander."[55] Illusion depended on that cluster of abilities that the ancients and early moderns glossed as rhetorical control.

Mancini's model of the singer-as-orator underlay the entire basis of eighteenth-century singing manuals. Tosi, in his *Opinioni de' cantori*, had emphasized not just the singer's delivery but processes of exchange, despite carping over abuses of the modern style exploited by singers to capture applause and kudos with shows of surpassing difficulty: "[Y]ou ask for the Vivat almost out of charity—the Vivat that you realize you do not deserve. In return you ridicule your patrons if they do not have enough hands, feet, or voices to praise you."[56]

53. *Practical Reflections*, 65. "Attenti pure al discorso d'un buon Oratore, e sentirete quante pose, quante varietà di voci, quante diverse forze adopra per esprimere i suoi sensi; ora inalza la voce, or l'abassa, or l'affretta, or l'incrudisce, ed or fa dolce, secondo le diverse passioni, che intendere muovere nell'Uditore" (*Pensieri, e riflessioni pratiche* [1774], 150). The same was said by Saverio Mattei (Fabbri, "Saverio Mattei," 611–29).

54. *Practical Reflections*, 65. "La virtù, e la forza d'una parola non rilevasi sempre dalla di lei sola natura, ma ben spesso la maniera, con cui viene proferita gli leva, ovvero aggiunge forza" (Mancini, *Pensieri, e riflessioni pratiche* [1774], 149, art. 13). The 1777 edition replaces "con cui viene proferita gli leva, ovvero aggiunge forza" with "con cui viene proferita le toglie, ovvero le aggiugne forza" (*Riflessioni pratiche*, 219).

55. *Practical Reflections*, 65. "Recita bene un Attore allor quando, investendosi forte del carattere di quel Personaggio, che rappresenta, lo spiega al naturale e con l'azione, e con la voce, e cogli affetti propri, e con tanta chiarezza lo ravviva, che l'Uditore dice, questo veramente è, per ragion d'esempio, questo è Cesare: questo è Alessandro" (Mancini, *Pensieri, e riflessioni pratiche* [1774], 148, art. 13). The passage is essentially unchanged in the edition of 1777.

56. Quoted from Agricola, *Introduction to the Art of Singing*, 207, who adds, "This concerns the Bravo and Eviva yelling, the clapping of hands and the noises that occur in Italian theaters when

If this was a sin for Tosi, it was far worse by the time Mozart was writing for Milan. Like the arias of his then contemporaries—Guglielmi, Piccinni, Misliweček, and di Maio—Mozart's arias often committed the sin of difficulty. Difficulty gave singers a way to make their mark in the professional world as they personified struggle triumphant through transcendent impersonations of royals, heroes, and beleaguered lovers.

THE SINGER AS MAGUS

When the English physician John Moore traveled Italy in the mid-eighteenth century, he translated his observations of Italian singers through their miraculous effects on audiences. Of Rome he wrote,

> The sensibility of some of the audience gave me an idea of the power of sounds, which the dulness of my own auditory nerves could never have conveyed to my mind. At certain airs, silent enjoyment was expressed in every countenance; at others, the hands were clasped together, the eyes half shut, and the breath drawn in with a prolonged sigh, as if the soul was expiring in a torrent of delight. One young woman, in the pit, called out "Oh Dio, dove sono! Che piacer via caccia l'alma?" [O God, where am I! What pleasure ravishes my soul!].[57]

Like many others on the Grand Tour, Moore ascribes to Italian listeners passions of mythical proportions. For Moore, operatic singing manipulates listeners' emotions as it stages the preeminence of singers, in line with an operatic marketplace that saw performative power directly in the power of performing persons. Of course singers in this configuration were boxed into an ironic position, since they often impersonated the same monarchs whose economic and political power on the stage of Realpolitik made possible their engagement at "princely" fees. That ability to impersonate them—and thus to be fetishized in a new world of commodities—also allowed singers to usurp power and charisma (both symbolic and real) that had properly belonged to the monarch, for whom exploiting the emotions of crowds through sound, image, and gesture had been power writ large over the body social. No wonder political authorities and cultural commentators tried to limit the power of singers.

The listening body of Moore's account is not just a social one, however; it is also individual. Both the body social and the individual body could react with sighs, drooping eyelids, clasped hands, with souls "ravished," "expiring in a tor-

a singer has performed anything that seems worthy of applause" (207 n. f). [Dieses bezieht sich auf das *Bravo* und *Eviva*-Schreyen, auf das Händeklatschen und Geräusch, so sich in den italiänischen Schauplätzen erhebet, wenn ein Sänger irgend etwas vorgebracht hat, das des Beyfalls würdig scheint (Tosi and Agricola, *Anleitung zur Singkunst*, book 8, "Hauptstück," 198 n. f).]

57. Moore, *A View of Society* 2:85–86. The bracketed translation is Moore's own.

rent of delight." In this Moore also throws into relief a double subjective process that singing could touch off: that sense of losing the self ("Oh God, where am I!") and at the same time joining a collective, where reactions are shared by "every countenance." It was precisely those moments of collective effervescence that could convert individual experience into a more and more powerful communal experience, and thus reexcite individual experience in a seemingly endless spiral.

Touching off such a process was no easy matter. It could easily elude the singer or slip away in the twinkling of an eye. Indeed, the very promise of a magical transformation depended on the fact that it could not, and was not, to be taken for granted. Only the singer who succeeded in transforming listeners and somatizing passions in them was a sorcerer of the soul. This was an idea that took hold well before pyrotechnics became the signature of operatic singing at midcentury, especially owing to the powers of one man, Farinelli. Shortly after his operatic debut at age fifteen in 1720, Farinelli had come to be "distinguished throughout Italy by the name of *il Ragazzo*, the *boy*" (as in "boy wonder"), as Burney reported in a famous anecdote. "His powers were regarded as miraculous," so much so that in the spring of 1732, at the age of twenty-seven, he was called to Vienna, where he sang privately for Emperor Karl VI at the court of Vienna. Still casting himself forty years later, in the early 1770s, as the deferential subject, Farinelli explained to Burney that the emperor, ostensibly under the sway of an incipient French ideology of naturalism, had admonished him to desist from his constant virtuosic artifices in favor of a more pathetic style. And he added that "his Imperial Majesty [had] condescended to tell him one day, with great mildness and affability, that in his singing, he neither *moved* nor *stood still* like any other mortal; all was supernatural."[58]

Many a traveler to Italy was struck not just by the passions of Italian audiences but by their magical symbiosis with the passions of the performers. Jean-Pierre Grosley noted that rituals of encoring were touched off by clapping, which in turn produced infinite variations of the aria encored aimed at impassioning the audience still further—touching off further passions in singers and thus collective effervescence, provoking more clapping, sometimes even additional encores, more collective emotion, leading to more clapping, and so on and so forth. Each time the phenomenon erupted anew, Grosley explained, the orchestra would return to the ritornello while the singer would

> [walk] about in a circle, and sing the favourite *arietta* the second time. This is sometimes repeated even to the fifth or sixth time; and in these repetitions it is, that the singer exerts every resource of nature and art, to surpass himself in each repetition, by the variety of gradations which he introduces into the trills, modulations, and whatever belongs to the expression. Slight and quick as some of these gradations may be, not one of them escapes an Italian ear: they

58. Burney, *The Present State of Music in France and Italy*, 153–54; cf. Farinelli, *La solitudine amica*, letters 17–21. The idea that in his youth Farinelli spent heavily on ornaments became a trope in eighteenth-century writings (e.g., Marpurg, *Historisch-kritische Beyträge*, 233–34).

> perceive them, they feel them, they relish them with a delight, which in Italy is called the *foretaste of the joys of Paradise.*[59]

This "foretaste of paradise" was the warrant of an efficacious partnership in which the singer's virtuosity pulls the listeners into a dialogue and induces a state of rapture (at least when it works). The famous account by Burney cited in chapter 1 of Farinelli's contest with the trumpeter—recently relocated to the mise-en-scène of a lowbrow town square in Corbiau's 1994 film *Farinelli*—underscores the agonistic dimension of such an exchange (a theme I resume in chapters 4 and 5). It underscores the potential of exchange to breed conflict and invite conquest, and to engage interlocutors in multidirectional transactions, from performer to performer and performer to viewer.[60] By Farinelli's time hardly any arias had obbligato accompaniments with trumpet, nor did all that many have obbligato accompaniments with any instrument, so the potential for competition was normally restricted to besting fellow cast members on a given evening (as Rauzzini tried to do with de Amicis), or besting listeners' memories of past performances (as Farinelli claimed to do with others)—particularly of the same aria or a new setting of a given text. Farinelli begged not to sing an aria for Arbace identified with his rival Giovanni Carestini (Il Cusanino), partly because during Carnival 1730 both were famed Arbaces in different settings of Metastasio's *Artaserse*, Carestini in Vinci's setting for Rome and Farinelli in Hasse's setting for Venice.[61] Many singers matched Farinelli's level of pride (often with less justification), and some, like Rauzzini, tried directly to provoke audiences to spur them on. Caffarelli did so often by amusing the stalls, sometimes with gross treatment of other singers, which included surprising one prima donna in a duet with a part she had never heard before.[62]

The classic instance of a singer succeeding in having the audience urge him on is Farinelli's celebrated performance of "Son qual nave che agitata," again retold by Burney:

> In the famous air *Son qual Nave*, which was composed by his brother Riccardo Broschi, the first note he sung was taken with such delicacy, swelled by minute

59. Grosley, *New Observations* 2:234. "Alors l'Orchestre revient au prélude, le *Castrato* se repromene circulairement, & reprend l'Ariette qu'un nouveau battement de mains fait recommencer. Cela se répéte quelquefois jusqu'à cinq ou six fois; & c'est dans ces reprises, que le Chanteur épuise toutes les ressources de la Nature & de l'Art, par la variété de nuances qu'il répand sur les tons, sur les modulations, & sur tout ce qui tient à l'expression. Quelque legères que soient ces nuances, aucune n'échappe aux oreilles Italiennes: elles les saisissent, elles les sentent, elles les savourent avec un plaisir appellé en Italie, l'avant-goût des joies du Paradis, qui en aura sans doute d'équivalentes pour les Nations dont les organes sont moins sensibles à l'expression harmonique" (*Nouveaux mémoires* 3:96–97).

60. It was precisely to this that the reformer Francesco Algarotti strenuously objected (*Saggio*, ed. Bini [1763], 30–33; passage included in Treitler, *Strunk's Source Readings*, 919).

61. Earlier Farinelli called Carestini "maledetto tal castrato" (*La solitudine amica*, 87).

62. On Caffarelli's behavior, see Heartz, "Caffarelli's Caprices," chap. 11.

degrees to such an amazing volume, and afterwards diminished in the same manner to a mere point, that it was applauded for a full five minutes. After this he set off with such brilliancy and rapidity of execution, that it was difficult for the violins of those days to keep pace with him.[63]

Burney was probably characterizing the ensemble of performances that Farinelli executed in a pasticcio of *Artaserse*, with music by his brother and by the famous Hasse, first given at London's Haymarket on October 29, 1734.[64] A version of the aria including Farinelli's ornamentations is preserved at the Österreichische Nationalbibliothek of Vienna in a presentation manuscript (Vienna 19111) dedicated by Farinelli himself to Empress Maria Theresia on March 30, 1753.[65] Evidence from the dedication and score gives an idea of how Farinelli's execution astounded with its uniqueness, including his remarkable vocal "estensioni," passagework, and cadenzas, all of which he rubricated in Vienna 19111 with ink and underlining. His performances would have played on the prior expectations of listeners, who had generally heard plenty of other simile arias on ships, storms, and shipwrecks and, in this instance, would have linked them with the opera's young hero Arbace from *Artaserse*.[66]

Son qual nave che agitata	[I am that ship which, agitated
Da più scogli in mezzo al mare,	By reefs in the midst of the sea,
Si confonde e spaventata,	Confounded and startled,
Va solcando in alto mar.	Goes ploughing through deep waters.

63. Burney, *An Eighteenth-Century Musical Tour in France and Italy*, 154. The aria was written by Riccardo in 1734 for insertion in Hasse's *Artaserse* and survives in MS A-Wn 19111 (hereafter Vienna 19111), fols. 38r–55v; facsimile reproduction in Schmitz, *Die Kunst der Verzierung*, 76–93.

64. On date and attribution see Freeman, "Farinello and His Repertory," 327 n .69 and 328.

65. A piano-vocal edition of Farinelli's aria can be found in Haböck, *Die Gesangskunst der Kastraten*. The dedication reads: "Sacra Reale Cesarea Maestà: Pieno di confusione, e di gloria per la benignissima ricordanza, che la Cesarea Maestà vostra si degna di conservare della mia profonda venerazione, ed incoraggito dalle sicurezze avutene da Monsignor Migazzi, ardisco presentarle in questo libro una piccola scelta di quelle ariette, che per una serie non interrotta di molti anni anno servito in bocca mia al privato sollievo di questi adorabili Sovrani miei Clementissimi Benefattori la musica di esse, cui sacrifai per passatempo i voli del mio capriccio, e particolarmente quella delle tre prime destinate alla sola mia abilità (qualunque ella siasi), rinovando forse nella mente della Cesarea Maestà vostra la idea della estensione, e delle altre qualità della mia voce, servirà talvolta a renderle meno noijosa la pena, che mi lusingo si vorrà prendere di ripassarle, al quale oggetto ho creduto di doversi inserire in note di color rosso, ed in strisce volanti alcuni dei molti cambiamenti ne'passaggi, e nelle cadenze. Sarà mia gran sorte, se onorandole Vostra Maestà di una benignissima Occhiata nei pochi istanti di riposo, che le permettone le vaste cure dell'Impero, si degnerà di ricercare in esse qualche ristoro alle sue gloriose fatiche, e riconoscere in me la continuazione di quell'appassionate Ossequio, con cui prondamente mi umilio."

66. A few Metastasian examples of the many simile arias on the ship and the sea include "Senza procelle ancora" (*Alessandro nell'Indie* 2.4), "Vo solcando un mar crudele" (*Artaserse* 1.15), "Siam navi all'onde algenti" (*L'olimpiade* 2.5), "Son qual per mare ignoto" (*L'olimpiade* 3.5), and "Con le procelle in seno" (*Ezio* 3.3). Almost every opera has at least one.

Ma in veder l'amato lido	But in seeing the beloved shore,
Lascia l'onde, il vento infido	It leaves the waves, the faithless wind,
E va in porto a riposar.	And comes to rest at port.][67]

Personified through the standard image of the ship, Farinelli nevertheless personalized his brother's music with a panoply of his own devices that his audience could decode—even the London audience for whom the aria was written to insert in the pasticcio-revival of Hasse's opera—manipulating these devices to surprise, anguish, and delight them.[68] The opening ritornello cued them into what the rocky seas had in store for the singer as metaphorical vessel: the rushing scales in the violins' opening bars; the wave-like sextuplet arpeggios following the central half cadence; the plunging glissandi and stormy leaps that ushered him in (example 2.2). His opening bars extended the object of the metaphor with a simple elaboration of f′ leading to a sostenuto on the motto "Son qual nave." The f′ on "na-" lacks a tenuto sign, but the sustained-note accompaniment under it indicates a *messa di voce ad libitum* for the singer. Since the public had been cued (indeed, prefigured and accompanied, as I have argued) by the orchestra, it needed only to hear Farinelli's renowned command over the *messa di voce* (which was probably undecorated in the first go-through of the A section), to know that stormy passaggi and devilish cadenzas lay in store.[69] This was a feat that he combined with exceeding virtuosity and one in which he was unsurpassed.

> There was none of all Farinelli's excellencies by which he so far surpassed all other singers, and astonished the public, as his *messa di voce,* or swell; which,

67. I give here a condensed version of the text from Vienna 19111, which has extensive repetitions and variations that defy a standard stanzaic layout. A version of the aria printed by John Walsh with the rubric "Sung by Sig. Farinello in Artaxerxes" in *The favourite songs in the opera call'd Artaxerxes* ([1735]; facsimile edition Bologna: Forni, 1980) is more streamlined, with textual variants and a different B section musically.

68. Hasse's version of *Artaserse,* as well as settings by others, is discussed in chapter 6 below.

69. Mancini says that the *messa di voce,* a swelling and diminishing of vocal power, should usually be applied at the beginning of an aria, on tenuti, or the beginnings of cadenzas. "Ordinariamente questa messa di voce deve porsi in uso nel principio d'un Aria, ed in una nota coronata; e similmente è necessaria nel preparare una cadenza: ma un vero, ed ottimo Professore ["artista" in 1777 ed.] se ne serve in qualunque nota di valore, che trovi anche sparsa in qualunque musical Cantilena" (*Pensieri, e riflessioni pratiche* [1774], 100, art. 9; *Riflessioni pratiche* [1777], 147; *Practical Reflections,* 44). Thus *messe di voce* can generally occur on any long held note or any opportunity to hold a note for a long time (e.g., a pregnant pause). Mancini frets about singers, especially young ones overreaching their skills, who fake or mangle the *messa di voce* because they are ignorant about conserving breath, and therefore end the cadenza without a trill and replace the final held note with many (*Pensieri, e riflessioni practiche,* 100–105; *Riflessioni pratiche,* 147–51; *Practical Reflections,* 44–45). In the late seventeenth century, the Englishman John Evelyn already wrote admiringly of the soprano castrato Siface's *messa di voce* as "extending and & loosing a note with that incomparable softnesse, & sweetnesse" (*The Diary of John Evelyn,* 864). See also Malkiewicz, "Zur Verkörperung des Kastraten."

EXAMPLE 2.2. Riccardo Broschi, "Son qual nave che agitata," mm. 1–24

From the pasticcio *Artaserse* (London, 1734). Short score based on Vienna 19111.

EXAMPLE 2.2. *(continued)*

> by the natural formation of his lungs, and artificial economy of breath, he was able to protract to such a length as to excite the incredulity even in those who heard him; who, though unable to detect the artifice, imagined him to have had the latent help of some instrument by which tone was continued while he renewed his powers of respiration.
>
> Of his execution the musical reader will be enabled to judge by a view of the most difficult divisions of his bravura songs. Of his taste and embellishments we shall now be able to form but an imperfect idea, even if they have been preserved in writing, as mere notes would only show his invention and science, without enabling us to discover that expression and neatness which rendered his execution so perfect and surprising . . . and his taste and fancy in varying passages were thought by his contemporaries inexhaustible.[70]

After elaborating his opening sostenuto, Farinelli launched the aria proper with a relatively measured, syllabic delivery of stanza one (a1), evidently venturing his first melisma at "spaventata" (mm. 33–35) with an initial deflection to the dominant. He pushed harder toward the dominant in a longer melisma on "mar" (mm. 37–42) before coming to another tenuto on V of V (m. 43, possibly embellished in performance, though not in Farinelli's exemplar). By the time he reached the last melisma in a1, the violins were rushing with him in scalewise unisons and thirds as he flew toward the big perfect cadence in the dominant key of C (m. 51), then left the orchestra to churn away (R2) during the accolades of the crowd.

Unfolding the stanzaic repetitions with none of Mozart's concern for binary formal symmetries, Riccardo Broschi supplied music for two more principal

70. Burney, *A General History of Music*, 2:790.

statements (totaling three in all), which progressively intensified the process of expansion and elaboration heard in a1. Quite possibly these strategies were the direct result of Farinelli's collaboration with his brother, as suggested by Vienna 19111. The first stanzaic repetition (a2) generates a melisma on "mar" whose eleven measures (mm. 77–87) double the size of the longest previous melisma (in a1, mm. 37–42) and would have showcased Farinelli's astonishing vocal range. The next and last statement (a3) furnished two more mammoth melismas, each one more staggering than the previous, with undulating figuration on the verse-ending "mar." The first one (mm. 100–111), again eleven measures long, had Farinelli depicting the sea with an octave descent by half notes, leaving ample room for ornamentation and improvisation; the second moved into a passage of rapidly stuttering vocal repetitions against the violins' stormy glissandi (derived from R1), and culminated finally in waves of descending thirty-second-note vocal figuration leading to a tenuto (with room for a cadenza); and the last (mm. 118–39) had him climax with an incredible twenty-two measures of vocal acrobatics, double the size of any previous melisma, with gruppetti, scalar passaggi, and rapid-fire note repetitions. Even on the first go-through of the A section, then, the length of the final melisma grew in size over the course of the verse repetitions, from six measures to eleven to twenty-two.

We are lucky enough to know from the horse himself that Farinelli made these exploits even more extravagant in the reprise. Example 2.3 shows the last melisma of the A section as it appears in Farinelli's gift to the empress. Two staff lines (placed above the basso continuo) are assigned to the vocal part, the lower one for the "essential" score, original to his brother and presumably representing A in its first performance, and the upper one for the elaborated version, presumably for the reprise. Many of the embellishments for the former are so elaborate that it seems impossible anything could be added. But amazingly, for the last melisma Farinelli managed to fit in new trills (toward the beginning) and new waves of thirty-second notes (around the middle, mm. 123–27). He put more metric kick into the figuration by inverting the original form of the rhythmic motive from ♪♫ to ♫♪ (with sixteenths shifted to the downbeat) and adding trills to eighth notes (mm. 131–36, toward the end of the melisma).[71] Finally, just before the cadenza (mm. 137–39), he exploited his tremendous tessitura, which ranged from alto through soprano, to soar up two octaves from e to f″. And to top it all off, he extended the whole feat with a cadenza at the end of the reprise.

To his listeners, Farinelli's powers of execution must have seemed to grow with each lashing of the waves. Continuing his encomium on Farinelli's "Son qual nave," the performance of which remained legendary forty years after the fact, Burney commented:

> In short, he was to all other singers as superior as the famous horse Childers was to all other running-horses; but it was not only in speed that he excelled,

71. The figure appears as ♪♫ at the beginning of measure 132, but this is clearly a copying error (tacitly corrected in Haböck, *Die Gesangskunst des Kastraten*, 184).

EXAMPLE 2.3. Riccardo Broschi, "Son qual nave che agitata," mm. 117–39, with embellishments by Farinelli in upper line for reprise of A section

(continued)

EXAMPLE 2.3. (*continued*)

EXAMPLE 2.3. (*continued*)

(*continued*)

EXAMPLE 2.3. (*continued*)

> for he had now every excellence of every great singer united. In his voice, strength, sweetness, and compass; and in his stile, the tender, the graceful, and the rapid. Indeed he possessed such powers as never met before, or since, in any one human being; powers that were irresistible, and which must have subdued every hearer; the learned and the ignorant, the friend and the foe.[72]

His control over audience response through the wizardry of vocal gymnastics and his touching manipulation of affect marked him as a kind of Orphic magician who not only amazed and delighted, but "subdued every hearer." Antoine François Prévost extended the magical metaphor in his *Le pour et contre* (Paris, 1735) by declaring, "a spell draws the crowd to Farinelli's [show]."[73] He was the man who could tame wild beasts, stop Sisyphus from pushing his rock, put Charon to sleep, and make the implacable Furies weep.[74]

72. Burney, *An Eighteenth-Century Musical Tour in France and Italy*, 154.

73. Translated in Deutsch, *Handel*, 390.

74. On an engraving of Orpheus dating from around 1737 long associated with Farinelli, however, see McGeary and Cervantes, "From Farinelli to Monticelli," who convincingly reassign the male figure in the image to castrato Angelo Maria Monticelli.

Two features are common to these reports: one, viewers are transfigured by their experience of performers, and two, their transfiguration is presumed to take place within a specific set of viewing conditions. Apropos, recall that performers delivered arias from downstage center in direct address. Until later in the century, set designs pointed only referentially to the subjects they invoked, lacking a dynamic sense of lived space and a regard for the relation of architectural proportions to human forms. With wings and backdrops largely static and continuities between acts and numbers kept to a minimum, there was little *onstage* to divert spectators' attentions from performers. Singers could and did temper viewers' sense of them *as performers*, portraying characters and their emotions to create theatrical illusion through their own visibly performative bodies. Indeed, as Burney insisted, acting was part of an Italian singer's power to enchant.[75] Nevertheless, it seems evident that in viewers' perceptions, beneath their guise as characters, singers were always starkly manifest as real persons. The viewing self could dissolve fully into the performance at certain moments not despite this fact but because of it.

Fervent in their devotion to performers, spectators until at least midcentury could easily overcome—indeed probably enjoyed—the visual disjunction of males singing female roles and vice versa.[76] Grosley wrote about the production of Hasse's *Demofoonte* in Naples 1758, for example:

> [A]t the arietta *Misero Pargoletto*, in which Timante speaks to his son, whom he holds in his arms, there was not a dry eye in the house: the whole expression of this *arietta* was that of nature: the very French who were present overlooked the awkward phyz [*sic*] of the Soprano, who acted Timante, and the disagreement of his voice with the enormity of his stature, of his arms and legs, and wept as cordially as the Neapolitans themselves.[77]

75. Burney, *An Eighteenth-century Musical Tour in France and Italy*, 278: "With regard to this last charge it is by no means a just one; for whoever remembers Pertici and Laschi . . . or has seen the Buona Figliuola there lately, when Signor Guadagni, Signor Lovatini, and Signor Morigi were in it, or in the serious operas of past times remembers Monticelli, Elisi, Mingotto, Colomba Mattei, Manzoli, or, above all, in the present operas has seen Signor Guadagni, must allow that many of the Italians, not only recite well, but are *excellent actors*." Burney was countering Joseph Lalande, who claimed that "the fine voices in an Italian opera are not only too few, but are too much occupied by the music and its embellishments to attend to declamation and gesture" (*Voyage en Italie* 5:444).

76. This is well argued by Freitas, "Sex without Sex," and "The Eroticism of Emasculation," 196–249. Casanova plays on the eroticism of males who seem female or females or turn out to be male, most famously in his tale of "Bellino" (*Histoire de ma vie*, vol. 2, chaps. 1 and 2). See also Martinelli on Mingotti's trouser role (chap. 1, n. 50, above).

77. Grosley, *New Observations* 2:234. "[L]es larmes se mêlèrent aux applaudissemens dans l'Ariette connue, *Misero Pargoletto*, que Timante adresse à son fils qu'il tient dans ses bras: l'expression de toute cette Ariette étoit celle de la Nature: les François présens à ce spectacle, oublièrent eux-mêmes l'air gauche du *Soprano* qui remplissoit le rôle de Timante, & la dissonance de sa voix avec l'énormité de sa taille, de ses bras, de ses jambes, pour mêler leurs larmes â celles des Napolitains" (*Nouveaux mémoires* 3:96).

Presumed was intangible nature whose representation involved an art that exceeded the limits of the written and seen, a set of immaterial conditions that let spectators peer past the visible, whether or not the visible was fully agreeable on its own terms.

This intangibility was the reason Mancini insisted that the extraordinary art of singing could never be captured in notation. "Take . . . an aria sung by the celebrated Farinelli, with those variations he used to embellish it separately written out. We will certainly discover from this his talent, his knowledge, but we cannot ascertain what was his precise method, which made his execution so perfect and amazing, for this cannot be expressed in notation."[78] Mancini explained:

> In all the liberal arts . . . pupils depend very much upon the knowledge of the master, and his good will to teach; but in singing schools, everything depends on it. . . . [A] great singer cannot leave posterity a memorial of that inspiration, that method, that grace, and that skill with which he alone embellishes his singing. One finds . . . vocal music written by the greatest masters, and perfectly executed by a celebrated singer; but in such a monument one finds only the concept of a simple cantilena, or a simple passage indicated, enough to let the great singer have full liberty in embellishing the composition in accord with his talent. Thus if the pupil wishes to take this as a model, he sees it only as a skeleton, and it neither reveals by what means, with what fire, nor with what skill it was set forth, and ought to be executed.[79]

78. *Practical Reflections,* 14. "Prendiamo, a cagion d'esempio, per mano un'aria cantata dal celebre Farinello, ed abbiasi anche separatamente in scritto quella variazione, di cui se n'è egli servito per abellirla. Noi scopriremo certamente in quella il di lui talento, la di lui scienza, ma non potremo per questo indovinare qual fosse il suo preciso metodo, che rese sì perfetta, e sì sorprendente l'esecuzione, giacchè questo non può essere spiegato con le note" (Mancini, *Pensieri, e riflessioni pratiche* [1774], 32; *Riflessioni pratiche* [1777], 51; the 1777 edition replaces "per abbellirla" with "per renderla più bella" but has no other substantive changes).

79. Translation adapted from *Practical Reflections,* 13–14. "In tutte le arti liberali dipende molto dalla scienza del Maestro, e dalla di lui buona volontà d'istruire, la riuscita dei scolari; ma nella scuola del canto ella ne dipende intieramente." He continues, "Non si hanno, nè si possono avere in questa gli anzidetti monumenti, per la ragione, che un bravo Cantante non può lasciare ai posteri una memoria di quell'estro, di quel metodo, di quella grazia, e di quella condotta, con i quali era egli solito abbellire il suo canto. Si trova . . . della Musica vocale scritta da bravissimi Maestri, e perfettamente eseguita da qualche celebre Cantante: ma in un tal monumento non ritrovasi che concepita una semplice cantilena, che accennato un semplice passaggio, giust'appunto per lasciare al bravo Cantante la piena libertà d'abbellire la composizione a suo talento, e però, se uno scolare vuol prendere questa per modello, non la vede che in ossatura, nè può da quella rilevare con qual metodo, con qual brio, e con qual condotta sia stata, e debba essere eseguita" (*Pensieri, e riflessioni pratiche,* 30–32). In the equivalent passage in the 1777 edition (49–51), Mancini changes "ma nella scuola del canto ella ne dipende intieramente" to "quasi tutto il successo dipende dai maestri" (49) but otherwise the passage is almost identical.

RUBBING INTO MAGIC

The remarks of Mancini and Grosley bring us back to the formal argument developed earlier to ask how these dimensions of operatic experience square with the formal mechanics of the seria aria. We saw in chapter 1 that the performative approach of Stanley Tambiah assembles several components of ritual action in constructing its theory of ritual efficacy. Asking how different formal patterns serve as pliable aesthetic vehicles for the enhancement of various performative rites, Tambiah invokes examples such as "parallelism" (following the linguist Roman Jakobsen) as a means of structuring oral recitation of couplets (a a′ b b′, etc.) and "formulaic recitation" using improvised word repetition and reordering. We might even wonder if such structural devices have certain broad counterparts in opera seria arias, especially in the extended text-repetitive exemplars of circa 1750–90 that were described rhetorically in terms of tonal-functional periodicity by late-eighteenth-century music theorists. Without pushing such relationships too far, it is nevertheless worth noting that each genre combines different aesthetic media with formal patterning to enact a kind of ritual, which in turn depends on those combinations for its efficiency, magical or quasi-magical. To this extent, the intangible character of performance, and the feelings it can arouse, are not irreconcilable with the concrete processes that bring them about, and "magic" is no longer simply the stuff of dreams, hallucinations, and rumors. To the contrary, repetitions of formal patterns, built upon their antecedents through a variety of sensory media, become tangible means of stirring the senses into states of enchantment.

Tambiah and Gell (following Malinowski) both point to the physical manipulations performed by Trobriand garden magicians, especially as they practice repetitive chanting, but they do so toward different ends, Gell focusing on technical virtuosity to enthrall and daunt a rival, and Tambiah on the magical execution of formal patterns in the service of ritual efficacy. Of the two, Tambiah's is the more pragmatic, even though it omits the aesthetic questions raised by Gell, and certainly the more performative. Let us try, then, to translate from tubers to song the specific question Tambiah raises of how formal patterning relates to magical effects and contemplate further his crucial notion that ritualized action combines the variant and the invariant.

* * *

I have argued that the formal patterning of a standard da capo aria was largely predictable because conventional. Listeners knew that as an opera progressed, arias would emerge in a particular (if variable) order and include certain types, which in turn followed stock internal patterns and styles. By the time the Neapolitan school of Leo, Vinci, and Pergolesi was flourishing in the 1720s, they knew that most times a singer took center stage they could expect a five-part da capo, with at least two principal statements of stanza 1. Secondary characters and lighter or fleeter moments might call for cavatinas (a single stanza). We should not underestimate the theatrical vitality of other kinds of departures from the norm: the opening ritornello omitted to move straight from recitative to solo aria; aria endings dovetailed into the ensuing recitative or sinfonia; recitative used in an aria's midsection; an aria placed at the beginning of a scene (*Didone abbandonata* 3.8); choruses used in act 1 (*Adriano in Siria, L'olimpiade*), characters changing address in midcourse (*Ezio* 2.13, where the protagonist alternates between addressing his beloved and his tormenting sovereign). But there was much else that listeners could take for granted. They also knew that principal characters would tend to arrive first and deliver large entrance arias, and they knew that singers would probably not fire off their most excited bravura material until the middle of the second act. They knew that they were unlikely to hear the same instrumental scoring in immediate succession if it involved the addition of wind color, and they knew that they certainly should not hear the same key twice in a row, nor the same emotion, aria type, or character delivering an aria (though all might happen on rare occasions).

These elements were structural at the broadest temporal level of operatic experience. At the more immediate level of the aria, listeners were acculturated to verse repetitions within arias that proceeded by convention from more thematic material at the beginning of a stanzaic statement and more ornate material toward the end. Within this process, they expected verse statements to be most stable harmonically and thematically at the beginning of a1 and to stretch out the anticipation of resolution through a slowed harmonic rhythm in the progression from subdominant to dominant to the tonic cadence in the singer's approach to a principal ritornello.

Predictable as these may have been, how would singers have wooed listeners without them? We have already seen in the brief discussion of "Il tenero momento" how an individual verse statement could start with measured declamation of thematic material and culminate in florid passaggi over a tautly slowed harmonic rhythm. By the middle of the century, when composers had expanded the da capo to encompass as many as four or five statements of the first stanza in A (and no fewer than two),[80] arias could repeat this process with different harmonic goals. Once there were as many as three or four statements of the first stanza, the relationship between words and notes became more abstract, resulting in a less intimate or at least less direct link between words and notes, but arguably the abstraction promoted a purely sensual lyricism even more than otherwise. Words assumed new phenomenal, imagistic, and symbolic func-

80. In 1756, the anonymous author of *Lettre sur le méchanisme* satirized this length and abstraction in Italian opera, locating it in the ills of virtuosity and alleging that the leads' arias, of difficult execution, were the focus of all, that the public reserved for them all its attention, that a few words could support a quarter hour of music, and that one stanza of four lines and twenty syllables took seventeen minutes, twelve of which dwelt on the syllable A. He went on about cadenzas, calling them violinistic *roulemens* in which the singer makes himself admired the more he varies them, and continued by complaining about practices of aria substitution and scenography that countered verisimilitude (33–35).

tions as they lost their more referential one. Repeated verse statements created a start/restart effect that in the best of cases could mesmerize listeners as each succeeding musical variation glossed the text with new repetitions and fragments and with its own tonal directionality. The phenomenon can be visualized in example 2.4, which shows the vocal lines of each of four statements of stanza 1 in Mozart's entrance aria "Il tenero momento" from *Lucio Silla* of 1772 (superimposed one upon the other). These numerous repetitions gave audience members a many-sided look at the single state encapsulated in the first short stanza, with the singer functioning as master artist of verbal/sonic variation. Ventriloquizing the dramatic poet and composer, he or she worked to call forth a particular feeling or image: the sighing breeze or the trilling bird, the tender heart, the battered sails. In a show of hubris, a singer might claim to steer his ship through the most menacing waves, stalk his prey with the stealth of a lion, or proudly succumb to the vagaries of the heart. Astonishing passages and delicate figuration gave proof of moral sway and authentic feeling. Through each stanzaic statement, the crowd's nervous energies were collected and released, playing on the rhetorical directions of words but in the end—especially in the mid- to late eighteenth century—moving them away from meaning to sheer sensation and syntax.[81]

* * *

Listeners who went nightly to an opera looked at arias as if through a prism, hoping for some special difference at each performance. As Grosley noted, differences could consist of a "variety of gradations which [the singer] introduces into the trills, modulations, and whatever belongs to the expression." Most pervasive were surface ornaments, typically with quicker rhythmic denominations, and most spectacular, the cadenzas.

Ritually speaking, cadenzas were the most celebrated of what Tambiah would call the "variant" side. Although often prepared in advance, most pedagogues continued to agitate for improvised cadenzas well into the second half century, and to insist at minimum that cadenzas be made to *seem* improvised. Tosi is the first of the eighteenth-century bel canto teachers to call in print for improvisation and to emphasize an extemporaneous manner of expression, despite other grievances with modern singers. As rendered by his contemporaneous translator Galliard, "[I]s it not worst of all to torment the hearers with a thousand cadences [cadenzas] all in the same manner? From whence proceeds this sterility, since every professor knows that the surest way of gaining esteem in singing is [through] a variety [literally, fecundity] in the repetition?"[82] Agricola was even

81. See further in Feldman, "Staging the Virtuoso," 174 and passim.

82. Tosi, *Observations on the Florid Song*, chap. 8, §13, p. 136. "E non sarà forse peggior d'ogni difetto il tormentare gli ascoltanti con mille cadenze tutte fatte a un modo? Da che procede questa secca sterilità, se ad ogni professore è noto che per farsi stimar cantando, il mezzo più efficace è la fertilità dei ripieghi?" (*Opinioni de' cantori*, ed. Leonesi [1904], 106).

EXAMPLE 2.4. Wolfgang Amadeus Mozart, “Il tenero momento,” superimposition of four statements of the first quatrain, A section, vocal line only

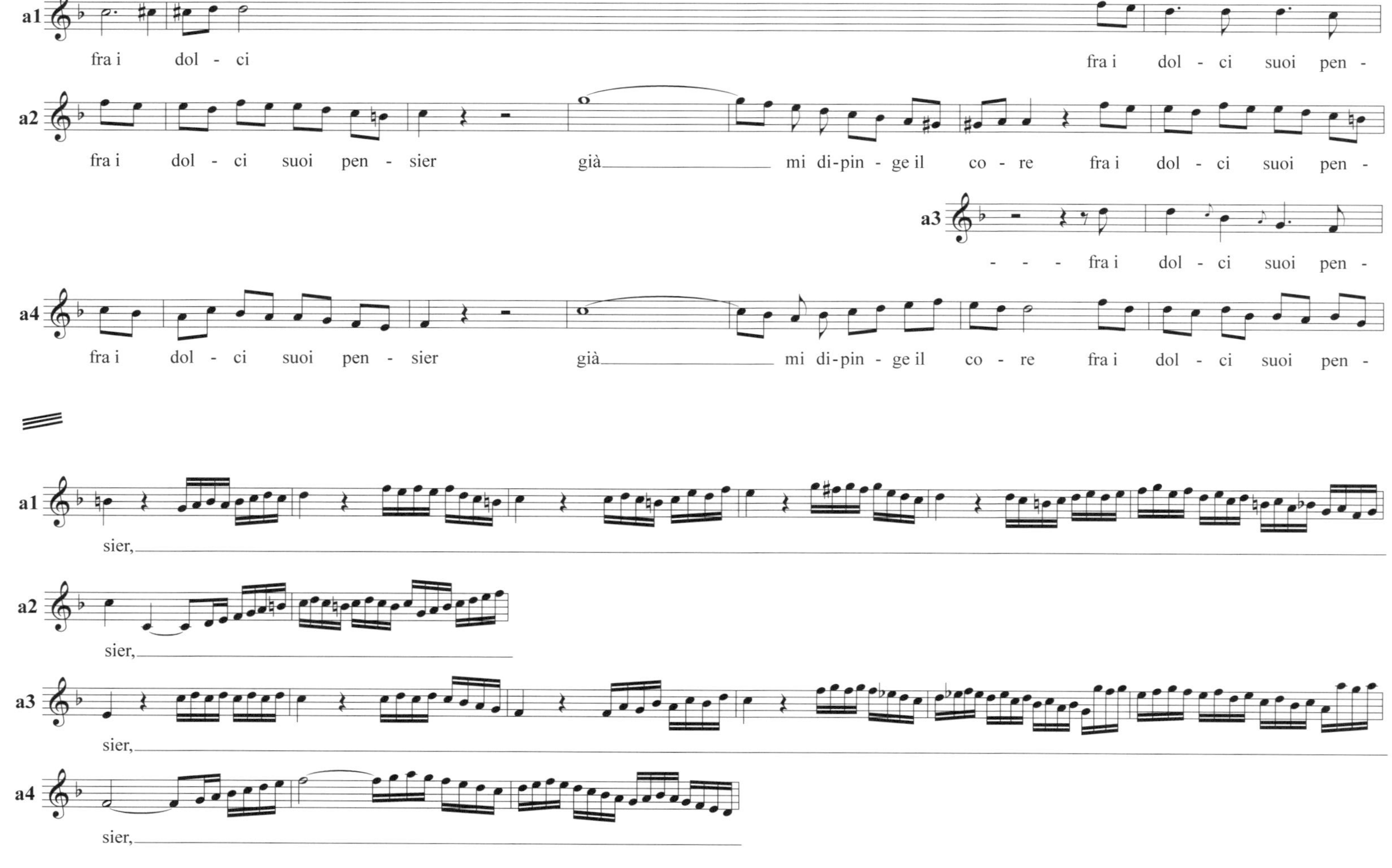
a1
fra i dol - ci
fra i dol - ci suoi pen -
a2
fra i dol - ci suoi pen - sier già mi di-pin - ge il co - re fra i dol - ci suoi pen -
a3
- - - fra i dol - ci suoi pen -
a4
fra i dol - ci suoi pen - sier già mi di-pin - ge il co - re fra i dol - ci suoi pen -
a1
sier,
a2
sier,
a3
sier,
a4
sier,

(continued)

EXAMPLE 2.4. *(continued)*

a1

fra i dol - - - ci suoi pen - sier.

a2

fra i dol - - - ci suoi pen - sier.

a3

fra i dol - - - ci suoi pen - sier.

a4

fra i dol - - - ci suoi pen - sier.

more emphatic in his much expanded and annotated translation of Tosi into German from 1757, extending Quantz's treatise on flute playing and eighteenth-century performance style. Demanding that the cadenza be improvised, Agricola found Tosi too soft on the point—and too hard on all sorts of modern cadenza practices: "Tosi is thus an enemy of our modern improvised cadenzas. . . . It is true that one would rather hear no cadenza at all than a poor one that is often rushed through. Now and then many a singer spoils all the good that he has achieved in the aria with an absurd ending. It is really burdensome for those who are poor in invention, not wishing to repeat the same one again and again, to have to create new cadenzas so often."[83]

This was the down side of improvising cadenzas, but for Agricola the up side was the whole point:

> It is also true, on the other hand, that a fiery person of talent can take his listeners by surprise and add, so to speak, a new degree of strength to the passion the aria is intended to arouse. He can bring to the ear of the listeners certain notes that were not always permissible in the aria by . . . clothing them in . . . a skillful cadenza, and thus he can acquaint the listeners with the entire range of his voice. The surprising, as well as the expected, has a place in music. As long as reasons for the cadenza are to be found that are not absolutely outweighed by reasons against them, a singer is not to be reproached for not letting slip through his fingers an opportunity to give free rein to a felicitous idea.[84]

"The surprising, as well as the expected, has a place in music." Here Agricola stresses the twin poles of the extraordinary and the ordinary, the variant and the invariant, arguing that their fluctuation is not just desirable but essential. His views were shared by all the famous singing masters and other pedagogues of performance in the 1750s through the 1780s, explicitly in Carl Philipp Emanuel

83. Agricola, *Introduction to the Art of Singing*, 210. "Herr Tosi ist also ein Feind unserer heut zu Tage noch üblichen willkührlichen Cadenzen . . . . Est ist wahr, es gehen viele Misbräuche dabey vor, deren einige unser Verfasser mit gutem Rechte getadelt hat. Est ist wahr, daß man oft est lieber gar keine, als eine so schlechte und so oft durchgepeitschete Cadenz zu hören wünschet. Mancher Sänger verderbt durch ein ungereimtes Ende bisweilen alles, was er in der Arie etwan noch Gutes vorgebracht hatte. Manchem, der an Erfindungen nicht reich ist, gereicht es wirklich zur Last, wenn er oft Cadenzen machen, und doch nicht immer eben dasselbe wieder sagen will" (Tosi and Agricola, *Anleitung zur Singkunst*, 203).

84. Agricola, *Introduction to the Art of Singing*, 210–11. "Est is aber dagegen auch wieder wahr, daß ein feuriger Kopf dadurch seine Zuhörer unvermuthet überraschen, und der Leidenschaft, deren Erregung die Absicht der Arie gewesen, gleichsam noch einen neuen Grad der Stärke zusetzen kann. Er kann gewisse Töne, deren Anbringung ihm in der Arie nicht allemal erlaubt gewesen, in eine geschickte Cadenz eingekleidet, den Zuhörern zu Ohren bringen, und diese also mit dem ganzen Umfange seiner Stimme bekannt machen. Das Wunderbare kann ja sowohl als das Wahrscheinliche auch in der Musik seinen Platz finden. So lange also, als noch Gründe für die Cadenzen zu finden sind, welche von den gegenseitigen nicht ganz und gar überwogen werden; so lange ist es auch einem Sänger nicht zu verargen, wenn er diese Gelegenheit einem glücklichen eigenen Einfalle freien Lauf zu lassen, nicht aus den handen gehen läßt"(Tosi and Agricola, *Anleitung zur Singkunst*, 203).

Bach's *Versuch über die wahre Art das Clavier zu spielen* (Berlin, 1753) and in the reformist treatise *Anweisung zum musikalisch-zierlichen Gesange* (Leipzig, 1780), chapter 7, by German *Singspiel* composer and pedagogue Johann Adam Hiller.[85]

How often cadenzas were truly improvised extemporaneously is hard to say. Farinelli and certain other singers were renowned for doing so,[86] but it is clear that many others used a variety of written cadenzas from night to night and others hardly varied theirs at all. Caffarelli evidently could not perform one night in Naples because he had lost his written-out cadenzas.[87] Some professional singers, and perhaps amateurs, collected albums of cadenzas, an exemplar of which is preserved in Special Collections of the Joseph Regenstein Library at the University of Chicago (MS 1267).[88] Others were given cadenzas while students or budding professionals. Mozart created at least two sets of embellishments for his young love Aloysia Weber in 1778 to groom her for the Italian stage. In one he supplied ornaments and cadenzas for a da capo aria by Johann Christian Bach, "Cara la dolce fiamma" (from *Adriano in Siria*), which is heavily ornamented in the first A section alone and still more so in the reprise, especially in anticipation of phrase endings (see example 2.5). For the B section, he supplied only cadenzas, two of them, presumably so Aloysia could vary hers from one performance to another but also have two cadenzas ready if asked to encore the aria on the spot.[89] The other aria by Mozart that survives with a pair of embellishments was for the A section and reprise of an "aria Cantabile," "Ah se a morir mi chiama" (K. 293c) from his *Lucio Silla*.[90]

85. See Bach, *Essay on the True Art of Playing Keyboard Instruments*, 379–86. Hiller excused singers who indulged in long and colorful cadenzas, since "it is not infrequent that the best, most masterly performed arias are not applauded, whereas the cadenzas of the most mediocre singers draw the loudest applause. Thus the singer has good reason, at the end of the aria, to solicit applause from the audience, even if he has to force the occasion" (*Treatise on Vocal Performance*, 122). [Man muss ihnen diesen Irrthum einigermaßen zu gute halten, da es sich nicht selten zuträgt, dass die beste, meisterhaft vorgetragene Arie nicht applaudirt wird, da hingegen die Cadenz des mittelmäßigsten Sängers den lautesten Beyfall nach sich zieht. Dieser ermangelt daher auch nicht, wenigstens am Ende der Arie, und sollte er auch die Gelegenheit dazu mit den Haaren herbey ziehen, eine Auffoderung an das Auditorium gelangen zu lassen (*Anweisung zum musikalisch-zierlichen Gesange*, book 7, "Von den Cadenzen," §3, p. 110).] Hiller added that Johann Mattheson in *Der Vollkommene Capellmeister* of 1739 called this a "farewell bow" ("un Abschiedscompliment"), offered by the singer to his listeners.

86. On Farinelli, see Burney, *General History of Music* 2:781, 788–93, 800, 814–17, 909, 919. Burney provides Farinelli's "divisions" sung in England (831–32), as well as a rendition of his singing of Riccardo Broschi's "Son qual nave" (833–38).

87. Heriot, *The Castrati*, 149–50.

88. See Brown, "Embellishing Eighteenth-Century Arias," 270–71 and passim.

89. A transcription of the original vocal line and much of its embellishment by Leopold or most probably Wolfgang can be found in Crutchfield, "Voices," 306–9 (with inclusive discussion on 304–10). For a complete edition of J. C. Bach's "Cara la dolce fiamma," see *Adriano in Siria*, 325–45. See Mozart's letter to his father of February 14, 1778, in Mozart, *Briefe* 2:226–27; Anderson, *Letters of Mozart*, 447–48.

90. Technically a dal segno aria, "Ah se a morir" is transcribed in nearly complete form from A-Sm (with tacit corrections) in Neumann, *Ornamentation and Improvisation*, 231–33. Mozart called it an "Arie mit ausgesetztem gusto" (an aria with variants dictated). His own copy of his embellish-

EXAMPLE 2.5. Johann Christian Bach, "Cara, la dolce fiamma," mm. 1–3 (incipit), from *Adriano in Siria*, with embellishments probably by Wolfgang Amadeus Mozart, vocal line

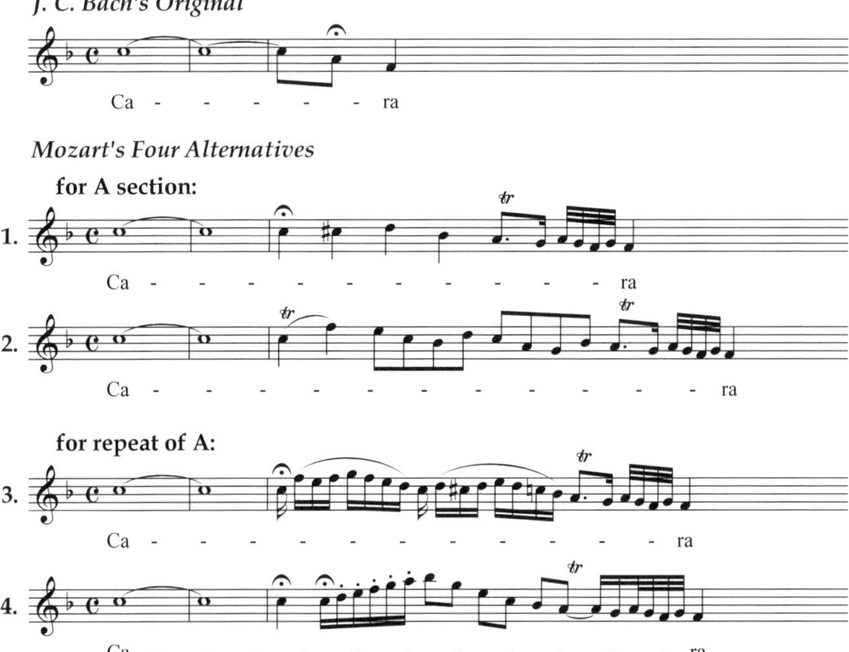

Original version by Bach in top system; Mozart's four embellishments for A section in second and third systems (A); and Mozart's embellishments for reprise of A in fourth and fifth systems (A′). Transcribed from A-Sm, copy in the hand of Leopold Mozart.

To memorize her diverse cadenzas, Madame Mara had her bravura piece from Gazzaniga's *Gli argonauti* copied out with four empty staves above the voice part, on which she wrote out four different ornamented versions, thus allowing her to feign improvisation. By using them on successive nights during the run of the opera, she secured her triumph over her rival Banti, who sang all her arias "by rote as she had learned them." Mara declared unabashedly that her performance brought the same people to the theater night after night because "one could hear something new every evening."[91]

A strong advocate of the importance and viability of improvising cadenzas, Agricola argued that it was probably impossible

> to teach someone to memorize clever ideas beforehand, because both the writing and the teaching are *partly elicited and partly determined by circumstances and opportunity*. Through diligent reading and observation of the clever ideas

ments for Aloysia's singing of "Non so d'onde viene" (K. 294) also survives; see Mozart, *Neue Ausgabe sämtlicher Werke* II.7.2, no. 19, pp. 41–58, plus Mozart's 1783 revision of the ornaments in the appendix (ibid., 151–66).

91. Riesemann, "Ein Selbstbiographie der Gertrud Mara," cols. 11–12. Significantly, Mara recounted this late in the century when improvisation had waned.

> of others, however, one can awaken, sharpen, and improve his own wit, and . . . control [it] by [following] the dictates of his own reason. In the same way, one can develop his own musical wit by attending carefully to the clever ideas of other good singers. All that remains is to show him the pitfalls to be avoided and to put before him, as guides, the precepts of good and reasonable taste. Whoever is already possessed of a fruitful inventive faculty, familiarizes himself with my observations concerning the improvised cadenzas, and listens attentively and diligently to good singers and instrumentalists will, in a short time, have an overabundance rather than a dearth of cadenzas, *even if he does not possess a single one that has been written down.*[92]

If an improvised cadenza was not an option—or, less commonly, where improvising cadenzas was inadvisable, as in double cadenzas (i.e., in duets), which Agricola thought could hardly ever be done with success—a cadenza could still be carried off well because the composer would arrange it "in such a way that it [would] not be apparent to the listener that it [had] been memorized."[93] All cadenzas were to give the effect of being improvised, whether they were or not.

There were no hard and fast rules about the various places where cadenzas were or were not to be added, except that they were expected at the end of the reprise of the A section at an absolute minimum. Tosi's remarks show that a practice had developed by the early eighteenth century of adding cadenzas to the ends of all three main sections of the da capo aria:

92. Translation adapted from Agricola, *Introduction to the Art of Singing,* 212 (emphasis mine). "Wer das bisher gesagete genau überleget, wird einsehen, daß es nicht wohl möglich ist allgemeine gute Cadenzen vorzuschreiben; so wenig als es möglich ist, jemanden witzige Einfälle vorher auswendig zu lehren. Denn eins und das andere wird durch die Umstände und die Gelegenheit theils hervor gebracht, theils bestimmt. Durch fleitziges Lesen und Beobachten der witzigen Einfälle anderer aber, kann einer seinen eigenen Witz erwecken, schärfen, und verbessern; so wie er ihn durch die Vorschriften der Vernunft in Ordnung halten kann. Auf gleiche Art kann ein Sänger, seinen musikalischen Witz, durch fleitzige Anhörung der witzigen Einfälle anderer guter Sänger auch bilden. Man hat nichts weiter nöthig, als ihm die Abwege zu zeigen die er zu vermeiden hat, und ihm die Vorschriften des guten und vernünftigen Geschmacktes dabey zum Leitfaden anzuweisen. Wer also die allgemeinen Beobachtungen, welche wir hier über die willkührlichen Cadenzen überhaupt mitgetheilet haben, sich wohl bekannt machet, und dabey gute Sänger und Instrumentisten fleitzig und aufmerksam höret, dabey auch selbst eine fruchtbare Erfindungskraft besiztet; der wird in kurzer Zeit an guten Cadenzen eher Ueberfluß als Mangel haben: sollte er auch gleich keine einzige in Noten aufgeschriebene besitzen" (Tosi and Agricola, *Anleitung zur Singkunst,* 205–6). Agricola looked with a jaundiced eye on the collections of written-down cadenzas amassed by some Italian singers: "[T]he listening music lovers, if they have considered it worth their while to read what I have written, will be able to determine rather well the value of most of the cadenzas that many of our Italian singers so avidly collect." [Die zuhörenden Liebhaber der Musik werden indessen, aus dem, was ich bisher gesaget habe, wenn sie es durchzulesen anders der Mühe werth achten, ohngefähr den Werth der meisten Cadenzen vieler unserer wälschen Sänger, welche aufzusammeln manche von ihnen so begierig sind, bestimmen können (ibid., 206).]

93. "Er wird sie schon so einzurichten wissen, daß es doch nicht ein jeder Zuhörer merken könne, daß sie auswendig gelernet worden sey" (ibid., 205).

> Every *Air* has (at least) three *Cadences* [*Cadenzas*], that are all three final. Generally speaking, the Study of the Singers of the present Times consists of terminating the *Cadence* of the first Part with an overflowing of *Passages* and *Divisions* at pleasure, and the *Orchestre* waits; in that of the second the *Dose* is encreased, and the *Orchestre* grows tired; but on the last *Cadence,* the Throat is set a going like a Weather-cock in a Whirlwind and the *Orchestre* yawns. But why must the World be thus continually deafened with so many *Divisions?*[94]

Laying aside his laments, what is most revealing in Tosi's explanation is the notion that as a whole the cadenzas will tend to mount both in surface activity and in the extent to which the singer overshadows the instruments. As each cadenza became thicker, more impassioned, and more ecstatic, the singer could increasingly surpass the orchestra and stir up the public. Moreover, the resulting crescendo of tension by means of surface activity, made by suspending resolution of the tonic six-four or dominant seventh chord (in essence over the course of the entire aria), would militate against surface-level repetitions and segmentation of the aria, with the whole effect heightened by the labor and triumph involved in taking the cadenza in a single breath. (The rules were not hard and fast, as Howard Mayer Brown demonstrates in his analysis of Faustina Bordoni's aria, discovered by George Buelow, which has a cadenza ending the B section that is not on a I^6_4 or V chord and a cadenza ending the reprise of A that outlines IV.)[95]

In 1723, Tosi still longed for a return to the metered cadenzas of the seventeenth and early eighteenth centuries. Those "out of Time" cadenzas rankled him no end. But by the time full-blown Neapolitan opera seria came into its own in the 1720s, the cadenza evidently had full metric liberty.[96] As Agricola put it, "[N]o rhythmic movement is to be observed therein," for "[i]t must seem as though the singer has been overcome by passion in such a way that he could

94. Tosi, *Observations on the Florid Song,* 128–29. "Ogni aria (per lo meno) ha tre cadenze, che sono tutte e tre finali. Lo studio dei cantori di oggidì (generalmente parlando) consiste nel terminare la cadenza della prima parte con un profluvio di passaggi ad libitum, e che l'orchestra aspetti. In quella della seconda si moltiplica la dose alle fauci, e l'orchestra s'annoia; nel replicare poi l'ultima dell'intercalare si da fuoco alla girandola di Castel San Angelo, e la orchestra tarocca. Ma perché mai assordare il mondo con tanti passaggi" (Tosi, *Opinioni de' cantori,* ed. Leonesi [1904], 101).

95. Brown, "Embellishing Eighteenth-Century Arias," 262–63.

96. "If inventing particular cadences without injuring the time has been one of the worthy employments of the ancients (so-called) let a student revive the use of it, endeavouring to imitate them in their skill of somewhat anticipating the time. Remember that those who understand the art of gracing do not wait to admire the beauty of it in a silence of the bass" (Tosi, *Observations on the Florid Song,* chap. 8, §17, p. 60). [Se l'inventar cadenze particolari senza offesa del tempo è stata una delle degne occupazioni dei chiamati antichi, chiunque studia la rimetta in uso, procurando d'imitarli nell'intelligenza di saper rubare un po' di tempo anticipato, e di ricordarsi che i conoscitori dell'artificio non aspettano di ammirare la bellezza nel silenzio dei bassi (Tosi, *Opinioni de cantori,* ed. Leonesi [1904], 107).] The unmetered cadenza was the rule well before Agricola's time, with the rarest exceptions (see Agricola, *Introduction to the Art of Singing,* 29, 205, and 211; *Anleitung zur Singkunst,* 195–96, 204).

not possibly be thinking of being limited by the rhythm."[97] This meant that the performer could gather a head of steam in the cadenza, with scales, trills, and other figures ripped off over the static seventh or six-four chord, before letting it out at the banal, metered reentry of the orchestra. With multiple cadenzas, it also meant that each exultant rise and ensuing collapse of the singer could outshine the previous one, a series of greater and greater triumphs arching over the performance before the singer's exit.

Tosi's recommendations generally correspond to those of other theorists as well as those we can discern from musical evidence. By the time Quantz wrote his treatise on flute playing in 1752, the total of three cadenzas lamented by Tosi had often grown in number (although Quantz's ascetic eye looked askance at this).[98] There were now sometimes five cadenzas, and there is evidence that even more were added in certain cases. A famous example with no less than eleven cadenzas, sung by Farinelli in Geminiano Giacomelli's "Quell'usignolo che innamorato" from the opera *Merope*, survives written-out in Vienna 19111.[99] The poetic text of the aria justified the extravagance expressively if nothing else did, since it was a trope on the most extravagantly melodious of all creatures, "That nightingale in love, who, when he sings alone from branch to branch, explains the cruelty of his fate."[100] Singers were expected to listen closely to the actual song of birds, if we believe Ludovico Zacconi (1558–1627), and many, like the castrato Filippo Balatri (1682–1756), who prided themselves on their adeptness in imitating them.[101] Still, "Quell'usignolo" must have outdone them all. Four cadenzas were added to the A section, one following a fermata at the end of the first poetic line, one following a1, one following the end of the first poetic line in a2, and one at the end of A as a whole (not to mention an *ad libitum* passage "a suo piacere" toward the beginning of the last statement in

97. Agricola, *Introduction to the Art of Singing*, 211. "Deswegen darf auch . . . gar keine Tactart darinn beobachtet werden. Es muß scheinen als wäre der Sänger von der Leidenschaft so durchdrungen, daß er darüber nicht mehr auf eine eingeschränkte Tactbewegung denken könnte" (Tosi and Agricola, *Anleitung zur Singkunst*, 204).

98. Brown, "Embellishing Eighteenth-century Arias," 259–60.

99. A-Wn, MS 19111; piano-vocal arrangement in Haböck, *Die Gesangskunst der Kastraten* 1:140–52. Farinelli sang at least four or five arias regularly each night for King Philip V of Spain (and more altogether). On February 16, 1738, he wrote, "Every blessed evening I gulp down eight or nine arias with no respite!" [Mi bevo tutte le sante sere 8 in 9 arie in corpo, non c'è riposo (*La solitudine amica*, 143–44, and see Carlo Vitali's commentary, 219–20).] Of the various arias he sang repeatedly during the years that overlapped with Philip's reign (1737–46), it seems that only "Quell'usignolo" was invariably included; see Freeman, "Farinello," 307–9, esp. n. 29. On its cadenzas, see Brown, "Embellishing Eighteenth-Century Arias," 264.

100. Here I differ from Brown, "Embellishing Eighteenth-Century Arias," 262–64.

101. Cf. Zacconi, *Prattica di musica* 1:58 (chap. 66, "Che stile si tenghi nel far di gorgia, & dell'uso de i moderni passaggi"), where Zacconi claims that we should listen to the beauty of figuration done by birds, which ravish the heart, and the discussion in Filippo Balatri's autobiography, *Frutti del mondo*, 256 (an abridged edition of the manuscript in G-Mb, Cod. It. 39, 67 and passim).

A).[102] Brown doubted whether Farinelli could have taken some of the cadenzas in "Quell'usignolo" in a single breath, but given how multipartite some of them are, the question may well be whether he would have elected to.[103]

FRAME

We have seen that when opera seria arias are cast into the theoretical lot of performance, aria scores can be reconceived as composers' templates for the stimulus and response of human passions that took place during operatic events. Auditors provide a counterweight to our dependency on scores. By attending to them, the practice of close reading acquires new vitality. As scores become hieroglyphs for a communicative language between singers and spectators, they turn from frozen specimens to living tissue, richly laced with the nerves and capillaries of social space.

I would like finally to situate the interactions of this social space within the conceptual sphere of what I call the "frame." By "frame" I mean first of all the metaphorical and pragmatic boundaries within which stage events were experienced, in a sense roughly parallel to Erving Goffman's usage in *Frame Analysis*.[104] But I also have in mind the enclosure and separation of performative events from the viewer. As a spectacle form, opera seria necessarily restricts the viewer's experience of the entire event—in this instance, the opera and intermezzi and all of the media deployed to stage them—to a state of "once-remove."

"Frame" conceived in this way underscores a limit. Through recurrent formalizing gestures and strategies of segmentation, opera seria performances imposed an inviolable distance between the stage and the house, disallowing the possibility of sustained absorption in an alternate reality and restricting the transmission of cultural messages and aesthetic experience.[105] Those nonsegmentary elements of the performance that I have underscored were not without effects:

102. See the modern edition in Haböck, *Die Gesangskunst des Kastraten*, 140–52, with added ornamented vocal parts and cadenzas.

103. On the cadenzas in "Quell'usignolo," which are not as long as some others, see Brown, "Embellishing Eighteenth-Century Arias," 164. On Farinelli, we have the testimony of Quantz, who heard him in Italy in 1725–26 and called his breath control "extraordinary" (as Marpurg reports in his biography of Quantz, *Historisch-kritische Beyträge*, 233–34). Sacchi speaks of Farinelli's breath control in the *messa di voce*, famously in Porpora's "Alto giove" (*Vita del cavaliere Don Carlo Broschi*, 36–37). See also Farinelli's own remarks about the three *messe di voce* he sang for Emperor Karl VI, letter of March 31, 1732, in *La solitudine amica*, 99. A summary of the unique techniques of breath control is given in Celletti, *A History of Bel Canto*, 109–11. See too Crutchfield, "Voices," 310. The *Lettre sur la méchanisme* in 1756 still assumes a single breath for a cadenza (34–35).

104. See *Frame Analysis*, where Goffman uses the notion of frame to designate the contextual boundaries within which daily social interactions are ritualized.

105. Analogous interpretations of the spectatorship of early cinema are put forward by Gunning, "The Cinema of Attractions," 56–62.

they could convey an underlying sense of overall dramatic progress and potentially stir spectators into a lather of emotion or sensual pleasure. But they did not alter the intractable condition of parataxis that was endemic to opera seria and the distance it imposed.

I suggest that this distance did not preclude interaction, however, but instead regulated it. As we have already seen and as countless other eyewitness reports tell us, audiences normally had a vigorous voice in the opera house. The cadential drives, vocal pyrotechnics, tutti flourishes, and noisy ritornellos deployed in the traditional opera seria aria were strategically mobilized to choreograph both its delivery and reception, simultaneously staging the singer's performance and molding the demonstrations of the crowd. Arias thus operated doubly, shaping the rhetorical energies of verse through musical phrases delivered by the singer while tacitly inscribing the viewer's reactions in the singer's rests and the music of the band. The singer's relationship with viewers was typically interactive, addressed to them even when it remained more or less within the frame of the performance (at least before the ascendancy of a naturalistic style of acting relatively late in the century). Sometimes singers were simply indecorous, even by eighteenth-century standards.[106] A concomitant of these interactions was to force the viewer away from the possibility of continuous spectating—a possibility that, by the 1750s and 1760s, was beginning to be articulated as an ideal and then had to be reconciled with existing modes of performance and viewing. To this extent, the concept of frame points paradoxically both to the formal-expressive structures that *governed* audiences' interactions with arias and (as I have claimed above) to formal-spectatorial norms that consequently *distanced* audiences from the stage events as a whole.

This contradictory condition of the frame—at once regulating and disabling viewer involvement—is epitomized within the aria itself. As each aria ruptures the narrative flow, pushing the audience repeatedly outside the stream of dramatic action (one it was often inclined to forgo anyway), it invites the audience into another drama: the formally closed, suprarational realm of song.

106. "The great singers in Italy . . . do not themselves always take the trouble to act: when they do, it's sometimes in a way that is quite familiar and not very respectful towards the spectators; they greet people they know, even in the middle of their performance, without fear of displeasing the audience whose indulgence has long authorized this abuse; it can also be attributed to the meager attention paid to the performance if there is an unbearable noise either in the pit or the boxes." [Les grands acteurs en Italie . . . ne se donnent pas la paine de jouer toujours eux-mêmes; quand ils le font, c'est quelque fois d'une façon très-familiere & très-peu respectueuse pour les spectateurs; ils salient les personnes de leur connoissance, même au milieu de leur jeu, sans crainte de déplaire au public, dont l'indulgence autorise ces abus; on peut aussi attribuer au peu d'attention qu'on donne au spectacle, où l'on fait un bruit insupportable, dans le parterre, où l'on est assis, soit dans les loges (LaLande, *Voyage en Italie* 7:207–8).] There are many other such observations, especially of singers like Caffarelli (on whom see Heartz, "Caffarelli's Caprices"). The composer Galuppi had to deal with one castrato who refused to sing one of his arias during a performance, whereupon he sang it himself. The audience loved it, so the castrato was induced to announce that he could do even better and with that proceeded to win their acclaim. The story is recounted in Barbier, *The World of the Castrati,* 109.

CHAPTER 3

Programming Nature, Parma, 1759: First Case Study

"Let us hope that Fable may . . . so submit to the purifying processes of Reason as to take the character of exact history." PLUTARCH, *Theseus*[1]

"Myth can be as fertile a field for lyric theater as history. . . . The misfortunes of Phaedra and Daphne can move us to tears as easily as those of Merope and Dirce. Does it matter whether the tears and joys of humankind . . . are stirred by history rather than myth in a theater dedicated to our amusement? We should take up Euripides and the most famous authors who, in their tragedies, applied themselves to fabulous subjects invented to render nature in all its truth." CARLO FRUGONI, preface to *Ippolito ed Aricia*, 1759[2]

On May 2, 1759, the duchy of Parma caused a stir among European elites by staging a French-styled mythological opera in its public theater, the Regio Ducal Teatro. The opera was *Ippolito ed Aricia,* with libretto by the court poet Carlo Frugoni and music by court composer Tommaso Traetta.[3] Originally, it was to have opened on May 1, the duke's nameday, but the performance was put off for a day because the prima donna complained of a cold.[4]

Ippolito ed Aricia was adapted with extensive modifications from *Hippolyte et Aricie,* the famous *tragédie en musique* composed by Jean-Philippe Rameau in 1733 on a libretto by the abbé Simon-Joseph Pellegrin, who in turn had drawn on Racine's *Phèdre* of 1677.[5] Ever since the Arcadian Academy's reform of the

1. Plutarch, *Theseus* 1:1, in Dryden, *Plutarch's Lives.*

2. Original libretto reprinted in Brown, *Italian Opera Librettos,* vol. 14 (hereafter cited as *Ippolito* libretto).

3. The Regio-Ducal Teatro had been built as a public theater (then called Teatro Ducale) by the indigenous Farnese dynasty in 1689.

4. Attested by Antonio Sgavetti, the court chronicler (Sgavetti, May 3, 1759). The date of May 9 usually given is wrong. The prima donna was Caterina Gabrielli, "La Coghetta" (cf. n. 60 below). Francesco Maria Hasse wrote to Giammaria Ortes from Vienna, February 28, 1761, to say that Gabrielli was "bravissima" but didn't always sing (Pancino, *Johann Adolf Hasse e Giammaria Ortes,* 72–73).

5. Facsimile of the autograph score in D-B Mus. MS 21995, reprinted in Brown, *Italian Opera,* ser. 2, no. 78, ed. Weimer (hereafter *Ippolito* score). On manuscript sources, see Binetti, *Tommaso e Filippo Trajetta,* 72; Riedlbauer, *Die Opern von Tommaso Trajetta,* 149; and Loomis, "Tommaso Traetta's Operas for Parma," 45–46. A performance was recorded at the Festival Valle d'Itria, Martina Franca, Puglia, Italy (summer 1998), David Golub, conductor (Dynamic, CDS 257/1-4 DDD, 2000). For Rameau's score and commentary on different versions, see Rameau, *Oeuvres complètes,* vol. 6. A

lyric stage decades earlier, Italian opera had favored ancient history over myth. There were plenty of exceptions—among Metastasio's operas, for example, *Didone abbandonata, Achille in Sciro,* and *Ipermestra*—but the center of gravity in Italian opera remained ancient history. Yet the men who masterminded *Ippolito* were after much more. The opera was the brainchild of the powerful minister of state Guillaume du Tillot, who had reached Parma in the retinue of the Francophile Don Filippo of Spain after the Spanish Bourbons were awarded the duchy in 1748 by the treaty of Aix-la-Chapelle, reclaiming it from the Austrians, who had ruled since the end of the Farnese dynasty in 1731.[6] Du Tillot was a fanatical culturalist of an authoritative bent. He had the touch of megalomania needed to effect sweeping reforms, and the idea to mount *Ippolito ed Aricia* came about just after he had spent a decade plotting to raise the cultural capital of the duchy by means of lavish theatrical pieces. The opera was also his chance to realize the dreams he shared with operatic reformers across Europe, in particular their prime spokesman, Francesco Algarotti, who longed to revise the lyric stage by mixing the euphonious passion of Italian arias with the purportedly "naturalistic" continuities of French opera. So styled, opera was to retain Italianate melody—meaning arias—while integrating the great scenic tableaux of French *tragédie en musique,* with its dramatic orchestral recitatives, choruses, and ballets. Following the premiere of *Ippolito,* Du Tillot wrote Algarotti proclaiming their success. "Our opera is what I predicted: it enchants the nation. As you know, I thought that by leaving in it the taste and music [of the Italians] . . . one could enrich it. . . . [I]n the end . . . we succeed; and I remind myself that I owe you a part of my courage."[7]

ENTER NATURE

The aesthetic vision over whose triumph Du Tillot exulted had its primary ideological expression in Algarotti's *Saggio sopra l'opera in musica.* Algarotti had returned to Italy after spending time in Paris (1735–36), where he shared quar-

---

new critical edition is underway, Rameau, *Opera omnia,* in which the 1757 revival of *Hippolyte* appears as ser. 4.6 (2005); the 1733 version, ser. 4.1, is in preparation. Recent recordings include Les Arts Florissants, William Christie, conductor (Erato, 1997 CD 15517), and Les Musiciens du Louvre, Marc Minkowski, conductor (Archiv-Produktion, 1995, CD 445 853-2). An important new cultural treatment of *Hippolyte et Aricie* in the context of the ancien régime is Thomas, *Aesthetics of Opera,* chap. 5.

6. For a succinct explanation of power rivalries and redistribution of lands to Spanish and Austrian powers between 1713 and 1748, see Symcox, "The Political World of the Absolutist State," 116–18.

7. "Nôtre Opéra est ce que j'avois prévu, il enchante la nation. J'avois conçu, vous le savez, qu'en lui laissant son gout et sa musique . . . , on pouroit l'enrichir. . . . enfin . . . nous triomphons: et je me souviens que je vous dois une partie de mon courage" (Algarotti, *Opere* 15: 359–60). Closely paralleling these comments is an anonymous review sent to Marmontel and published in the *Mercure de France* in July 1759; see Heartz, "Traetta in Parma," app. 2, 271–92. Heartz provides essential background on the making and make-up of the opera.

ters with the reform dramatist Voltaire, afterwards spending thirteen years at the reformist court of Frederick the Great in Berlin (1740–53) from where he made trips to the progressive electoral court of Dresden. When he got to Italy for good, he was shocked by the state of Venetian public opera and in 1755 issued his *Saggio* as an anonymous broadside on the whole institution. The cognoscenti of Parma seconded his views warmly. Frugoni himself thanked him in March 1756, partly on behalf of Du Tillot, for bringing opera back to "truth." He sympathized with Algarotti's hopes that opera's disparate elements would someday be made to harmonize, though suggesting that Algarotti's own attempt at a libretto (on Iphigenia, included with the *Saggio*) was overly idealistic.[8] Partly as a response to the Parmesan reception and partly as a specific response to their mounting of *Ippolito ed Aricia*, Algarotti in 1763 revised his *Saggio* and published it under his own name.[9]

At its foundation lay the idea that opera should banish the artifices of baroque spectacle opera—not so much the marvelous machines as the sensible and narrative disjunctions that had long been tolerated in Italy's festive theaters. Gone would be the extraneous ballets wedged between acts of an opera, men dressed in women's clothing, scenic perspectives ill-proportioned to human forms, jolting shifts from simple recitative to elaborate arias, poetry mangled by word repetitions and littered with extravagant passaggi. Algarotti claimed that when various elements did not accord, the possibility of illusion would vanish—hence the coordination of text and music, opera and ballet, gesture and meaning, vocal sound and physical sight was essential to producing a harmony of elements.

> Indeed, if we consider what little effort [is] put into the choice of a libretto, or a plot, almost nothing into how the music will fit the words, and nothing at all into the truthfulness of the manner of singing and reciting, the link between dances and stage action, stage designs, and even how theaters themselves are properly constructed, it is quite easy to see how any theatrical presentation,

8. "Che volete voi che io vi dica del libretto vostro, che voi meglio di me conoscete? Io lo trovo degno del vostro genio. Non si può pensar meglio per ridurre il dramma vostro musicale a quella varietà ed a quella convenevolezza, che ancor gli manca. Diletterebbe molto più, se negli abiti, nelle scene, nei balli quel carattere si conservasse, che ai vari soggetti dee darsi, e se tutto avesse con la rappresentazione quel rapporto, che si conviene, e se in fine la musica dipingesse le parole del poeta. Voi mostrate come i precetti vostri si possano felicemente eseguire; e piacesse alle muse che d'ogginnanzi gli scrittori drammatici vi prendessero per guida e per maestro! Ma il reo costume troppo è signore dei musicali spettacoli in Italia." [What might I say to you about your libretto, which you know better than I do? I find it worthy of your brilliance. One could not think how better to convert your musical drama to that variety and decorum that it still lacks. How much more it would delight if it were to preserve in the costumes, scenery, and ballets that character with which one must endow various subjects, and if everything were appropiately integrated into the opera, and finally, if the music were to depict the words of the poet. You show how your precepts can be successfully executed; and may it please the muses if nowadays dramatic writers should take you for their guide and maestro! But bad habits are too much the master of musical spectacles in Italy! (Frugoni to Algarotti, letter of March 23, 1756, in Algarotti, *Opere* 10:62–63).]

9. Facsimile of both editions in Algarotti, *Saggio*, ed. Bini.

> which should by nature be among the most delightful, turns out to be insipid and tedious. Because of the confusion created among its various parts, not a shadow of imitation remains; illusion, which can be born only of a perfect accord between its parts, vanishes completely; and opera, one of the most artful contrivances of the human spirit, turns into a composition that is languid, disconnected, inverisimilar, monstrous, grotesque, and deserving of all the nasty things that are said about it and of the censure of those who hold pleasure to be that serious and important thing that it is.[10]

That opera *was* a form of illusion was not at issue. The task was how to make it more convincingly so.

Central to this goal was Algarotti's call for the use of Greek myth. Ancient mythology offered a *fons et origo* of the human condition. With seemingly primordial links to language, its use in opera was put forward as a way to allow singing to enhance communication. Yet nature's only imaginable incarnation was one of classical simplicity, a conception not unlike that of the Arcadian Academy and Metastasio. Decades earlier they had expelled the comic-cum-serious admixtures, numerous subplots, and huge casts of seventeenth-century opera. But for Algarotti and his kind the main trouble were the virtuosi, still beloved by audiences but largely anathema to the reformists: "For one hundred rhapsodists of common cloth—those who cram in whatever is least suited—one manages only with great difficulty to find one who uses learning to unite taste with elegance and naturalness, and in whom proper discretion restrains fantasy."[11] The criticism went back at least as far as Ludovico Antonio Muratori's *Della perfetta poesia italiana* (1706), but it had reached a strident pitch by Algarotti's time.[12]

10. "Anzi se vorremo por mente come pochissimo travaglio ei sogliono darsi per la scelta del libretto, o sia dell'argomento, quasi niuno per la convenienza della musica colle parole, e niuno poi affatto per la verità nella maniera del cantare e del recitare, per il legame dei balli con l'azione, per il decoro nelle scene, e come si pecca persino nella costruzione de' teatri, egli sarà assai facile a comprendere qualmente una scenica rappresentazione, che dovrebbe di sua natura esser tra tutte la più dilettevole, riesca cotanto insipida e noiosa. Colpa dello sconcerto che viene a mettersi tra le differenti parti di essa; d'imitazione non resta più ombra, svanisce in tutto la illusione che può nascer solamente dall'accordo perfetto di quelle; e L'Opera in Musica, una delle più artifiziose congegnazioni dello spirito umano, torna una composizione languida, sconnessa, inverisimile, mostruosa, grottesca, degna delle male voci che le vengon date e della censura di coloro che trattano il piacere da quella importante e seria cosa ch'egli è" (Algarotti, *Saggi*, ed. da Pozzo, 149–50).

11. "Per cento rapsodisti di luoghi comuni, o d'infarcitori di ciò che meno conviene, ne riesce a gran fatica un solo che con la dottrina riunisca il gusto, con l'eleganza la naturalezza, e in cui la propria discrezione imbrigli la fantasia" (Algarotti, *Saggi*, ed. da Pozzo, 171). An important precursor of Algarotti's *Saggio* was Charles Blainville's *L'esprit de l'art musical* of 1754. On the deployment of *tragédie en musique* to enhance the nation, see Isherwood, *Music in the Service of the King;* Klingsporn, *Jean-Philippe Rameau;* Burgess, "Ritual in the *Tragédie en Musique*"; Couvreur, *Jean-Baptiste Lully;* Chae, "Music, Festival, and Power"; Apostolidès, *Le roi-machine;* and for the late sixteenth and seventeenth centuries, van Orden, *Music, Discipline, and Arms.*

12. Sergio Durante shows that the debate actually reached back to the seventeenth century: see "The Opera Singer," 368; "Vizi privati e virtù pubbliche," 415–24; and "Theorie und Praxis der Gesangsschulen," 59–72.

Condemning anything deemed overly complex, Algarotti advanced the austere ideology of a "naturalist" project. True affinity with "nature" was to preclude wanton displays of prowess or spontaneity, except in the most rarefied forms, for nature's simplicity hinged on its stature as the supreme moral paradigm for what was good and right, and obedient to sound moral prescription.[13] Thus Algarotti's naturalism could no longer tolerate the grotesque fancy of the marvelous manifest in Italianate vocal virtuosity, even though he did accept French-styled spectacle with magic transformations, appearances, and pageants. Furthermore, the sensory continuities he demanded could only be marshaled by a dominant authorial voice—something advocated by early-eighteenth-century reformers but never widely attempted. In his vision, composers and (above all) poets were to reign supreme, while costly singers—with their capricious exhibitionism, prêt-à-porter arias, and stock costumes—had to be held at bay.

In this guise, the naturalist program did not push *against* precepts of imitation, but reiterated, following d'Alembert's early avowals in his 1751 *Discours préliminaire de l'Encyclopédie*, that their success *hinged* on imitation. As d'Alembert put it, "Any music that does not portray something is only noise; and without that force of habit which denatures everything, it would hardly create more pleasure than a sequence of harmonious and sonorous words stripped of order and connection."[14] For d'Alembert, the fact that common listeners were apt to miss the manifold ways that music imitated nature only underscored the central problem that music, as the least *naturally* imitative of all the arts, was prey to the disorders of the nonimitative.[15] Thoroughly cosmopolitan in his orientation, Algarotti vouchsafed the same, quoting Daniel Webb's treatise on painting in support of it.[16] Yet he also argued that once music was combined with poetry, and still more with painting, it could enter a powerful partnership. That partnership was opera, where music, text, and scenery could be arranged in perfect harmony, so much the better to work upon the senses whence our perceptions of imitation first arise.

Since Italian opera to that time had thrived on rapid production systems, which suffered from an unequal distribution of resources heavily weighted toward star singers, stock scenery and costumes had become veritable necessities. To that extent, *Ippolito ed Aricia*, with its rich and varied stage pictures treated as integral to a unified aesthetic program, was a true novelty, especially for a commercial theater. Its sets, custom crafted by Francesco Grassi, were probably inspired in part by the archaeological discoveries of Herculaneum (1738) and Pompeii (1748), resulting in a fusion of virtuosic baroque perspectives with

13. See the introduction to Daston and Vidal, *The Moral Authority of Nature*.

14. D'Alembert, *Preliminary Discourse*, 39. "Toute musique qui ne peint rien, n'est que du bruit; et sans l'habitude qui dénature tout, elle ne ferait guère plus de plaisir qu'une suite de mots harmonieux et sonores dénués d'ordre et de liaison" (d'Alembert, *Oeuvres*, 1.1, 39).

15. D'Alembert claimed that in the hierarchy of imitative faculties vaunted by each art, music is inferior to poetry, as poetry is inferior to painting, concluding: "Enfin la musique . . . tient le dernier rang dans l'ordre de l'imitation" (*Discours préliminaire*, 38, in *Oeuvres* 1.1, 39).

16. Webb, *Remarks on the Beauties of Poetry*, quoted in Algarotti, *Saggio*, ed. da Pozzo, 158, n. a.

neoclassical motifs.[17] Its costumes, on the other hand, fashioned by Giovanni Betti, were doubtless sumptuously of their time, stiff, scintillating, and profligate; and so too the nine elaborate divertissements choreographed by ballet master Pietro Alovar, who hailed from the Frenchified dance center of nearby Turin. Visual evidence for all of these is lost, but surviving court documents, principally a *vestiario* (wardrobe inventory) from 1759 and forty-three receipts paid to fabric makers,[18] verify that far from a neoclassical aesthetic, costumes (unlike sets) were still steeped in the baroque trappings of whalebone, wigs, embroidery, and brocade (and for dancers, heels and in some instances even masks). True neoclassical stage dress had to wait for Calzabigi and Gluck's 1762 production of *Orfeo ed Euridice* in Vienna, and in Italy much longer, probably as late as the 1790s. Even in France, it was not until 1759 that the Comédie-Française adopted a measure of local historical and geographical color in its costuming.[19] Hippolytus, Aricia, Phaedra, Theseus, and the whole parade of characters largely inherited from Euripides were all of them still baroque subjects, regulated and constrained in their corsets and panniers to model good conduct for the viewers of an absolutist duke. Besides, an immense pannier was good for propagandizing, for impressing toney hometown girls and gawking tourists, even if it could never match the awe factor of bel canto.

The cornerstones of Du Tillot's program were artistic integrity, unity of production means, and enforced audience absorption, a triad on which he insisted throughout the 1750s in his dealings with the Regio Ducale Teatro, and with increasing moral authority and practical controls. Especially abhorrent to him was the fragmentation of interests that plagued Italian impresarios, whose artistic decisions lay ever at the mercy of economic constraints and public opinion.

17. Mercedes Viale Ferrero believes Grassi inspired Fabrizio Galliari's scenography at the royal theater in Turin after 1760, so Galliari's drawings might serve as references for imagining Grassi's, now virtually all lost. See Galliari's neoclassical sketch of a "Bosco sacro a Diana" for a production of *Ifigenia in Aulide* done at Turin's Teatro Regio in 1762, reprinted in Viale Ferrero, *La scenografia*, 160, plate 60; and see Viale Ferrero's *Storia del Teatro Regio di Torino*, vol. 3, plate 22B and passim. On an emergent verisimilitude, see Viale Ferrero, "Stage and Set," 22–30 and passim; and Heartz, "From Garrick to Gluck."

18. "Inventario Generale di tutto il Vestiario del Teatro ed utensigli dello stesso magazino, che si ritrovano Esistenti doppo l'Opera della Primavera dell'anno 1759" (*Vestiario* in PAas.AdT88; payment receipts in PAas.Cfb932.4). On the advent of neoclassical stage dress, see Heartz, *Haydn, Mozart, and the Viennese School*, 207–9, and Hansell, "Theatrical Ballet," 198–250, and 202 n. 68 on Alovar (Pierre Alouard). Archival material is valuable for reimagining historical costumes because contemporaneous engravings (e.g., of singers pictured as operatic characters or scenes for literary editions)—heavily mediated by exigencies of visual genres—are often misleading as actual stage evidence. See, for example, the engraved frontispiece to Favart's parody of Lully's *Armide*, *Cythère assiégée* (Brussels, 1748, based on Boucher's painting *Armide et Renaud*), which shows a draped seminude female figure at a time well before Greek drapery had made its way onto staged human figures (reproduced in Heartz, *Haydn, Mozart, and the Viennese School*, 171; my thanks to Bruce Alan Brown for clarifying the sources).

19. Bergman, *Lighting in the Theatre*, 175–76.

Thus, unlike most court ministers, who left the brass-tacks business of arranging seasons, hiring artists and staff, and running the theaters to hired subordinates, Du Tillot began to intrude on day-to-day production shortly after he arrived in Parma.[20] Ever more zealous to construct a resplendent image of the court and finding the impresario's mediation particularly inimical to his goal of reconciling the glories onstage with the comportment of the ducal audience,[21] he alienated the impresarios who worked for him in the early 1750s. In 1753, he dismissed the last impresario entirely and took over their work himself, becoming a minister who was both director of court entertainments and de facto impresario of the public theater. This was a breach of any precedent, but it allowed him to put all of Parmesan spectacle in his own grip. It also cleared the way to installing the Algarottian idea that princely theater should serve as an enlightened school of morality and to ameliorating the global disjunction between its content and its function.[22] As the ultimate arbiter of all matters concerning the theater, artistic, financial, and political, Du Tillot was finally, and uniquely, poised to enact Algarotti's agenda of reorganizing management, restoring public order, and reforming artistic content.

In the years 1755–58, theatrical offerings at the ducal theater alternated between old-styled opera seria, spoken theater, and ballet, the last two given by an imported French troupe led by director-choreographer Jean-Philippe Delisle. Delisle's company brought Parma the dazzle of French ballet and the "naturalism" of new English-inspired French acting styles, retooled after the teachings of the Shakespearean David Garrick. By late 1758, an original French opera was even mounted: Rameau's *Castor et Pollux* (Paris, 1737), which would be reworked, like *Ippolito*, into an Italian version as *I Tindaridi* in 1760. The result was a theatrical menu that allowed Parmesans to indulge a taste for French cultural production beyond anything usual elsewhere on the peninsula, without relinquishing their steady diet of Metastasian opera seria.[23]

REMAKING VIEWERS

With Algarotti's close counsel, Du Tillot launched *Ippolito ed Aricia* as his first major project in operatic reform. At once a glamorous experiment and an homage to Parma's duke, the opera was to inaugurate the Ascensiontide season on Filippo's nameday as part of an annual cycle of festivities that merged the Christian calendar with a new Bourbon monarchical liturgy (see fig. 3.1.). Where

20. Ferrari, Mecarelli, and Melloni, "L'organizzazione teatrale parmense," 357–80.

21. Ibid.; also Ferrari, *Spettacoli drammatico-musicali,* 73 and passim.

22. Ferrari, "La compagnia Jean Philippe Delisle," in 163–210, notes the presence at Parma during this time of Saverio Bettinelli, whose moralistic philosophy led him to pronounce bluntly: "Le Théâtre doit être l'école de la vertu et tribunal incorruptible, où les crimes sont punis, l'innocence vengée, et les passions tournées à notre utilité" (166).

23. See Ferrari, "La compagnia Jean Philippe Delisle."

IPPOLITO,
ED
ARICIA
TRAGEDIA

Da rappreſentarſi

NEL REALE TEATRO
DI PARMA

*NELLA PRIMAVERA DELL' ANNO
MDCCLIX.*

Nuovamente compoſta, e adattata
alle Scene Italiane

DAL SIG. ABATE FRUGONI

REVISORE, E COMPOSITORE
DEGLI SPETTACOLI TEATRALI DI S. A. R.,
E SECRETARIO PERPETUO
DELLA SUA REALE ACCADEMIA
DELLE BELLE ARTI.

Nil deſperandum TEUCRO *Duce*, *& Auſpice* TEUCRO.
Horat. Od. VII. lib. I.

PARMA,

NELLA REGIO-DUCAL STAMPERIA MONTI
IN BORGO RIOLO.
CON LICENZA DE' SUPERIORI

xiij

MUTAZIONI DI SCENE.

NELL' ATTO PRIMO.

Tempio magnifico di Diana.

NELL' ATTO SECONDO.

Veſtibulo della Reggia di Plutone.
Reggia di Plutone.

NELL' ATTO TERZO.

Gabinetto d' Aricia.
Cortile nel Palagio di Teſeo con veduta di Mare.

NELL' ATTO QUARTO.

Introduzione agli Appartamenti di Aricia.
Selva conſacrata a Diana con veduta di Mare in lontananza.

NELL' ATTO QUINTO.

Gallerìa terrena.
Gran Giardino delizioſo Sacro a Diana, che introduce a i Boſchi di Aricia.

Inventore delle ſuddette Scene &c.

Il Sig. Franceſco Graſſi Parmigiano, Architetto, ed Ingegnere Teatrale all' attuale Servigio di S. A. R., ed Accademico Profeſſore di Proſpettiva della ſua Reale Accademia delle Belle Arti.

ATTO

FIG. 3.1. Libretto title page and list of scene changes for Abate Frugoni and Tommaso Traetta's *Ippolito ed Aricia* (Parma, 1759). The opera is noted as "newly composed and adapted for the Italian stage." Harvard Theater Collection, Harvard University. Reproduced by permission.

six to eight weeks was normally the maximum length of time for preparing a new opera in Italy, *Ippolito*, with its unprecedented nine changes of scenery and twenty-seven different costume designs, was readied over several months—pace Frugoni, who protested having too little time to write the libretto.[24] Those months saw the court humming with excitement, conscious that *Ippolito* was to represent a totally new type of drama. During late winter and spring, brilliant, luxurious fabrics, sequins, feathers, notions, gloves, silk leaves, and shoes were purchased in great numbers from the finest fabric makers and artisans. There were dedicatory sonnets circulated in broadsides, and residents were urged to rent rooms to the many "Signori Forastieri" who were to be welcomed for the occasion.[25] The battles and triumphs that often occurred in the featured opera seria of a wealthy court were to be replaced by sumptuous stagings of chorus and dance integrated into the drama in the French manner of divertissements.

Yet as opening day approached, a new sobriety fell over the town. Traditionally in Italy, festivities that served to solemnify a court also gave people a certain license to disorder, at the least when not in the presence of monarchs. Such were the paradoxes of absolutist politics. In Parma, to the contrary, the court's new emphasis on magnificence merged with unheard-of demands for good behavior. Viewers were now to gaze upon the ducal stage, the better to embellish its glittering court.

Efforts to control audience behavior had actually begun shortly after Du Tillot's arrival in Parma, but at first they focused mainly on nights when the court was in attendance. On October 4, 1749, an official "Avviso Per l'Opera da farsi in Musica" demanded that audiences show "due respect, which is not compatible with the racket, pounding, crying out, babbling, and other excesses" that were alleged to have been taking place (see the appendix to this chapter). From then on, no one was to "clap their hands, make noise, shout out 'Viva,' or similar things, nor make poundings and clamor or such actions deviating from the respectful behavior that the Royal Presence of the Prince calls for." Significantly, however, on nights when the "Royal Personage" did not enter the theater, "simple words of 'Viva,' and applause and clapping of hands [would be] . . . permitted, . . . there still being prohibited any other act . . . [or] disorder that [might] . . . proceed from continuous babbling."

Throughout the 1750s, attempts at regulation continued through a series of official advisories that forced viewers to pay better attention to the stage. On November 19, 1756, the court chronicler Antonio Sgavetti bemoaned the severity of the new regime:

24. On the time it generally took to compose an opera, see Surian, "The Opera Composer," 336–39. Writing to Algarotti on February 1, 1759, Frugoni claimed three months before the premiere that the libretto was already half-written, though this proved a slight exaggeration (Heartz, "Traetta in Parma," 278–79).

25. I-PAas, *Raccolta manoscritti*, b. 73; I-PAp, W** 24115, *Gridari degli Stati di Parma*, March 30, 1759.

> This morning they posted the *avviso* [specifying] how the nobility and others must conduct themselves at the opera and comedies—this being with such respect and reverence that I believe God would be content to be respected thus in his own church. No one may speak, no one may wear a hat, no one [may wear] a sword except officers of the court and nobility, and no visits are to be allowed from box to box.[26]

In the same year, Casanova ripped through the town on one of his many escapades and laid waste the haughty decorum insisted on by the new monarchs. Ever the Swiftian ethnographer, he asked the Parmesans if they were pleased to have become subjects of the Spanish Bourbons and offered this little vignette as one reply:

> Pleased? It has put us all in a perfect maze; everything is upside down, we don't know where we are. Happy days, when the house of the Farnese reigned, you are no more! Day before yesterday I went to the theater, and Arlecchino had everybody laughing fit to burst; but guess what—Don Filippo, who's our new Duke, tried so hard to keep from laughing that he made faces; and when he couldn't hold in any longer he put his hat in front of his face so no one could see him roaring. Somebody told me that laughing spoils the grave countenance of an Infante of Spain, and that if he let it be seen they'd write to his mother in Madrid and she would think it dreadful and unworthy of a great prince. What do you think of that? Duke Antonio—God rest his soul!—was a great prince too; but he laughed so heartily you could hear it in the street. We're brought to such confusion as nobody could believe.[27]

26. "Anno affisso l'aviso questa matina del modo si dovrano contenere la Nobiltà ed altri che si portarono à Teatro per le Opere, e Comedie starasi con tale rispetto, e riverenza, che io credo si contenterebe Iddio di essere rispetato così nella Sua Chiesa, cioè che niuno parli, niuno porti il capelo, niuno con spada salvo quelli di Ufizio della Corte e Nobiltà, non ametendo visita fra un palchetto al'altro" (Sgavetti, November 19, 1756).

27. Casanova, *History of My Life*, 3:48. I cite from the translation of Trask for its lively rendering of the sense of the text. [Contents? Nous nous trouvons tous dans un vrai labyrinthe; tout est bouleversé, nous ne savons plus où nous sommes. Heureux temps, où régnait la maison Farnèse, tu n'es plus! Je fu avant-hier à la comédie, où Arlequin faisait rire à gorge déployée tout le monde; mais devinez: Don Philippe, qui est notre nouveau duc, se tenait de rire tant qu'il pouvait, faisait des grimaces; et quand il n'en pouvait plus il mettait son chapeau devant son nez pour qu'on ne le vît pouffer. On m'a dit que le rire déconcerte la grave contenance d'un Infant d'Espagne, et que s'il se laissait voir on l'écrirait à Madrid à sa mère qui trouverait cela abominable et indigne d'un grand prince. Qu'en dites-vous? Le duc Antoine, Dieu veuille avoir son âme, était aussi un grand prince, mais il riait de si bon coeur qu'on en entendait les éclats dans la rue. Nous sommes réduits à une confusion incroyable. Depuis trois mois, il n'y a plus personne à Parme qui sache l'heure qu'il est." (Casanova, *Histoire de ma vie*, 47–48.)] The Farnese dynasty died out with Antonio in 1731, twenty-five years before the supposed conversation, so Casanova's interlocutor would have been up in years. Don Filippo's mother, Elisabetta Farnese, was a *parmigiana*, but had marrried King Philip V of Spain in 1714 and become thoroughly Spanish Bourbon.

Carlo Goldoni reported much the same when he was called to write for Parma in March 1756, resulting in his fantastically popular *La buona figliuola*, initially set by Duni. Stunned by the silence in the theaters, Goldoni recalled:

> I saw the Comédiens François for the first time. I was enchanted with their acting, and I was stupefied by the silence that reigned in the hall. I don't remember the comedy performed that day, but seeing in one scene the amorous male ardently embracing his beloved, this action, this imitation of nature—permitted the French but prohibited to Italians—pleased me so much that I cried out "Bravo!" with all my strength.
>
> My indiscreet, and unknown, voice shocked the silent assemblage. The Prince wanted to know from whence the voice arose. I was named and the surprise of an Italian author was excused. This escapade meant my general presentation to the public. I went to the foyer after the show and saw myself surrounded with numerous people.[28]

In Parma, even the preeminent Italian comedian was a bull in a china shop. Far from popular expression ratifying theatrical festivity, it was treated as a malady to be cured. Only then could social divisions be properly highlighted and rigidified.

Like all theaters, the Regio Ducal produced its social hierarchies in physical space. From a large royal box, centrally situated in the deepest curve in the hall, the audience radiated outward. Initially, the royal box swallowed a space three tiers high and four boxes across, with elaborate architectural ornaments, but the Bourbons had it artfully shrunken to a space two tiers high by two boxes wide in order to accommodate six added boxes in an attempt to ensure that all nobles and a greater number of the wealthy middle class would have their own boxes. The redesign (fig. 3.2), offered by machinist Pietro Fontana, came with an accompanying text promising that it would help maintain decency by containing the plebeians in the uppermost tier. Whatever the cause for persuasion, whether expansion or containment, the problems were deemed dire enough to justify the shrinkage.[29] The result was evidently graced with its final glory, possibly around 1759 or 1760, when the brilliant artist and official architect of the duchy, Ennemond Alexandre Petitot (1727–1801), redecorated the scaled-down

28. "[C]'étoit pour la premiere fois que je voyois les Comédiens François; j'étois enchanté de leur jeu, et j'étois étonné du silence qui régnoit dans la salle: je ne me rappelle pas quelle étoit la Comédie que l'on donnoit ce jour là; mais voyant, dans une scene, l'amoureux embrasser vivement sa maîtresse, cette action, d'après nature, permise aux François et défendue aux Italiens, me plut si fort que je criai de toutes mes forces, *bravo*.

"Ma voix indiscrette, et inconnue, choqua l'assemblée silencieuses; le Prince voulut savoir d'où elle partoit; on me nomma, et on pardonna la surprise d'un Auteur Italien. Cette escapade me valut une présentation générale au Public; j'allai au foyer après le spectacle; je me vis entouré de beaucoup de monde" (Goldoni, *Mémoires* [1787], 2:254, from chap. 31; cited from Goldoni, *Tutte le opere* 1:377–78).

29. See Carpanelli, "Architettura dei teatri di Parma," 25–44, esp. 38.

FIG. 3.2. Pietro Fontana, two drawings of the ducal box in the Regio Ducal Teatro, Parma, showing its original configuration (*left*) and its reconfiguration by shrinking its size in order to add six additional boxes for patrons (*right*), 1750s. Archivio di Stato, Parma, Spettacolo a Parma e Piacenza, busta 4. Prot. N. 5254/V.9.3. Reproduced by permission.

FIG. 3.3. Ennemond Alexandre Petitot, design for the redecoration of the ducal box at Parma, ca. 1759–60. Museo Glauco-Lombardi, Parma. Reproduced by permission.

ducal box using winged angels holding aloft the ducal crown, swept up by scalloped drapery folded with a masterful nonchalance (fig. 3.3).[30]

In a general way, the hierarchies of audience boxes relative to the ducal box corresponded ideologically to hierarchies within the drama, where they flowed downward from the goddess Diana to a royal parental couple (Phaedra and Theseus), thence to the eponymous young princely lovers, the queen's confidante Enone, and on to various choral groups—stand-ins at different hierarchic ranks for a wider set of constituencies roughly representing the "populace." Among the last were priestesses, furies and dryads, sailors and sailorettes, hunters and huntresses, shepherds and shepherdesses. Mutual viewing between stage actors and social actors secured their social and moral bonds, emphasizing continuities

30. Alternatively, it may be that Petitot's design actually replaced Fontana's, but the evidence is unclear. See Bédarida, *Feste*, 71, plate 51 and accompanying note.

between public, court, and spectacle that were always being enhanced under Bourbon rule through "improved" public decorum—never more so than in the period when *Ippolito* was produced. But of course displays of compliance were also essential to embellishing an absolutist monarch. Sometime early in 1759, Du Tillot ordered that a notice be printed praising the public's good conduct but paradoxically warning that anything less would no longer be tolerated (fig. 3.4), especially as the theater was physically attached to the ducal apartments.[31]

> The wise admonitions given in past years for good comportment have recently produced an excellent effect in this Royal-Ducal Theater, which nowadays is becoming one of the greatest moral decency. [Our theater] both bears witness to the clear idea of that respect that must be [shown] to a place by a public not disjoined from the royal residence and excites much more in the mind of everyone the perfection of a work greatly harmonized to the Sovereign Will. Thus [the work] comes to merit a beneficial applause, and one fitting in virtuous and reasonable persons.

We can easily infer from this that despite Du Tillot's tyrannical controls over all aspects of the theater—strong enough to have provoked Delisle to desert Parma in disgust the year before—audience infractions had never altogether abated. Therefore, even in the duke's absence, the same notice forbade those signs of approbation and censure that Italian audiences were long accustomed to producing through the instruments of body and voice.

> Since . . . the prudent orders referred to are directed toward . . . maintaining all necessary modesty during the performances—[and] so that execution of the above-mentioned excellent commands not be suspended, even on evenings when it please the Royal Sovereign not to attend the theater—one and all are reminded of the prohibition against every sort of noise and pounding, which are more the testimony of popular and inconsiderate tumult than a sincere token of applause inspired by merit.

Most particularly, audience members were to forestall all physical participation until after the end of each number, and "only at a few moments and with all moderation clap their hands and thus applaud the solo singer after he had ended his song, and not before, *taking care however to abstain from using the voice in any manner*" (emphasis mine).

By suppressing the visceral part of the body social so conspicuous in most Italian theaters, the court tried to reproduce the allegedly well-regulated political body of the ducal court while promoting the illusions it conjured up on the stage. New artistic ideals in this way were inseparable from a new aesthetics of power brought in by the Bourbons, which made spectators into public signs of

31. The same was true of the San Carlo, though the palace there was on a much larger scale. The decree is undated, but almost surely dates from early 1759, as Marchesi also believed ("Il Teatro Ducale," 68). See Feldman, "L'opera seria," 132.

AVVERTIMENTO

Per la Conſervazione del buon Regolamento di queſto Regio-Ducal Teatro.

E Saggie provvidenze date negli Anni ſcorſi per il buon Regolamento di queſto Regio-Ducal Teatro, ànno in appreſſo cagionato quell' ottimo effetto, che in oggi viene di eſſere un Teatro compoſto della maggiore morale decenza; e dà evidentemente a comprendere la ſtabile idea di quel riſpetto, che dal Pubblico deveſi ad un luogo non disgiunto dalla Regia Abitazione: ed eccita molto più nell' animo d' ogn' uno la perfezione d' un' opra molto conforme alla Sovrana Volontà, e che viene di meritarſi un' applauſo aſſai giovevole, e proprio delle oneſte, e ragionevoli Perſone.

Siccome però le accennate provvide Diſpoſizioni ſono dirette al fine di conſervare in tempo delle Recite tutta la neceſſaria modeſtia, così perchè non reſti mai interrotto il corſo del ſuddetto ottimo regolamento anche nelle ſere, nelle quali piacerà a Reali Sovrani di non intervenire al Teatro; Viene preſentemente la Generale Direzione de' Regio Ducali Teatri nella determinazione di rammemorare a tutti la proibizione di ogni qualunque ſorta di ſtrepiti, e dibattimenti, che ſono piuttoſto un Teſtimonio di Popolare, ed inconſiderato Tumulto, che un ſincero contraſegno d' applauſo ſpettante alla virtù; E confondendo in tal maniera, e ſenza miſura la debita approvazione, con l' indiſcretezza, giungono a far disdoro al guſto di una Adunanza conoſcitrice del merito, e della virtù medeſima, e ſembrano piuttoſto amanti dello ſtrepito, che di animare, e far coraggio alli Virtuoſi Attori, e conſeguentemente intenzionati a diſturbare l' attenzione degli intelligenti Spettatori.

Senza però togliere a queſti la facoltà conceſſa di poter ſaviamente in aſſenza de' Reali Sovrani fare applauſi a chi ſe ne fa degno; E perchè poſſano in tale particolare congiontura dare il loro modeſto contraſegno dell' interno Muſicale diletto, ſi fà ad Eſſi di nuovo paleſe, che in pochi momenti unicamente, e con tutta moderazione potranno battere palma a palma; ed applaudire così al Virtuoſo Cantante dopocche avrà egli terminato il ſuo Canto, e non prima, con avvertenza però di aſtenerſi ad eſercitare in tutte le forme la voce, per non dare alcuno benche menomo incentivo a Quelli, che abuſivamente toſto profittono d' ogni ſemplice, ed innocente eſempio.

Da queſte reiterate, e di già pubblicate ammonizioni ſi promette la ſuddetta Generale Direzione in tutto il corſo delle correnti Recite una continuata dimoſtrazione di vero oſſequio, ed inalterabile Venerazione alla Reale Padronanza; ed alla riſpettabile nominata Parte della Regia Sua Caſa.

FIG. 3.4. "Warning about the preservation of good behavior in this Royal Ducal Theater" (Avvertimento per la conservazione del buon regolamento di questo Regio-Ducale Teatro), 1759. Archivio di Stato, Parma, Spettacolo a Parma e Piacenza, busta 1. Prot. N. 5254/V.9.3. Reproduced by permission.

moral rectitude, signs of the reason, harmony, and respect that the duchy epitomized and that it was capable of cultivating. Spectating, in short, helped consolidate images of monarchical rule by showing, and showing off, how literate, cultivated, and attentive were the monarch's subjects, subsuming the process of viewing into the interests of rule.[32]

"CRUEL PHAEDRA!": *IPPOLITO ED ARICIA*

Given these pretensions, the appeal of Racine's *Phèdre* and Rameau's *Hippolyte et Aricie* as sources for a prestigious new undertaking is not hard to see. The court's attempt to align social hierarchies with public behavior, and those in turn with the propositional content of the operas performed, co-opted the French court model as artillery against native theatrical traditions, which were then under international fire from elites. These alignments were above all about social distinction, of associating and disassociating in advantageous ways by means of aesthetic choices.[33] They were about putting status on display. Distinguished was not just the court from the ranks of the audience but the court from the common horde of other Italian theaters, even royal ones, and even the court within its own ranks, as seating arrangements in the ducal box attest (fig. 3.5).[34] The Phaedra myth had been absent from Italian operas during the eighteenth century, aside from an *Ippolito* given in Milan in 1745 and dedicated to delegates of the ruling Austrian empire, plus four other, relatively minor, ones.[35] But reformist ideologies, much as they sought prestige in myth and Frenchness, also began seeking a new richness of operatic subjects in the second half century, and in this reformers from Parma were also taking part.[36] Phaedra and Hippolytus offered such richness along with a new mythological cachet, redolent of the cultural distinction and purportedly better-behaved audiences at the Paris Opéra, but also a rich legacy of literary sources reaching back to Euripides.[37] For

32. On such mechanisms under Louis XIV, see n. 11 above. For the middle of the eighteenth century on into the nineteenth, see Johnson, *Listening in Paris*, who stresses a transition at the Paris Opéra from relatively less attention to greater attention among audiences. Johnson's yardstick of France differed greatly from Italy in geography and character, of course, as French travelers always remarked.

33. On the discriminations of taste, see Pierre Bourdieu, *Distinction*.

34. See Marchesi, "Il Teatro Ducale," 61–92 Giovanni Montroni gives a concise explanation of organization and hierarchy within the Spanish Bourbon court, in "The Court," 22–43, esp. 34–37. On the architectural and performative dimension of princely theatrical display, see Alice Jarrard's *Architecture as Performance*, esp. chaps. 3 and 4.

35. A glance at Sartori, *I libretti italiani*, confirms how the Hippolytus/Phaedra myth penetrated settecento opera. Paisiello's *Fedra* is the only opera so titled in the eighteenth century (see chap. 8). A Ph.D. dissertation-in-progress by Philine Lautenschläger, "Phädra-Vertonungen" (University of Heidelberg), promises to treat settings of the myth by Rameau, Traetta, and Paisiello.

36. See Chegai, *L'esilio di Metastasio*, 91–93 and passim.

37. I use "distinction" here in Bourdieu's sense. See Bourdieu, *Distinction*.

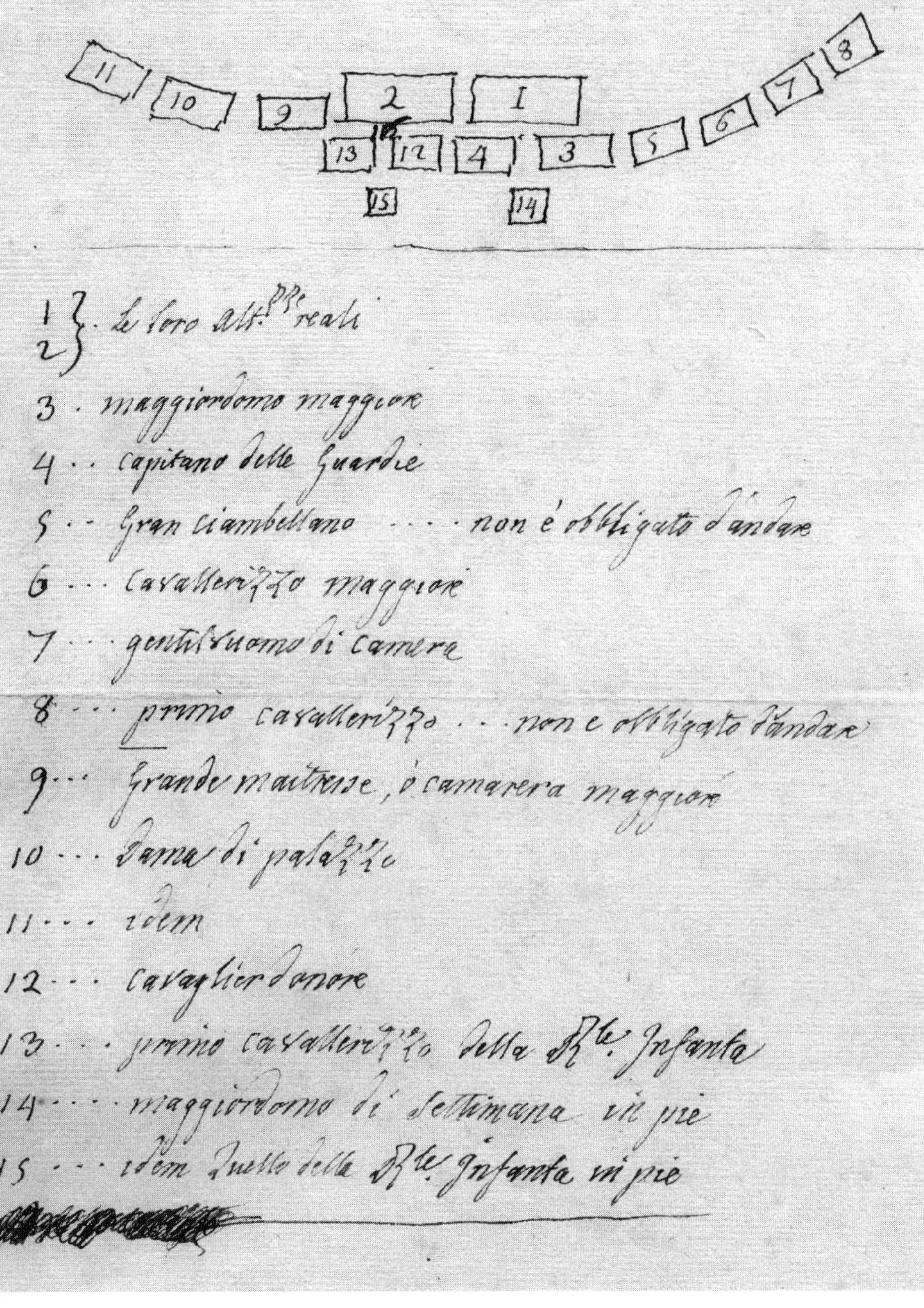

1
2 } Le loro Alt.ze reali

3 . maggiordomo maggiore

4 .. capitano delle Guardie

5 .. Gran ciambellano .... non è obbligato d'andare

6 ... Cavallerizzo maggiore

7 ... gentiluomo di camera

8 ... primo cavallerizzo ... non è obbligato d'andare

9 ... Grande maitresse, ò camarera maggiore

10 ... Dama di palazzo

11 ... idem

12 ... Cavaglier d'onore

13 ... primo cavallerizzo della R.le Infanta

14 ... maggiordomo di settimana in piè

15 ... idem quello della R.le Infanta in piè

FIG. 3.5. "Distribution of places that the principals, charges, and the rest of the court service should occupy whenever the Royal Sovereigns are present in [the ducal box at] the theater" (Distribuzione de luoghi, che devono occupare le Primarie, Cariche, ed il resto del Servigio, allorché Li Reali Sovrani si trovano in Teatro). Archivio di Stato, Parma, Spettacolo a Parma e Piacenza, busta 1. Prot. N. 5254/V.9.3. Reproduced by permission.

this, Parmesan audiences had been primed by recent performances of French spoken tragedies by the Delisle troupe, including performances of Racine's *Phèdre* and Pradon's *Phèdre et Hippolyte.*

Yet Frugoni's libretto gave the myth a form that took leave of previous literary traditions, changing events and characters in a way that altered its basic propositions about nature and human nature. In the Frugoni/Traetta opera, nature ended up less a manifestation of external causes that beset humankind—as it had been with the Greeks and had still been with the French in the seventeenth century—than it was a set of forces internal to humans. Idealized principles of human nature and natural phenomena were deployed to give shape and logic to human forces, fitting nature to the same standards of reason and harmony as the duke's subjects.

The job of delineating these principles first fell to Frugoni. Even as Algarotti was serving as a kind of oracle and propagandist for the whole project, Frugoni was artfully dodging his hints that one of his own libretti be staged by claiming that he was already well along in the work of adapting and amplifying Pellegrin's borrowings from Racine, especially for acts 3 and 4.[38] Some of the elements of the myth that Frugoni preserved were of course canonical, to wit: Hippolytus is a devotee of Diana's (Artemis's) cults of chastity and the hunt and a lover of horses; his stepmother, Queen Phaedra, suffers from a catastrophic love for him; his father Theseus, king of Athens, becomes enraged, wrongly believing that Hippolytus has tried to seduce Phaedra in his absence; at last Hippolytus dies beneath the hooves of his own horses, who rear up in fear of a sea monster sent forth by Neptune at Theseus's behest. Racine's central alteration of Euripides had consisted in giving Hippolytus a love interest—Aricia by name—rendering the hero far less fanatical in his devotion to chastity than Euripides had made him but more humanly fallible as a son, since Aricia is the last survivor of the race of Pallas, his father's "mortal enemies." Here court opera and spoken drama could join hands.

Where nature and human nature were at stake, however, differences between the two were greater. Racine had reduced the supernatural to some mere allusions (to Hades, the sea monster, and the deities) without allowing any of them onstage. By contrast, both operatic versions reinstate the supernatural—in the Parmesan case, without Rameau's mythical prologue (already dropped from the Paris revival of 1757)—while also stressing romantic love, and in ways that are germane to the new operatic role of nature. Both retain Euripides' Artemis in the figure of the goddess Diana. And *Ippolito* keeps *Hippolyte*'s underworld through the entirety of act 2, which concentrates the supernatural in the form of a marvelous congeries of grotesque figures and motifs, reanimating the seventeenth-century tradition of depicting Pluto and Proserpina in Hades. In plate 1, Pluto lords over Hades with his torch and dagger, surrounded by bats and serpents. The reconstruction, by Gabrielle Feldman, draws on both

38. See Frugoni to Algarotti, February 2, 1759, in Algarotti, *Opere* 13:96.

the wardrobe inventory contemporaneous with the production, which shows him to have been clothed in brilliant reds and blacks, and an unbroken lineage of theater sketches dating from the seventeenth century.[39] In preserving the elements of supernature, Frugoni pointedly followed the French operatic tradition codified by Quinault and Lully in the 1670s, which specifically legitimated the *merveilleux* for musical theater, even as he moved closer to an eighteenth-century rationalized view of nature. In addition to eliminating Rameau's allegorical prologue, he also got rid of the storm and sea monster of act 4 and the appearance of Neptune in act 5, keeping only Diana's descents in acts 1 and 5 and the appearance of Pluto, Proserpina, and Mercury, along with their demons and furies, in act 2.[40] Frugoni's conception, like the French opera, focuses more on the plight of the young prince and on his beloved, as victims of Phaedra's fatal love, than on the psychology of the queen, as Racine had done. By bringing Aricia into parity with Hippolytus, a particular geometry of human relations emerges, better suited to the requirements of court opera than of spoken tragedy. Dramaturgical supremacy is assigned to a sympathetic young couple who

39. The reconstructions offered here attempt to combine scholarly evidence with the artist's imagination. We make no attempt at thoroughgoing historical accuracy for these reconstructions, but rather hope to breathe life back into the rich visual tradition of *Ippolito*, which is otherwise wholly lost. To this end, we also used contemporaneous stage costumes and aristocratic fashions from France and Italy as references for French and Italian noble dress and theatrical sketches from the Paris Opéra, whose designs had currency at the French-influenced court of Parma. Important among the latter were designers Jean-Baptiste Martin (flourished 1748–57) and Louis-René Boquet (1717–1814), and still, albeit to a lesser extent, the earlier Claude Gillot (1673–1722). The stage iconography for Pluto, and for inferno scenes generally, was highly consistent over the seventeenth and eighteenth centuries. A late seventeenth-century inferno scene showing Pluto with bats, snakes, demons, and furies exists in a colored drawing attributed to the seventeenth-century designer for the Opéra Jean Berain (1640–1711); see Reade, *Victoria and Albert Museum: Ballet Designs*, plate 45, and more generally Gorce, *Berain*. Similar iconography appears in Italy a hundred years later in a drawing designed by Leonardo Marini (engraved by Gizzardi) showing a demon in an Armida opera, *Abiti antichi di diversi nazioni* (Turin, 1770); reproduced in Sadie, *New Grove Dictionary of Opera* 3:217; cf. Viale Ferrero, "Leonardo Marini," in *La scenografia*, 68–70. PAas.AdT88 describes Pluto's costume as being "di raso ponsò guarnito di riporti di tela d'oro, siniglione ponsò, e nero, Frangia d'oro, intornati li riporti di galone d'oro" (of bright red satin trimmed with embroidery of cloth of gold, bright red and black chenille, gold fringe and appliqué turned with gold piping). "Tela d'oro" was a very luxurious fabric with gold threads. "Siniglione" had a velvet chenille cord in the weft and was used for trim. My thanks to Margaret Rosenthal for help with translations of some terms for fabrics. In *Ippolito* libretto, 15, Teseo is pursued by a fury with a torch in hand. The wardrobe inventory also shows that for the furies the wardrobe had seven costumes of black and poppy-red velvet chenille and black roan cloth ornamented with appliqué of poppy-red taffeta and turned out with silver piping. There were also large masks and hats for demons, plus thirty-nine serpents and forty *maschere serie* for furies (PAas.AdT88), which must have been used in the first divertissement in act 2, as well as ten scarlet red shoes specially produced for the opera (PAas.Cfb932.4, no. 17). For Martin's engraved images of both a demon and a fury, see Fischer, *Les costumes*, 69.

40. Reform operas at both Parma and (shortly thereafter) Vienna reintroduced the underworld to Italian opera. The librettos of Metastasio and other historicizing reformers had of course excised it in the early eighteenth century in the interest of verisimilitude.

are politically necessary to help guarantee monarchical succession and aesthetically necessary to its efficacious representation and internalization by viewers. That young couple stands in for unsullied nature itself.

To see how this is so, let us consider certain details of Frugoni's story. When *Ippolito ed Aricia* opens, Aricia, secretly in love with Ippolito (Hippolytus), is seen lamenting the sorrowful fate assigned her by Teseo (Theseus). She is to pledge herself to the goddess Diana so that chastity and childlessness will end her lineage. But Diana's priestesses recoil from "sacrificing" one whose heart is bound in love, causing Fedra (Phaedra), who rules in Teseo's absence, to fly into a rage on her very first appearance. Fearless Teseo has meanwhile descended to the underworld in hopes of recovering his friend Peritoo (Perithous) from the clutches of Pluto. Teseo's mission fails, but in a prescient development he gains passage back to the living through the intervention of his father, Neptune.

Greater troubles await Teseo on earth, and they extend the mechanisms whereby sexual attraction, filial duty, and paternal supremacy will all implicitly tie human nature to a purportedly natural world. As act 3 begins, Fedra confides her love for Ippolito to Enone (Oenone) and demands an audience with the young prince. Once Ippolito arrives (3.4), she recounts to him a vision in which he appeared to her as a new Teseo (her real husband still believed dead). Her confession of love launches the drama's central dramatic crisis: Ippolito rebuffs her in horror, and as she grabs his sword to kill herself, he wrests it from her in a famous *coup de théâtre* at the same moment that Teseo returns.

The plot thickens when Enone exploits Teseo's confusion to insinuate—more directly than she does in Racine—that it was Ippolito who tried to seduce the queen (3.7). Enraged, Teseo seeks vengeance on Ippolito through Neptune. Fedra becomes desperate (4.2), but since Ippolito will not stoop to incriminating her, he flees the Arician groves for a life of exile only to meet death by the shores of Neptune's sea (so we will learn from Teseo at the start of act 5). Fedra enters dying of poison to confess her wrongs, whereupon Teseo rushes off to forgive Aricia.

The story has yet to resolve, but the rest concerns only the fate of the young lovers, extending certain facts of kinship that have already been placed tacitly before us. First, we have learned that Teseo lies in the thrall of his father, Neptune, who, myth has it, had promised him three wishes.[41] Relying on him, Teseo relies at once on natural forces (Neptune as god of the sea) and on the force of paternal authority (Neptune as pagan surrogate for a masculine Christian god and simultaneously father to the lesser because mortal son). It follows that Ippolito's accession should depend as much on Teseo's grace as Teseo's claim to rule does on Neptune's. Second, we have learned that Ippolito is not, as in ancient myth, a chaste hunter, disdainful of female flesh and therefore infuriating to the libidinous goddess Venus, but as in Racine a man of flesh and blood,

41. An alternative version of Theseus's parentage (probably later) has King Aegeus as his father (Plutarch, *Theseus*, 3 [incl.], in Dryden, *Plutarch's Lives*).

PLATE 1. Pluto in Hades, shown in red and black with pitchfork, bats, and serpents, for *Ippolito ed Aricia*, act 2. Watercolor with pen and ink on paper. Imaginative reconstruction by Gabrielle Feldman. Reproduced by permission.

PLATE 2. Sketch of Aricia in pearl shot silk for *Ippolito ed Aricia*, act 3. Watercolor and charcoal pencil on paper. Imaginative reconstruction by Gabrielle Feldman. Reproduced by permission.

PLATE 3. *Ippolito and Aricia* in woodland finery, conjoined in Ippolito ed Aricia, act 5. Watercolor and charcoal pencil on paper. Imaginative reconstruction by Gabrielle Feldman. Reproduced by permission.

PLATE 4. Choral dancer on heels, informal pose, *Ippolito ed Aricia*, act 5. Watercolor and charcoal pencil on paper. Imaginative reconstruction by Gabrielle Feldman. Reproduced by permission.

a potential father himself, and thus a worthy successor in the dynastic lineage. Paternity here is the supreme instrument of generation and a complex ideological engine of social stress and resolution.

Yet the ideology of paternity is fraught with contradiction, caught between the mystified claims of absolutism and the moralized premises of enlightenment reason. Though nearly a whole act remains following Teseo's departure after 5.2, both he and Fedra—in a total breach of Racine's play—disappear suddenly and forever from the stage, superseded by the sheer triumph of romantic love as the socially well-ordered path to virtue.[42] In this scheme, Ippolito must ascribe to a "natural" order allegedly determined by laws of *human* nature, which he and Aricia alone most ideally succeed in realizing. Their good "nature" is not *acquired* (as that of Parma's viewers was made to be), but seemingly belongs to that sense of the natural as something that is prior to all else. In this sense, their triumph recalls Jean Ehrard's point that although early- to mid-eighteenth-century empiricists like Condillac—teacher from 1758 to the young prince of Parma—insisted that ideas were *learned*, they nevertheless tended to sculpt the man of nature in abstract, ideal form. A "phantom of universal man" persists over, against, perhaps even in response to the eighteenth-century "cult of facts."[43] Its result, I would argue, is a paradoxical ratification of old beliefs in innate human nature, even as the latter is tested, moralized, and dramatized according to new normative models—models that were just then being instantiated by the insistence that better attention be paid to the stage.[44]

* * *

With this in mind, let us turn momentarily to our neglected queen, for in her person lies one key to the conception of human nature suggested by the musical universe of the opera. Fedra's name is maligned before she is even seen: "l'empia

42. Frugoni begins act 5 with a new mise-en-scène, a ground-floor gallery where the dialogue between Teseo and Fedra takes place. In Pellegrin's version, the change of scenery had occurred, most atypically, only in 5.3, while the beginning of the act, where the libretto reads "le théâtre ne change qu'à la troisième scène," continued with the scenery used at the end of act 4. As early as the first season in 1733, however, *Hippolyte* responded to public criticism of this breach of the traditions of the *liaison des scènes* and *liaison de présence* by dropping the first two scenes of act 5 and beginning immediately with scene 3. Geoffrey Burgess offers an analysis of this change, arguing that it not only preserved unity of place but mollified the subversive political effect of banishing the king before the opera's denouement ("Le théâtre ne change," 275–87). Indeed classic Metastasian opera seria consistently kept the monarch in play until the end of the opera, when he often conferred marital rights on his dynastic successors or performed some other act of judgment and resolution.

43. Ehrard, *L'idée de nature*, 251–52. On Condillac's tenure at Parma, see dal Pra, "Il *Cours d'études* di Condillac," 25–46, esp. 25–27.

44. An argument for the contingency of facts in the enlightenment that also addresses anxieties about the unreliability of nature is offered by Daston, "Enlightenment Fears," 115–28. Daston also demonstrates the ineluctable ties between eighteenth-century practices of attention and notions of nature in "Attention and the Values of Nature," chap. 4 of *The Moral Authority of Nature*.

Fedra"—cruel Phaedra—Aricia exclaims in a recitative that precedes their first encounter in 1.4. When in the next instant, Fedra first appears, she is in extremis, imploring the gods and scheming to ensure Aricia's sacrifice to the cult of virgins. With rising fury, she sees she will be foiled by Diana's priestesses, who shrink from inducting one bound in love. Her rage boiling over, she curses the divine powers with a triadic dotted-note fanfare in recitative, accompanied by rising orchestral glissandi and rapid tremoli (example 3.1): "So! Why do you still wait? May the fatal trumpet sound and, at my nod, rousing arms and warriors, give the horrible signal; and may my voice fell altar and temple with deadly havoc. Wicked ones, tremble all. I knew to predict the crime. May a vain power perish—perish, oppressed, which wrongly denies homage to kings and offends their glory." (E ben, che più si tarda? Suoni la fatal tromba, e al cenno mio / destando armi, e guerrieri / dia l'orribile segno, / e con funesto scempio / cada alla voce mia, l'altare e il tempio. / Perfidi, tutti si tremate. Io seppi / prevedere il delitto. Oppresso pera, / pera un vano poter, che mal contende / ai re l'omaggio, e la lor gloria offende.)[45] This is one of only a handful of obbligato recitatives in the opera, despite all the reformist posturing around *Ippolito*, and it is worth noting where they occur. The first comes, quite unusually, just as Aricia first appears, staging her with tenderly Lombard rhythms, always minor-leaning and sweetened with appoggiaturas. Another is used for Fedra's dramatic speech at the start of act 3, a third for Teseo's invocation to Neptune to kill Ippolito (4.4), and a final one for Aricia's reaction to Ippolito's death (5.3). The last three all arrive at dramatic highpoints, and the last two are both prompted by a pictorial mise-en-scène. Teseo gets agitato scales and fantastic arioso writing for his act 4 speech, and Aricia in her grief in act 5 is lulled to sleep by the rustle of murmuring breezes. Thus Fedra's act 1 obbligato is no musical commonplace. Nor is it so much pictorial as utterly oratorical, at least until she exits to the sound of a trombone. Furthermore, her first terrifying appearance brings with it one of the opera's very rare instances of forward continuity, with the orchestra anticipating the trombone by entering midverse on a portentous "tromba" halfway through the recitative.

Far from winning sympathies, Fedra alienates them.[46] She is not the woman immortalized by Euripides and Racine but the one newly born of eighteenth-century opera, a mad virago of a queen. More than victim, she is victimizer, a psychic cousin to the Electra of Mozart's *Idomeneo*.[47]

45. *Ippolito* libretto, 9, from 1.4; music in *Ippolito score*, 101–5.

46. For an account of such differences between Racine's Phèdre and the operatic Phèdre of Pellegrin and Rameau, see Norman, "Remaking a Cultural Icon," 225–45.

47. Like Electra, she has fateful ties to Atreus, who, as vengeance for bedding with his wife, fed to his brother his brother's own children and unleashed chaos on their descendants for generations to come. Electra was his grandchild (as was Theseus) through Agamemnon, and Phaedra was his aunt by marriage, since her brother Catreus was father to Atreus's wife, Aerope. Theseus's mother, Aethra, was also daughter of one of Atreus's brothers. For Charles Dill, the Phaedra of French opera is one of Rameau's "imaginary monsters" ("Rameau's Imaginary Monsters," 433–76).

EXAMPLE 3.1. Tommaso Traetta, obbligato recitative for Fedra, "Suoni la fatal tromba" (preceding the sinfonia for Diana's descent by Rameau), mm. 94–114

From *Ippolito ed Aricia* (Regio Ducal Teatro, Parma, Ascension 1759), 1.4. Short score based on D-B, MS 21995.

(*continued*)

EXAMPLE 3.1. (*continued*)

In ancient myth Fedra's kin had been vexed by a gale of woes, and Frugoni's preface underscored them. She conceived for Ippolito an "illegitimate fire," much as her mother, Pasiphae, he noted, daughter of Apollo the Sun, was given to "unjust flames."[48] Recall that Pasiphae was plagued by Neptune's curse on her husband Minos, king of Crete, who had kept a beautiful bull given him by the

48. *Ippolito* libretto, viii–ix.

god rather than sacrificing it to honor him. In punishment, Pasiphae lusted after the bull and gave birth to the Minotaur, that extreme incarnation of human animality and reminder of a kinship between that which should ever be kept apart. Worse still, the rampant sexuality Neptune's wrath aroused in Pasiphae wreaked havoc beyond her own person. Fanned by the flames of the sun, sexual misfortune spread to her daughters to ensure the efficacy of the curse.[49] Pasiphae's older daughter Ariadne fell passionately in love with Theseus before Phaedra did, and so procured for him the secret map that led him through the labyrinth to the sleeping Minotaur and out again. Many Athenians had died in the Minotaur's labyrinth before young Theseus slew it and carried Ariadne off to sea, only to desert her, mad with grief, on the shores of Naxos. Thus temperance and tranquility were alien to the women of Minos, and the carnal surplus that had filled Pasiphae with dark desire endured as a family flaw.[50]

Without the specific chain of cause and effect (leading to cause, leading to effect, and so on in an endless regress), no curse could have the same devastating power as one that persists beyond its original victim; nor would it have the same power to discourage future lapses. Still, in ancient mythical tradition, latent afflictions typically needed divine agents to arouse passions in the persons of successive generations. For Phaedra's passion, Euripides had given clear cause, and Racine followed suit: her crazed love for Hippolytus was kindled by a jealous Aphrodite (Venus) in order to retaliate for Hippolytus's devotion to Artemis (Diana), rival goddess of chastity.[51] Whether her love is also perverse because it displaces higher love for lower lust, or because it places love on the wrong object, may be uncertain in the classical tradition of spoken theater; but as an immediate cause of Phaedra's woes, neither Euripides nor Racine leaves the wrath of Aphrodite/Venus in doubt, least of all to Phaedra, who is as crushed by the goddess's curse as she is powerless to defeat it.

Here, then, is the crux of differences between the spoken and lyric traditions at hand. By insisting on external cause, the Phaedra of Euripides and Racine becomes the tool of a god's will, a puppet on Venus's stage (or a "projection" of Ve-

49. The large amounts of taffeta purchased for costumes were probably for Fedra. They have no clear place in any choral scene but were used in a contemporaneous production to costume Bacchantes (PAas.AdT88, 12) with whom Fedra could have been assimilated typologically.

50. Cf. Euripides, *Hippolytus*, 337–43.

51. Euripides' prologue begins with Aphrodite/Venus declaring her vengeance. Frugoni adds another strand: Venus was indignant with the Sun (Phaedra's grandfather Zeus, Apollo in Roman tradition) for having discovered her furtive amours with Mars and therefore resolved to kindle unjust flames in Pasiphae, Ariadne, and Phaedra to get back at him (*Ippolito* libretto, viii–ix). Euripides had only hinted at this, having Aphrodite note that Artemis is Zeus's daughter (*Hippolytus*, 15).

Racine's preface to *Phèdre* (19) states directly that *only* external provocation of the gods can account for Phaedra's infatuation with Hippolytus, for "when she is forced to disclose it, she speaks with such embarrassment that it is clear that her crime is a punishment of the gods rather than an urge flowing from her own will" (lorsqu'elle est forcée de la découvrir, elle ne parle avec une confusion qui fait bien voir que son crime est plûtot une punition des dieux qu'un mouvement de sa volonté).

nus on earth, as Walter Burkert would have it).[52] Like all mythological mortals, Phaedra is prey to the whims and fancies of the gods. But her predicament is far worse than that of many others, since a divine curse—that most formidable of ancient causes—lies on her father's head and fire courses through her mother's veins. Past and present conspire to overwhelm her.

From this helpless fate the lyric tradition extended by Frugoni largely departs. Omitting Pellegrin's prologue and many other allusions to Venus, Frugoni held onto the curse of Venus only in scattered hints. Yet it is important to note that even in the revisions of Pellegrin/Rameau's version Venus's agency had been attenuated, and in a manner that probably paved the way for Parma. Originally *Hippolyte* had made Phaedra's victimization by Venus explicit, not just with the prologue, but with the direct address Phaedra makes to Venus at the dramatic apex of the opera in her great act 3 monologue (3.1), so heartbreakingly rendered by Rameau in rich harmonic language, "Cruelle mère des Amours," continuing, "Ta vengeance a perdu ma trop coupable Race; / n'en suspendras-tu point le cours?" (Cruel mother of Love, your vengeance has sent my too-guilty race astray. When will you ever give up this course?)[53] With this address to the goddess, the monologue clings to those personifications that peopled the seventeenth-century imagination. Perhaps it is not so surprising, then, that the shelf life of the original version was seemingly short. Charles Dill notes that "Cruelle mère" was likely replaced early on with a different monologue, "Espoir, unique bien d'une fatale flame," printed in an appendix to the original 1733 score.[54] "Espoir" stresses longing rather than tragic destiny, and insofar as it deals in personifications, it personifies an abstraction (Hope) instead of a goddess. In a further move away from acknowledging Venus's work, both monologues were gone from the libretto made for the 1742 revival, replaced musically by a dramatic but wordless orchestral *ritournelle*, which modulates extensively from D minor and back before yielding to Phaedra for the short, uneventful recitative with which she comments on her unhappy luck in having Theseus return. One further reduction in Venus's influence was to come at the Opéra with the 1757 revival, from which, as we've seen, the prologue was dropped completely.[55] The implied power of gods—and arguably of the higher authorities whom they allegorized—was thus much diminished and the story demagicalized in spite of its supernatural elements, in keeping with the spirit of opera in both France and Italy during the 1750s and 1760s.

52. Burkert, *Structure and History*, 111ff.

53. Thus the French original (1733) frames Venus's agency in the idiom of the marvelous. In addition to 3.1, see Phèdre's arias in 4.2 and in 5.1 where she says "Heaven placed this gloomy ardor in my heart."

54. Dill, "Pellegrin, Opera, and Tragedy," 247–57, esp. 254–55, and *Monstrous Opera*, 73–76. Claudio Gallico, "Cori a Parma," 82, establishes that Frugoni drew primarily from the 1742 version for the choral sections, although we will see that Frugoni also drew on the 1757 version.

55. Rameau's prologue—baldly supernatural and allegorical—included an appearance by Venus's son Cupid, who invades Diana's groves and threatens to start amorous wars.

Those thin allusions to Venus's agency that were retained in *Ippolito ed Aricia* are insufficient to project Phaedra's ills as a psychic battle against external forces and are outdone, finally, by her own mean-spirited self-display. By comparison with the Phaedra of Euripides and Racine, Frugoni/Traetta's Fedra is less victimized by inner torment and more vindictive in her own right. She is vindictive *by* nature—her own poetic and musical nature—not merely *because of* it, she herself an embodied force of nature more than a mere figuration, instrument, or extension of the physical world. Perhaps, as Catherine Cole has suggested, she is a countertype to the idealized eighteenth-century vision of human nature, one who evokes, in her errancy, a proto-Christian notion of the Fall.[56]

PASTORAL REDEMPTION, OR THE OLD ORDER RESTORED

Why these different conceptions of nature, and why do they matter for shifts in eighteenth-century opera? We have seen that by contrast with the Euripidean legacy, the Phaedra of mid-eighteenth-century operatic fame is out of tune with a fundamentally harmonious world, a world proposed by opera (and especially opera seria) in which social harmony is bolstered by prescribed yet putatively abiding and natural moral principles. Intrigues and travails may abound, but in the end harmony rules. As a result, Phaedra can only be made truly mad by her own natural origins (not the evil of divine forces) and, in consequence, by her own inner nature. Implied in this "operatic" view is that natural origins provide explanations for actions that cannot be healed in the breach except by moral learning—a rather fated view not as regards events per se but as regards the influence of human nature on events and the influence of events on human destiny.

Cathérine Kintzler has argued about *tragédie en musique* that in trying to represent the miraculous in a quasi-naturalistic way, it pursues a "logic of the supernatural," one that takes reflection of nature to a metaphysical level.[57] We see something of this in *Ippolito*. Through a charismatic exemplification of ideal types and opposites the impossible norms of human nature it proposes in its school for virtue reiterate static old ideas of human nature as innate. In this optic, Phaedra is not so much unnatural as she is a figure who acts against human nature *as it is supposed to be*, namely, good by definition—or tautologically speaking, "natural."[58]

The opera thus reproduces the general moral economies that ruled eighteenth-century opera seria, wherein an ethical hierarchy was partially correlated with a cast hierarchy. Starring soloists were oftentimes intrinsically virtuous characters, or more often only mildly or temporarily flawed, especially earlier in the

56. Private communication, May 25, 2005.

57. Kintzler, *Jean-Philippe Rameau* and *Poétique de l'opéra français*.

58. See Cole, "'Nature' at the Opéra," chap. 5.

century, while characters with insuperable moral limitations or those that were downright evil were more apt to be secondary. Married women, widows, and mothers were the exception rather than the rule in the Italian tradition, but when they did appear they were prime candidates for moral disorders. Fedra, of French origin, is all three.

Even though Fedra is dramatically central in *Ippolito ed Aricia*, she is secondary in the cast hierarchy—an unthinkable idea in Racine's terms. Ippolito and Aricia, by contrast, as those destined to restore moral order, are the primo uomo and prima donna. The implied future of the crown, they must be young and inherently good. The bold character contrasts the opera sketches make Aricia the virtual female antonym of Fedra. A conventional leading lady, Aricia must bear the traits of virginity, virtue, and honor that suit her to wed the prince and eventually inherit the throne. Further, since her royal claims are predicated on her capacity to share the task of reestablishing concord, she must always maintain at least a modicum of restraint and self-possession, even in her most anguished moments.

The totality of these criteria is expressed in the paradoxical (if not atypical) totality of arias for the leading lady, which range from the innocent tempo di minuetto of "Prendi Amor, prendi pietoso" (1.7) to the delicate and affecting cantabile aria "In questo estremo Addio" (4.6) to the brilliant coloratura of "Va dove Amor ti chiama" (3.2)—an eleven-minute showstopper, which (typical of bravura arias) was situated midway through the opera. If Traetta satisfied his audience by giving them the euphony and melody they so loved, in "Va dove Amor ti chiama" he also gave them the fireworks they expected from a great diva. Ultimately they allow Aricia to upstage Fedra both with delicacy of manner and with imperiousness and heroism of temperament. Indeed Fedra has just opened the act with an obbligato recitative ("In qual mare d'affanni") in place of Phèdre's celebrated "Cruelle mère" but then proceeded to a prosaic simple recitative with Enone before delivering an aria marked "Andante grazioso" in lilting *senari* ("Povero core," 3.1).

Frugoni had already given Aricia clear dynastic reason for eclipsing Fedra. In the recitative leading up to "Va dove Amor," responding to Ippolito's announcement of his departure for Athens to secure for her the throne (at a point when he believes Teseo dead), she exclaims: "You have complete power over me. You fill me with unaccustomed hope. *I glow in the heat of your noble power and feel myself grow stronger.* Go where heaven and your heart may take you. My thoughts, my vows, will follow you faithfully. Go now, my love, and may you accomplish the great deed. *Conquer, triumph, and return amid the acclaim of men and gods to crown my fate and yours*" (3.2).[59] Fidelity, submissiveness, forbear-

59. Emphasis mine. "Tutto su me tu puoi. Tu mi ricolmi / d'inusitata speme. Ardo al bel foco / del tuo nobil valore e di me stessa / sento farmi maggior. Va dove il cielo e il tuo core ti guida. I miei pensieri, / i voti miei ti seguiran fedeli. / Vanne, mio bene, e il gran disegno adempi. / Vinci, trionfa e torna / fra il plauso dei mortali e degli dei / a coronare i tuoi destini, e i miei."

ance, higher purpose, and honor—all of which mark her as an enlightened heiress apparent—converge with a telos of personal and political transformation, rubbed into magic by the friction of her explosive virtuosity. Through the heat of Ippolito's divinely ordained power, the diva extraordinaire Caterina Gabrielli (Aricia) could gather strength for her surpassing display, a C-major aria di bravura 279 measures long.[60]

Va dove Amor ti chiama,	[Go where Love calls you,
Dove ti guida il fato,	Where fate leads you:
Va di costanza armato	Go armed with constancy
A trionfar per me.	To triumph for me.
Vendica un sangue oppresso:	Avenge my oppressed race,
Rendimi al trono mio;	Restore my throne;
Ma su quel trono istesso	But on that very throne
Voglio regnar con te.	I want to reign with you.]

Thickly scored with oboes and horns, the aria spins out two much-extended statements of the first stanza, with rising string scales charging up to "dove ti guida il fato," chromatically inflected to $\flat II_6$ of V on "Va dove Amor ti chiama" (m. 60), slid onto a diminished seventh chord at "chiama" (m. 61), and followed with hugely long, fiery melismas repeated over "trionfar" to end each statement (example 3.2). Aricia/Gabrielli went on to deliver two cadenzas in the A section, on "fato" and "trionfar," not even imagining what she may have done in her reprise.

Thus, exactly two acts after Fedra bursts forth craving vengeance, Aricia establishes herself disarmingly as Fedra's positive inverse. From a diffident damsel she rises up to join hands with Ippolito against an evil queen and realize her own manifest destiny. Because of this, the lion's share of the opera's arias belong to her unapologetically, signifying her fittingness—as character and inseparably as prima donna—for the role marked out for her. The stunning arias of Gabrielli justify Aricia's divinely sanctioned role in the political order, just as Aricia's prominence in the political order justifies Gabrielli's dominance of the cast.[61] Descriptions left in the wardrobe inventory underscore this dual preeminence. In the first half of act 3, set in Aricia's apartments, she was likely clothed in pearlescent shot silk, much like the princess of Parma who stands behind her parents in Giuseppe Baldrighi's ducal family portrait, first painted in 1758 (cf. plate 2 and fig. 3.6).

Although Aricia must unite with Ippolito in order to promote natural

60. On Gabrielli, see Ademollo, *La più famosa delle cantanti italiane*, and Croll and Brandenburg, "Gabrielli," 396–97. Numerous accounts confirm her nature as tempestuous and finicky (Pancino, *Johann Adolf Hasse e Giammaria Ortes*, 72–73).

61. More typically, the prima donna is introduced with an entrance aria di mezzo carattere or an aria tenera.

EXAMPLE 3.2. Tommaso Traetta, aria for Aricia, "Va dove Amor ti chiama," mm. 38–70

From *Ippolito ed Aricia* (Regio Ducal Teatro, Parma, Ascension 1759), 3.4. Short score based on D-B, MS 21995.

52
me, va di co-stan-za ar-ma-to, do-ve ti gui-da il
pf
pf
dolce
+Ob., Hn.
56
fa-to, do - - - ve ti gui - da il fa - - - - - - - - to,
pf
sf
dolce
60
va do-ve A-mor ti chia - ma, a tri-on-far per me, a tri-on-
64
far, a tri - on - far per
68
me, a tri - on - far per me.
f
f

FIG. 3.6. Giuseppe Baldrighi, portrait of the ducal family of Parma, shown with musical scores, bound and unbound, and a lute. The royal princess stands behind the settee. Oil on canvas, 1758, with later additions. Galleria Nazionale, Parma. Reproduced by permission.

harmony in the kingdom—an operatic imperative with patent political valence—the couple nevertheless mediates between different, if overlapping, conceptions linking nature to rule. In one conception, consolidated by Louis XIV in the seventeenth century, monarchs are divinely ordained and implicitly point to a Christian god whom they exemplify on earth. In another more modern one (virtually pan-European), sovereigns are nature's purest subjects. The latter conception could only exist in a world in which God as an autonomous entity had been widely subsumed into nature, nature itself divinized, and sovereigns' collaborations with God thereby reimagined as collaborations with divine nature.[62] It is this conception that informs the end of act 5, evoked here visually in plate 3, which shows Aricia passing her liminal woodland days in hunting gear of rich-hued finery with an immense pannier, the better to suit her to her future prince. Against this courtly/pastoral backdrop, Ippolito is adorned with neoclassical motifs, tokens of sympathy with the out-of-doors. His sandaled buskins of blue satin crisscross his calves in Grecian style, like those of a prince drawn by Boquet, and his costume, said to be *à la grecque*, is covered with sky blue satin and ornamented with silver-threaded appliqué using red gems and sequins.[63]

62. A synthetic account of this development in philosophical texts is Becker's "The Divinization of Nature," 47–61.

63. "Un abito da uomo di raso celeste alla Greca guarnito con riporti di lama d'argento, e mosaico di lustrine, petto, maniche e reversci di sames d'argento con riporti di Talchi rossi, e lustrine, suoi calzoni dello stesso raso, per Signor Elisi." [A man's costume of pale blue satin *à la grecque* trimmed with silver-threaded appliqué and a mosaic pattern of sequins; chest, sleeves, and linings of silver Venetian satin; an appliqué of red gems and sequins; his shoes of the same (pale blue) satin; for signor Elisi (PAas.AdT88).] Satin, as used for both Hippolytus/Elisi and Aricia/Gabrielli, was always highly luxurious because extremely perishable, and would have been especially so in the presence of stage lighting. "Sames" was a Venetian satin. Silver Venetian silk is also noted in PAas. Cfb932.4, no. 30. For images of male princes attired *à la grecque* see Fischer, *Les costumes,* 91, upper left-hand plate. The red-and-pink dress and coat for Aricia in plate 3 is based on a costume for Gabrielli inventoried in PAas.AdT88 (act unspecified). "Un abito da Donna di raso color di rosa con ornamenti o sia agremani da Favella [bavella], color di rosa contornate di Frangietta d'argento, guarnizione di Gazza Bianca a' fiori lustrine, suo Corsetto, per la Signora Gabrieli." [A woman's costume of pink satin with ornaments or embroideries in pink; finished with floss silk thread; embroideries of pink edged with silver fringe, decorated with white egrets and sequined flowers on the bodice; for Signora Gabrielli.] Floss thread was made of raw silk. It had more body than regular thread and was used for embroidery. "Gazza" can mean magpie or egret but "gazza bianca" suggests white egret. Women's panniers had reached maximum size at this time: see a design of circa 1750 by Boquet (active at the Opéra from 1748) showing a princess being made a declaration by a prince (reproduction in Sadie, *New Grove Dictionary of Opera* 1:978), where the hoopskirt extends outward three times the width of the singer's body on either side and is adorned with highly elaborate embroidery of rocailles and garlands. Great amounts of whalebone were purchased for *Ippolito* to construct hoops, as noted in PAas.Cfb932.4. Whalebone, still very fashionable, was not to undergo attack until late in the century, as discussed in the last section of chapter 8 below, "The Family of Opera." Baldrighi's royal family portrait (fig. 3.6) is an excellent reference for the dress of the royal figures in *Ippolito,* showing the highly rococo style then in vogue (see Pisetzky, *Storia del costume in Italia,* vol. 4, which greatly helped our study, especially plate 7, with commentary on p. 18).

By act 5, the dancing choruses of quasi humans from acts 1 and 2—fauns and dryads, demons and furies—have given way to dancing sailors (act 3), hunters (act 4), and finally shepherds (act 5), emblems of a pastoral and purportedly more human nature, though still artificial enough to perform on heels, with women wearing immense hoopskirts (see plate 4).

Viewed in the traditional terms of Italian opera, this dynastic imaginary demands that both principals sing with the highest and nimblest voices in the cast. Not only was Aricia a top-billed coloratura but Ippolito was a soprano castrato, played by Filippo Elisi, who was prized not for coloratura (like most of that time) but for expressiveness.[64] Bearing the signature of her ultimate fall, Fedra as seconda donna could equal neither Aricia's prowess nor her vocal graces. Already mother and wife, her sexual and procreative powers realized, she is hellishly bent on obliterating Aricia's hopes and bending Ippolito to her will.

Fedra is Fury incarnate from her first number, "Furie del cor geloso" (example 3.3), a rage aria that sets off in F major with mad arpeggios, seething by measure 5 under violin tremolos. Though F major was associated with contradictory ethoi over the course of the eighteenth century, earlier eighteenth-century theorists like Rameau identified it with "furies and tempests" (*Traité de l'harmonie*, 1722).[65] This accords with Fedra's general disharmony with idealized nature, as projected through her heavier vocal quality and instrumentation by comparison with Aricia, and by her intemperate keys and tempos by comparison with Diana.

Tellingly Fedra's rage alone disrupts the sonic and visual tropes of melancholy pastoral that frame act 1. Note that after Aricia's initial recitative opens the opera, Ippolito sings an aria of liquid cantabile marked "Andante grazioso" in the pastoral key of B flat, "Se ai vaghi lumi tuoi," continuing, "Cara, m'accese amore, / Chiedi ad Amor se puoi / Tutto sperar da me" (Dearest, if your lovely eyes have ignited my love, ask Cupid if you can hope for everything from me). Accompanied by pure legato and imbued with Lombard rhythms, the aria is touchingly *galant* (example 3.4). Enter Diana's priestesses in a soothing choral siciliana with flute accompaniments in compound meter, again "Andante grazioso" and continuing the Lombard rhythms (example 3.5). From here onward, the entire tableau is cast in a pastoral idiom: the priestesses' "grazioso" dance (borrowed from Rameau); the grand priestess's triple-meter aria-with-chorus, "Soggiorno amabile" ("Andante grazioso" again, and still in G) leading to her solo dance and the priestesses' choral dance ("grazioso"), both in G minor

64. See Monson, "Elisi, Filippo," in *Grove Music Online*, which quotes Thomas Gray from 1761. On the cast, see Loomis, "Tommaso Traetta's Operas," 39–46.

65. Rita Steblein summarizes characteristics associated by different eighteenth-century theorists with F major ("Key Characteristics," 291–92). Among Rameau's contemporaries, F major was associated with fury and quick-temperedness (Marc-Antoine Charpentier, ca. 1692), majesty and gravity (Rousseau, 1743 and 1768), and hunting (Kirnberger, 1769). By contrast, Mattheson said it was capable of expressing "the most beautiful sentiments in the world" (*Der vollkommene Capellmeister*, 338). After 1770, F major seems more often to have been heard as calm, beautiful, or of mixed character.

EXAMPLE 3.3. Tommaso Traetta, aria for Fedra, "Furie del cor geloso," mm. 1–15

From *Ippolito ed Aricia* (Regio Ducal Teatro, Parma, Ascension 1759), 1.6. Short score based on D-B, MS 21995.

EXAMPLE 3.4. Tommaso Traetta, aria for Ippolito, "Se ai vaghi lumi," mm. 1–6

From *Ippolito ed Aricia* (Regio Ducal Teatro, Parma, Ascension 1759), 1.2. Short score based on D-B, MS 21995.

(also from Rameau);[66] Ippolito and Aricia's worried recitative exchange, with Fedra *in disparte,* followed by the priestesses' chorus in a forthright C major, declaring Aricia unsuited to the role of priestess.

As much as Fedra bursts this pastoral frame like a tempest, Diana's calm, expressed with sunny keys and moderate tempos, intercedes to restore and reinforce it at both the opera's outer ends (see tables 3.1 and 3.2). Ushered in by Rameau's thunderous sinfonia ("ton[n]erre"), in essence a prolonged dominant on G, Diana finally lands her chariot on the tonic of C major. Note that she appears only in acts 1 and 5. She defines a problem and resolves it, authoring the temperate world of which she is the supreme authority. Her act 1 appearance brings her on in full court, summoned by her priestesses with a great clap of instrumental thunder and attended by a cortège of fauns and dryads. With all arrayed about her, she declares that souls must live free, allowing Aricia to renounce her cult and roam her forests as a huntress, reassuring Ippolito of his good standing, claiming disdain only for evil, and allowing the first act to end finally with a series of choral dances by the fauns and dryads, who are richly feathered in their verdant woodland but still formally masked *à la baroque* and most certainly heeled like dancers at the Opéra.[67]

66. Virtually all of the instrumental music in the divertissements comes straight from Rameau, notwithstanding Traetta's denial of ever having seen Rameau's score, as voiced in a letter printed in Mannheim in 1760 (quoted and translated in Loomis, "Tommaso Traetta's Operas," 19–20).

67. Masks are listed in PAas.AdT88. PAas.Cfb932.4 shows payment for numerous feathers (no. 22), green leaves (nos. 21 and 24), and white shoes for zephyrs (nos. 18 and 24). Compare the

EXAMPLE 3.5. Tommaso Traetta, chorus of priestesses with solo grand priestess, "Soggiorno amabile," mm. 1–15

From *Ippolito ed Aricia* (Regio Ducal Teatro, Parma, Ascension 1759), 1.3 Short score based on D-B, MS 21995.

Where Fedra represents nature-gone-mad, in defiance of true "nature," Diana is the epitome of nature-made-reasonable-and-pure. She is doubly superior, both a higher authority within her sylvan polity and an authority superior in natural type. As high priestess of an ideal natural order, a kind of fairy queen who puts all right, she is anything but Euripides' goddess of the wild woods, the bloodthirsty Artemis who promises to avenge the death of Hippolytus by declaring, "The wicked we destroy, children, house, and all."[68]

---

faun by Claude Gillot and the faun and dryad by Martin reproduced in Fischer, *Les costumes*, 59 and 71, respectively, and Reade, *Victoria and Albert Museum: Ballet Designs*, plate 57 (attrib. P. Lior, ca. 1744).

68. Euripides, *Hippolytus*, 1341. Artemis's subjects appeased her by offering sacrificial victims. See Frazer, *The Golden Bough*, 1–9; Burkert, *Structure and History*, 111–22, and *Greek Religion*, 149–52; and esp. Vernant, *Mortals and Immortals*, chaps. 11–14, explicating Artemis's status as a goddess of

Table 3.1. Musical plan for act 1 of Frugoni and Traetta's *Ippolito ed Aricia* (Parma, Ascension 1759)

Section	*Characters*	*Keys*	*Expressive markings*	*Scoring*
Aria	Ippolito	B-flat major	Andante grazioso	str
Coro e danza	Sacerdotesse	G major	Grazioso	str, fl
Aria + Coro→	Gran Sacerdotessa	G major, D major→	Andante grazioso	str
→Danza	Gran Sacerdotessa	G major	[Andante grazioso]	str
[Danza]	Gran Sacerdotessa	G minor	[P]oco allegro	str, fl
Coro→	Sacerdotesse	C major	Andante comodo→	str
Coro	Sacerdotesse	C major	[P]iù andante	str
[O]bbligato recitative	Fedra			str
[S]infonietta				str, tr
Aria + Coro	Sacerdotesse + tutti	G major	Allegro spiritoso	str, hn, ob
"To[n]nerre"→		G major	Presto	str
Aria	Diana	C major	Andante brillante	str
Aria	Fedra	F major	Presto	str, hn, ob
Aria	Aricia	A major	Andante comodo	str
Danza	Fauni, driadi	G major	Allegro→	
[Danza]	Fauni, driadi	G minor	Largo staccato	str
[Danza]	Fauni, driadi	G minor	Primo rondò	solo vln, bass
[Danza]	Fauni, driadi	G major	Secondo rondò	str

Vestiges of a less controlled Diana echo in the deliciously chaotic world of seventeenth-century opera, whose gods are prey to human foibles. In Cavalli's *La Calisto* (Venice, 1651), Jupiter dresses up as Diana to seduce one of her virgins, and Diana herself ends up falling for Endymion. By contrast, the eighteenth-century Diana is a displaced figure of enlightenment authority who suffuses her woods with peace and temperance, order and reason. By 1759, her authority also depended on her ability to keep one foot in the woods and one in the metaphorical town, mediating between eighteenth-century conceptions of nature and culture. Ambivalent in her relationship to nature, she both stands within it and subdues it. Small wonder that Fedra, who cannot be subdued, also cannot be saved, even—or especially—in the empire of opera seria, which rarely let a monarch die. In order for nature to realize its reasonable, concordant side, Fedra had to be tamed. But since her flames were irreducible, they could only be extinguished.

Correspondingly, Ippolito could not display the emotional excess flaunted by Fedra, as Hippolytus does in Euripides. Where Hippolytus is a cultic devotee of Artemis—radical in his idolatry and fanatically committed to chastity, railing against the female sex—Ippolito cannot express his devotion to Diana through cultic chastity, any more than the prince of Parma could express religious sentiment by becoming a priest or a monk. (Indeed Condillac, who arrived in Parma

boundaries—between youth and adulthood, self and other, wildness and tameness, strangeness and familiarity—securing but also shepherding passage between them.

Table 3.2. Musical plan for act 5 of Frugoni and Traetta's *Ippolito ed Aricia* (Parma, Ascension 1759)

Section	*Characters*	*Keys*	*Expressive markings*	*Scoring*
SCENA				
[O]bbligato recitative	Aricia			str
Cavata	Aricia	F major		muted str, hns
Sinfonia	[for Diana's arrival]	G major	Allegro	str, hns, obs
Aria	Diana	G major	Andante	str, fl, hns
Duet	Ippolito, Aricia	A major	Andante grazioso	
Danza	[shepherdesses' arrival]	A major	Musette	vla, ob, bn, bass
Coro		D major		str, ob, hn
Danza		A major		violetta with str
Ciaccona		A minor		vla, ob, bn, bass
Prima gavotta		A major	Presto	vlns, fl, bns
Seconda gavotta		A minor	Presto	vls, fl, violetta

in 1758, warned princes and specifically the prince of Parma in his *Cours d'études* against excessive religiosity.)[69] Like Parma's prince, Ippolito had to be fully of this world, especially the world of the court. In helping him to attain Aricia's hand through legitimate means, Diana recalls that ancient strain of Artemis's legacy that sometimes made her out as a protector of marriage and a goddess of fertility.[70] Here again looms the narrative of court opera: the leading man is destined for the leading lady and an all-powerful monarch eventually abets their union, however much she or he first stands in the way. Darker forces have to be fended off—diminished, checked, or eradicated—before the union can be achieved. At last the heroic young couple, having passed through their trials by fire, unite to preserve the most wholesome strain of royal blood genealogically available. Theirs is a festive triumph of kinship in the service of kingship.

But it is still a mystified and extraordinary order proposed, with no pretensions to the rough-hewn neoclassical "naturalism" of later eighteenth-century operas, evinced in the kind of jagged caves, rocky precipices, and towering ruins seen in Antonio Jolli's designs for Naples (1762–77). Here instead nature is bound to the French court, of which Filippo and his wife, daughter of Louis XV, were a decided part. We do well to remember that Algarotti was a courtier, Du Tillot a court administrator, Frugoni the court poet, and Traetta the court composer. Even Gabrielli was made court singer shortly after *Ippolito* was staged—an honorific, since opera seria singers on the active circuit were largely touring freelancers, but one that nominally formalized her abiding relationship to the

69. Arguments against fanaticism abounded in eighteenth-century Parma, in particular, from the moralizing philosopher Severio Bettinelli.

70. See Detienne, "The Powers of Marriage," 395–97; Frazer, *The Golden Bough*, 8–10 and passim.

Parmesan court. If it was unclear how a naturalistic stage would work at court, "the natural" was nevertheless complicit with Bourbon politics. In his *Saggio*, directed both to Parma and to a much wider European readership, Algarotti urged that costumes accord with scenery and come close to the customs of the times and nations depicted, since nothing helps more to transport a spectator:

> [Y]et . . . they should never be permitted to put pipes into the mouths, and Dutch breeches on the posteriors of Aeneas' Trojan companions. But, in order that dresses should be appropriated according to the custom of a country, and be well fancied at the same time, the assistance of a Julio Romano, and a Tribolo, would be wanted; because in that article they have given proof of their skill; or at least it would be necessary that the persons who superintend the wardrobe-department, were blessed with a kindred genius to those eminent artists.
>
> It would have been still more necessary for our modern painters to copy after a San Gallo and a Peruzzi, because we consequently should not see in our theatres the temple of Jupiter or Mars bear a resemblance to the church of Jesus, nor would the architecture of a piazza in Carthage have a Gothic complexion; for, in all scene-painting, the costume and propriety must be united. The scenery is the first object in an opera that powerfully attracts the eye, that determines the place of action and co-operates chiefly to the elusive enchantment, that makes the spectator imagine himself to be transported either to Egypt, to Greece, to Troy, to Mexico, to the Elysian Fields, or even up to Olympus.[71]

When he revised the work, he added to his critique the authority of d'Alembert's *De la liberté de la musique* of 1759, which claimed that owing to the ridiculous gods and heroes at the Opéra, even one of their great artists, most cognizant of "la belle nature," had renounced serious spectacle in favor of comic.[72] Yet tellingly, Algarotti cautioned that visual elements could only match their historical referents "il più che sia possibile" (as much as possible), for theater needed license to be make-believe and to avoid pedantry and rigidity.

Modest and ambivalent, these pleas parallel the equivocal juxtaposition in *Ip-*

71. Algarotti, *Essay*, ed. Burgess, 47–48. "[S]e non si esige da' nostri Canziani ch'e' taglino le vesti all'antica, così per appunto come le ci vengono descritte dall'erudito Ferrario, non dovriano né meno farsi lecito di dare a' compagni di Enea la berretta e i braconi alla foggia olandese. Perché i vestiti fossero costumati insieme e bizzarri, ci vorrebbono i Giulî Romani e i Triboli, che diedero prova anche in tal genere del loro valore; o almeno faria mestieri che i nostri uomini al vestiario fossero inspirati dal genio di quegli eruditi artefici. E molto più faria mestieri che dagli di odierni pittori seguite fossero le tracce di un San Gallo e di un Peruzzi, perché ne' nostri teatri il tempio di Giove o di Marte non avesse sembianza della Chiesa del Gesù, una piazza di Cartagine non si vedesse architettata alla gotica, perché in somma nelle scene si trovasse col pittoresco unito insieme il decoro e il costume. Le scene prima di qualunque altra cosa nell'Opera attraggono imperiosamente gli occhi e determinano il luogo dell'azione, facendo gran parte di quello incantesimo per cui lo spettatore viene ad esser trasferito in Egitto o in Grecia, in Troia o nel Messico, nei campi Elisi o su nell'Olimpo" (Algarotti, *Saggi*, ed. da Pozzo, 175–76).

72. Artist not cited; see d'Alembert's *De la liberté de la musique*, note to art. 14; reprinted in Launay, *La querelle des bouffons* 3:2199–282, at 410 n. e in facsimile (-3:2230).

polito of the marvelous with a newly rationalized view of nature: on one side the artificial wonders of Gabrielli's astounding virtuosity, Elisi's castrato soprano, and the Busby-Berkeleyian scenic extravagance; and on the other the harmonious woods, the expulsion of allegory and the supernatural by eliminating the prologue, the sea monster, and the display of Neptune, and by retaining Diana's descent and Theseus's trip to Hades.[73] In these paradoxes, "nature" implies a prescriptive moral order. Ostensibly, of course, Algarotti's pleas were historicist: costumes, scenery, and voices had to accord not just to promote abstract dramatic harmony and illusion, but to lend verisimilitude to a coherent narrative. But Algarotti refused to push this historicism too far. To have done so would have undermined the monarchical interests of a court that required universalist conceptions—stable, not relativized—to undergird what still had to be asserted as a divinely ordered world.

* * *

Where did this leave opera lovers who craved bel canto, adored spectacle, and longed for the frisson of magical transport that came from listening to a great singer?

One might have expected Frugoni's verse and Traetta's music to have introduced tableaux, divertissements, and dramatic obbligatos in a way that worked to dampen opportunities for applause and vocalizing. There are some, but they are few. Fedra's outburst in 1.4 dovetails midsentence from simple recitative into trumpet-accompanied obbligato, continues with a trumpet fanfare on her final chord, moves into a fugal chorus, and then catapults to the sinfonia that accompanies Diana's descent. In a climactic moment in 5.2, Aricia reacts to news of Ippolito's death with a passage of obbligato that starts unconventionally with a sinfonia (Rameau's), incorporates it into her ensuing monologue, and after a passage of pictorial arioso on the murmuring breezes that puts her to sleep, is awakened with a vivacious sinfonia heralding Diana's return. But these were exceptions to the rule, and strikingly, both are dynamic scenic complexes that are juxtaposed with the stolidity of Diana. Apart from them, all of the arias in the opera are exit da capos with conventional ritornello structures; and far and away, most recitatives are simple ones that lead to arias, even at such dramatic moments as Fedra's outburst at Ippolito for allowing Aricia to refuse the priesthood, Teseo's plea for death in the underworld (2.1), Ippolito's exchange with Aricia before his departure (4.5), and Teseo's report to Fedra of Ippolito's death (5.1). Where dramatic enhancement and greater continuity might have been elected, it was usually forgone or, if present, was pictorially inspired. Fedra's speech at the beginning of act 3 is an exception, and yet it quickly fizzles into simple recitative and an aria di mezzo carattere in quinari unmistakably crafted

73. Chegai aptly calls the Parmesan initiative a reform "with short legs" (*L'esilio di Metastasio*, 92).

for a secondary character.[74] There was no attempt at the radical continuities of that most famous of reform operas, Calzabigi and Gluck's *Orfeo ed Euridice*, nor those that Traetta himself later essayed in *Armida* (Vienna, 1762) along with Durazzo and Migliavacca, with Gabrielli in the title role, nor those that Traetta explored with Verazi in *Sofonisba* (Mannheim, 1762), Coltellini in *Ifigenia in Tauride* (Vienna, 1763), and most especially Coltellini (with Gabrielli again) in *Antigona* (St. Petersburg, 1772).[75]

Perhaps what was at issue was defined most decisively by the court chronicler, who wrote on May 3, 1759, that besides the fabulous visual spectacle, no one could talk of anything in Parma but La Gabrielli, who "sang like an angel."[76] The reception of *Ippolito*, like the opera itself, was conservative. Vested in Italianate vocal traditions that extend even to such atavistic elements as a Handelian church-styled fugato chorus for the priestesses, the opera recalls the pomp and artifice of the old law for which they stood.[77] We might therefore see the project as an attempt—with mixed results—not so much to change the cultural ways of the old regime as to safeguard it by sprucing them up.

74. In the live recording of *Ippolito* (see n. 5 above) the audience applauds after every closed number and most vigorously—and vocally—after Aricia's, sung by Patrizia Ciofi.

75. See Heartz, "Traetta in Vienna," 293–12. On important parallel developments in Turin during the 1760s, see Butler, *Operatic Reform*.

76. Sgavetti made similar entries on May 4, 23, 24, 27, 29, etc. To my knowledge comments on audience reactions other than those cited herein have not come to light.

77. Heartz, "Traetta in Parma," 281.

APPENDIX: DECREE ON AUDIENCE BEHAVIOR, PARMA, OCTOBER 4, 1749

AVVISO Per l'Opera Buffa da farsi in Musica per quest'Autunno.[78]
Ed. 4 ottobre 1749; Parma, Real Ducal Stamperia in Borgo Riolo.

Essendo piaciuto all'*Altezza Serenissima Reverendissima* di accordare all'Impresario, che nel suo Ducal Teatro si rappresenti quest'Autunno un'Opera Buffa in Musica, e volendo che in detto Teatro si osservi il dovuto rispetto, ciò che non è compatibile colli schiammazzi, battimenti, grida, mormorìo, ed altri eccessi, che si sono sperimentati nel decorso delle Rappresentazioni passate: Inerendo quindi alle *Regie* determinazioni, ed in nome del Clementissimo Padrone si comanda doversi eseguire, quanto qui abbasso resta disposto.

Primo. Non sarà permesso a qualunque Persona di qualsivoglia grado, condizione, trovandosi *Serenissima Altezza Reverendissima* in Teatro battere le mani, far rumore, dar voci di Viva, od altre simili, nè fare battimenti, strepito, o simiglianti moti alteranti il rispettoso contegno, che esige la *Reverenda* Presenza del Principe.

Secondo. Quando poi nel Teatro suddetto non intervenisse la Reale Persona, si permettono a' Concorrenti le semplici voci di Viva, e di Applauso, e battimento delle sole mani, restando proibito qualunque altro atto, come altresì qualunque disordine, che possa provenire da un continuato mormorio, o dalle frequenti voci.

Terzo. Avendosi date le provvidenze, affinchè il Teatro resti illuminato per ogni parte, si proibisce quindi il potervi entrare Persone, Servidori, Lachè, o qualunque altro con fanali, e con torcie di qualunque specie, nè servirà di scusa, o pretesto qualunque ragione o motivo, che si potesse, o volesse addurre.

Quarto. Non sarà permesso a' Soldati, Milizie, Servidori di Livrea, e qualunque altro Inserviente il poter entrare nella Platea, nè stare nell'Interiore de' Palchetti, sì appiedi, che seduti, finchè i loro Padroni vi giungono, nè prima, ne dopo sotto qualunque motivo, o pretesto.

Quinto. Sulle considerazione poi di non esser possibile per ora dar la destinazione de' Palchi tutti, e particolarmente del Pianterreno, ed Ordine Reale, ma doversi indugiare per una nuova disposizione fino all'arrivo di *Serenissima Altezza Reverendissima* la Signora Infanta Sovrana, si è venuto in sentimento di dichiarare, che li soddetti due Ordini Pianterreno, e Reale siano egualmente nobili, ed effetto possa la Nobiltà servirsi de' medesimi, il prezzo de' quali si è, come resta appiedi del presente.

78. I-PAp, W** 24115, *Gridari degli Stati di Parma.*

Sesto. Si avverte, che a nissuno di qualunque grado, e condizione sarà permesso il pretendere per nissun pretesto si scrivi alla Porta il Biglietto dell'Entrata, perché certamente sarà rifiutato; e questo in virtù del pregiudizio sperimentato per il passato dall'essersi fatto Vacchetta alla Porta.

Settimo: Si avverte di più che come verrà data dal Sig*nor* Intendente Generale di questa Corte Messer Du Tillot una lista di quelli dovranno essere esenti di pagare l'entrata al Teatro, e la quale sarà affiso in stampa, non potrà nissun altro per qualunque pretesto pretendere d'esser esente.

Ottavo. Il Secondo, e Terz'Ordine de' Palchi sono dati per Impresa a' Distributori de' Biglietti, così essendo piacciuto al detto Impresario; onde quelli che ne vorranno affittare giorno per giorno, faranno Capo da' suddetti.

Nono. Le recite di detta Opera saranno distribuite in numero di quaranta per l'Autunno, e se mai accadesse, che per ordine di *Serenissima Altezza Reverendissima* dovesse la Compagnia trasferirsi a Piacenza, li Palchi si pagheranno *pro rata* di quelle Recite, che si faranno.

Decimo. Essendosi finalmente presa la più esatta cura di stabilire interinalmente il prezzo de' Palchi, sì del Pianterreno, Ordine Reale, che degl'altri, e così pure de' Viglietti dell'Entrata, e Sedere, durante le Rappresentazioni dell'Opera Buffa: Così i biglietti d'entrate, e Sedere durante le Rappresentazioni dell'Opera Buffa: Così non resta, che di stabilire il prezzo de' Rinfreschi, e Generi, che si esiteranno privatamente in Teatro, e la loro perfetta qualità, e condizione, di cui se ne farà avvertito il Pubblico con Tariffe separate, quali si dovranno giustamente da chichessia osservare.

Prezzi de' Palchi

Ordine Reale, e Pianterreno	Zecchini 3.
Second'Ordine	Zecchini 2.
Terz'Ordine	Zecchini 1.
Entrata della Porta	Lire 3.
Per il Sedere	Lire 1.

Quali Prezzi restano così fissati, nè sarà in libertà dell'Impresario di prendere più di quanto viene di sopra espresso.

Parma 4. Ottobre 1749

Don Pietro Serou Controlor in absenza di Messer Du Tillot Intendente Generale della R. Casa.

In Parma, nella Reale Ducal Stamperìa Monti in Borgo Riolo.

CHAPTER 4

Festivity and Time

"There is no serious opera . . . but in carnival time." CHARLES BURNEY, *An Eighteenth-Century Musical Tour in France and Italy*[1]

Reforms in Bourbon Parma were caught between an ambivalent ideology that venerated and moralized the natural and a practice of rule predicated on energetically deploying the artifices of festivity.[2] In the end, the two were not easy to arbitrate. Like other absolutist governments across the peninsula, the Bourbons held onto the fabulous, even as they attempted social reforms within and without the theater. In that way, the miraculous body of the sovereign could be suffused into the landscape and body of his people. Later in the century, as the character of Italian festivities became less fantastical, rulers sometimes invoked economic and ideological reforms to justify a reduction in festive practices. Reformist Tuscany under Habsburg archduke Peter Leopold, for instance, introduced a new constitution in 1779 that reduced the number of feast days (with a correlated increase in working days) in keeping with broader moves toward separation of church and state.[3] A model for such reductions had already been launched in Habsburg Vienna under Maria Theresia, one that Joseph II extended in 1776 when he eliminated Italian opera from the Burgtheater as being too lavish and brought it back in 1783 only in the guise of the less extravagant opera buffa. But since festivities were fundamental to maintaining absolutist pecking orders, governments had to scale back judiciously (in Joseph's case,

1. Burney, *An Eighteenth-Century Musical Tour in France and Italy*, 66.

2. The term "festivity" here covers the vast range of practices and forms variously indicated by "feast," "feasting," "festival," and even "celebration." There is no English equivalent to the versatile term in romance languages: *festa* (Italian), *fête* (French), *fiesta* (Spanish), etc.

3. Litchfield, *Emergence of a Bureaucracy*.

at a time when shoddy management had caused interest in Italian theater to decline among Viennese nobles). And as they scaled back, they had to replace festivities with other premises and other modes of rule—nationalism, religious piety, economic egalitarianism, austerity, state-supported welfare, education, and public works. Moves to suppress festivities were particularly unwelcome in Italy and, moreover, they had no measurable effect on numbers of Italian opera houses or numbers of productions, both of which grew apace throughout the century.

The standard history of festivity in eighteenth-century Europe provides a global point from which to view the Italian terrain. According to this account, absolutist rulerships siphoned off much festive life from cities by draining autonomy and vitality from civic administrations, guilds, confraternities, and other urban societies that had thrived in the late middle ages and Renaissance, and concentrated controlled festivities near the physical bases of rule.[4] As absolutist governments lost ground in the eighteenth century, they were increasingly pressed to reconcile the fundamental paradox of how to display largesse by producing and permitting festivity while still wielding authority in the face of potential license. The usual solution, we are told, was to regulate (and sometimes help finance) festivities in public spaces—town squares, watersides, churches, and theaters—using laws and intermittent edicts while turning a blind eye to as much disorder as a system founded in idioms of domination could endure. At the same time, rationalist tendencies and reformist programs of government caused gradual reductions in festive life.

An edict on masking produced by the court of Parma on July 18, 1728, speaks to the earlier part of this story. The occasion for festivities was the wedding of Duke Antonio Farnese to Enrichetta d'Este, and featured Frugoni and Leonardo Vinci's opera *Medo*, designed by Pietro Righini. As a wedding, the event was linear and historical in nature rather than cyclical, not least because in 1728 masking had been totally banned in Parma for the previous forty-six years. Posted as a broadside throughout the town, the edict gestured ostentatiously toward the advent of a new regime and good new times, even as it insisted strenuously on maintaining order and social hierarchy.[5] His "Serene Highness, wanting this city to have masking in conjunction with the joyful events made to solemnify his wedding on the sumptuous entrance of [his betrothed] the Serene Madame Duchess," had ordered "the illustrious governor to make a public avviso" to that

4. Mercedes Viale Ferrero follows these tendencies in Italian staging devices and architecture, quoting Emanuele Tesauro's *Il cannochiale aristotelico* (Turin, 1670), which explains that sumptuousness and magnificence *had* to be concentrated within the sovereign because he was their very fount (Viale Ferrero, *Feste delle Madame Reali di Savoia*, 63). On the paradigmatic case of Louis XIV, see Apostolidès, *Le roi-machine;* Burke, *The Fabrication of Louis XIV;* Marin, *Portrait of the King;* and Chae, "Music, Festival, and Power."

5. I-PAp, W24115, vol. 42 (1720–39), *Grida per le maschere*. The court chronicler Borra noted only occasional mild infractions against the long-standing prohibition against masking, on which see Allegri, "Introduzione allo studio degli apparati," 30 n. 18. See too Botti, "Il 'Medo' di Pietro Righini," 223–38.

effect. Full license was thereby given to every subject to go masked "every day of the *allegrezze*, both morning and evening, beginning on the day . . . after the solemn entrance of the . . . duchess, and lasting until the final day, . . . save Fridays and the mornings of feast [holy] days." A long list of proscriptions followed, each one accompanied by a threat. Anyone who went masked on unauthorized days would do so "under pain [of a fine] of fifty gold scudi and three lashes of the whip to be given in public." No one was to rove the city in groups larger than twelve or "wear the dress or appurtenances of . . . monks or nuns, pilgrims and hermits, or collars, girdles, . . . crowns or other things belonging to a religious state, or . . . wear any style representing any kind of ill-virtue," or "wear a mask in church, cloister parlors, monasteries, or convents." No one was to "carry any kind of arms" (extensively detailed), throw confetti, sing lewd songs, toss chamber pots or other foul things, or accompany others who did any of the above, or make others do so (e.g., servants), both offenders and those with or near them being subject to the same penalties. Nor was anyone to speak or act immorally, provoke brawls or disorders, cause others to be dishonored through slander, or "go to the public offices of lawyers, medical doctors, or Jesuit priests" where they might "bother and disturb anyone, either scholars or readers or masters." Half an hour before sunset all persons of whatever station had to remove their masks and fake beards from their faces, and not carry them unless they were also carrying a light.[6] Furthermore, no costumes or masks could be purchased from anyone but the so-called impresario of masking, who was licensed by the government. Punishments were applicable to infractions of virtually all of the above, administered at the discretion (*arbitrio*) of the sovereign—not the sovereign himself, of course, but the strong arms that extended the will of his corporeal body. And all carried the same penalty, reiterated with the iteration of each prohibition.

The proscriptions thus covered a whole clutch of interlocking aims, dramatizing the tension between largesse and rule. Masking was to produce the mark of festivity without actually letting the world turn upside down. Collective violence was preempted by the prevention of crowds and arms, irreverence by the prevention of religious motifs, obscenity, and profanity, disorder by the protection of sobriety and industry, inversions of social hierarchy and decorum by the complete control of costumes. Far from suspending the official life through the carnivalesque, the proscriptions gave officialdom ways to sustain it.

For the most part the threats were ritual ones. They can be found repeated in substance (if not at such length) in many other *gride, avvisi, bandi, editti,* and *proclami per la maschera* issued at regular intervals for the length and breadth of the peninsula, from Venice and Milan to Rome and Naples, from Turin and Genoa to Bologna and Ancona.[7] They did set the stage for some arrests, and

6. On time-reckoning in Italy, see Blackburn and Holford-Strevens, *Oxford Companion to the Year*, 662.

7. At Parma, for instance, *gride per la maschera* began after 1728 to be posted at least twice yearly, at Carnival and often again at Ascensiontide.

certainly there was widespread use of arbitrary force, corporeal punishment, and detention. But arrests too were often ritual in nature. As John Rosselli has shown, they were mostly attempts to secure conventional shows of compliance, contrition, and pleas for mercy. They sought to reproduce the hierarchy that made the ruler out as the parent and the subject the child. Only occasionally were they first stages in criminal prosecution. And aside from a night or two in prison, even punishment was comparatively rare—often carried out mainly to set a public example for others and flaunt the power of the ruler or ruling group to exact justice arbitrarily.[8]

Still, edicts like these reveal fears of crowd action that often did erupt in both squares and theaters. Even in Du Tillot's time—when official forces were marshaled against traditional popular behavior and subjects were largely excluded from production mechanisms—paying customers had enough tooth to vent their frustrations in the opera house. By the end of this chapter, I will have proposed that an effective antidote to disorder, within theaters and without, was a tolerance of festivity. The contrast between Parma and Rome here is instructive. After 1728, masking at Parma went from atrophy to hypertrophy,[9] from a condition of prohibition to its repeated licensing throughout the year, and greater success in maintaining order followed suit. At Rome, theater and masking were normally licensed for only eight to ten days annually during Carnival, and by contrast with Parma's opera houses, Rome's were the wildest in Europe.

This is just one index of how the larger flux of temporal events shaped opera and festivity. Festivity by its nature was always a condition written over life *for a time*, in contrast to other conditions at other times. It could produce the illusion of an eternity—an eternity variously marked by pleasure, gratitude, and merriment, or alternatively by revenge, abandonment, and terror—but only if it was normally absent. The contrast was dramatically articulated within the fluctuating rhythms of the Catholic year, which swung from great periods of celebration (Nativity, Easter) to periods of solemnity or penitence (Advent, Lent), each sustained for lengths of time that corresponded to their relative level of importance in the hierarchy of the church, but also tempered by vestigial pagan festivities, the most salient of which was Carnival. The many edicts posted at times of theatergoing and festivity, while they did mean to avert the worst disorders, also served to announce times when disorder *was* the time.

TIME AND THE CALENDAR

The start of Carnival festivities was generally signaled by the opening of a town's theater, and theater was their supreme sign. Even when masking time and theater time were not perfectly coterminous, they were symbolically inextricable. In 1795 an anonymous text called *Amours and Adventures of Two English Gentle-*

8. See Rosselli, *The Opera Industry.*

9. Allegri, "Introduzione allo studio degli apparati," 21.

men in Italy was published by a pair of rakish young men who traced these elisions in a comical description of their Carnival intrigues in Venice:

> Almost every one is so disguised in Habit, that there is no knowing any by their Dress, when they appear in the *Piazza*, or at the *Redotto*, a large publick Building, divided into seventy Rooms, where is Gaming, choice of Sweet meats, Wines, all sorts of Fruits, and variety of Entertainment and a free Conversation with any one: Every Night is spent at Comedies, Operas or at some noble Venetian's House, who gives a Ball. By this you may imagine the scene of intermixt pleasure, jumbled together without any Regulation.[10]

Carnival was the central theater season, and the fulcrum of the church year was the conjunction of Carnival with Lent, when a raucous Mardi Gras yielded to the stillness of Ash Wednesday. Periodicals and travelers repeatedly affirm that the opening and closing of theaters heralded the coming and going of Carnival, that as much as Ash Wednesday meant the stilling of Carnival, theater openings meant its awakening. On January 13, 1748, the official Roman weekly *Diario ordinario di Roma* (known as *Chracas*) reported, for instance, that to give a start to the public "divertimenti" of the upcoming Carnival, performances had already begun in public theaters.[11] Four decades later, in 1788, Goethe declared, "The Carnival [at Rome] really starts with the opening of the theatres at the New Year."[12] Since Rome was exceptional in delaying licensed Carnival activities outdoors so shortly before Lent, theater there was a particularly crucial beacon of Carnival, a sign of its preparation but also a sign that Lent was not far off.

Opera as a lyric genre marked the condition of festivity more strongly than any other types of theater because it most thoroughly transcended the ordinary—and opera seria above all. With its ravishing voices, grand triumphs, battles, and ballets, opera seria was festivity in a high register and as a consequence was often licensed at only one theater per town at a time.

For theatrical purposes, Carnival in Rome and elsewhere was conventionally extended backward not just in spirit but in deed to December 26, St. Stephen's Day, in contrast to the official outdoor festivities, which at Rome usually began on or shortly before January 17, the feast of St. Anthony of Egypt (or the Desert).[13] Outside Rome, as the century progressed, new theaters were built, and competition for singers and other personnel stiffened, additional theater seasons were added in autumn, during Ascensiontide, or even summer. There were special events too, such as weddings or visits by royalty or foreign dignitaries. And increasingly eighteenth-century monarchical cities used festive, or quasi-festive periods of the church calendar for routine annual celebrations of dynas-

10. *Amours and Adventures*, 10. The book plays Carnival off against the genre of adventure tales (note its subtitle: "*The Duels They Fought; the Dangers They Escaped; and Their Safe Arrival in England*").

11. *Diario ordinario (Chracas)*, no. 4755, 9–10.

12. "Schon von dem neuen Jahre an sind die Schauspielhäuser eröffnet, und das Carneval hat seinen Anfang genommen" (Goethe, *Italienische Reise*, 522).

13. Rosselli and MacNutt, "Season," 281–83.

tic birthdays and namedays, as monarchs folded celebrations of themselves and their dynasties into the annual rhythm of religious liturgy and pagan holidays.

Most notable was Naples under the Bourbons, which began its winter season on King Charles's nameday, November 4, stopped for Christmas, and reopened on December 26 for "Carnival"—a much longer Carnival than that at Rome, but likewise started earlier in theaters than out-of-doors.[14] Habsburg influenced, this Bourbon liturgy was tantamount to a political usurpation of the long-standing church calendar by the new monarchical calendar, as Paolo Fabbri has underscored, and in this respect was echoed by the Bourbon calendar at Parma under the rule of Carlo's brother.[15] In both cities, the Bourbons placed overwhelming stress on a new cyclical rhythm based in dynastic events and milestones that were interspersed throughout the entire year. At Naples, the Bourbons virtually ignored the traditional suppression of festivity during Advent through a nearly continuous recognition of birthdays and namedays from November 4 through Fat Tuesday, not counting the added season of opera seria at Ascension. And they also repeated Viennese practice by celebrating Queen Amalia's nameday with opera in summer.[16] Other commemorations of the dynasty included operas given on namedays of past rulers, solemnified through their linkage to births of saints, and special operas for Bourbon treaties with allied states. All of these strategies used the calendar to collectivize the Neapolitan populace around a Bourbon consciousness.

The practical and symbolic consequence of the Bourbons' long winter opera season was a central, extended period of festivity surrounding either side of the winter solstice. This focal point coincided with the density of well-off visitors in the city, as with Carnival elsewhere. Hence in 1769, the traveler Jean-Pierre Grosley could highlight the place of opera seria at the top of the festive hierarchy: "The opera [seria] at Naples acts from St. Charles's day to Lent, and three times a week: the other parts of the year are left to the comic opera, and a play not like that of the other parts of Italy [i.e., the comic intermezzo], which is also acted by Italian players in foreign countries."[17]

14. Morelli, "Castrati, primedonne e Metastasio," 33–60.

15. There are parallel examples, especially Habsburg ones, of dynastic calendars that were blended seamlessly, and virtually equaled in symbolic weight, the church calendar. For Joseph II's propagation of a rubricated calendar, showing all of the royal birthdays and namedays in red, see Tanzer, *Spectacle mussen seyn*, 106–24.

16. Fabbri, "Vita e funzione di un teatro pubblico," 61–76. For the operas given each year at the San Carlo, with their opening dates, see *Il Teatro di San Carlo* (vol. 1, ed. Ajello et al.; vol. 2, ed. Roscioni). In addition to the November, Carnival, and Ascension seasons, the operas for Maria Amalia's birthday were staged annually on July 10 and cantatas for Carlo III's birthday on January 20 and (later) for the birthday of his son Ferdinand IV on January 12. November 4 openings occurred at other monarchical theaters where Charleses were installed too, notably the Vienna of Karl VI, Mannheim of Karl Teodor, and Stuttgart of Carl Eugen, but not with the same changes to the winter and summer seasons that occurred at Naples.

17. Grosley, *New Observations*, 2:235. "L'Opéra joue, à Naples, depuis la S. Charles jusqu'au Carême, à trois représentations par semaine. Les autres tems de l'année sont remplis par l'Opéra-

Operatic histories have never interpreted the alliance between winter and the central calendrical phase of operatic production in connection with older calendrical customs, but the web of pagan associations was rich and stubborn. Within the prodigious annual cycle of Neapolitan celebrations, winter was the focal point, coinciding not just with the greatest presence of well-to-do visitors and noblemen, but with an extended period of opera seria and related festivities that preceded the winter solstice and that (as elsewhere) almost immediately followed it. The routine labeling of the winter opera season as "Carnival" the day after Christmas, both in official notices (e.g., libretti, broadsides) and unofficial references (periodicals, letters, travelers' diaries), gave it a pagan charge and placed that most vaunted of theater seasons in a metonymic relationship to Carnival all told. Importantly, the winter solstice invited different emphases from the vernal equinox, which was associated not with the start of Carnival but with its culmination and the approach of Lent—hence with pagan revels leading to the renewal of Christianity. Different calendrical systems made these contrasts clear. March 1 as start of the year was closer to the vernal equinox, which had constituted the traditional beginning of the pagan year and signaled the chasing out of winter and inauguration of spring, whereas January 1 was closer to the winter solstice, the onset of winter, and the birth of Christ.

In either case, festivity during winter had meant the possibility of rebirth and renewal as far back as ancient times. As E. O. James has argued, the very fact that the Nativity was observed at the winter solstice, which had associations with the wild but propitiary Saturnalia of ancient Rome, meant to ensure the rebirth of the weakening Sun, "brought it into very intimate association with the mythological victory of light over darkness and of the rebirth of the sun as the author and giver of light."[18] Old agrarian and other seasonal associations of nature lingered in popular consciousness, rural and urban, during the eighteenth century, especially among rural immigrants to the city, the baronage, and others of the ruling class. The last typically made annual excursions in autumn for the hunt, around which were elaborate rituals and accompanying portraiture that emphasized the juxtaposition of life and death.[19] In urban opera seria, standard

---

Bouffon & par Comédie qui n'est point celle que l'on trouve dans le reste de l'Italie, & que les Italiens portent dans les pays Etrangers où ils sont des théâtres" (*Nouveaux mémoires* 3:97). As comic opera was never done at the San Carlo, Grosley can only be referring to the comic intermezzo. Regular Ascension seasons began to take place in 1745–46, except for 1755–60 when spring operas were seemingly displaced to early summer. See *Il Teatro di San Carlo* (vol. 1, ed. Ajello et al.; vol. 2, ed. Roscioni).

18. James, *Seasonal Feasts*, 231. Saturnalia ended on December 23. James's assumption of a loose association between these festivities does not presuppose a causal, historical relationship of the kind some writers on Carnival have protested (see Clemente, "Idee del carnevale," 11–35, esp. 21–25), but proposes the survival of an associative relationship. Similarly, the November 4 start at Naples and elsewhere coincides roughly with the northern European Yuletide starting in mid-November.

19. Depictions of rulers engaged in the hunt were standard in royal portraiture; see Francesco Liani's portraits of Charles III and Queen Maria Amalia of Saxony and of Ferdinando IV as a grenadier (Mancini et al., *Il Teatro di San Carlo*, 1:35, 39, and 63).

scenic components included tamer elements of nature, like gardens with fountains and verdant triumphal landscapes, but the prodigiously popular ballets between acts often dwelt on pagan and bucolic themes.[20] Literal exemplars staged at the San Carlo include a ballet for Carlo's birthday in 1746 entitled *Festività di Bacco*, two ballets for Advent in 1761—*Feste saturnali* and *Carro di Bacco*—and in 1768 an *Allegro baccanale tra paesani e pastori*. Clearly these were entrée- or divertissement-type ballets, suites of dance curios rather than new-styled narrative ballets; and their themes hovered between the high-flown, rather antinaturalistic world of opera seria and a whole parallel universe of earthy dialect operas, cantatas in dialogue, works on pastoral themes, vernacular comic operas, and dialect plays.[21]

Among pagan festivities that came to be folded into early Christian liturgies, those of Christmas had historically been the most musical—we need think only of medieval Nativity plays with music, or worldly Christmas songs, many comical and irreverent in tone, sung on streets, in courts, and in churches (much as church hymns and other religious songs could conversely be sung to secular, even clownish or bawdy words).[22] And the Christmas season had traditionally also seen the celebration of a whole array of rites that turned the ordinary world upside down. Most striking was the Feast of Fools, which emerged in the early Middle Ages (and still lives on in rural France, and to a lesser extent England), celebrated by schoolmen and lowly clerics on the feast of St. Stephen (December 26), the feast of St. John (December 27), the feast of the Holy Innocents (December 28), New Year's Day, and Epiphany (January 6).[23]

The almost universal start-up of opera's Carnival season on December 26 should be understood as an extension of these traditions. Like Carnival generally, opera not only allowed for make-believe, a social time outside of normal time, and a degree of insubordination; it also lit up the frigid darkness of winter at a time, seasonal and historical, when light was scarce, supplying visual brilliance and motion to compensate for the cold air and shorter (and drier) food selections. By association, light connected opera mythically with a victory over darkness at the same time as it animated a world that would otherwise have

20. For examples of such "natural" elements, see the scenic designs reproduced in ibid., 1:22, 27, and 17, respectively.

21. Recently the Cappella della Pietà dei Turchini, directed by Antonio Florio, has been reviving Neapolitan dialect works to great effect. On eighteenth-century spoken dialect comedy in Naples, see Naddeo, "Urban Arcadia," 41–65.

22. Bakhtin, *Rabelais*, 79.

23. Ibid., 74–75; Heers, *Les fêtes des fous;* James, *Seasonal Feasts*, 278–80; and Gaignebet with Florentin, *Le carnaval*. On the present-day endurance of temporal and symbolic aspects of festive calendars in rural Italy, see Grimaldi, *Tempi grassi*. Other festive seasons also had traditional associations with mockery and laughter, such as Easter (less focused on music than on storytelling and anecdotes). See Bakhtin, *Rabelais*, 78, who also shows that the close connection between laughter and seasonal rhythms was still well-understood in the eighteenth century, including the traditional *risus paschalis*.

been rigid and dense. Charles Burney wrote about an opera he attended for the "great festival of St. Charles and the King of Spain's name-day,"

> It is not easy to imagine or describe the grandeur and magnificence of this spectacle . . . : The court was in grand gala, and the house was not only doubly illuminated, but amazingly crowded with well-dressed company. In the front of each box a mirrour, three or four feet long, by two or three wide, before which are two large wax tapers; these, by reflection, being multiplied, and added to the lights of the stage and to those within the boxes, make the splendour too much for the aching sight.[24]

Animated by flickering candles and reproduced by mirrors, brilliant light replicated the multiple sightlines of sociability that were fundamental to festivity in the opera house. Like many other accounts, Burney's also stresses how thoroughly lighting calibrated the status of an event.[25] As a sign of the times, dazzling light was an ongoing desideratum, a utopian dream relinquished only of financial necessity or to tone down less significant events in comparison with more significant ones.

Even when chiaroscuro lighting was advocated by opera reformers who favored naturalism later in the century, Italian productions usually preferred brilliant light. In 1787, the "splendour" Burney described was still not "too much" for the Neapolitan theater architect Vincenzo Lamberti, who (quite unusually) devoted the whole sixth chapter of his 1787 treatise *La regolata costruzion de' teatri* to illumination, and in a way that shows the continued import of light in the late settecento. Progressive in his scientific understanding of light and acoustics, Lamberti was troubled by the consumption of air—and hence sound—by existing light sources. He reckoned that at the San Carlo of his time there were in the footlights alone some 232 oil lamps with wicks and 712 about the stage all told, including lamps in the six wings, the grand total of which he estimated as the equivalent of about 2,848 candles—probably a conservative calculation, even for the stage and wings.[26]

Lamberti was not impervious to the naturalistic views of reformers, who had moved very far from the "painted light" on wings and backcloths and center-stage lighting described by Swedish architect Nicodemus Tessin the Younger in 1687–88 and far too from the simple chiaroscuro lighting that had been intro-

24. The work was Metastasio and Jommelli's *Demofoonte* (Burney, *An Eighteenth-Century Musical Tour in France and Italy*, 277). Compare comments by the tenor Michael Kelly, *Reminiscences*, 23, and Jommelli, cited in McClymonds, *Niccolò Jommelli*, 73. I take up the magical and communicative dimensions of Burney's comment in Feldman, "Magic Mirrors," 423 and passim. On brilliant lighting at Genoa, see the Marquis d'Orbuscan, *Voyage d'Italie* (1749), in *Mélanges historiques*, 1:2.

25. Compare descriptions from Rome in the time of Urban VIII of celebrations of the feast of Saints Peter and Paul and the anniversary of the pope's coronation (which produced lighting for one night each) with the observances surrounding the actual coronation of a pope (which produced lighting for three nights running). See Hammond, *Music and Spectacle*, 120.

26. Lamberti, *La regolata costruzion*, lvi (and see n. 30 below).

duced to complement perspectival sets shortly after Tessin's time. In reformist approaches of the second half of the eighteenth century, atmospheric lighting was gradually replacing the glitter-and-glitz approach of baroque theater.[27] The cosmopolitan Algarotti advocated an uneven distribution of light to further the illusion of a "vue optique" by means of oiled papers that could make images appear softer, warmer, more distant, and altogether more poetic.[28] Jean Georges Noverre, as early as his *Lettres sur la danse, et sur les ballets* of 1760, had similarly advocated the introduction of painting-inspired tableaux vivants involving an uneven distribution of light, varied in intensity, and shaded for perspective, recommendations he subjected to technical refinements in his *Observations sur la construction d'une salle d'opéra* of 1781. Other Frenchmen, such as the theater architect Charles-Nicolas Cochin and literatus Jean-François Marmontel, also followed suit.[29] In all these reformist approaches the general tendency was to dim the hall, shade the backstage, and animate the side wings to the extent technically possible, thus imposing a separation between the stage and the house capable of giving viewers an incipient sense of the proverbial fallen wall and making a disdain for footlights almost unavoidable.

Lamberti not only recognized such directions but was acutely aware of new scientific research on electricity and light, evinced by the meticulous calculations he made, which accorded with new, contemporaneous urges to measure and expand existing light in industrial workplaces and urban thoroughfares. What is notable in Lamberti's agenda is that all such knowledge converged with his pragmatic quest for lighting that was cheaper, cleaner, safer, and acoustically more sympathetic (oil lamps gave off horrendous amounts of smoke) at the same time as he continued to assume the need for a blaze of illumination that was just as great as it had been under Carlo III—something that was indeed to go largely unchallenged in Italian theaters for decades to come. To achieve those ends, Lamberti advocated using reflectors to retain "luminous flux" while improving the quality and output of light with fewer light sources.[30]

27. Bergman, *Lighting in the Theatre,* 176.

28. See the French edition, *Essai sur l'opéra,* 150ff. (quoted in Bergman, *Lighting in the Theatre,* 180).

29. Discouraged by small French halls, Noverre advocated fewer but wider wings to emphasize the width of the stage picture and make it more illusionistic (as against symmetrical and perspectival sets), with continued modeling on paintings. See too Cochin's 1781 treatise *Lettres sur l'opéra.*

30. As Bergman has written, the challenge of lighting the auditorium was "insoluble as long as . . . [it] was to fulfill the double function of festival hall and optical spectators' room, an auditorium with an audience visible to all those in the boxes and at the same time a darkened room where the interest had to be concentrated on the illusion of the stage" (*Lighting in the Theatre,* 185; also 209 and passim). See as well Penzel, *Theatre Lighting;* Saunders, *A Treatise on Theatres;* and Langhans and Benson, "Lighting." Bergman reckons that Lamberti undercalculated the amount of light around the stage, since concealed light sources behind separate set pieces formed part of the *scena per angolo* (210). Battens were often used in Italian opera houses, too, as shown in the records of a legal suit in Rome between Federico Capranica and the lighting contractor Ferri concerning his duties at the Teatro Capranica (June 16, 1723, I-Ras, Camerale 3, facs. 2131, Teatro Capranica, no. 1). Ferri was re-

Lamberti's views confirm that even late in the century light in Italy remained obligatory as a sign of festivity, even though—indeed because—it was very expensive,[31] and despite the gradual encroachments of illusionistic principles. In Rome and most other Italian cities, the chandelier was usually extinguished once the show began (unlike in pre-1760 France). But this was done only to save money in a nation where the proliferation of theaters meant constant competition, and competition for resources posed the constant threat of financial loss to rulers, municipalities, families, and societies. Boxholders had to compensate for lack of light by lighting their own boxes, by decree when festive occasions demanded it. To add to the panorama of flickering light, people in the parterre might also be permitted to use little bougies, ostensibly to follow the libretto but with the further motive of enhancing the total spectacle.[32] If light could be multiplied and, especially, if it could be squandered, its value as surplus beyond utility was increased—a desire shared by impresarios, makers, backers, and patron-spectators.[33]

If anything, the bravura required by the hyperproduction of light set itself up not in sympathy with the natural light of the sun but against it, since the proposition of the ruler (or, by substitution, the ruling class) as the ultimate source of light—hence the giver of life and power and protector of lesser humankind—lay at the base of absolutist allegory. This of course had its immediate antecedent in the panoply of symbolic devices surrounding the person of the *roi du soleil*, Louis XIV. But its symbolic force extended far further back in space and time. When light was figuratively "bestowed" by rulers or ruling bodies through their licensing of festivity, the populace was generally eager to accept its own duties in producing light along with other festive embellishments. Writing about Fat

sponsible for lighting "all the borders with tallow candles, to illuminate the proscenium with 150 oil lamps with two wicks [etc.]" (tutti i celi con candele di sego, illuminare le boccature del Palco con coccioli di sego vergine in numero 150 a due stuppini).

Bergman reminds us that the lighting described by Tessin, author of a rare seventeenth-century treatise on lighting, was impoverished compared with a theater like the San Carlo, which was "ablaze with light" (*Lighting in the Theatre*, 95ff. and 209).

31. Apropos, see Allegri, "Introduzione allo studio degli apparati"; Agazzi, "Feste e macchine di fuochi," 81–116; Salatino, *Incendiary Art;* and Boorsch, *Fireworks.*

32. See Cagiano de Azevedo, "I viaggiatori francesi," 89–99, who notes that Roman boxholders, like others in Italy, furnished their own decorations and lighting whether they owned or rented (93). Compare observations on their travels in Italy by the abbé M. Richard (*Description historique*, 5:177) and Pierre Jacques Onésyme Bergeret de Grancourt (*Journal inédit*, 184). The latter observed that only in ambassadors' boxes "il est permis qu'il y ait des bougies allumées à des bras, vis-â-vis des glaces et, pour parler lumières, il est toléré que dans le parterre ceux qui veulent ont une petite bougie pour suivre le livre de l'opéra, ce qui fait une multitude de petites lumières, ainsi que dans plusieurs loges." [one may hold in one's hand little lit bougies, alongside a sorbet, and speaking of lighting, in the parterre whoever wishes may hold a little bougie in order to follow the libretto, which makes for a multitude of little lights, not just in the various boxes.]

33. Allegri, "Introduzione allo studio degli apparati," 23–24. Compare Bataille's theories, discussed below (chap. 6).

Tuesday in Rome, Goethe noted that, in addition to the proliferation of candles, "balconies are decorated with transparent paper lanterns . . . and all the windows, all the stands are illuminated, and it is a pleasure to look into the interiors of carriages, which often have small crystal chandeliers hanging from the ceiling, while in others the ladies sit with coloured candles in their hands."[34]

Because opera and Carnival were reciprocally produced at the apex of the festive calendar, dazzling light combined with the most sumptuous resources that could be mustered.[35] In prestigious cities, this meant engaging top singers, in contrast to cities that hired singers of the second rank or waited to mount their best productions in lesser seasons when they could capture the best voices with less competition. But displacing the operatic highpoint of the year to a season other than Carnival had affective and symbolic consequences for the overall rhythm of the calendar. Secondary cities like Bologna, to say nothing of Vicenza, Monza, Piacenza, and the like, had to modify or sacrifice the usual temporal contrasts between parts of the year.

FESTIVE REALMS / FESTIVE SPACES

Theater and festivity were inseparably bound up, then, with the social organization of time, within which there were times of greater or lesser prohibition and freedom.[36] But the dichotomy by no means lined up in so simple a way as to make prohibition tantamount to penitential and reverential time (a time, for example, like Lent, when no sex or meat-eating was allowed in Catholic states), or make freedom tantamount to festivity and irreverent time (a time like Carnival when animals were traditionally torn apart for meat). The whole history of medieval and early modern festivity fused religious and "pagan" forms, especially in early modern Italy, despite enlightenment ideologies that tried to pry them apart. Thus it is important to think not in modern terms that oppose the holiday and the holy day, but in terms that recover the dynamic, reflexive involvement

34. Goethe, *Italian Journey,* 467. "Die Balkone sind mit durchscheinenden Papierlaternen verziert . . . und es sieht sich gar artig in die Kutschen hinein, an deren Decken oft kleine krystallne Armleuchter die Gesellschaft erhellen; indessen in einem andern Wagen die Damen mit bunten Kerzen in den Händen zur Betrachtung ihrer Schönheit gleichsam einzuladen scheinen" (Goethe, *Italienische Reise,* 549).

35. This was the reason Mozart and others saw composing opera seria as the highest honor. Mozart forever longed for the sunny years of 1770–72 when he wrote for Milan's royal theater. See the discussion in chapter 2 above on his arias from *Lucio Silla,* about which later told his father, "Do not forget how much I desire to write operas. I envy anyone who is composing one. I could really weep for vexation when I hear or see an aria. But Italian, not German; seriosa, not buffa" (Mannheim, February 4, 1778, in Anderson, *Letters of Mozart,* 462). "[V]ergessen sie meinen wunsch nicht opern zu schreiben. [I]ch bin einen jedem neidig der eine schreibt. [I]ch möchte ordentlich fur verdruß weinen, wenn ich eine aria höre oder sehe. [A]ber italienisch, nicht teütsch, serios nicht Buffa" (Mozart, *Briefe* 2:254).

36. See Bakhtin, *Rabelais,* 80–81.

of feasts and festivities at once in the sacred and the irreverent, the licit and illicit, in extraordinary versus ordinary time, in the inverted and the playful, and finally to consider how the presence or absence of special media—music, dance, and light—engages them.

In Émile Durkheim's classic *The Elementary Forms of Religious Life*, the *fête* is that which is the object of prohibition, something that cannot be performed in the wrong time or in ordinary circumstances. It also represents the eternal, and as such, the sacred. On this view, the *fête* is not just a transgressive time of abandonment or a time of holy celebration, but something that exists within what Durkheim calls "indivisible time," a time outside of time itself—even if ultimately time must be divided rhythmically *in time* by interruptions and articulations without which its content would be indistinguishable. *Fête* in this Durkheimian sense does not point to conventional forms of worship—certainly not in a Christian guise, although that was one of the meanings it had long since taken on by the eighteenth century—but to time *felt* as eternal. We might add to this Norbert Elias's point in his essay on time that festivity is always bound up in a social sense with time, especially in the absence of the many measuring instruments that nowadays shadow us everywhere. Festivity made it possible to perceive articulations in time not just through natural phenomena but through the phenomenon of the social collective.[37]

Like time, space can be sacralized by the festive, since the process of entering a festive space involves an exiting, temporal and physical, from the everyday. Whether the space in question is a theater that runs on festive time, an outdoor apparatus, a decorated city center, the route of a royal procession, or a baptism, wedding, funeral, or mass celebrated in church, festive spaces all propose a quality of being outside of ordinary time. They all renounce real historical referents, which are then reworked or somehow mythologized, locating their protagonists in eternal time. This view of festivity underlay the sociology of Durkheim and his younger cohorts Hubert and Mauss in the early twentieth century, and has continued to do so in the work of Elias, Claude Gaignebet, and others.[38]

Historically, of course, relationships between spectators and the spaces they encounter have undergone sweeping changes. Luigi Allegri, who studies outdoor ephemeral apparatuses in eighteenth-century Parma, glosses two space/spectator relationships by differentiating "object apparatuses" (*apparati-oggetti*) from "backdrop apparatuses" (*apparati-sfondi*).[39] Object apparatuses were quintessentially seventeenth-century and involved large continuous spaces filled

37. Elias, *Time*, 54–56 and passim. Some theorists of time and festivity have concentrated on passages from sacred to profane and back. Edmund Leach aligns such passages with the opposed behaviors common during the apogee of festivity, largely manifested as "role reversal"—women dressing as men, people walking backward, etc.—thus putting the sacred/profane opposition into infinite regress by invoking a temporal pendulum (Leach, *Rethinking Anthropology;* cf. Cocchiara, *Il mondo alla rovescia*).

38. Hubert and Mauss, *Sacrifice;* Elias, *Time;* and Gaignebet, *Le Carnaval.*

39. Allegri, "Introduzione allo studio degli apparati," 15.

with things (the city dressed up with banners, drapes, and kiosks). Backdrop apparatuses involved things placed in space and viewed from afar (funerary catafalques, ephemeral fireworks machines, hackney horses, and the like). For Allegri, object apparatuses place certain events, such as weddings and triumphal entries, *within* a space, while backdrop apparatuses give the space of an event a *definitive setting*. The first protrudes, convex, into a viewer's bodily space; the second, concave, pulls the eye into *it*. Where the seventeenth century transformed whole city spaces by modifying them physically and symbolically and turning the city itself into a masquerade, the eighteenth century increasingly inserted festive apparatuses into city space as a particular garb or dress or situated them acontextually as scenic backdrops for events.

As baroque uses of architectural ephemera to restructure existing architectonic space declined in the eighteenth century, the backdrop apparatus won out. The apparatus gradually turned into a thing to view and those in its midst the viewers. "The apparatus [of the eighteenth century] becomes ever less a machine in which to enter and ever more an object to contemplate in a situation of separation with respect to it."[40] The history of the apparatus thus indexes the emergence of the so-called Western viewing subject, whose lived surroundings are no longer so much transformed by baroque magic as defined and demarcated for the eye's appreciation, whether outdoors or in. Already by the early eighteenth century, the festive apparatus—notably those by the stage designer Ferdinando Galli-Bibbiena (1657–1743), author of *L'architettura civile* (Parma, 1711)—had become a stand-in for spaces that surround it. It was more alike in its effects to Bibbiena's famously stereoscopic, angled stage sets with Albertian vanishing points, as seen in his study from 1711 (fig. 4.1).[41]

Eventually, through these shifts, a new distance emerges between viewer and viewed. The stage becomes a stereoscopic space whose planes the viewer cannot rationalize. Discouraging a true sense of spatial alterity, both the new outdoor apparatuses and contemporaneous stage sets exploit the *scena per angolo*. Both are seen at an angle and in a constant "condition of relativity and partiality" that puts distance between viewer and viewed. As the everyday is given an alternative face, viewed spaces produced by the eighteenth-century *apparatore/scenografo* are no longer so much transformed as neutralized (in the case of the outdoor apparatus) or demarcated (in the case of the theater stage).[42] Insofar as the apparatus and the stage share these conditions, they do so through the person of the *apparatore*—the maker of apparatuses—who provides continuity throughout the seventeenth and eighteenth centuries by maintaining a production shop (typically a hereditary family business) in which he squirrels away festive materials in various modular forms for both outdoor apparatuses and indoor theater sets: statues, architectural elements, festoons, drapes, and so forth.[43]

40. Ibid., 18.

41. See also Lenzi et al., *I Bibbiena*, 247, catalog entry by Alessandra Frabetti.

42. Allegri, "Introduzione allo studio degli apparati," 20–21.

43. Cf. Botti, "Pietro Righini," 139–62.

FIG. 4.1. Ferdinando Bibbiena, "Study no. 68 to draw a stage, hall, or room seen at an angle," ca. 1711. Staatliche Graphische Sammlung München, Inv. No. 35316 Z. Reproduced by permission.

Tracing the history of the outdoor apparatus as it crisscrosses theater history, we see an eventual shift from a panoptic situation of multidirectional viewing, anticipated by the apparatus, to a situation of more unidirectional viewing that opposes extreme continuity between stage and hall. Ironically, this shift not only turns the common horde from participants into spectators but makes the literate elite population who are able to read accompanying texts more privy to the particular meanings of poetic compositions, plot descriptions, prefaces, cast lists, and scenic descriptions. Instead of promoting fraternity within the collective, it encourages elites to sequester themselves in the salons, gardens, atriums, balconies, and theaters that are variously assigned to *feste* and celebrations.[44] Witness the observations of the Milanese poet Giuseppe Parini: "Behold, it is Carnival time, and in which of the year's seasons . . . are greater follies created by men? Bacchus now circles round . . . and his heart is stricken by Venus who . . . has her son with her. The triumphant crowd follows him and laughs. You, [Muse,] laugh at the rascally crowd . . . . *But we do not really rub shoulders with the plebeian madness: let us go there where the rich and noble assemblage gathers. They are going into the theater.*"[45]

By encouraging movement indoors, growing eighteenth-century strictures against festivity edged toward viewable planes, promoting the very phenomenon of theater at the same time as theaters were sprouting up all around Italy.[46] There is a parallel history in the relationship to theater of European monarchs. In the seventeenth century, the young Louis XIV, Carlo Emanuele II of Savoy, and Emperor Leopold I occasionally played roles in their own theaters (unlike their successors), moving fluidly from the position of spectator to that of spectated and back.[47] Additionally, many monarchs moved from sitting conspicuously toward the front of their halls (typically rectangular salons) to occupying royal boxes enclosed on three sides and situated amid the similar but smaller

44. Routine religious festivals with apparatuses brought otherwise segregated social classes into contact. The court was almost never party to subaltern festivities—popular rites or performances of low comedic troupes, marionettes, minstrels, acrobats, and tumblers in open markets—but could watch from afar, as Princess Isabella did when *ciarlatani* performed in the piazza at Parma in 1760 (Allegri, "Introduzione allo studio degli apparati," n. 61). Very occasionally popular forms ascended to the court or nobility, but more typically they were disdained, or repressed through protests or incarcerations, common with rites of burying Carnival, the *rogo della vecchia* or effigy of the old hag (ibid., 28).

45. "Or ecco il Carnesciale; e in qual dell'anno / stagione . . . / spropositi maggior gli uomini fanno? / Bacco or va intorno: lo spumoso greco / ne l'agita bollendo; e 'l sen gli sferza / Vener ch'ignuda e calda il figlio ha seco. / Seguelo il volgo trionfando e scherza. / Scherzi [Musa mia] il volgo profano; . . . *Ma noi non già de la pazzia plebea / frustiam le spalle: andiam là 've s'aduna / e la ricca e la nobile assemblea. / Andiancene al teatro*" (Parini, "Il teatro," vv. 1–8, 19–22, in *Poesie e prose*, 275–76; emphasis mine). Goethe gives another instance of declining outdoor festivity, reporting in 1778 that only the lower classes, not the nobles, still fancied horseracing on the Corso (*Italian Journey*, 449; *Italienische Reise*, 523).

46. See also Fagiolo dell'Arco and Carandini, *L'effimero barocco*.

47. Goloubeva, *The Glorification of Emperor Leopold I*, 41 and 106.

boxes of their inferiors. In both developments, the stage becomes the viewed space of the imaginary, the play, and the players, rather than a space that fuses doers with viewers. Since Italian theaters were becoming ever more large, numerous, and publicly accessible, the base, infecting elements of festivity could best be contained by enclosing people within them. This was happening at the same time as rawer elements of old outdoor festivities were being suppressed in favor of the more genteel, or at least controllable, ones of indoor theater, in keeping with Elias's "civilizing process." Here the history of Venetian Carnival is instructive. In the Middle Ages and Renaissance, the centerpiece of the city's Carnival involved chasing live pigs, killing them, and distributing them to noblemen in Piazza San Marco; by the eighteenth century the earlier pig slaughter was gone, and much of the merriment it had "cooked up" was rechanneled for consumption by natives and tourists in public theaters, which had grown to seven or eight by midcentury.[48] The mayhem of older street scenes and the playfulness of seicento court theaters were absorbed into what the protagonists of the *Amours and Adventures* grouped together as "Comedies, Operas or . . . some noble Venetian's house."

* * *

This riot of different phenomena raises the question of what is meant by "festivity" and its various aliases—ceremony, *fête,* feast, festival—particularly within a changing political world in which authorities routinely co-opted the unofficial life. Why heap under a single umbrella this untidy congeries of forms and activities, from festivities as a tenor of life, to feast days, to *fêtes* and festivals as events?

One reason is that we are speaking of a range of lexical and cultural histories with different valences, and yet strong continuities, at least before the later eighteenth century rendered festivity problematic. Nevertheless, for heuristic purposes, it is useful to note a gross political distinction often identified between two seemingly opposed realms of festive life. The one associated with the spirit of the carnivalesque, and made famous in the interpretation of Bakhtin, refers to a time and a mode of sociability when normal rules of life are challenged, transgressed, overturned, and reinvented. This is the traditional and (loosely speaking) popular form of festivity. The other, associated with celebratory and ceremonial modes of cultural production, manifested society's collective ideals or ruling ideologies as they were synthesized and held up for public display. This is festivity in its official guise.

A casualty of the Soviet politburo, Bakhtin spoke disparagingly of the second of these as a travesty of the carnivalesque brought on by the strangling effects of state bureaucracy in precisely the period that concerns us here:

48. See Muir, *Civic Ritual,* 156–81, and *Ritual in Early Modern Europe,* 87–89; as well as Burke, "The Carnival in Venice," 183–90.

> During [the seventeenth and eighteenth centuries] . . . we observe a process of gradual narrowing down of the ritual, spectacle, and carnival forms of folk culture, which became small and trivial. On the one hand the state encroached upon festive life and turned it into a parade; on the other hand these festivities were brought into the home and became part of the family's private life. The privileges that were formerly allowed the marketplace were more and more restricted. The carnival spirit with its freedom, its utopian character oriented toward the future, was gradually transformed into a mere holiday mood. The feast ceased almost entirely to be the people's second life, their temporary renascence and renewal.[49]

Bakhtin's vision of Carnival swept Western scholarship off its feet when it appeared in English translation in 1968. By the mid-1980s, on the eve of Eastern Europe's communist collapse, his lament had been taken up as a requiem of postmodern ideology and left-leaning political critiques. For Umberto Eco, for instance, Carnival itself was merely a form of "authorized transgression."[50] Yet the attenuated festivity that Bakhtin describes has to be understood not just with respect to broad historical tendencies in festive production, but also as a description of what were merely the outward expressions of sanctioned forms. As the examples of opera houses prove, many eighteenth-century institutions of festivity were not easy for officialdom to tame. Notwithstanding their efforts, it was hard for rulerships to overpower local practices, not least those of opera, for the obvious reason that opera was commercially run and marked by publics, managers, and owners that were highly varied.[51] The institution of opera seria in particular, dominated by singers and fans, was imbricated in many other social practices that overspilled official sanctions and meanings. Nor was it in the interests of most governments to subjugate the will of operagoers ceaselessly to their own ends. As we will see in chapter 8, in the last analysis, it was less the absolutist state that encroached on operatic festivity than the new middle-class enlightenment ideals of community, self-discipline, and civility, and a new ideology of labor. Remarkable in the phenomenon of opera seria is its very heterodoxy, its ability to be neither a ceremonial form of festive spectacle nor a festive suspension of social norms but an amphibious mixture of both. It was a utopian image of the present seen through the past—thus a ceremonial medium—but also an assertion about the past that was undermined by the unwieldiness of the present-tense event.

In this sense, opera seria combined what Bronislaw Baczko has called a *fête chaude*, a "hot festivity" in which a collective spontaneity and sentiment corre-

49. Bakhtin, *Rabelais*, 33.

50. Eco, "The Frames of Comic Freedom," 1–9.

51. Rosselli, *The Opera Industry*, claims that commercial theaters linked with monarchies generally had messier administrations of opera than those that weren't. Hence Frederick the Great's Berlin had better success in constraining audiences than Parma did, and the management of operations at the San Carlo in Naples was even worse than at a typical family-run theater in Rome or Venice.

spond to the notion of an ideal, imagined time, and a *fête froide*, a "cold festivity" so wholly exploited by bureaucratic institutions as an instrument of politics and ideology that nothing can ever really happen to the imagination or sentiment of the collectivity. Baczko's analysis runs hot/cold because it deals with French revolutionary *fêtes*, yet it nevertheless helps define the relevant poles in the complex structure of a late absolutist institution.[52] Opera seria had its "cold" qualities, but it was a very long time before they killed it off. Its longevity must have come from an ability, characteristic of any viable festivity, to act as a transformative force. We have seen instances of this force in singer/audience interactions, visual infatuation with spectacle and dance, and in the sociabilities of the institution. Strikingly, the last of these had an existence in the physical marking of operatic time. At a given hour after the show, or a given evening, the parterre (literally, "at earth" level and thus plebeian, but architecturally speaking, floor level below the boxes) could become the *terre*, effectively a piano nobile that served as a gala ballroom, where it was then the place to be and be seen. To create it, workmen would typically extend the stage horizontally outward by elevating the floor of the parterre to produce the form shown in figure 4.2, something they could manage with miraculous speed. Alternatively, steps could be added along the sides of the back hall, creating a split-level ballroom with a sunken section at parterre and stage levels (fig. 4.3) from which attendees could move up and down. Either way, this conjuring act dropped the usual plane of the piano nobile down from the lower balconies to the level of the stage, to which the parterre was conjoined, with accompanying restrictions on nonnobles descending to the ballroom space. On special nights, when balls or gala operas took place—sometimes on separate evenings, as seen in the season schedule in figure 4.4—boxes could also be changed into little mise-en-scènes (*palchini*) through the addition of extra lights, curtains, vases, and tribunes. These mimicked the large "boxed" stage used by the performers, the *palcoscenico*, literally "scenic box" or "stage box," thus suggesting a circuit of ministages throughout the theater, as rendered in Giorgio Fossati's engraving of a Venetian theater (fig. 4.6 below). In Rome, theater boxes were the indoor counterpart to outdoor balconies along the streets, which could conversely be transformed into theatrical boxes by adding columns, lights, flowers, drapes, and sashes.

As surely as puddles of rain or piles of snow marked the time and space of winter, these transformations marked the space-time of festivity in the settecento city.[53] But the transformative role of operatic festivity was also marked on the body. The face could be hidden, re-formed, or revealed on a moment's notice. Sara Goudar, the Irish social climber who wrote about opera and Carnival in the 1770s, had herself pictured in her book on Neapolitan Carnival dressed for

52. Baczko, *Lumières de l'utopie*, 278; in English as *Utopian Lights*, 212–13. Baczko is specifically speaking of Michelet's views and not attempting to apply them doggedly. Cf. Stallybrass and White, *The Politics and Poetics of Transgression*.

53. See Munn, "The Cultural Anthropology of Time," 93–123.

FIG. 4.2. Masked ball at the Teatro San Carlo, Naples. Probably nineteenth century, artist unidentified. Italian Theater Collection. By permission of the Research Library, Getty Research Institute, Los Angeles (P980004).

FIG. 4.3. Masked ball for the birth of Ferdinand IV, son of Carlo III, Teatro San Carlo, Naples, with steps added at the rear of the hall. Engraving, possibly by Giuseppe Vasi, 1747. From *Narrazione delle solenni feste* . . . , plate 9, no. 3755. By permission of the Fondazione Giorgio Cini, Venice.

AVVISO AL PUBBLICO.

Sapendo la Maestá del Re quanto sieno graditi al Pubblico i Festini nel Real Teatro di S. Carlo, è venuto perciò, usando gl' atti di sua solita Real Munificenza, in permettere i medesimi nel venturo Carnevale. E siccome è sua Real Intenzione che tali Festini sieno eseguiti co' dovuti riguardi, e proprietà; così per evitare qualunque disordine, e confusione, che potesse mai insorgere, ha voluto per mezzo di quest' Avviso si facciano noti ad ogn' uno que' regolamenti, che la M. S. ha prescritti, e che debbansi inviolabilmente osservare.

Avendo la M. S. considerazione pe' Proprietarj de' Palchi del Real Teatro, ordina perciò, che ne' giorni de' Festini sia ciascun Proprietario preferito, godendo il suo Palco corrispondente. Considerando inoltre che il dippiù de' Palchi debbon ben' anche restar occupati per render vieppiù luminosa la Festa, ha quindi ordinato che quelli si godano ancora da coloro, che se gli truovano affittati per intiero, o per metà, dovendogli godere colla stessa legge, che si costuma per le Opere; ben' inteso però che così a' Proprietarj, che agl' Affittuarj, non sarà lecito l' ingresso senza provvedersi de' Viglietti.

Li Viglietti si dispenseranno nella porta di mezzo del Real Teatro dalla mattina per tutta la notte, alla ragione di carlini cinque l' uno. E siccome per li Proprietarj, e Fittuarj de' Palchi viene proibito l' ingresso, senza provvedersi de' Viglietti, così deve intendersi ben' anche pel dippiù delle Persone, che vorranno concorrere nella Platea, o ne' Palchi, venendo impedita a chiunque l' entrata, senza l' esibizione del Viglietto.

Gl' Abiti di Maschera saranno decenti, e proprj, o di Caratteri, o in Dominò, o in Bautta alla Veneziana, o Pulcinella, purchè siano di seta. Avvertendosi ogn' uno, che non ostante d' aver pagato l' importo del Viglietto, sarà escluso, qualora comparirà con Maschera di Paglietta, o con ogn' altra specie di Bautta, o Maschera foggiata con mantelline di Donne.

Chiunque vorrà uscire dal Teatro per rientrarvi deve riscuotere il Controviglietto, avvertendosi che senza la restituzione del medesimo sarà proibito il rientrarvi.

Essendosi nell' ultimo Festino celebrato in detto Real Teatro sperimentata la gran confusione ne' Corridoj, tanto di persone d' Anticamera, quanto di Livrea, e considerandosi da S. M. che una persona d' Anticamera, ed una di Livrea possa esser sufficiente per ciaschedun Palco; ha perciò ordinato che si dia un solo Viglietto per ciaschedun Palco per una persona d' Anticamera, ed un altro distinto per una sola persona di Livrea, formandosi un luogo espressamente per tutte l' altre persone di Livrea, acciò non stiano esposte in mezzo della strada per la rigidezza dell' Inverno.

Si avverte ancora, che si daranno rigorosi ordini alle Sentinelle, tanto delle Porte, che de' Corridoj, acciò invigilino di non far entrare per servizio delle cene nel Real Teatro fuoco di qualunque specie, e ciò per evitare qualunque incomodo, e disordine.

Li giorni destinati pe' Festini si ravvisono nella controscritta nota.

Sarà permesso ad un ora di notte, e non prima alle Maschere di poter entrare nel Teatro, cioè tanto nella Sala di ballo, che ne' Palchetti, e comincerà il Festino circa le due, e durerà fin tanto che vi sarà nella Sala numero sufficiente di Maschere, che vogliono continuare le Danze, a riserba dell' ultimo giorno di Carnevale, che si terminerà ad ora competente per evitare lo scandalo di vedersi a giorno Maschere per la Città.

Con Licenza de' Superiori.

N O T A

DELLE OPERE, E FESTE DI BALLO

DA CELEBRARSI

NEL REAL TEATRO DI S. CARLO

Da' 30. del prossimo entrante mese di Dicembre a tutto il Carnevale del venturo anno 1782.

DECEMBRE 1781.

30. Domenica *Festa di Ballo*.

GENNAJO 1782.

3. Giovedì *Festa di Ballo*.
6. Domenica *Festa di Ballo*.
12. Sabato *Opera nuova*.
13. Domenica *Festa di Ballo*.
14. Lunedì *Opera*.
15. Martedì *Opera*.
19. Sabato *Opera*.
20. Domenica *Opera*.
21. Lunedì *Festa di Ballo*.
22. Martedì *Opera*.
23. Mercordì *Opera*.
24. Giovedì *Festa di Ballo*.
26. Sabato *Opera*.
27. Domenica *Festa di Ballo*.
28. Lunedì *Opera*.
29. Martedì *Opera*.
30. Mercordì *Festa di Ballo*.
31. Giovedì *Opera*.

FEBRAJO:

2. Sabato *Opera*.
3. Domenica *Festa di Ballo*.
4. Lunedì *Opera*.
5. Martedì *Opera*.
6. Mercordì *Festa di Ballo*.
7. Giovedì *Opera*.
9. Sabato *Opera*.
10. Domenica *Festa di Ballo*.
11. Lunedì *Opera*.
12. Martedì *Festa di Ballo*.

FIG. 4.4. "Avviso al pubblico," Naples, December 30, 1781. The schedule listed at the right for the upcoming Carnival, alternating operas and gala balls, includes no less than twelve balls. Collection of Sergio Ragni. Reprinted by kind permission.

the opera and holding a removable mask (fig. 4.5). In keeping with her theatrical theme, the architectural frame of the portrait was turned into a festive box, adorned with mask, flowers, instruments, and a musical score.[54]

In sum, the institution of opera seria served a special function in mediating between the various modes and valences of festivity that punctuated the urban calendar. It distinguished pagan holidays from religious liturgy from new and changing monarchical liturgies. It mediated between governmental directives, ecclesiastical forces, noble culture, and popular subversion. And because it moralized the sociopolitical order in a didactic way, it could mediate between festive and penitential modes.

But opera seria pulled two ways. Its mediating ability could be enlisted to signal sacrifice, even as it deflected a penitential role. When weather in Rome grew very bad in the winter of 1742, for instance, comedies were suspended at the theaters of the Tordinona, the Valle, and the Pace as a way to show repentance and plead for mercy, but opera seria—pretending to a higher moral and social plane—was still allowed to go on in the elite theaters. At other times, opera seria had to add its weight to shows of mourning, penitence, and pleas for clemency by closing down altogether. In 1735, all Roman theaters stayed shut owing to the death of Queen Clementine (Polish consort of the exiled Catholic king James III, the "Pretender"); and on January 28, 1740, they were closed in midseason to seek mercy on behalf of the ailing pope Clement XIII. They closed again to show penitence in 1744 when epidemics were spreading in Sicily and southern Italy. And when jubilee years came around (e.g., in 1750), Carnival celebrations were suspended altogether, allegedly to make the appropriate symbolic sacrifices, but certainly also to divert all possible attention and resources to pontifical celebrations.[55]

Other theater closings were ordered explicitly to rebuke or prevent disorders. The Alibert and Argentina were closed by papal ordinance in 1733 when there were disputes over the assignment of boxes. They reopened on February 10, 1734, but for the next three years the Tordinona alone was allowed to put on opera seria.[56] This was a hedge against aristocratic fractiousness and a

54. Discussed in Croce, *Aneddoti e profili settecenteschi*, following p. 64 and passim.

55. Valesio, *Diario di Roma*, writes on the closing of Roman theaters in 1735 and 1740 and also reports on closings related to epidemics, as do the *Diario ordinario* (*Chracas*) and numerous broadsides published by the government (cf. Cagiano de Azevedo, "I viaggiatori francesi," 89–99). On suspensions for pontifical celebrations, see Rinaldi, *Due secoli di musica;* Clementi, *Il carnevale romano;* and Fagiolo dell'Arco and Carandini, *L'effimero barocco*. Theaters were also closed on Fridays, saints' days, and some other feast days (e.g., Purification), though exceptions led to performances in November, May, and even July. From 1730 until circa 1800, two theaters usually mounted opera seria, but only during Carnival. The Alibert had spring seasons only in 1731, 1732, 1738, and 1780, and not for opera seria. See de Angelis, *Il Teatro Alibert o delle Dame*.

56. See Cametti, *Il Teatro di Tordinona* 1:14–19; Antolini, "Rome"; and Pirrotta, "Metastasio e i teatri romani," 30. In 1740, an edict ordered that the Capranica, Argentina, and Alibert alternate in producing opera seria, taking turns by lot, with the one remaining closed receiving compensation. In

FIG. 4.5. Sara Goudar, "en habit de masque." From *Rélation historique des divertissements du carneval de Naples; ou, Lettre de Madame Goudar sur ce sujet à Monsieur le Général Alexis Orlow* (Lucca, 1774). By permission of Randolph-Macon College, McGraw-Page Library, Special Collections.

reprimand of it. More serious disorders were feared in the same theaters when Clement XIII died on February 6, 1740, and theaters remained closed not just to show respect and mourning but because crowd violence traditionally erupted during the interregnum. Particularly in Rome, extreme swings of behavior within the *longue durée* were ritual marks of theatrical life, much as extreme swings of behavior marked linear events and other cyclical events throughout the year. Perhaps they were an instance of the phenomenon that Norbert Elias has proposed for earlier societies in which time-consciousness at the immediate level of the hour and the minute was less marked and continuous than now (and individuals consequently more easily given to impetuous outbursts of exuberance or violence).[57]

UNBRIDLING THE HOLY CITY

In the splendid account of a famous traveler, a king is derided and insulted. Pulcinella is cuckolded, beaten, and defiled. He multiplies himself as a couple or a whole crowd, and reappears as a woman. Men in the guise of oversized women embrace their own sex and take liberties with women. Cross-dressed women mock the power of men. Maskers become beggars seeking alms. One reveler wearing a two-faced mask gets stuck in the crowd. "Nobody knows which is his back and which is his front or whether he is coming or going." On Fat Tuesday, as this sea of humanity flows to high tide, revelers snuff out each other's candles with shouts of "Death to anyone who isn't carrying a candle!" (Sia ammazzato chi non porta moccolo).[58]

1755, another edict ordered that only the Alibert and Argentina produce opera seria, most regularly the Argentina, usually two per season, each including ballet intermezzi.

57. Elias associates extreme swings of behavior with the discontinuous timekeeping of earlier societies, where people were unconstrained by the continual compulsion to remind themselves of time through mechanical instruments kept on their persons (*Time*, 22–27).

58. Goethe, *Italian Journey*, 450–54, 460; *Italienische Reise*, 525–30, 538, esp.: "Hier kommt ein Pulcinell gelaufen, dem ein großes Horn an bunten Schnüren um die Hüften gaukelt. Durch eine geringe Bewegung, indem er sich mit den Weibern unterhält, weiß er die Gestalt des alten Gottes der Gärten in dem heiligen Rom kecklich nachzuahmen, und seine Leichtfertigkeit erregt mehr Lust als Unwillen. Hier kommt ein anderer seines Gleichen, der bescheidner und zufriedner, seine schöne Hälfte mit sich bringt. Da die Frauen eben so viel Lust haben, sich in Mannskleidern zu zeigen, als die Männer sich in Frauenskleidern sehen zu lassen, so haben sie die beliebte Tracht des Pulcinells sich anzupassen nicht verfehlt, un man muß bekennen, daß es ihnen gelingt, in dieser Zwittergestalt oft höchst reizend zu sein" (526). On women mocking the power of men, Goethe comments, "Now and then one sees one of the Fair Sex, sitting in a box, dressed up as an officer and displaying her epaulettes to the public with the utmost self-satisfaction; and already the number of carriages driving up and down the Corso is beginning to increase" (*Italian Journey*, 448) [Man sieht hie und da in den Logen eine Schöne, welche als Offizier ihre Epauletten mit größter Selbstzufriedenheit dem Volke zeigt. Die Spazierfahrt im Corso wird zahlreicher; doch die allgemeine Erwartung ist auf die letzten acht Tage gerichtet (*Italienische Reise*, 522).] Writing from Rome on January 22, 1764 (*Voyages d'Italie* 1:197), the abbé Coyer made similar comments: "Not only does everyone who belongs to the ecclesiastical hierarchy wear the ecclesiastical habit, from the pope on down to the *bedeau* [lowly

These are the characters who people Goethe's Roman Carnival. They are figures of symbolic inversion, abusers and abused, who look beyond pleasure and folly for what the great folklorist Paolo Toschi called "ritual madness," a madness that often leads to violence. At least this was the case until insubordination was temporarily quashed by the Napoleonic invasion in 1798.[59]

It is worth pausing to look more closely at the situation in Rome, because nowhere else was theater so totally identified with Carnival, or so strongly identified with transgression and abuse.[60] Rome distended the usual tension between license and control to its extreme. Expansive and crowded, refined and riotous, the most penitential of cities and the most subversive, the most rule-bound and the most anarchical, contrasts at Rome were heavily correlated with ritual fluctuations throughout the year. They also differentiated periods lasting for years and decades, especially different papacies, which varied considerably in the relative leniency or austerity shown toward theater.[61]

Chracas, a mouthpiece of the government, was constantly reiterating the status of Carnival as a controlled festivity. On February 15, 1749, at the same time as it announced the official beginning of Carnival activities with horse races on the Corso and the opening of the season's second opera, it greeted readers with a veiled threat—something that could double as a safety measure:

> On Saturday, during the day, His Holiness went to watch the usual Litanies of the Madonna at Santa Maria Maggiore; His Most Eminent Royal Highness and Cardinal the Duke of York was there as well.
>
> *Along the Corso on the morning of the same day, by order of the Governor, there was a public whipping of two thieves; then in the later afternoon Carnival began,* although with very cold, rainy weather expected there was little thronging of maskers and carriages; and towards evening, with the usual formalities, the eminent house of Rospigliosi won the Barbery [horse] race.
>
> On the same evening the second opera, called *La Semiramide riconosciuta*, by the celebrated Abbot Pietro Metastasio, opened in the Teatro delle Dame by the Orti di Napoli.[62]

servant], but also the whole Curia, solicitors, lawyers, and judges, plus doctors and various foreigners, to save money or gain easier entrance to houses." [Non-seulement tout ce qui tient à la Hiérarchie ecclésiastique, depuis le Pape jusqu'au Bedeau; mais encore tous les Curiaux, Procureurs, Avocats, Juges; mais encore les Médécins & quantité d'Étrangers, par économie, ou pour trouver des entrées plus faciles dans les maisons, prennent l'habit ecclésiastique.]

59. Babcock, *The Reversible World* and "Arrange Me into Disorder"; Toschi, *Le origini del teatro italiano*, chaps. 5–9; and Clementi, *Il carnevale*.

60. See Fagiolo, *La festa a Roma*, for visual iconography of official religious and political festivities.

61. Cagli, "Produzione musicale," 1–21, begins with the burning down of the Tordinona in 1697, the result of "elderly moralism [in a] pontifical gerontocracy"; see also Cametti, *Il Teatro di Tordinona*, vol. 1, chap. 8, and Ademollo, *I teatri di Roma*, chap. 22.

62. "Sabato il giorno la Santità di Nostro Signore andò ad assistere alle solite Litanie della Madonna a S*anta* Maria Maggiore; per la qual divozione vi fù ancora Sua Altezza Reale Em*inatissima* il Sign*or* Cardinale Duca di Yorck.

* * *

Notwithstanding voices of intimidation, festivities in Rome, as elsewhere, were only partially controllable. A double rhythm of prohibition and transgression underwrote the edicts issued periodically by the government to forestall "abuses" in the theater. Printed annually just after New Year's, an edict of the kind was affixed to the governor's palace, the Campo dei Fiori, and the doors of all theaters with the warning that every person was "bound [by it] as if he had been personally informed." Characteristically, the edict of January 4, 1749, listed proscriptions that echo the *gride per la maschera* published in Parma (and in many other cities), pronouncing extreme controls on all aspects of opera and operagoing, from content to timing, comportment, and crowd control (see the appendix to this chapter). Renewing all previous edicts as an expression of papal will, it began by giving the source of the dictates as the Roman governor and vice chamberlain (that is, of the Apostolic Chamber, where he reported directly to the pope).[63] The initial stress was on "a virtuous and licit entertainment in the performance of operas, comic or tragic." Operas were subject to scrutiny and censorship, and could only be staged if deemed "laudatory." Performances were not to begin less than two hours or more than two and a half hours after sunset (i.e., between about 7:00 and 7:30 p.m.) under pain of a fifty-scudi fine.[64] The impresario was legally bound to maintain within and without the theater the familiar desiderata of "buon' ordine, e regolamento" and to prevent and denounce any disorder through vigilance and impartiality, on pain of fines or corporal punishments. He and all performers had to behave with "modesty and respect" in both deed and word, subject to the same vague but potentially corporal penalties.[65] Prostitutes and women of ill repute could not legally attend the theater under pain of the whip (though very many did), and anyone who took them there risked five years in the galleys.

"La mattina del detto giorno nella strada del Corso per ordine del Governo fù dato il publico castigo della corda a due ladri; nel dopo pranzo poi si principiò il Carnevale, benché con poco concorso di maschere, e carozze al passeggio, atteso il tempo assai rigido, e piovoso; e fattasi verso sera, con le solite formalità, la corsa dei Barberi conquistò il Palio quello dell'Ecc*ellentissi*ma Casa Rospigliosi.

"La sera medesima nel Teatro detto delle Dame agl'Orti di Napoli andò per la prima volta in scena il secondo dramma intitolato *La semiramide riconosciuta* del celebre Sign*or* Abb*ate* Pietro Metastasio" (*Diario ordinario* [*Chracas*], no. 4926, February 15, 1749, 2–3; emphasis in translation mine).

63. The governor shared civil and criminal jurisdiction with the Capitoline tribunal headed by the senator of Rome. See Re, *Monsignor Governatore*, and Nussdorfer, *Civic Politics*, 51 and chap. 4. Nussdorfer reports (52 n. 19) that Giovanni Battista de Luca, in his *Il dottor volgare* (1673), thought the governor had more spies than other Roman officials, lay or ecclesiastical, and so could catch more criminals. See also Gross, *Rome*, chap. 2.

64. Theater hours went from about an hour past the sound of the Ave Maria (usually half an hour past sunset) until about midnight. Time-reckoning in eighteenth-century Italy can be notoriously difficult (Bouquet, *Il teatro di corte*, 214–23, esp. 215–16; Talbot, "*Ore italiane*," 51–62).

65. To my knowledge, no instance of corporal punishment being enacted on a singer or impresario has ever come to light.

As in Parma and elsewhere, fighting and arms were forbidden, except for nobles carrying swords, their requisite accoutrement in the old regime. Punishments for infractions were meted out according to station: the laity to be punished with death for inflicting injuries (even light ones) and ecclesiastics with life in the galleys.

Other proscriptions having specifically to do with audience behavior resemble those that were tightening around the same time in Du Tillot's Parma. Spectators, reads the 1749 edict,

> are prohibited from making commotion, noise, whistling, and other indecent acts, both in exiting and entering [the theater], . . . when the opera is performed, or from disturbing actors or forcefully demanding the repetition of an aria, or a recitative, just as castrati and actors may not repeat their speech or aria beyond what is determined in advance by the composer, under pain to actors and castrati at the arbitrary will of his illustrious Signoria and others, of three strokes of the whip and other corporal penalties, even serious ones, also with respect to ecclesiastics, to be inflicted and imposed immediately, with no other proceeding but the testimony summarily heard.
>
> And because some people show no respect or adherence to any order, attending the opera just to bother people and the castrati who are singing, making commotion and noise by stomping their feet and clapping their hands both in the parterre and in the boxes—[they are subject to] . . . three strokes of the whip, even given right away in public, and other serious corporal penalties as imposed above, with only a summary trial and with the ability to proceed ex officio and by inquisition.

Rules of masking were not specified, but reference was made to a separate set of masking ordinances that also had to be obeyed in the theater. Finally, there was the usual long litany of regulations for coachmen and other traffickers, likewise subject to arbitrary whipping in public, which could be given at the mere report of a traffic guard.[66]

One purpose of regulating starting times was to control public action, especially of lowly clerics and others of like station, by governing the proportion of leisure time as measured against work time and worship time. Prohibiting encores, noise, and vocalizing meant policing crowd violence and minimizing perilous factionalism. It also made it possible to trim expenses by snuffing the lights at a scheduled hour, with hopes that order would hold. In principle, regulations could apply to virtually all the constituencies who participated in operamaking, operagoing, and conducting operagoers in conveyances to and fro. Indeed, control of crowds extended explicitly beyond spectators' obligation to obey governmental decrees to the preventive actions of performers, management, impresarios, and anyone else who might have a hand in crowd actions or be attributed with responsibility for them. The whole was fitted up with a caul

66. Bad traffic and unruly drivers were legion in early modern cities, and coachmen the continual focus of fights and disorders. See Farinelli's anecdotes in *La solitudine amica*, 85–86.

of morality, but in reality, since Roman theaters thrived in the breach, there was little effort to enforce prohibitions, at least among elites.

What made Roman theaters sites of such legendary crowd commotion were the notorious minor abbots who littered the parterre. Goldoni related on joining his wife at the Alibert in 1758 that "the pit at Rome . . . was dreadful; the abbés decide in a vigorous and noisy manner."[67] So fearsome was their reputation that Alessandro Verri, a Milanese long resident at Rome, could lament in a letter to his brother Pietro on January 20, 1770, "here there's the custom of dismissing a castrato when he's not liked. Three are being sent away, and Manzuoli will be coming. . . . He has never wanted to sing at Rome, saying that he was highly thought of everywhere and didn't want to end up being booed by four abbots."[68]

But the problem was not just those idle (often unwilling) victims of minor orders. Goldoni added about the Argentina that "there are no guards or police; and hisses, cries, laughter, and invectives resound from all quarters of the house."[69] Waging wars of passion over composers, productions, singers, and singing styles were rowdy elements of the population from many different walks of life and social echelons. Burney left one of the more textured, impartial accounts of the Roman scene when he visited for the second time in early winter 1773:

> There is . . . in this city more cabal than elsewhere, and party runs higher. It is generally supposed, that a composer or performer who is successful at Rome, has nothing to fear from the severity of critics in other places. At the opening of an opera, the clamour or acclamation of the company frequently continues for a considerable time before they will hear a note. A favourite author is received with shouts of *Bravo! Signor Maestro. Viva! Signor Maestro.* And when a composer is condemned by the audience, it is with discrimination in favour of the singer, by crying out, after they have done hissing, *Bravo pure il Guarducci!* (Bravo! however, Guarducci) and on the contrary, if the performer displeases in executing the music of a favourite composer, after they have expressed their disapprobation of him, by hissing, they cry out *Viva pure il Signor Maestro!*[70]

Extreme reactions, from very hot to very cold, figure repeatedly in accounts of Roman operatic reception. Burney's *General History of Music* tells the famous

67. "La parterre de Rome est terrible: les Abbés décident d'une manière vigoureuse et bruyante" (Goldoni, "Prefazioni di Carlo Goldoni," in *Tutte le opere* 1:404–5; in English as *Memoirs of Carlo Goldoni*, 326).

68. "[Q]ui v'è l'usanza di congedare un musico, quando non piaccia. Tre se ne mandano via; e verrà Manzoli. . . . Egli non ha mai voluto cantare a Roma, dicendo ch'egli era stato considerato dapertutto, e che non voleva finire ad esser fischiato da quattro abati" (Verri and Verri, *Carteggio* 3:165–66, referring to Giovanni Manzuoli, who sang in Mozart's *Ascanio in Alba* in Milan, 1771).

69. "[I]l n'y a point de gardes, il n'y a point de police; les sifflets, les cris, les risées, les invectives retentissoient de tous les côtés." Continuing he wrote, "Mais aussi, heureux celui qui plaît aux petits collets: je vis, dans le meme Théâtre, l'Opéra de *Ciccio de Mayo,* à la premiere representation" (Goldoni, "Prefazioni," in *Tutte le opere* 1:405; *Memoirs of Carlo Goldoni*, 326).

70. Burney, *An eighteenth-century musical tour in France and Italy*, 303.

story of Pergolesi, who set Metastasio's *L'olimpiade* with great passion and commitment for the Tordinona in 1735. Although by midcentury he would be canonized by audiences and critics throughout Europe, his effort was received with coldness because he was a newcomer to Rome, despite his previous success in Naples.[71]

Many of the opera wars turned on the voice of the singer or the voice of the crowd. Some were mainly private, like the one that broke out between several castrati in autumn 1752 over the registers of singers' voices, as Girolamo Chiti reported to Padre Martini.[72] Others found their way onto the streets. In 1784, a correspondent for Carl Friedrich Cramer's Hamburg periodical, *Magazin der Musik,* claimed a Roman audience would not even applaud an opera that hadn't already been given to acclaim in Naples and even booed some that had. If impressed, they might applaud so long that candles had to be relit. When they really loved an opera, they would put the composer on a chair and carry him through the streets, but this was no guarantee of success next time. The correspondent claimed this had happened to Jommelli one year, yet the following year he had to sneak out of the theater to avoid the wrath of the crowd.[73] Perhaps the correspondent was simply echoing Romans' own mythology about themselves, but it lived on. As late as 1805, after the rise and fall of Napoleon's Repubblica Romana, the Englishman Peter Beckford still wrote, "The Romans are severe critics. Their manner of hissing is particularly formidable; and when that is no longer permitted, they are very ingenious in finding a substitute—they sneeze—*Evviva! Grazie!*—and will thus make civility answer the purpose of the highest impertinence."[74]

The reports of Cramer's *Magazin* and Beckford's letter may be exaggerated—certainly Cramer's correspondent delivers his report as something learned secondhand, and both have a mythologizing air. But separating fact from mythology is impossible, especially as crowds were compelled to live up to myths about themselves, and in any case, various evidence makes it clear that the behavior of Roman publics easily spilled into violence. Maria Grazia Pastura Ruggiero reports that the court records of the governor's criminal tribunal are filled with

71. Burney says Rome didn't want composers and singers who hadn't already been successful elsewhere: "The Romans . . . received his opera with coldness; and the composer being a young man but little known, they seemed to want to be told by others that his Music was excellent, and would soon, by the admiration of all Europe, make them ashamed of their injustices and want of taste" (Burney, *General History of Music* 2:921).

72. I-Bc, I.6.62 (= Schnoebelen, *Padre Martini's Letters,* no. 1559). See Petrobelli, "Un cantante fischiato," 363–76; della Seta, "Il relator sincero," 73–116; and Cametti, "Critiche e satire teatrali," 1–35; the three-part study by Celani, "Musica e musicisti"; Celletti, "I cantanti," 101–7; and Pejrone, "Il teatro attraverso i periodici romani," 599–615.

73. In noting the savagely fickle behavior of Roman audiences, the anonymous correspondent prefaced his remarks with a standard myth about the Romans' special sensitivity to music. See Cramer, *Magazin der Musik* 2.1:50–53 (July 9, 1784).

74. Beckford, *Familiar Letters* 2:282.

imputations and testimony by Romans and foreigners of every class, recounting incidents in the parterre, corridors, and boxes of the opera houses and the streets outside. They involve not just abbots and callow youths but lackeys and vassals, who fill the corridors, stealing time, quarreling, drinking, occupying empty boxes, or playing quarters (*squarci*) in doorways of boxes while awaiting their masters' orders[75]—all true to form in a city where theatrical broadsides and pamphlets, pasquinades, and other invective genres were long-lived traditions.

Why these incessant reports of abuse? Why the ritual folly, madness, and even violence?

Crowd noise and crowd action were power, and Romans had few chances to exercise it throughout the year. To do so was to make use of a peculiarly Roman right to judge, a domain in which they had an international reputation to keep up. Moreover, Romans were venting themselves against the oppressive machinery of an absolutist papal autocracy that pressed on their lives day in and day out. In an important sense, abuse of composers and singers in the opera house was a displacement of ill will toward authorities who were politically far higher than any musician. The authorities were many and their representations variously mediated. They included the papal prince himself, who, unlike monarchs abroad, almost never attended the theater but was in every sense the head of a political monarchy powered by an elaborate state machine; and they included the total system of power and prestige that surrounded the papacy: the cardinals' college, the heads of tribunals, the monsignor governor and his deputies (treasurer, clerks, and auditor of the chamber). Less directly, they also included the powerful foreign embassies and their delegates, foreign monarchs in residence (like James III, Queen Clementine, and the Duke of York), the prestigious Académie Française and its members, and a host of grandees and eminences who periodically visited from abroad. Many of these luminaries had special, often permanently designated boxes, and libretti were regularly dedicated to them.[76] Hissing, booing, sneezing, shouting, stomping, brawling, and mob action were all challenges directed at these higher powers and the "old law" for which they stood. They allowed the lowly clerical class, and even well-

75. See Pastura Ruggiero, "Per una storia del teatro pubblico," 453–86, esp. 484–85, and "Fonti per la storia del teatro romano," 505–87, who is in turn indebted to de Domenicis, "I teatri di Roma." Cf. Rosselli, *The Opera Industry* (synthetic, but rich and precise).

76. This was so even though the Roman theaters of the delle Dame and later Argentina dedicated operas to James and Clementine at the general rate of one each per season between 1721 and 1730, culminating in Metastasio's most popular operas, *Alessandro nell'Indie* and *Artaserse* during the 1730 season, and again from 1738, when, following Clementine's death, operas at the newly refurbished delle Dame were again dedicated to James and their two sons. The Stuarts added the monarchical prestige that the pope's physical absence left unfulfilled. But when they kept crowds waiting, dined when no one else could do so, or brought courtiers who dressed too sumptuously, they also caused resentment. See Clark, "The Stuart Presence at the Opera at Rome," as well as Boiteux, "Il carnevale e le feste francesi a Roma"; Cagli, *Le muse galanti;* and Petrocchi, *Il teatro a Roma.*

off but unwashed youths, to be hoisted up as temporary sovereigns—effigies of an iconic, princely kind.

The fool is crowned; the king is uncrowned. So wrote Goethe.[77] At Rome there is a repeated, abrasive rhythm of crowning and uncrowning, with a long history that predates the history of opera and continues to shape it via singers, spectators, and composers. Effects on the papal monarchy and its subjects were inevitable. For when the crowned are uncrowned, some kind of ritual conflagration eventually follows as the wintry night of Carnival makes way for the rebirth of spring.[78]

These rituals of abuse have important Roman precedents in rites surrounding the Vacant See, the interregnum between the death of one pope and election of another.[79] Periods of the Vacant See were particularly volatile times in Rome and its outlying states because the papal monarch was elected by conclave, not handed down through inheritance, and because the conclave convened only after the pope died. When that happened, he and his key nephews (who were part of his dynastic power and hope for familial succession) were gone without replacement, old scores were settled, and legendary violence broke out. Laurie Nussdorfer has described the interregnum as the time of a new regime when the "expectations of deference and courtesy flowing upward from inferiors to superiors who dispensed favors and protection in exchange were suspended. The demand that subjects obey the will of the prince no longer had meaning; there was no one figure to be courted, placated, or accommodated. Political styles did an about-face: insults and self-assertion replaced compliments and submission, Roman traditions of political protest, rituals of inversion tenaciously observed over the centuries, open—even violent—jurisdictional conflict, and satire and mockery swept to the fore."[80] The shift of rule was mandated by law and by tradition. When the pope died, a series of official actions immediately ensued that radically reduced the power of the state until the Holy Spirit, through the work of the College of Cardinals, elected the next pope. No new laws could be promulgated, no tribunals held, most curial officials lost power, the ring that the pope used to seal briefs was ritually broken along with the matrix that formed the lead stamps that he used for papal bulls, and prisoners were led out of prison houses by the *caporione* of each prison.

Most relevant to our themes and also strongly founded in tradition, sponta-

77. Compare *Amours and Adventures* (7), which describes Carnival as "a farewell to Flesh before the time of Lent; a mighty Junket and Mummery; an hodgepodge of Diversion, before Fasting and Penitence; a Surfeit, for which Lent is the Physick. It is something like the Old *Roman Saturnalia,* when all the Rabble of *Rome,* were suffered to make Mirth with vile Buffoonery by Authority: It is a large Bartholomew Fair, or Days of Privilege, when every Man plays the Monster, or *Jack Pudding,* that pleases him best; and the Gallantry is esteemed by the Greatness of the Foolery and Extravagance."

78. See Bakhtin, *Rabelais,* chap. 3.

79. See Nussdorfer, *Civic Politics,* chap. 14; and earlier, Spinelli, *La vacanza della sede apostolica.*

80. Nussdorfer, *Civic Politics,* 228.

neous rites of popular violence that went unimpeded by authorities took place during interregna. The most striking of these were ritual sacks of the goods and property of cardinals. Carlo Ginzburg and his seminar at Bologna have shown that these sacks continued from medieval times into the eighteenth century and involved extreme forms of disorder and violence.[81] Sacks had specific material goals in the spoliations involved, but like abuse in the theater they also served a cathartic role. In both cases, the ritual abuse of a "feasting" crowd did the work of correcting an imbalance: in the case of sacks, imbalances of riches and power; in the case of abuse, of power and honor. And like the sack, when the ritual abuse ended—in our case, with the end of Carnival—the local identity and hierarchy of the place were reaffirmed.

The most anarchical of Carnival rites emerged (or perhaps was resuscitated) at Rome in the latter half century. Called the rite of the *moccoletti* (from *moccolo*, candle), it first appeared in the 1760s, and by 1773 was used along the whole of the Corso.[82] The rite of the *moccoletti*, as suggested by Goethe's description above, was a game, visual, gestural, and oral, in which, on the eve of Lent, revelers celebrated by quickly passing lit candles or lanterns between one another. The lights resembled torches used in funerals—hence were signs of death—and the game involved trying protect one's own light while extinguishing that of someone nearby and uttering the formula "Sia ammazzato chi non porta moccolo." In the eighteenth century, the symbolic significance of killing off the old life to bring in an auspicious new year was still alive. As a propitiary ritual insult, "Sia ammazzato" (literally, "be killed") was tantamount to our "break a leg."[83] It would have resonated in the popular imagination with other propitiary and expiatory rituals of Carnival: beating and killing the effigy of a pregnant old hag; wearing the ominous medieval clerical outfits of the *tabarro* (in Rome) and *bauta* (in Venice); and, not least, disrupting opera houses, ritually "killing off" a rival composer or unpopular singer, chasing a composer out of a theater, but finally extinguishing Carnival antics and reinstating order by the time Lent dawned.[84]

* * *

Whether speaking of the sack, the *moccoletti*, or the theater, all of these rites must have an aleatory dimension, not just an abusive one, for unpredictability represents both the expected exercise of a customary right and the production of something extraordinary because unexpected. The fact that theater and Car-

81. Ginzburg et al., "Saccheggi rituali," 615–36.

82. See Clementi, *Il carnevale*, 162–63; and Boiteux, "Il carnevale e le feste francesi," 321–71, esp. 353.

83. See also Ginzburg et al., "Saccheggi rituali," 621–22.

84. Pagan Carnival had been loosely elided in the collective imagination of city people with the death and rebirth of Christ commemorated at Lent and Easter, even as the classical and medieval meanings of Carnival endured through traditional revelries at the vernal equinox.

nival came around so seldom made this only truer, as Alessandro Verri seems to declare to his brother Pietro in a letter of January 10, 1770:

> The place is in the usual ferment over the Bacchanals: after ten months without public spectacle of any sort, the people of Quirinius race with unbelievable breathlessness to fill the theaters, of which this year there are a good eight. . . . The operas being two, with two different companies formed by the impresarios, they give rise to emulation, party politics, and factions; and applause, hissing, and hooting resound all throughout these vast halls.[85]

Verri may have characterized his fellow operagoers as debauched and belligerent, but he added that at a given moment their passions could be softened, and wild calls alternate with utter silence:

> [T]here is much intelligence and sensibility to the music. The daring gestures, the support of the orchestra, the flights of brilliance by the *maestro di cappella* [Monza] are suddenly accompanied by a universal, passing uproar, as suddenly a profound silence descends [on the hall].[86]

As domination and submission fluctuated with shifting favor and disfavor, rituals hardened and disintegrated by turns. The positions of the perpetrators and those on whom their acts were perpetrated lived on the knife-edge of change. Much as the Carnival king becomes the fool and the fool the king, at the Roman opera the victor becomes the loser, the master the slave, the hero the villain, and back again. At Carnival, time was always in a state of becoming, because such transformations were the magical effects of a festive time and mood. Unlike the linear events of papal interregna and the spoliations of cardinals' homes, demonstrations at the opera often involved no real passage to new pragmatic conditions or permanent new identities, but rather a periodic, cyclic renewal of possibility, later remembered for its individual character and only occasionally for changes in actual structures. Thus, the marginal state of the abbots is suspended but returns with Lent; the noble youths are untethered and then fastened back into place; the Argentina conquers the Alibert one Carnival year, but loses the cup the next.[87] The effect of the rites was partial, involving

85. "Il paese è nel solito fermento de' baccanali: dopo dieci mesi che non vi è spettacolo pubblico di nissuna sorte, il popolo Quirino corre, con un affanno incredibile, a riempire i teatri, che questo anno sono ben otto. . . . Le opere essendo due, e diverse le compagnie d'impresari, ne nasce l'emulazione, lo spirito di partito, e le fazioni e gli applausi e le fischiate e gli urli fanno risonare questi vastissimi teatri" (Verri and Verri, *Carteggio* 3:155). Quirinus was the ancient military leader of Rome, thus "People of Quirinius" functions metonymically for "the Romans."

86. "Generalmente, v'è molta intelligenza e sensibilità alla musica; i tratti arditi, i rinforzi d'orchestra, le scappate di genio del maestro di cappella vengono subito accompagnate da uno schiamazzo universale e momentaneo, perchè subito succede un profondo silenzio" (ibid., 156).

87. Writing from Rome on March 7, 1746, Girolamo Chiti stated bluntly to Padre Martini that "the Alibert was bested by the Argentina" (l'Alibert fù vinto dal Argentina), adding about Jommelli, "I pity that cunning Jommelli: he adapted himself to the bad taste of Roman theaters" (Lo com-

temporary suspension of moral laws and laws of state, and above all renewals of social promise, reminders that everyone has a time, that that time will return, that abstinence will lead to surfeit, continence to indulgence, propriety to impropriety, and constraint to freedom.

At Rome these dynamics were permanently implicated in the formidable hierarchies of social life, whose reputation ran as high and nasty as the city's rituals of abuse. A suggestive incident took place at the Argentina, when on January 2, 1792, the Roman governor made a huge stink for not having been sufficiently honored when his carriage got caught in a bottleneck.[88] Years earlier, on March 3, 1773, Alessandro Verri complained to Pietro, after a particularly enervating Carnival, that the lengthy balls at Rome were afflicted by terrible exaggerations of social hierarchy. The reason Roman balls were boring and sorry compared with those at Milan, he said, was that they exacted so much attention with so little to gain. "The first objection" was that the noblemen,

> who put on the balls with their own money, make a separate room for the nobility. Two of their men stand at the doorbell like Minos and Radamanthus, in order to judge severely the purity of the souls, and see that the citizen class can't go in. As a result, so as not to be mortified by this humiliating distinction, the rich female citizens don't show up. Few women are left in the pure palisade of these noblemen, because there are few girls who dance, and the rest of the ball consists of badly dressed girls in the style of our "roasts."[89]

These hierarchies were so ingrained that the nobles refused to put new wealth on a par with old and went out of their way to disavow the upwardly mobile. Beckford, trying to make his way as a foreigner, lamented the nobles' offishness, calling Rome "the chief residence of pomp, punctilio, and nastiness."

> You arrive at an immense palace; ascend a magnificent, but dark staircase, frequently crowded with poor, and always covered with dirt. You pass through a number of large, lofty, but uncomfortable rooms, full of servants and depen-

patisco, Jomella furbo: si adattò al gusto cattivo di Roma teatrale). From I-Bc, I.2.20 (= Schnoebelen, *Padre Martini's Letters*, no. 1234).

88. Pastura Ruggiero, "Per una storia del teatro pubblico," 485.

89. "La prima obbiezione è perché i cavalieri, che fanno a loro spese la festa, formano a parte una sala per la nobiltà. Stanno al cancello due di loro, qual Minosse e Radamanto, a giudicare della purità delle anime severamente, cosicché la cittadinanza non vi può entrare. Ne viene per conseguenza che le cittadine ricche non compariscono per non avere la mortificazione di questa umiliante distinzione. Rimangono poche dame nel purissimo loro steccato, perché poche sono le giovani che ballano, il rimanente delle festa sono ragazze malvestite all'uso dei nostri detti *arrosti*" (Verri and Verri, *Carteggio* 6:27). Pietro Verri had written of Milan, "I vostri divertimenti mi pare che siano violenti; sino le quattordici ore ballare, è veramente troppo; le nostre feste da ballo, presentemente, sono assai più ragionevoli" (3:197). [Your festivities seem too extreme to me. To dance until the wee hours is truly too much. Our balls at present are much more reasonable.] Pietro explained that their balls in Milan now took place only on Thursdays and went from "mezz'ora di notte" until "un po' prima di mezzanotte" (3:198). On class distinctions at Milanese balls, cf. 6:182–83.

> dants of different denominations. After a long and disagreeable march, your name constantly repeated till you are tired of hearing it, you arrive at length at the door of the room where the company are assembled, and there your name is announced for the last time. The lady of the house receives you at the door; you make a bow, she makes a curtsy, and you are then left to shift for yourself as at other great assemblies.[90]

The hierarchical fabric of Roman life was interwoven with the elaborate pecking order of the papal bureaucracy, which had evolved by the eighteenth century into the principal template of modern state bureaucracies. Although obliged to stand for piety, the papal see was a major exemplar—perhaps *the* exemplar—of absolutist statecraft in a modern monarchical guise.[91] Yet as Mona Ozouf has written, "Traditional festivities were the realm of distinctions" without which distinctions of power and rule were enfeebled.[92] Contrasts of order and disorder, piety and irreverence, were only as extreme as contrasts of social and political rank.

LAUGHTER, RIDICULE, CRITIQUE

The opera seria stage furnished innumerable sources of laughter, often animated by the very vanities of the institution, its pretensions to pomp, dignity, and moral superiority. In the *Lettre sur le méchanisme* of 1756, the author gives an instance of this in the sopranos' "trick of the train." Onstage princesses were distinguished by their attendance by little pages, whose job was to restore the position of their trains whenever they moved out of place. In keeping with real-life protocols, two pages were assigned to each princess, but as the author wrote, "Nothing is more pleasant than the constant movement in which these little scamps run after the singer when she turns a lot. Sometimes their activity puts them in a sweat, embarrasses them; their awkwardness always makes for laughter. It is a farce that often singularly distracts the spectator in highly pathetic situations."[93] As recounted in chapter 1, audiences also roared their appreciation at the ridiculous prompter who mouthed the music of a missing singer in Milan and was assaulted in jest by a frustrated tenor, and at the castrato who first refused to sing an aria by Galuppi but who, after the composer began in consternation to sing it himself, went on to upstage him.

Laughter had a dimension of competition and often nastiness, a response to agonistic struggle that could bring on awe and cheers. It was cathartic, especially for opera seria with its factionalism and cabals. In the most notorious of cases,

90. Beckford, *Familiar Letters* 2:280.

91. See Prodi, *Il sovrano pontefice* (in English as *The Papal Prince*), and Nussdorfer, *Civic Politics*.

92. Ozouf, *Festivals of the French Revolution*, 3 (translation here is mine).

93. *Lettre sur le méchanisme*, 33.

the castrato Caffarelli, during the production of an opera by Latilla at the San Carlo in January 1741, reportedly "engaged in malicious behavior [*discolezze*] disturbing the composure of other singers, making lascivious gestures to one of the female performers, speaking from the stage with auditors who were in theater boxes, echoing phrases sung by others, finally refusing to join in ensembles with other singers."[94] Several years later, during the Naples performance of Hasse's *Antigone*, he unexpectedly changed the music of a duet in such a way that the soprano had to improvise a whole new rhythmic structure at each verse statement and again at the da capo; and each time she tried again to adapt to his changes, he made dramatic demonstrations to her with his hands and mouth of the correct rhythm, in full view of the audience.[95] If only performances had been documented then as well as they were a century later, we might know better whether spectators laughed with Caffarelli or booed. Probably he got mocking laughter out of his own faction, even if he risked disapprobation from the authorities and from the party of the soprano (and even if he risked punishment from the former, which he sometimes got). As reported by spectators of a quarrel he had with the poet-impresario Metastasio during a rehearsal at Vienna, Caffarelli's violent antics provoked terror and then "horse-laughs."[96] Audiences at performances also routinely laughed at singers when they stumbled on props or passagework, and they laughed at faulty machinery and sets. Collective and uncontainable, laughter was the underbelly of the opera.

The satire on the "trick of the train" tells not just about public laughter, but opera as grist for the literary laughter of savvy readers. Many eighteenth-century accounts of operatic laughter are doused with moralism but redeemed by the literary craft of anecdote and parody. The *Lettre sur le méchanisme* masqueraded anonymously as a factual account mixed with critique, though it was actually unabashed satire. If its author was really the librettist Calzabigi, as Heartz believes, then we are indeed dealing with an acknowledged master of literary craft.[97] And while the passage about the princesses' trains recounts the mocking laughter of a public, it also manifests the fact that by the eighteenth century, opera was a major impetus for laughter that only partly belonged to a public collectivity. There were also private publics who read about opera aloud in groups at home, and there were private individual readers.

Operatic satire was essayed in 1715 with Pier Jacopo Martello's *Della tragedia antica e moderna*, published in Rome, and codified in 1720 with the shriveling *Il teatro alla moda* by the Venetian nobleman Benedetto Marcello. After they ap-

94. Quoted from Heartz, "Caffarelli's Caprices."

95. Heriot, *The Castrati*, 145–46, quoting the impresario Saverio Donati. In Florence, Donati threatened to make the castrato Egiziello sing out of tune (ibid., 116). Even when Caffarelli was punished with house arrest, he was always quickly back on stage. Cf. Farinelli, *La solitudine amica*, letters 37, 39, 53–55; and Heartz, "Caffarelli's Caprices."

96. The term is Burney's, from his translation of Metastasio's letter, July 5, 1749 (*Memoirs of . . . Metastasio* 1:274).

97. On this attribution, see Heartz, *Haydn, Mozart, and the Viennese School*, 158–64.

peared, a few other such works followed suit,[98] but mostly operatic satire crept into letters, treatises, and even novels (much as allusions to opera crept into literary satires). That changed in 1749 when Zaccaria Seriman, offspring of a rich Catholic Armenian family that had migrated to Venice via Persia in 1698, published his *Viaggi di Enrico Wanton alle terre incognite australi, ed al paese delle scimie, ne' quali si spiegano il carattere, li costumi, le scienze e la polizia di quegli straordinari abitanti* (Journeys of Henry Wanton to unknown Australian lands, and to the land of the monkeys, explaining the character, customs, sciences, and regulations of its extraordinary inhabitants). An admirer of Italian enlightenment thought and a student at the Studio of Padua, Seriman composed the work as a satiric, journalistic novel, publishing the first edition in two volumes and expanding it to four for a later edition of 1764.[99] In the *Viaggi* Seriman claims to have found a lost manuscript by a London traveler, Enrico Wanton ("wanton Henry"), and to follow, à la *Gulliver's Travels*, Wanton's fantastical journey to a land of apes. Along the way, the simians engage in a whole gamut of human social customs, each of which, seen from the alterity of Wanton's vantage point, prompts new philosophical musings on the deterioration of modern life. Eighteenth-century editions included some thirty-two engraved illustrations by Giorgio Fossati showing quasi simians in eighteenth-century dress (posed in contrast to Wanton and his sidekick, Roberto—the only full-fledged humans) and fully engaged in human actions.[100]

By volume 2, chapter 6, Enrico and Roberto are getting ready for the opera season. Roberto prepares Enrico by telling him it is the custom of the land to put on "certain spectacles, in which some raucous action is depicted that happened in ancient times"[101]—a reader's cue that the opera to be imagined is a self-important opera seria, not opera buffa. Roberto adds that extraordinary efforts

98. Notable later examples are the Baron Friedrich Melchior von Grimm's *Le petit prophète de Boehmischbroda* (1753), and the *Lettre sur le méchanisme*. On Martello see Weiss, "Pier Jacopo Martello on Opera."

99. After its original publication in Venice, the work was often reprinted elsewhere—Naples 1750 and 1756, Berna 1764 (in reality Treviso, according to Pagetti, *La fortuna di Swift*, 83), and throughout the nineteenth century. A Spanish translation appeared in 1778, reprinted until 1880 (see Parenti, *Un romanzo italiano*, 27). The 1764 edition is considered the most authoritative and complete and appears without illustrations in a modern edition published in 1977. I have examined the 1749 and 1764 editions and cite from the latter. Opposite the title page of the 1764 edition is an engraved frontispiece showing Seriman holding quill and map with the rubric "Enricus Wanton Anglus." An epigraph reads "*Non cuivis Lectori, Auditorique placebo: Lector, & Auditor nec mihi quisque placet.* Owen. Ad Henr. Pri. Lib. 3 Epig. 124" (A1v). Seriman translated and edited Latin, French, and English. A polygraph, he wrote an opera seria libretto in 1747, *Caio Marzio Coriolano*, judged as poor by Giammaria Ortes. See White, *Zaccaria Seriman;* Torcellan's review of White, "I viaggi di Enrico Wanton," 165–70; Ortolani, "Un romanzo satirico," 97–133; and Pagetti, *La fortuna di Swift*, esp. 82–94.

100. Seriman, *Viaggi* (1977), 2:568 n. 35.

101. "Appresso noi si usano certi spettacoli, ne' quali si rappresenta qualche azione strepitosa avvenuta nel tempo antico" (Seriman, *Viaggi* [1764], 2:93).

will be made to transport the audience to an elsewhere: side curtains painted to create verisimilitude, singers in sumptuous dress, and passions rung out with great verve. Is the point of all this simply to interest the audience in falsehoods, Wanton asks, as if false appearances were real? The question launches a comical account of frenzied preparations for the Venetian opera season: the "inexpressible pleasure" of securing a box, finding a rich woman to gain admission, and not least, procuring the right mask. Befuddled Wanton is told he can't get in without one, but the mask his friends offer him only fits an ape.

Included in the chapter is an illustration that counts among the most reprinted in recent writings on eighteenth-century opera, proffered more than once as a "typical" Venetian opera house in action (fig. 4.6). But the joke turns out to be on us, since no one seems to have noticed that most of the spectators (and possibly the soprano) are masked apes.[102] The only non-apes in the audience are Wanton himself, standing to the right in the parterre, and his Virgil, Roberto, at his side. The more legible of the two, Wanton faces us wearing the *bauta*-style mask that typifies Venetian Carnival (*not,* in his case, adapted to simian form). He marvels that the very friends who prepared so obsessively for the night are barely interested in the actual opera, which anyway is full of patent incongruities.

> From the start this habit of masking seemed to me a strange and incongruous thing, but then I became tolerant of using it, and finally enjoyed it. In such garb I was then led to the theater. My reader, you might believe that I am about to describe what I saw that night, but I urge you not to expect this of me, as I did not perceive anything but confusion and tumult. A loud noise and the continuous sounds of various instruments suffocated the various voices of the actors, all of whom were singing, whether weeping or consoling, in chains [or] . . . on the throne. I noticed that those who were declaiming (male and female) had fine voices. I observed that the sets flew, the trees walked, lights were projected from the ground, that the same characters were transported from city to country, or to far-off places, from one moment to another, without ever discovering how this enchantment was wrought. The costumes were utterly ludicrous, such that no painter even of the most perturbed imagination has ever conceived anything of the kind. They were so weighted down with precious stones that had they been natural instead of fake, the value of a kingdom would not suffice for one costume. Everything was reduced equally to the verisimilar and the believable. Certain dances, interspersed between the songs, were indeed quite expressive, it being easier to express a lascivious act than an honorable sentiment. The height of eccentricity was an endless, overwhelming whispering while the opera was being staged and a profound silence when not the hearing but the eye was charged to enjoy the dance. I observed finally

102. See, e.g., Zaslaw, *The Classical Era,* 46, and Buelow, *The Late Baroque Era,* 87. Throughout the 2,385 pages that make up the 1764 *Viaggi,* only a few pictures show protagonists without monkey faces.

FIG. 4.6. Giorgio Fossati, engraving of a fictitious Venetian theater. From Zaccaria Seriman, *Viaggi di Enrico Wanton* (Venice: Giovanni Tagier, 1749). By permission of Miami University, Special Collections, Oxford, Ohio.

> that during the opera all the ladies turned their back to the stage and their face toward the spectators, a haughty show of disdain for the spectacle that they had so ardently longed for.[103]

Bakhtin tells us that after the sixteenth century, Rabelais's carnivalesque images turn into satire at the hands of his imitators. His "two-poled encompassing grotesque" loses its inner core, as the positive pole becomes an abstract idea and the "material lower bodily stratum," previously linked to Rabelaisian physicality and exaggeration, is rechanneled into moralistic caricatures.[104] By now reams have been written on the utopian urges that mark Bakhtin's history of laughter—so startlingly original and erudite but freighted as history by the negative telos that always lurks near utopian ideals. For Bakhtin laughter by the eighteenth century became dogmatic and private, negative because itself a negation.

> The seventeenth century was marked by the stabilization of the new order of the absolute monarchy. A relatively progressive "universally historic form" was created and was expressed in Descartes' rationalist philosophy and in the aesthetics of classicism. . . . [T]he new official culture . . . differed from the ecclesiastic feudal culture but was also authoritarian and serious, though less dogmatic . . . . In [it] . . . there prevails a tendency toward the stability and completion of being, toward one single meaning, one single tone of seriousness. The ambivalence of the grotesque can no longer be admitted. The exalted genres of classicism are freed from the influence of the grotesque tradition of laughter.[105]

103. "Strana, ed incommoda cosa riuscivami quella maniera di maschera da principio, l'uso poi me la fece tollerare, e finalmente gustare. In tal arnese dunque fui condotto al Teatro. Crederà forse, il mio Lettore, che io sia per descrivergli ciò, che abbia veduto in quella notte; non lo attenda da me, che non rilevai che confusione e tumulto. Uno strepito acuto, e continuo di suoni di vari istromenti, soffocavano le voci degli attori, che tutti cantavano, e quando piangevano, e si consolavano, e fra catene, e sul trono. Notai, che i recitanti e maschi e femmine avevano una voce sottilissima. Osservai, che le fabbriche volavano, che gli arbori camminavano, che nascevano i lumi dal terreno, e che gli stessi personaggi da un momento all'altro erano trasportati dalla città alla campagna, o in altri discostissimi luoghi, senza scoprirsi come si formasse quell'incantesimo. I vestimenti erano affatto grotteschi, e tali, che da niun pittore di sconvolta immaginazione n'erano stati ideati de' simili. Questi erano carichi di pietre preziose a tal segno, che se fossero state naturali, e non finte, non basterebbe il valore di un regno per prezzo di un solo vestito. Tutto era ridotto al verisimile, ed al credibile sopra lo stesso piano. Certe danze intrecciavano i canti, e queste danze infatti erano alquanto esprimenti, essendo più facile cosa l'esprimere un' atto lascivo, che un sentimento di onore. Per colmo di stravaganza regnava un bisbiglio eterno allor quando si rappresentava l'azione, ed un silenzio profondo allorchè l'occhio, e non l'udito era chiamato a gustare le danze. Finalmente feci riflesso che tutte le dame nel tempo della recita rivolgevano il dorso al palco, e la faccia agli spettatori, dimostrazione fastosa del disprezzo di uno spettacolo, che avevano desiderato con tanto ardore" (Seriman, *Viaggi* [1764], 2:103–6).

104. Bakhtin, *Rabelais,* 62 and 119.

105. Ibid., 101–2.

Bakhtin's view resonates with the history of European laughter, but opera seria diverges from it in several ways. First, operatic laughter and its darker cousins, abuse and even violence, did not go underground to purely private realms but endured in the theater, where some persons were in public view and others retreated to the semiprivacy of their boxes and preened for one another, and in the salon, where people read libretti and satires, talked by the hour, and sang or listened to opera arias. Second, the commercial nature of settecento opera tempered its whole dynamic, which encompassed classical ideals of decorum, politesse, courtly etiquette, honor, and heroism on one side and abuse, ridicule, noise, and laughter on the other—both poles of the same social universe. Laughter in the large, jostling spaces of the opera house, poised at the center of social and political life, was real and collective. And third, insofar as laughter and festivity more broadly were attenuated over the course of the eighteenth century, it was not just by the stranglehold of absolutisms. Rationalists of the enlightenment often saw in festivity little but vice, sloth, enthusiasm, ignorance, fanaticism, disorder, violence, and superstition. When it came to feasting, many rationalists stood ironically on the same side of the fence as certain religious reformists whose critiques date back at least to the fifteenth century, and were especially prominent in the seventeenth.[106] In a wonderful meditation on the embattlements of early modern festivity over several centuries on into the time of Napoleon, Yves-Marie Bercé has shown some of the historical antecedents and political correlates of these rationalist reservations. Jean Gerson, for instance, proposed a reduction of the number of feast days in the early fifteenth century at the Councils of Reims and Constance—this in a period when more than one out of every three days was a feast day—by arguing that there were too many of them to be properly observed. On the other hand, the Barberini pope Urban VIII (reigned 1623–44) made festivity into a thing of explicit monarchical control when he assigned the papacy the right to designate, delimit, and define the sanctioned feast days.[107]

By the eighteenth century, many governments across Europe were trying to squeeze festivity down to size through a concrete reduction of feast days. A well-documented example explored by Gerhard Tanzer comes from the realm of Maria Theresia at Vienna. There festivity from the early eighteenth century on was mainly manifested in masked balls, but in 1746 the then empress began to have specific rules for donning masks, which resemble Italian ones in making illegal anything lewd, disorderly, or imitative of religious attire. Similarly, the number of holidays in Vienna decreased radically over the course of the century (as in many other Catholic cities). In the first half of the century, there were eighty feast days, including Sundays plus about twenty-eight others (saints' days, Circumcision, Epiphany, the feast of the conversion of St. Paul, Easter, St. George's Day, All Saints', All Souls', and the local St. Leopoldstag, to name

106. Ozouf, *Festivals of the French Revolution*, 1–4.

107. Bercé, *Fête et révolte*, 136–50.

a few).[108] Maria Theresia introduced a major reform of these holy days in 1754 when some of them became half holidays: feast days for Saints Paul, Matthias, Joseph, and James; Easter Monday and Tuesday; St. George's Day (March 24), Pentecost Monday and Tuesday, the feasts of St. John the Baptist (December 27), Mary Magdalene, and a number of others. On a half holiday, people could work in the morning and go to mass in the afternoon. At first the motivation was ostensibly to reduce manifestations of the profane on sacred days by reducing the amount of secular time, thus strengthening the distinction between *Freizeit* and *Andachzeit* (free time and prayer time). Markets could still be open on half holidays, but taverns were closed. This would have satisfied Voltaire, who believed that the profusion of feast days was the fault of innkeepers looking to promote a sort of religion of lazy peasants and workers who wanted nothing better than to get drunk and commit crimes on their time off (and were therefore doomed to stay poor).[109] In 1771, Maria Theresia received a papal bull mandating that all but a few of these half holidays be eliminated, but Joseph II later reinstated some of them and liberalized observance of holy days in a general effort at reform. Other such actions were taken across Europe throughout the later eighteenth century. On February 5, 1790, in a wave of reformist austerity, for instance, the Roman custom of the *moccoletti* was banned by Monsignor Ranuccini.[110]

The exemplary Italian case of reform-contra-festivity was that of Habsburg Tuscany under Grand Duke Peter Leopold, model of a reforming sovereign. After assuming power in 1765, just after the Great Famine, he worked on agrarian reform, freeing the grain trade by ending provisioning systems, dividing common lands, and selling off grand-ducal estates to produce more food through a new class of independent smallholders in place of poor tenant farmers. In 1779, he introduced a new Tuscan constitution, the first and only in Italy, which dissolved monasteries but promoted extreme piety while also reducing the number of feast days in order to increase the number of working days, as his mother had done—changes that were supremely unpopular. Similar reductions of feast days were sought in many parts of France, often by moving saints' days to Sundays to kill two birds at one blow and thus increase the number of available workdays.

Such reductions were typically avowed as ways to prevent the profane from contaminating the sacred, though their real goal—even in Catholic states, where saints' days were largely preserved—was to prevent saints' days from being spent drunk and idle or getting into trouble. Here, then, was the preliminary modern separation of feast day from festive day, the holy day from the holiday, and here too the "disenchantment of the world."[111]

108. Tanzer, *Spectacle müssen seyn,* 102.

109. Voltaire's *Dictionnaire philosophique portatif* appeared in 1764; there is a definitive edition of 1769 under the title *La raison par alphabet* (and see the modern edition of 1954).

110. Clementi, *Il carnevale* 2:209, and Volterra, "Il carnevale romano sotto Pio VI," 128–32, esp. 138.

111. The premise of the separation of sacred and secular holidays underlies Bercé, *Fête et révolte,* and de Grazia, *Of Time, Work, and Leisure.* The term "disenchantment [*Entauberung*] of the world"

NATURE REVISITED

Clearly the rationalist argument against festivity was articulated neither along axes of power and centralization nor of confession. On the materialist end enunciated by Montesquieu, the argument favored labor, capital, utility, efficiency, and productivity (in all of which the merchants of Protestant lands, which had eliminated some fifty feast days, had outpaced the Catholics). On the ideological end enunciated by Voltaire, the argument favored reason and order.[112]

Less explicitly, festivity for most rationalists was an offense against nature. We will see in chapter 8 that the operatic figure that came to emblematize such an offense was the castrato, increasingly attacked in the later eighteenth century. But such attacks were part of a more general crisis. As tolerance for old festive forms of transgression, collective effervescence, and unauthorized invention were waning, changing views of nature were used to justify a sense that the people's festivity was cause for fear and loathing, or to justify the paradoxical view that odious behavior at festive times was *overly* natural. As Alessandro Verri wrote on December 28, 1773,

> We are in a state of pure nature. It has already been three nights that one hears of people being caned, wounded, cloaks and hats stolen, women insulted and abducted in various part of the city. They're not always petty thievings, but quite often ferocious abuses with no theft, and the roughnecks are many and sometimes in a band. Tonight in my district the arm of a boy was almost completely severed. It seems that the raging madmen have been let out of the insane asylum. Truly, for it's all done according to a grand design [gran bel regolamento].[113]

Feeling crushed by the impending Carnival and distilling that most polyvalent of terms into a pejorative, Verri made "nature" synonymous with the ancient practices of misrule linked with Epiphany.[114] We do not know if those who pro-

comes from Max Weber; see *The Essential Weber,* 238, and Whimster's definition of it as "literally . . . de-magicalization. It is a product of religious and scientific *rationalization* that removes the original, naïve and direct attitude of humans to the world and to community" (408).

112. Montesquieu, *De l'esprit des lois* (in English as *The Spirit of the Laws*); Voltaire, *Dictionnaire philosophique.* Alternatively Rousseau claimed festivity made people want to live and work in the first place, that it was the foundation of sociability and hence civilization. The view permeates his utopian vision of the origins of music in the *Essai sur l'origine des langues,* often condescendingly so (*Essay on the Origin of Languages,* 307). Ozouf, in the introduction to *Festivals of the French Revolution,* gives background to the debates.

113. "Siamo nello stato di pura natura. Sono già tre notti che si sentono gente bastonata, ferita, ferraioli, cappelli rubati, donne insultate e rapite in varie parti della città. Non sono sempre latrocinî, bene spesso feroci insulti senza furto ed i grassatori sono molti e talvolta in truppa. Questa notte nel mio distretto è stato tagliato quasi di netto un braccio ad un ragazzo. Sembra che sieno usciti dallo spedale i pazzi furiosi. In verità che è un gran bel regolamento" (Verri and Verri, *Carteggio* 6:160).

114. The Lord of Misrule was a mock king or farcical devil type who traditionally ruled during the Christmas season, especially from New Year's to Epiphany (James, *Seasonal Feasts,* 278–79). In

duced this particular "state of pure nature" came from subaltern or elite classes, but abusive rituals in and around opera houses were not just the work of minor clerics, coachmen, footmen, chambermaids, and garbage collectors, but also of hotheaded aristocratic sons and other elites who acted like hooligans in festive times. Little wonder that Verri's ironic "gran bel regolamento" played on the language of official edicts that tried to tame festivity into some kind of magnificent order.

* * *

Like many of his confreres, by 1773 Alessandro Verri was fed up with the whole business of Carnival and even opera in its then-present form, which had become repellent and demystified. A reformed opera might have worked for him, but not the Roman fare. And as Mona Ozouf has written, "For those who resist the spell of illusion, the whole machinery creaks; the effects become tawdry, incongruous, ridiculous."[115] This is how it was for the abbé de Mably at the Paris Opéra, for other rationalists who came to disdain the "magic" of brilliant festivities, and for many observers on the street or in the lineaments that ran from the street stage to the stage house.[116]

We might ask whether the ambivalent nature of opera seria is betrayed by satire and laughter, whether it set out to affirm the absolutist establishment but ended up unsettling it. The relationship of opera seria to the sociopolitical establishment was decidedly ambidextrous, negating and reinstantiating it. It was implicated in what Peter Stallybrass and Allon White have called an "inner complicity of disgust and desire which fuels . . . crises of value" in a double motion that includes the positive that is asserted and its negation through inversion.[117]

December 1981, my stepdaughters, while attending the Rhyl School in the Chalk Farm neighborhood of north London, still learned a jaunty traditional song about the Lord of Misrule, which started "At Christmastime I'd like to be / The Lord of Misrule 'til Epiphany."

115. Ozouf, *Festivals of the French Revolution,* 2.

116. Mably, *Lettres à Madame la Marquise.*

117. Stallybrass and White, *The Politics and Poetics of Transgression,* 20; and earlier, Babcock, *The Reversible World.*

APPENDIX: EDICT ON ABUSES IN THE THEATER, ROME, JANUARY 4, 1749

Editto sopra gl'Abusi ne' Teatri.[118]

Dovendosi per benigna permissione della Santità di Nostro Signore dare un'onesto, e lecito divertimento con la recita dell'Opere, o siano Comedie, e Tragedie, Monsignor Illustrissimo, e Reverendissimo Cosimo Imperiali di Roma, e suo Distretto Governator Generale, e *Vostro* Camerlengo a fine che ciò succeda nelle lodevoli dovute forme per l'autorità del suo Officio, e per comandamento avutone a bocca da Sua Santità, rinovando in prima tutti gli Editti sopra tal'emergente altre volte emanati, quali vuole, che abbiano intieramente il suo vigore, come se fosse il tenore de' medesimi nel presente individualmente, e specificamente espresso, ingiunge più specialmente le seguenti disposizioni.

Primieramente, che l'Opere, e Comedie, o altro divertimento non possino farsi senza la licenza in scritto di sua Signoria Illustrissima, e non possino recitarsi, che nelli luoghi destinati, e non possino principiarsi prima di un'ora e mezza, ne doppo le due, sotto pena di scudi cinquanta per ciascuna volta da applicarsi ad arbitrio di Sua Signoria Illustrissima.

Che nelle Porte, e Teatri si debba tenere dagl'Impresarii buon'ordine, e regolamento, e succedendo sconcerto, debbano denunziarlo, perché possa darvisi il suo riparo a tempo, e se tali disordini saranno causati dalle negligenze, mal'ordine, o parzialità, si procederà contro d'essi stessi alle pene gravi anche corporali, da regolarsi secondo le circostanze de' fatti, e qualità delle Persone.

Che li medesimi Impresari, Comici, e Musici debbano contenersi con tutta la modestia, e rispetto nelle loro azzioni, e parole, senza offesa né diretta, né indiretta ad alcuno sotto l'istesse pene.

Si proibisce a ciascuno di qualunque condizione, stato, e grado anche Ecclesiastico, privilegiato, ed esente di poter portare dentro li Teatri alcuna sorte d'Armi, benché ne avessero la licenza, eccettuata la Spada, sotto pena della Galera per sette anni: e di commettere alcun contrasto, o risa, nè dentro li Teatri, né fuori in sue vicinanze sotto la medesima pena in caso, che non v'interceda sangue, contusione, o percossa, poichè in tal caso, ancorchè l'offesa fosse leggiera, e senza sangue, e contusione, la pena sarà della vita, rispetto alli Delinquenti Secolari, ed in quanto agl'Ecclesiastici della Galera perpetua.

Si proibisce ancora alle stesse Persone di sopra espresse il fare strepito, rumore, fischiate, e fare atti indecenti, sì nel uscire, ed entrare, che nel tempo, che si recitano l'Opere, o con disturbare i Comici, o con pretendere forzarli alla replica dell'Arietta, o parte recitata, come parimente si proibisce alli Musici, e Comici di replicare la parte, o Arietta più di quella regola prefissale dal Compositore, sotto pena alli Comici, e Musici ad arbitrio di Sua Signoria Illustrissima, ed agl'altri di trè tratti di corda, ed altre pene corporali anche gravi respetti-

118. I-Ras, *Collezione di Bandi*, vol. 86.

vamente agl'Ecclesiastici da infligersi, ed imporsi ancora subito non con altro Processo, che con Testimoni sommariamente sentiti.

E perché alcuni si avanzano senza rispetto a disturbare sì le Persone, stanno al'Opera, sì ancora li Musici, che cantano, anche con far strepito, e rumore nel battere tanto colli piedi, quanto con le mani, e nella Platea, e nelli Palchetti eccedentemente, e fuori d'ordine, si proibisce a ciascuno di fare simile sorte di rumore, e strepito sotto pena di trè tratti di corda da darglisi anche subito in publico, e d'altre pene corporali anche gravi come sopra da imporsi con il solo Processo sommario, e colla facoltà ancora di procedere ex officio, e per inquisizione.

S'ordina in oltre, che nell'entrare debba ciascuno come sopra specificato ubbidire alla Maschera con andare nel luogo, che di mano in mano sarà trovato vacante, e doppo essersi accommodato non debba senza urgente necessità più moversi.

Non sia lecito a Donne Meretrici, e di mal'odore portarsi alli medesimi Teatri, sotto pena della Frusta, e chi le condurrà della Galera per cinque anni.

Di più vuole, ed ordina a tutti, e singoli Cocchieri di qualsivoglia sorte, e condizione, & ad ogn'altra persona, che guidi, e conduca Carozze, o Cocchi d'ogni sorte, che nel portarsi a' Teatri conduchi il suo Cocchio senza farlo correre, ed affrettar gl'altri, che fossero avanti, né tenti levare il suo luogo a nessuno, e si astenghi di far strepito, forza, violenza, rissa, o contrasto così di parole, come di fatti, ma debba guidare, & accostare il suo Cocchio al luogo destinato con quiete, ed in tempo opportuno, & abile, e subito smontate le persone, che conduce, debba, se non è impedito, ritirare il Cocchio in largo, e distante dal Teatro per non far confusione, e dare impedimento à gl'altri. E con l'istesso ordine, quiete, ed attenzione debba poi, finita l'Opera riaccostare il Cocchio, e prendere le Persone, che deve condurre, volendo Sua Signoria Illustrissima, che tutti i Cocchieri siano tenuti ad ubbidire esattamente agl'ordini, che verranno dati loro dagl'Offiziali, e Soldati, già incaricati d'invigilare al buon servizio della Nobiltà, che vorrà intervenire a' Teatri sudetti, sotto pena in ogni contravenzione alle sudette cose di tre tratti di corda in pubblico, ed a questo basterà l'assertiva di uno degl'Officiali sudetti, o vero la semplice relazione, ed esame de' Birri, nel caso però, che per colpa di ciascheduno di essi restasse offesa qualche Persona, debba soggiacere ad altre pene maggiori arbitrarie, oltre le pene contenute ne' Bandi Generali, e particolarmente emanati sopra simili materie.

All'osservanza del sudetto Editto vuole Sua Signoria Illustrissima, che sia ciascuno tenuto, benché Persona come sopra Ecclesiastica, ed esente, e che di procederà per inquisizione, & ex officio, e che il presente Editto affisso, che sarà al Palazzo del Governo, e nella Piazza di Campo di Fiore, e nelle Porte de' Teatri, obblighi ciascuno, come se le fosse stato personalmente intimato. Dato dal Palazzo della nostra Residenza questo dì 4. Gennaro 1749.

Cosimo Imperiali Governatore, e Vice-Camerlengo.

Bernardino Rossetti Notaro per la Carità.

[etc.]

In Roma 1749. Nella Stamparia della Reverenda Camera Apostolica

CHAPTER 5

Abandonments in a Theater State, Naples, 1764: Second Case Study

The year is 1764, Carnival in Naples at the royal palace. The opera *Didone abbandonata,* Virgil's tale of the virtuous queen abandoned on the shores of Carthage, text by Metastasio, music by Traetta. Outdoors the king will stage a series of utopian rituals of abundance, bestowing victuals on beggars to be plundered with carnivalesque abandon for a chorus of onlookers. Meanwhile, a state of acute famine, the worst in memory. Seemingly disconnected, these events conjoined a set of symbolic practices and social tensions that struck the heart of the Neapolitan monarchy in the age of enlightenment. The monarchy was choked with contradictions. The city, it claimed, was blessed with manna, yet the city had no bread. The king would put all right, but the king was still a boy. The governors were the king's men, but one of them ran the state.

This chapter asks how ideas about princely virtue changed their register when circumstances put them under extraordinary pressure. It follows conceptions of monarchy through encounters indoors at the opera and outdoors in spectacles for the masses. Following the departure of Carlo III, who became king of Spain in 1759, the kingdom was left with the hard-nosed Tuscan Bernardo Tanucci as prime minister and regent for Carlo's eight-year-old son, Ferdinando IV (1751–1825). The Great Famine of 1763–64 caused the regency's first major crisis, and it was not quickly allayed. Things got much worse over a long period of time before they got better, and when riots and looting broke out during Carnival, royalist politics were put in tension with the reformist agenda of the modernizing state. Yet Naples under the Spanish Bourbons remained to all appearances, as Clifford Geertz termed nineteenth-century Bali, the archetypal "theater state." It was capital of a kingdom that expressed itself in pageantry, court ceremonial, and pomp, that carefully staged its every drill and procession, its curtsies and hand waves, coach rides and cavalcades. Pageantry dramatized the kingship's ruling ideology of "social inequality and status pride," consolidating its power through an annual liturgy of elaborately articulated public spectacles. Indeed, spectacle not only theatricalized the king's *possession* of power, it was central to the means through which it was gained and maintained.[1]

This focal reality held true despite the fact that by 1734, when Carlo III's accession as king of Naples and the Two Sicilies displaced the Austrian Habsburg viceroys, old ideas of monarchy were forced to converge with new ideologies and political machines—machines of modern statecraft and ideologies of reform. Naples was home to vital enlightenment thinkers, French-influenced but also strikingly independent, who offered penetrating critiques of everything from bureaucratic, institutional, and administrative structures to systems of trade, civic life, economic reform, and political theory. Members of this intelligentsia, notably the famed economist Antonio Genovesi (1712–69) but many others too, agitated for reforms and succeeded in posing pragmatic challenges to some of the crustier tenets of Bourbon absolutism. Nevertheless, monarchical theatrics continued to dramatize myths of royal generosity in scenes staged in the opera house and on the square, encouraged by the general favor felt for the kingship among Neapolitans, including progressives. To be sure, there was resistance to Bourbon sovereignty among the feudal faction of the aristocracy, but city nobles joined enlightenment thinkers and others in viewing the Bourbons as liberators from the vassalage they had suffered from 1707 to 1734 in the yoke of Austrian oppressors, and before then, for two hundred and four years under a Spanish rule that gave them no king. The fact that their new king was foreign mattered little.[2] For Neapolitans, Bourbon kingship meant independence and a king to call their own, and it enabled the dynasty to win both popular and governmental cooperation in centralizing spectacles of power increasingly in and around the royal palace and the king's physical person. Even under Ferdinando, whose period of regency (1759–67) suffered a demonstrable weakening of absolutism, the king continued to have broad-based support, if only because he was Carlo's son, a monarch in whom "the Kingdom had not only its 'own king,'" as with Carlo, "but also a 'natural' king."[3]

1. "Court ceremonialism was the driving force of court politics; and mass ritual was not a device to shore up the state, but rather the state, even in its final gasp, was a device for the enactment of mass ritual" (Geertz, *Negara,* 13). See also Montroni, "The Court," 22–43, esp. 32–34.

2. Fundamental are Croce, *Storia del regno di Napoli;* translated as *History of the Kingdom of Naples,* esp. 168–70; Imbruglia, *Naples in the Eighteenth Century;* Venturi, "Il movimento riformatore degli illuministi napoletani," 198–224; *Settecento riformatore,* vols. 1 and 2; and with Giarrizzo and Torcellan, *Illuministi italiani,* vol. 2, *Riformatori napoletani* (originally published 1962).

3. Rao, "The Feudal Question," 106.

COMPOUNDS OF ROYALTY

The king's palace formed an extensive network of spaces that elaborated royal power. At the heart of the palace complex, overlooking the bay of Naples, stood the monumental edifice built by the Spanish in the early seventeenth century, which nestled the court in a compound of royal apartments, galleries, salons, banquet halls, atriums, meeting chambers, the court theater, and inner courtyards. From the main structure, additional spaces projected north and west of the bay into the city's reach to mediate between court and public, including gardens and parks, the late-medieval Castel Nuovo, the great city square then known as the Largo del Palazzo (later named the Piazza del Plebescito), and, affixed to the north side of the palace itself, the colossal Real Teatro di San Carlo (fig. 5.1).[4]

Added by Carlo to the architectural complex of the royal palace, the San Carlo opened in 1737 as the largest and most sumptuous theater in all of Europe.[5] Still standing relatively unchanged today, the stage of the theater measures an impressive 33 × 24 × 70 meters, and with its present seating arrangement holds some 2,400 persons.[6] As we saw in chapter 4, the theater throughout the eighteenth century remained unabashedly pledged to Bourbon glory and to the privileged classes, with an exclusive, and unusual, menu of opera seria used to articulate the annual lineup of Bourbon celebrations centering on dynastic birthdays and namedays.[7] Its suggestions of divine kingship were brash and concerted, not least in naming the theater for the temporal king by calling on the immortality of his eponymous saint.

Reinforcing the San Carlo's articulations of royal power were the most stellar singers to be had, a large orchestra of over fifty players, magnificent decorations, scenery, and spectacles, and the brilliant candlelight that flickered famously on

4. Touring Club Italiano, *Napoli e d'intorni,* 97–110.

5. Croce, *I teatri di Napoli,* remains essential. Originally published in installments of the *Archivio storico per le provincie napoletane* (1889–91), Croce's work appeared in a second revised edition, which he emended and made more readable, cutting some documents. The latter appeared in 1992, taking account of Croce's emendations from the third and fourth editions (1926 and 1947). Croce cites many archival sources since lost in the bombings of World War II. Key postwar studies of eighteenth-century Neapolitan opera include Robinson, *Naples and Neapolitan Opera;* Greco and Catone, *Il teatro del re;* Mancini et al., *Il Teatro di San Carlo;* Ajello et al., *Il Teatro di San Carlo;* and Degrada, "L'opera napoletana," 237–332.

6. Nowadays the 2,400 seats break down into approximately 600 in the parterre and 1,800 in boxes, but in the eighteenth century the totals could be even higher, since there was a variable number of places, both in the numbers of seats and the amount of standing space (see Mancini et al., *Il Teatro di San Carlo* 1:26).

7. The only other theater that staged opera seria exclusively during this time period was the Regio at Turin, on which see Bouquet, *Il teatro di corte,* 214–23; and Butler, *Operatic Reform.* Other theaters, for example, in Rome 1734–37, did so only temporarily (see chap. 4, n. 56 above).

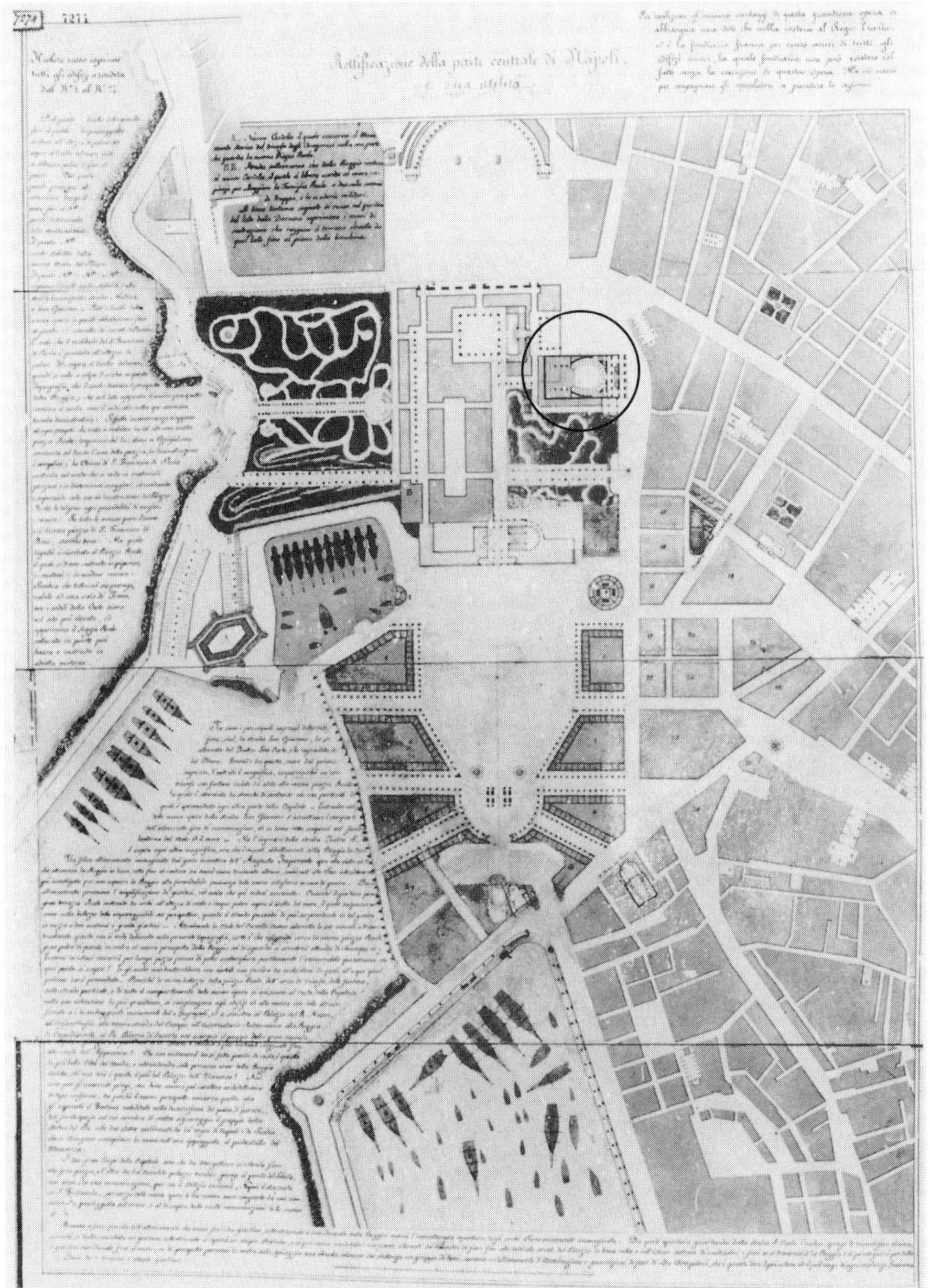

FIG. 5.1. Antonio Nicolini, project to reconstruct the surrounds of the royal palace at Naples, early nineteenth century. The Teatro San Carlo (circled) is shown embedded in the royal complex, jutting out from the palace. Museo di San Martino, Naples. Reproduced by permission.

court festivals before mirrors suspended from each box.[8] In the midst of these acoustic and visual signs, the king was given a decided spatial focus through the placement of his immense box. Towering two stories high in the second and third tiers, dead center opposite the stage, the king's box amassed his public around him like attendees at court. Particularly ingenious in this display was a system of moveable, gilded pieces, assembled from carved wood strung together with wire to form a trompe l'oeil of lushly draped glittering fringe. The fringe edged the royal box and extended to the uppermost perimeter of the theater in a kind of double choreographic frame, incorporating in a single, continuous symbolic system the different social ranks that comprised the king's body and that in turn his body encompassed. (Compare figures 1.1 and 5.2, and see a detail of the fringe to the side of the royal box in figure 5.3.) Thus, the raw symbolic machinery of absolutist spectacle was called on to articulate social hierarchies in a way that mimicked habitats and privileges outside the theater, especially in giving the illusion of being powered, and dwarfed, by the royal box. This was eighteenth-century opera in its paradigmatic royal form, the whole body politic symbolically gathered under a single roof and ubiquitous to the public eye. It was the essence of what Apostolidès has called in the France of Louis XIV "le roi machine."[9]

Not surprisingly, then, the San Carlo put heavy emphasis on Metastasio's tales of benign and divinely inspired kingship, tales the poet had first begun crafting while resident there in the 1720s and ones that remained dear to the city as the creations of a kind of native son.[10] Let us return to 1763–64, when the ideal of divine kingship was placed in relief early in the opera season with a staging of Metastasio's *L'olimpiade* as set by Pietro Guglielmi (1728–1804). The opera was mounted in the same autumn season that opened with Caterina Gabrielli singing music by Traetta, as she had done so stunningly at Parma in 1759. This time she sang Traetta and Gianambrogio Migliavacca's *Armida*—a prima donna vehicle that had seen success when it was created for her at Vienna's Burgtheater in January 1761 and opened in Naples on October 30, 1763. In 1763–64, Gabrielli sang exclusively at Naples.[11] Besides *Armida* and *L'olimpiade* (November 4, 1763), she sang in three additional operas by Metastasio: *Issipile* (December 26, 1763), *Didone abbandonata* (January 20, 1764), and *La Nitteti* (May 30, 1764). Among these *L'olimpiade* was, symbolically speaking, the monarchical centerpiece. Notwithstanding the terrible crisis of famine that had set in, it was jointly dedicated

8. Bergman, *Lighting in the Theatre*, 208–21, and chap. 4 above.

9. Apostolidès, *Le roi machine*.

10. See Fabbri, "Vita e funzione," including a list of Metastasian operas staged at the San Carlo in the eighteenth century (2:65–66); Galasso, "Metastasio e Napoli," liii–lxxvii; and Cotticelli and Maione, "Funzioni e prestigio del modello metastasiano a Napoli," 281–321.

11. Indeed, she sang nowhere else through Carnival 1767; see Croce, *I teatri di Napoli* (1992), 242–45, esp. 244. On the Naples performance of *Armida*, see *Il Teatro di San Carlo* (vol. 1, ed. Ajello et al.; vol. 2, ed. Roscioni, 38). On the original Viennese *Armida*, see Heartz, "Traetta in Vienna," and Dunlap, "Armida and Rinaldo."

to King Carlo (now of Spain) for his nameday and to his twelve-year-old son, already king of Naples and the Two Sicilies during the regency.[12]

Seen in this light, the story of *L'olimpiade* has particular poignancy. A young Cretan, Licida, turns out inadvertently to have wronged his best friend, Megacle, during the Olympic Games. Licida curses the gods, incurs the king's ire, and finds himself banished from the kingdom. When he goes mad and tries to commit regicide, he is caught, enchained, and sentenced to die. To this point the opera looks like a cautionary tale, but in Metastasio nothing is ever so simple. Set in motion in the opera's last scenes is a social transformation for which the royal heart proves an important medium. King Clistene charges the priest with slaying Licida on the altar with the sacred ax, but before the priest can do so the king realizes that the traitor is his long-lost son whom he believed he had disposed of after the Delphic oracle prophesied that the son would grow up to commit parricide. What triggers this realization and motivates the king's final act of redemption is not immediately transparent, but mystified and mystifying, even to the king himself. It expresses itself in sensate, irrational form, even though its real origin is the king's prescient nature. To express it, Metastasio gave Clistene an impassioned recitative followed by a text calculated to prompt a moving aria, "Alcandro lo confesso—Non so d'onde viene." The text is the same one set in February 1778 by Mozart for Aloysia Weber and by many others before and after—in the loose translation of Metastasio's contemporary John Hoole: "Whence can these tender passions rise? This warmth that thro' my bosom flies, This new, but pleasing pain? Sure pity never could impart Such strong emotions to the heart, That thrill thro' ev'ry vein."[13] Divinely inspired, the king's recognition enables him to grant rightful spouses to his son and to his son's friends, forcing Licida to marry the princess to whom he is betrothed but has been disloyal and allowing Megacle to marry the woman (Aristea) whom both friends have loved.

In this way quandaries of kinship are resolved, but not public accounts or the future of the crown. Duty still demands that the king slay the wayward son, and only through Megacle's persuasion is he convinced to let the public judge what the common good requires. The opera ends as King Clistene appeals to public judgment, answered by a chorus of devoted priests and subjects: "May the delinquent son live so that an innocent parent not be punished through him." As Elena Sala di Felice shows, *L'olimpiade* is an exception that proves the rule that the king always has the last say. In the end, Clistene presides but is deprived of his astral investiture, since it is only the dramatic expedient of the setting sun

12. The music for Guglielmi's *L'olimpiade* survives at P-La, and the libretto at I-Mc. An Avvertimento by the impresario Gaetano Grossatesta states, "Quel poco che vedrai cambiato in questo rispettabilissimo Dramma, si è composto dal Direttore di esso, per ordine ricevuto . . . ." Of the little written on Guglielmi's important opere serie, see DellDonna, "The Operas of Pietro Alessandro Guglielmi."

13. Metastasio, *The Works*.

FIG. 5.2. Royal box at the Teatro San Carlo, Naples. Photograph from the cover image of *Il Teatro di San Carlo, 1737–1987*, ed. Franco Mancini, Bruno Cagli, and Agostino Ziino (Naples: Electa Napoli, 1987), vol. 1. Reproduced by kind permission of the publisher.

that makes his royal mandate in Olympia expire, returns power to the hands of the people to whom he appeals, and thus allows a happy resolution.[14]

14. Sala di Felice, *Metastasio*, 163, quoting Clistene's speech, "Io son custode / Della ragion del trono" (3.6), in Metastasio, *Opere* 1:624. Sala Di Felice shows that Clistene makes legalistic discourses late in the game, like Metastasio's Artaserse—"Esecutor geloso / delle leggi io sarò . . . " (*Artaserse* 3.8; *Opere* 1:409) and Tito (*Clemenza di Tito* 3.7; *Opere* 1:742). They testify to what she deems a "garantista" conception of monarchical power—before which all subjects are equal in their remote distance—though one that might better be called "contractualist" in this instance since it is bilateral, as Sergio Durante has noted (personal communication, September 28, 2005).

FIG. 5.3. Teatro di San Carlo, Naples. Close-up of the system of gilded fringe that surrounds the royal box and upper perimeter of the theater. Photograph by Gabrielle Feldman. Reproduced by permission.

The result is a hesitant assertion of the happy alliance between royal power and public assent, whose combined powers are used to put aright the social order even as the libretto suggests predictably that royal prerogative is inalienable and social hierarchy inevitable.[15] Yet the ambivalent relationship advanced between kingship and society resonates disarmingly with real monarchical politics at Naples and their representations. Much as King Clistene embodies contradictions between clemency and severity, personal power and empowerment by a collective, so Neapolitan kingship—particularly in the period of the regency—embodied a tension between largesse and severity, even brutality, and moreover, between increasing state control and an ideological field that still asserted the king as the ultimate source of generosity and good.

THE SACK OF THE BEGGARS AND THE GIFT OF THE KING

All Neapolitan idioms of festivity were tensed within these contradictions, but in 1764 festive representations of kingship made pointed efforts to downplay them even as political events made them impossible to hide. During Neapolitan Carnival, when opera seria had its principal season, the fiction of sovereign generosity and abundance was traditionally elaborated in various outdoor rituals. The official Carnival season extended through four successive Sundays, on each of which the king would appear on his royal balcony to bestow food on the city's beggars, who gathered before him in the great piazza that faced the palace, the Largo del Palazzo (fig. 5.4). Fronting the palace, a vast architectural structure would be erected many stories high, decked with allegorical and mythological figures bearing food and gazing down upon livestock, fountains of wine, and rivers of milk. Both the architecture and the event were known as the *cuccagna*, after the fabled utopian land of leisure and plenty (*le pays de cockaigne* in French). Although the structure took months to produce, it was almost wholly ephemeral. On the first Sunday of Carnival, and by royal sanction, it was ritually sacked by the males of the beggar class, who stripped it of comestibles, leaving it much the worse for wear. The structure was patched of any injuries and the same exercise repeated on three subsequent Sundays leading up to the beginning of Lent.[16]

15. Joly, *Dagli elisi all'inferno*, 87–88, stresses the king's recourse to the public to synthesize the otherwise irreconcilable demands of personal feeling and obligations of state. See also Maeder, *Metastasio*.

16. Further examples appear in Mancini, *Feste ed apparati*. See Serao, *Il paese di cuccagna;* Mancini, "Le maschere e i carri di Carnevale," 51–62; Camporesi, "Carnevale, cuccagna e giuochi di villa," 57–97; Cocchiara, *Il paese di cuccagna*, 159–87; del Giudice, "Mountains of Cheese," 11–63, in *Imagined States* (a work richly illustrated with images and folklore and which del Giudice generously shared with me before publication); and the brilliant historical-literary account of Camporesi, *Il paese della fame*, chap. 3, in English as *The Land of Hunger*. An eighteenth-century description of Neapolitan Carnival appears in Goudar, *Relation historique*, 10–15.

FIG. 5.4. Royal balcony facing onto the Piazza del Plebescito, once called the Largo del Palazzo. Viewers looking toward the balcony from the piazza would see the western edge of the Teatro San Carlo to the left. Photograph by author.

Contrary to the utopian myth of spontaneous luxury it proposed (and far indeed from the inverted social order that Bakhtin dreamed of), the festival epitomized Umberto Eco's notion of "authorized transgression."[17] Indeed, the tradition was an invented one, originally transferred to Naples from village rites by the Spanish viceroys, who, starting in 1672, had arranged for chariots, triumphs, and floats owned by the guilds and corporations to process annually in quadrilles, grouped formations of guilds and tradesmen in their different dress and colors, along the via Toledo, the city's main drag. At that time *cuccagna* did not yet signify an object placed centrally in the palace Largo. Instead *cuccagne* were decorative structures that were carried by mobile Carnival vehicles (*carri*), which they perched magnificently, and precariously, atop.[18]

Already in the 1670s, the festival of the *cuccagna* was conceived at Naples in highly scopophilic terms. The original edict specified that it would consist of "eating by the plebeians *in view of* the competitors, knights, ladies, and his Excellency himself" (the last of whom ate in front of others at tables set up in corridors at the opera where they were served whole meals—thus redefining the relation of the consumer to power).[19] As these hybridized *carri-cuccagne* became more elaborate and thus heavier over time, they posed dangers to the crowd. Therefore they had all but ceased to be mobile by the time of Carlo III, being set up after 1746 within the palace Largo, which they would circle round gingerly rather than joining in the actual street processions. In a final act of Bourbon centralization, in 1759 the mobile *carri* were eliminated altogether, leaving only the vast stationary *cuccagne* to serve as elaborate allegorical fantasies. An engraving by Giuseppe Vasi of a design by scenographer Vincenzo Re (flourished at the San Carlo 1740–62) shows the beggars waiting to sack the *cuccagna* (fig. 5.5); another by Antonio Baldi on a design by Sanfelice Ferdinando shows them in the midst of a sack (fig. 5.6).[20]

The new form of the *cuccagna* complemented the Bourbon program of centralization in much the same way as the Teatro San Carlo, consolidating power around the king's residence. Indeed as already seen in chapter 4, the media of centralized spectacle were even produced by the same persons, scenographers whose workshops created stage sets as well as outdoor *apparati* for architectural ephemera.

Also increasingly centralized were methods of financing the *cuccagna* and rituals of exchange imposed upon it. In the seventeenth century, the *carri* (and later *carri-cuccagne* hybrids) had been administered by neighborhood administrations and guilds. Gradually the government-assigned deputy to the plebeians,

17. See Eco, "The Frames of Comic Freedom."

18. See, for example, the images in Mancini, "Le maschere e i carri."

19. Quoted from Scafoglio, *La maschera*, 11 (emphasis mine). On nobles eating at the San Carlo outside their boxes, see Mancini et al., *Il Teatro di San Carlo* 1:10.

20. My sincere thanks to Dottoressa Azzinari of the Archivio di Stato di Napoli for bringing the Vasi engraving to my attention and copying it for me.

the so-called Eletto del Popolo, made the guilds' participation in the festivals of the *cuccagna* mandatory on pain of paying exemption fees.[21] And by Bourbon times, the guilds were forced to split the expense of the vast stationary *cuccagne* with the king, even though they no longer had a part in their production. Other spontaneous festive forms also diminished around the same time, including carriages and foot traffic of the masked nobility, who now spent more time indoors, particularly in the theater.

Analogously, the processions that led up to the ritual sack had turned by Bourbon times into an elephantine relic of popular sovereignty, capped by a set of hardened rites that honored the king beneath his balcony. Entering the palace Largo on each of the four successive Sundays, the cavalcades and quadrilles would turn twice around the square before pausing under the royal balcony where the king awaited them. The consuls of the guilds and the Eletto del Popolo presented various broadsides to the king, poems of homage and declarations of loyalty printed on silk with elaborate borders of artificial flowers, paper copies of which were sold for cheap to members of the crowd. In response, the king might toss coins to the maskers. Next the head of the beggars would bear himself before the king and pronounce an address in his praise, followed by songs and dances done in the king's honor by maskers of the quadrilles. Finally, there were fireworks prepared by the masked processioners and acrobatics done with flags. It was only after this preliminary sequence of rites was over that the king signaled the royal guard to fire the shots that allowed the sack to start.

The ritual sequence that prepared the sack would thus seem to embody a particular but classic instance of Marcel Mauss's general theory of gift exchange.[22] The people made gifts to the king of their loyalty, obeisance, servility, and praise. These were not materialized, apart from a few festive forms and objects (broadsides, masks, *carri*, quadrilles, flags) so much as performed through a mélange of poems, songs, dances, and gestures. The king "reciprocated" in more material forms (money and victuals) and in far greater abundance than what he received, in keeping with his status as the idyllic source and epitome of abundance itself. The asymmetry was tangible evidence of the king's surfeit and his miraculous nature.

To be effective, such an exchange had to be eminently visible, open to scrutiny and affirmation. It was, and was part of, what Mauss would have called a "total social phenomenon," as well as a "system of total services," first in the sense that the exchange reproduced metaphorically the collective kinship structure presupposed by the Bourbon dynasty and state, and second in that it reproduced (if generally) the implications of the kingdom's highly stratified economy. The king appeared as father of all, the nobles as "sons" and "daughters" of the royal household, the civilian classes (artisans, professionals, merchants, and

21. See Calabria, *The Cost of Empire*.

22. Mauss, *The Gift*.

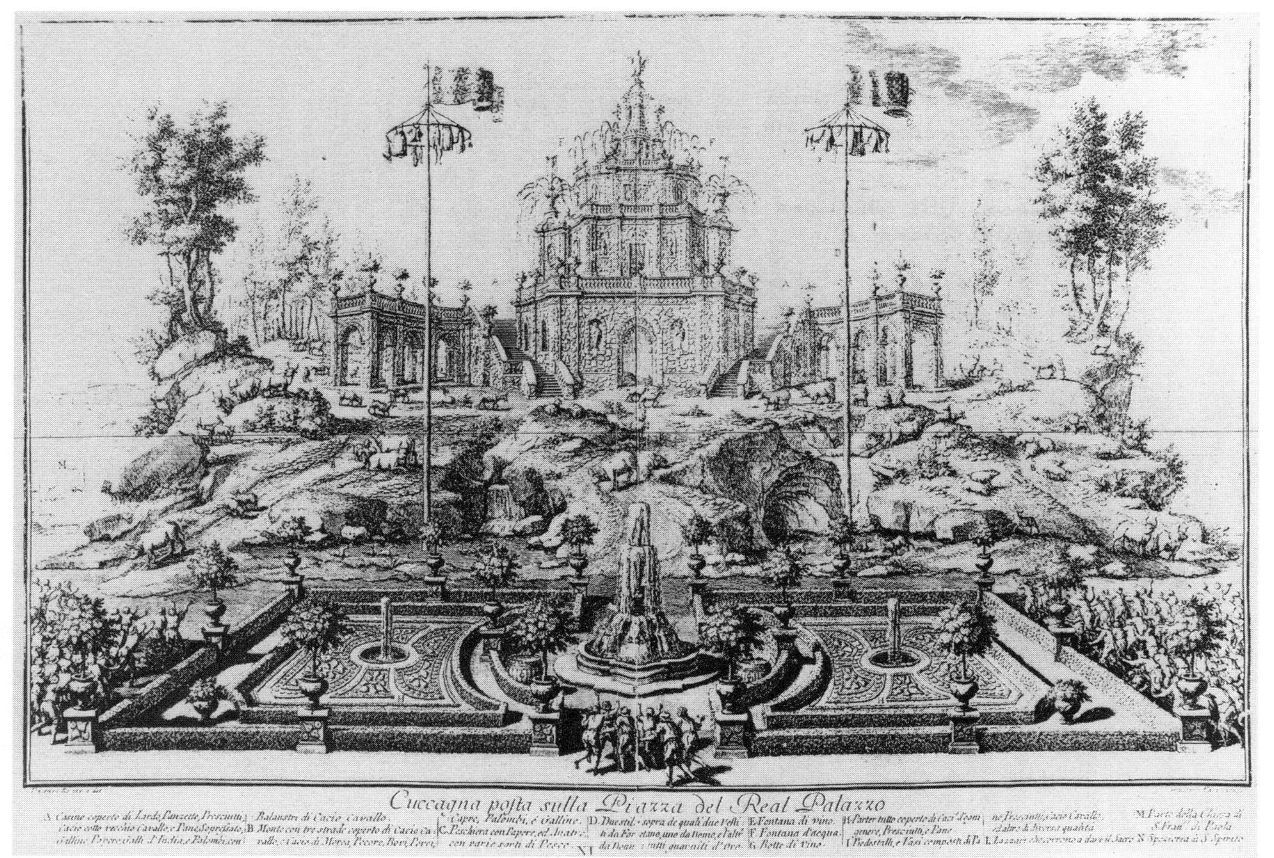

FIG. 5.5. "Cuccagna posta sulla piazza del Real Palazzo." Beggars waiting to sack the *cuccagna* designed by the scenographer Vincenzo Re. Engraving by Giuseppe Vasi, before 1762. The legend at the bottom reads: "A. House covered with bacon fat, pancetta, and prosciutto, aged cacio cavallo [a cheese], bread, and sorpresatto [a kind of sausage], hens, geese, Indian hens, and ring-doves, with balustrades of cacio cavallo. B. Mountain with three streets covered with cacio cavallo and cacio di morca, sheep, oxen, pigs, goats, ring-doves, and hens. C. Fish pond with geese and ducks, and various sorts of fish. D. two poles from which are suspended two foreign costumes (one man's, one woman's), all covered with gold. E. Fountain of wine. F. Fountain of water. G. Cask of wine. H. Terrace level completely covered with cheeses of every kind, prosciutto, and bread. I. Pedestals and vases made of bread, prosciutto, cacio cavallo, and other kinds of foodstuffs. L. Beggars who run to make the sack. M. Part of the Church of San Francesco di Paola. N. Apothecary di Santo Spirito." Archivio di Stato, Naples, Archivio Borbone, vol. 2514, tavola 11. Reproduced by permission.

FIG. 5.6. Beggars sacking the *cuccagna* designed by Sanfelice Ferdinando. Engraving by Antonio Baldi, ca. 1740. Società Napoletana per la Storia Patria, Naples. Reproduced by permission.

scholars) as figurative servants of the central dynastic house, and the beggars as its figurative slaves. Such at least were the general correlations to be drawn.[23]

But the exchange also diverged from the classic Maussian gift in that the fiction that the gifts given and received were voluntary ones was barely maintained, if at all, even as an appearance. The point is not simply that the exchange was not voluntary, which is obvious and axiomatic in a Maussian exchange model of any sort, but that they relinquished (or ignored) a principle basic to a standard strategy of exchange: that of making exchange *appear* voluntary. Nor, as we will see, was there much attempt to make the dream of bounteous distribution real, and thus encumber the recipients with real debt as a result of the gifts.[24]

In this way the Bourbon *cuccagna,* by contrast with its original medieval and rural forms, was not a utopian dream, but as the anthropologist Domenico Scafoglio has insisted, a festival of limits. To understand this point, we need to look at the reception of the king's gifts by his poorest subjects in the sack generally and specifically in 1764, something that has received a penetrating reading by Scafoglio and a rich if somewhat more schematic one by Laura Barletta, among others.[25] Scafoglio has noted that by contrast with its Bourbon form, the *cuccagna* in medieval myth and festival was a variant of the Golden Age, the utopian dream of a totally egalitarian land of plenty and leisure for all. In this sense it was both materialist and sensualist, the folklorish underbelly of intellectualist utopias (and a somewhat blasphemous takeoff on Christian paradise). Over time this totalizing character diminished, so that by the sixteenth century the *cuccagna* was reduced to a simple dream of food. Yet it was food aplenty, not food for few.[26] By contrast, the Bourbon *cuccagna* retained only the illusion of boundless abundance. An elaborate array of mythological personifications (Saturn, Ceres, or Virtue, as Nature transcendent) would be encrusted onto an architectural fantasy (a *paradiso* of papier-mâché in 1764, for instance, or temples and pyramids in other years) in order to encourage identifications of the Bourbon reign with the Golden Age, filtered through a classical cover that could render the idioms of the populace in the language of gentlemen.[27] At the same time, severe class stratifications were put on display as a curious middle class ogled the beggars from the edge of the great piazza while the nobility kept court

23. The elision of beggars and slaves may seem extreme, yet the only other group who could legally join in the sack were male slaves of the royal household.

24. I suggest below, however, that economic and political pressures on the Bourbons to modernize precluded the Geertzian possibility that ceremonious displays of generosity were simply ends in themselves. Compare Geertz's claim that for the kings of Negara "power served pomp, not pomp power" (*Negara,* 13), but also the persuasive counterclaims of Wiener, *Visible and Invisible Realms.*

25. Scafoglio, *La maschera,* and Barletta, *Il carnevale del 1764,* chaps. 2–5. See too Allocati, "La panificazione a Napoli," and Venturi, "1764," 394–472.

26. Beautifully demonstrated in Camporesi, *Il paese della fame,* chap. 3.

27. On the 1764 cuccagna, see Scafoglio, *La maschera,* 65, quoting Florio. No exact details of this cuccagna survive, since the various chroniclers, gazetteers, and travelers reporting on it arrived too late to see it (ibid., 65–66). On the king as Saturn, see Barletta, *Il carnevale del 1764,* 3.

along the balconies of the royal palace. By means of this social choreography the event paralleled the hierarchical class relations and paradoxical assertions of abundance found in the opera house. Nor was the real lack of sufficient victuals mere happenstance. It was essential to the entire festivity, because it allowed the lowest order of persons to be watched in a competitive spectacle of scratching and clawing, antagonized by the lack of enough to feed all the beggars who carried out the sack (estimated upward of 12,000 to as many as 20,000, counting only the men of the beggar class, whose women and children thronged the sidelines).[28]

Moreover, in order to reach the fabled land, participants had to make their way perilously through rivers and moats. Reportedly there were some who held to low ground and dove after livestock, and others who managed to reach the main structure. Only the most athletic attempted to climb tall tree trunks or poles (see fig. 5.5), which often bore victuals in greatest numbers. Scafoglio stresses that with the contestants wet and crowded, and food draped at high vertical reaches, the sack became a dangerous exhibition of pratfalls, tumbles, and slips performed at great speed, and the *cuccagna* itself a backdrop to urgent consumption.[29] The event was thus fundamentally agonistic—not just a sequence of assault, struggle, sack, and slaughter but a grotesque mimesis of old-styled carnivalesque gorging and intemperance. And that agonistic dimension in turn highlighted the success of the organizers in appearing to extend wealth to the base and unruly with well-managed results.

DIDONE ABBANDONATA: AGONISM AND EXCHANGE

Two aspects of opera seria performances at Naples had striking counterparts in the agonism of the sack. For one, the San Carlo was as noisy and disorderly

28. Although the quantity of comestibles and livestock distributed on the four Sundays of Carnival sounds high, even during the famine of 1764 (when it included 1,157 rolls of meat, 194 ducklings, 261 doves, 20 pigs, 14 lambs, etc.), the quality was evidently poor and the numbers of beggars participating much too great to be accommodated (see Barletta, *Il carnevale del 1764*, 33).

29. See Scafoglio, *La maschera*, 228, and the contemporaneous Saint Non and Chamfort, *Voyage pittoresque* 1.1:250. The Marquis de Sade claimed it took eight minutes to "destroy" it (*Voyage d'Italie*, 441). In 1766, the abbé Richard elided the *cuccagna* as a "species of costumed theater" with the proximity of the opera house and stressed the great number of cavalry installed to control the populace: "On appelle cocagne une espèce de théâtre dressé dans cette place, vis-à-vis du grand balcon du vieux palais, garni du haut en bas, de pains, jambons, cervelats, saucissons, boeuf, lard, & autres viandes sallées. Il y a quelques spectacles relatifs à cette fête pendant lesquels le peuple s'assemble; quand ils sont finis, au signal que le Roi donne, on abandonne au peuple le pillage de la cocagne. Pour éviter autant qu'il est possible le désordre inséparable de ces fêtes tumultueuses, il y a des détachemens considérables de cavalerie & d'infanterie postés dans la place même pour contenir le peuple. C'est dans cette place qu'est la porte principale du grand théâtre, qui n'a rien de plus remarquable que son étendue qui est proportionnée à la nombreuse population de la ville, & sur-tout à la grande quantité de noblesse qui l'habite" (*Description historique* 4:111–12).

as any comparable theater in Italy (even those in Rome), marked by conflicts both among publics in the hall and between publics and singers. Infamous cases involved the celebrated Caffarelli, whose antics put him under house arrest in 1741 despite his immense popularity with the public, and the high-strung Gabrielli, who was notorious for her whims and outbursts.[30] For another, the San Carlo staged more than its share of astonishing battle scenes. In 1774, the demimondaine and tireless operagoer Sara Goudar, in her long description of Neapolitan Carnival, directly elided battle scenes staged for highbrows at the opera with a belligerent heroism among the beggars at the sack:

> [T]here is something better at this opera house than singing or dancing. They fight as if in a war. Corps of troupes arrange themselves in pitched battles; a siege is seen carried out by the book . . . but with real soldiers practiced in military arts. All the combatants are superb and suit the grandeur of the rest of the spectacle.[31]

Where staged battles gave elites spectacles for gawking visual consumption, highly mediated with respect to life outside the theater, sacks of the *cuccagna* involved beggars in real-life struggles that in turn offered spectacle to the upper classes. Yet Goudar, from her spectatorial position, explained the sack and its aftermath essentially as symbolic action.

> Since the Beggars have their heroes too, they fix their imaginations on certain [allegorical] figures, representing peace or war, of which to take possession. At the moment of the sack the most ambitious leave the bread and geese to race straight to glory: they fly toward the flagpole and try to take possession of it; they raise it as a trophy in their houses.[32]

30. On the misbehavior of Caffarelli and others, see Heartz, "Caffarelli's Caprices"; Croce, *Aneddoti e profili settecenteschi,* 45–50; and chap. 4 above, n. 95. Croce also describes Gabrielli's audacious behavior and some of the conflicts it caused in the 1763–64 season (*I teatri di Napoli,* ed. Galasso, 242–45).

31. "[I]l y a quelque cose [sic] de mieux dans cet Opéra, que des chants & des danses. On s'y bat comme à la guerre. Des Corps de troupes y donnent des bataille rangées: on y voit un Siège fait dans le régles; . . . mais de véritables Soldats exercés dans l'art Militaire. Touts les Combattans sont superbes & repondent à la grandeur du reste du spectacle" (Goudar, *Relation historique,* 10).

32. "Comme les Lazarons ont aussi leurs héros, ceux-ci ont fixé leur imagination sur les figures, qui selon les dessein du Tableau, représentent la paix ou la guerre pour s'en saisir. Au moment du pillage le plus ambitieux laisse le pain & les oyes pour courir droit à la gloire; il vole vers l'Etendart, & cherche à s'en emparer; c'est un trophée qu'il élève dans sa maison" (ibid., 18). Many libretti show that real fencing masters were hired to carry out these onstage battles, as seen in Grosley's description: "Le spectacle est varié par des marches, des batailles, des triomphes: le tout exécuté en grand & dans le plus grand. Les batailles se donnent entre de nombreuses troupes de Maîtres d'Escrime, qui distingués par de riches uniformes, ont l'air de se batter réellement, le cliquetis de leurs armes se mêlent en mesure au jeu de l'Orchestre: ces batailles sont mêlées de Cavalerie montée sur des chevaux des écuries du Roi & des premiers Seigneurs de Naples. Dans les triomphes, le char est traîné par les plus beaux chevaux du Roi, caparaçonnés aux frais des Entrepreneur" (*Nouveaux mémoires* 2:94; *New Observations* 2:232).

The French traveler Jean Claude Richard de Saint Non seconded Goudar's account by reporting in his *Voyage pittoresque* of 1781–86 that the most triumphant sackers would be carried aloft by their companions, with heroes sometimes retaining their status within local neighborhood social groups through most of the year.[33] If these accounts can be believed, then the costumes atop the poles in figure 5.5 served as victory garb for whichever beggars succeeded in capturing them, and the agonism of competition, engineered to confer or deny prestige, must have loomed large over popular Neapolitan festivities. Viewed as such, hierarchies were not just reinforced and reinstated top to bottom but urged on by rivalries within ranks. What bound them all together was a common message: that there were many who needed care, and that the care of many was ultimately assured by the greatness of one. The idea was patently rhetorical, of course, since it was the more powerful members of each class and especially the most powerful classes who actually benefited most from exchange with the king.

* * *

Some details about the famine and its historical background are instructive here, since Bourbon festivity converged with political tensions that were heightening during the regency and spiked when famine first struck. The effect of that convergence was to reanimate a centuries-long history of Neapolitan conflict between the nobles and the ruler dating back to times when barons still held fully autonomous fiefs—a history that had been pacified when Carlo III ascended the throne and was reantagonized in 1759. With Carlo's boy child as heir and the tough-minded Tanucci as regent and prime minister, relations between the state and the nobility worsened, the more so with the onset of crisis. Important here is that eighteenth-century Naples was already plagued by a split political consciousness—as kingdom, city-state, and nation-state—so it was inevitable that in a state of crisis the regency would find itself splintered and sluggish in its response.[34] Tanucci's politics combined royalist fervor with a reformist policy of free trade, designed to encourage production. Both proved impediments to easing famine,[35] which was largely met with the government's mystified claims of abundance, accompanied by refusals to fix prices against extortionists, prohibit export, or find grain from other sources. By contrast with the noble Eletti, who saw their role in terms of an older ideology of noblesse oblige that caused them to advocate for civic interests by opposing export and price-fixing,[36] Tanucci wanted at all costs to unshoe positions that ran counter to his reformist

33. Saint Non, *Voyage pittoresque* 1.1.250.

34. Venturi, "1764," 395.

35. See Villani, "Una battaglia politica," 611–66.

36. On the splintering at the time between nobles, nation-state, and city-state in Naples, see Venturi, "1764," 395.

ideals. His populism was utterly wedded to principles of absolute monarchy, of which he was chief protector, but both populism and royalism worked against traditional privileges and abuses by barons and other nobles.[37]

Famine had already set in by June 1763 when calamitous rains ruined crops, making vegetables scarce and grapes unusable, and creating desperate shortages of grain for humans and livestock. Initially there was little pursuit of material remedies. As the Venetian ambassador wrote home, "[T]he countryside and particularly certain provinces [have] . . . suffered very grave troubles as a result of rains and hail that fell, desolating the poor inhabitants, [so] the court has ordered that public prayers be said for nine continuous days [a novena] during which theaters and all other public spectacle will be suspended."[38] By July and August, the agitated urban populace was crying out against specific names in the Council of the Regency, accusing them of sending grain out of the kingdom. When the king appeared for his devotions at the church of Santa Maria del Carmine on August 9, a group of women shrieked that people were dying of hunger and demanded that he restore abundance and hang the Eletto del Popolo.[39]

In later August the city did start to purchase grain from ovens managed by the Eletti at the same time as it made avowals to its detractors about the advantages of free commerce, in accordance with the reformist line. Some antiexport measures were taken, but they were modest. Most tellingly, the government made no direct admission that there was true famine until late October and November, and even went on claiming that it could face famine reasonably well as it had in 1759 when Tanucci had gotten grain from Puglia. Historians have argued that the famine was in this sense met with a juridical, moralizing mentality, one that failed to stop prices from rising or make provisioning any easier, though it did prompt the Council of the Regency to use coercive measures of intervention. On October 31, Tanucci issued an edict prohibiting extortionist prices, and since he expected some quarters to ignore it, he also started having grain confiscated. This prompted elected city nobles to hire a lawyer against him—a poor match, it seems, for someone so powerful who was managing the state through continual correspondence with Carlo in Spain. In mid-December, Tanucci took the urgent decision to fight avaricious hoarders who were jacking up prices by sending a commissioner, Pallante, into the provinces to root out the grain he believed they were hiding and stabilize prices.[40]

37. Villani, "Una battaglia politica," 616–17, and Venturi, "1764," 397 and 404. Tanucci's role in monitoring these developments locally and developing strategies with the king in Spain can be traced in his correspondence in I-Na, Archivio Borbone, 1:18. See Tanucci, *Epistolario*, vol. 12; Ferrari, *1763–1764, Bernardo Tanucci;* and Mincuzzi, *Lettere di Bernardo Tanucci.*

38. Quoted in Villani, "Una battaglia politica," 616–17.

39. Venturi, "1764," 401 n. 29. This occurred at the spot where the popular revolt of Masaniello had taken place a century earlier.

40. On the October edict, see Vinciguerra, "La reggenza borbonica," 81, and de Renzi, *Napoli nell'anno 1764*, 139–40; on the nobles' attorney, see Scafoglio, *La maschera*, 57ff.; and on the Pallante commission, Tanucci, *Epistolario* 12.2:691–96 (December 20, 1763).

Though Pallante had been a councilor of the royal agency, he was a mere functionary and instrument of the government.[41] His real job was to vindicate the state by confuting with facts the "highly prejudicial, artificial famine spread throughout the realm of there not being sufficient grain for the sustenance of the populace and for agriculture" and to correct with all necessary "rigor" the "wickedness" that was responsible for creating a state of famine. Tanucci's reports to Carlo about Pallante's work testify to the powers of mystification that royalist politics exploited but to which they were also prey. In keeping with symbolic messages expressed in the opera house and elsewhere, Tanucci continually claimed a state of abundance and liberality in the kingdom and characterized famine as a consequence of negative forces that needed to be purged from the realm.[42] Only in January 1764, when thousands upon thousands of country people poured into the city in search of bread, did he finally acknowledge a crisis.

* * *

Hence the crisis rehearsed tensions between the emerging state apparatus and royal absolutism itself,[43] tensions that were encompassed and condensed in the king's opera house with its compound of commercial, royal, and state management, its mixed audience, and its multiple symbolic orders. Even as the San Carlo dramatized royal magnanimity, like other royal settecento theaters, its organization and administration epitomized the convergence of disparate interests,[44] with private enterprise running head to head with both royal initiative and control and aristocratic interests. The initial underwriting of the theater, for example, was split: one third of its financing came from the king and two-thirds from the sale of boxes to nobility in the first four tiers. In March 1737, the king entrusted general control over all theaters to a governmental appointee whose activities were subject to royal approval (the Uditore dell'Esercito), and in an elaborate contractual agreement with the court he engaged Angelo Carasale as impresario. Carasale thus became contractor of singers, dancers, and numerous other personnel whom he supervised and whose interests and demands he mediated with those of the court and nobility. He was also charged with collecting annual levies from boxholders and managing finances in other ways, but *not* with making delicate decisions about special privileges, such as who should re-

41. Venturi, "1764," 402, who notes that he was not a magistrate.

42. Barletta, *Il carnevale del 1764*, 9 and passim. Scafoglio points out that this action of sending a government functionary from the capital to root out trouble was (paradoxically) modeled on tradition-bound measures taken against bandits (*La maschera*, 60–61).

43. See Barletta, *Il carnevale del 1764*, 37.

44. For a general account of these conditions in Italian theaters, with emphasis on the late eighteenth and nineteenth centuries, see Rosselli, *The Opera Industry;* for specifics on the mid-eighteenth century, see Piperno, "Opera Production to 1780" (in addition to the literature cited in n. 5 above). On the San Carlo specifically, see esp. Mancini, "La storia, le vicende amministrativi," 9–24.

ceive the preferred boxes nearest to the king's. The court pointedly maintained its pragmatic and symbolic powers by retaining fifteen boxes along the second tier for the king's guests. For a time, after Carasale's mysterious imprisonment and death in 1741, the court assumed a larger share in the theater's administration, but in 1747 management was again given to a private person, a notary named Diego Tuffarelli engaged to manage the theater's capital at substantial risk with only a minor subsidy (3,200 ducats) from the royal government.

This contrast between new forms of commerce and capital and old forms of patronage intensified during the regency. In 1759, the then impresario, a dancer named Gaetano Grossatesta, consented to stay on for four additional years without any subsidy but merely the promise of a royal "gift" whenever the show were to please his majesty. To avoid the risk of sudden bankruptcy, he immediately struck out clauses in performers' contracts that furnished them with new costumes, which meant they either had to wear old costumes from the theater wardrobe or use their own. This was far from following the latest standards of operatic reform, but it was well in line with Tanucci's belt-tightening economic reformism. The impresario who took over in 1763, the castrato Giovanni Tedeschi (called "L'Amadori"), encountered even worse financial conditions with equal responsibilities for keeping the books in the black. Paradoxically, though, the impresario's powers if anything were lessened during the same time, since Carlo had established a committee in January 1760, the Giunta dei Teatri, to tighten controls. Now it was the Giunta that selected singers and dancers—sometimes at huge fees that caused great hardship to the impresario—and the Giunta that also reviewed the theatrical calendar.[45]

* * *

With these tensions in mind, let us reenter the opera house in 1764, where on January 20, the third opera of the San Carlo Carnival season, *Didone abbando-*

45. The edict is preserved in Gatta, *Reali dispacci* 2:14–15, "Della Giunta de' Teatri. I. Il Re fa una Giunta per li Teatri. Considerando il Re che non sia di poca importanza il ben condurre la economia del Regal Teatro di *San* Carlo, e regolarne a dovere il sistema; e volendo che non solo sieno maneggiati gli affari con quella esattezza e proprietà, che richiede il regal servizio, ma si promuova ancora con particolar cura tutto ciò, che possa influire al maggior decoro e alla magnificenza maggiore del pubblico spettacolo, ha risoluto che si tratti e proponga avanti di me da *Vostra Signoria* Illustrissima, dallo Uditore dello Esercito, e da *Don* Bernardo Buono, tutto ciò, che sia più proprio ed espediente, così toccante allo affitto, che si stimerà convenire, come allo scegliere e fermare Cantanti, e Ballerini, e generalmente tutto ciò, che riguarda la economia, regolamento, e direzione del Teatro; rimanendo a me il carico d'informare la Maestà Sua di quel, che si stimerà conveniente, per attendere le sovrane risoluzioni. A qual effetto nella Regal Segreteria di Stato si unirà *Vostra Signoria* Illustrissima, lo Uditore dello Esercito, e *Don* Bernardo Buono, qualunque volta lo richiederà la urgenza de gli affari, per trattarsi gli affitti, per farsi le accensioni di candele, e tutto in somma quel, che occorrerà per la economia del Teatro. Ben inteso che, per quel, che tocca ad affari di giustizia, nulla s'intenda alterato dal sistema finora osservato. Di regal ordine lo prevengo a *Vostra Signoria* Illustrissima, perche eseguisca la sovrana risoluzione nella parte, che se spetta. Palazzo, 18. di Gennaro, del 1760. Bernardo Tanucci."

LA DIDONE
ABBANDONATA
DRAMMA PER MUSICA
Da rappreſentarſi nel Real Teatro di S. Carlo
nel dì 20. Gennajo 1764.
Per ſolennizzarſi il giorno natalizio
DELLA CATTOLICA MAESTA'
DI
CARLO III.
AUGUSTO MON[...]
SPAGN[...]
ED ALLA
DI
FERDINANDO IV.
NOSTRO AMABILISSIMO SOVRANO
DEDICATO.
IN NAPOLI MDCCLXIV.
PER VINCENZO FLAUTO
Impreſſore di Sua Maeſtà.

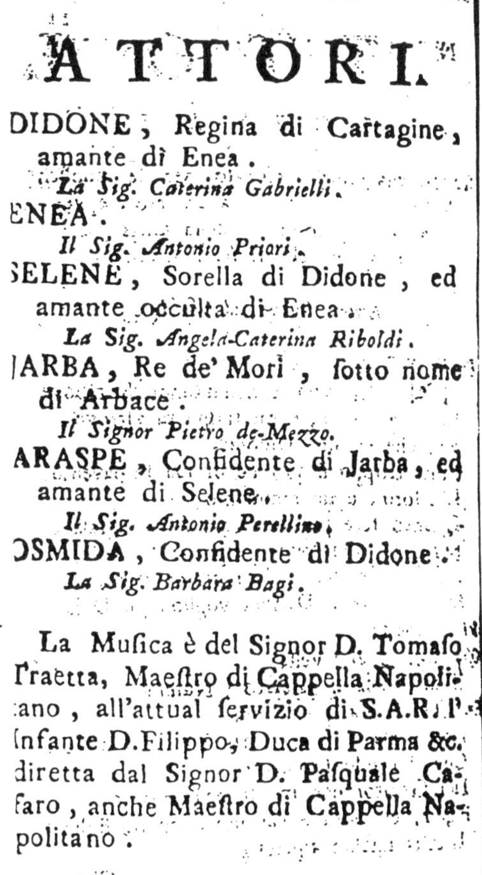

ATTORI.
DIDONE, Regina di Cartagine, amante di Enea.
La Sig. Caterina Gabrielli.
ENEA.
Il Sig. Antonio Priori.
SELENE, Sorella di Didone, ed amante occulta di Enea.
La Sig. Angela-Caterina Riboldi.
JARBA, Re de' Mori, ſotto nome di Arbace.
Il Signor Pietro de-Mezzo.
ARASPE, Confidente di Jarba, ed amante di Selene.
Il Sig. Antonio Perellino.
OSMIDA, Confidente di Didone.
La Sig. Barbara Bagi.

La Muſica è del Signor D. Tomaſo Traetta, Maeſtro di Cappella Napolitano, all'attual ſervizio di S.A.R. l'Infante D.Filippo, Duca di Parma &c. diretta dal Signor D. Paſquale Caſaro, anche Maeſtro di Cappella Napolitano.

ATTO

FIG. 5.7. Unique copy of title page and dramatis personae from the libretto of Metastasio's *Didone abbandonata* as set by Traetta for the Teatro San Carlo, Naples 1764. By permission of the Music Division, the New York Public Library for the Performing Arts, Astor, Lenox, and Tilden Foundations.

nata, was premiered. It was a gala night, celebrated with brilliant candlelight throughout the theater and the addition of a three-voice cantata because, as the title page of the libretto announced, the date marked the birthday of Carlo III in the annual liturgy of theatrical events (fig. 5.7).[46] The prima donna Gabrielli was at that time undisputedly the most coveted diva of the day, and the opera reportedly a "great success," "praised by all."[47] Anton Raaff (1714–97), the fa-

46. The *Cantata a tre voci per festeggiare nel Real Teatro di San Carlo il felicissimo giorno natalizio di sua maestà* (Naples, 1764) had Gabrielli as Tetide (Thetis, wife of Titan, lord of the river Ocean, and herself a Titan), Caffarelli as Paleo, and del Mezzo as Orfeo, with music by the Neapolitan Pasquale Cafaro.

47. *Diario ordinario (Chracas)*, no. 7278, February 25, 1764: "Napoli 7. Febraro. Fu posta in scena in questo Reale Teatro il Dramma intitolato *la Didone abbandonata,* e Domenica sera essendovi intervenuto il nostro Sovrano a goderla, che riuscì di universale approvazione al gran concorso." On

mous tenor, had written Padre Martini the year before giving his own reasons: "Gabrielli is a huge hit and the Neapolitans are fanatical about her. I had never seen her like this before—she knows how to sing. She has enormous ability . . . but sang like a beast, always out of tempo, either rushing or slowing down."[48] For a singer of Raaff's generation, at that time forty-nine years old as against her thirty-two, Gabrielli's performance style was over the top. She was spectacle incarnate—exactly what Naples loved, as proved by the unabated succession of spectacles that went on even in the winter of 1764, when in addition to opera, the public was "impatiently" awaiting wedding celebrations at the theater for the king's sister's marriage to Peter Leopold, archduke of Austria, including three public balls.[49] The French abbé Coyer, meanwhile, scurrying between his hotel and the theater all through Carnival 1764, described extravagances at least as grand as usual: "[O]n one side [of the stage] one could see Aeneas with the Trojan fleet and on the other [the Moorish king] Jarba with his Africans and elephants. . . . [T]he famous Gabrielli . . . plays the role of Dido; pious Aeneas would have to have quite a lot of devotion to resist the charms of her voice and figure!" Famine, Coyer quipped wryly, "does not diminish the fury of spectacles a bit, because the bons vivants are not yet hungry."[50]

Of course there were strategic motivations for continuing with festivities, since they helped maintain appearances of business-as-usual even as threats to public disorder were mounting precipitously. Confirmation of this comes from the royal architect Luigi Vanvitelli (1700–1773), who spent night after night at the opera. On the Saturday before the first *cuccagna* was to take place, February 11, he wrote his brother that the people were going mad from lack of bread. "Famine worsens. In the provinces they are dying of hunger and run to Naples

Gabrielli's performances at the San Carlo, Peter Beckford wrote: "It was here, in the year 1766, I first saw GABRIELLI, who possessed qualities for the Stage that have never been equalled since. Her action was as interesting as her voice was charming, and both were perfect. Though not a first rate beauty, she was handsome enough; and was amiable and seducing beyond most of her sex" (*Familiar Letters* 2:382–83). In a letter to Padre Martini, Domenico Vittozzi gave her an enthusiastic mention for her part in the opera at Naples later that spring (I-Bc, I.23.49, Naples, May 28, 1764 = Schoebelen, *Padre Martini's Letters,* no. 5625). On Gabrielli, cf. chap. 3 above.

48. "Qui la Gabrielli fa fracasso, li Napoletani ne sono fanatici, io non l'avevo mai si veduta, si intende cantare . . . ha una grande abilità . . . cantò come una bestia, sempre fuor di tempo, ora stringendo, ora allargando" (Anton Raaff to Padre Martini, July 11 (12?), 1763, I-Bc, I.4.97 = Schnoebelen, *Padre Martini's Letters,* no. 4246).

49. *Diario ordinario* (*Chracas*), no. 7275, February 18, 1764, 12: "Napoli 31. Gennaro. Con grandissima impazienza si attendono da questo Pubblico le magnifiche feste, che dovranno farsi nella fine del presente Carnevale per le felicissime nozze della Reale Infanta Sorella del nostro Sovrano coll'Arciduca Pietro Leopoldo di Austria, attesi li reali preparativi, che si osservano per questo Reale Teatro, dove vogliano, che seguiranno 3. publiche feste di ballo."

50. "[O]n y voit, d'un côté, Énée aves Les Troyens et sa flotte; et de l'autre, Jarbe avec ses Africains et ses éléphants. C'est la fameuse *Cabrielli,* qui fait le rôle de Didon; il faut que le pieux Énée ait bien de la dévotion pour résister aux charmes de sa voix et de sa figure!" (letter 30, February 11, 1764, Coyer, *Voyage d'Italie* 1:422–43). "On laisse le peuple s'arracher la farine & le pain; cela ne diminue rien de la fureur des spectacles; parce que la bonne compagnie n'a pas encore faim" (ibid., 421).

to find grain that isn't there. May God preserve us from some great trouble!"[51] By that same evening, trouble was already upon them. The next day he continued: "Yesterday evening . . . at [two and a half hours past sundown] the beggars sacked the *cuccagna*, which was supposed to be sacked today [Sunday] at about 2 p.m. Afterward they began to loot some stores on the via Toledo, from there carrying platforms and wood from the *cuccagna*, which is very large and costly."[52] Some grain was expected from the islands, he added, but not enough, nor could it be milled and made into bread soon enough for all who were coming to get it in order to avoid dying of hunger. By now the city had swelled by some 50,000 people.

* * *

Coyer and Vanvitelli were typical of other upper-class chroniclers, including various foreign ambassadors, who were spending the evening at the San Carlo when sacking and looting broke out. For them the opera house proved a filter for the crisis, since opera reproduced the insuperable nature of kingship, metaphorically and narratively, and allegorized the king's largesse. That night Coyer restaged the scene of rioting—"It is 9 p.m. in the evening; two more lines . . . but what do I hear? . . . an extraordinary noise in the streets, the shops . . ."—then commented the following Sunday on the surprising "ordre dans le désordre."[53] Vanvitelli for one did not hide his contempt for popular defiance that questioned royal perfection: "The great abundance in which people are used to living in the kingdom leads to commotion and a penchant for thieving, to which the *popolo* are most inclined, since [from lack of] bread they have sacked everything else."[54] The government knew what was coming but still held fast to the ideology of royal generosity by deciding earlier that day to proceed with the first day of the *cuccagna*, despite rumblings among palace domestics who knew that a premature sack was imminent.[55]

51. "La carestia qua si avvicina; nello Stato si muore di fame, e corrono in Napoli per ritrovare quel grano che non vi è. Iddio ci preservi da qualche grande inconveniente!" (Vanvitelli, *Le lettere* 3:115–16).

52. "Ieri sera, Sabato, alle 2½ di notte, i lazzari diedero il sacco alla cuccagna, la quale doveasi saccheggiare oggi alle 21 ore. Dopo ciò incominciarono a dare il sacco ad alcune botteghe di Toledo, indi a portar via le tavole e [i] legni della Cuccagna, la quale è grande assai e costa del denaro" (February 12, 1764, Vanvitelli, *Le lettere* 3:117).

53. "Il est neuf heures du soir; encore deux lignes, je vous quitte . . . Mais qu'entends-je? . . . une rumeur extraordinaire dans les rues; des boutiques . . ." (letter 30, February 11, 1764); second quote from letter 31, February 20, 1764 (Coyer, *Voyage d'Italie*, vol. 1).

54. "La molta abbondanza, nella quale sono avvezzi a vivere nel regno tutto produce il clamore, e l'indole delle ruberie, alle quali il popolo è inchinatissimo, produce il disordine, perché dal pane hanno saccheggiato il resto, cioè i denari delle botteghe andate a sacco" (letter of February 12, 1764, Vanvitelli, *Le lettere* 3:118).

55. So reported the French ambassador Durfort. Durfort left the court theater and headed to the San Carlo where he reported that "il s'éleva dans la salle un très grand bruit qui fit un effet considérable sur la plus part des personnes qu'elle renfermait; on vint appeler tout ce qu'il y avait de

Once underway, the uproar unraveled the performance of a comedy in the little court theater and the opera at the San Carlo. Vanvitelli went on:

> Yesterday at . . . [the San Carlo] people were terrified and the opera went awry. The voice of whoever sang trembled; the dancers' legs trembled, the players' view of their notes danced on the parterre; some wanted to flee and others stopped for fear of shooting. There was murmuring among ladies in the boxes; some left suddenly on foot, others halted. In sum, imagine what a burlesque it was, notwithstanding which the performance continued, with everything done wrong and no one any longer caring. But it finished in such a flash that one might well believe that they had crossed the Rubicon in every manner, and it [all] turned into total disorder.[56]

A number of operagoers had been warned by servants and coachmen in attendance, who knew what was coming and who ran out to view the angry mob throw itself on the empty *cuccagna*. In the ensuing commotion, some stealing took place in the theater itself.

The initial government response was mild: troops shot in the air to disperse the mob, arrested nineteen, and one person was found dead of unreported causes. But the tumult continued through Sunday (when of course there could be no *cuccagna*), and some stores were again looted in the late afternoon. On the following Monday, the regency had three of the arrested from the previous Saturday conducted stripped to the waist through the streets, where they were whipped and then led to jail, "publicly and after a brief trial," as Tanucci put it, later to be sent to the galleys.

After order was restored by the strong arm of the law, the government had to decide whether to proceed with the next three *cuccagne*. Tanucci, as an engineer of economic reform, hated excess, dissipation, and disorder and had actually cut Carlo III's expenditures by nearly half. But as a staunch royalist, he also believed that men of high affairs should countenance spectacle in order to flatter the people and reinforce royal power.[57] For him the *cuccagna* was the opiate of the masses. It required a royal show of wealth and charity to make real its political claim of tolerance. Thus, in the end, the nobles in the Council of the Regency prevailed over him to go forward, in keeping with Mauss's dictum

---

militaires et quant ils furent sortis on ferma les portes du spectacle" (quoted in Barletta, *Il carnevale del 1764*, 13).

56. "Ieri sera, sabato, al teatro tutto il popolo era sbigottito, e l'opera andiede a traverso; chi cantava, le tremava la voce; ai ballerini tremava le gambe, ai suonatori ballava la vista delle loro note alla platea; chi voleva fuggire, e chi il timore delle scioppettate arrestava. Alle dame ne palchetti vi era un sussurro, chi andiede via subito a piedi, chi arrestò; in somma, figuratevi cosa fu la commedia, la quale, nonostante, si seguitò a recitare, sbagliata tutta e senza che niuno più vi badasse. Però finì prestissimo, onde è da credere che si saltavano i fossi d'ogni genere, ed era divenuta in perfettissimo disordine" (Vanvitelli, *Le lettere* 3:118).

57. Scafoglio, *La maschera*, 43.

that a gift expected must be bestowed in order for the authority of the giver to be maintained.[58]

Of course there was also the Maussian problem that in order for the gift to be successful, the exchange of which it is part needs to be complete. To this effect, Coyer observed that the court was less afraid that great masses of disorderly plebeians would arrive to sack the *cuccagna* than they were that the plebeians would skip their appointment altogether.[59] Were they to have abandoned the exchange, they would have asserted the demise of royal power, even if they could not exercise power themselves. The nobles in the Council of the Regency pushed to resume the ritual, and on the subsequent Sunday the heads of the people, presenting the silken broadside to the king, declared themselves having had no part in the tumults that had ruined the first *cuccagna*, and the next three Sundays went off with perfect tranquility.[60]

* * *

All of the symbolic strategies in play here juxtaposed the violence, antagonism, and hunger of the lower classes to the surplus and luxury of the upper classes. The *cuccagna* was an icon of bacchic excess, the existence of which was supposed to have been made possible by a hierarchy topped by the expansive authority and generosity of the king. At this higher end of royal festive production sat opera seria, which not only had its most sumptuously dynastic incarnation in Bourbon times but one of its primary birthplaces in pre-Bourbon Naples—an "origin" that had acquired a mythical status by the mid-eighteenth century.[61]

Traetta's *Didone abbandonata* epitomizes this excess in sonic form, even as it betrays a decline in Neapolitan musical vigor.[62] Gabrielli's passaggi typify the century's most extreme, with a style of coloratura that disregards reforms that were then beginning to reduce (or at least temper) singer-driven coloratura at

58. Mauss, *The Gift*, 13–14 and passim.

59. Quoted in Scafoglio, *La maschera*, 51.

60. On the post-February 11 events, see Barletta, *Il carnevale del 1764*, 14–17. *Chracas* dispatched the following (*Diario ordinario*, no. 7285, March 14, 1764): "Napoli 21. Febraro. Ricorrendo Venerdì l'anniversario della nascita del Reale Infante D*on* Francesco Saverio, Fratello del Re nostro Sovrano, vi fu gala alla Corte avendone ricevuti Sua Maestà li complimenti da questa Nobiltà, Ufficialità, e Ministero. Domenica seconda di Carnevale si vidde dinanzi al Reale Palazzo la seconda Cuccagna rappresentante: *Bellorofonte sul Cavallo Pagaseo nel Monte Elicone:* E tra le altre l'abbondanza de commestibili fu universalmente aggradita per la vaghezza del disegno, e saccheggiata dal minuto popolo nel dopo desinare con tutta la più desiderabile quiete." The entry of March 21, 1764 (no. 7288), reads: "Napoli 28. Febraro. Il nostro Sovrano gode perfetta salute, angustiatissimo bensì dalla penuria in cui trovasi il suo Regno di vettovaglie sebbene non ha mancato la Maestà Sua di prendere quei spedienti più propri per sollevarlo da tali miserie. Viddesi non ostante Domenica scorsa la solita Cuccagna per la terza volta, ripiena di ogni sorta di Comestibili, e saccheggiata precedente il solito segno del Re con tutta quiete, e pace."

61. See di Benedetto, "Music and Enlightenment," 13–53 and 137–38.

62. I-Nc, MS Rari 7.9.20–22, score for 1764 Naples performance, which I use here.

places like Vienna and Stuttgart. Algarotti's *Saggio* had first been published nine years earlier, Gluck's *Orfeo* staged in Vienna in 1762, and Traetta and Gabrielli had collaborated on their French-styled reform operas at Parma in 1759 and 1760 and at Vienna in 1761 and 1763 (*Armida* and *Iphigenia in Tauride*).

Already in act 1, Gabrielli's "Son regina e son amante" (1.5)—a declarative first-person text from Metastasio's original that asserts her sovereignty as queen and lover—is as profligate in its virtuosity as the act 3 aria Traetta had given her in *Ippolito*. With doubled oboes and horns in her cortege, she is an icon of royal power and pomp. Jommelli had given Dido a new-styled pomp when he did his third setting of *Didone* the year before, on a text modified by the reforming poet Mattia Verazi for Duke Carl Eugen at Stuttgart. With strong dynamic contrasts and crescendos, dramatic polarities of upper and lower string writing, highly innovative ensembles, and strong orchestral color, including extensive writing for solo winds, winds in dialogue, and winds used to enhance inner string writing, Jommelli's setting for Stuttgart was practically the antithesis of Traetta's for Naples.[63] Traetta's Dido by comparison was an old-fashioned opera queen, given, therefore, like her interlocutors, to a discrete succession of poses. In 2.3 she bared another one, that of the tempo di minuetto in delicate cantabile, "Ah! non lasciarmi, no," in which, pleading with Enea not to leave (example 5.1), she proved herself not just a model of bravura but an icon of human frailty. With dolcissimo melodies, chromatically inflected, reverse dotted, and softened with grace notes, with drooping appoggiaturas and throbbing syncopations, she emerged as an emotive, anguished monarch who could force her listeners to hold their breath till their ribcages practically felt like bursting. And then, only a few scenes later, she returned with another round of fireworks, "In tanto tormento" (2.12), placed in its bravura slot midway through act 2. The "fireworks" metaphor is apt, as fire—love fire and death fire—were the opera's principal tropes. They were the spark that a Gabrielli could bring it, a specially female spark, uncontainable, changeable, ruinous.

Gabrielli's opulence added up to pure personal power, conveyed in a surpassing show of indefatigable passagework, rife with high C's and prefaced by a huge opening ritornello scored for transverse flutes and a violin obbligato that played her off in dashing style, trading figuration with her and underpinning her by thirds (example 5.2). All in all, the opera stacks up one huge da capo upon another, scaling back only for the secondary singers. The opera even forgoes the dal segno, often imposed by the mid-1760s as a modest restraint on immense midcentury da capos to prune back the overgrown A section on its return. And it includes cavatinas a mere three times.[64]

63. See Tolkoff, "The Stuttgart Operas of Niccolò Jommelli," chap. 3, 115–38, and chap. 6, and Heartz, *Music in European Capitals*, 468–73. Tolkoff shows well how thoroughly Jommelli's Stuttgart works were music for connoisseurs, with rich instrumentation, extensive obbligato recitatives, inventive aria forms, and the like, and how little favored they were by Italian listeners with their more traditional tastes (chap. 2).

64. One for Iarba in act 1 and one each for Osmida and Didone (the famous "Va crescendo" in act 3).

EXAMPLE 5.1. Tommaso Traetta, aria for Didone, "Ah! non lasciarmi, no," mm. 1–24

From *Didone abbandonata* (Teatro San Carlo, Naples, Carnival 1764), 2.3 (vol. 2, 5r–v). Short score based on I-Nc, MS Rari 7.9.20–22. *(continued)*

EXAMPLE 5.1. (*continued*)

In keeping with this vocal extravagance, *Didone* received a lavish staging, not just with the elephants that Coyer reported (doubtless manmade, but nevertheless visually impressive),[65] but also a huge field of supernumeraries leading tigers and lions, military guard performing in great battle scenes (e.g., 3.2), and mise-en-scènes that utilized vast perspectival sets of Carthage showing public squares, seaports, and palaces. Designed by Antonio Jolli, principal scenographer to the San Carlo, the sets embodied the neoclassical monumentality that had become the theater's standard after the death in 1762 of Vincenzo Re. Adding to the operatic spectacle were three ballets performed by eight soloists and a corps of ten, one between each of the acts plus a set of lighter pantomime ballets following the opera's end in addition to the cantata given on opening night.[66]

Luxury was a flashpoint in Italian enlightenment discourses of the time, and in Gabrielli's form, opera seria was its very sense and symbol. But the great Italian writers who engaged the problem of luxury (*lusso*)—Pietro Verri (1728–97) and Cesaria Beccaria (1738–94) in Lombardy, economists Antonio Genovesi (1712–69) and Ferdinando Galiani (1728–87) in Naples—fretted along with

65. An elephant was in fact given to Carlo III by the Great Sultan. It was described in 1742 and appeared at the San Carlo in 1743 (Croce, *I teatri di Napoli* [1891], 2:342–43), but there is no evidence of multiple elephants having been on stage.

66. See Mancini, "Antonio Joli," in *Il Teatro di San Carlo* 3:37–48. The subject of the first ballet was the building and sculpting of Carthage, that of the second the entourage of Jarba. Jolli did the scenography for both. Comic intermezzi were abolished from the San Carlo after 1741, as they were at Turin and later elsewhere (Robinson and di Benedetto, "Naples").

EXAMPLE 5.2. Tommaso Traetta, aria for Didone, "In tanto tormento," mm. 79–110

From *Didone abbandonata* (Teatro San Carlo, Naples, Carnival 1764), 2.12 (vol. 2, 44v). Short score based on I-Nc, MS Rari 7.9.20–22.

(*continued*)

EXAMPLE 5.2. (*continued*)

EXAMPLE 5.2. (*continued*)

many others over its relationship to public good and happiness. They deemed luxury a wondrous if sometimes corrupting influence in the arts, and puzzled over its moral ambiguities.[67] In his *Saggio,* Algarotti implied that *lusso* was politically contradictory, something that could engender the virtue of a splendid court spectacle, felicitously joined to royal pomp, or the performative vice of high-paid singers who corrupted verisimilitude with their excessive ornaments. By 1772 Antonio Planelli advocated an austere operatic aesthetic of leaner notes, simple, sober, and stripped of surface gloss, to convey illusion and harness morals—a kind of aesthetic antiluxury.[68]

But in Naples 1764, such ideas were still inaudible and invisible. As savvy and reform-minded as Tanucci was, pragmatically speaking, ideas of the kind did not concern him or those responsible for producing opera. In fact, paradoxically, the decision to mount Traetta's *Didone* gave the lie to royal luxe and royalist hype (and gave Dido's suicide a deadly valence even beyond the usual) since, although Traetta had originally set the libretto for Venice in 1757, where the lead was sung by Rosa Curioni, the Neapolitans used a revision he had made for Milan and Gabrielli in 1763. Rather than commissioning a new setting, in other words, as normally done for Carnival by the great court-run public theaters, they played it penny-wise by utilizing a preexistent score, cut and revised by their local chapelmaster, Pasquale Cafaro. (A *protesta* published at the front of the libretto apologized for condensing act 2 with a duet for the leads at the end and for cutting a good deal of recitative throughout—practices that were utterly typical.)[69] What was saved was evidently spent to hire the same leading lady used in Milan, who was paired with a primo uomo of only average consequence, Antonio Priori. In his "triumph" aria "A trionfar mi chiama" (3.6), Priori—playing Aeneas on the verge of conquering the Sabines and founding

67. Verri, "Considerazioni sul lusso," 155–62; and Galiani, "Digressione intorno al lusso." Very valuable is Wahnbaeck, *Luxury and Public Happiness* (on Naples, 66–69). See too Frascani, "Il dibattito sul lusso," 397–424.

68. *Saggio,* ed. Bisi (1763), 17; di Benedetto, "Music and Enlightenment," 138–41, gives a fine analysis of Planelli's aesthetic.

69. See Riedlbauer, *Die Opern,* 112–20 and 369–78; Fabbri, "Vita e funzione."

the city of Rome—mustered a vocalism that fell far short of Dido's. And the tenor Pietro de Mezzo as Jarba, threatening to burn Dido's palace in his famous "Cadrà fra poco in cenere" (3.15), had to depend for much of his menace on the "noisy" Neapolitan basses about which Burney had complained (see chap. 2 and example 5.3). To boot, the ballets were evidently unrehabilitated entr'acte-type suites, and the musical prologue by Gian Francesco di Maio added for opening night "very bad," if we believe the opinion of Vanvitelli.[70]

How poignant that the proud San Carlo would have revived with little change an opera that had already been revised in the previous year for its old Habsburg rival, the Regio Ducal Teatro, seat of the archduchy of Milan. Ironically, though, *Didone abbandonata* was not the typical tale of absolutist magnanimity, but of the Phoenician queen deserted and disconsolate on the shores of Carthage. Within the Metastasian canon, with its relentlessly happy endings, *Didone abbandonata* is of course unique: Metastasio's first libretto, from 1724, it was among his few to celebrate a female monarch, and his only thoroughgoing lyric tragedy. To older audience members at the San Carlo, who had seen the story set to different music in previous seasons, Dido cut a familiar figure.[71] She was an emblem of royal valor, whose high-minded principles in the midst of private grief spoke tacitly to her regard for public trust. In the private realm, she is shown as doubly valorous, since she rebukes the bids of the tyrannical king of the Moors, Jarba, for her hand in marriage against threats to usurp her kingdom—and this after Aeneas has already announced his departure from Carthage, where he abandons her.

Yet it seems just as telling that Dido's repudiation of Jarba also portrayed her as the royal personification of shrewd exchange. As early as 1.5, Jarba arrives posing as his own deputy to offer gifts of "spoils, gems, treasures, men, and beasts . . . , [as] tokens of [Jarba's] greatness" and openly declaring their potency: "In the gift one learns the nature of the giver" (literally, "what the giver is").[72] But Dido is too sharp for that and deflects his self-congratulation: "In my accepting the gift, your lord receives [my] great mercy. But if he is no wiser, that which is now a gift may turn into an homage [to me]."[73] When Jarba, still disguised, tries to coerce her, maintaining that Carthage was Jarba's "gift" to her, she corrects him: "You confuse the sale with the gift."[74] She bought Car-

70. Cf. Riedlbauer, *Die Opern*, 370 n. 133.

71. The libretto had been performed in settings by Hasse in Carnival 1744 and Lampugnani in Carnival 1753. Its original setting was premiered at Naples's San Bartolomeo.

72. "Queste, che miri intanto / spoglie, gemme, tesori, uomini e fere, / che l'Africa soggetta a lui produce, pegni di sua grandezza in don t'invia. / Nel dono impara il donator qual sia."

73. "Mentre io ne accetto il dono / larga mercede il tuo signor riceve. / Ma s'ei non è più saggio, / quel, ch'ora è don può divenire omaggio."

74. Jarba: "Ti rammenta, o Didone, qual da Tiro venisti, e qual ti trasse / disperato consiglio a questo lido, / che fu questo, ove s'alza / la superba Cartago, ampio terreno, / dono del mio signore, e fu . . ." Didone: "Col dono / la vendita confondi . . ." In the Naples 1764 libretto, the following lines are cut after "a questo lido" and before "[che] fu questo": "Del tuo germano infido / alle barbare voglie, al genio avaro / ti fu l'Africa sol schermo e riparo."

EXAMPLE 5.3. Tommaso Traetta, aria for Jarba, "Cadrà fra poco in cenere," mm. 1–12

From *Didone abbandonata* (Teatro San Carlo, Naples, Carnival 1764), 3.15 (vol. 3, 37r–38v). Short score based on I-Nc, MS Rari 7.9.20–22.

thage with her own assets spirited away from Phoenicia: "Carthage is a 'gift' at the price of my treasures," she insists with irony, "and not in fact [a gift] of your king."[75] Having purchased her "liberty," she will not now trade it for "chains" (vv. 170–72).

75. "Dalla reggia di Tiro / io venni a queste arene / libertate cercando, e non catene. / Prezzo de' miei tesori, e non già del tuo re Cartago è dono."

APOCALYPTIC ENDINGS

Had Tanucci's partisans listened to Dido—and to be sure they all knew her speeches whether they listened or not—they would have heard at once a lesson on the compromised nature of the gift and a canny view of commerce. In parrying Jarba, Dido insists on a marketplace notion of exchange. She is a Phoenician, after all, practiced in the trade and commerce that Tanucci was trying to promote, but also wise to the potential avarice behind the gift. Like Dido, some observers may have wondered whether "gifts" distributed by the king asked more in compliance and fidelity than they gave in return. Dido is sure that they do. In her final hour she rails at Jarba, "You have no pity on an abandoned woman." Moments before pitching herself into the flames of her burning palace, Dido depicts the sacrifices she has made as offerings unredeemed. With Carthage burning, unmoved by pleas to yield and forsaken by family and friends, she at last cries out, "What did I do, evil gods? I did not stain your altars with profane victims, nor make them smoke with impure flames! . . . What *gods* [are these]? They are idle names, chimeras dreamt, or else unjust" (3.16).[76]

These lines preface her final *scena*—at midcentury an unconventional yet traditional, theatrical, and highly anticipated solo vehicle for the leading lady. Preceded by racing scales and tremolos she erupts in the plaintive key of E flat,[77] "Ah, what have I said, unhappy me," and then exclaims on a plunging diminished fifth, surrounded by upward violin glissandi, "to what excess has my fury driven me." As she presses on—"Oh God! my horror grows. Everywhere I look death and terror appear before me"—she modulates to C minor, passing through a flat-six chord over "morte" and tumbling through a melodic minor seventh to land in B flat on the lines, "The palace trembles and threatens to fall."[78] Finally, having delivered the libretto's famous cavatina, the tremolos reintensify, and she plummets a last time from A flat to B flat above middle C (now V of E flat), crying out, "Let Carthage fall, let the palace burn, and may its ashes be my tomb (fig. 5.8.)."[79]

Dido's final appeal and immolation, turning herself into the medium of sacrifice as a last appeasement to the gods, resonates chillingly with the desperate turn Carnival took in the days before Lent. On March 5, the Sunday of the final *cuccagna*, seven or eight hundred women begged the archbishop to initiate a novena, nine days of religious devotions that would suspend the culmination of Carnival. And on March 7, the popular classes obtained an injunction against

76. "[C]he feci, empi Numi! Io non macchiai / con vittime profane i vostri altari, / né mai di fiamma impura / feci l'are fumar per vostro scherno. . . . Che dei? Son nomi vani, / son chimere sognate, o ingiusti sono." (This is identical to 3.19 in Metastasio, *Opere* 1:51.)

77. See Steblein, "Key Characteristics," 277–78.

78. "Ah! che dissi infelice! A qual eccesso / mi trasse il mio furore! / Oh Dio! Cresce l'orrore. Ovunque io miro, / mi vien la morte, e lo spavento in faccia. / Trema la Reggia, e di cader minaccia" (Metastasio, *Opere* 1:52).

79. "Precipiti Cartago / arda la reggia, e sia / il cenere di lei la tomba mia."

FIG. 5.8. Dido throwing herself into the flames of her burning palace. Frontispiece to act 3 of *Didone abbandonata*, designed by Pietro Antonio Novelli, engraved by G. Zuliani. The caption quotes the end of the opera, "May Carthage fall, may the palace burn, and may its ashes be my tomb." From Pietro Metastasio, *Opere del signor Ab. Pietro Metastasio, poeta Cesareo: Giusta le correzioni e aggiunte dell'autore nell'edizione di Parigi del 1780* (Venice: Antonio Zatta, 1781), vol. 1. Hagerty Archives—HistBook ML49.A2 M44 v. 1. Image courtesy of Drexel University Archives, Philadelphia.

parties and dances, shutting down the usual consummation of Carnival on Fat Tuesday. It was the first in a series of penitential initiatives among the popular classes in which women and children processed bareheaded and barefooted, singing prayers and religious songs to the patron saint of Naples, San Gennaro, in hopes of alleviating the famine. Famine now came to be seen as the retribution of a terrible god of pre-Christian times, and as subject to the same charges of collective guilt as any natural disaster.

Scafoglio has argued that the rites that emerged in the midst of this Carnival-turned-Lent were not simply versions of Lenten penitence pure and simple but reproduced the function and spirit of Carnival itself.[80] The protagonist of the now "Lenten" Carnival, however, was Christ, impersonated by beggars bearing crosses. Adorning their loose locks with crowns of thorns, they traversed the city's streets and piazzas, weeping and crying out. This mimicking of the sacrificial Christ utilized a mechanism of identification by which Christ took on what Émile Durkheim interpreted as a task of redemption by means of sacrificial expiation with an identified body.[81] The body with which the Neapolitan masses identified was mutilated and dismembered, like the effigy of the murdered man traditionally carried about during Carnival to guarantee rebirth the following spring. And like the carnivalesque effigy of the murdered man, it helped to conjure up, but then finally to expunge negative elements of violence and disorder through rituals that sought to reestablish order and peace.[82]

In part, the common people by becoming Christ figures also effectively martyred themselves for the sake of an ideology that venerated the good king—a divine king who mediated between an enigmatic God and everyday people. In doing so, they reasserted beliefs in the king's paternalistic largesse, his forbearance, and the impossibility of his guilt. For the moment, old regime–style tolerance paid off.

In saying so, however, I do not wish to reduce the crisis of old-regime politics highlighted in the collision of opera, Carnival, and the Great Famine of 1764 to a set of final answers. The disparate strands drawn together out of these events seem to me to set in relief a set of tensions inherent in the institution, symbols, and narratives of opera seria, and inherent as social and political forms in the absolutist polities that promoted opera seria and other festivities. The ground on which monarchy of the old order could shore itself up through cultural production had become increasingly fraught, even in Naples, which might easily seem to have been impervious to those tensions. And opera seria was perched on that shaky ground.

As a text, *Didone abbandonata* resonates with the crisis faced by royalist poli-

80. Scafoglio, *La maschera,* 86–87. Most contemporary evidence is based on the eyewitness accounts of the Piemontese ambassador Lascaris.

81. Durkheim, *Elementary Forms,* book 3, "The Principal Ritual Attitudes," and esp. chap. 2, part 1, "The Elements of Sacrifice," and chap. 5 on piacular rites of mourning for deaths and calamities.

82. As the ambassador from Piedmont said, "the Savior . . . was turned into a thousand pieces, everyone wanting a portion," like miraculous relics (in Scafoglio, *La maschera,* 87).

tics in 1764. Predating the years when Metastasio consolidated his representations of the ideal monarch and the reputation as its main mythographer that he established after taking up his position as imperial court poet in Vienna in 1730, *Didone* revealed a more fragile, impermanent, marginal, feminine, and avowedly mythical view of monarchy. In this respect, it was suitable for a time when the display of hierarchy was threatened even as it was being choreographed for public consumption.

CHAPTER 6

Myths of Sovereignty

"Sons, I am no less father of the kingdom than of you." SIROE, from act 1 of Metastasio's *Siroe*[1]

"A king is the creature par excellence of the miracle; in his person he concentrates the virtues of a miraculous presence." GEORGES BATAILLE, "Sovereignty"[2]

"Myths are made up of actions that include their opposites within themselves." ROBERTO CALASSO, *The Marriage of Cadmus and Harmony*[3]

Naples was the representative kingship in the southern peninsula after 1734, approached in stature only by the kingdom of Savoy in the north. It epitomized a monarchy wherein the king stood front and center to his people, in ideology, symbol, person, space, and time; it epitomized the festivity of the old order through the king's legitimation of crowd rituals, indoors and out; and it epitomized an attachment to traditional narratives of the sovereign in its avid recycling of the Metastasian canon. Naples made flesh the image of the omnipotent, providential king. Yet we have seen that that image cracked under the pressure of hard political facts involving the regency, a growing state machine, and the cataclysmic events surrounding the Great Famine. The *cuccagna* showed off the old order but unmasked its reforms and the state that authorized them, exposing the representation of the *popolo* by a puppet and the evacuation of lifeblood from the guilds. As the rites of gift exchange between king and people became empty, the symbolism of royal paternity, with its implications of kinship for the body social, inevitably came unmoored. Efforts to make exchange seem voluntary, or give it an aura of real largesse, had in any case been feeble at best.

Still, I have argued that festivities indoors and out managed to accommodate certain real expression, especially in the agonistic mechanisms that organized them: in competitions over conveyances, dress, decoration of boxes, and mask-

1. "Figli, io non son del regno men padre che di voi" (*Siroe* 1.1, in Metastasio, *Opere* 1:71).

2. Bataille, "Sovereignty," part 3 in *The Accursed Share*, 2:211; originally published as "La souveraineté" in *Oeuvres complètes* 8:243–395.

3. Calasso, *The Marriage of Cadmus and Harmony*, 280.

ing, in rivalries between singers and the efforts of fans to exalt or debase them; in demonstrations of class differences, frenzied pillaging of the *cuccagna*, penitential processions, and people's threats to official restrictions. These mechanisms had many and complex functions. They provided diversion and, inseparably, the machinery of exchange that was fundamental to spectacle. They paid tribute to sovereign and state, highlighting shifting hierarchies while reaffirming the old social order. And they proclaimed officially—if vacuously—that subjects of the king had certain freedoms, even if those freedoms were mystified and often undermined. Several generations of Neapolitan reformers, from Genovesi to Galiani and Filangieri, were repeatedly disappointed by the slow progress of reforms in law, economics, public works, education, and services, increasingly so after the devastating famine, although there were small gains, especially in the gradual erosion of feudalism.[4] Meanwhile, for some the practices and spaces of opera continued to supply possibilities of agency and vitality of expression, at least intermittently. A decade after the famine, Naples was temporarily in the operatic vanguard, issuing Planelli's treatise on operatic reform in 1772 and staging Calzabigi and Gluck's revised *Orfeo ed Euridice* in 1774 at the royal theater, along with five other reform operas in the same decade.[5]

Thus, while Naples saw some aspects of old-styled sovereignty come undone, others remained relatively secure. These paradoxes are just one instance among many of conservatism in eighteenth-century Italy surviving, indeed flourishing, under pressure. The present chapter asks how opera helped sovereigns to thrive, acting as a filter for identifications of sovereigns by subjects, whether in kingships, republics, or vassal states, and how the growing state machine complicated operatic assertions about subject/sovereign relationships. My claims are that opera seria succeeded in mediating feelings about absolute sovereignty by propagating itself, narratively and performatively, as myth; that to understand opera seria one must understand its mythical nature; and that understanding its mythical nature means grappling with its principal mythographer. So doing, we can start to see how opera seria in Italy cooperated in allowing old-styled sovereignty to survive even the French spirit of revolution, and how it managed to endure (however changed) through at least the time of Rossini, despite the lather of reformist thinking among opera-loving intelligentsia.

OF MYTH AND THE MYTHOGRAPHER

A mythographer in the Homeric sense is one who makes a redaction to a mythical body of stories or creates his own. In either work, the mythographer endows his material with ideological form and at the same time makes it efficacious for

4. Venturi, "The Enlightenment in Southern Italy," in *Italy and the Enlightenment*, 198–224.

5. Gialdroni, "La musica a Napoli," 75–143; di Benedetto, "Music and Enlightenment," 147–50; and Tufano, "*Le nozze di Orfeo e Partenope*."

his own and later generations.[6] To succeed as myth, stories must stake certain fundamental cultural claims but also encompass ambiguities sufficient to allow them to circulate widely, to be retranslated, recast, and hence made susceptible to varied reuses and interpretations. This is why students of myth generally hold that a given "text" (written or oral) meets the criteria of myth only if it encourages distinct, even opposed readings—readings from which different meanings can be drawn as it travels through different historical settings.[7] Only in that way can myths live on, being taken as new signs, or signs of new portents, histories, symbols, ideologies, and other things in new contexts. Only then do stories constitute "myths" worthy of the name. For myths are not particular tales, in and of themselves. At most they are uses of tales that are taken to be traditional, disseminated as such, and deployed for political or other kinds of legitimating purposes.[8] Often they become the stuff of which political, religious, or (from the later eighteenth century onward) national ideologies are built.[9] In this sense, myths are privileged narratives.

But their immediate audience will not necessarily understand and label as myths any stories that meet these criteria—at least not as myths in the often-pejorative sense of fables or falsehoods, of things removed from present reality that were once believed but no longer are, or no longer should be. In fact they may even understand what we would call a myth as historical truth. In this sense, as I noted in chapter 1, what is called history (or reporting, or speech making) fits Mircea Eliade's definition of myth as an exemplary story that warrants, even demands, being "recited," "proclaimed," "shown." As Eliade says, stories can function as myths if they incorporate a "fabulous time of origins" (not the "time of fabled origins") and try to make their audience "in a certain way 'contemporary' with the events that are evoked," causing it "to share in the presence of . . . Gods or Heroes."[10] Conversely, audiences may label such stories "histories" if the stories' pedigree and truth claims meet the going cultural criteria for the historical genre. Many myths and histories flow into one another like seas of the same ocean. In this chapter, I will stress this fact to argue that

6. This definition stands in contrast to the mythologist, who studies myth, as richly sampled in Feldman and Richardson, *The Rise of Modern Mythology.*

7. Doniger, *The Implied Spider,* 2, and chap. 4, "Micromyths, Macromyths, and Multivocality"; Lincoln, *Theorizing Myth,* 54; and Calasso, *The Marriage of Cadmus and Harmony,* 280–81.

8. Doniger is "less interested in dictating what a myth *is*" than "exploring what myth *does*" (*The Implied Spider,* 1). For her myth is "a story . . . sacred to and shared by a group of people who find their most important meanings in it" and concerns "an event that continues to have meanings in the present because it is remembered" and "is part of a larger group of stories" (2).

9. Lincoln, *Theorizing Myth,* 53–54 and passim, develops this idea in relation to early German romantics such as Herder, who follow Vico's climatological analysis (*Scienza nuova,* 1715) by theorizing myth as a resource for collective identity, transmission of tradition, cultural knowledge, and history. Lincoln's definition is intentionally and shrewdly metadefinitional (hence somewhat mythological itself): myth is not a usage, but a variety of ways that the word, concept, and category have been utilized or invoked (ix).

10. Eliade, "Toward a Definition of Myth," 4–5.

while opera seria was born of a shift in Italian opera from frequently staging stories derived from mythical traditions to largely staging stories gleaned from histories, it was equally born from turning histories into myths.[11]

* * *

Eighteenth-century writers had a complex relationship to myth. Many rationalists, like Voltaire, were wary of it, much as they were wary of festivity, as something caught up in superstitions and idolatry.[12] Others saw myth as key to high ideals (like Noël-Antoine Pluche with his astral theories) or used myths to find romance in primal symbols and forces (like the alchemist Antoine-Joseph Pernety, for whom they bore occult meanings).[13] Those who were fans of myth often operated under the spell of exoticism, infatuated with the rituals and beliefs of newly discovered "primitive" peoples who were brought into European consciousness by explorers such as Richard Blome, Willem Bosman, and especially Père Joseph Lafitau and expressed in the vibrant anthropological philosophies of Giambattista Vico. Still, all eighteenth-century commentators would have agreed that *mythos* was fable or fiction, as opposed to *logos* and *historia*, which pointed to reason and truth. In thus devaluing *mythos* in favor of *logos*, they were also heirs to a particular fossilized form of Plato's condemnation of poetry in book 10 of the *Republic*.

The lineages of these distinctions cannot be pursued here. Suffice it to stress that in a century at once attracted and repulsed by various mythical forms, the lines between collectors and scholars, inventors and propagators, were often thin. In the realm of poetic production, we might imagine a spectrum with

11. See Bellina and Caruso, "Zeno e Metastasio," 239–312. Weiss, "Baroque Opera and the Two Verisimilitudes," shows how history entered seicento opera in mythical, miraculous form, and was smoothed of wonders only in Zeno's later libretti, which disregarded the Arcadians' desire for spoken historical tragedy. The notion of Metastasian theater as mythical appears (briefly) only in Coscia, "La scena del mito," 323–33, mostly apropos the "myth of *romanitas*" (329–30). Dumézil's remarkable study, *The Archaic Community of the Romans*, shows the process of making myth into history by those who, directly or indirectly, provided many of the sources for opera seria plots (see esp. vol. 1, chap. 6) Dumézil's comparatist methods have spawned various critiques, notably by Arnaldo Momigliano, *Roma arcaica*, and recently Alexandre Grandazzi, *The Foundation of Rome* (chap. 3), but all seem to presume the soundness of the history/myth nexus.

12. Eliade cautions, however, that Voltaire and Bayle would not have seen as "myth" various contemporary phenomena as we might nowadays—phenomena including enthusiasm, prophecies, apocalyptic beliefs, or messianic ideologies associated with monarchs, for example, Frederick II, who was thought to have bound together elements of the cosmos (Feldman and Richardson, *The Rise of Modern Mythology*, xv).

13. In *L'histoire du ciel* (1739), Pluche argued from monotheism, interpreting (and forgiving) myth as a form of symbolic communication. In contrast, in *Les fables égyptienne et grecque* (1758) and *Dictionnaire mytho-hermétique* (1787), Pernety wove allegorical interpretations meant to show myth as an arcane language of early Egyptian alchemists who wanted to conceal their knowledge, and hence as a vehicle of transcendent truths hiding in material forms.

James Macpherson (1736–96) concocting the myth of Ossian on one side and Metastasio his drammi per musica on the other. In the early 1760s, Macpherson announced that he had translated the poetry of a blind third-century bard and pumped it full throttle into the rising Scottish nationalism of his day. As a mythographer, Macpherson was highly attuned to what his readers wanted to believe, and he succeeded in translating their longings into a seemingly authentic text, only decades later derided as invention.[14] By contrast, Metastasio had fashioned an operatic poetics that largely renounced mythical stories in favor of heroic histories passed down by the likes of Plutarch, Livy, Herodotus, and Cassius Dio. Designed to edify the minds and souls of auditors and shield them from false examples, Metastasio's outward intentions could not have been more different from Macpherson's. His work followed the larger classicizing project of the Arcadians, who took aim at the unruly mixture of genres and characters, comic and serious, pagan and modern, of seventeenth-century opera, and replaced it with regularity and morality—extraordinary mortals installed over "improbable" immortals—and hence with exemplary historical prototypes.

Yet Metastasio was arguably the most successful mythographical poet of his time, and certainly of opera seria. Born Pietro Trapassi in 1698 to a working-class family, he was taken as a small child under the wing of the musical and well-connected Roman aristocrat Pietro Ottoboni.[15] By age ten, he was dazzling Roman elites with brilliant poetic improvisations and was given up by his poor grocer father for adoption by the erudite jurist Gianvincenzo Gravina. A Greek scholar, literary theorist, and classical tragedian, Gravina raised the boy in the bosom of the Arcadians. At fourteen, Metastasio was taken to Calabria to study with Gravina's cousin Giorgio Caloprese, a prominent Cartesian philosopher and important conduit to Italy of Cartesian thought.[16] En route home, Gravina and Pietro sojourned at Naples, where the young poet allegedly improvised forty stanzas before Vico on the given theme of "La magnificenza dei principi e le sue lodi" (The magnificence of princes and their praises), a feat that launched his fame abroad as a stupendous performer of poetry and established his credentials as a royal laudator. Two years later, in 1714, he took minor orders at the Lateran Basilica in Rome, continued to study, compose, and interact with the Arcadians, and in 1715 was crowned by Gravina with his Greek name (Trapassi translated into Metastasio).

As a staunch moralist, Gravina shielded the boy from the grittier Latin and vernacular classics, but Metastasio sought them out anyway, adding Ovid, Tasso, and Marino to his personal canon, along with Homer, Virgil, Horace, and

14. Lincoln, *Theorizing Myth*, 51, and Trevor-Roper, "The Highland Tradition of Scotland," 15–41. The Ossian myth touched the Italian stage too (Chegai, *L'esilio di Metastasio*, 116–19, and Tufano, "La via ossianica all'esotica," the latter of which I have not been able to read).

15. On Metastasio's Italian career, see Franchi, "Patroni, politica, impresari," 7–48. Biographies include Neville, "Metastasio," and Brunelli's opening essay in Metastasio, *Opere* 1:xi–xlix. See Neville, "A Metastasio Database," for an important compilation by the University of Western Ontario.

16. Lomonaco, "Tra 'ragione poetica' e vita civile," 165–202.

Ariosto. His close contacts included the moralizing reformer Ludovico Antonio Muratori, the literary theorist Pier Jacopo Martello (who proposed new metric principles for tragedy), and the philologist Giovanni Mario Crescimbeni (also an avid correspondent with the Venetian Arcadian literato and librettist Apostolo Zeno). In April 1718, shortly after Gravina's death, Metastasio was formally inducted as an Arcadian, but some of his modern leanings put him at odds with the Arcadian cohort.[17] He migrated to Naples in 1719, soon started his operatic career, and stayed until 1728, when he returned to Rome, only to transfer just two years later to the post of imperial court poet at Vienna, where he remained for some fifty-two years until his death.

Metastasio's extraordinary success built on his having thoroughly internalized Cartesian morality and ideology, combining them with an immediacy of poetic inspiration and a keen sense for theater. With his gifts for lyricism, staging, and dramatic tension, and as an improviser and aficionado of epic ottava stanzas, long recited in oral traditions throughout Italy, he had a performative mind through and through and he understood intimately the relationship of text to audience. He had even studied music for a time with Porpora, and years later told Casanova "that he had never written . . . [an aria] without setting it to music himself," adding that he almost never showed his music to anyone.[18]

Between 1723–24 and 1771, Metastasio codified a body of stories that embodied the fantasies of foundation, morality, and selfhood of European society like none other and were disseminated more widely than any other stories of their time.[19] Their proliferation, even into the nineteenth century, has become a perfunctory entry in histories of music, yet it was utterly phenomenal. Across

17. He would thus have been familiar with Crescimbeni's *La bellezza della volgar poesia* (1700) and Muratori's *Della perfetta poesia italiana* (1706). On Metastasio among the Arcadians, see Nicastro, *Metastasio e il teatro*, 11–60; Freeman, *Opera without Drama*; Binni, *L'Arcadia e il Metastasio;* and Acquaro Graziosi, "Pietro Metastasio e l'Arcadia," 48–61.

18. Casanova continues, "and he laughed heartily at the French for believing that it is possible to fit words to a tune composed beforehand. He made a very philosophical comparison: 'It is,' he said, 'as if you said to a sculptor "Here is a bit of marble, make me a Venus which will show her expression before you have carved her features."'" (*History of My Life* 3:221). "Il me dit en suite qu'il n'avait jamais fait une ariette sans la mettre en musique lui-même, mais qu'ordinairement il ne montrait sa musique à personne; et il rit beaucoup des Français qui croient qu'on puisse adapter des paroles à une musique faite d'avance. Il me porta une comparaison très philosophique:—C'est, me dit-il, comme si on disait à un sculpteur: voilà un morceau de marbre, faites-moi une Vénus qui montre sa physionomie avant que vous ayez développé ses traits" (*Histoire de ma vie* 3:341). See also Heartz, "Metastasio, 'Maestro dei Maestri.'"

19. Mladen Dolar conceives opera's origins in the paradox of absolutism, foundational to which is a mythical past that enables fantasies of bourgeois society, allowing "transcendence and utopian reconciliation" (Žižek and Dolar, *Opera's Second Death*, 16–17). Cf. Lévi-Strauss, for whom music, like myth, was "a machine to suppress time" and for whom the music/myth marriage was therefore made in heaven (*The Raw and the Cooked*). Salazar, *Idéologies de l'opéra*, like Dolar, proposes opera as a miniature of absolutism wherein the king is both privileged viewer and central hero. See also for the French domain Isherwood, *Music in the Service of the King;* Couvreur, *Jean-Baptiste Lully;* Burgess, "Ritual in the *Tragédie en Musique*"; and Chae, "Music, Festival, and Power."

western and eastern Europe, and as far abroad as the Americas, Metastasio's tales were reworked in hundreds upon hundreds of new operatic settings by different composers (four hundred, conservatively estimated, plus many more anonymous ones), commissioned by different patrons and impresarios, and sought out by different bodies of listeners and readers—sometimes with, more often without, his approval.[20] The settings total close to a hundred apiece for the most popular libretti—*Alessandro nell'Indie* and *Artaserse* had about ninety each, not counting anonymous settings and innumerable adaptations to other genres—and commonly there were upward of twenty-five to fifty operatic settings of his other libretti. His texts were translated into English, Portuguese, Danish, and Swedish (to name a few) for purposes of both reading and for setting afresh, pulled into parts of opere buffe, made into satires, turned into ballets, and reworked into cantatas, *feste teatrali, serenate,* as well as the later and gutsier *azioni drammatiche.*[21] They were extracted for settings as concert arias, duets, and ensembles (some with orchestral and others keyboard accompaniment), turned into vocal suites (divertimenti vocali or notturni), and eventu-

20. In parts 1 and 2 of his *Bibliographia dramatica,* Reinhart Meyer provides extensive statistical evidence on the proliferation of Metastasian opera in various dramatic, generic, and material forms to about 1750, with volumes on later decades in preparation. Meyer's article "Die Rezeption der dramen Metastasios," 419–24, lists 226 different mountings of *Artaserse* alone (in contrast to *Grove Music Online,* which lists about 100 operatic settings). On the poet's virtual commissioning of his works, see Chegai, *L'esilio di Metastasio,* 13, and Metastasio, *Opere,* vols. 3–5, passim. As discussed in letters of January 30, 1751, on *Didone abbandonata,* and of February 23, 1756, on *Alessandro nell'Indie,* Metastasio shortened texts for Farinelli's Madrid audience, who had just recently been acculturated to opera seria (Burney, *Memoirs of . . . Metastasio* 1:394–95 and 2:117), but he answered the Countess of Sangro's request for cuts abrasively (see n. 36 below).

21. On translations of his texts, see, e.g., de Brito, *Opera in Portugal;* Michael Burden, "Twittering and Trilling," 615; Boyd and Carreras, *Music in Spain;* Stonehouse, "*Demofoonte* and Democracy," 135–54. Many translations used facing pages (typical, for example, is the Danish *Didone abbandonata . . . da rappresentarsi sul Regio Teatro Danese* of 1762). Metastasio editions entered private American libraries, and whole operas were performed in Latin America: *Alessandro nell'Indie* and *Didone abbandonata* as set by David Perez and *Artaserse* by Giuseppe Scolari opened the Casa de Opera da Praia in Bahia, Brazil, for the Portuguese Infanta Donna Maria's marriage to Prince Don Pedro in 1760; amateurs performed an anonymous setting of *Demofoonte* in Maranho, Brazil, in 1786 (de Brito, *Opera in Portugal,* 82–83); *Artaserse* was performed on the Portuguese Atlantic island of Madeira in 1759 (ibid., 83); Louis Antoine de Bougainville heard "plays by Metastasio" in Rio de Janeiro in 1767; and Piccinni's *Didone* was staged in Havana in 1776 to open the Coliseo Theater (Diniz, "A musica na Bahia colonial," 93–116; Brasil, *A musica na cidade;* and Mendoza de Arce, *Music in Ibero-America,* 221–38). Davies shows extensive reworkings of Metastasian arias for devotional purposes at Durango in "The Italianized Frontier," chap. 4. In North America, Metastasio was performed as songs (see Meredith, "The Old World in the New," 155–70; see also Summers, "Opera Seria in Spanish California," 269–90). Among the satires are *Il conclave dell'anno mdcclxxiv dramma per musica da recitarsi nel Teatro delle Dame,* text adapted from Metastasio, music attributed to Piccinni, though Albert Schatz thought that Sertor had written it and "used the two names then most in vogue" (Sonneck, *Catalogue of Opera Librettos,* 307). Among many others, the ballets include, famously, Carlo le Picq's ballo "tragicoeroico" (Naples, 1779).

ally condensed into the darker dramma serio or the bloody two-act tragedia per musica of the late eighteenth century. The most celebrated performances were generally professional ones, but the texts were also staged and sung by amateur courtiers (e.g., *Il re pastore* and *L'eroe cinese*), academy members, and schoolboys. They were put on as spoken theater without music, turned into prose, used as inspiration for instrumental music and, from the eighteenth century and onward into the latter part of the twentieth century, were also reincarnated as outdoor *tournées* and puppet shows.[22] The stories were used as the bases for pasticcios concocted by stringing together Metastasio's arias in settings by various composers, sometimes also expanded with settings of texts by other poets. And printed editions of the texts were copiously collected for reference and silent reading by book owners as far flung as Mozart in Vienna and Thomas Jefferson in Virginia.[23] It is hard to think of another Italian poet who so dominated music and vernacular culture after Petrarch, and none who was a dramatic poet. In the aggregate of these different forms and media, Metastasio's writings came to form what Andrea Chegai has called a "giant hypertext."[24]

What qualified the Metastasian corpus for this extraordinary dissemination and reworking—a reworking that itself drew off of earlier French spoken tragedies by Racine, Pradon, and most especially their towering predecessor Corneille, as well as libretti from the generation of Zeno, and that subsequently generated countless imitations and rewritings in its own and later times? And what can justify the claim that Metastasio's texts were mythical, since only a few were based on legends and none displayed pagan deities or magic onstage?

22. In defending poetry and censuring modern singers in response to the Chevalier de Chastellux (whose treatise privileged music), Metastasio claimed, perhaps in a moment of ire, that his own dramas were better "when declaimed by comedians, than when sung by musicians" (letter of July 15, 1765, Metastasio, *Opere* 4:398; Burney, *Memoirs of . . . Metastasio* 2:318). Chegai cites a review (*Gazzetta universale*, 1800) that praised a performance of *Nitteti* by the Compagnia Comica del Regio Teatro degl'Intrepidi, arguing that spoken shows were done by amateurs because professionals associated Metastasio with music (*L'esilio di Metastasio*, 16 and n. 13). On his travels in Italy, Burney never heard of Metastasio being performed without music; probably it only happened in private academies and homes, though in Vienna spoken shows occurred at the Kärntnerthor (Zechmeister, *Die Wiener Theater*, 203, 251, and 401). Cf. Neville, "Metastasio: Beyond the Stage," 87–109, esp. 99. On Metastasio's works as prose, see Metastasio, *Opere* 1:1476, and as outdoor entertainments, Morelli, "Maggio e melodramma," 167–86, with special attention to reworkings of *Demofoonte*. See Chegai on early nineteenth-century Metastasian *tournées* (e.g., *Didone*, *Ezio*, and *Tito* at Rimini, 1826) and on comics who performed Metastasio in piazzas (*L'esilio di Metastasio*, 16 and chap. 1, n. 33). Antonio Sgavetti tells of a Metastasian marionette opera in Parma's Teatrino della Corte, March 26, 1761. The violin virtuoso and composer Giuseppe Tartini may have taken inspiration from *Didone abbandonata* in writing his Sonata for violin and keyboard in G minor, op. 1, no. 1, published in 1734, which later took on the nickname "Didone abbandonata." See d'Alembert, *De la liberté de la musique*, 455–57; in Launay, *La querelle des bouffons*, 3:2275–77.

23. Neville, "Metastasio."

24. Chegai, *L'esilio di Metastasio*, 37. Maeder explores Metastasio's influence in Italian opera through much of the nineteenth century (*Metastasio*, chap. 10).

THEMISTOCLES, HERO

Metastasio's dramaturgy took it as axiomatic that poetry stood above, or at least prior to, music, acting, scenography, and costume design (for him, dancing hardly counted at all). As an octogenarian, Metastasio summarized this viewpoint for the young Turk Mattia Verazi (ca. 1730–94), an avant-garde Roman poet working at Mannheim and later Munich who had just dedicated to him his *L'Europa riconosciuta*. "In this [libretto] I found my Signor Verazi always the equal of himself—fluid, pleasing, clear, and rich with that enviable fecundity of invention that constitutes the most useful merit of dramatic poetry and communicates itself to all the subordinate arts employed to follow it."[25] For Metastasio, it was the poet's charge to control all possible gestural and scenic aspects of stagings through his dialogue and stage directions.[26] Far from merely presuming the priority of the poet in the lineup of theater personnel, he exercised what Elena Sala di Felice has called textual "totalitarianism," which tended to engulf future stagings and discourage later writers from recasting themes he had already taken up.[27] Nevertheless, and perhaps ironically, it was precisely these presumptions that went hand in glove with an immediate consciousness of performance. It combined with Metastasio's sense of the living stage, of deft character contrasts, finely tensed plot developments, and with his exquisite rhythmic and sonic ear, all of which left him few competitors for many decades.

We can get a good idea why Metastasio dominated the stage by comparing his Viennese *Temistocle* (staged with Antonio Caldara's music in 1736) with Zeno's *Temistocle* for Vienna written thirty-five years earlier (an *azione scenica* originally set by Marc'Antonio Ziani and later, in 1718, by Porpora).[28] Both recount the exile from Athens of Themistocles, the Greek hero whose power and fame allegedly so aroused the envy of his countrymen that he had to find ref-

25. "Trovai in quello il mio signor Verazi sempre eguale a se stesso, fluido, felice, chiaro, e ricco di quella sua invidiabile fecondità di fantasia che fa il più utile pregio della poesia drammatica e che si comunica a tutte le arti subalterne impiegate a secondarla" (letter of September 3, 1778, Metastasio, *Opere* 5:526). See McClymonds, "Transforming Opera Seria," 119–32.

26. Metastasio sometimes gave stage directions in dialogue: e.g., *Temistocle* 2:1 (Metastasio, *Opere* 1:887), where Temistocle describes his surrounding decor; *Achille in Sciro* 2.1 and 2.7, where Acade and Ulisse describe sound worlds; *Achille* 2.8, where Achille announces throwing away his lyre (see Sala di Felice, *Metastasio,* 35–37). Metastasio often did not share the extensive stage directions that he kept, and the quantity of stage directions in author-approved editions of his works varied widely. For example, there are many in *Nitetti* 3.6 (*Opere* 1:1237–39), particularly concerning passions to be affected, and quite few throughout *Ciro riconosciuto* (cf. Savage, "Staging an Opera," 591–94).

27. Sala di Felice views this totalitarianism as part of Metastasio's vision of the text itself, as something that projects itself indefinitely in time "to dominate every future scenic realization of the text" (*Metastasio,* 19).

28. *Raccolta di melodrammi seri* 2:3–44. See Freeman, "Apostolo Zeno's Reform," 321–41, countered by Weiss, "Teorie drammatiche," 273–96, who shows that Zeno, like other Arcadians, produced libretti on fables rather than histories.

Table 6.1. Dramatis personae in Zeno's and Metastasio's libretti for *Temistocle*

Zeno, Temistocle *(1701)*	*Metastasio,* Temistocle *(1736)*
Artaserse, king of Persia, approves love between Temistocle and Palmide	**Serse,** king of Persia
Temistocle, Athenian hero, in love with Palmide	**Temistocle,** Athenian hero
Palmide, princess, in love with Temistocle	**Aspasia,** daughter of Temistocle, attendant of Rossane
Eraclea, daughter of Temistocle, ambivalent about Clearco's love	**Neocle,** son of Temistocle
Cambise, the king's favorite, jealous of Temistocle and in love with Palmide, who disdains him	**Rossane,** Persian princess in love with Serse and envious of Aspasia
Clearco, "Athenian" ambassador, in love with Eraclea	**Lisimaco,** "Greek" ambassador
Arsace, captain of Artaserse's guard, nonplussed by the king's regard for Temistocle	**Sebaste,** the king's confidante

uge at the court of the king of Persia—Artaserse (Artaxerxes) in Zeno's version based on book 1 of Thucydides' *Historiae,* and Serse (Xerxes) in Metastasio's based on Plutarch's *Lives,* which allegedly corrected Thucydides. In Zeno's plot, Artaserse steals thunder from the denouement by condemning the hero to death in a showy aria text midway through the opera (2.4) when Temistocle refuses to help battle Athens. Only at the very end of the opera is the king so impressed with Temistocle's honor that he suddenly relents, without prompting (3.10). Much of Zeno's drama hangs in limbo with little tension, apart from action that turns on conflicted loyalties to a beloved versus the king or *patria* or to one *patria* versus another (Temistocle calls himself "son of Athens" [2.4]). Zeno plays out these conflicts with five characters in addition to Artaserse and Temistocle (table 6.1): Cambise, the king's favorite, jealous of Temistocle and unrequitedly in love with the Persian princess Palmide; Palmide, who loves Temistocle, as he does her; Eraclea, Temistocle's daughter; Clearco, an Athenian ambassador who aims to bring Temistocle back to Athens and who is (mostly) unrequitedly in love with Eraclea; and a military captain, Arsace.

Palmide's main preoccupation is that Temistocle might love Athens more than he does her (2.5), and she is right. His passion is diluted by tedious complaints that the king's approval of their love contradicts his demand that Temistocle betray Athens, since betraying Athens would make the Athenian hero an unworthy lover (though he and Palmide still manage to sing a big love duet near the end of act 2). In act 3, a sudden turnaround makes everybody admire Temistocle and brings the two couples together: Temistocle with Palmide (hence Athens with its enemy Persia) and Clearco with Eraclea (hence the hero's daughter with his homeland). Zeno paints none of the other Persian men strongly enough to engender much dramatic action or character contrast. Cambise loves Palmide but is only pallidly envious of her love for Temistocle, and at the bottom of the cast hierarchy Arsace is a mere go-between with little mind of his own (as in

2.7). Formulaic and propositional, the drama ends with the Persian subjects singing an encomiastic chorus.

Metastasio puts more at stake for Temistocle by giving him a son and daughter (Neocle and Aspasia) instead of a love interest, and sets extra landmines for him by including two conspirators against the throne as against Zeno's one: the princess Rossane (in love with King Serse but attended by Temistocle's daughter, whom she envies as a possible rival) and the king's confidante, Sebaste (who envies Temistocle's friendship with the king). A further threat to Temistocle's life is the Athenian ambassador Lisimaco, whose explicit job is to have the hero returned to Athens to stand trial. Temistocle's children provide an audience for his enlightened speeches of self-abnegation in the face of public duty, and allowed Metastasio to raise the specter of a parent about to be executed. The introduction of a second conspirator allowed him to draw a stronger contrast than Zeno had between heroism and treachery, exploring the perils of envy that plague great heroes and finally untangling the plot in a neat denouement.

Both texts, Zeno's and Metastasio's, situate the turning point of the plot at the moment when the king demands that Temistocle join forces with him to conquer Athens. But once Zeno's hero refuses, things lumber along as the Persians, Palmide, Cambise, and Arsace, make a series of sententious reflections on Temistocle's strength in the face of death, interspersed with minor love incidents. Zeno's version bludgeoned its viewers with a dull and unsympathetic image of patriarchy as Temistocle makes a show of paternal power in the middle of act 3 by forcing his daughter's hand to Clearco's in order to recement his alliance with Greece. And gradually—through the combined force of Temistocle's hubris, the laments and (later) supplications to the king of nearly all the other characters, and Temistocle's final acknowledgment that though the king's sentence is just, he has no alternative but to kill himself—Artaserse's royal ire turns into love and admiration. Zeno ends by having the king pardon Temistocle and sending the Athenian ambassador off to expunge hatred in Greece.

Unlike Zeno's drama, what is critical to Metastasio's is Temistocle's own agency. After the king demands that he take up arms against Greece and is refused (2.7–8), the business of setting up the denouement is left largely to the protagonist, who brings it about through a brilliant *crescendo di azione*. Told by Sebaste in 3.1 that he must either swear a public fealty to Persia at a burning altar or else face certain death, Temistocle hesitates. His heroism can allow him to die in a public act of loyalty to the fatherland—even at the cost of disloyalty to the sovereign who has given him refuge—but it cannot allow him to die in infamous obscurity. He withholds his ultimate answer by promising only to appear at the altar ("Verrò"), but as soon as Sebaste leaves he tells his children secretly that once there he plans to choose death instead of making the expected oath—a theatrical plan if ever there was.[29] Accordingly, Temistocle's monologue

29. First he gets their assurances of loyalty (3.3): "Do you know what exact obedience the command of a father requires?" to which they reply, "It is a sacred bond. It is an inviolable law." (Te-

EXAMPLE 6.1. Antonio Caldara, aria for Temistocle, "Ah, frenate il pianto imbelle," mm. 7–16

From *Temistocle* (Burgtheater, Vienna, 1736), 3.3. Vocal line from A-Wgm, MS IV.1966.

ascends into flights of poetic lyricism as he declares that his legacy to them will be virtue, glory, heaven, and his example, climaxing finally in a stern aria of reproach to his weeping daughter:

Ah, frenate il pianto imbelle;	[Oh cease your fragile tears,
Non è ver, non vado a morte;	It's not true, I go not to death,
Vo del fato, delle stelle,	I go to triumph over
Della sorte a trionfar.	Fate, the stars, and fortune.][30]

Indeed, it was exactly the hero's triumphant martial spirit that Caldara's setting stressed melismatically when it was performed at the Burgtheater in 1736 (example 6.1).

By 3.6, Rossane, repentant, proves to Serse that his life is in danger. The king confronts Sebaste—"Non tremar, vassallo indegno, / È già tardo il tuo timore" (Tremble not, unworthy vassal, / Your fear is much too late)—in Caldara's setting, a rage aria seething with orchestral tremolos throughout its whole length (see example 6.2). With the stage set for Temistocle's *coup de théâtre,* the scene shifts to the burning altar (3.9), readied for his oath. By then, Temistocle's appearance has become a charged event, made more so by keeping him offstage for several previous scenes. Before the rite begins, the king moves to embrace the hero in a gesture of trust, only to have Temistocle draw back, declaring himself still unworthy. As the sacred cup is prepared, he holds it aloft and turns majestically to address the spectators: "I promised to come but not to swear an oath."

mistocle: È noto a voi / a qual esatta ubbidienza impegni / un commando paterno? Neocle: È sacro nodo. Aspasia: È inviolabil legge.)

30. Afterward, his son's aria announces his new inspiration to virtue, "Di quella fronte un raggio" (3.4), while the daughter follows with a "feminine" aria patetica of desperate indecision, "Ah! Si resti Onor mi sgrida / Ah! Si vada . . . Il piè non osa" (3.5; ellipses in original).

EXAMPLE 6.2. Antonio Caldara, aria for Serse, "Non tremar, vassallo indegno," mm. 5–9

From *Temistocle* 3.6. Short score based on A-Wgm, MS IV.1996.

Hear me, Serse,
Listen to me, Lisimaco; you
people who look upon us, listen
to Temistocle's meanings, and may you all bear
witness and be their custodian. An adverse fate
wants me as an ingrate and a traitor.
Besides these two counts of guilt,
no arbiter of my choice remains
but life,
that free gift of Heaven. To stay true to myself
and not commit a crime, I see no other path
than the path of the tomb, and that I choose. (*draws a vial of poison from his breast*)
May this readied poison, which has
kept me company in my painful exile,
complete its work. May the sacred
liquor, the sacred cup (*he lets [the poison] fall into the cup*)
act as its ministers, and may all the gods bear witness
to the offering of this voluntary victim of faith, gratitude, and honor,
may everyone aid the gods. . . .
(to Lisimaco) You, Lisimaco, my friend,
reassure our fatherland of my loyalty, and plead for grace
for my ashes. Should I have a tomb where I have left behind
the cradle, I will forgive all the injuries to my fate.

(to Serse) You, great king, do not repent
of your beneficence, for which you will receive mercy
from an admiring world. What
I can do for you meanwhile (oh harsh fate!) is simply
to confess and die. Merciful gods,
if the final vows of innocent souls
have any rights in heaven,
may you protect the destiny
of your Athens, and care for
this king, this kingdom, and
inspire in the heart of Serse a sense of
peace with Greece. Ah! Yes, my king, may your scorn
and my life end at the same point.
Children, friend, Sire, *popolo,* farewell![31]

Temistocle lifts the cup to drink the poisoned liquid. Serse intervenes, trying to reappropriate the king's position as royal arbiter of men's fates. Yet it remains our hero who fashions himself—through his spectacular, histrionic staging of virtue, redeemed before the whole panoply of classes and social relations—as protagonist of an extraordinary myth. Caldara set Temistocle's entire speech in simple recitative but endowed it with an oratorical style that finally refers power back phenomenally into hero's domain, a position Metastasio spelled out by having Temistocle declare: "Serse, you cannot take death from me. This is the only power not allowed monarchs" (3.11).[32] Compared to the styles Caldara assigns to Serse, Aspasia, and Lisimaco, all of whom interject recitatives at various moments in the scene, Temistocle's recitative—like his aria to his daughter—is stolidly stepwise and evenly paced.[33]

31. "Sentimi, o Serse; / Lisimaco, m'ascolta; udite, o voi / Popoli spettatori: / di Temistocle i sensi, e ognun ne sia / testimonio e custode. Il fato avverso / mi vuole ingrato o traditor. Non resta, / fuor di queste due colpe, / arbitrio alla mia scelta, / se non quel della vita, / del ciel libero dono. A conservarmi / senza delitto altro cammin non veggo / che il cammin della tomba, e quello eleggo. . . . *(trae dal petto il veleno)* / Questo, che meco / trassi compagno al doloroso esiglio, / pronto velen l'opra compisca. Il sacro licor, la sacra tazza *(lo lascia cader nella tazza)* / ne sian ministri; ed all'offrir di questa / vittima volontaria / di fé, di gratitudine e d'onore, / tutti assistan gli dèi. . . . *(a Lisimaco)* Della mia fede / tu, Lisimaco, amico, / rassicura la patria, e grazia implora / alle ceneri mie. Tutte perdono / le ingiurie alla fortuna, / se avrò la tomba ove sortii la cuna. / *(a Serse)* Tu, eccelso re, de' benefizi tuoi / non ti pentir: ne ritrarrai mercede / dal mondo ammirator. Quella, che intanto / renderti io posso (oh dura sorte!) è solo / confessarli e morir. Numi clementi, / se dell'alme innocenti / gli ultimi voti han qualche dritto in cielo, / voi della vostra Atene / proteggete il destin, prendete in cura / questo re, questo regno; al cor di Serse / per la Grecia inspirate / sensi di pace. Ah! sì, mio re, finisca / il tuo sdegno in un punto e il viver mio. / Figli, amico, signor, popoli, addio! *(Prende la tazza)*" (Metastasio, *Opere* 1:916–17).

32. "Serse, la morte / tormi non puoi: l'unico arbitrio è questo / non concesso a' monarchi" (ibid., 917). Sala di Felice, *Metastasio,* uses the neologism "arbitro-re" for the king who decides life and death.

33. A-Wmg, MS IV.1996, pp. 292–98.

* * *

Metastasio's letters betrayed an ambivalence toward the work. "[T]his accursed *Temistocle* was my scourge because of the very simplicity of its intricacies and the need to carve everything out of a single hero."[34] It was unusual to feature a primo uomo with no love interest, a feat Metastasio repeated only in *Attilio Regolo* (completed in 1740, but owing to the emperor's death, not performed until 1750).[35] Nevertheless, when asked years later by the Countess of Sangro to reduce the libretto for a Neapolitan summertime performance, Metastasio was irked. "Mutilating it would be a savagery worthy of an Ezzelino or a Mezentius obliging a father to mangle his own son. . . . [I]t's pointless to ask corrections of someone who did not notice any errors in it when he first wrote it . . . [and anyway] a Burchiello in your midst will be much more useful than a Sophocles far away."[36] A true child of the living theater, Metastasio shows himself partial to his intractable hero, yet upholds the pragmatic view that adaptations have to be made on the spot. Indeed, during the years when Metastasio worked in Vienna, he personally inspected the stage of the garden theater La Favorita, checked stage machinery on site before mounting the spectacular *licenze* offered monarchs at the ends of operas, debated with costume designers and tailors, requested mock-ups of set designs from Lorenzo Quaglio, kept *direzioni* for some operas (beyond what appeared in his texts), and prepared and rehearsed stagings. He had first learned stage directing hands-on from La Romanina, the Roman soprano/director and Metastasio's great friend Maria Benti Bulgarelli, for whom he later wrote stage directions (she contributed two scenes to *Didone*, which she premiered). For Metastasio, being a top stage director was inseparable from being a top librettist, two jobs that were traditionally managed by one hand.[37]

Being ever conscious of the text as something malleable, meant for living, breathing people to perform and hear, Metastasio did modify his libretti to suit the very different institutions and audiences in Farinelli's Madrid during the 1740s and 1750s, and he helped Hasse (much esteemed by him) to stage his libretti at Dresden. But his primary tasks were to ensure a best possible first performance and a best possible written text, suited to innumerable future stagings in a world where adaptations were desirable and virtually preordained. Amazingly suasive, Metastasio's texts became choice vehicles for singers, spec-

34. "Questo maledetto *Temistocle* . . . è stato il mio flagello . . . L'impegno è grande per la semplicità del viluppo, e per la necessità di cavar tutto dal solo carattere dell'eroe" (letter of September 29, 1736, Metastasio, *Opere* 3:143).

35. Reinhard Strohm views the two operas as a "dramatic duality" ("Dramatic Dualities," 559).

36. "Quando fosse necessario mutilarlo, sarebbe barbarie degna d'Ezelino o di Mesenzio l'obbligare un padre a storpiar . . . il proprio figliuolo . . . è vano il dimandar correzione a chi non ha conosciuto gli errori quando l'ha scritta . . . [e] un Burchiello presente sarà molto più utile che un Sofocle lontano" (Metastasio, *Opere* 3:790).

37. Savage, "Staging an Opera," 583–95; Heartz, "The Poet as Stage Director"; and Joly, *Dagli elisi al inferno*, chap. 4 (on *Nitteti*).

tators, and producers (princes, academists, noble *comitati*, impresarios), leagues beyond their competitors in the contest for textual iteration that was endemic to opera seria and that blasted the popularity of the genre across Europe. With ever more impresarios at work, many of whom could scarcely afford to sink money into new stage sets, finance new libretti, or risk hiring traveling singers—singers who would not know the texts they were to sing, would have little time to learn them, and often preferred to minimize the recitatives and insert their own arias anyway—there were practical imperatives as well as artistic and political ones that led to a state of affairs in which Metastasio's libretti virtually colonized Italian opera for some decades.

A factor of no small relevance to this phenomenon was Metastasio's uncanny feel for mass desire, for how to penetrate collective consciousness in ways that could cut across particular occasions, local conditions, and national frontiers. Shaping mass audiences and sentiments across linguistic boundaries and making ideology heartfelt—this was his mother's milk.

Revealing on this score is a letter to La Romanina about the reception of *Demetrio*, which had just premiered at Vienna in 1730.

> Last Sunday, my opera *Demetrio* was performed . . . with such success, that *the oldest people in the country assure me, they never remember approbation so universal. The audience wept at the parting scene; to which my most August patron was not insensible. And not withstanding the great respect for the Sovereign, in many of the recitatives, the applause of the theatre was not restrained by his presence.* Those who were before my enemies, are now become my apostles. I am unable to express to you my surprise at this success, as it is a gentle and delicate opera, without those bold strokes which produce great effects; *nor did I believe it adapted to the national taste.* But I was mistaken. The entire audience obviously understood it, and *they repeat parts of it in conversation, as if it were written in German. My master began to show his satisfaction, from the end of the first act, and afterwards spoke it openly to all around him.* The music is of the most modern kind that Caldara has composed.[38]

The letter is a pithy condensation of Metastasio's mythopoetics. In delivering its parable of sovereignty, his opera created a collective effervescence that celebrates and endears sovereignty, but also oversteps it. Karl VI was so moved

38. Burney, *Memoirs of . . . Metastasio* 1:76–77 (emphasis mine). "Domenica scorsa andò in scena il mio *Demetrio* con tanta felicità, che mi assicurano i vecchi del paese che non si ricordano di un consenso così universale. Gli ascoltanti piansero alla scena dell'addio: l'augustissimo padrone non fu indifferente: e non ostante il gran rispetto della cesarea padronanza, in molti recitativi il teatro non seppe trattenersi di dar segni della sua approvazione. Quelli che erano miei nemici sono diventati miei apostoli. Non vi posso spiegare la mia sorpresa, perché, essendo questa un'opera tutta delicata e senza quelle pennellate forti che feriscono violentemente, io non isperava che fosse adattata alla nazione. Mi sono ingannato: tutti mostrano d'intenderla, e ne dicono i pezzi per le conversazioni come se fosse scritta in tedesco. Il padrone cominciò dalla fine del primo atto ad assicurarmi del suo cesareo gradimento, e poi lo dimostrò a tutti spiegandosene con quelli co'quali ne ha parlato. La musica è delle più moderne che faccia il Caldara" (Metastasio, *Opere* 3:58–59).

and the audience so swept away that even though the monarch's prerogatives dictated that his people imitate his actions, determining when spectators would and would not be animated by applause, the emperor in this instance let them override him. The result was an instance of communal exhilaration, a "universal approbation" that exceeded anything in the memory of even "the oldest people in the country." What allowed all this was the transmission of grand ideology through intimate sentiment—unleashed by means of Metastasio's moving verse, Caldara's "modern" score, and (presumably) the delivery of the performers.

In a trenchant passage on the sovereign ideal in *Demetrio*, Jacques Joly argues that, unlike Racine's plays for Louis XIV, Metastasio's libretti foreground human subjects before whom the sovereign assumes responsibility in the name of a public trust.[39] Queen Cleonice (in love with Demetrio disguised as the humble Alceste) is so wholly "servant of [her] own subjects" that she is effectively the supreme subject of subjects, especially as she wants passionately to exist not just as an instrument of public necessity but as a person. I would add that in *Demetrio*, Metastasio adapted eighteenth-century norms of sovereignty to new enlightenment ideals, brilliantly manipulating a mechanics of public identification that was already facilitated by the commercial opera house.[40] Subjects here stand at the crux of such identification, but only insofar as they command internal alterations in rulers. Synthesized with this sovereign-subject relation, and adroitly reworked, is also an idealized conception of love drawn from the old Platonic and courtly Provencal traditions of the *donna angelicata*. From this synthesis of love and the throne—the love felt by persons and the throne commanded by metapersons and empires—emerges melodrama with a vengeance.[41]

HISTORY AS MYTH

Ironically, the most compelling eighteenth-century account of why Metastasio's tales had such unparalleled magnetism (even if it also tried to acknowledge Metastasio's faults) was written by a Jesuit who had fled to Italy after expulsion from Spain in 1767. Stefano Arteaga's famed history of Italian opera, *Le rivoluzioni del teatro musicale italiano dalla sua origine fino al presente*, revised and published between 1783 and 1788, devotes a chapter nearly eighty pages long to arguing that the very perpetuity of opera as an institution had been ensured by

39. Joly, *Dagli elisi al inferno*, 18–19.

40. Joly stresses Metastasio's choice of a woman, hence a subject, for this role. Cleonice's hesitation between kingdom and love is outlined immediately in her aria "Fra tanti pensieri" (1.3), with B section "Le cure del soglio / Gli affetti, rammento: / Risolvo, mi pento: / E quel che non voglio / Ritorno a voler."

41. See Joly, *Dagli elisi al inferno*, 28; Vieira de Carvalho, "From Opera to 'Soap Opera,'" 41–61; and Žižek and Dolar's general argument in *Opera's Second Death*.

Metastasio's singular ability to unite beauty and emotion with historical truth.[42] Where fables had deprived opera of any proper order or common sense, history gave opera regularity.[43] This was an old truism by Arteaga's time, but he went on to elaborate in considerable detail how musicality, passion, and philosophy (founded in historical truth) united in Metastasio with his decisive sense of dramatic logic. No poet, he claimed, had ever been endowed with Metastasio's ear for music, his ability to "adapt with singular dexterity the diversity of meters to the various passions." No poet had previously succeeded in so artfully fitting metric lengths to dramatic declamation. None had so skillfully deployed short verses for languorous affects, apt for those moments when the weary soul doesn't have the strength to finish a thought,[44] nor managed to turn short verses like this one into expressive virtues:

Oh che felici pianti!	[Oh what happy tears!
Che amabile martir!	What pleasurable suffering!
Purchè si possa dir:	As long as one can say:
Quel core è mio.	That heart belongs to me.][45]

Nor had any so perfectly deployed full, fast, energetic verses when characters express courage:[46]

Fiamma ignota nell'alma mi scende	[An unknown flame descends into the depths of my soul.
Sento il Nume: m'inspira, m'accende,	I feel the Deity: he inspires me and ignites me
Di me stessa mi rende maggior.	And makes me greater than my own self.
Ferri, bende, bipenni, ritorte,	Shackles, blindfolds, axes, chains,
Pallid'ombre, compagne di morte	Pale shades, companions of Death:
Già vi guardo, ma senza terror.	I look upon you now, but without terror.][47]

For Arteaga, it was an article of faith that Metastasio should have refused "the deliriums of ancient mythology" (read "fable and fiction") to draw near the "leaves of tragedy," and with a translinguistic lyricism utterly apt for the melodramatic muse. His success rested on skill at making *filosofia* come alive on stage, giving ideology an ear and a soul.[48] Philosophy in his hands was spared the

42. To explain Metastasio's universal success, Arteaga needs to "esaminar . . . partitamente i mezzi ond'egli è arrivato a rendersi lo scrittore unico, e privilegiato dei musici, e la delizia delle persone gentili" (*Le rivoluzioni* 1:335).

43. Ibid., 345.

44. "[A]dattando con singolar destrezza la diversità dei metri alle varie passioni, facendo uso dei versi curti negli affetti, che esprimono la languidezza, allorché l'anima, per così dire, sfinita non ha forza, che basti a terminar il sentimento" (ibid., 337–38).

45. *Zenobia* 2.5, in Metastasio, *Opere* 1:947.

46. "Dei pieni, rapidi, e volubili dove si esprime il coraggio" (Arteaga, *Le rivoluzioni* 1:337).

47. *L'olimpiade* 3.4, in Metastasio, *Opere* 1:622.

48. Arteaga, *Le rivoluzioni* 1:345–46.

dust of schoolish learning and "sophistic stupidity." It "worked its way through all the myriad faculties that give access to human knowledge, like the universal soul of the Pythagoreans, without enslaving itself to the charms of eloquence or the graces of harmony." Seneca by comparison was like a "boy who's just gotten out of the lyceum."[49]

> What dramatic poet has heretofore succeeded better? Looking at ethics, or the part of philosophy that scrutinizes and reinforces the duties of man . . . (the only study that merits attention from a sentient being), who has made himself more worthy than he? Is the fact that he has depicted the virtue of ethics with the most pleasing of colors not shown in the magnificent exemplars that he proposes for us to imitate, or the important maxims he has scattered throughout his works, or the persuasive, irresistible ways that he disposes the heart to receive them?[50]

Was not the exemplar of exemplars Metastasio's Titus, "delight of the human race," "true father of his subjects, model for the subjects of the king, the man [like Trajan] . . . born to honor human nature and represent the divine"?—the model for transcending impossible conflicts, the supreme philosopher-king, virtuous for the sake of public happiness.[51]

But Arteaga also emphasized how Metastasio's operas broadcast the exemplarity of royal subjects and republican citizens. "Do not the encomiasts of freedom . . . feel joy on contemplating their Regulus, their Cato [heroes of his republican operas]? And Siroe, Timanthès, Svenvango, Ezius, Arbaces, and Megacles: do they not make us prize the human species more highly? Does one not rejoice at being human knowing that Themistocles has been one's company? Does everyone not . . . wonder on hearing the lofty sentiments the poet puts in their mouths in the most delicate situations a hero can confront?"[52] In

49. "[M]a quella aurea e divina, che internandosi agguisa dell'anima universale dei pitagorici per entro a tutte le facoltà dell'umano sapere, non ischiva di travestirsi sotto il fascino della eloquenza, o sotto i vezzi dell'armonia affine di stillare più soavemente negli animi la verità" (ibid., 347). "Armonia" here denotes euphony, but is charged with Pythagorean cosmic harmony. On Seneca, see ibid., 349–50.

50. "Qual poeta drammatico ha ottenuto ciò finora meglio di Metastasio? Se si riguarda la morale, ovvero sia quella parte della filosofia che disamina e fortifica i doveri dell'uomo . . . la sola [scienza] che meriti di occupar i riflessi di un Essere pensante, chi se n'è renduto più benemerito di lui? Che ne ha dipinta la virtù con colori più amabili o si ponga mente ai magnifici esemplari, che egli propone alla nostra imitazione, o le massime importanti quà e là sparse nei suoi componimenti, o la persuasiva, irresistibil maniera colla quale dispone il cuore a riceverli?" (ibid., 347).

51. "Non è egli le delizie dell'uman genere nei suoi scritti, come già fu sul trono? Non apparisce forse il vero padre dei suoi vasalli, il modello dei re cittadini, l'uomo . . . nato ad onorare l'umana natura, e a rappresentar la divina?" (ibid., 347–48). Cf. Rao, "Enlightenment and Reform," 229–52, esp. 230.

52. "Gli encomiatori della libertà . . . non sentono eccitarsi all'eroismo contemplando il suo Regolo, e il suo Catone? E Siroe, Timante, Svenvango, Ezio, Arbace, e Megacle non fanno sì, che s'abbia in maggior pregio l'umana spezie? Non si gioisce di esser uomo sapendo di aver avuto per

fact, Metastasio's operas were even more prone to venerate heroes than monarchs, as ideal subjects who served as models for others. The hero could trace an upward moral trajectory whose span might outstrip the monarch's, becoming, like Ezius or Themistocles, the very model for a king, or end up through a twist of fate as heir to the throne, like Timanthes. He could also embody heroism to such a degree as to emerge through a fated revelation, out of hiding, disguise, or mistaken identity, as the true king, like Demetrius (alias Alcestes), Achilles (disguised as the girl Purrha), Cyrus (as Alcaeus), or Licidas (hidden as an infant). In this sense, the hero was a subjective mirror for the prince—literally the subject struggling valiantly through life's travails who is held up to the prince as an exemplar. And as an ideal model to the king's people, both in the drama and within the theater, as well as in the republic of letters, the hero gave resonance to the people's status as subjects.[53]

But the paradigm of exemplarity is hardly unambiguous—something that is also central to the mythical status of the Metastasian libretto. Ideologically the king is revered as king, no matter what his kingdom. Since the people create him as ruler, he depends on their loyalty; and the more he extracts in loyalty and generosity the more he owes in return.[54] Still, the people's loyalty is widely confused and tested, including by a general reverence demanded of them toward all kings. Moreover, though the king is the paternal figure par excellence, natural fathers demand loyalty too. The choices heroes face between the dual poles of duty to one's king and to one's natural father are nearly irresoluble (witness *Artaserse*), so that potential conflicts often cause kings, like heroes, to make disloyal acts or commitments of the heart, ones that eventually have to be called to account and compensated. And just as the fatherly king and natural father demand loyalty, so too the fatherland. The Persian king who is sovereign over the exiled Temistocle commands him to loyalty, but by the same token is refused it for the sake of the fatherland (2.8). Arteaga reiterates the king's surprise—"What do you love so much in Athens?"—and Temistocles' response:

> Everything, Sire:
> the ashes of my ancestors,
> the sacred laws, the tutelary gods,
> the language, the customs;
> the sweat that it cost me;
> the splendor that I drew from her;
> the air, the tree trunks, the earth, the walls, the stones.[55]

---

compagno Temistocle? Non sentesi ognuno compreso da meraviglia . . . ascoltando l'elevatezza dei sentimenti, che gli mette in bocca il poeta in una delle situazioni più delicate, che possano presentarsi ad un Eroe?" (Arteaga, *Le rivoluzioni* 1:348).

53. Cf. Hortschansky, *Opernheld und Opernheldin*, and Heller, "Reforming Achilles," 562–81.

54. Cf. Sahlins, "Poor Man, Rich Man, Big-Man, Chief," 71–93.

55. "Tutto, signor: le ceneri degli avi, / le sacre leggi, i tutelari Numi, / la favella, i costumi, / il sudor che mi costa, / lo splendor che ne trassi, / l'aria, i tronchi, i terren, le mura, i sassi" (Metastasio, *Opere* 1:900).

Based on strict codes of honor and glory, Temistocle's totalizing loyalty involves higher authorities (the goddess Athena), countrymen, and land in an indivisible triad, one that makes inevitable his disloyalty to the adoptive sovereign.

Whether or not ideological constraints are absolute, for Arteaga loyalties are always arbitrated by passion: "What do you *love* so much in Athens?" Passions are not just media within the drama, however—love for the sovereign, the father, or the fatherland as emotions *acted out* on stage. They are inspirational for viewers, "magnificent exemplars that [Metastasio] proposes for us to imitate" in life. "What forms his main characteristic, that which makes him the delight of sensible souls and demands above all the universal recognition of readers for the tears he has drawn . . . is the art of moving the affections."[56] Repeatedly Arteaga stages scenes of conflict illustrating to the eye and ear Metastasio's perfect technology of identification, which disposes viewers and readers to open their hearts—"men because they find there the true copy of the original inside themselves; women because no other writer acquaints them better with the surprising power of their beauty and sex."[57]

> No one before Metastasio has felt so much in his philosophy of love . . . , which . . . has never been painted with more genuine colors, making visible the most hidden feelings, simplifying the most complex, unmasking the most illusory appearances. . . . No one possesses such eloquence of the heart, nor knows better . . . how to move affections, develop interests, and test them . . . , revealing distinctly the circumstances that occur simultaneously in an action, gathering them all in the event, probing the most immediate, expeditious motives, most compatible with a person's character, and most tied to his particular interest.[58]

For Arteaga, Metastasio's supremacy in this transcendent mythopoesis is obvious in the tools he gives others: writers, listeners, readers, composers, singers, and scenographers. "Reading nearly all the scenes, observing most of the recitatives and especially arias and duets, it's clear what copious sources of expression, what inexhaustible sources of tragic sensibility he has revealed to

56. "Ma quello che forma il suo carattere dominante, quello che gli rende la delizia delle anime sensibili, e che esige principalmente l'universale riconoscenza dei lettori per le lagrime, che ha cavate . . . , si è l'arte di muovere gli affetti" (Arteaga, *Le rivoluzioni* 1:360).

57. "Gli uomini perché vi ritrovano la vera copia dell'originale, che hanno dentro di sè. Le donne perché niun altro scrittore fa loro conoscer meglio la possanza sorprendente della bellezza, e l'ascendente del loro sesso" (ibid., 367).

58. "Niuno ha sentito tanto avanti quanto Metastasio nella filosofia dell'amore, filosofia . . . la quale . . . ha dipinto con più genuini colori, ora rendendo visibili e sentimenti più ascosi, ora semplificando i più complicati, ora smascherando le più illusorie apparenze. . . . Niun'altro possiede in sì alto grado l'eloquenza del cuore, nè sa meglio di lui porre in movimento gli affetti, inviluppar gl'interessi, e metter l'uno a cimento coll'altro, rilevar distintamente le circostanze, che concorrono in un'azione, radunarle poi tutte nell'occasione, spiar i motivi più immediati, i più spediti, i più confacenti col carattere della persona, e più legati col suo particolar interesse" (ibid., 368–69).

composers . . . . Hardly an aria in a hundred does not describe a situation, develop a character, or exhibit a varied affect."[59] This kaleidoscope of sentiment, somatized in the auditor through a singer who hews to the composer, starts in the lineaments of Metastasio's text, superlative in the art of pathos, in "the philosopher's tears on the miserable destiny of virtue, the mental transitions, the reticences, the incredibly fast, almost imperceptible journeys of the passions."[60] The encomium culminates in a feverish rhapsody extolling Metastasio's dramas as windows for the beleaguered mortal onto man's origins in God.

> The imagination of the virtuous man—besieged by the sight of vice triumphant, weary of wandering through a world where nothing is offered . . . but oppressors and oppressed, bewildered by cries of calumny that smother . . . the timid sighs of the innocent, drained . . . by the dealings of men he finds so often weak or evil or petty or brutal—consoles itself with the writings of this loveable poet, wandering off to an imaginary world that restores him after the vexations suffered in the real one. There he enjoys a less tempestuous sky, breathes a more worthy air, and converses with men who honor the divinity, so that flashing before his eyes he sees that primitive light of the great and beautiful that attests to his heavenly origins.[61]

We are apt to see ironies in this insistence that only historical truth will allow emotional catharsis and identification—indeed in the assertion that historical truth exists—but eighteenth-century critics did not. Furthermore, even in the Italy of Arteaga's time, sovereigns were fundamentally transcendent beings whose existence, metaphysically or symbolically at least, was divinely ordained. And yet, whether bested by heroes or tempted by human desires, sovereigns were also understood to be bound to that order. In this, their representations by Metastasio and his contemporaries still mimicked the pagan deities of Greek drama who are typically prey to earthly desires and envies: Zeus or Dionysus, who dally on earth with damsels or boys, or Aphrodite who retaliates against

59. "Si leggano quasi tutte le scene, s'osservi gran parte dei suoi recitativi, e in principal modo le arie, e i duetti, e si vedrà quai copiosi fonti di espressione, quali miniere inesauribili di tragica sensibilità abbia egli aperte ai compositori . . . . Appena in cento si troverà un'aria, che non rappresenti una situazione, che non isviluppi un carattere, che non esibisca una varia modificazione di affetto" (ibid., 362).

60. "Le lagrime del filosofo sul misero destino della virtù. Le transizioni mentali, le reticenze, i rapidissimi, e pressoché impercettibili passaggi delle passioni" (ibid., 364).

61. "L'immaginazione dell'uom virtuoso attediata dall'aspetto del vizio trionfante, stanca di vagar per un Mondo, dove altro non s'offre . . . che oppressori ed oppressi, sbigottita dagli urli della calunnia, che soffogano . . . i timidi sospiri della innocenza, annoiata . . . dal commercio dell'uomo, quale il ritrova comunemente, o debole, o maligno, o piccolo, o brutale, va per consolarsi agli scritti di questo amabile poeta, come ad un Mondo immaginario, che la ristora delle noie sofferte nel vero. Ivi gode d'un Cielo men tempestoso, ivi respira un'aria più degna di se: ivi conversa con uomini, che fanno onore alla Divinità, onde si scorge balenare sugli occhi quella luce primitiva del Grande, e del Bello, che attesta la sua origin celeste" (ibid., 349–50); cf. Doniger's theory of microscopic and telescopic levels of myth (n. 7 above).

females for personal wrongs.[62] In both cases, the divine and transcendent merge with the personal and banal. Like the gods of Greek mythology, the Metastasian sovereign provides viewers with an encompassing model that draws together public and private, inner and outer lives, humble concerns with high and mighty ones. In them lies a contrast between the good of a perfect, higher order and the disorderly travails of the immediate and mundane.

Not all libretti of the time were monarchical, of course, so not all predicated such contrasts directly on divine prerogatives (striking counterexamples in Metastasio include the republican libretti *Catone in Utica* and *Attilio Regolo*). But they did all assume the pervasive existence of a highly asymmetrical world. That upper classes had special prerogatives—social privileges, tax exemptions, lesser legal penalties, and so on—was a given. The subject's role was to avoid or correct ubiquitous moral and emotional pitfalls, following old feudal norms of honor and glory. Hierarchy in this world system implied that natural relations of lineage, ethnicity, and blood had to be respected if political order was to be maintained and sentimental dilemmas resolved. Here again, the ideological meets the sentimental, the transcendent the ordinary. Metastasio elaborated on the logic of this world order in a famous letter of 1749 to Hasse concerning his *Attilio Regolo*. The dramatis personae in the opera function, he explained, as symbolic members of a Roman body politic, with the inner character of Regolo—not a king but a great Roman hero—forming an exemplar of Roman nationhood: "a great commander, good citizen, and affectionate father." Regolo's affectionate nature was not "distinct from his country, or otherwise among the blessings or evils of life." Rather, all of these traits together "eventually contribute to the welfare or injury of that whole of which he considered himself a part." Thus, much like a monarch, Regolo was a microcosm of Roman nationhood as well as a metonym of it.[63] These premises changed over the course of the century, of course, and were already under scrutiny in the 1720s by the likes of Giannone in Naples when Metastasio wrote his first libretti. But the footings of the old order were deep and change was slow.[64]

FOUR SOVEREIGNS AND TWO HEROES

The Exemplary Prince and the Loyal Son: Artaxerxes and Arbaces

Metastasio's *Artaserse,* indebted to Corneille's *Le Cid* and the most popular of all Metastasio's stories, is the classic exemplar of the broader myth of sovereignty perpetuated in opera seria. The opera was first performed in Leonardo Vinci's setting for the Teatro delle Dame in Rome on February 4, 1730, and, remarkably,

62. Dazzling on these themes is Calasso, *The Marriage of Cadmus and Harmony.*

63. See Burney, *Memoirs of . . . Metastasio* 1:315–31; quote on 317.

64. Cf. Rao, "Enlightenment and Reform," and Venturi, *Italy and the Enlightenment,* passim.

less than two weeks later in a new setting by Hasse at the Teatro San Giovanni Grisostomo in Venice, with text already revised by Giovanni Boldini.[65] Not surprisingly, each setting was adapted for different star singers, but extraordinarily for opera seria, both Vinci's and Hasse's settings were restaged many times in subsequent decades to become true classics, what Reinhard Strohm has called "the single most substantial tradition in eighteenth-century opera seria."[66] Already in 1731, Vinci's setting was restaged for Carnival in Fano with some original cast members, and then in Ferrara where Farinelli migrated to play Arbace (Arbaces) opposite his then frequent cast partner Vittoria Tesi Tramontini, prompted by the connections of his principal patron, Count Sicinio Pepoli, with the marquis Guido Bentivoglio d'Aragona, grandee of Spain. Farinelli was so invested in Hasse's setting that he wanted to sing Hasse's recitatives in Ferrara and refrained only because the literary-minded Bentivoglio thought it a travesty to mix different composers' works, as happened regularly elsewhere.[67] In London, where pasticcios were in vogue, Hasse's setting was mounted in 1734 with added arias by Farinelli's brother, Riccardo Broschi. Remountings in Graz and St. Petersburg in 1738 were closer to Hasse's Venetian version, but in 1740 and 1760 Hasse himself completely reset *Artaserse* for Dresden and Naples, respectively, and both saw subsequent restagings elsewhere. Fascinating in this whole phenomenon is that even though particular locales did make adaptations that responded to local political demands—like the Venetian version of 1730, which minimized references to royalty and kingdom[68]—even more often the libretto roamed from city to city with relatively little done to accommodate local political circumstances but much to accommodate local production needs (a matter on which plenty of research remains to be done). The payoff for continual resettings of *Artaserse* was high, especially for inaugurating new theaters as the libretto often did.[69] Singers always already knew its lines, something that was critical when producers were trying to open a new building on top of the typically frenetic business of mounting an opera, and moreover, the narrative was widely regarded as exemplary.

Artaserse typifies Metastasio's plots in oscillating continually between the demands of public duty and private desire, a tension that can only be subdued by resolving the fate of lovers who surround the monarch and his family. This is

65. Metastasio, *Opere* 1:355–414. On Vinci's and Hasse's settings, see Heartz, *Music in European Capitals*, 92–98, 309–21, and "Hasse at the Crossroads," 24-33; Meikle, "Leonardo Vinci's *Artaserse*"; Sprague, "A Comparison of Five Musical Settings"; Strohm, *Opernarien* 1:67–70, 2: 135–38, 175–76; and Markstrom, "The Operas of Leonardo Vinci." Copies of Hasse's three settings, for Venice (1730), Dresden (1740), and Naples (1760), are at US-BEm.

66. Strohm, *Dramma per musica*, 78.

67. Farinelli, *La solitudine amica*, 91–92, 198.

68. See Heartz, *Music in European Capitals*, 312–16, on Boldini's revision of "Per quel paterno amplesso" and the two settings.

69. E.g., *L'Artaserse dramma per musica da rappresentarsi nel teatro novellamente eretto . . . nella città di Cremona il carnovale dell'anno mdcclix* (Brescia, 1749). See also chap. 7 below.

a process that tests the monarch's authority, especially in deciding affinal relations, and ultimately affirms it. The principal problem is delineated at the outset when the reigning king Serse (Xerxes) is mysteriously murdered offstage. Through this action his son, Artaserse, becomes heir to the throne at the same time as he is embroiled in one of the opera's two love interests: one his own love for a noblewoman, Semira; the other his sister Mandane's love for Semira's brother, Arbace. Hence a symmetrical alliance between the two families, one royal, one noble, plays out in a familial exchange of young lovers and concomitantly between different social levels. The prospects of the lovers are throughout confounded by a drawn-out crisis initiated by Arbace's and Semira's father, Artabano, who secretly murdered Serse (so we later learn) in order to defend Arbace's honor against doubts cast on his fittingness as a suitor for Mandane's royal hand.

Thus the story poses directly the absolutist problem of the paterfamilias. How can absolute loyalty to each father, natural and political, be maintained in the face of demands that negate one another? How can Arbace stand true to his consanguineal father (who has framed him as murderer for strategic reasons) and yet stand true to his murdered king and to his prince—also friend and soon-to-be (fatherly) king? By extension, how can Mandane be loyal to her beloved Arbace, who desires to be her spouse and thus head of her nuclear family, yet also remain loyal to her murdered father? How can the social order manage to reproduce itself in the face of ineluctable conflicts, which always involve competing genealogical paradigms? Framed more broadly, how can loyalties to the practical and ideological exigencies of the broader father relation be upheld in the face of these conflicting demands?

The liminal figure in the conundrum is not the royal Artaserse but the heroic subject Arbace, a fact that explains why the tale emphasizes throughout the terrible ambiguity of the father as both biological and symbolic figure. Once the scent of guilt descends upon Arbace early in act 1, his exculpation, and the agonizing dilemmas of conflicted loyalty he has to undergo to achieve it, become keys to a general pacification of everyone in the realm. Only when he is exonerated can the way be cleared for the two marriages, which allow the opera to end with the populace singing the praises of King Artaserse. Analogues to these dilemmas can be found in numerous other Metastasian plots in which a virtuous but beleaguered novice proves to be upwardly mobile, and thereby also serves as an ideal object of identification by the new bourgeois viewing subject—Megacle in *L'olimpiade*, for instance, or the eponymous hero in *Ezio*. Arbace braves his trials throughout precisely so that he can establish his credentials as a worthy initiate into manhood and hence, beyond the reach of the text, as a candidate for paternity. All of the principal players undergo their own trials by fire, of course, the women included, but Arbace's rage fiercest. Because of that, he also experiences the most dramatic rite of passage, a passage that is possible only once virtue, severely tested, triumphs by paying tribute simultaneously to multiple father figures. This is consistent with many other Metastasian plots in which

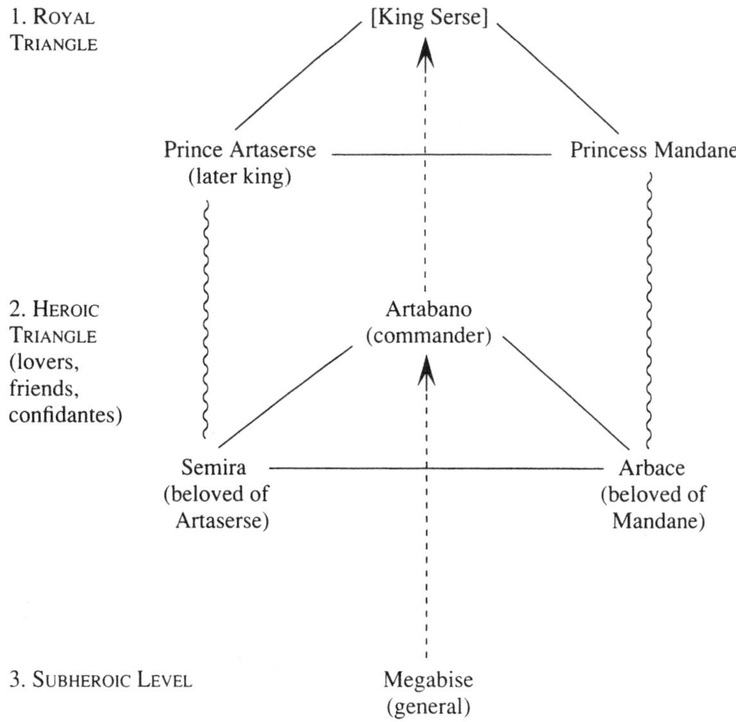

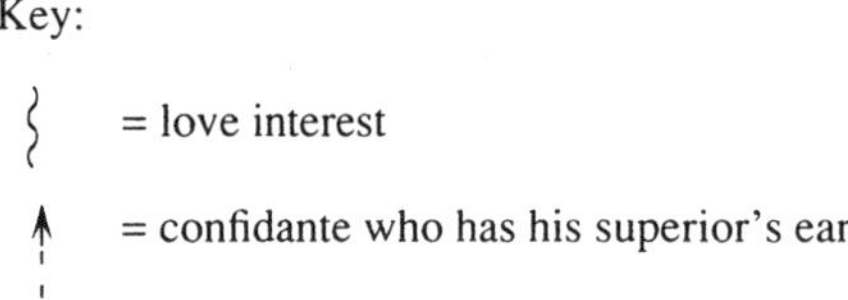

FIG. 6.1. Political, affinal, and sentimental relationships in Metastasio's *Artaserse* (Rome, 1730). Diagram by author.

females can, and usually do, inhabit a liminal role, protecting ethnic or patriotic interests and undergoing limited moral evolution, but do not act as leading figures of moral transformation. In this sense the prima donna was normally a *suddita seconda* as far as sovereignty went. She was a partner in realizing the succession of the dynasty, but only rarely was she a unilateral moral being.[70]

In the midst of trials like Arbace's, conflicts are mediated through an ethical hierarchy with obligations that point ever upward from lovers, friends, counselors, and confidantes, to fathers, brothers, and sisters, and finally to kings. As a rule kings trump kin, and kin trump nonblood relations in resolving conflict, as indicated in figure 6.1. Accordingly, the moral prerogatives postulated through this scalar movement also place public concerns above private ones, with the

70. Exceptions include *Demetrio*'s Cleonice, plus Didone and Zenobia.

king at the apex as public representative of wider social interests. Larger clan relations bind king and kin as well as other alliances to help ensure the perpetuity of the patriarchy as a whole.

The king alone among all figures occupies at once the two categories of sacred and profane. Still hewing roughly to medieval and early modern tradition (as described most famously by Ernst Kantorowicz), he is human with respect to person but still quasi-divine with respect to office, the guarantor of divine will and the purveyor of divine providence. Even though the king is no longer divine in a legal sense (as he had been in old English and French traditions), the settecento sovereign continued to be loosely associated with notions of divine ordination and right, which, despite their increasing erosion, still underlay popular consciousness.[71] In *Artaserse*, the king's link to the sacred is directly embodied in various symbols. When Artaserse attains the crown, he bestows sublime love on the people in exchange for their earthly loyalty (3.11). In the midst of the rite, he is to drink from a "sacred cup" by which he imbibes the eternal polity into his body and consolidates his connection to the sacred.[72] Mediating the two realms, his double position between sacred and profane is intended to aid in securing new affinal relations, new princely offspring, and thus the general harmony and durability of the kingdom. The sacred part of the king is that which is the kingship. To that extent the king *is* the realm—the kingdom.

As a being, the king thus forms an earthly link to the sacred through the totality of his subjects, whose virtues are concentrated in the young hero. Toward the end of the drama (3.10), this link is affirmed in the last major twist of Metastasio's plot, when Arbace's sword becomes the divine rod of iron that breaks the back of his father's duplicitous accomplice, Megabise, who has been conspiring to rouse the people against the king. Megabise is the traitor so often needed in Metastasian myth, the dark side of the social order as against Arbace's bright side.[73] Accordingly, Mandane's report that Arbace has bested Megabise before the populace is decisive in resolving dilemmas of alliance because it offers proof positive that the young hero has caused divine providence to shine on the new reign.

71. Foundational is Kantorowicz, *The King's Two Bodies*, which shows that medieval Europe conceived the king's bodies as having separate temporalities. By the eighteenth century, however, the king was no longer ideologically eternal. (But compare France's attempt to use royal effigies to continue effecting royal continuity and eternity at the time of Louis XIII, as discussed by Giesey, "The King Imagined," 41–59.) Valuable on rituals surrounding the king's body is Bertelli, *The King's Body*. Useful cross-cultural differentiations are treated in Feeley-Harnik, "Issues in Divine Kingship," 273–313, and Cannadine and Price's introduction to *Rituals of Royalty*.

72. The scene is dense with signs of the king as a divine father surrogate, and spectacular enough to win audience attention. Metastasio's stage directions place Artaserse before the populace for a magnificent coronation scene with a throne laid with crown and scepter and a burning altar adorned with a simulacrum of the sun, proclaiming "A voi, popoli, io m'offro / Non men padre, che re. Siatemi voi / Più figli, che vassalli" (To you people, I offer myself, no less a father than a king. May you be more sons to me than vassals), after which an attendant brings the sacred cup.

73. See Joly, *Dagli elisi al inferno*, 64–65, and Metastasio, *Opere* 3:73.

When Vinci's setting premiered in Rome, Arbace was embodied by the soprano castrato Giovanni Carestini ("Il Cusanino"), who made especially famous the aria "Fra cento affanni e cento" (Amid hundreds and hundreds of woes [1.2]), a response to his father's first rejection.[74] Carestini also made famous the plaintive aria at the end of act 1, "Vo solcando un mar crudele" (I go ploughing a cruel sea), which delineated the figure of the son torn between father and sovereign. The latter became a virtual prototype for all future arias that cast the singer as a sailor buffeted by stormy seas, a metaphor that encapsulated the very ethos of settecento culture. In the most celebrated work of the Italian enlightenment, Cesare Beccaria's *Dei delitti e delle pene* (Of Crimes and Punishments [1764]), the same metaphor was deployed to allegorize the enlightenment sense of awakening as "a tempest and storm of passion churning up the waves, only to feel their blows more violently."[75] Fittingly, Grétry called Vinci's "Vo solcando" "the first *tableau* that was made in music." It is an aria that paints the hero's plight with ascending trilled whole notes (most probably ornamentation vehicles, at least in the da capo), wide vocal spans and leaps, prolonged harmonic suspensions, and agitato figuration in the violins.[76] Yet "Vo solcando" was cut from Boldini's revised version for Hasse—perhaps, as both Cheryl Sprague and Daniel Heartz have conjectured, to allow Francesca Cuzzoni, starring as Mandane, to end the act—while just before hers the incomparable Farinelli was given a new aria, "Se al labbro mio non credi" (excerpt in example 6.3). A gorgeous Largo in $\frac{6}{8}$ in the unusually pathos-filled key of F minor, the aria became inextricably linked with Farinelli's name, sung by him in the London staging of the opera, which used added numbers by his brother and was commemorated and circulated in Walsh's *Favourite Songs in the Opera Call'd Artaxerxes* (London, [1735]). As Anne Desler has noted, the flavor of Farinelli's Arbace was cantabile, thus reshaping him into a *galant*, implicitly virtuous lover.[77]

In a letter to Sicinio Pepoli of September 26, 1731, Farinelli declared that while he was willing to sing Carestini's "Vo solcando" in private circumstances, he would never sing it in the theater:

> As for the arias, I'll bring them along with me since I haven't had time to have them done as I would like. Regarding the one Signor marchese Bentivoglio wants, "Vo solcando il mar crudele," I beg your Excellency to persuade him that in the privacy of his chamber or outside the theater I'll sing it as many times as he commands me to, but inside the theater I implore you to leave me free not to sing it. For as long as I've been in this business there has never been a single occasion on which I've sung others' arias on the stage, especially those of that conceited person [Carestini]. I myself enjoy the fact that others sing my

74. See Meikle, "Leonardo Vinci's *Artaserse*."

75. Venturi, "Cesare Beccaria," in *Italy and the Enlightenment*, 154–64, esp. 155–56; originally published as "Cesare Beccaria," in Fubini, *La cultura illuministica in Italia*, 120–29.

76. See Heartz, *Music in European Capitals*, 95–98.

77. Ibid., 309, and Sprague, "A Comparison," 44. Desler, "From 'Oh virtù che innamora,'" 117–38.

EXAMPLE 6.3. Johann Adolphe Hasse, substitution aria for Arbace/Farinelli, "Se al labbro mio non credi"

From *Artaserse* (Venice, 1730). Facsimile from Walsh, *Favourite Songs in the Opera Call'd Artaxerxes* (London, [1735]), first page. By permission of the British Library.

> arias in the theater and thus give me the pleasure of hearing them, as has often happened to me, so I do not want some vainglorious person to be able to boast that Farinelli sings his arias.[78]

Farinelli had already risen to the level of being imitated by other singers and would risk reversing the trajectory in a demeaning way were he to do so himself. "Se il labbro mio non credi" and others of Arbace's helped consolidate Farinelli's rising image as the virtuous young hero/lover. The formidable Farinelli became the myth of Arbace, or the role of Arbace became the mythical Farinelli.[79] Farinelli/Arbace's rival Carestini never rose mythically to the same height, even though Vinci's opera had as good an afterlife as Hasse's.

The Conquering Lover-King: Alexander the Great

Artaserse epitomizes a didactic move in contemporaneous libretti whereby sovereignty is celebrated by condensing ideal virtues in a central royal figure, who in turn helps instill them in his subjects. This move was anticipated in *Alessandro nell'Indie.* Written for the Roman Teatro delle Dame, it was premiered for the opening of Carnival on December 26, 1729, also in the setting by Vinci (composer of both operas for the theater's 1729–30 season), and was repeated innumerable times throughout Europe in different settings thereafter.[80] (Versions of the libretto that have been revived in modern times include Hasse's *Cleofide* of 1731 and Handel's *Poro* of 1735.) But Metastasio's Alexander the Great is prone not just to Artaserse's error of apprehension but to an error of desire, of wanting the wrong woman. He falls in love with the Indian queen Cleofide, who is beloved by King Poro, ruler of a part of India that Alexander has just conquered. The error of desire is a necessary one, and common to Metastasio's sovereigns. In Alexander's case, it is indivisible from the king's role as a warrior and conqueror, hence necessary in affirming his very status as king. Yet his desire for the women of ethnic others is continually tensed between his conquering side and his more irenic, forgiving, and moral one.

78. "Circa le arie le condurrò meco, mentre non ho avuto tempo di farmele fare a mio modo, per l'aria che desidera il signor marchese Bettivogli 'Vò solcando il mar crudel' supplico Vostra Eccellenza a persuadere il suddetto Cavaliere, che in stanza o fuori di teatro la canterò quante volte il medesimo mi commanderà, ma per cantarla in teatro la prego a lasciarmi in libertà, mentre da che faccio la professione, non v'è stato mai caso ch'io abbia in scena cantata arie altrui massimamente di quel soggetto glorioso, sicché io godo che gl'altrui cantano le mie in teatro ed io aver il contento d'ascoltarle, come più volte mi è successo e così, non desidero che qualche soggetto vanaglorioso si possa vantare che Farinello canti le sue arie" (Milan, September 26, 1731, in Farinelli, *La solitudine amica*, 89–90).

79. Durante, "The Opera Singer," notes that singers often became identified with specific roles, even when singing them in different settings and productions.

80. On the early phase, see Strohm, "Metastasio's *Alessandro nell'Indie*," 232–48, and Cummings, "Reminiscence and Recall," 80–104.

These principles fit into a royal picture that displays the monarch on a larger map of sovereignty whose coordinates include competitors, winners and losers, rival clans and nations, usurpers and allies, and many others: marriageable women, siblings, friends, military officers, confidantes, betrayers, all figures who help realize the claim that sovereignty must exist over and against any and all possibilities of alternative sovereignties. There is always a mythical sovereignty that is Ours and other less legitimate ones that are Theirs. Who exactly Ours is is not so important. It may be an immediate symbolic forebear, Greek or Roman, or a more distant one—Persian like Artaserse, Carthaginian like Dido, Syrian like Demetrio and Cleonice, Iberian like Radamisto, or even a Chinese regent like Leango. Whatever the case, Our sovereign will often establish himself by claiming land and women through his peregrinations in a larger world (though, as we will see, also by renouncing land and women at appropriate times). In this, the sovereign fulfills his role as a charismatic center of symbolic power who carries out extraordinary exploits and mobilizes key events to secure status (not unlike more recent monarchs in East Africa and Morocco, for example).[81] In one prototype of Metastasio's libretti (including *Adriano in Siria,* discussed below), representations of royalty are spatialized along an axis of the West and the rest—of the ideal, would-be Christian monarch and the heathen, barbarian other.[82] By claiming the other's women, the "Christian" monarch carves his mark on the proprietary tree at the same time as he extends the imaginary map of Christendom through an allegory that throws him face to face with a distant spirit familiar (here, the Indian king). Metastasio's enlightenment ethics also turn this into the king's encounter with the weakness of his own passions. If properly managed, those passions can utilize ethics and reason to make ethnic/social bonds appear inviolable, but in order to recognize them as such the Metastasian monarch must typically err beforehand. Such erring allows him, following good mythical form, to encompass the other within the self. Thus Poro is encompassed within Alexander, much as Shinzon, the "Star Trek Nemesis," is encompassed within Picard, commander of the starship *Enterprise,* who discovers in Shinzon an enemy literally wrought from Picard's own self.

Prima facie, it may seem ironic that for Alexander to recognize his own weakness, he needs inspiration from the jealous, hotheaded heathen king of India, who has none of Alexander's rationalizing temperament. But Poro makes up for his intemperance with valor and a thoroughly uncompromising nature that ends by teaching Alexander what he cannot learn otherwise. Prisoner of the Greek king on our first encounter with him (1.1), Poro wants to die precisely in order to deprive Alexander of his greatest prize. Alexander can only best Poro

81. See Geertz, "Centers, Kings, and Charisma," 121–46. Geertz extends Max Weber's theories of charisma, in *Max Weber on Charisma and Institution Building,* and Shils, "Charisma, Order, and Status," 199–213.

82. This spatialization takes dramatic place in *Attilio Regolo,* where the hero's character is directly opposed to those of his North African captors.

by recognizing Poro's heroism, giving up his bourgeois desire for Poro's beloved, and returning her to her rightful mate. So doing, the Macedonian king ensures his own position as dispenser of mercy and clemency while finding compensation for the return of the woman he desires in the respect he earns from his rival for such an enlightened gift ("La man che lo diede / Rispetta nel dono" [2.12]).[83] This is the ultimate mythical reminder that Alexander is Ours and Porus Theirs—that according to the world of reference we are handed, Alexander rules and Porus is ruled. The exemplarity of the tale has its ideological center in Alexander's capacity to form a totality of good and evil, to pass from flawed to less flawed, to comprehend others within himself, and finally to instruct those who at first instruct him.

By losing in love, the king wins. He remains isolated, unsocializable in a sense, but thereby individual like none other (much as Titus does in renouncing Berenice). Metastasio's male monarch does not marry; he only marries off. He is a unique being, with unique connections to the cosmos, and as such must "sacrifice the uniqueness of every other"—not literally, as Agamemnon sacrifices his daughter, but symbolically in that every other gives up his or her own uniqueness in order to imitate him.[84]

* * *

Not long after the Venetian success of *Artaserse*, in September 1731, Hasse made a sensational debut in Dresden at the court of elector Frederick Augustus, "the Strong" (also king of Poland), with a setting of Metastasio's *Alessandro nell'Indie*, heavily revised by Michelangelo Boccardi and renamed *Cleofide* to highlight the diva who played her, Hasse's wife, Faustina Bordoni. On the libretto's title page, Cleofide (and by extension, Faustina) received equal billing with the king, who in turn got added value through the honorific "Re delle Polonie, Elettor di Sassonia, Sempre Grande e Invittissimo" (always great and most invincible—which was not actually the case).[85] Remarkably, the very focus of the opera thus shifted from the male monarch to the female star, epitomizing the nature of opera seria to behave like a prism that could be turned this way or that. Indeed, when the story was again rewritten to feature the famed alto castrato Senesino (Francesco Bernardi) as Porus in Handel's London production of 1731, the title given the opera was *Poro*. Porpora's *Poro* (Turin, 1731) followed suit, Carl Heinrich Graun's *Alessandro e Poro* (Berlin, 1744) gave the Macedonian and Indian kings equal billing, and Agricola's *Cleofide* (Berlin, 1754) harkened back to the

83. An intriguing reading of relationships between mercy, clemency, and entreaty is offered by Nagel, *Autonomy and Mercy*.

84. Calasso, *The Marriage of Cadmus and Harmony*, 115. In this reading of Alexander's sacrifice, I differ with Wiesend, "Der Held als Rolle: Metastasios Alexander," 139–52, who sees in Alessandro an "identification-figure" whose very passivity signifies the old order and explains the king's frequent secondary status in the cast hierarchy.

85. Title page reproduced in Heartz, *Music in European Capitals*, 322; discussion on 321–28.

practice of Hasse. All of these operas represent a drift away from the eponymous ruler, most often played by a tenor who ranked below the two leads in the cast hierarchy.

We are reminded of Roberto Calasso's view that mythical stories are branches of a family and that elements of a myth are travelers on its branches (hence the bull that carries Europa, that mates with Pasiphae, that fights Theseus, that causes Ariadne's anguish, that alerts her to Dionysius's wiles, that inspires her dual cult at Crete (for a joyous and grieving Ariadne), and so on.[86] But there is also something else at work. Sovereignty constitutes an encompassing social field that resides not just in the sovereign but in those who partake of exchange with him or her. Ultimately, acts of mercy take place that exchange "the divine in man . . . for the human in the deity, or its earthly representative, the monarch."[87] Following this logic, starring singers become axes of sovereignty, markedly so in stories in which they impersonate sovereigns. In *Cleofide* (2.6), the Indian king and queen join hands in marriage and pray to their gods to protect them:

Sommi Dei, se giusti siete	[Great gods, if you are just
Proteggete il bel desio	Protect the precious longing
D'un amor così pudico	Of a love so pure.]

Even though more travails await them, they are graced for the moment by this sweet and serene *preghiera a due*, rich with parallel thirds in the unusual and bright key of E.

A Hapless Emperor: Hadrian

Metastasio made a particular enlightenment confection of his broader principles when he depicted the exploits abroad of the emperor Adriano (Hadrian). A sovereign who storms onto foreign ground without checking his amorous feelings (as Alexander quickly did), unable to temper his desires for the woman of the other, may find that his projects of political expansion fail from the inside out. This is the decidedly eighteenth-century message of *Adriano in Siria*. Remarkably, despite its unattractive depiction of monarchy, it was composed for the nameday of Karl VI in Vienna, and first played at the Hoftheater in a setting by Caldara on November 4, 1732. The tale takes place in Antioch, Syria, where the conquering Adriano falls for the imprisoned Syrian princess Emirena, thus betraying his long-standing engagement to the Roman Sabina, niece of his predecessor Trajan (Marco Ulpio Trajan, d. 117 AD). Opening with an ostentatious

86. In Calasso's gendered view of family, the bull is the contrary of women, as bulls regenerate on earth while women lift off or disappear from it (*The Marriage of Cadmus and Harmony*, 1–18).

87. Žižek and Dolar, *Opera's Second Death*, 20.

act of imperial largesse, staged in blockbuster style with the victorious emperor held aloft over shields of his chorusing soldiers, Adriano concedes peace to the vanquished peoples and invites to Antioch "all the princes of Asia," notably Emirena's father. The usual complications get in the way. Emirena loves and is loved by the Parthian prince Farnaspe. Her father, Osroa (Osroes), king of the Parthians, rejects Adriano's overtures of accord between Asia and Rome—offered partly to secure Emirena's hand—and instead penetrates Antioch in disguise. Meanwhile, Adriano's dutiful bride-to-be, Sabina, her name and ancestry aligned with the foundation of Rome and Roman glory, arrives from their homeland knowing nothing of the new love triangle that has formed.

Amazingly, it turns out that every last character is prepared to sacrifice private desires to public duty sooner than Adriano is. The ideal emperor represented at the outset—a victorious sovereign symbolized through military trophies, arms, and spoils, and praised by the onstage chorus of Roman soldiers as "il duce" and "il padre" in whom "the whole world puts its faith"—turns out to be chimerical. Adriano's passions have strayed far from the sovereign mark, failing the enlightenment standards of selfhood and state, and he barely comes center by the story's end.

In this perverse landscape, personal choices are pulled up out of a stubble field of harsh social constraints. Whatever is desired always seems most wrong and least attainable. The problem is not constraint alone, but a new set of terms under which personal desire exists. In part they involve what Joly identifies as the libretto's obsessive concern, "the problematic of the heart" and the new urgency of individual human passion within a larger field of social mores.[88] At the very beginning, Adriano asks Farnaspe if he "loves" Emirena. Sabina wants Adriano's "heart" more than she wants the empire (1.11). In response Adriano restages the scene of his falling wrongfully in love with the Syrian princess, playing the part of a man so vulnerable and pitiable that his defenses simply collapsed. Persisting with her unshakeable loyalty, Sabina—an utterly symbolic figure—afterward tells the counselor Aquilio in an agitated aria of direct address (3.1):

Digli ch'è un infedele;	[Tell him he's a traitor.
Digli che mi tradì	Tell him that he betrayed me.
Senti: non dir così:	Listen: don't tell him that:
Digli che partirò;	Tell him that I will leave.
Digli che l'amo.	Tell him I love him.]

Sabina's text is one of such emotional flux and reversal that it even inverts the prosodic conventions of Metastasian poetry (which were practically unchangeable) with three decisive tronco verses (accents on the final syllables, "tradì,"

88. See Joly, *Dagli elisi al inferno*, 55–56 and passim, which argues for an autobiographical reading.

"così," "partirò," vv. 2–4) preceding a final piano verse (accent on the penultimate syllable, "l'amo," v. 5)—a softening metric (and inversion of the usual metric emphases) that lyricizes her surrender to love.

Needless to say, such expressions are not just about personal love. They point to a specifically bourgeois variety of sentimentality that serves as a persistent filter for issues of state, something that overshadows concern for public duty when it ought instead to bow to it and in the sovereign's case basically eclipses it.[89] That Adriano's position was a subjective projection on Metastasio's part is clear from a letter he wrote La Romanina on July 4, 1733, asking that she read and reread the following speech from *Adriano* 3.3:

> Ah, you know not what a war of thoughts agitates my soul. Rome, the Senate, Emirena, Sabina, my glory, my love. I have all of these. I would like to harmonize them all. I find in all of them some reef to fear. I choose, I repent, then I'm full of regrets for having repented. At the same time, I am so weary of long doubting that I can't distinguish good from evil. In the end I find myself pressed by time, and I decide for the worst.[90]

"The good that I would I do not; but the evil which I would not, that I do"—so wrote Paul in a letters to the Romans (Rom. 7:19). And Metastasio to La Romanina, again on *Adriano:* "I am in an abyss of doubts."[91]

From this evidence, it would be easy to deduce that Metastasio's third libretto for imperial Vienna—performed for the traditional opening of the winter season celebrating the emperor's nameday, and thus high in status—subverted the principles of enlightened sovereignty that Metastasio was brought to Vienna to sustain. But I think the truth is otherwise. In *Adriano in Siria* we encounter a sovereign who, like Alexander, combines two significant characteristics: (1) he appears as a conqueror who comes from the outside; and (2) as such he virtu-

89. For the later eighteenth-century history of theatrical sensibility, see Vincent-Buffault, *A History of Tears*, and chap. 8 below.

90. "Ah! Tu non sai / qual guerra di pensieri / agita l'alma mia! Roma, il Senato / Emirena, Sabina, / La mia gloria, il mio amor, tutto ho presente: / Tutto accorder vorrei: trovo per tutto / qualche scoglio a temer. Scelgo, mi pento; / poi d'essermi pentito / mi ritorno a pentir. Mi stanco intanto / nel lungo dubitar, tal che dal male / il ben più non distinguo. Al fin mi veggio / stretto dal tempo, e mi risolvo al peggio" (Metastasio, *Opere* 1:564).

91. Asking her if she wanted to suggest the theme of his next opera, Metastasio continued: "Ah, don't laugh saying that sickness is in the bones, for the choice of a subject certainly merits this agitation and uncertainty. My lot is that the uncertainty must be resolved in an absolute way, and there's no chance of avoiding it. Were it not for that, I'd be doubting till Judgment Day and then I'd start up again. Read the third scene of the third act from my *Adriano*, observe the character that makes the emperor what he is and you'll see my own." [Oh non ridete con dire che la malattia è nelle ossa, perché la scelta di un soggetto merita bene questa agitazione e questa incertezza. La fortuna mia si è che bisogna risolversi assolutamente, e non vi è caso di evitarlo. Se non fosse questo, dubiterei fin al giorno del giudizio, e poi sarei da capo. Leggete la terza scena dell'atto terzo del mio Adriano: osservate il carattere che fa l'imperatore di se medesimo, e vedrete il mio (*Opere* 3:85).] The context was persistent physical ailments and hypochondria, which Metastasio links with his spiritual condition.

ally ignores social mores that demand respect for preexistent affinal bonds, regardless of the hierarchical positions of those who hold them. In a brighter, or more innocent, view of sovereignty than Metastasio stages here, Adriano would transform these initial conditions by adapting more decisively to mainstream mores, as Alessandro does. He would renounce his transgression sooner, more willingly, and more easily, with less ill effect. The episode would then suggest merely the initial phase in a larger implied narrative, and a less ambiguous one. Instead, the libretto telescopes Adriano's final epiphany so radically as to paint him as a failed sovereign. Only in the last two scenes does Adriano suddenly admit to his weaknesses, make Emirena's father again king, rejoin Emirena to Farnaspe, absolve Aquilio in an act of clemency, and reaccept Sabina. His transformation is feeble at best.

Seemingly *Adriano in Siria* thus conflates the enlightenment idea of the monarch as an instrument of clemency with the Pauline idea (Rom. 13:1–7) that all kings are divine, regardless of whether they are good or bad, because their power comes from God—an idea still viable during Metastasio's time insofar as the sovereign's relationship with God was privileged.[92] Still, there is no escaping the fact that here Metastasio has distended the dilemma of sovereignty to an extreme. Will the sovereign, who stands outside of society at some initial stage in a process of assimilation into the social order, ultimately be incorporated into it? Or will he never be more than a powerful outsider, whose domestication and thus incorporation is permanently incomplete, in whom negative and positive elements always coexist, and who is therefore in continual imminent danger of being disempowered?

The answers to these questions are as ambivalent as Metastasio's representation of sovereignty all told. Through Adriano's transgressive nature, he models those traditional monarchs who move from a phase in which, having first stood outside the body social, they are then assimilated into it; and who, by standing outside their own society as conquerors of another one, are effectively brought "home," redomesticated on foreign turf.[93] He typifies monarchs who are not just warriors and conquerors, but are sexually transgressive. Among Roman precedents, there were examples aplenty in Plutarch's *Lives* and elsewhere. Ro-

92. That Metastasio should simultaneously have approved and disapproved his characters (their deeds, beliefs, natures) is consistent with his position as mythographer. Doniger notes that it is precisely because "myths span a wide range of human concerns and human paradoxes" that they are highly "translatable," susceptible to continual cross-cultural adaptation and thus appropriate for comparison (*The Implied Spider*, 84 and passim). For Lévi-Strauss, too, translatability was the essence of myth.

93. African studies have analyzed much ethnographic/historical data on the origins of kingships in acts of conquering, e.g., Vansina, *L'évolution du royaume*, on the military conquests of acephalous Hutu farmers by pastoral Tutsi in Rwanda (East Africa), and Goody, *Technology, Tradition, and the State*, on the ascendancy to the status of kings of West African Savannah tribes by belligerent, commercial, land-based nobility who built kingdoms through plunder and trading (notably, of African slaves for European guns).

mulus, for instance, was a conqueror from abroad who was raised by a courtesan (Acca Larentia) and founded the Roman kingdom through the rape of the native Sabines, much as the usurper Amulius raped his own niece (see *Romulus* 4.2 and 4.3). Indeed, Metastasio's own *argomento* published with his *Romolo ed Ersilia* of 1765 acknowledges that Romulus sanctioned, and even sanctified, abduction and rape, suggesting by way of an excuse that he made "virtue" out of a necessity.

> The extraordinary and fortunate valor of fierce youth that was gathered together to form the nascent city of Rome quickly filled all the bellicose neighbor nations that went by the name "Sabine" with a jealous sense of competition. Before long the Romans perceived that the glory of such fortunate beginnings would end in the course of a single epoch were they not to succeed in equipping their own lack with foreign wives, sweetening through blood ties the adverse minds of the conquered, and stabilizing the great hopes of Rome with numerous progeny. They therefore asked insistently for the hands in marriage of Sabine girls, but had all their requests proudly rejected. Offended by the obstinate refusals, prompted by fear of perishing, and authorized by Greek examples, they agreed to obtain by force what had been denied by their entreaties. And during the timely competition of the annual games that sanctified Rome in honor of Neptune, they executed the famous rape, so well remembered in every century.
>
> Romolo, who would have tried in vain to stem the tide of a people who were not yet docile but rather provoked and bellicose, knew how to find a use for his royal virtues even in the breach of them. He delivered the raped girls into the custody of wise matrons, and did not marry them off until, conquered by their generous welcome, by affectionate persuasion, and by the respect and merit of the husbands offered them, they consented voluntarily to the proposed marriages, which in those days were done by his command in the manner of sacred rites and were publicly celebrated with the greatest pomp permitted during the tenuous beginnings of Rome.[94]

94. "La straordinario e fortunato valore della feroce gioventù, che si raccolse a formar la nascente Roma, riempì ben presto di gelosa emulazione tutte le vicine bellicose nazioni che componevano il nome sabino. S'avvidero in breve i Romani che la gloria di così fausti principii sarebbe nel corso d'una sola età terminata, ove non riuscisse loro di supplire alla scarsezza delle proprie con le spose straniere, di raddolcir coi legami del sangue l'animo avverso de' confinanti, e di stabilire con numerosa prole le vaste speranze di Roma. Richiesero perciò instantemente in ispose le donzelle sabine, ma furono per tutto le istanze loro alteramente rigettate. Offesi dagli ostinati rifiuti, spinti dal timor di perire, ed autorizzati dai greci esempi, convennero d'ottener con la forza ciò che si negava alle preghiere; e nell'opportuno concorso degli annui giuochi che in onor di Nettuno si solenizzavano in Roma, eseguirono il celebre ratto, tanto in ogni secolo rammentato.

"Romolo, che avrebbe tentato in vano di fare argine all'impeto d'un popolo non docile ancora, irritato e guerriero, seppe trovare impiego alle sue reali virtù, anche ne' trascorsi di quello. Consegnò in sacro loco le rapite donzelle alla custodia di pudiche matrone; né dispose di esse, fin che vinte dalle generose accoglienze, dalle affettuose persuasioni, dal rispetto e dal merito degli offerti sposi, non condescesero volontarie alle proposte nozze, che furono poi per comando di lui, a tenore de' sa-

Metastasio's protestations notwithstanding, Romolo's case is worse than Adriano's, where imperial aims are eventually checked by the fusion of old feudal codes of honor with enlightenment norms of reason. Adriano fails as emperor because, as he admits to Sabina (2.3), he is traitorous in love, like a badly errant knight. Ultimately the feudal ideal of honor is at risk. Small wonder that the Parthian "other" Emirena doubts that any concept of honor applies among the Romans (1.4), a doubt that anticipates a glaring reversal of the usual relation of Roman ethics to that of the "barbarians." The latter are identified with erotic rather than heroic love but, ironically, can muster self-control when necessary to face off Roman oppression, unlike Adriano, over whose inner self erotic passion exercises a barbaric tyranny. In the end, it is Sabina who must teach honor to Adriano, and almost too late—perhaps a weak position for a Roman emperor, but a strong statement for eighteenth-century Europeans about the vitality of the sovereign within his royal family and by extension his "family" of subjects (and vice versa). The heart pangs of the sovereign could thus be assimilated to those of the bourgeois spectator and to a new mass sentimentality, which identified with the sovereign through the wondrous spectacle and fantasy of opera.

* * *

Adriano in Siria began life as a dynastic opera when first staged in Vienna for Karl VI's nameday, but at its premiere Metastasio was already apologizing for the fact that Adriano is a cad (as Sabina herself suggests when he fails to greet her in 1.8). The initial staging ended with this disarming recitative in the *licenza*, addressed to the emperor:

> Emperor, fear not; Adriano does not dare compare himself to you. He makes not a model, but a spectacle of himself when his vicissitudes are bared before your eyes. The likeness would be quite untrue, and the differences between you, Sire, are quite clear. The throne gave light to him; it receives light from you. He was sometimes great and just; you are always so. He subdued his own emotions; you avert them. He chose belatedly the paths of honor; you chose them from your earliest days until your first dawn. He admired the earth, you the world adores.[95]

---

cri riti, e con la maggior pompa permessa allora ai tenui principii di Roma, pubblicamente celebrate" (Metastasio, *Opere* 1:1295). The incidents do not appear in the text of Metastasio's *Romolo ed Ersilia*, but they were part of its mythical background for audiences, who also would have encountered the *argomento* in reading versions of Metastasio's complete works.

95. "Cesare, non turbarti; a te non osa / somigliarsi Adrian. Quando al tuo sguardo / le sue vicende espone, / fa spettacol di sé, non paragone. / Troppo minor del vero / l'immagine sarebbe; e troppo chiare, / Signor, fra voi le differenze sono. / A lui diè luce il trono, la riceve da te. Fu grande e giusto / ei talvolta, e tu sempre. I propri affetti / ei debellò, tu li previeni. Ei scelse / tardi le vie d'onor, tu le scegliesti / de' giorni tuoi fin su la prima aurora. / Lui la terra ammirò, te il mondo adora."

If the audience had to be told in front of the emperor that the depiction of Hadrian was his near opposite, why was Hadrian chosen to celebrate Karl VI in the first place? Why subsequently did *Adriano in Siria* often function as a monarch's opera—set, for instance, for the birthday of Elisabetta Farnese, queen of Spain and mother of Carlo III, on a much-revised text in Naples, 1734, by Pergolesi, and for the much-feted Mannheim marriage of Wittelsbach princess Amalia Augusta of Zweibrücken to Elector Frederick August of Saxony by Ignaz Holzbauer in 1768–69? And why, moreover, was it evidently attended by monarchs galore? (Johann Christian Bach's 1765 setting for London was twice attended by King George III and Queen Charlotte.)[96]

A clue to these paradoxes lies in Metastasio's response to Giuseppe Riva's criticism that it was inverisimilar to have Sabina listen to the advice of Aquilio—who tells her that she should be true to Adriano and make him ashamed of his infidelity (1.10)—given that Aquilio, a mere confidante and tribune, secretly loves her. "Poor Sabina," Metastasio wrote,

> has no reason to hope either for Adriano's love or his interest in saving appearances of decency. Still, she retains a thread of hope . . . of succeeding by surrendering and tolerating. She seizes on this advice both because there is no other and also because it agrees with the character I endow her with from start to finish. Observe that any time . . . I make her inflamed at the wrongs she suffers, I immediately have her reflect and correct herself, returning to her natural prudence and tolerance—qualities that are necessary . . . so that spectators can believe her capable of the extraordinary generosity with which she untangles the opera; qualities that made me reject, as destructive to those same qualities, the expedient of having her depart out of jealousy, on her own counsel, though I wrote that in the first draft . . . . Since by reducing her to such resolve, one would have to suppose her not just jealous but proud, intolerant, and wild—something I neither want nor ought to do.[97]

Sabina was seconda donna in the cast hierarchy but "first lady" politically speaking, and thus an important medium for viewer identification. Because she epitomizes the virtue and temperance of Roman womanhood, she is wholly

96. Bach, *Adriano in Siria* in Warburton, *The Collected Works of J. C. Bach.*

97. "[A]lla povera Sabina non rimane ragione di sperar nè su l'amore di Adriano, nè su la cura del medesimo di salvar l'apparente onestà. Eppure le rimane qualche filo di speranza. Dee esser quello di poter vincer cedendo e tollerando. Questo è il consiglio al quale si appiglia, sì perché non ve ne sono altri, come perché si confà col carattere ch'io le do dal principio . . . sino al fine. Osservate che, qualunque volta, per non fingerla insensibile, io la faccio scaldare su i torti che riceve, faccio che immediatamente rifletta e si corregga, ritornando alla naturale sua prudenza e tolleranza. Qualità che . . . sono necessarie, perché possano gli spettatori crederla capace della straordinaria generosità che usa nello scioglimento dell'opera. Qualità che mi hanno fatto rigettare, come distruttive delle medesime, l'espediente di farla partire per motivo di gelosia e di proprio consiglio, benché nel mio primo scenario io l'avessi scritto . . . . Poiché, per ridursi a tale risoluzione, bisogna supporla non solo gelosa, ma altiera, intollerante e violente; il che io non voglio, né debbo" (letter of September 20, 1732, Metastasio, *Opere* 3:74–75).

"ours." In correcting herself, she corrects the emperor and corrects us all. (How many elected "sovereigns" of own day rely similarly on their wives?) Her self-correction also balances the fact that the young dynastic couple, ever important, are not Ours but Theirs, even though, as primo uomo and prima donna who will be conjoined at the end, they are assimilated to, or even surpass, the virtues of the imperium and are empowered through an abundance of impassioned song. Indeed, when Pergolesi set the opera in 1734 with the wild and wildly popular soprano castrato Caffarelli playing Farnaspe, the text was radically altered to showcase him.[98] All his arias had new texts, lengthy music, and special techniques and colors (one with obbligato oboe, another with double orchestra), especially at the ends of acts 1 and 2.[99] Only ten of the original twenty-six arias survived the revision, and that a mere two years after Metastasio wrote it.

After two more years, with the aid of his countryman violinist/composer Francesco Maria Veracini, Farinelli took up the heroic role while making the biggest operatic splash ever to hit the shores of the English isle. Two of his arias, "Son sventurato ma pure stelle" (Metastasio's) and "La ragion, gl'affetti ascolta" (newly written) framed Walsh's *Favourite Songs in the Opera called Adriano by Sig.r Francesco Maria Veracini* published in January of 1736.[100] The first, a tempo di minuetto, was much more singable by amateurs than the typical Farinelli aria. The inner pages of Walsh's volume were devoted to the arias of other singers: alto castrato arias for Senesino/Adriano (the added "Prendi, o cara," which gave buyers the bonus of alternate voice parts in a lower range, and Metastasio's "La ragion, gl'affetti"); one number sung by the flexible bass Antonio Montagnana/Osroa, "Non si ritrova" (Metastasio, 3.6); Francesca Cuzzoni's "Quel cor che mi domasti"; and Senesino/Adriano and Francesca Bartolli/Emirena's reinserted duet "Prendi o cara." Thus, for the price of Walsh's print, you could be an Adriano, an Emirena, a Farnaspe, or even an Osroa, which effectively meant you could play Senesino, Cuzzoni, Bartolli, or Montagnana playing one of their parts, or even pretend to be Farinelli. Alternatively, you could listen to your friends impersonate your favorite singers playing one of their signature roles. And if you had really good means, you might even be able to invite the Farinellis, Senesinos, and Cuzzonis to your own place, so long as there were enough diamond-studded snuffboxes to go around.

Proud Hero and Imperial Autocrat: Aetius and Valentinian III

Ezio premiered at Rome's Teatro delle Dame on December 26, 1728, in a setting by Pietro Auletta and was reset about forty times, most famously by Han-

98. Heartz, "Caffarelli's Caprices."

99. See Pergolesi, *Adriano in Siria*, vol. 3 in Monson, *Pergolesi: Complete Works;* di Benedetto, "Dal Metastasio a Pergolesi," 259–95; and Heartz, *Music in European Capitals*, 114–15.

100. Copy at F-Pn, Vm3 226; see Smith and Humphries, *A Bibliography . . . of John Walsh*, entry no. 1501, 333–34.

del. The drama stands apart from the others we have considered in announcing a simple if frightening fact: that sovereignty could encompass such a range of opposites—good and evil, order and disorder, stability and instability—that it might in the end be simply bad. By Metastasio's measure, Valentiniano (Valentinian III) is an autocrat staring blankly out of the pages of history. No sooner does the young hero Ezio (Aetius) return from conquering Attila the Hun, to the general acclamation of all and bearing spoils of war (weapons, insignia, and slaves [1.2]), than the emperor accuses him of treason. Ezio is fanatically devoted to honor, glory, the monarch, and empire (1.3, 3.1), but like Temistocle and other heroes he is marred by pride (1.3, 1.9, 2.13, 3.6). When the emperor learns that Ezio thinks he can still have Fulvia for himself, he turns violently against him, believing him an insolent traitor who is plotting against him, and puts him in chains.

Ezio occupies the middle "heroic" rank in the political hierarchy (cf. fig. 6.1), as does his beloved Fulvia, but, like the siblings Arbace and Semira in *Artaserse*, both Ezio and Fulvia have the moral potential to be pulled up to the sovereign level. Conversely too, the older occupant of their rank, Fulvia's father, Massimo, a Roman patrician, has the potential to be pulled morally downward, like Arbace's father, Artabano, because he protects their interests too zealously—in this case prompted by an old score he wants to settle with the emperor.

At the crux of the narrative is the balance of power. Ezio is idolized by the people as a virtual sovereign, and he acts the part by wanting his Fulvia despite Valentiniano's prerogative as the actual sovereign. The emperor for his part longs for the kind of bourgeois love that is the privilege of his subjects, causing him to lament the throne as "an unhappy gift for those close to it" (1.9).[101] Things are further complicated by his love for Fulvia because, as a feudal-styled unattainable lady with respect to his abject love for her (1.3, 2.12–13), she is effectively sovereign over him.

Yet ultimately Valentiniano does resist both his own tendencies to tyranny and her power to subjugate him, as he imagines pervasive threats to his sovereignty but nonetheless declares that "Heaven defends the lives of monarchs" (2.2).[102] The logic of sovereignty thus remains essentially ambivalent, symbolically and practically, attempting to transform a moral negative through a catharsis and turning an unattractive autocrat into a modest exemplum whose wrongs teach his vassals about love and redemption in the face of loss. His sister tells him, "May your vassals learn what the heart of an emperor is" (3.2).[103] Plagued at last not by the hero but by his own antonym, Massimo, Valentiniano finally sees through a glass, darkly but clearly enough to trade the hand of Fulvia and Ezio's freedom for the truth. Through this simple exchange, the

101. Metastasio, *Opere* 1:208.

102. Ibid., 215.

103. "I tuoi apprendano qual sia d'Augusto il cor" (Metastasio, *Opere* 1:239).

hero is again reassured, albeit at the final hour, that life is a "gift" from the sovereign (3.6).[104]

Such reassurance in turn ensures the sovereign's unique power to produce that sudden shudder of awe that Paul Veyne called a "psychic frisson,"[105] yet still fulfill the minimal conditions of being a man, a subject himself—conditions that were especially critical to the eighteenth century. In a surprising sense, Valentiniano stands at the brink of Rousseau's modern man of *The Social Contract*, or the man manifest in Foucault's "modern" episteme. But he remains a mythical man, mythical because on the one hand the icon of a great generality—an abstraction—and on the other minutely subjective in trying to scrutinize his own motives and passions. He is what Wendy Doniger has deemed typical of myth, at once a telescope, grand and remote, and a microscope, intimate and personal. In this he also participates in what is most intrinsic to myth itself—subjective experience, ordinary feeling, personal encounter with great events, and what Doniger calls the implied message of "this could happen to anyone"—as well as the abstract, objective, formal, generalizable, cosmic. It is this double view, from close up and afar, that makes Metastasio's representation of sovereignty mythical. It was this that allowed him to recast the libretto for a production at the king of Portugal's new theater in 1755 (with an added, rather generic *licenza*), and that sometimes disposed him to sanction others' revisions, as he did with Saverio Mattei's insertion of a quartet for the San Carlo production of 1774—even at the cost of dropping arias.[106] Italian singers and composers made Ezios and Valentinianos as famous abroad as legends of them were at home. A Londoner who went theatergoing in 1732 would have recalled them in Handel's incarnation, with Senesino as Ezio and the female contralto Anna Bagnolesi, no less, as Valentiniano in a trouser performance; and a Londoner in the 1760s would have encountered them for the price of two shillings and sixpence by purchasing a copy of Bremner's *The Favourite Songs in the Opera Ezio*.[107] Having Bremner's print was like downloading the redoubtable Tenducci singing Ezio's "Belle luci che accendete," an added "rondeau" for two violins and continuo composed by Vento, and the great Manzuoli singing Ezio's newly fashioned complaint "Recagli quell'acciaro" (2.6) in a dramatic setting by Pescetti. Theoretically the buyer could replay "Recagli quell'acciaro" ad infinitum, each time rehearing the wronged hero give his sword up to the emperor with the

104. Recall Porus in *Alessandro nell'Indie* 2.12.

105. Veyne, *Le pain et le cirque*, 587; in English as *Bread and Circuses*.

106. Letters to Giuseppe Bonechi, May 24, 1755, and to Saverio Mattei, September 18, 1774, in Metastasio, *Opere* 3:1015 and 5:308.

107. Bagnolesi had previously played the role in Milan in Carnival 1730 opposite the castrato Carlo Scalzi (who had himself played Valentiniano the previous year at Rome), and she played Valentiniano again in Turin in 1731 opposite Farinelli's Ezio in the setting by Riccardo Broschi. Indeed, she seems to have initiated a partial tradition for having the role played by a female, as Elisabetta Ottini played it in Hasse's Naples setting of 1730 (also opposite Scalzi as Ezio), and in 1738 Mariana Marini played Valentiniano in Lampugnani's Venice version.

words "Take this weapon, which defended the throne, remember who I am and see him blush," accompanied by thirty-second-note violin glissandi and wide declarative leaps that explode in the *seconda parte* into melodic twelfths (example 6.4).[108] They could replay the heartbreaking "Non so d'onde viene" as scored by Johann Christian Bach (the text Mozart outfitted some years later for his beloved Aloysia Weber): "I know not whence this tender feeling comes, this strange movement born in my breast." Likewise a Frenchman who had traveled abroad might discover his favorite *Ezio* arias in the delightful periodical *Journal d'ariettes italiennes des plus célèbres compositeurs avec les paroles italiennes et François, la basse sous le chant et toutes les parties séparées pour la facilité de l'éxécution*, published by Bailleux in Paris between 1779 and 1795. And still others could find similar pleasures in Italian aria series published for fortepiano, with guitar accompaniment, and even cittern, or in aria series that supplied subscribers with full sets of parts.

THE KING COMETH

Having looked at Metastasio's sovereigns in various guises, we can distill several basic principles. The protagonist, whether king or hero, is transcendent. The hero is a prototype for the sovereign and vice versa. Each encompasses good and evil, order and disorder in different measures, but is ultimately a figure who learns, teaches, and reforms. Subjects are crucial to this process. By experiencing through word and tone a ritual iteration of these transcendent movements, by watching their visual display and various physical embodiments and witnessing their sonorous variations in innumerable performances—settings, resettings, restagings, readings, rereadings, revisions, and recastings of all kinds—spectators bore witness to miraculous sovereignty while participating in a new but already quite definite expression of bourgeois sentimentality, both of which were continually reaffirmed and reinternalized.

The portraits drawn above hardly exhaust the eighteenth-century variants on operatic sovereignty, even confining for heuristic purposes our search in this chapter to Metastasio's own libretti. Some monarchs are creatures of disguise, who reveal their royal nature through an inexorable process that leads to their eventual recognition (Alceste in *Demetrio*, Alceo in *Ciro riconosciuto*).[109] Others, more hieratical, are driven by sacrificial imperatives (Clistene in *L'olimpiade*, or the eponymous Demofoonte—both gerontocratic figures who at first are projected as hardened to human needs). Quite different are monarchs who represent extreme sacrifice of the self, ruling over their own passions with classical restraint in the spirit of Corneille and Descartes (Titus in *La clemenza di Tito*, or even the more vulnerable Cleonice in *Demetrio*, and heroes like Regulus in the

108. The copy in F-Pn, D.4632 (2) (RISM B.II.1, 175), gives a provisional date of 1765. The text there is identical to Metastasio's.

109. Joly, *Dagli elisi al inferno*, 18–19.

EXAMPLE 6.4. Giovanni Battista Pescetti, aria for Ezio/Manzuoli, "Recagli quell'acciaro"

From Metastasio, *Ezio* 2.6. Facsimile from *The Favourite Songs in the Opera Ezio* (London: R. Bremner, [1765?]). By permission of the Bibliothèque Nationale de France.

(*continued*)

EXAMPLE 6.4. (*continued*)

EXAMPLE 6.4. (*continued*)

(*continued*)

EXAMPLE 6.4. (*continued*)

republican opera *Attilio Regolo*). Still others are shepherd-kings who come to herd their flocks with the aid of idyllic nature (Alceste again, and especially the Aminta of *Il re pastore*). Taken collectively, these figures show that eighteenth-century society did not refuse the dark side of sovereignty but folded it in dialectically with the bright.[110]

Writing in a land saturated with foreign conquerors, Metastasio could not have ignored qualms over foreign despotism (in the Hobbesian sense of government established by subjugation from outside, or even in La Bruyère's or Pierre Bayle's sense of government whose subjects suffer in a state of excessive servitude and want). What he offered instead was an ingenious and sensuous because thoroughly musical form of pacification. Situated in a seductively lyrical world, Metastasio's sovereigns, like the subjects who are constrained to copy them, must all sooner or later mobilize an unerring government over the passions as part of a larger didactic pursuit of *virtù*, and yet cannot so without also experiencing and expressing them.[111]

Metastasio's Cartesian mentor Gregorio Caloprese—whom the poet said still lived and breathed in him in adulthood[112]—had explained the reason that knowledge of the passions is philosophically and socially necessary.

> [T]hings . . . are known only by those things that comprise them. Empires are founded on cities, and cities are recognized as being composed of nothing but men . . . [so that] to want to know the nature and origin of empires . . . it is necessary before anything else to investigate what spiritual constitution men have from nature, and what principles move them to act. . . . [A]ll the rules of civil jurisprudence take a different path according to the different idea, whether good or evil, that we have of these principles and of this constitution of the soul.[113]

110. Even more striking are denouements wherein sovereigns are unworthy—*Siroe, Ciro riconosciuto*, and *Ipermestra*—and where the king may cede all power voluntarily by conferring *lui* on his successor, as happens in *Ciro* (Metastasio, *Opere* 1:863); see Sala di Felice, *Metastasio*, 157–59.

111. Joly, *Dagli elisi al inferno*, chap. 2, "Un'ideologia del sovrano virtuoso," 84–94. The Viennese triptych of 1731–33, *Demetrio, Adriano in Siria*, and *L'olimpiade*, are all dedicated, Joly argues, to finding balanced solutions to educating audiences on government of the self and others, without forgetting the ideological sides of questions. Joly claims that in its working out of these themes, *Demetrio* had proposed a conciliatory model between empires of the heart and the world, whereas *L'olimpiade* offered an extreme reconciliation between justice and the happiness of subjects. By contrast, *Demofoonte*, in political encounters between the old king and the young people, concedes nothing to the affections or to the heroic youth who requests a human version of sovereignty that would leave more open the discussion of the prerogatives imposed by power. For Joly, the implacable Demofoonte is the negative inverse of Karl VI (102–3), as Metastasio writes to the emperor in the *licenza* (*Opere* 1:691): "Qualunque eccesso /rappresentin le scene, in te ne scopre / la contraria virtù" (Whatever excess the scenes represent, the opposite virtues are found in you). Cf. Neville, "Moral Philosophy in the Metastasian Dramas," 28–46.

112. Giarrizzo, "L'ideologia di Metastasio," 43–77.

113. "[L]e cose . . . non si conoscono se non per quelle che si compongono, e gl'imperii son fondati su le città, e le città non d'altro che d'uomini composte si ravvisano . . . , a voler conoscere la

Underlying this axiom, as Giuseppe Giarrizzo has shown, is a Cartesian epistemology that presupposes a foundation of certain knowledge tempered with constant doubt: *Ego cogito, ergo sum.* Caloprese reasoned that there are bad, uncivilized men who create empires of pain because they live in fear of others. Following an inexorable telos, they are driven by a mechanics of evil that can be set in motion at any time. Consequently, all states require virtue as a conscious moral corrective. The greater the consciousness of virtue, the greater the general happiness and the more virtue perpetuates itself. Caloprese's model for such a state was the Roman republic, seat of loyalty, strength, justice, liberality, and above all Ciceronian moderation. To temper the lure of evil with good, Caloprese viewed public laws based on moderation as essential.[114]

But striking in the Metastasian legacy is the fusion of this moral philosophy with a mythical view of the past, and of the sovereign as an immediate projection into the present of a past that exalts but also distances him. Again, such a fusion echoed contemporaneous political ideology as compressed by the great political theorist Montesquieu in his *Spirit of the Laws* (1748), book 6, chapter 21, "On the Clemency of the Prince," which argued that since monarchs gain love and glory through mercy, they must maintain a position distinct from that of anyone else in the realm—a position that puts them beyond comparison and allows them to pardon subjects who must break laws for the sake of honor (and thus in a sense to transcend the law).

> Clemency is the distinctive quality of monarchs. In a republic, which has virtue as its principle, it is less necessary. In a despotic state, where fear reigns, it is used less . . . . In monarchies, where one is governed by honor, which often requires what the law prohibits, it is more necessary.
>
> Monarchs have so much to gain from clemency, it is followed by such love, and they draw such glory from it, that it is almost always a fortunate thing for them to have occasion to exercise it; and one can almost always do so in our countries.[115]

Montesquieu's claim implies a benevolent, mythical counterpart to the Hobbesian contractualism underlying Metastasio's texts. In the *Leviathan* (1651) Hobbes

---

natura ed origine degli imperii . . . prima d'ogni altra cosa fa d'uopo d'investigare qual costituzion d'animo abbiano l'uomini sortito dalla natura, e quali sono *i principi per li quali si muovono ad operare;* . . . tutte le regole della civil prudenza prendono diverso camino secondo la diversa idea, o buona o rea, che noi abbiamo di questi principî e di questa costituzion d'animo" (ibid., 44).

114. See Ferrara, "Gregorio Caloprese," 11–23.

115. Montesquieu, *The Spirit of the Laws,* 94–95. "La clémence est la qualité distinctive des monarques. Dans la république, où l'on a pour principe la vertu, elle est moins nécessaire. Dans l'État despotique, où règne la crainte, elle est moins en usage . . . . Dans les monarchies, où l'on est gouverné par l'honneur, qui souvent exige ce que la loi défend, elle est plus nécessaire . . . . Les monarques ont tant à gagner par la clémence, elle est suivie de tant d'amour, ils en tirent tant de gloire, que c'est presque toujours un bonheur pour eux d'avoir l'occasion de l'exercer; et on le peut presque toujours dans nos contrées" (Montesquieu, *Oeuvres complètes,* 331).

had stressed the necessity of a covenant, or contract, of every man with every other man in order to ensure the viability of the commonwealth—literally, "common wealth"—

> in such manner, as if every man should say to every man, *I authorise and give up my right of governing myself to this man, or to this assembly of men, on this condition, that thou give up thy right to him, and authorize all his actions in like manner.* This done, the multitude so united in one Person, is called a commonwealth, in Latin civitas. This is the Generation of that great leviathan, or rather (to speak more reverently) of that *Mortal God* to which we owe, under the *Immortal God,* our peace and defence.[116]

Hideako Shinoda argues that while there is a powerful, hierarchical relationship between the parts that make up Hobbes's "Mortal God" (i.e., sovereign), there is no intrinsic relation between him and the "Immortal God" (i.e., God in heaven).[117] In Shinoda's reading what is symbolic for Hobbes is that the "Mortal God" is at the same time an "Artificial Man," one in which "*the sovereignty is an artificial soul,* as giving life and motion to the whole body."[118] By contrast with the "Artificial Soul," the "Artificial Man" introduced into Hobbes's contractualist world system represents a new mechanism, constitutive of the state and identified with the physical and material world. Having thus asserted the king as head of a universe in which God has in a sense retreated, Hobbes's theory eventually opens the way, Shinoda argues, to the emergence of an autonomous state. Before that state would come fully into being, of course, a century and more of absolutist ideology dominated Europe, notwithstanding challenges from enlightenment thought, bourgeois systems, urges, and ideologies, new forms of capital, exchange, urban and ecclesiastical reform, and political strife. And during that time, Hobbes's theory held remarkable ground, founded as it was head to toe on a political body that had the sovereign at its head and as its soul, distinct from man. Yet even if the sovereign could not be equated with men and women—as was still true for Montesquieu a century after Hobbes—it is men and women who are the living limbs (quite literally, the legs and feet) of the "Artificial Man" (the state) and thus the people whom the prince in an eighteenth-century vision must serve.[119] This was certainly so in the ideological terms evinced in Metastasio's elders and peers Giannotti and Muratori, which

116. From part 2, *Of Commonwealth,* chap. 17, art. 13, in Hobbes, *Leviathan,* 109.

117. Shinoda, *Re-examining Sovereignty,* 14. Jean Bodin's *On Sovereignty* (1576) had earlier called sovereignty "the absolute and perpetual power of a commonwealth" (*république*). But inasmuch as Bodin saw his prince as being above positive law because expected to act in accordance with higher, divine laws in line with secular power, the prince was God's image on earth in a way that Hobbes's prince was not (13).

118. Hobbes, *Leviathan,* 3 (emphasis mine); Shinoda, *Re-examining Sovereignty,* 14.

119. Pictured on the title page of Hobbes's *Leviathan,* originally published in English by Head in 1651; see the 1994 edition (lxxviii), for a reproduction.

have their mythical counterpart in Metastasio's *patria*—exalted even as the modern state was oiling its new gears.[120]

To return to Montesquieu, then, the lower members of the political body—ruled as opposed to ruler—also secure the state *absolutely*, but unlike in Hobbes they do so through a feudal mentality anchored in love of glory and honor and expressed in a hierarchical, obedient relation to civil order.

> In moderate states [as opposed to despotisms] love of the homeland, shame, and fear of blame are motives that serve as restraints and so can check many crimes. The greatest penalty for a bad action will be to be convicted of it.[121]

The feudal subject's love of honor should be greater than his love of comfort, fame, or lucre. This corresponds to Metastasio's subject and his image of the monarch, who has absolute power but is providential in guaranteeing the public good and has respect for the rational and natural sanctity of laws.[122]

Giarrizzo has made the interesting suggestion that the relatively untamed quality of Metastasio's Italian libretti—*Didone* (1724), *Siroe* (1726), *Catone in Utica* (1728), *Ezio* (1728), *Semiramide* (1729), *Alessandro* (1729), and *Artaserse* (1730)—reflects in each case various manifestations of power conceived as glory, but that, different from his later ones, glory requires extraordinary sacrifice. Glory "exalts the hero but sacrifices the man" (or woman). Hence glory may lead to suicide in the face of a conquering power (Dido and Cato), extreme self-abnegation in the face of conflicting loyalties (Arbace), or the sacrifice of love for honor (Alexander, Titus), duty (Cleonice), and often both. In a 1790 engraving from *Tito* that opens act 3, the emperor declares, "Let it be noted in Rome, that . . . I know all, absolve all, and forget all" (fig. 6.2). In *Artaserse*, challenges to the monarchical self and its ultimate subordination had peaked, whereafter, having reached the Habsburg court of Vienna, Metastasio turned more consistently and thoroughly to self-control rewarded with happy endings.

But the doubt that emerges so strongly in *Adriano*, like the resistance to good of the emperor in *Ezio*, shows that the monarch remains an ambivalent figure, though a totalizing and mythical one. Adriano as conqueror transgresses

120. See in particular Muratori's last work, *Della pubblica felicità* (1749), esp. chap. 1. By the later 1760s, the famine had shown that even good government could not stay the course of nature's storms. Debates on sovereign jurisdiction and powers were reignited, fueled also by Rousseau's notion of the *patria* as a community founded on virtuous pursuit of public good and public happiness through good laws. By the 1770s, Rousseau's ideas were widely applauded in Italy, expressed in the Milanese periodical *Il Caffè* and the Este legal code implemented in Ferrara in 1771 (Rao, "Enlightenment and Reform," 237–46).

121. Montesquieu, *The Spirit of the Laws*, book 6, chap. 9, p. 82. "Dans les États modérés, l'amour de la patrie, la honte et la crante du blâme, sont des motifs réprimants, qui peuvent arrêter bien des crimes. La plus grande peine d'une mauvaise action sera d'en être convaincu" (Montesquieu, *Oeuvres complètes*, 318).

122. Sala di Felice, *Metastasio*, 159–60, also hints at the importance of current debates on jurisprudence, e.g., Giannone's *Istoria civile* (Naples, 1723) and Muratori's *Della pubblica felicità*. Cf. Metastasio's letter to Saverio Mattei, October 1775, in *Opere* 5:363, and Ferroni, "Il Metastasio napoletano," 203–22.

FIG. 6.2. Engraving for the opening of act 3 of *La clemenza di Tito*, captioned with Titus's words: "Let it be noted in Rome that I am the selfsame man, that I know all, that I absolve everyone, and that I forget everything." From Metastasio, *Drammi scelti dell'abbate Metastasio* (Venice: Antonio Zatta & figli, 1790), p. 396. The New York Public Library, Astor, Lenox, and Tilden Foundations.

sexually, as Valentiniano fails morally. From being militaristic, untamed, evil or defiant beings, such monarchs turn regularly into tamer, more ordered, and honorable ones. To turn back the circle, only by allowing space for disordered monarchs can ordered ones exist and thrive. This is so in Metastasio's main mythohistorical handbook, Plutarch's *Lives*, where the Roman king Numa Pompilius, relatively tame compared with his predecessors and successors, is preceded by Romulus (who conquered the Sabines and raped their women in founding Rome) and succeeded by the violent Tullus Hostilius (true to his name). Similarly, though Tullus Hostilius precedes the usurping regicide Ancus Marcius, the latter does eventually introduce new forms of social order, or at least more ordered rules regarding war. Thus Plutarch models the progress of monarchs from wild states, incompatible with social norms, to peaceful ones, in ways that make the totality of negative and positive manifest over the course of a sovereign's reign or between reigns—all requiring recognition by subjects who sanctify and legitimate monarchs for the sake of the social order.[123]

Such popular recognition is familiar from Metastasio. Artaserse is given a

123. Identification of such oscillations is characteristic of the analytical style of Dumézil, *Archaic Roman Religion*, e.g., 1:276–77; see also Palmer, *The Archaic Community of the Romans*, 1.

coronation that resonates with the Roman rite of inauguration, which involved conferral of the imperium that in Rome turned the king into an earthly echo of Jupiter. Clistene in *L'olimpiade* (3.6) is elided visually with Jupiter through his descent from the steps of the god's great temple, surrounded by the populace and a chorus of sacrificial priests. Clistene, in particular, moves over the course of a few scenes from stern and terrible judgments to benevolent ones. And it is the people who stand witness to his elision with Jupiter and who publicly proclaim the pardoning of his son.

* * *

Metastasio's mythical views of sovereignty existed in counterpoint to the historical sovereign allegorized in his Neapolitan and Roman libretti and lauded in his Viennese *licenze*. I have stressed the mythical over the historical function in this chapter not to forget the more grounded lessons of earlier chapters and the concrete ways that Metastasian opera was poised between fixity and variability, but to show how its myth-making was key to its power, to its almost hypnotic iterability and endless adaptability to different variables and contingencies.[124]

No wonder Metastasio could be relatively cavalier about his sovereigns' fates on the eighteenth-century stage. Especially as he aged, he was more occupied with how his texts were handed down in print, and how his own literary reputation would be established in the great expanse of ancient and modern literary traditions, than with the countless performances of his libretti across Europe.[125] This is nowhere clearer than in his lengthy paraphrase and commentary on Aristotle's *Poetics, Estratto dell'Arte poetica d'Aristotile e considerazioni su la medesima*, completed in 1773 and first published in 1782.[126] The *Estratto* declared that the dramma per musica was full-fledged tragedy, the most perfect in history, not least because fully sung. Eighteenth-century opera lay at the apex of the great Greek tradition, it claimed, extending fully the "immemorial custom" of delivering tragedy using number and meter.[127] Piero Weiss has proposed that Metastasio advanced such an idea notwithstanding obvious historical truth, and at a time when the *Poetics* was simply outmoded, because doing so was a way to fashion a pedigree for opera seria that gave legitimacy to Metastasio's entire life work.[128] Yet with characteristic introspection, Metastasio made his motives

124. Compare Chegai, *L'esilio di Metastasio*, 13, who notes opera seria's ability to confront contingent exigencies without experimenting, and to operate on principles that balance alterity against familiarity.

125. On Metastasio's preoccupations with editing and publishing his *oeuvre* see Savage, "Staging an Opera," 591. Rosy Candiani discusses the contrast between the relative quiet of the literary world regarding Metastasio's work and the clamor of his publics, in *Pietro Metastasio*, 227–41.

126. Metastasio *Opere* 2:957–1117.

127. Ibid., 970.

128. Weiss, "Metastasio, Aristotle, and the *Opera Seria*," 385–94. Metastasio tried to have the same precepts put forward in Ranieri de' Calzabigi's preface to the Paris edition of his works from 1755 (in *Poesie del signor Abate Pietro Metastasio*, ed. Calzabigi).

transparent: "The sole aim of my work has been the restless desire to justify myself in my own eyes insofar as possible, as I am naturally . . . less gentle than any of my critics."[129] At the core of what followed this preface was an assessment of opera seria as an improved variety of mythical Greek tragedy: opera seria expanded the limits of Aristotelian catharsis to include not just terror and pity but tenderness and love; it bettered Greek morality by stressing virtue and self-sacrifice; it eased the tyranny of the unities by softening shifts in temporal perspective with scenic changes; and it minimized superstitiousness immanent in Greek choruses by favoring the verisimilitude of a single singing/speaking voice.[130]

If Metastasio's motive here was his own immortality, he knew that the "ineluctable destiny" of his words was that they be "absorbed and estranged in spectacle," losing their sacredness in circulation.[131] Beyond this, the varied recitation of his texts also ritually reiterated the monarch's moral/political function. As Sala di Felice has shown, to repeat the operas was also to enunciate again and again their function as the monarch's tool and spread news of his greatness far and wide. Metastasio openly avowed as much in the *licenza* to his highly imperial *L'olimpiade*, premiered for the empress's birthday on August 24, 1733:

> I formed vows in my mind, but they issue from my mouth; I know not from what magic, my vows transformed in your praise. . . . Heaven produces great souls to all our profit. Why do they hide their light, if it teaches the good path to others? Praises of the one who reigns are a school for his servants. The great exemplum loves, corrects, persuades, teaches. Not all reside near the source—a good reason to quench the thirst even of those who are distant. Ah, someone who obeys the gods and instructs mortals by singing the praises of royalty is not wrong![132]

For Sala di Felice, *L'olimpiade* is the apex of Metastasio's work in constructing "fables [that were] deliciously pathetic but at the same time invested with a social function that is no less meaningful for being skillfully disguised."[133] Yet by assigning himself the role of mediator between the throne and its subjects, Metastasio is also able to endow his monarchs with a magical instrumentality

129. "Il solo oggetto del mio lavoro è stato l'inquieto desiderio di giustificarmi, quanto è possibile, con me medesimo, che sono naturalmente il men discreto . . . di tutti i giudici miei" (Metastasio, *Opere* 2:960).

130. Glossed in Weiss, "Metastasio, Aristotle, and the *Opera Seria*," 390–94.

131. Sala di Felice, *Metastasio*, 15.

132. "Voti in mente io formai: ma dal mio labbro / escon, per qual magia dir non saprei, / trasformati in tua lode i voti miei. / L'anime grandi / a vantaggio di tutti il Ciel produce. / Nasconderne la luce / perché, se agli altri il buon cammino insegna? / Le lodi di chi regna / sono scuola a chi serve. Il grande esempio / innamora, corregge, / persuade, ammaestra. Appresso al fonte / tutti non sono. È ben ragion che alcuno / disseti anche i lontani. Ah! Non è reo / chi, celebrando i pregi / dell'anime reali, / ubbidisce agli dèi, giova a' mortali" (Metastasio, *Opere* 1:633).

133. Sala di Felice, *Metastasio*, 151.

that overshoots their absolute, visible, or otherwise tangible qualities. He makes himself the bearer of that magic, as Bernini, Lully, or Quinault were the messengers and makers of Louis XIV's power.

Only such an understanding can address the range of site-specific political yokings found for any Metastasian libretto, from the closest (made by means of *licenze*, adaptations of recitatives and arias, ballet intermezzi, and so on, to suit local circumstances and ideologies) to the loosest and least natural (republican operas staged in monarchies, monarchical operas in republics, sacrificial operas in centers of political reform). For all the republican operas that were staged at Venice, there were numerous monarchical ones (and for all the monarchical ones at Naples, no lack of republican ones). To insist that Metastasian stories had to suit specific polities and occasions in order to be politically meaningful misses the mythical point. Much as Roland Barthes asked how so many meanings had been inferred by the French from the single photograph of the black soldier saluting the French flag,[134] we might ask how so many meanings were inferred from the parable of the youth torn between father and sovereign, or the parable of the monarch who renounces his desire for the other's women.

BATAILLE'S SOVEREIGNS: A POSTSCRIPT ON IDENTIFICATION

According to Georges Bataille, the distinctive character of sovereignty lies in those who possess it, their quality (French, *aspect*) and especially their relation to other beings rather than their rank, prerogatives, properties, or conditions per se.[135] This "quality" may pertain not just to kings but to a variety of creatures: rulers, divinities, and even everyday mortals not necessarily vested with any official authority but with a supreme autonomy from the subordinated demands of utility. The sovereign being is marked by signs of a life free from existence as a mere series of functions, applications, and services enacted in respect of something higher. On this view, and in the broadest sense, we might say that a poor man might bear the marks of sovereignty, and so might a lion, so long as their fundamental condition opposes itself to the servile condition of the bourgeois person. For that which is sovereign within Bataille's "economy of consumption" is whatever part lies beyond "servile utility"—that which opposes "The Accursed Share" (*La part maudite*, accursed or godforsaken), the title under which Bataille's theories of "general economy" were collected and made famous in English. Sovereignty, as a condition, is marked by the consumption of wealth and surplus for the sake of pure enjoyment, beyond what is useful. It is marked by a transutilitarian orientation. "Life *beyond utility* is the domain of sovereignty."[136]

134. "Myth Today," in Barthes, *Mythologies*, 109–59.

135. Bataille, "Sovereignty," 248–51; original, somewhat differently organized, in Bataille, *La part maudite*, 47–225.

136. Ibid., 197ff.

Yet the enabling condition of Bataille's sovereignty is the miraculous production of surplus. That is the basis for wonder, or more precisely the anticipation of wonder, which is more powerful than wonder itself. It is wonder that allows delight and a transcendent state that cannot be attained while toiling away for future benefit, wonder that requires an unfettered existence situated in present time. Since the sovereign is infused with the divine, moreover, he must bear the quality of the miraculous that makes divinity what it is—hence his symbiotic relation to festivity as the material embodiment of a miraculous surplus.

This in turn is critical to perceiving the sovereign as a medium of identificatory projections gratifying to the subjects who labor for him. Only through a focus on the miraculous does the sovereign come to be seen not as an object but as a subject.[137] And it is that identificatory process of, and satisfaction in, recognizing oneself (*se reconnaître*) that renders efficacious the mechanisms of miraculous festivity, which appear to the sovereign's subjects as having been conjured up by him.

Furthermore, the miraculous that sustains the sovereign's status, which in turn can thrust his subjects into the moment, operates in conjunction with the divine on a so-called principle of ambiguity, on the ambiguous force that is always met by a counterforce—birth by death, pleasure by displeasure, beauty by ugliness, refinement by barbarism or obscenity. The principle of ambiguity explains the metamorphoses of winter into spring, barbaric violence or obscene humor to serene contemplation and obedience, transgression to law. Within this flux of antitheses, constantly folding in on themselves, the sovereign looms as an encompassing principle.

Crucial to this operating principle is the sovereign approach to knowledge—knowledge more as a form of unknowing than of knowing, as a form of anti-knowledge, a refusal or resistance to know or be known. Being given *in time,* knowledge itself (Bataille argues) can never be inherently sovereign, since sovereignty plays out not in the experience of time-in-motion but in the static celebration of the moment. That moment, like the quality of the miraculous that is commensurate with the sovereign, is an eternal moment of festive oblivion, of embracing sovereignty as the font of surplus and delight.

* * *

Things get more complicated when the identificatory mechanisms are channeled through a surrogate—the singer—who begins to accrue the properties and material luxuries of political sovereigns. Opera ranks among festivities vested in the sovereign character through and through. It constitutes the miraculous as the moment realized in strong emotions, which opera seria in its classic phase projected in bel canto arias, manifestations of personal power and luxury that could persuade audiences not through any natural illusion or progression, but through the sheer miracle of their presence. The performance of emotions

137. Ibid., 240

was the performance of a power uniquely capable of awakening untapped sentiments in listeners. In a time when most still sought "the sign of royal authenticity," strong emotions came charged with the feeling that the object of all acts and works was to attain the miraculous—a feeling that focusing on utility would destroy, but immersion in wide-eyed sensation could promote. For Bataille, therefore, sovereignty, as a condition allied to useless splendor, resisting the banal exigencies of mere utility, refuses reduction to labor or reason alone. This is why the king's festivity signifies a kind of universal sovereignty, itself already implied in the impulses of the masses. The monarch and the splendor that surrounds him satisfy his subjects' desire to gaze upon a miraculously limitless experience, a condition that manifests the sovereign for the benefit of those for whom surplus will never be attainable and who will never accrue sovereignty as their own condition.

In Bataille's scheme, all these mechanisms depend on a logic of identification, since the sovereign can only assume objective existence through reference to a deep subjectivity in his admirers (literally, those who gaze on him, *mirarlo*), whose gaze he attracts. But the direction of this process is nearly inverted in what Bataille calls "traditional sovereignty," since "the masses see the sovereign as the subject of whom they are the object."

The flaw in this model—utopian and idealizing—is too obvious to belabor. Clearly when Bataille argues that reason and understanding in our age are assigned to the domain of consciousness, privileged over the domain of the sovereign moment (moments like laughter, happy tears, disbelief at death, in short, the moment-in-time), he is speaking in the ungrounded zone of geohistorical time if it is the zone of history at all—in epistemic time rather than the fine grain of historical facts. Perhaps this is ironic in that Bataille reached his universalist view through his own subjective contemplation of existence, using personal instinct in lieu of particularizing data.[138] Clearly, too, no one has ever gained or maintained political, perhaps even existential sovereignty, without planning, counting, and calculating to reinforce such a position. The question then is whether a concern for time and a sovereign state are incompatible, even antithetical. Or whether the very question is chimerical.

They are not antithetical, I would argue, if sovereignty is understood as a play of fantasies and illusions among subjects located in a hierarchically ordered world. In fact, Bataille's singularly brilliant realization was that what the sovereign represents, in whatever form, is the *inner experience* of the observing, laboring subject. The sovereign is the intermediary of the subject's inner experience, and succeeds in representing it through "sensible, emotional contact" in which the "state of mind of the sovereign, of the *subject*, is *subjectively communicated* to those for whom he is sovereign."[139] On such a view, sovereignty is effective only when subjects identify with the sovereign. To carry this off, objects that

138. Ibid., 241.

139. Ibid., 240, 242, and see also 243.

mediate this intersubjective communication must not appear as such, because sovereignty is an existential condition both of the sovereign and of those for whom she or he is sovereign.

Only on the hard ground of real political exchange, rather than in the pliant space of subjective experience, is sovereignty antithetical to a concern for time. For amid such political realities, no "sovereign state of mind" can be communicated to the sovereign's subjects without the mediation of many pragmatic facts and actions. Certainly if the issue concerns the existential condition of sovereignty during the European period of absolutism when the projection of sovereign images was increasingly disjunct from their reception by observing subjects, time served the sovereign state of mind through rigorous, tyrannical, self-consciously orchestrated schemes.

Time in the opera house came to be radically reworked in the decades that followed the heyday of the Metastasian canon. The bumpy realities and openly unreal time effects caused by stop-and-start aria forms, dramaturgical sectionalism, opera acts knocking into ballets, all accompanied by disjoined and disproportioned physical and perspectival space, were gradually abandoned for "naturalistic" temporal progressions of more seamless aria forms, ensembles, scenic tableaux, integrated ballets and choruses, and accompanying perspectival changes.

Yet Bataille's theory of sovereignty is useful precisely because it is a "general" one, rather than one that is politically or historically specific, much less a general theory of sovereign rule. It focuses on subjective relations that sovereignty sets in motion. The very thing that makes its claims maddeningly impressionistic, ungrounded, and uncoordinated for historical purposes also gives them considerable grit for thinking about sovereignty as part of the dynamics of opera seria as a floating signifier, highly generalized as an expression of sovereignty in myriad adaptations. It is useful precisely in thinking about how audiences and producers drew such different meanings from the operas' forms and symbols.

CHAPTER 7

Bourgeois Theatrics, Perugia, 1781: Third Case Study

"Music, theater, and dance. These are just some of the ingredients of the sparkling Umbrian summer.

"The tip of the diamond is sure to be Umbria Jazz . . . which will transform Perugia into a citadel of music." Preview of the annual "Umbria Jazz" festival, Perugia[1]

On New Year's Eve 1781, a professor of medicine and botany stood before an academy of citizens from the small hill town of Perugia to congratulate them on the opening of their theater. Middle-class residents of a papal outpost numbering no more than about 18,000,[2] they had formed a theatrical society four years earlier and built a magnificent theater that well surpassed in size that of their noble rivals. By the time they met for their general assembly following the autumn season, Annibale Mariotti had been their president for three years and could plume congratulations on his flock while remembering the many trials they had borne on the road to triumph.[3]

Mariotti spoke in the language of Metastasian simile, of the weary helmsman buffeted by tumultuous seas, fighting the waves, threatened by harsh reefs and deep vortices, his sails torn and his masts downed, packing his speech with quotations from the "Italian Sophocles" (see the appendix to this chapter). Echoing the Aeneas of Metastasio's *Didone* (3.1), who on leaving the shores of Carthage looks ahead wistfully to the day when he will recount his past travails, Mariotti

1. "Musica, teatro e danza. Sono solo alcuni degli ingredienti della frizzante estate umbra.

"Punta di diamante si conferma Umbria Jazz; . . . trasformerà Perugia in cittadella della musica" ("Non solo jazz").

2. Bonazzi, *Storia di Perugia* 2:443, estimates a population at the time of 12,000, which may well be low; Mariotti himself spoke of 18,000 residents in 1781 (see n. 40 below).

3. On Mariotti (1738–1801), see Antinori, "Notizie per la vita del dottor Annibale Mariotti," ix–xxii; Ferrini, "Annibale Mariotti," 3–118, and *Deputazione per la Storia Patria di Umbria* 99 (2002). Mariotti published on many intellectual topics beyond theater, medicine, and botany, for example, in 1788, nine essayistic letters on Perugian graphic arts up to Vasari's time in *Lettere pittoriche perugine*.

declared that victory had finally come for his fellow *soci*, and they could at last recall the perils they had met while longing for its arrival. He reminded them that they had no sooner conceived the idea of leaving the unhappy soil of their subordination, where the pride of others had condemned all their "thoughts of a [theater based in] virtuous common delight and erudite pleasure" to "harsh servitude," than false smiles had appeared on the nobles who thought that the high seas would always be theirs to rule over with their niggling little boat. The society had had to obtain affirmation from their "sovereign authority," the pope, who controlled the laws that granted everyone equality on the high seas, but even at that, they had first had to overcome many obstacles. They entrusted themselves to a god greater than any being on earth and began the difficult labor of contriving a well-planned fleet. At last all was readied and nothing left but to set sail, yet still there were those who forced them to return to the papal throne for permission to sail on. Wandering off course in the dark of night, at the mercy of the waves, agitated by fierce winds, they struck insidious quicksands and wondered—as Vitellia did when she renounced her troth to Titus (*La clemenza di Tito* 3.11)—if they had risked turning their treasured hopes into ballast like a sailor carried off to a distant shore. Now their only task was to meet the winds with courage, like Ezio's beloved Fulvia (*Ezio* 1.13), who had had to fend off the furious overtures of a tyrannical emperor, repairing their damaged ship, reordering their sails, and putting them on a happier course once the angry winds died down.

* * *

Mariotti's speech was given on the heels of a jubilant opening season, preceded by several turbulent years of building and preparation. The theater that had swept them onto this course is now called Teatro Comunale Morlacchi, a name that dates from the later nineteenth century.[4] Foot traffickers passing the theater in present times might notice announcements of prose plays, less often concerts. Only occasionally will they find operas or ballets. In early summer, on the other hand, the Morlacchi is briefly absorbed into a popular panoply of musical festivities, as kiosks, banners, posters, and sound stages spring up throughout the town's piazzas and alleys in anticipation of "Umbria Jazz." For ten days each July, the town is outfitted "not just as a festival but as a *festa* [party]," as an estimated 200,000 visitors jam-pack the old Etruscan town (see figs. 7.1 and 7.2).[5] I'd been passing through in 2000 on an artist's permit courtesy of the staff that was hosting my partner, who was playing the Teatro Pavone—once the

4. The *boccascena* presently measures 10.5 meters across and the stage 20 meters wall-to-wall. For other specifications see the Web site of the Teatro Stabile dell'Umbria, http://www.teatrostabile.umbria.it/canale.asp?id=33 (accessed January 25, 2003).

5. Zwerin, "Jazz Alive and Kicking," 10, notes 4,400 in attendance at Keith Jarrett's concert at the Giardino del Frontone in 2001. Comment by Marija Šarač, staff member, Umbria Jazz (July 14, 2003).

FIG. 7.1. Perugia city center. Early morning during Umbria Jazz 2003, looking onto kiosks set up in the main piazza. Photograph by author.

FIG. 7.2. Teatro Pavone outfitted for Umbria Jazz 2003. Photograph by author.

exclusive theater of the Perugian nobility and like the Morlacchi an exquisite eighteenth-century horseshoe.[6] Perugians at the start of the twenty-first century were still justifiably proud of their theaters. They were proud that they could

6. Unlike the Morlacchi, which stages live performances, the present-day Pavone is mostly used as a movie theater.

present indoor jazz events in no less than two lush, mint-condition settecento opera houses, and once they saw how enchanted I was with them they were kind enough to regale me with historical lore and impromptu tours.

Each of the theaters is ringed with five tiers and lavishly decorated, like so many prodigies of Italian theater architecture.[7] I was struck to learn that the Morlacchi, largest of the festival's indoor venues, had originally been built under the exclusive aegis of the bourgeoisie, who named it Nuovo Teatro Civico del Verzaro. These middle-class Perugians, officially called *cittadini* or members of the *secondo ordine*, had embarked on the enterprise as a way to establish the autonomy of their class while surpassing the Pavone, which had first been built by the nobles in 1723 and was rebuilt in 1773 just eight years before the opening of the Civico (for the interior of the Pavone, see figure 1.7 above). As an index of grand eighteenth-century narrative history—bourgeois initiative trouncing old aristocratic privilege—the events seemed almost too good to be true. I spent that first visit to Perugia searching the theaters' archives and quickly learned what any student of Perugian history would already have known: that the town had been a hornet's nest of class conflicts for many a century, and that any history of lyric theater in late-eighteenth-century Perugia would also have to be a history of those conflicts.

A THEATER FOR THE MIDDLE CLASS

Many of the theaters springing up in Italy during the later eighteenth century grew from collaborations between noblemen and rising members of the middle class, or from projects undertaken by nobles whose ranks were beefed up by wealthy merchants and professionals, men who had purchased titles in the recent past when the Italian economy was in a steep decline.[8] At nearby Amelia, for instance, a group of nobles and bourgeoisie joined together in 1780 to begin plans for building what stands today as the Teatro Sociale, a beautiful three-tiered theater with forty-four boxes and a *boccascena* (stage opening) measuring just 6.5 meters across.[9]

The *cittadini* of Perugia embarked on a very different course. Despite Perugian precedents for joint academies of nobles and *cittadini*,[10] they fashioned

7. The fifth tier of the Pavone was a true peanut gallery and nowadays is used only for technical equipment. It never had boxes, so in that sense was never actually a separate "tier."

8. I discuss the historical cause célèbre of Venice below (chap. 9); see also Tenenti, *Venezia e i corsari, 1580–1615*, available in English as *Piracy and the Decline of Venice;* Davis, *The Decline of the Venetian Nobility;* and Rapp, *Industry and Economic Decline.*

9. Dimensions are available on the Teatro Stabile dell'Umbria Web site, http://www.teatrostabile.umbria.it/canale.asp?id=76 (accessed January 25, 2003).

10. Cf. Atlas, "The Accademia degli Unisoni," 5–23; and Pimpinelli, *I riti nell'Arcadia Perugina.* Documents relevant to the opening of the Teatro Civico are preserved in I-PEc, *Atti.* On the theater's archive, see Ventura, *Teatro Francesco Morlacchi;* and on its history, Guardabassi, *Appunti storici;* see also three short titles by Iraci, "Il Teatro Morlacchi," 5–13, "Perugia—Accademia Civica," and "Can-

their own society, the Società per l'Edificazione di un Nuovo Teatro, gathering twenty shares from twenty founding members and convening a general assembly on December 21, 1777. The moment had particular significance since the nobles had recently renovated and reopened their Teatro Pavone to much fanfare. Since the city formed part of the Papal States and was thus effectively part of the papal kingdom, with all its populace subject to papal will, the society had to have the pope authorize the building project and any major aspects of the theater's operation.[11] A *supplica* had been sent the previous October to the pope's decision-making body, the Sacra Consulta, through the Perugian governor (a Roman bureaucrat) and the regional archbishop, which pleaded to let the "honored Cittadini" build a theater, using their own money, for "comic, tragic, and dramatic shows and . . . other virtuous academic functions" (Comiche, Tragiche e Drammatiche rappresentazioni e . . . altri accademici onesti esercizi)," mounted at "the usual times" of year—meaning especially Carnival. The theater of the nobility was too cramped to hold the throngs of people who wanted to attend it, they claimed, and besides, the civic theater was to enshrine a new morality of "honest pleasure and love of virtue."[12]

Early on, the governor sent a memo to the pope supporting the idea on grounds that the nobles had been staging only "opere serie e burlesche in musica" (in short, only opera) while the "people" also wanted "comedies, tragedies, and similar *accademici esercizi*" (plays in addition to operas, plus concerts, cantatas, and the like). What was more, one could not "force the proprietors of all those boxes [at the Pavone] to meet every request" for seating and risk spoiling the beauty of their theater and lowering its status.[13] The governor rightly anticipated resistance. On January 14, he received notice from Rome that the Sacra Consulta wanted to put the matter to the nobles to see if they had anything contrary to say.[14] Between January 28 and early February 1778, the nobles responded nervously to the Sacra Consulta, trying to plant seeds of doubt about the proposition while establishing a basis for their own future demands without actually taking an opposing stand:

> [A]lthough the present [noble] Theater . . . has always been and is presently commercial and large enough for the City of Perugia, and its boxes have been and are given by the Owners to anyone who requests them . . . [and although]

---

tanti e danzatrici," 16–19; and most especially Brumana's recent "Il dramma per musica *Artaserse*," 239–78, which Professoressa Brumana kindly shared with me as I was writing this chapter.

11. On the papal monarchy, see Prodi, *The Papal Prince*, and on Perugia within its Papal States, Black, "Perugia and Papal Absolutism," 509–39. More broadly, see Anderson, *Lineages of the Absolutist State*, chap. 6.

12. Original in I-PEc, *Atti*, filza 1, "Supplica per la Costruzione del Teatro," which declares the theater "troppo angusto per il numeroso concorso di tutto quel Popolo che ama di intervenire."

13. I-PEc, *Atti*, filza 1, from the "Monsignor Governatore," who argued that other, smaller cities already had two theaters; undated memo antecedent to the main decision-making phase of the process.

14. I-PEc, *Atti*, filza 1, February 11, 1778.

> many of those boxes are available for sale today, nevertheless the Academy members in no way oppose the building of a new theater, having complete faith that this will in no way prejudice the usual and habitual rights granted to them. This is what the members of the Academy have resolved by unanimous consensus.[15]

Permission to build the new theater was therefore granted the *cittadini* by the Sacra Consulta on February 7, 1778.[16]

In truth, not only was the advent of a rival theater directly implicated in the long history of severe strife between the nobles and the people who stood directly beneath them in the Perugian class hierarchy, but the theater also went against immediate noble interests, financial and symbolic, especially given the size of the town. At the time the Teatro Civico was built, there were just fifty noble families left in Perugia. Most of them were concentrated in five parishes, including San Martino del Verzaro in the *rione* (district) of Porta Sant'Angelo, where the new theater was to stand. The area was also highly populated by *cittadini*,[17] some of whom had intermarried with nobles, especially in the previous century when marriage markets and bridewealth had shrunk across Italy with the general economic decline and nobles had had to pump up their numbers with citizens from the *secondo ordine*.[18]

Nowhere was this more evident than behind the scenes of the Pavone. Like the Civico, the Pavone was run by an academy, the Accademia dei Nobili del Casino. *Casino* then meant "box," or literally, "small house," loge, lodge, or club, often implying a private men's club (sometimes a brothel). A *casino* could only be sold to a male classified as a *gentiluomo* or a *civile*.[19] Thus when applicants of ambiguous status petitioned to join the Accademia dei Nobili, members who reviewed the petition would take the measure of the man using his ancestry,

15. "[Q]uantunque il presente Teatro . . . sia stato sempre e sia al presente venale e capace per la Città di Perugia, e i Palchi di questo siano stati dati e si diano da i Sig*no*ri Accademici Padronali a quelli che loro ne hanno fatta istanza; e sia ancora che molti di d*ett*i Palchi siano resi in oggi vendibili; tutta volta i Sig*no*ri Accademici non si oppongono punto alla Edificazione di un nuovo Teatro sulla certa fiducia, che questo niente pregiudicherà a quei dritti soliti, e consueti a Loro competenti. Questo è quanto hanno risoluto i Sig*no*ri Accademici d'unanime Consenso" (I-PEc, *Atti*, filza 1, undated). Pascucci, *La Nobile Accademia del Pavone*, 20, cites the nobles' *Atti accademici*, minutes of January 28, 1778 (in I-PEas, which now preserves the Pavone archives, currently in reorganization and inaccessible when I wrote this chapter). My thanks to Professoressa Brumana and Dottoressa Clara Cutini Zazzerini, director of the Archivio di Stato, Perugia, for this information.

16. I-PEc, *Atti*, filza 1, 6r (original) and 8v (copy). The *cittadini* reported on February 15, 1778, that the Sacra Consulta had ordered that the noble class be consulted in order to clarify any "ambiguities" (I-PEc, *Verbali*, 3r–3v).

17. Chiacchella, *Ricchezza*, 53, 199, and passim (information based on a census of 1782).

18. Volpi, "La crisi della nobiltà," 361–406.

19. Pascucci, *La Nobile Accademia del Pavone*, 18 and n. 2, citing the *Atti accademici* of 1726. Pascucci's work was printed during a bicentennial celebration of the theaters in 1927, which produced the fascist leaflet *Nella celebrazione del Teatro Pavone* and other minor writings. See Piergiovanni, "Il Teatro del Pavone," 28.

wealth, and current family status. Decisions about his admissibility were ad hoc and ad hominem.

Later in the eighteenth century, the Accademia dei Nobili made its admissions criteria more regular and more stringent, seemingly in response to dilution in its ranks. Applicants began having to give evidence of *vera civiltà* (with the emphasis on *vera*). It was no longer enough, as before, to show sufficient means and ancestral purity—for example, not having worked in the trades. Minimally an applicant had to be the "son of a noblewoman and married to another noblewoman," pay the academy 300 scudi, and have an annual income of at least 1,000 scudi. Fixed in an assembly of the Nobili on September 20, 1775, these three criteria were prompted by the case of an applicant who allegedly enjoyed an income of 2,000 scudi, which had been deemed enough to excuse the nonnoble origins of his mother as long as no forms of trade (*arti mecchaniche*) had been practiced by his father and grandfather—an exception that tested the rule.[20] If suitability for noble status within the nobles' academy was thus judged through a combination of income, class, and pedigree (the second based partly on marital ties and the latter two both taking into account work), a history of nonparticipation in trades remained an immutable factor. These norms were apparently so rigidly observed that one man who had requested admission in 1784 was denied it until his marriage to a noblewoman had taken place. Specific requirements of noble affiliation became determinants of class, and class status became a necessary (if not sufficient) condition for admittance. So distinct was the mark of membership in the academy, which sat in judgment on numerous applicants, and so salient its arbitration of admissions that in 1823 the city's magistrate could describe it as "another distinct class of Nobility, legally recognized as such," in contrast to the patriciate and the *nobiltà perugina*, only without some principal prerogatives of the actual nobles.[21] The nineteenth-century Perugian historian Luigi Bonazzi stressed the historic importance of certain *cittadini* having been admitted to the nobles' academy, precisely because their admission established a precedent whereby a given *cittadino* could thenceforth be counted as a nobleman.[22]

Ironically, though, however much such blurrings broke down class barriers, they also reantagonized and recemented old rivalries that extended back to the Middle Ages, rivalries that in modern times had always exacerbated the jealousy of the nobility over their perceived rights to mount and host opera. The long view of history is revealing here. The Comune of twelfth-century Perugia had been governed by males of a wealthy middle class, called the *popolo grasso* or *popolani*, people of learning and political acumen who lived well by manufacturing, trade, and other kinds of commerce.[23] Together they had formed an

20. Quoted in Pascucci, *La Nobile Accademia del Pavone*, 19.

21. Ibid. 19, 20; cf. Bonazzi, *Storia di Perugia* 2:639.

22. Bonazzi, *Storia di Perugia* 2:639–40 and chap. 28.

23. The principal Perugian histories, Pellini's *Della historia di Perugia* and Bonazzi's *Storia di Perugia*, side mainly with the nonnobles.

iron-fisted, prosperous oligarchy that included the nobles only minimally, since noble wealth was primarily land-based. But by the early thirteenth century, the powers of the *popolo grasso* were waning, and they had begun protesting against special privileges that made nobles immune to taxation. In the mid-thirteenth century, the Comune was taken over by the *popolo minuto,* artisans and shopkeepers who were often aligned with the nobles in fierce power struggles against the *popolo grasso.*[24]

Eventually the *popolo grasso* acquired the nickname "Raspanti," an epithet that most probably alluded to the cat's claw adopted as their emblem in the fourteenth century.[25] Across the centuries, they lost and regained power many times vis-à-vis the nobles, and with each loss or gain the loser suffered a bloody expulsion. Such extreme patterns of strife and factionalism extended to factionalism between noble families too, something that lay the city open to unhappy and changeable forms of rule: absentee *seigneurs* in the fifteenth century and the papacy, via arbitrament, in the earlier sixteenth and as absolute ruler beginning in 1540—not surprisingly in a city that was already papal-dependent and staunchly pro-papal, Guelf, that is.[26] When Perugia was finally yoked to the papacy through formal incorporation into the Papal States, factionalism was subdued to an extent. In any case, the monied middle and noble classes had grown more alike by the seventeenth century (much as in many other Italian cities): the nobility was tainted by commerce and trade, even when it tried through matrimonial strategies and political alliances to sustain its markers of "pure" group identity, and the *cittadinanza* was modeling itself widely after the nobility, going so far as to make itself appear fixed and exclusive by means of a *chiusura,* a legal closing of its ranks.[27]

Nevertheless, mutual suspicions were alive and well in the eighteenth century when the theaters were built. Even in the 1870s, Bonazzi said he heard old men reminisce that during the years when the Civico was founded and long

24. As elsewhere, nobles (also called *magnates* in this period) were immune to taxation because included within feudal aristocratic ranks (or knighthood). Generally, though not always, the nobles opposed themselves to the *popolo grasso,* who formed an elite subset of the wider group known as the *popolo.* The understanding of who was counted among the *popolo* in medieval Perugia was evidently highly varied and complex. In the late Middle Ages the meaning of *popolo* was social and juridical, encompassing every person outside the ranks of the nobles living within communal jurisdiction. On various groups and their histories in political governance within the *popolo,* see Grundman, *The Popolo at Perugia,* and for terminology, see also Heywood, *A History of Perugia,* 42n.

25. Felice Ciatti claimed the term alluded to the city's arms, a griffin with claws raised to strike (*raspare,* "to claw"), but that explanation is currently not well accepted (*Delle memorie annali* 1:44).

26. The cycle peaked from the late fourteenth to the late fifteenth century and only abated when the noble Degli Oddi were expelled in 1488. The previous *seigneur,* Braccio Fortebracci, exercised agency through lieutenants, but after 1488 the rival Baglioni ruled Perugia with the virtual dictatorship of "Ten," they and their adherents holding all seats (see Black, "The Baglioni as Tyrants," 245–81, and "Comune and the Papacy," 163–91).

27. Chiacchella, *Ricchezza,* 197, and Irace, "Il nobilato a Perugia," 35–40. Relevant to the fifteenth-century prehistory is Frascarelli, *Nobiltà minore e borghesia.* For a similar phenomenon in later sixteenth-century Venice, see Grubb, "Elite Citizens," 339–64.

FIG. 7.3. Entrance tickets to the Teatro Civico del Verzaro, Perugia, showing Ctesibius's famous pump with plunger and valve and the motto "Haud natura negat" (Nature in no way forbids it). Biblioteca Augusta Comunale, Perugia, Archivio Morlacchi, Manifesti. Reproduced by permission.

afterward, three-quarters of the litigations in Perugia had been between the two theaters.[28] Sometimes recollections of old conflicts must have been quite specific, as when Mariotti, ruminating over the theater's inscription and emblems, wrote in his notes, "The device of the Academy to be placed on the facade can have as its ornament a griffin on one side and on the other a daring cat"[29]—an idea that that may well have been abandoned because the allusion was so obviously hostile, but one that highlights the continued symbolic alignment of the *cittadinanza* with the Raspanti and with the popular party politics that had animated the *popolo grasso* in the fourteenth century.

As Francesco Guardabassi stresses, the elision between the *cittadini* and the Raspanti was also repeatedly manifested in other ways, particularly in the device and motto adopted by the Accademia del Teatro Civico. The device consisted of the pump with plunger and valve made famous by the Alexandrine mathematician and inventor Ctesibius. To ancients and moderns both, it signified mechanical genius. The image was printed on every entrance and exit ticket issued by the academy with the complementary motto "Haud natura negat" (Nature in no way forbids it), reminding the public through a venerable ancestry that their "industry" and learning could prevail over mere privilege (fig. 7.3).

These were the principal meanings on which Mariotti expanded (anonymously), at the beginning of his long preface to the libretto of *Didone abbandonata*, which opened the theater on September 17, 1781.

> Animated by an honest wish to relieve their spirit from certain serious pursuits, to which either their talent or genius or condition obliged them, and by the pressing desire to open up a new field to the youth of their Class . . . , some Perugian Cittadini have established an Academy . . . and . . . given as its emblem a Hydraulic Pump of Ctesibius with the motto *Haud Natura Negat*, which they have intended as a response to the common presumption of their lacking real talent, which many adduce to justify with ill-intended humility their own sloth and aversion to making an attempt at any honest assessment of talent and diligence.[30]

28. Bonazzi, *Storia di Perugia* 2:462.

29. "L'impresa dell'Accademia da porsi sulla facciata può avere per ornamento da una parte un Grifo e dall'altra un Gatto ardito" (in Guardabassi, *Appunti storici*, 15). The griffin was the emblem of the city. On these symbols and their history see Pellini, *Della historia*, book 8, part 1, and on the griffin, Marinelli, "Lo stemma di Perugia," 22–27.

30. "Animati alcuni Cittadini Perugini da onesta brama di sollevare lo spirito da quelle serie occupazioni, alle quali o il lor talento, o il loro genio, o la lor condizione li vuole obbligati; e presida desiderio di aprire un nuovo campo alla Gioventù dell'Ordine loro . . . ; stabilirono una Accademia . . . ; e le diedero [il nome] per Impresa un ANTLIA IDRAULICA CTESIBIANA, col Motto HAUD NATURA NEGAT, con cui intesero di rispondere all'ordinario pretesto della insufficienza del proprio ingegno, che molti adducono per giustificare con male intesa umiltà la propria infingardaggine, e la ripugnanza che hanno dal cimentarsi a qualunque onorata prova di talento e d'industria" (unsigned preface by Mariotti, who composed all the society's published writings during his presidency, *La Didone abbandonata*, iii).

Advanced in opposition to detractions by the nobility, the motto and the device of the pump set middle-class industry against smug noble indolence. At the bottom of Mariotti's copy (preserved at the Biblioteca Augusta Comunale, Perugia), he footnoted by hand the word "infingardaggine" (sloth) with the words "difficultatis patrocinia praeteximus segnitiae = Quintilio *Isti. Orat.* Lib. 2 Cap. 20," misremembering the location but not the quote: "The plea of difficulty is a cover for sloth."[31]

One paradox in all of this is that even though by early 1781 the society was ready to put these challenges in black and white, its dealings with the nobles were marked by constant fears of publicness and publicity. There is no small irony here. A society of middle-class Perugians might have displayed enough generosity to argue, on implicitly egalitarian grounds of natural law and natural right, that the privilege of running a theater was the proper province of anyone and should thus be open, but Mariotti instead urged members to adhere to a code of secrecy. Even as he longed to share, and share in, the edifying project and sociabilities of theater, he continued to characterize the nobles as "adversaries" from whom the society's strategies should be hidden.[32] Meanwhile its adroit lawyer in Rome, Giovanni Battista Zanobetti, begged that its members avoid gossip as perilous to their cause, declaring that he hadn't explained *why* there had been a delay in approving the constitution because his "imprudence would have ruined everything" and asking Mariotti to persuade his colleagues "that there were certain fearsome adversaries" and that he should "implore the deputy not to gloat over the matter and the members not to exult and celebrate their triumph." He also promised that a license to open the theater in the autumn was forthcoming, and repeated: "[F]or goodness sakes, let them show no signs of triumphing."[33]

The problem reared its head again in summer 1781 with the question of printing the academy's newly approved constitution (something that was ultimately avoided until 1803), and this time Mariotti made secrecy his rallying cry.

> As for the idea of printing our constitution, I cannot fully approve of it. As soon as it's made public (and it will be made public as soon as every individual in the Academy has a copy) the whole world will know our Society's system. Now this is what I would like them never to know. Let them make a thousand copies of the Pontifical Brief and distribute those to every café in Perugia. Here is the beauty. Our constitution has been approved by the Sovereign authority, and

31. Quintilian, *Istitutio oratoria* 1.12.16. My thanks to Shawn Deeley for identifying the correct location.

32. See I-PEc, *Carteggi*, anno 1781, Mariotti to Rosa; *Atti*, filza 10, Mariotti to Rosa; and *Atti*, filza 11, Mariotti to Rosa (June 30, 1781); and see Guardabassi, *Appunti storici*, 26: "Vi dirò di più in strettissima confidenza che il prefato soggetto con segretezza mi ha comunicato la lettera di proprio pugno di Mons*ignor* Governatore diretta a questo Mons*ignor* Segretario, prevenendolo di questa da Lui penetrata Idea e chiedendo riparo per qualunque disordine che dubita possa nascere in una azione in cui non vi è tutto il buon consenso fra la Nobiltà e la Cittadinanza: amico, segretezza in questo Articolo."

33. I-PEc, *Carteggi*, anno 1781, letter of January 24.

> these articles are known only to few of us. *The more the cherished state of the mystery increases, the more it's venerated.* In my view politics demands that the curiosity of those who are not our friends never be satisfied without a positive advantage to us. I remember having read in Chambéry's dictionary regarding the Freemasons that although their laws are secret, it's well known that they possess a high degree of virtue—that is, secrecy. I should like this maxim of secrecy in minor matters too, and because of that I like it even more in those matters that are surrounded by hundreds and thousands of curious people who could compromise them.[34]

For Mariotti and like-minded thinkers, secrecy operated on a principle of supply and demand in which value inhered in scarcity. The smaller the supply of knowledge, the more demand for it would increase, and with that its value. And the more its value, the more it would become a fetish object desirable to others. As a theme, secrecy and mystery had many manifestations in bourgeois strategies of the later eighteenth century. Among the Freemasons, it brokered a new form of privilege—a way to be counted among the select and a means of protection from forces of opposition. Thus "mystery" was not just valued as the ideological basis for initiation into occult knowledge, rites, and cosmic secrets, Sarastro-like, but was foundational to a proto-bourgeois quest for rank and respect—perhaps Sarastro-like too, but not prompted by infatuation with the occult merely for its own sake. In manifesting this bourgeois leaning, Mariotti must have been influenced as well by an encyclopedist spirit and by the same political impulse to counter traditionalist opposition that informed the actions of numerous secret societies prior to the French Revolution (as Guardabassi alleged).[35]

* * *

Given this background, it makes sense that the sudden erection of a theater by the *cittadini* raised hackles among the nobility, who saw themselves as symbolically and pragmatically on top and who had long hosted the city and its visitors

34. "Circa il pensiero di stampare le nostre costituzioni, io non so pienamente approvarlo. Subito che si son fatte pubbliche (e si son fatte pubbliche subito che ne ha una copia ogni individuo dell'Accademia), tutto il Mondo sa il sistema della nostra Società. Or questo è quello che a me piacerebbe che non si sapesse mai. Si faccian pur mille copie del Breve Pontificio, e si spaccino pure per tutti i Caffè di Perugia. Qui consiste il bello. Sono approvati dalla Sovrana Autorità i nostri capitoli; e questi Capitoli non si sanno se non da pochi di noi. Più cresce la rispettabile condizione del Mistero; e più il Mistero si fa venerando. Secondo me, la politica vuole che non si appaghi mai senza un nostro positivo vantaggio la curiosità di quelli che non son nostri amici. Mi ricordo di aver letto nel dizionario di Chambery sul proposito de' Liberi Muratori, che rimanendo tuttavia segrete le loro leggi, si sa a buon conto che possiedono in alto grado una gran virtù, cioè la segretezza. Questa massima della segretezza mi piace anche ne' piccoli affari; e perciò mi piace anche piu in quegli affari che hanno cento, e mille curiosi, che potrebbero pregiudicarli" (I-PEc, *Atti*, filza 11, undated letter by Mariotti; cf. the analysis in Guardabassi, *Appunti storici*, 17).

35. Guardabassi, *Appunti storici*, 18.

in spectacles and festivities. In fact, in 1737 the nobles had actually been assigned public monies by a city prefect to put on spectacles, something they did during Carnival and when dignitaries were visiting.[36]

So when the nobles answered the Sacra Consulta in that fateful winter of 1778 by averring their "faith" that the citizen's theater would "in no way prejudice the usual and habitual rights granted" to themselves, they had very specific rights in mind and were well aware of potential challenges to their own power and status. In fact, immediately after the Civico opened in autumn 1781, the nobles tried to prevent it from reopening for the prime season of Carnival. Mariotti got wind of the fact in mid-October and dashed off a preemptive petition to the governor saying he had heard prose would be performed at the Pavone come November and, far from objecting, simply hoped there would be no petition against their own theater staying open at Carnival. By early November, it was clear that the nobles were filing just such a petition, and Mariotti blew up. Charging them with "bad faith" and intent to damage the *cittadini* rather than show "upright principles of equity and propriety for each class of persons," he entered a litany of grievances, including the nobles'

> strange interpretations of sovereign decrees, their unceasing accusations against our conduct, and their vaunting of absolute despotism over our theater—a despotism asserted to make us eventually repent of having opened it—and a hundred other actions, all directed at disrupting our peace and provoking . . . our rancor. All that we are gladly prepared to forget, as we declare ourselves [ready] to respect everything that issues from reputable subjects, reflecting only that the spirit of party, the cultivation of motives for disdain, the lack of concern for others' woes, [the habit of] going headlong one's own way and not abiding by laws established by the most venerated authority are *not* and will never be the ideal means to maintain and promote public tranquility. To the contrary, proceeding with respect owed to superior orders, obeying laws to the letter, desiring that all conform to these, pleading with most reasonable moderation: we believe all these to be things that should not merit others' indignation and spite, but should be sought and welcomed in every society since they keep good order and public peace.[37]

36. For example, when the archduke and archduchess came from Milan in May 1780 (I-PEc, *Atti*, April 26, 1780).

37. "[L]asceremo ben volentieri di comentare alla *Eccellenza Vostra* le strane interpretazioni dei Sovrani decreti, le insussistenti accuse della nostra condotta, il vantamento di un assoluto dispotismo sopra il nostro Teatro, dispotismo che si protesta di farci un giorno pentire di averlo aperto, e cento altre espressioni tutte dirette a inquietare la nostra pace e a provocare . . . i nostri rancori. Noi tutto ciò volentieri lasciamo di ricordare, perchè ci protestiamo di rispettare tutto ciò che procede da soggetti rispettabili e unicamente andiam riflettendo che lo spirito di partito, il coltivare i motivi di disgusto, il non curare i danni altrui, lo svolgere a suo modo o il non attender le leggi stabilite dalla più veneranda Autorità non furono e non saranno mai mezzi opportuni a mantenere e a promuovere la pubblica tranquillità; siccome, al contrario, il procedere col dovuto rispetto verso gli ordini superiori, l'ubbidire esattamente alle leggi, il bramare che tutti si conformino a queste, il prevalersi colla

"We are and take glory in being most respectful subjects of our sovereign," Mariotti added, and thus "in respecting his every law and following those regarding the theater that have been established by his supreme authority."[38] In this account, subjection and sovereignty were bedmates. The route to self- (and group) autonomy was to utilize obediently the mechanism of the sovereign state and the directives sent down by its head. Rather than presuming a sovereign place for himself and his fellow *soci*, Mariotti's bid to have the theater reopen for Carnival tried to reinforce the alliance of sovereignty with the nonprivileged status of citizen subjects over and against old aristocratic claims founded on sheer class privilege.

One of the citizenry's most astonishing counterassaults on the nobles, born during the summer of 1781 in the wake of rising tensions that were putting the intended autumn opening of the Civico in jeopardy, came to light only by chance, or perhaps as a result of bad political maneuvering. An earthquake had shaken Umbria during the previous Pentecost season, and the *cittadini* thought the nobles were exploiting it by intriguing with the papal bureaucracy to have the opening of their theater postponed by up to a year, perhaps longer, to show repentance for divine displeasure. Mariotti's anxiety meter was on a steep rise by late June, when he began to decry the new machinations against the *cittadini* and even question privately the integrity of the papal prince.

> Here it's taken as certain that the pope wants to suspend all public entertainments in Umbria for at least a year because of the earthquakes in Città di Castello. . . . Should the prohibition be aimed directly at our theater, as some say, it will be utterly humiliating. . . . After such expenses, so much thinking, so many steps taken on the word of the prince! . . . Before long Rome will understand that it's all the work of diabolical malice, not zeal or religious piety.[39]

più discreta moderazione dei propri diritti, crediamo essere tutte cose che non debbano meritare l'altrui indignazione e dispetto, che anzi debbano procurarsi e gradirsi in ogni Società, perchè si mantenga il buon ordine e la pubblica pace" (I-PEc, *Atti*, filza 16, December 8, 1781, addressee possibly the secretary of state, cited from Guardabassi, *Appunti storici*, 39).

38. "Noi siamo e ci gloriamo di essere rispettosissimi sudditi del nostro Sovrano, e come tali ci gloriamo di rispettare ogni sua legge e di seguire sul particolare del Teatro quelle che dalla sua suprema autorità vennero stabilite" (in Guardabassi, *Appunti storici*, 40). Mariotti added in another memo the same day that the *cittadini* were "hated" by some nobles, that their theater had already been let to an impresario who was planning to mount a comedy with musical intermezzi, and that actors had already been contracted (I-PEc, *Atti*, filza 16, December 8, 1781). The academy put on Cimarosa's *Il pittor parigino*, a comic *intermezzo in musica a cinque* done in Rome at the Valle in 1780 (see Brumana and Pascale, "Il teatro musicale a Perugia," 132). A copy at F-Pn, Mus. MS D.2141–42, shows it to be a fairly developed work.

39. "Qui si dà per cosa certa che il Papa voglia sospendere per un anno almeno nella Provincia dell'Umbria, stante i terremoti di Città di Castello, tutti i pubblici divertimenti . . . se mai la proibizione fosse immediatamente diretta al nostro Teatro, come dicono alcuni, questa sarebbe una cosa per noi troppo umiliante. . . . Dopo tante spese, dopo tanti pensieri, dopo tanti passi fatti sulla parola del Principe! . . . [N]on ci vorrà molto perché Roma capisca, che tutto è opera di vera malignità diabolica, e non di zelo, e di pietà religiosa" (I-PEc, *Atti*, filza 11, Mariotti to Rosa, June 30, 1781).

On July 24, convinced the opening would be suppressed, Mariotti was convulsive with outrage. He blustered that the earthquake had damaged nothing in Perugia, nor had its bishop said a single devotion for it: "The truth is that this quake was so light that of 18,000 persons not a thousand felt it, so much so that we could have 17,000 testify to the complete reverse of what our adversaries want to prove. The greatest proof of the truth ought to be the conduct of the bishop. After the quake on Pentecost he ordered that thanks and prayers be given in all the churches for nearly an entire, continuous month. For this [last] one not a single bell rang and no devotions were made."[40]

Meanwhile Mariotti continued looking for a suitable dedicatee for the opening. The deputies had already dismissed the idea of a foreign dignitary or monarch,[41] fearing it would alienate any remaining goodwill at Rome, and decided to try for an acceptance from Pope Pius VI's prince-nephew Luigi Braschi and his wife. This was shooting high and demanded a delicate touch, so Mariotti offered to write to Braschi himself.[42] Whether ultimately he did so, the academy was evidently rebuffed, and nothing remains of the scheme but fragmentary notes, together with drafts of dedicatory material intended for the libretto that include a shockingly unguarded poem by academy member Giuseppe Ludovisi:

Since you, Immortal Couple, with your goodwill,
so freely share the inestimable gift of your favor,
may the new stagings, which imitate truth,
issue forth happily, proud of their fate,
and may the entire Civic Theater exult
that the eminent name of the Braschi lineage,
honor of Lazio and love of Italy,
should be a shield and shelter against every fear.
Nay, may the blessed daughter of the illustrious Italic Muse—
sober of countenance and mistress of virtue, her
feet adorned with Sophoclean buskins
with the agile, dancing crowd following her—

40. "[L]a verità si è che questo Terremoto fu tanto leggiero che di 18. mila persone non lo sentirono mille, tantoché noi potremmo avere 17. mila attestati che proverebbero tutto il contrario di ciò che provar vogliono i nostri Avversari. La maggior prova della verità sia però la condotta del Vescovo. Pel Terremoto del giorno della Pentecoste, si è durato per suo ordine a fare ringraziamenti, e orazioni quasi per un mese continuo in tutte le chiese. Per questo ultimo non è stata sonata una campana, non si è fatta niuna devozione" (I-PEc, *Atti*, filza 10, Mariotti to Rosa, July 24, 1781). Mariotti wrote to Rosa again on July 28 over a rumor to disallow the Civico from opening (ibid.). For further on these summer episodes, see Guardabassi, *Appunti storici*, 19–25.

41. In correspondence with Rosa, Mariotti had also urged secrecy in advocating against a foreign dedicatee (i.e., one from outside the Papal States) as displeasing to the pope (I-PEc, *Atti*, filza 11, June 30, 1781).

42. Mariotti wanted Rosa to include the verses with the offer to the Braschi of the dedication and was even willing to ask them himself: "[I]o son tanto ardito, che non avrei difficoltà di scrivere io stesso una Lettera al Principe don Luigi, per chiedergli a nome dell' Accademia la permissione di questa dedica" (I-PEc, *Atti*, filza 10, Mariotti to Rosa, July 18, 1781).

no longer delay her kind appearance.
Under your auspices she will suddenly hear
an approving sound moving
through the gilded loges, and henceforth
the populous arena of the theater will reverberate
with thousands and thousands of happy applauds.
For, Great Couple, should you arrive
with your sovereign look and bearing,
intent on our wishes,
forgetful of the Tiber and its splendors
to rejoice in the sonorous evening hours,
then our humble homage will already be rewarded,
and in the brilliance of your unexpected light
the festivities on stage, made with such industry,
will become even greater.
No longer will "Wicked Envy, who with her crooked teeth
has no fear of lying," be seen,
insulting and proud, "making an implacable war."[43]

Bristling just under the surface was a shocking subtext: should papal power grace our halls, we'll be only too glad to kiss the chastened ass of our noble foes. By association with the dedicatees, papal protectors were turned into swords of protection against malevolent noble enemies. Alliances and antagonisms both resonated with long-standing conflicts in Perugian history, one class conniving with a hierarchically nonadjacent one against another (nobles with the old *popolo minuto* against the *cittadini* and vice versa; the *cittadini* with papal authorities against the nobles). For *cittadini,* coalitions so structured made it possible to circumvent the nobles and link themselves directly to the papal monarchy, much as nobles over past centuries had, conversely, refused alliances with the *popolo grasso* in favor of the more proletariat *popolo minuto.*

43. "Progetto di dedicare il primo libretto dell'opera alli Principi Braschi, e lettera de la Dedica . . . : 'Poichè del favor tuo facil comparti / l'inestimabil don, Coppia immortale, / Escan pur liete di lor sorte altera / Le novelle del vero emule scene, / E tutto esulti il Civico Teatro / Che il nome eccelso della Braschia stirpe, / Onor del Lazio e dell'Ausonia Amore / Fia contro ogni timor scudo e riparo. / No, più non tardi in sua gentil comparsa / L'alma figlia d'illustre itala Musa / Grave per sensi, e di virtù maestra, / Ornata il piè di sofoclèo coturno, / Cui siegua la danzante agile schiera. / Sotto gli auspici tuoi muover d'intorno / Alle dorate Logge udrà repente / Un suono approvator, che quindi allegra / Ripeterà fra mille plausi e mille / La popolosa teatrale arena. / Che se, gran Coppia, a' voti nostri intenta, / Immemore del Tebro, e de' suoi Fasti, / Le notturne a bear ore canore / Verrai col guardo e col Sovrano aspetto / Il nostro ossequio umìl già tutto ottenne / E le sceniche feste industriose / Al folgorar d'inaspettata luce / Diverran di se stesse allor maggiori, / Nè più vedrassi insultatrice e fiera / "Col dente reo far implacabil guerra / La bieca Invidia che mentir non teme."'" (I-PEc, *Atti,* filza 13; punctuation slightly modified). A transcription appears in Guardabassi, *Appunti storici,* 24, but with "L'alma figlia" wrongly transcribed in the masculine, as Lucia Marchi observed (private communication). According to Guardabassi, the quotation in verses 28–29 comes from Carlo Frugoni.

* * *

Two coincident struggles developed around 1780 between nobles and *cittadini*. First, Mariotti was distressed over the "miserable band" of Milizie Urbane being assigned to act as the Civico's military guard, and fearing noble conspiracies, he asked sources in Rome if there were any further "strange doings" to which the theater was vulnerable. The quality of the military guard was a sign of status in an elegant theater, and also made it possible to control crowds with dignity.[44] Mariotti insisted that the impresario would need guards minimally at every indoor post. Facing obstacles from Rome (despite already agreed-upon terms), he vociferated to get troops from the Soldati Corsi rather than the urban militia or the Presidio delle Fortezze (also far less elite).[45]

Second, the nobles continued to see it as their exclusive right to host nontheatrical entertainments (*veglioni*) such as balls and benefits on grounds of custom, claims rebutted by a group of *cittadini* in a memo to the governor some years after the theater first opened. Unable to invoke privilege, they asked to mount *feste* based on past precedents, reinforced by ideologies of "natural liberty" similar to those Mariotti had invoked in his Metastasian speech to the general assembly:

> *The natural liberty* to give commercial *feste di ballo* during Carnival time, whether in public or private places, which everyone possesses who is armed by the local authority with the right licenses, was never called into doubt in the past. Even in Perugia such a liberty was always respected, both in the years when the old theater called the Pavone, belonging to the Accademia dei Nobili del Casino, was being restored and in later times, after the hall was in its present elegant form. Many Perugians know this who have enjoyed similar public spectacles in the two theaters Graziani and Vincioli and the palaces of the Vermiglioli, degli Oddi, and Ranieri—the memory of the *festa* given in the last of these in 1780 being quite fresh—something to which those who had an interest in the enterprise can give ample testimony . . . . Nor did the Sacra Consulta ever doubt this in its responses (i.e., *Servetur Solitu*) to the petitions of any of the impresarios who have worked in the Teatro Civico del Verzaro in recent times.
>
> Yet no less than the last impresario of the above-mentioned Teatro Pavone presumed in the noted petitions to create an extraordinary monopoly according to which public *feste di ballo* could only be given there. The Accademici del Civico Teatro were shocked by the odious word. And *to guarantee their own*

44. Mariotti didn't want the society paying for "twenty miserable soldiers" simply because it was at the mercy of Perugian noble officials (I-PEc, *Atti*, filza 16, Mariotti to Ippolito Vincenti in Rome, December 18, 1781; cf. Rosselli, *The Opera Industry*, chap. 4).

45. I-PEc, *Atti*, filza 12. Mariotti complained around late winter 1781 (undated letter to the governor), then on August 25, 1781 underscored that the Accademia Civica had never asked for anything else, as the Sacra Consulta seemed to think, while manifesting total subordination to the papal authority and "supreme will."

> *natural liberty,* strengthened by particulars in their laws, which the immortal Pius VI has graciously condescended to confirm, they humbly lay the most spirited supplications before the Sacra Consulta; so that, eschewing every sinister, ill-founded interpretation, that supreme assembly might declare them licensed, with the same dependence owed to anyone who oversees matters, to put on some public commercial *feste di ballo* in said theater at Carnival time.[46]

There were modest attempts at reconciliation between the two theaters into the 1780s—attempts, for example, at coordinating use of impresarios. But because the vexed question of *veglioni* kept rearing its ugly head, nothing long-lasting ever took root. The nobles continued to insist on their exclusive right to host *veglioni,* referring to custom and to reservations that they had voiced obliquely back when they were first asked to state their views on the construc-

46. "Non si è mai in addietro rivocato in dubio la natural libertà, che ha ognuno, il quale munito sia delle opportune licenze del superiore locale, di dare in tempo di Carnevale delle venali Feste di Ballo, sia ne privati, sia ne pubblici luoghi. Anche in Perugia è stata una tal libertà mai sempre rispettata tanto negli anni ne' quali si ristaurava l'antico Teatro denominato del Pavone di spettanza dell'Accademia de' Nobili del Casino, quanto ne successivi dopo di essere stato questo ridotto nell'odierna elegante forma, e lo sanno quei Perugini in gran numero i quali hanno goduto di simiglianti publici spettacoli quando ne *due Teatri Graziani,* e *Vincioli,* e quando ne Palazzi Vermiglioli, degli Oddi, e Ranieri, essendo assai fresca la memoria della Festa datasi in quest'ultimo nell'anno 1780, delle quali fa ben ampla testimonianza chi ha avuto interesse nell'impresa . . . . Neppure la Sagra Consulta ne ha punto dubitato ne suoi Rescritti, '*Servetur Solitum,*' a petizione di qualcuno degl'Impresari che ne' recenti tempi hanno agito nel Teatro Civico in *via del Verzaro.*

"Nulla però dimeno dall'ultimo Impresario del sudetto Teatro del Pavone si è preteso di costituire negli accennati Rescritti una insolita Privativa per cui quivi solamente dar si possano delle pubbliche Feste di Ballo: all'odioso nome si scossero gli Accademici del Civico Teatro, e per garantire la propria connatural libertà fiancheggiata ancora dalle particolari di loro leggi, che l'Immortal Pio VI ha avuta la degnazione di graziosamente confermare, umiliano le più fervide suppliche alla Sagra Consulta, perché, a scanzo di ogni sinistra mal fondata interpretazione, venga dichiarato da quel Supremo Consesso essere loro lecito colla dovuta dipendenza da chi presiede di dare in tempo di Carnevale nell'anzidetto Teatro delle publiche venali Feste di Ballo" (I-PEc, *Carteggi,* anno 1780; memo undated, unsigned; emphasis mine). The document is filed with papers from 1780, but was certainly written some years after the opening of the Civico, perhaps as late as the 1790s.

Guardabassi (*Appunti storici,* 42) cites the following related document (which I have not located), evidently from the same period: "Noi sottoscritti, in ossequio della verità facciamo fede ed attestiamo che ne trascorsi anni, in tempo di carnevale, si sono fatti dei festini pubblici venali in maschera, i quali da noi perugini si chiamano veglioni, quando nel Teatro Graziani, quando nell'altro Teatro Vincioli, quando nell'antico palazzo della nobile famiglia Vermiglioli e quando nel palazzo del nobile Sig*nor* Conte Ferdinando Degli Oddi di b.m.; nel carnevale poi dell'anno 1780 diversi pubblici veglioni in maschera come sopra furono ancor fatti nell'antico palazzo del defunto Nob*ile* Sig*nor* *Conte* Mario Ranieri." [We the undersigned, being deferential to the truth, avow and attest that in past years at Carnival time, masked parties, public and commercial, which we Perugians call *veglioni,* were held in the Teatro Graziani, the Teatro Vincioli, the old palace of the noble Vermiglioli family, and the palace of the noble Count Ferdinando Degli Oddi di b.m. In Carnival 1780, various public masked *veglioni* like those above were still held in the ancient palace of the now deceased nobleman Count Mario Ranieri.]

tion of the Civico. And to the incredible consternation of the *cittadini*, they apparently succeeded in retaining exclusive rights to give balls through the end of the century.[47]

WHAT CLASS IS OUR GENRE? REWORKING *ARTASERSE*

From the very beginning of his presidency in 1779, Mariotti regarded the Civico as the pet project of the *secondo ordine*, a way to improve its status through an institution to the "benefit of our class."[48] In 1780 his agenda was carved into the theater's facade in the form of a Latin inscription, painstakingly crafted through months of correspondence with a scholar in Rome.

> NUMINI MAJESTATIQUE PII VI PONT. MAX.—
> CORPORATI CIVES PERUSIAE AUGUSTAE ORDINIS
> SECUNDI—LEGIBUS AD INCREMENTA ARTIUM
> BONARUM—EX AUCTORITATE OPTIMI PRINCIPIS
> CONSTITUTIS—CURIAM PIAM COETIBUS CONSESU
> DEDICARUNT—ANNO MDCCLXXX.

> The citizen body of the Secondo Ordine of Perusia Augusta
> have, unanimously and in accordance with the laws
> established by the authority of the Prince for the
> advancement of the fine arts, dedicated this pious hall,
> built with funds bestowed for the purpose of holding
> gatherings of the enlightened, to the divine will and
> majesty of Pope Pius VI in the year 1780.[49]

Though the Civico foregrounded the citizen class in word, in deed its members used opera seria unabashedly to mimic the hierarchical world of the nobility and monarchy. The opening season featuring Metastasio's vastly popular *Didone abbandonata* and *Artaserse* betrayed this aristocratic emulation, if nothing else did.[50] Small wonder there was frustration at being unable to give balls.

Notably, at the time when the Civico opened, the Pavone had recently put on several serious operas: Metastasio's *Alessandro nell'Indie* and Zeno's *Quinto Fabio* for the theater's reopening in 1773, and later Metastasio's *Demofoonte* (1776) and *L'olimpiade* (1778), and the somewhat more vanguard *Medonte, re di Epiro*

47. See Pascucci, *La Nobile Accademia del Pavone*, 12, which I have found nothing to contradict.

48. I-PEc, *Carteggi*, anno 1779, "al beneficio del nostro ceto" (undated).

49. The epigraphist was Stefano Antonio Morcelli, a librarian. Documents about the inscription are preserved in I-PEc, *Atti*, filza 11. On the theater's architecture, see Bonaca, "Il Teatro Civico." My sincere thanks to Courtney Quaintance for locating Dottoressa Bonaca and to Bonaca for sharing portions of her thesis.

50. In addition, as discussed below, a third, new libretto was written for it, also a dramma per musica, though it was ultimately thrown aside in favor of *Artaserse*.

(1778) by Giovanni de Gamerra in a setting by Giuseppe Sarti that featured castrati Giuseppe Aprile and Girolamo Crescentini. As discussed further in chapters 8 and 9, the canons of Metastasian opera seria were starting to break down in these years, with new poetic forms, dramaturgical ploys, scenic tableaux, and so forth, at the same time as the kinds of stage settings were expanding. Looking throughout Italy, one finds, first, an increase in the numbers of mythological operas, starting with Frugoni and Traetta's at Parma and including Vittorio Amedeo Cigna-Santi and Ferdinando Bertoni's *Iphigenia* at Turin (1762) and a host of *Orestes* that followed in the 1770s. In addition, there were pre-Columbian settings like *Motezuma* (e.g., by Cigna-Santi and Gian Francesco di Maio at Turin, 1765), romances based on Ariosto and Tasso featuring Armida (Gianambrogio Migliavacca and Traetta, Vienna, 1760; Francesco Saverio de Rogatis and Jommelli at Naples, 1770; Jacopo Durandi and Pasquale Anfossi, Turin, 1770; Durandi and Antonio Sacchini at Milan 1772; de Rogatis after Durandi as set by Giuseppe Gazzaniga, Rome, 1773; Giovanni Bertati and Johann Gottlieb Naumann in 1773), Rinaldo (Antonio Tozzi's setting after Bertati, Durandi, and de Rogatis), as well as Ruggiero (Metastasio and Hasse, Milan, 1771). There were settings from the "native" perspective, for example, Durandi and Paisiello's *Annibale in Torino* (Turin, 1771) and Verazi and Michele Mortellari's *Troia distrutta* (Milan, 1778). Latterly there were also exotic settings, like Calzabigi's and Pietro Morandi's *Comala* after Ossian, done in Senigallia in 1780.[51] Developments abroad, especially at Vienna and Stuttgart, influenced Italian opera from the outside in—most notably, Calzabigi and Gluck's *Orfeo ed Euridice* (Vienna, 1762), Marco Coltellini and Traetta's *Iphigenia in Tauride* (Vienna, 1763), and Verazi and Jommelli's *Fetonte* (Ludwigsburg, 1768).

But there was nothing more commonplace, even around 1780 and especially in smaller cities, than using Metastasian texts, which had come to function almost as fakebooks for the many poets who recast them in continual glosses both from their originals and from certain previous, usually prominent reworkings. Between 1773 and 1782, the Pavone staged non-Metastasian operas aplenty, but mostly in the cheaper and generically more populist (and often more progressive) genres of opera buffa or dramma giocoso.[52] The pattern echoed many noble theaters elsewhere, including (though less so) Rome, which was an operatic pipeline to the Pavone, and later the Civico.[53] Venice during the same decade saw more of a divide between those theaters that put on opera seria (still called dramma per musica) and those that put on opera buffa. The nobles' Teatro San Benedetto mounted nothing but opera seria, for example—generally three or four a year—while the Teatro San Moisè, the San Samuele, San Cassiano, San

51. See Ferrero, "Stage and Set," 1–123; Chegai, *L'esilio di Metastasio*, chap. 3; Joly, *Dagli elisi al inferno*, part 2; Conti, "*Amiti e Ontario* di Ranieri di Calzabigi," 127–55; and Tufano, "La via ossianica."

52. See Brumana and Pascale, "Il teatro musicale a Perugia."

53. Three operas staged at the Pavone between 1773 and 1780 were performed shortly beforehand at Rome, others at Venice, Florence, or Vienna (ibid.).

Giovanni Grisostomo, and San Salvador typically mounted opere buffe, drammi giocosi, *farse* (one-act musical comedies performed at the end of a play), and comic intermezzi (although some occasionally did do serious operas, particularly the San Moisè, which in some periods gave almost one a year). The reasons for such divides were largely financial, but as we have seen, they had strong symbolic valences relative to class divides.[54]

Nevertheless, by 1781 alignments of class with genre, and with them alignments of class with opera seria, were undergoing changes. The dramma giocoso had risen geyser-like to popularity twenty years earlier when Piccinni and Goldoni's distressed damsel hit the stage in *La buona figliuola* (Rome, 1760), and had given new focus to intense middle-class emotion in the opera house.[55] Tugging at the hearts of the masses, lovelorn arias, fraught with sighing appoggiaturas, augmented sixth chords, and delicate, thinned-out textures, became the rage. The dramma giocoso was hardly a call to arms, but it did put opera seria on the spot. Paolo Gallarati has argued that it changed opera seria by teaching audiences to be touched and moved, to weep and cry out.[56]

Yet when the *cittadini* of Perugia chose to emphasize the tradition of what they called "opera regia" (royal opera) or "opera seria" over opera buffa or dramma giocoso,[57] they were pointedly opting *not* to mute their secondary class status but to try beating their superiors at their own game. To this end, Mariotti wanted to ring the changes of social betterment on the venerable strains of ancient history. Alessio Lorenzini served as chief architect and academist Baldassare Orsini as chief painter, but even so, in decorating the theater the society took pains to have its builders follow details of Mariotti's symbolic plans from the most minuscule to the most majuscule (no trace of which survive in the theater's present-day, restored form).[58] Among his preliminary sketches from 1778 is a portrait gallery of sixteen canonical dramatists, ancient and modern, that would limn the theater's inner vault in three-meter-high ovates: the Greeks Sophocles, Euripides, Aristophanes, and Menander, enumerated in Mariotti's sketches in careful Greek capitals (fig. 7.4); the Romans Seneca, Terence, and Plautus; the Italians Trissino, Metastasio, Goldoni, and Fagioli; the French

54. Wiel, *I teatri musicali veneziani.* Of course Metastasian opera was economical because recycled. Apropos, the Civico borrowed funds at 3.5 percent interest to purchase the costume wardrobe of the Eredi Angelucci of Rome, previously owned by the Teatro delle Dame (I-PEc, *Atti,* 39r, assembly of June 25, 1781). It is not clear what the relationship was between this purchase and the attribution in the libretti of fall 1781 of costumes to Giovanni Battista Falconi, Vincenzio Damora, and Giuseppe Bonaventura.

55. Piccinni, *La Cecchina,* ed. Weimer, published in facsimile in *Italian Opera, 1640–1770,* ser. 2, no. 80. See Castelvecchi, "Sentimental Opera," chap. 2. Immensely popular was the beleaguered La Cecchina's number "Una povera ragazza" (see Stenzl, "Una povera ragazza," 81–97).

56. Gallarati, *L'Europa del melodramma.*

57. I-PEc, *Atti,* filza 10, Mariotti's letter to the underdeputy of Perugia of March 7, 1781; Guardabassi, *Appunti storici,* 22. The term "opera seria," which they also used, still made no appearance on the title pages of libretti and rarely on scores but had been in common parlance.

58. Bonaca, "Il Teatro Civico," 73–89, esp. 84, and 128–36 on later redecorations.

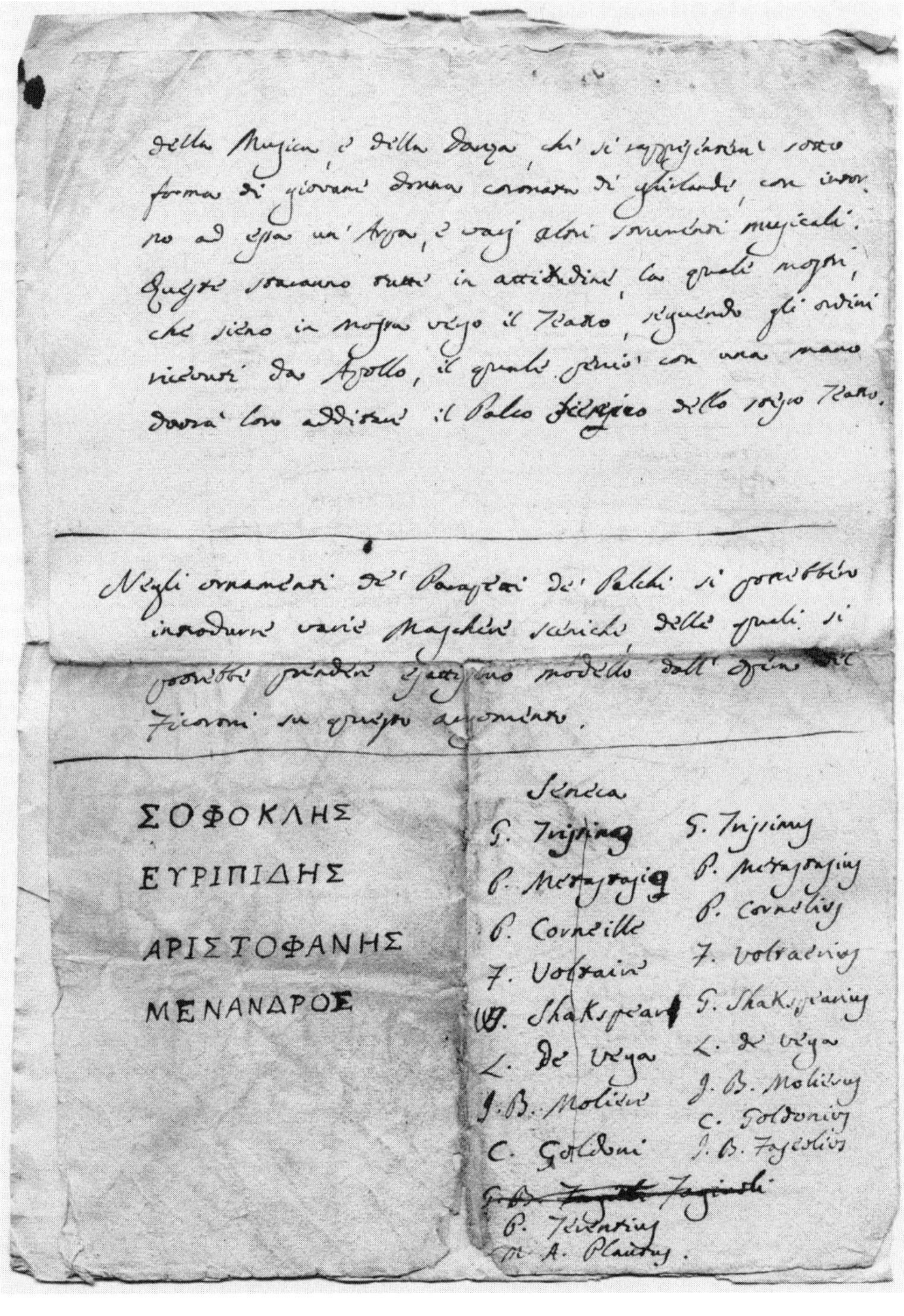

della Musica, e della Danza, che si rappresentano sotto forma di giovani donne coronate di ghirlande, con intorno ad esse un'Arpa, e varj altri strumenti musicali. Queste staranno tutte in attitudine, la quale mostri, che siano in mossa verso il Teatro, seguendo gli ordini ricevuti da Apollo, il quale perciò con una mano dovrà loro additare il Palco Filarmonico dello stesso Teatro.

Negli ornamenti de' Parapetti de' Palchi si potrebbero introdurre varie Maschere sceniche, delle quali si potrebbe prendere esattissimo modello dall'opera del Ficoroni su questo argomento.

ΣΟΦΟΚΛΗΣ
ΕΥΡΙΠΙΔΗΣ
ΑΡΙΣΤΟΦΑΝΗΣ
ΜΕΝΑΝΔΡΟΣ

Seneca
G. Trissino
P. Metastasio
P. Corneille
F. Voltaire
W. Shakspeare
L. De Vega
J. B. Molière
C. Goldoni
~~G. B. Fagiuoli~~
P. Terentius
M. A. Plautus

G. Trissinus
P. Metastasius
P. Cornelius
F. Voltairius
G. Shakspearius
L. de Vega
J. B. Molierius
C. Goldonius
J. B. Fagiolius

FIG. 7.4. List of ancient and modern dramatists to be included in the gallery lining the vault. From Annibale Mariotti's preliminary sketches for the Teatro Civico, Perugia (1778). Biblioteca Augusta Comunale, Perugia, Archivio Morlacchi, *Atti*, filza 8. Reproduced by permission.

Corneille, Molière, and Voltaire; the English Shakespeare; and the Spaniard Lope de Vega.[59] Conceived in pairs by provenance and genre, the ovates were lined up along the frieze of the vault, with the effigies placed in bas-relief on a royal purple ground (figs. 7.5 and 7.6).

Much of the other decor was Mariotti's brainchild too. As ornaments for the parapets of the boxes, he proposed cameos of theatrical masks, some seven meters wide. He had already sketched the medallions on the vault over the parterre, which condensed the stages and forms of dramatic poetry into four personifications: Icarus sacrificing a goat to Bacchus (the first "germ" of drama), followed by Tragedy, Comedy, and Pastoral Fable (fig. 7.5, lower right-hand corner).[60] And at an early stage, he had conceived plans for painting the ceiling of the parterre in a way that would situate the theater in literary and mythical history. Included would be

> Apollo resting on clouds flanked on one side by Melpomene, goddess of tragedy, magnificently attired with buskins on her feet, a dagger in one hand, and a lyre in her other; and on his other side Thalia, goddess of comedy, as a young woman crowned with ivy, with a mask in hand and socks on her feet; and near them Terpsichore, goddess of music and dance, shown in the form of a young woman crowned with garlands, with a harp and various musical instruments about her.[61]

Pointing stageward, Apollo's command would be obeyed by the movement of the theatrical deities, representing Apollo as the sovereign will that impels theatrical action, or metaphorically as the absolutist cog that turns the operatic

59. The idea for decorating the parapets was based on Ficoroni's work: "Ne' 16. Ovali del primo giro, si potranno rappresentare in altrettanti cammei i piu eccellenti Tragici, e Comici che abbia avuto la Grecia, e il Lazio fra gli antichi; e fra moderni la Francia, l'Inghilterra, la Spagna, e la Italia" (I-PEc, *Atti,* filza 8). The Florentine Giambattista Fagioli (Fagiuolo, 1660–1742) was included to give good representation to the Italians among "some of the most renowned writers, tragic and comic, from the most cultivated nations," and make up an even sixteen. Modestly talented and famed, Fagioli wrote *rime giocose* and *capitoli* in a Berneschian mode and Molière-styled comedies. He was hardly the comic equal of Goldoni, and definitely not fit to compensate for omitting the likes of Racine, as Mariotti acknowledged (Guardabassi, *Appunti storici,* 27).

60. I-PEc, *Atti,* filza 8; cf. *La Didone abbandonata,* v, where Mariotti credits all the painters who worked under Orsini. The medallions in the vaults of Icarus, tragedy, comedy, and pastoral, plus the sixteen cameos of dramatists, were painted by academician Carlo Spiridione Mariotti (*La Didone abbandonata,* v–vi), unrelated to Annibale (Ferrini, "Annibale Mariotti," 112). Other vault painting is attributed to Perugians Vincenzio Monotti, Niccola Giuli, and Pier-Francesco Cocchi, painting on parapets of boxes, their scenic masks, and the proscenium ceiling to Giovanni Cappelli. Mariotti's preface celebrates the talents of Perugian *cittadini* and also attests to new interests in authorship and labor by attributing every decorative detail on the pedestals, the busts in the vestibules, stuccoed carvings, etc. Mariotti was besotted with the number of painters at work.

61. Orsini realized the scheme: "Opere sono del suo pennello la pittura della riquadratura della volta del vestibulo: le figure dello sfondato di forma ovale nella volta della platea, rappresentanti Apollo, Tersicore, Melpomene, e Talia" (*La Didone abbandonata,* v). The deities were seven meters wide, and two and a half high. See Mariotti's text in n. 62 below.

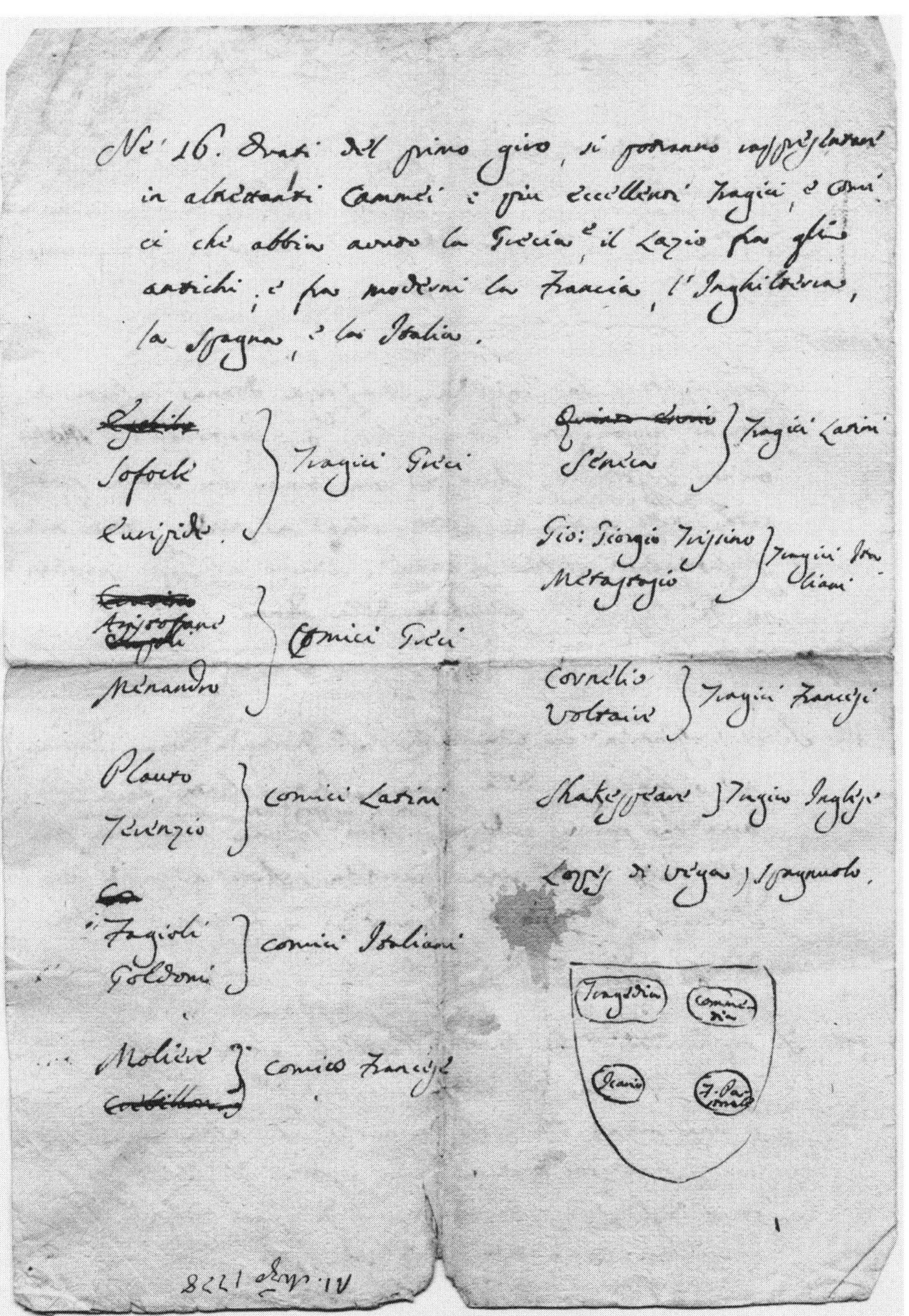
N.° 16. Ovati del primo giro, si potranno [illegible]
in altrettanti Cammei i più eccellenti Tragici, e Comici che abbia avuto la Grecia, e il Lazio fra gli antichi; e fra moderni la Francia, l'Inghilterra, la Spagna, e la Italia.

~~Eschilo~~ Sofocle Euripide } Tragici Greci

~~Cratino~~ Aristofane ~~Eupoli~~ Menandro } Comici Greci

Plauto Terenzio } Comici Latini

i Fagioli Goldoni } comici Italiani

Moliere ~~Crebillon~~ } Comico Francese

~~Quinto Ennio~~ Seneca } Tragici Latini

Gio: Giorgio Trissino Metastasio } Tragici Italiani

Cornelio Voltaire } Tragici Francesi

Shakespeare } Tragico Inglese

Lopez di Vega } Spagnuolo

Tragedia

Commedia

FIG. 7.5. Pairings within the portrait gallery and detail of medallions representing four categories of drama. From Annibale Mariotti's preliminary sketches for the Teatro Civico, Perugia (1778). Biblioteca Augusta Comunale, Perugia, Archivio Morlacchi, *Atti*, filza 8. Reproduced by permission.

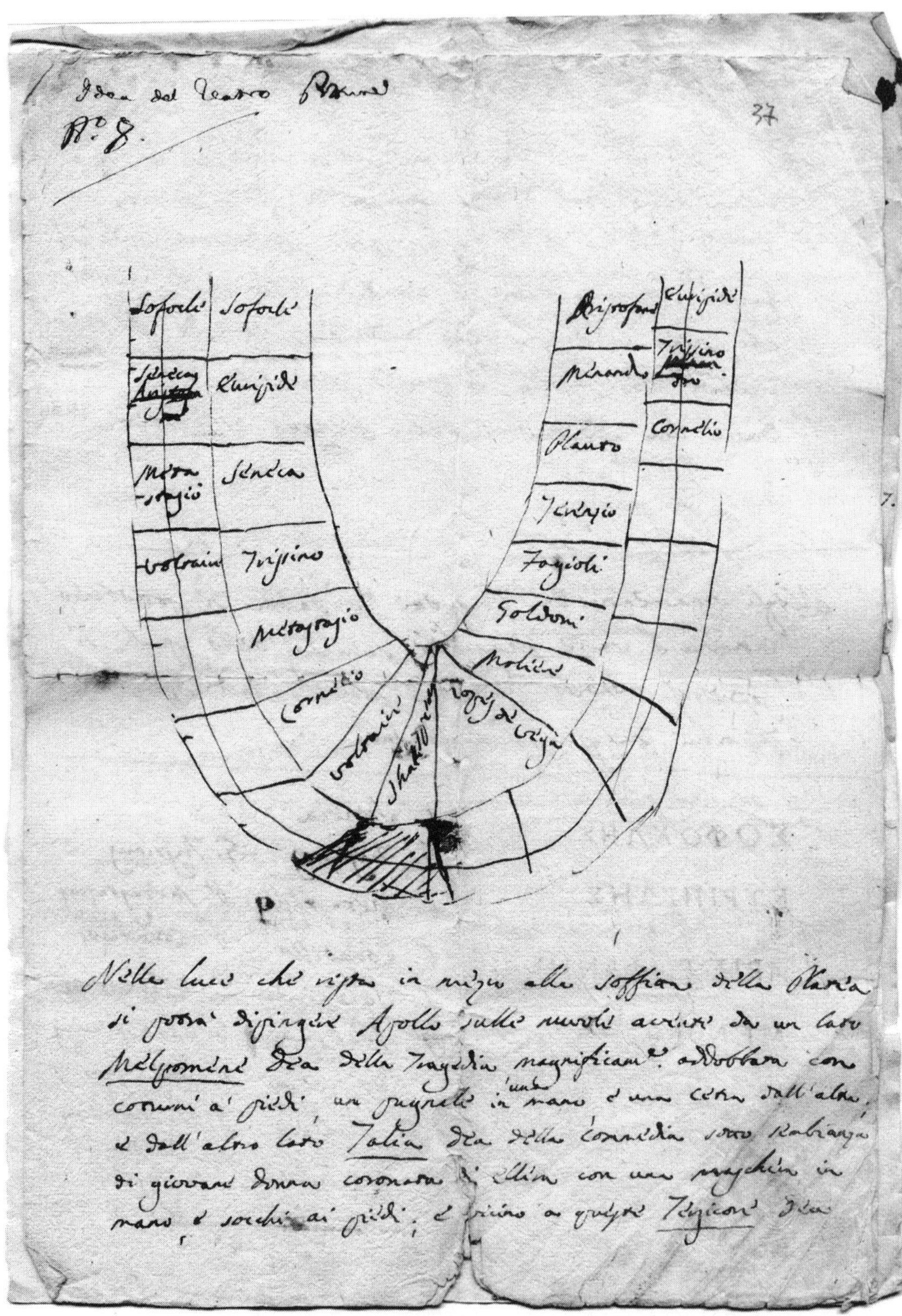

FIG. 7.6. Layout of the portrait gallery of dramatists intended to line the vault of the Teatro Civico in bas-relief. From Annibale Mariotti's preliminary sketches for the Teatro Civico, Perugia (1778). Biblioteca Augusta Comunale, Perugia, Archivio Morlacchi, *Atti*, filza 8. Reproduced by permission.

wheel.[62] But their progress along the proscenium ceiling was also meant to reveal personifications of a more mischievous kind—Bacchus, satyrs, and the bacchantes, associated from time immemorial with the pleasures, licit and illicit, of drama and music. As Apollo's deities finally passed bas-reliefs of ancient instruments on the pedestal columns that flanked the proscenium, their imagined advance down- and stageward would thus consolidate the marriage of drama with music.

Mariotti thankfully omitted ideological explications of his program from the libretto. His mood was Horatian, declaring that men are generally led to useful things by means of pleasure, which nothing can accomplish better than dramatic poetry, as its improvement of "the rough *popoli,* and those less enamored of fine studies" had often shown.[63] That heroic drama was elected for the opening of the theater was explained not as a prestige ploy but a matter of high-minded edification.

No one could deny, of course, that Metastasio's operas, however edifying, were the very stuff of prestige and trophies—something that absorbed the Accademia del Teatro Civico when it met in February 1781. At that time, the deputies reported that they had not yet hired many singers because everything needed to proceed from the choice of the "primo soprano"—of necessity a male singer (meaning castrato) since Roman edicts locally in effect prohibited women from the stage. The academy had been turned down by the famous castrato Luigi Marchesi, who had other obligations, and was stymied.[64] But it had pulled off a great coup in signing the renowned Giacomo David, who had much to do with the steep rise in prestige of the Italian tenor during the late eighteenth and early nineteenth centuries, and it had also engaged a fine dance troupe headed by Domenico Ricciardi.[65] Later the academy signed the other great tenor of the time,

62. "Nella luce che resta in mezzo alla soffitta della Platea si potrà dipingere Apollo sulle nuvole avente da un lato *Melpomene* dea della Tragedia magnificamente addobata con coturni a' piedi, un pugnale in una mano, e una cetra dall'altra; e dall'altro lato *Talia* dea della commedia sotto sembianza di giovane donna coronata di ellera con una maschera in mano, e socchi ai piedi; e vicino a queste *Terpsicore* dea della Musica, e della danza, che si rappresenterà, sotto forma di giovane donna coronata di ghirlande, con intorno ad essa un'Arpa, e vari altri strumenti musicali. Queste staranno tutte in attitudine, la quale mostri, che sieno in mossa verso il Teatro, seguendo gli ordini ricevuti da Apollo, il quale perciò con una mano dovrà loro additare il Palco lirico dello stesso Teatro" (I-PEc, *Atti,* filza 8).

63. *La Didone abbandonata,* iv.

64. "[P]erchè la scelta del primo soprano molto contribuir suole pel resto, rimane il tutto irresoluto ancora, ed a variazione soggetto" (I-PEc, *Verbali,* 37r, February 11, 1781).

65. See Borgato, "David, Giacomo," 140–42, and Forbes, "Davide [David], Giacomo," who claims his voice was flexible voice enough to "compete with the castratos in florid music and far exceed them in his dramatic intensity"—though the latter claim is impossible to substantiate.

The Civico's deputies promised outstanding singers and dancers (the latter from Ricciardi's company, said to have been a smash the previous year in Florence and Rome) (I-PEc, *Verbali,* 38r, February 11, 1781). Ricciardi also worked at Venice, where he did Sertor and Bianchi's *La morte di Cesare,* with interpolated chorus and ballet (see chap. 9 below), and Padua (Massaro, "Il ballo pantomimo," 215–75).

Table 7.1. Singers in the two casts of Metastasio and Rust's *Artaserse* (Perugia, autumn 1781)

*Singers**	Didone abbandonata	Artaserse *(first cast)*	Artaserse *(second cast)*
Luigi Andreani	Didone (prima donna)	Artaserse (secondo uomo)	Artaserse
Domenico Massi	Enea (primo uomo)	Mandane (prima donna assoluta)**	Mandane
Matteo Babbini	Jarba (tenore)	Artabano (tenore)	
Giacomo David			Artabano (tenore)
Domenico Bedini		Arbace (primo soprano assoluto)**	Arbace
Valeriano Violani	Selene (seconda donna)	Semira (seconda donna)	Semira
Francesco Cibelli	Araspe (secondo uomo)		
Giuseppe Hornung	Osmida (seconda donna)	Megabise (secondo tenore)**	Megabise

*Singers are listed in the order given in the libretti.

**Designation used in the broadside advertising the performance (fig. 7.7).

Matteo Babbini, who in the end sang tenor roles in both operas during the main season, Jarba in *Didone* and Artabano in *Artaserse*, and then handed off the latter to David for an added six performances—though not before David's attempt to renege had the whole town frothing with scandal.[66]

The cast that was finally assembled (see table 7.1) shows that what began as a simple matter of hiring a few stars ended in an inadvertent transformation of the genre. After signing David, the academy hired the soprano castrato Domenico Bedini (best known today for playing the role of Sesto in Mozart's *La clemenza di Tito* at Prague in 1791), though only for the second opera as the young Arbace in *Artaserse*, which had been inhabited by every stellar castrato since 1730.[67] A published broadside announcing the opera and naming him as "primo soprano assoluto" shows the academy promoting him as the Marchesi they had failed to get (fig. 7.7). A less renowned, if accomplished, castrato, Luigi Andreani, was engaged for the title parts in both season openers. In order to keep his position at the top of the social hierarchy in the dramatis personae, Andreani not only

66. Vacchelli, "Babini, Matteo," 789–90, and Forbes, "Babbini [Babini], Matteo." Babbini received 80 scudi (I-PEc, Archivio Morlacchi, *Contabilità, Libro di cassa redatti dagli eredi di Giovanni Piazza in occasione della costruzione del Teatro*, mar. 1778–dic. 1784). In the early years of the opera Artabano had often been sung by a castrato (Nicolo Grimaldi and Pellegrino Tomy in Venice, 1730 and 1734, respectively, and Senesino in London in 1734), but by 1750 and thereafter virtually all Artabanos were tenors: de Mezzo, Raaff, Domenico Panzacchi, Gaetano Ottani, Carlo Carlani, Giuseppe Tibaldi, Valentin Adamberger (Mozart's Belmonte), Domenico Mombelli, Giacomo Panati, Gaetano Scovelli, and Vincenzo Maffoli. When soprano Anna Morichelli Bosello sang the part in Rust's *Artaserse* at Florence's Pergola in 1783 she was the exception that proved the rule. Artaserse was cast variably but was typically a high voice and a minor singer, whereas Arbace was played by famous castrati throughout the century (in addition to Carestini and Farinelli, Egiziello, Tommaso Guarducci, Gaetano Guadagni, Tenducci, Gasparo Pacchierotti, Domenico Bruni, and Marchesi).

67. Perugia feted Bedini in 1781 and 1788 with a portrait and a canzonetta, respectively (Brumana, "Il dramma per musica *Artaserse*," 255–56, for the 1781 items, and d'Ambrosa, "Le opere metastasiane di Giacomo Rust," 48 n. 14, for those of 1788); cf. Durante, "The Chronology of Mozart's 'La clemenza di Tito,'" 560–94.

had to switch genders for the second opera but fall to a secondary position in the cast hierarchy. The distinctions in *Artaserse* between hierarchies of dramatis personae and hierarchies of cast are obvious from a comparison of figure 7.7 with figure 7.8. In figure 7.8, which shows the dramatis personae of the libretto, Andreani/Artaserse comes first in keeping with the literary tradition of listing the cast by social hierarchy within the drama, while the broadside in figure 7.7 lists him lower down and names him "secondo soprano." Serviceable but not stellar was also a third castrato, Domenico Massi, who sang Aeneas as primo soprano in the first opera and Mandane as "prima donna" in the second.[68] The five roles that remained between the two operas were covered by three minor singers, so that effectively Perugia ended up in the progressive position of featuring tenors even over leading castrati (only Bedini had anything approaching the prestige value of David and Babbini). Of the two tenor roles, moreover, only Artabano was even minimally redeemable in moral terms.[69] Iarba was downright evil. This meant not just the traditional cast hierarchy at odds in prestige with the hierarchy of dramatis personae, but a cast hierarchy at odds with the moral hierarchy of the characters—something with less precedent.

Yet this emphasis on the tenor—usually a darker or older voice in a genre still largely without basses, baritones, or amorous tenors—was out of keeping with the traditional character of the set numbers.[70] Only occasionally had tenors gotten starring parts earlier in the century, and then generally in outlying theaters when a tenor was the most prestigious singer available, not as a matter of course. Of the two operas done for the Civico's opening season, only one used an ensemble as large as a trio (*Didone*, finale, act 2), and each had only a single duet, placed in the age-old position at the end of act 1. The arias that studded the torsos of acts 1 and 2 were all exit arias, save Dido's cavatina "Va crescendo" (3.8), whose lack of an exit was original to Metastasio.

* * *

By far the more traditional of the two operas was *Didone*, set by the Perugian chapelmaster Francesco Zannetti, which started off the season.[71] Zannetti's

68. Massi (Masi) debuted only in 1779, in Rome, and through 1796 sang entirely in northern Italy. Initially he performed female roles, as was common among young castrati, especially in the Papal States, but after 1785 he took on male parts. Andreani (called alternately "di Fermo" or "di Roma") debuted in Rome in 1772 and through 1784 sang almost exclusively in female parts throughout Rome and the Papal States, retiring after 1787.

69. Rosselli gives an idea of how unusual it still was to feature tenors at the time, in *Singers of Italian Opera*, chap. 8. On basses in Metastasian opera—quite rare in Italy—see Jander et al., "Bass," and Durante, "The Opera Singer," 387 n. 112.

70. See Covell, "Voice Register as an Index of Age and Status," 193–210.

71. I-PEc, Archivio Morlacchi, *Commedie, drammi e spartiti manoscritti*, no. 2, "Spartito strumentale della *Didone* data per l'apertura del Teatro, musica di Francesco Zanetti" (20 parts, none vocal). The text is cued at set numbers but written out fully only in recitatives. On Zannetti and sources of

1781

IN PERUGIA NELL' AUTUNNO DEL MDCCLXXXI.

IN OCCASIONE DELL' APERTURA

DEL NUOVO TEATRO CIVICO DEL VERZARO

SI RAPPRESENTERA' PER SECONDO DRAMMA

L' ARTASERSE

POESIA DEL SIGNOR ABATE PIETRO METASTASIO ; MUSICA NUOVA DEL CELEBRE SIGNOR GIACOMO RUST.

ATTORI

Primo Soprano Assoluto SIG. DOMENICO BEDINI.	*Prima Donna* SIG. DOMENICO MASSI.
Primo Tenore SIG. MATTEO BABINI *Virtuoso di Camera di Sua Maestà la Imperatrice delle Russie.*	*Seconda Donna* SIG. VALERIANO VIOLANI.
Secondo Soprano SIG. LUIGI ANDREANI.	*Secondo Tenore* SIG. GIUSEPPE HORNUNG.

I BALLI saranno tutti d' Invenzione, e Direzione del Rinomatissimo Sig. DOMENICO RICCIARDI. Nel primo si rappresenterà la morte di Arrigo VI. Re d' Inghilterra: Il secondo sarà un Ballo villereccio con varj accidenti; E verranno eseguiti da' seguenti.

PRIMI BALLERINI SERJ

Da Uomo	*da Donna*	*Da Uomo*	*Da Donna*
Sig. Domenico Ricciardi	Sig. Giacomo Tantini	Sig. Giacomo Ricciardi	Sig. Teofilo Corazzi *già al servizio di S. M. Fedelissima*

PRIMI GROTTESCHI

Sig. Gregorio Grisostomi — Sig. Antonio Marassi — Sig. Carlo Sabatini — Sig. Gaetano Rubini

Sig. Giovanni Codacci

ALTRI BALLERINI

Sig. Michele Nota, Sig. Domenico Magni, Sig. Giuseppe Calvi, Sig. Antonio Cipriani.

FIGURANTI

Sigg. Federigo Federighi	Sigg. Antonio Silei	Sigg. Antonio Maraccini	Sigg. Domenico Simoncelli
Giovanni Bianciardi	Leopoldo Banchelli	Antonio Righi	Lorenzo Geri
Francesco Albertini	Luigi Gherardini	Gaetano Gherini	Vincenzio Giannozzi
Giuseppe Lena	Niccola Andreoni	Luigi Bianchi	Pietro Pieroni
Silvestro Andreoni	Antonio Mei	Giuseppe Bianciardi	Andrea Magrai
Andrea Ghedini	Luigi Boschi	Antonio Silvi	Michele Rossi

Il Vestiario è di vaga, e ricca invenzione de' Sigg. Gio: Battista Falconi, Vincenzio Damora, e Giuseppe Bonaventura.

Al primo Cimbalo Sig. Romualdo Rossi. *Al secondo Cimbalo* Sig. Francesco Basilj.

Primo Violino de' Drammi Sig. Francesco Rastrelli. *Primo Violino de' Balli* Sig. Melchiorre Ronzi.

Le Recite di questo secondo Dramma cominceranno la sera del dì 20. Ottobre, e proseguiranno fin verso la metà di Novembre; e saranno cinque in ogni Settimana, cioè nelle sere di Sabato, Domenica, Lunedì, Martedì, e Mercoledì; salvo il caso di qualche disgrazia. Quei Forestieri, che volessero portarsi in Perugia in tale occasione, potranno indirizzarsi alla Locanda del Sig. *Luigi Ercolani*. Quelli poi che bramassero separata Abitazione, potranno preventivamente avvisarne il Sig. *Antonio Grazioli*.

FIG. 7.7. Broadside announcing the upcoming performance of Metastasio and Giacomo Rust's *Artaserse*, Teatro Civico di Verzaro, Perugia (autumn 1781). Note that poet and composer receive equal billing and singers are listed by their preeminence as performers, not characters. Biblioteca Augusta Comunale, Perugia, Archivio Morlacchi, Manifesti. Reproduced by permission.

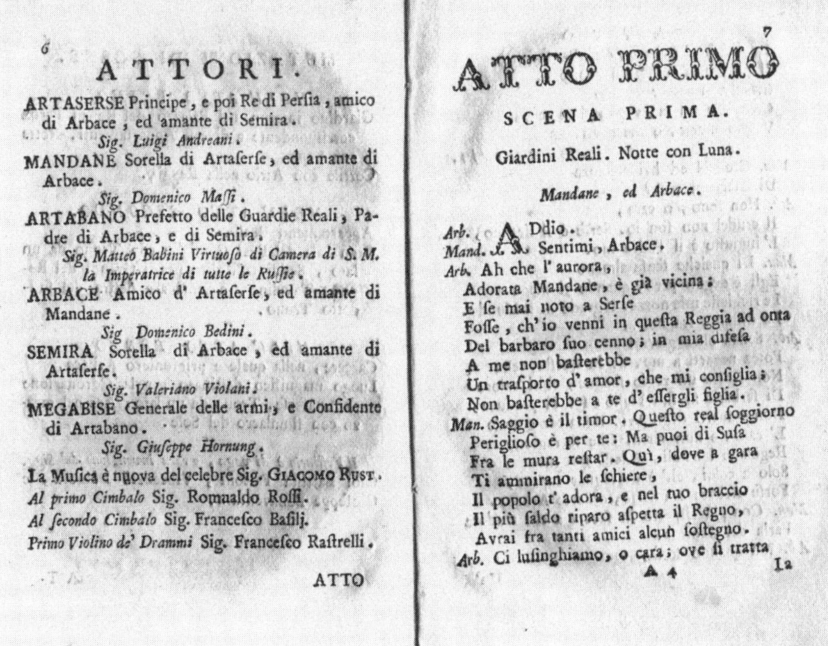

6

ATTORI.

ARTASERSE Principe, e poi Re di Persia, amico di Arbace, ed amante di Semira.
Sig. Luigi Andreani.

MANDANE Sorella di Artaserse, ed amante di Arbace.
Sig. Domenico Massi.

ARTABANO Prefetto delle Guardie Reali, Padre di Arbace, e di Semira.
Sig. Matteo Babini Virtuoso di Camera di S. M. la Imperatrice di tutte le Russie.

ARBACE Amico d' Artaserse, ed amante di Mandane.
Sig Domenico Bedini.

SEMIRA Sorella di Arbace, ed amante di Artaserse.
Sig. Valeriano Violani.

MEGABISE Generale delle armi, e Confidente di Artabano.
Sig. Giuseppe Hornung.

La Musica è nuova del celebre Sig. GIACOMO RUST.
Al primo Cimbalo Sig. Romualdo Rossi.
Al secondo Cimbalo Sig. Francesco Basilj.
Primo Violino de' Drammi Sig. Francesco Rastrelli.

ATTO

7

ATTO PRIMO

SCENA PRIMA.

Giardini Reali. Notte con Luna.

Mandane, ed Arbace.

Arb. ADdio.
Mand. Sentimi, Arbace.
Arb. Ah che l' aurora,
Adorata Mandane, è già vicina:
E se mai noto a Serse
Fosse, ch' io venni in questa Reggia ad onta
Del barbaro suo cenno; in mia difesa
A me non basterebbe
Un trasporto d' amor, che mi consiglia;
Non basterebbe a te d' essergli figlia.
Man. Saggio è il timor. Questo real soggiorno
Periglioso è per te: Ma puoi di Susa
Fra le mura restar. Quì, dove a gara
Ti ammirano le schiere,
Il popolo t' adora, e nel tuo braccio
Il più saldo riparo aspetta il Regno,
Avrai fra tanti amici alcun sostegno.
Arb. Ci lusinghiamo, o cara; ove si tratta

A 4 La

FIG. 7.8. Dramatis personae listed in the libretto for Metastasio and Giacomo Rust's *Artaserse* (Perugia, autumn 1781), where the hierarchy follows that of the opera, not the cast. Biblioteca Augusta Comunale, Perugia. Reproduced by permission.

setting was a mere revival of one he had written for Livorno fifteen years earlier (how far revised we cannot know, since the earlier libretto and score are both now lost).[72] For Perugia, Zannetti employed a good-sized and colorful orchestra, to judge from the twenty surviving parts from the 1781 version: five copies each of first and second violins, one each of first and second violas, and one of basses, plus one each of first and second oboes, first and second horns, first and second trumpets, and bassoons. Adding in the harpsichords—two of them, as listed in the libretto, probably to amplify the acoustics during the opening sinfonia and the ritornelli and orchestral interjections—plus the flutes called out in selected numbers within the oboe part (as in Enea's "Dovrei . . . ma no" [1.2]), the orchestra would have totaled between thirty-seven and forty-five players. This assumes at least two players each on winds and brass, with either separate flute players or more likely oboists doubling on flute and two cellos on bass. The Civico's orchestra would thus have been just slightly smaller than the one used at Dresden in 1771, larger than any of the London theater orchestras from the

his music see Fabbri, "Francesco Zannetti," 161–82, 172–73 on *Didone*. Mariotti's 1788 funeral oration, *Elogio funebre del Sig. Francesco Zannetti*, describes the composer as a musical polymath, superb contrapuntist, and concertato specialist.

72. My thanks to Dottoressa Cristina Luschi, Biblioteca Labronica F. D. Guerrazzi of Livorno, for information on the source situation there.

same period, larger even than Mozart's very colorful orchestra for *Idomeneo* at Munich, also in 1781, and about two-thirds the size of those used at the much bigger houses of Naples, Turin, and Milan (for example, when Mozart's *Lucio Silla* was done at the Regio Ducal Teatro in 1772–73).[73]

Nevertheless, some orchestral writing has a retrospective feel. The strings often follow the old five-part texture used by Lully and the Italians in the seventeenth century, including *divise* viola parts, in keeping with Zannetti's minimal use of ensembles and the libretto's avoidance of innovative meters in favor of settenari and ottonari with just a sprinkling of quinari and decasyllabi.[74] Only nine of Metastasio's arias were retained, on top of two that were revised, plus his act 1 duet, which was extended. Principal singers were outfitted in traditional style with the obligatory numbers of arias and dramatic effects distributed among them. Massi as Enea got an obbligato recitative at the opening of the opera plus two new arias (2.12 and 3.2), for example, both with more varied meters than Metastasio had used. The first accommodated his cantabile, and the second, marked "Andante," brought out his affecting side. Andreani as Didone got a new aria, "Se mi lasci, amato Bene" (2.7), three strophes long, but his dramatic thunder mainly came from Metastasio's legendary final *scena,* which was textually unchanged. Not surprisingly, Babbini, playing Jarba, got a new aria, "Agitato il core non sento," marked "Allegro Imperioso in C and common time ($\frac{4}{4}$)" to replace Metastasio's "Fosca nube il sol ricopra" (2.9). Judging from the parts, "Agitato il core" was probably a written-out bravura aria that gave Babbini's fans the dotted rhythms, triadic head motifs, and other paraphernalia expected from an enemy sovereign. Zanetti evidently gave "Fosca nube" his most creative scoring as well, having the bass drop out lengthily four times and giving the aria an obbligato bassoon part. And toward the end of act 2, all three principals got to sing a trio preceded by obbligato recitative (2.15).

These modifications, while hardly radical, kept pace relatively well with the general state of Italian musical directions in 1781. Unlike the case in mid-1760s Naples, by this time sonata-like arias, two-tempo rondòs, and ensembles

73. See Price, Milhous, and Hume, *Italian Opera* 1:286, 321; Spitzer and Zaslaw, *The Birth of the Orchestra,* 317–18, who deem "large" concert orchestras, starting in 1773, as numbering fifty-one to seventy-five players. On Italian opera orchestras, see 142–54, and on the orchestra at the Paris Opéra, 184–90. See also, by the same authors, "Orchestra," part 5, "18th Century," 723–28, esp. table 1 (726–27).

74. In a letter to Gaetano Martinelli, Jommelli complained about the deadening lack of metric variety in the aria texts of opera seria during his time (November 14, 1769, in McClymonds, *Niccolò Jommelli,* appendix 6, no. 10, 488–49; see also chap. 8, nn. 71–72 below). Relatedly, Planelli, *Dell'opera in musica,* 29–38, advocated reforming Italian opera by using varied meters within a given aria. Chegai cites an anonymous writer in the Roman *Giornale delle belle arti* (1784) who lamented opera seria's use of a single meter for many different affects (*L'esilio di Metastasio,* 22). On the increasing plurality of meters in the later eighteenth century, between and within arias, and the related importance of comic genres, see Fabbri, "Istituti metrici e formali," 63–233, esp. 192–214; in English as "Metrical and Formal Organization," 151–219.

had all effectively replaced da capos and even dal segnos with rounded A sections. As a result, opera seria had become less a form of exit opera than it had been, though exit arias were still abundant, especially in dramaturgically unrehabilitated opera houses. The genre was also somewhat more tableau-driven and formally continuous than previously, though not necessarily "reformed" in a Gluckian sense. Aspects of the *Didone* produced in 1781 were doubtless updated accordingly from Zannetti's 1766 Livorno version—the orchestra souped up and the arias, at the very least for Babbini (and probably Massi too), modified formally and dramatically.

Didone was probably mounted in a rush, with most of the energy spent on the ballets. The libretto looks hastily assembled (its signatures in the Perugia copy are gathered in the order A, D, C, B, and there are a number of typos). Babbini, as the nefarious Jarba, was the only major star in the cast, with three arias plus his part in the act 2 trio—only one less than Dido and Aeneas, respectively (each of whose totals include a short cavatina as against Babbini's full-length arias). Like *Artaserse* and most other Metastasian settings of the time, *Didone* chopped back the lush foliage of Metastasian recitative, radically reducing the discursive dialogue, including all of the references to gift exchange discussed in chapter 5. Metastasio's act 2 arias were all replaced and obbligato recitatives added (some probably tailored to fit the Perugia cast), but original Metastasian aria texts still fill up act 1, where only the duet is new, in a way redolent of productions from decades earlier. In addition, there are only five fewer set numbers total than in Metastasio's original (not including his *licenza*) as compared with eleven fewer in *Artaserse*.[75]

Typical of the 1770s, Ricciardi's ballets were evidently on a par with the opera itself.[76] A "grand" four-act ballet, *Il trionfo di Alessandro, o sia La prigionia di Dario* following *Dido*'s act 1—announced in the libretto with a seven-page program, practically the length of a separate *scenario*—was a rough Metastasian gloss filled with melodramatic action mimed by the soloists. As was typical, the ballet between acts 2 and 3, *Erminia abbandonata nelle isole del Canada*, was shorter (three scenes, accompanied by a two-page program), but was linked to the opera by extending its theme of abandonment—a progressive technique of narrative continuity.[77]

All in all, the ballets combined with the Metastasian operas to form a vast

75. For *Artaserse*, too, the set numbers totaled substantially less than Metastasio's original, nineteen as opposed to thirty-one, only nine of them Metastasio's, and the counts dropped further, to six, five, and six, respectively, in subsequent productions at Livorno, Florence, and Rome (see Brumana, "Il dramma per musica *Artaserse*," 266 and 268).

76. See the richly informative essay by Hansell, "Theatrical Ballet," 177–308. Both of the Civico operas had ballet intermezzi that included new music by Mattia Stabingher, costumes by Damora, Falconi, and Bionaventura (as for the operas), and sets, machines, and *scenari* designed by Antonio Stefanucci, who had worked for theaters in Rome and Mannheim.

77. Chegai, *L'esilio di Metastasio*, 165–83.

homage to the *cittadini* and the great tradition they were so grandly perpetuating. The programs and personnel lists show that both ballets were heroic pantomimes, combining French-styled narrative with whole-body dance of a kind then customary in Italy, though repressed for a time in the 1760s and 1770s in favor of more gestural dance à la the French reforms of Noverre.[78] The size of the ballet troupe, numbering thirty-four, would have been average only for the biggest Italian opera houses of the time; they would have been quite large for a provincial theater, and substantially larger than troupes used by major opera houses as recently as ten years earlier.[79] Included were four *ballerini seri* (soloists), four *primi grotteschi* (acrobatic dancers who played character types), four dancers listed as *altri ballerini* (presumably stars of the corps), and twenty-four *figuranti*. Audiences hungry for ballets got a two-for-one: continual melodrama mimed in the rhetorical style of the *danza parlante* plus the thrill value supplied by *grotteschi*. The first ballet also treated viewers to two huge battle scenes between the Macedonians and the Persians, after the last of which Alexander the Great forgave his foe Darius with a grand gestural display of magnanimity.

* * *

Originally, the second opera was supposed to have used a brand-new libretto, *Augusto in Perugia*, delineating the city's Roman myth of origins, according to which the emperor Octavian Augustus had besieged, conquered, and then pardoned his enemy Lucius at Perugia. Central to the myth was how Augustus dealt in the wake of victory with Caius Cestius, an "enterprising Perugian citizen" who burned down his own house because he could not suffer to see his homeland in Roman hands but inadvertently made an immense fire that swept across most of the city. Perugian civic mythology stressed not Cestius's patriotism per se but the fact that it prompted a sovereign act of clemency—the emperor's pardon of Cestius, along with all other rebels (or at least those who hadn't taken part in the death of his hero, Julius Caesar), and his permission to rebuild the city and rename it "Augustus." The myth was also one of *romanitas*, because it overrode—indeed eliminated through the conflagration, at least symbolically—the real historical roots of the city, which were not Roman but Etruscan, as testified by ancient Etruscan walls that still stand today.

Biancamaria Brumana provides a helpful account of struggles with the "thorny" libretto by Florentine poet Carlo Lanfranchi Rossi, who agonized over it in the summer of 1781 in a series of letters to the respected Roman composer

78. Giovanni-Andrea Gallini defended heroic pantomimes in his 1762 *Treatise on the Art of Dancing*. In 1763, Sara Goudar recuperated them against strong criticism in *De Venise: Rémarques sur la musique et la danse*. For a precis of Goudar's letter as it relates to ballet see Hansell, "Theatrical Ballet," 225–27.

79. Hansell, "Theatrical Ballet," 215–16.

Giacomo Rust. Although he had sent Mariotti at least two acts by mid-August, Lanfranchi complained that

> the characters in it, all heroic types and sublime, united in the gravity of the deed, do not admit of those affectations that the depraved modern taste aspires to, without which the most erudite works are condemned. Since I know you to be among the select of Apollo, I hope that you may find something good in my opera that justifies a poor poet who has wanted to do good and has neglected no effort to succeed in it. I would like it if this were enough to justify me with the highly reputable public of a city that is without doubt one of the oldest and most glorious in Italy.[80]

The poet continued to dawdle, however, and Rust fretted to Mariotti that he needed the finished text in good time to set it, and would also need Lanfranchi to be present in Perugia by the second half of August in order to make changes to the libretto as the music evolved.

In the end the libretto was never performed in Perugia, nor evidently elsewhere, even though it was ultimately completed, so it seems unlikely that it was dropped only because it was finished too late. Mariotti must have been as unenthused as Lanfranchi feared.[81] The drama is a shabby affectless Metastasian imitation, impoverished and wooden, and its symbolic valences probably seemed all wrong. Octavian Augustus stood at the heartland of the imperial system, persistently associated with the practice of consolidating Roman power by conquering provinces. He and the Roman imperium were strongly identified in local theatrical practice with the nobility, who had adopted Augustus as a sacred figure. Worse still, Augustus—at the root of the city's symbolic repertory—had been elided at the Pavone with the castrato Giuseppe Aprile when he had given a memorial concert there as recently as 1778 (see fig. 7.9).

In the end, the main hoopla of the season was reserved for the second opera,

80. "[I] caratteri di esso tutti eroici, e sublimi, uniti alla gravità del fatto, non ammettono quelle smorfie, che il depravato moderno gusto pretende, senza di che si condannano le opere più studiate. Ella, che so, essere dei prediletti di Apollo, spero, che ritroverà in questa mia opera qualche cosa, che giustifica un povero autore, che ha desiderato di far bene, e non ha omesso fatica per riuscirvi. Lo che vorrei, che fosse bastante a giustificarmi appresso il rispettabilissimo pubblico di una città, che senza dubbio è delle più antiche, e gloriose d'Italia." I-PEc, MS 1731, fasc. 1, 5r–6r, letter by Carlo Lanfranchi Rossi to Mariotti, cited and reproduced in Brumana, "Il dramma per musica *Artaserse*," 43, from which I quote.

81. A complete MS copy of the libretto survives with the papers of the Morlacchi (I-PEc, Archivio Morlacchi, *Commedie, drammi e spartiti manoscritti*, no. 1, "Augusto in Perugia dramma per musica di Carlo Lanfranchi Rossi gentilhuomo Toscano fra gli Arcadi Egesippo Argolide. 1781"; MS of act 1 in I-PEc, MS 1731, fasc. 1). A later theater deputy named Pacini, who sent Mariotti the original in 1794, blamed the whole debacle on Zannetti: "Among other blundering expenses of the Theater one can also count this one, for which the academy is indebted to Maestro Zannetti." Cited in Guardabassi, *Appunti storici*, 25: "Fra le altre spese spropositate del Teatro può contarsi anche questa, di cui l'Accademia è debitrice al Maestro Zannetti."

FIG. 7.9. Engraving for a memorial concert by castrato Giuseppe Aprile, Teatro Pavone, Perugia, 1778, with an artist's rendering of the proscenium and stage right. A standard, borne by a peacock, reads "Aprilem memorant." A bust of the emperor is emblazoned with the words "Augusto sacrum." Biblioteca Augusta Comunale, Perugia, Misc. II.4.14. Reproduced by permission.

Artaserse, set by Rust, which opened on October 20 (fig. 7.7), giving the composer equal billing with the *éminence grise* Metastasio. There were again two new ballets by Ricciardi. The first, a five-act "ballo eroitragico pantomime," *La morte di Arrigo Sesto,* ran wild with histrionic motifs: regicide by dagger, a burning palace, the king (Henry VI) staggering to his death beneath a clouded moon, icy stares of indictment, a grief-struck prince, thundering accusations from the king's grave, the usurper denounced.[82] The run included about thirty performances, which made it a big enough hit to be revived in Livorno, Florence, and Rome during the following two years (with Babbini recast in the first two and Bedini in Livorno, followed by Crescentini as Arbace in Florence, and Marchesi in Rome).[83] Brought in just for *Artaserse,* Bedini played Arbace in Perugia

82. The second ballet was a divertissement, *Villareccio, con diversi accidenti.*

83. Forty-six performances for the two operas combined was a considerable number. To date I have found no other direct evidence about their Perugian reception. The Livorno production took place at the Armeni, spring 1782; the Florentine production at the Pergola, Carnival 1783; and the Roman production at the Argentina, spring 1783 (Brumana, "Il dramma per musica *Artaserse,*" 254 and passim, and d'Ambrosa, "Le opere metastasiane di Giacomo Rust"; the latter gives detailed textual comparisons of versions from Perugia, Florence, and Rome but not Livorno). All these revivals had textual revisions, as usual.

against Babbini's Artabano until Babbini left following the end of the scheduled performances and David stepped in (see table 7.1 above).

David's performances were done in the teeth of his determination to break contract, but they proved a *succès de scandale*. Preceding them was terrific ferment in the academy, which viewed his actions as breaching a vow of theological proportions in ways that emphasized the struggle between singers as commodified subjects and sovereign citizens with new modes of enfranchisement, suggesting that contracted commerce entailed the sanctity of "the public faith." Eventually the mess was resolved in a compromise—announced bitterly by the academy in a public broadsheet—that had David singing an added six performances, from November 19 through 26.[84]

The score for the original Perugia version of *Artaserse* is presently lost, but thanks to its evident popularity, it engendered a good amount of piecemeal copying. At least eight numbers survive out of an original nineteen (see table 7.2), as Brumana has shown through her collation of sources.[85] Several survive in manuscript anthologies of arias from Rust's opera, and others as single manuscript copies or prints of individual numbers. All have earmarks of amateur usage, which establish that memory of the opera was perpetuated through domestic and concert uses in the years immediately following its performances in 1781–83 and on into the early nineteenth century (as was true with many operas).[86] Not

84. Copy in I-PEc, Archivio Morlacchi, Manifesti. For an account of the dispute, see Guardabassi, *Appunti storici*, 38, and Brumana, "Il dramma per musica *Artaserse*," 257–60. Two general assemblies in fall 1781 were devoted to trying to make David keep his contract or else offer a compromise. On November 4 the Civico voted unanimously to insist he keep the contract (I-PEc, *Verbali*, 52r–52v, relevant part reproduced in Brumana, "Il dramma per musica *Artaserse*," 258), and on November 25 it referred matters to the Venetian Council of Ten and Count Mario Savorgnan, *podestà* of Verona, where David had had gone to sing (53r–54r). David responded by petitioning the Umbrian governor to have him remunerated to the tune of 172 zecchini, but the general assembly refused and turned the affair back to Savorgnan.

85. Brumana believes a ninth number, an aria "dialogante" "Là tu vedrai chi sono" (in which Artabano addresses Serse before killing him), may have been performed at Perugia at the very beginning of the opera, since it appears with other surviving arias for Rust's *Artaserse* at I-PEsp collected by Laura Donini Montesperelli, who commissioned the copies ("Il dramma per musica *Artaserse*," 275 and 277; see also n. 86 below). The text is not in the printed libretto, so it must have been added after the libretto was printed or else have been cut just beforehand.

86. Donini Montesperelli owned a copy of Artabano-Babbini's big *scena*, "I tuoi deboli affetti—Ah che mi sento, oh Dio" (I-PEsp, MS M CXXX.5), possibly copied around 1781 (though the owner's name is in a different hand). In March 1786, it became widely available to amateurs through publication in the bimonthly Parisian music periodical *Journal des ariettes italiennes* (see table 7.2). Of three other surviving copies listed in table 7.2, one (from B-Bc) is a piano-vocal reduction for soprano of the published Parisian version, pitched to amateurs or small ensembles. Other evidence of the opera's domestic use may include copies of the duet "Se tu sapessi, o cara" made for Marietta Natali (HR-Dsmb) and the aria "E ben: va tu, crudele—Mia speranza, amato bene," also owned by Donini Montesperelli. Brumana supposes domestic use of the latter because it survives with three string parts in addition to the usual parts ("Il dramma per musica *Artaserse*," 270 n. 50). The source for "Mia speranza, amato bene" (2.4) at I-Tf is doubtless a nineteenth-century copy for use by the Tu-

surprisingly, those numbers with the longest shelf life were primarily the ones made famous by star singers. They include a decent share of obbligato recitative and arias in modern forms: Arbace's entrance aria "Quando sperai la calma" (1.2), a two-tempo variation on the famous "Fra cento affanni e cento"; Artaserse's sonata-like "Deh, respirar lasciatemi" (1.11); a multitempo duet for the two lovers Arbace and Mandane, "Se tu sapessi, o cara" (1.13), which replaced Metastasio's famous "Vo solcando un mar crudele" for Arbace at the end of act 1; Arbace's obbligato *scena* with rondò "E ben; va tu crudele—Mia speranza, amato bene" (2.4); his two-tempo aria "Per quel paterno amplesso" (2.10); and most famously Artabano's grand *scena* and two-tempo rondò "I tuoi deboli affetti—Ah, che mi sento, oh Dio" (2.14), preserved in five known sources.

Viewed together with the libretto, the surviving numbers reveal in essence an aria opera but an updated one that catered to modern sensibilities. The first and second acts carried all the dramatic weight while, typically for the time, the last was a virtual throwaway (even the famous dramatic crescendo of *Didone* lost a lot of its Metastasian buildup in Zannetti's version). With only two set numbers in act 3, including the final chorus, mandatory for *Artaserse,* the eviscerated last act was something of a way station en route to the new-styled two-act opera seria that was eventually to emerge in the 1790s. Rust's anonymous poet-reviser also streamlined and updated the text for modern tastes, cutting twenty-two of Metastasio's arias, replacing ten with brand-new or substantially revised poems, and keeping only seven in original form. For much of the simile and aphorism of Metastasio's (or Metastasian-type) arias, the reviser substituted direct diction, born out of the characters' immediate predicaments. What stayed intact were texts with nonstop propulsive rhetoric. The anguished "Deh, respirar lasciatemi" sung by Artaserse toward the end of act 1—"Ah, let me breathe free in a moment of peace, my reason cannot decide. I find in myself at once judge, friend, lover, and delinquent king"—was retained verbatim, for example. It was an aria that Rust was able to stage effectively with a breakneck "Allegro spiritoso" in the sonata-like form that had come into favor in the 1770s with Jommelli's late operas and Mozart's early ones, avoiding the tonic return until the first-stanza reprise (A′).[87]

Arias of the kind fed a new antisectionalist, proillusionist impulse—two desiderata that were formally at odds. A stunning exemplar was the show-stopping *scena ed aria,* "I tuoi deboli affetti—Ah, che mi sento, oh Dio," which Babbini made famous at the end of act 2, and which came to be associated with David in the source printed in Paris in 1786 as "chantée par Monsieur David."[88] The *scena* revisits the father who brashly imperils his son while defending his

---

rinese Accademia Filarmonica, with idiosyncratic scoring for strings and flute (omitting the original recitative, and oboe and horn parts). My sincere thanks to Alberto Rizzuti for procuring the source and sharing his insights on it.

87. Cf. chap. 2 above and McClymonds, *Niccolò Jommelli,* 234–44 and passim.

88. Facsimile of the opening page in Brumana, "Il dramma per musica *Artaserse,*" 276.

Table 7.2. Contents and sources for Metastasio and Rust's *Artaserse* (Perugia, autumn 1781)

Act/ Scene	*Incipit*	*Characters*	*Main features*	*Relation to Metastasio's text**	*Sources*
1.1	"Conservati fedele"	Mandane	First stanza = quatrain in ottonari; second stanza = tercet in settenari A major; Andante, $\frac{2}{4}$; 2 hns, 2 obs in I-Gc; 2 hns, 2 fls in HR-Dsmb	= Metastasio 1.1	I-PEsp, M CXXXVI.31, 3 str pts only; I-Gc, MSS R.2.2.24 (Rome, 1783); HR-Dsmb, 45.1264
1.2	"Quando sperai la calma"	Arbace	One six-line stanza in settenari A major (I-PEsp); Largo—Allegro; 2 fls and 2 hns in I-Rsc*	Textual variation on Metastasio 1.2, "Fra cento affanni e cento," whose first stanza is incorporated as lines 3–6 of the aria	I-PEsp, M CXXXI.16 (Rome, 1783); I-Rsc (Rome, 1783)
1.3	"Sulle sponde del torbido Lete"	Artabano	Two tercets of decasillabi Music lost	= Metastasio 1.3	
1.5	"Par che fugga ancor da lido"	Artaserse	Two quatrains of ottonari Music lost	Replaces Metastasio 1.5, "Per pietà bell'idol mio"	
1.6	"Sogna il guerrier le schiere"	Megabise	One stanza = three lines of settenari and one of quinari Music lost	= Metastasio 1.6, first stanza only	
1.7	"Bramar di perdere"	Semira	Two sextets of alternating seinari and quinari Music lost	= Metastasio 1.7	
1.11	"Deh, respirar lasciatemi"	Artaserse	First stanza = quatrain of alternating ottonari and settenari; second stanza = tercet of settenari C minor; Allegro spiritoso, C; 2 hns, 2 obs; pictorial setting	= Metastasio 1.11	I-PEsp, M CXXX.6 (Perugia, 1781)
1.13	"Se tu sapessi o cara"	Arbace and Mandane	Act-ending duet A major with expressive markings and time signatures shifting from Andante $\frac{3}{4}$ to Andantino $\frac{3}{8}$ to Allegro $\frac{4}{4}$;* 2 obs, 2 hns	New; replaces the last four arias in Metastasio's original as set by Vinci (1.12, 1.13, 1.14, 1.15), including the famous act-ending "Vo solcando un mar crudele" of Arbace; weaves in bits of Metastasio 1.14 (Mandane, "Dimmi, che un empio sei"),** but without Metastasio's dramatic energy	I-PEsp, M CXXVII.31; HR-Dsmb, 45.1263

(*continued*)

Table 7.2. (*continued*)

Act/ Scene	*Incipit*	*Characters*	*Main features*	*Relation to Metastasio's text**	*Sources*
2.1	"Or che freme irato il vento"	Megabise	Two quatrains of ottonari Music lost	New	
2.2	"Rendimi il caro amico"	Artaserse	Two quatrains of settenari A major; Andantino, $\frac{2}{4}$; strings only Aria d'affetto	First stanza = Metastasio 1.1; second stanza replaces Metastasio's with a prosodic sextet in settenari, "Compagni della cuna . . . "	I-PEsp, M CXVII.35; p. 1 reproduced in Brumana, "Il dramma per musica *Artaserse,*" 274
2.3	"Del mio paterno affetto"	Artabano	Septet in settenari plus quatrain in settenari Music lost	New	
2.4	"E ben; va tu, crudele—Mia speranza, amato bene"	Arbace	*Scena* [recit.] *ed aria* of three quatrains in ottonari Obbligato recitative precedes aria in A major, Largo, C; rondò in affective style Recitative uses strings only; aria adds 2 fls, 2 hns	New	I-PEsp M CXXX.4, collection of Laura Donini Montesperelli (also contains three additional pts, vlns 1 and 2, plus bass, possibly for domestic performance); I-Tf, aria only (entitled "Rondò"), 19th-century, MS 10.I.19-9, lacking hns and vlas, but with fls; imperfect copy with missing mm. between 3v–4r
2.5	"Tenta invano un'alma amante"	Semira	Two quatrains of ottonari Music lost	New	
2.6	"Odo del caro bene"	Mandane	Two quatrains of settenari Music lost	New	
2.10	"Per quel paterno amplesso"	Arbace	One quintain plus one quatrain in settenari E-flat major, first stanza Largo $\frac{3}{4}$; second stanza Allegro C; 2 obs, 2 hns	First stanza = Metastasio 2.11; second stanza new	*Journal d'ariettes italiennes dédié à la Reine*, no. 166 (Paris: Bailleux, Nov. 1785), 7 pts (RISM A.I, R 3248)
2.11	"Va tra le selve ircane"	Mandane	Two quatrains of settenari Music lost	Metastasio 2.12	
2.14	"I tuoi deboli affetti—Ah, che mi sento, oh Dio"	Artabano	Grand *scena* [obbligato recitative] *ed aria,* two quatrains in settenari Obbligato recitative in E-flat major , with al-	New; replaces Metastasio's aria for Artabano in 2.15, "Così stupisce e cade"	I-PEsp, M CXXX.5; G-B, Music MS 19143.3, dated Jan. 1789 by the scribe, 15 pts; *Journal*

Table 7.2. *(continued)*

Act/ Scene	Incipit	Characters	Main features	Relation to Metastasio's text*	Sources
			ternating Andante and Allegro assai, 2 fls and 2 hns; aria in C major, first stanza Largo, transitional Allegro, second stanza Presto, 2 obs, 2 hns		*d'ariettes italiennes dédié à la Reine,* no. 173, with title "Chantée par M.r David" (Paris: Bailleux, March 1786), 7 pts (including 2 obs and 2 hns); copy formerly in G-DO (Music MS 1698), evidently now sold (cf. Brumana, p. 274, n. 54); B-Bc, MS 5166, soprano and pf only (= short score), prob. copied from *Journal d'ariettes*)
3.1	"Non ho pace, mille pene"	Arbace	Quatrain plus couplet in ottonari Music lost	New; replaces Arbace's two arias in 3.1 (beginning and end of the scene respectively), esp. the latter	
3.10	"Giusto re, la Persia adora"	Chorus	Music lost	= Metastasio 3. 11	

Note: Unless otherwise indicated, instrumentation includes violin 1, violin 2, viola, and bass. Relationships to Metastasio's text refer to the modern edition, Metastasio, *Tutte le opere,* ed. Brunelli.

*On musical sources, see Brumana, "Il dramma per musica *Artaserse,*" 239–78. Where a single asterisk appears, I have relied on RISM and Brumana.

**For information about textual relationships to Metastasio, see d'Ambrosa, "Le opere di Giacomo Rust," esp. as double-asterisked.

honor. Metastasio's *Artaserse* began the precedent for having Artabano close act 2 alone, with a brief recitative bemoaning his quandary as his son's judge, followed by a simile aria ("Così stupisce e cade") that shakes off his fears like a "stunned shepherd" who is thrown to the ground by fear of a lightening bolt but rises up to count his scattered flock.[89] The Artabano set by Rust has no such

89. *Artaserse* 2.15, in Metastasio, *Opere* 1:399 (loose translation in Hoole, *The Works of Metastasio* 1:87). In Metastasio's 2.3, Artabano begins the scene with the incipit of a new aria used by Rust's reviser, "I tuoi deboli affetti," speaking to himself (*Opere* 1:383).

equanimity, and none of the luxurious distance that simile allows. Seared with remorse, Artabano indicts himself in unsparing self-address.[90]

SCENA [recitative]

I tuoi deboli affetti	Miserable Artabano, in the end you still
al fin pur senti, infelice Artabano.	suffer from your wretched affections.
Un innocente figlio	Evil parent, here is an innocent son
per te, reo genitor, ecco in periglio.	in peril for you.
Oh ciel, qual fredda mano	Oh heaven, what cold hand
mi s'aggrava sul cor?	consumes my heart?
Qual mi circonda di terribile orror	By the dark of night I hear what surrounds me
notte profonda ascolto, amato figlio.	with terrible horror, my beloved son.
I rimproveri tuoi, rabbia, vendetta,	Your reproaches, your anger, your revenge,
pentimento, pietà, vergogna, amore	repentance, pity, shame, love
mi trafiggono a gara	[all] pierce me by turns,
fin, mezzo al rischio estremo,	until, in the midst of tremendous risk,
ardir mi manca, mi confondo e tremo.	courage fails and confounds me, and I tremble.

ARIA

Largo—Allegro recitativo

Ah, che mi sento, oh Dio,	Ah, what do I hear, oh God,
Tenera voce al core?	A tender voice in my heart?
Deh, figlio, al mio dolore	Ah, my son, may you at least
Volgi uno sguardo almen.	Turn to glance at my grief.

Presto

No, che non ho più pace;	No, for I no longer have peace.
Fosco mi sembra il giorno.	Daytime looks to me like darkness.
Ho cento larve intorno,	I have a thousand spirits all about me,
Ho mille furie in sen.	A thousand Furies in my breast.

Rust exploited the large orchestra to color Artabano's grief with winds—two flutes and two horns in the recitative, two oboes and two horns in the aria—in 183 through-composed measures that climax in the newly popular two-tempo rondò.[91] Most compelling is the recitative, where the orchestra serves as a tool of conscience, memory, feeling, and foreboding. Articulated with winds lovingly exchanging thirds and sixths, its beginning makes recourse to an affective con-

90. Hasse's 1730 Venetian setting of Boldini's revision had already concocted a much more theatrical ending for Artabano's monologue, an obbligato recitative for the guilty father who imagines himself phantasmagorically trying to stop his son's executioner, replete with a ghost, a falling head, and the victim's sobs (see Heartz, *Music in European Capitals,* 317).

91. The two-tempo rondò first occurs in J. C. Bach, Galuppi, Piccinni, and Traetta during the 1760s and 1770s but was not common until the 1780s. Rust uses quite a few, to judge from surviving texts and arias. See Lühning, "Die Rondo-Arie," 219–46, and Neville, "Rondò," 656.

vention that has Artabano expressing self-pity ("infelice Artabano") in a drooping major sixth (m. 12) over an E-flat tonic pedal (example 7.1). The thought of his imprisoned son (vv. 3–4) opens a chink in his armor of self-possession, projected through a sustained augmented sixth chord (mm. 15–16). Gripped by the cold hand of death, he plunges down two diminished fifths (mm. 25–26) over a violent orchestral Allegro of tremolos and glissandi (mm. 22ff.), interrupted only briefly by the pathos of a chromatic Andante (mm. 29–31). A sea of feelings then wash over him—anger, revenge, repentance, pity, shame, love (vv. 9ff.)—that cause him to lose syntactic control, rushing through a rising harmonic sequence from B flat (V) to C (bVI) to D (VII) (mm. 32–43) with violin unisons crescendoing over an angular bass.

Cadencing on the dominant of VI (C major), the sequence sets the stage for Artabano's tender aria d'affetto, which tropes the filial voice he hears in his heart. Gone here is the use of poetic reference and analogy made famous by Metastasio, which Saverio Mattei still defended in the 1770s.[92] The light chromatic touch, falling in a diminished third on the invocation "Dio" (m. 60), the sighing violins of the "tenera voce" (mm. 61–63), the whirling kaleidoscope of motives and figures with their delicate shadings, sostenuti, and inflected passaggi sounding as Artabano pleads for his unseen son to behold his grief (mm. 65–84)—all these were touchstones of the newly heightened language of the here-and-now.

Once Artabano had idled in them, he went full-tilt from the Largo through a briefly uncertain Allegro recitativo (mm. 84–88) into the confident act-ending bravura of the second-tempo Presto. Most of the Presto is texted with the second quatrain, but before long it reintroduces a technique first ventured in the Allegro recitativo of freely drawing from earlier text for exclamations and vocatives: "figlio," "oh Dio," "Ah, che mi sento." Deployed first over a prolonged dominant pedal (mm. 100–107) and again in the retransition, they lead to the central C-major reprise of the main key, tune, and verse (example 7.2). Textual fragmentation works as the stuff of hesitation, ambiguity, uncertainty. It is a form of emotional spontaneity that mobilizes a decisive triumph of vocal bravura, as the primal parental grief is recast in a repetitive marcato gauged to solicit the roar of the crowd (example 7.3).

Whatever sacrifices were made in the Presto to public pleasure, both the obbligato recitative and the two-tempo rondò harnessed musical language in the interests of continuity and expressivity in a way that neither the more sectional and rounded da capo nor the dal segno could do, nor even the younger genre of through-composed sonata-like arias.[93] And they did so with a compelling musico-dramatic force that was to continue expanding into the nineteenth-century *scena* composed by the likes of Mayr, Paer, Donizetti, Bellini, and Verdi, induced in part by dilemmas of family (a theme I pursue in the next chapter). Family dilemmas had of course figured in Metastasio's dramas, but with a less

92. Fabbri, "Saverio Mattei," and di Benedetto, "Music and Enlightenment," 141–45.

93. See my discussion in Feldman "Staging the Virtuoso" and "Mozart and His Elders."

EXAMPLE 7.1. Giacomo Rust, recitative and aria for Artabano, "I tuoi deboli affetti—Ah, che mi sento, oh Dio," mm. 1–107

Obbligato recitative and opening of the primo tempo, Largo, from *Artaserse* (Teatro Civico del Verzaro, Perugia, autumn 1781), 2.14. Short score based on copy in D-B.

EXAMPLE 7.1. (continued)

(continued)

EXAMPLE 7.1. (*continued*)

EXAMPLE 7.1. (*continued*)

(*continued*)

EXAMPLE 7.1. *(continued)*

EXAMPLE 7.1. (*continued*)

(*continued*)

EXAMPLE 7.1. (*continued*)

EXAMPLE 7.2. Giacomo Rust, "I tuoi deboli affetti—Ah, che mi sento, oh Dio," mm. 133–39

direct rhetoric and emotional charge than in the newest drammi giocosi or in revisions of Metastasio for the later eighteenth-century stage. What then of the son? Arbace lay at the affective core of Metastasio's conception, already utilizing a more direct diction than the drama's other characters with only one out-and-out simile aria, "Vo solcando un mar crudele" (1.15). The reviser of the Perugian libretto retained parts of Metastasio's texts for two of Arbace's arias—"Quando sperai la calma" (1.2) and "Per quel paterno amplesso" (2.10)—and eliminated the simile aria to stress the "tender heart" of the son dwelt on by Artabano (example 7.1). Such tenderness was the very quality that Mariotti praised in Bedini in his light canzonetta of homage: "[W]hoever's not affected by Bedini's tender singing has an impenetrable soul or no heart in his breast."[94] The act 2 arias that preceded Artabano's big *scena*—"Mia speranza, amato bene" (2.4), also fronted by an obbligato recitative, and "Per quel paterno amplesso" (2.10)—both anticipated directly the theme of the compassionate son, wronged by his father and locked up awaiting execution in Orsini's penumbral prison.[95] "Mia speranza" echoed the father's interjection of "Oh Dio," emoting with Artabano's broken-syntax style. Where the father had cried out to the son, Arbace/Bedini

94. The poem is signed E.T., that is, Elpidio Trionio, Mariotti's Arcadian name. Pimpinelli's indices give all the names (Arcadian and non) of academy members with dates of entrance. Originally begun in the early eighteenth century, the Arcadia Perugina was revived in 1778 after a dormancy of thirty-four years. Its membership included nobles and members of the middle class—clergy, artists, and "new social elements tied to the University and free professions"—resulting in "rich interclass encounters" (Pimpinelli, *I riti,* 6).

95. Scenic sketches survive in Baldassare Orsini's 1785 work *Le scene del Nuovo Teatro del Verzaro,* copy in PEc; prison scene reproduced in Brumana, "Il dramma per musica *Artaserse,*" 263.

EXAMPLE 7.3. Giacomo Rust, "I tuoi deboli affetti—Ah, che mi sento, oh Dio," mm. 172–83

made a heart-rending tonic-dominant transition through a sustained chromatic envelope—again, culminating on an augmented sixth—to cry out "Il Padre!" (example 7.4).

Mia speranza, amato bene, Vo a morir, ma fido a te. Ah, son fiere le mie pene Quanto è bella la mia fé.	My hope, my beloved, I am off to die, but faithful to you. Ah, my pain is as fierce As my loyalty is fine.
Ma la sorte . . . il padre . . . oh Dio! Non temer. . . oh Dio. . . perché Tu non sai, bell'idol mio, Il mio caso, oh Ciel, qual è?	But my fate . . . my father . . . Oh God! Fear not . . . oh God . . . why Do you not know, my lovely idol, Oh heaven, what my fate holds?
Alme belle innamorate, Che vedete il mio cimento, Dite voi se ugual tormento Può soffrire un fido cor.	Beautiful souls, in love, Who witness my trial, Tell me if a faithful heart Can suffer such a torment.

EXAMPLE 7.4. Giacomo Rust, aria for Arbace, "Mia speranza, amato bene," mm. 22–30

From *Artaserse* (Teatro Civico del Verzaro, Perugia, autumn, 1781), 2.4. Short score based on I-PEsp, MS M CXXX.4.

When he got to "Per quel paterno amplesso," Rust souped up the melodrama with an added "padre, addio" in Bedini's first stanza, the accompaniment pulsating through a largo cantabile in E flat (example 7.5, page 2, second and fifth systems).

In lieu of anecdotal or other documentary evidence, the high survival rate of Bedini's arias speaks to the continued resonance with the public of the castrato as a young hero and Bedini's success in embodying him. Three of his four arias survive (all from acts 1 and 2), plus a duet with Mandane. There was nothing new in dramatizing the moral and sentimental progress of the young hero/castrato, but otherwise the slant here was on the moral position of the father—not metaphorically, as with the king, but literally—and on the triumphant tenor. The paternal crisis echoed the social crisis that had emboldened Perugia's citizens to determine their own theatrical fate, as the father was implicated, figuratively and literally, in the late-eighteenth-century problematic of how subjects were constituted and how they were cared for by a supreme fatherly sovereign. Arguably, it was for that reason that fathers (like sons) required redemption. In Perugia, the solution was to seize on a new ideology capable of converting the negativity of the father by asking the public to submit to the naturalist illusion, but then to awaken them from it by giving recognition to the real-life tenor as the true hero-to-come. Hence Mariotti's encomiastic meditation in a sonnet on Babbini's portrayal of Artabano, which asked listeners to wonder at his illusionistic powers, to hold them up to the light of truth and only then give themselves over to them, and to the passions their enchantments could elicit.

Is this Artabano? Is a traitor hidden
in such a fine cloak, under so sweet and calm
a demeanor? And has such a
thirst for rule penetrated his wicked breast?!

But am I raving? You alone, Babbini, can boast
of giving living form to a performed emotion,
and pressing on the hearts of others with new charms
through your assiduous deeds and your noble song.

It's your lips that envelope the stirred souls,
wherever they might wish, of anyone who hears you.
Thus, to the shame of truth, your fans fly with you into a passion.

But then, sensible to the skilled deception,
they admire all the more the power of your words,
and take pleasure and delight in the deceit.[96]

96. "Per l'egregio cantante Babini sostenendo la parte de Artabano nell'Artaserse": "Questi è Artabano? E in sì leggiadro ammanto / Sotto un sì dolce e sì sereno aspetto / Si cela un tradìtor? E giunge a tanto / Sete di regno in scelerato petto? / Ma che vaneggio? E' sol, Babin, tuo vanto / Con gli atti industri e col tuo canto eletto / Dar vive forme a un simulato affetto / E forzar l'altrui cor con novo incanto / E' il labbro tuo, ch'ovunque vuole, aggira / L'alma commossa di ciascun che t'ode, /

EXAMPLE 7.5. Giacomo Rust, aria for Arbace, "Per quel paterno amplesso," pp. 1–2

From *Artaserse* (Teatro Civico del Verzaro, Perugia, autumn, 1781), 2.10. Facsimile from *Journal des ariettes italiennes dédié à la Reine* (Paris), November 1785, no. 166:1–2. By permission of the Bibliothèque Nationale de France. (*continued*)

EXAMPLE 7.5. (*continued*)

WHETHER PURSES OR PERSONS

The men who built the Teatro Civico came from a working professional class. Most were untitled. Only a few went by *dottore, avvocato, capitano,* or *tenente.* Others were business people, merchants, or painters (Orsini, for example). Almost all performed labor for pay, with no expectation of privilege beyond the respect commanded as members of the *secondo ordine* and, for some, the titles they temporarily assumed as the society's *deputato, sovraintendente, computista,* or even *presidente.* To outstrip their rivals in the new public sphere and accumulate cultural capital, symbolic capital, and (not least) hard capital, they had to employ their every wit in the financially doomed enterprise of theater ownership. They also had to balance financial obligations continually against conflicting opinions, new modes of debate, and new ideologies of equity.

This set of challenges coalesced in the society's early years around voting and shareholding. The constitution of the society ensured that all members had voting rights, but how were rank and power to be represented internally? Each general assembly began with a roll call, and proceeded with motions from the floor, debated and voted up or down. In its original form, the system was simple. If you bought a box, you had also bought a share and you got a vote in the general assemblies. But as the society found itself increasingly pressed for funds, it needed to expand its ranks beyond its initial founding members in order to raise capital, complete the building project, and pay off loans. The only way to attract new members in sufficient numbers was to make shares more widely affordable. Half shares were created with a consequent expansion of corporate governance and diversification and a lessening of the prestige of ownership.

The first major proposal designed to address these problems was introduced at the eighth general assembly on May 16, 1779, when the bookkeeper, Francesco Bartoli, proposed a plan to reform the level of contributions by splitting shares beyond the then-current subdivision into halves to a further subdivision into quarters. The object was to allow new members to buy in more cheaply. Half a share would give members two votes and a quarter share one vote, while holders of full shares would be (re)assigned four votes, and so on. Whatever you gave in lucre was exactly what you'd get back in voting power. Bartoli also wanted to lower the annual assessment to 4 scudi per quarter share, so members who had previously been paying 26.40 scudi per full share would owe only 16 scudi. The plan was to raise capital by attracting new members, but also to make old members more likely to cough up payments on time (a major problem).[97] Not surprisingly, the proposal passed thirty-six to one.

One difficulty encountered immediately was that some shareholders feared

---

Sì che ad onta del ver con te s'adira. / Ma accorta poscia della dotta frode, / Vie più 'l poter delle tue voci ammira, / E dell'inganno si compiace, e gode" (Mariotti, *Versi e prose,* no. 21).

97. Two copies survive, one written by notary Francesco Mattei (I-PEc, *Atti,* filza 5, 18v–21r), another in the society's minutes (*Verbali,* May 16, 1779). For Guardabassi's interpretation, see *Appunti storici,* 34–35.

wide discrepancies in numbers of votes assigned would mean that groups of members—even groups in the minority—could easily band together to override any motion whatsoever. Hence a counterproposal was advanced at once that disallowed members to cast more than one vote if they held between one-quarter and three-quarters share and more than two votes if they held a whole share or more. The counterproposal aimed to limit coalition-building, but also to forestall a situation in which a sheer financial contribution could translate directly into votes. After a lengthy discussion, the counterproposal passed thirty-six to two.[98]

It was only because the society was a theatrical one, founded on ideologies that (tentatively, at least) favored class mobility and put its agendas of pleasurable entertainment, moral instruction, and artistic excellence over financial profit or even solubility, that such a motion could fly. A modern concept of corporate governance in the crude financial sense did not apply. At stake were honor and pride, learning and edification, emulation and competition (the latter with noble rivals at home as well as with rival towns), and not least a fledgling, if much contested, notion of equality among members.

Nevertheless, extensive revisions to Bartoli's proposal *and* its counterproposal were soon being plotted. Four members, including two deputies, wrote privately expressing outrage at the "impulsive and ill-considered resolution to reduce the [numbers of] votes of the *soci*" as being against the society's constitutional principles for assigning votes:

> The surprise of the undersigned members was truly great when news reached them that in the assembly held on the . . . [*sic*] day of last July, rashly, against all principles of reason and justice, the precipitous and ill-thought resolution was made to devalue and reduce the votes of society members in such a way that they could not exceed two in number for each individual regardless of his holdings.
>
> We have stated "against all principles of reason and justice," since it is not credible that those who attended such an assembly were not familiar with the Constitutions of the Academy, the various plans and resolutions recorded in its minutes, and the deeds executed on the occasions when theater boxes became the property of its members—all documents demonstrating that votes were always proportionate to the weight of the sums contributed and never to the number of individuals.

Power, and voting power, was supposed to have been factored in money, not bodies, ostensibly for the simple reason that no other method could attract and retain the necessary capital. "Given that for monetary reasons some members have the right to more than one vote, who," they chafed, "for heaven's sake, will it ever suit to allow other members to divest themselves arbitrarily of their vot-

98. I-PEc, *Verbali*, 20v–21r. Voting on the counterproposal took place under the old voting system, since the counterproposal was made at the same general assembly as the proposal (May 16, 1779).

ing power if they don't at the same time also relieve their fellow members of the extra amount they've had to pay in order to enjoy a greater number of votes?"[99]

On April 6, 1780, at the thirteenth general assembly, one of the deputies, Vincenzio Tini, who had been first among the signers of the above petition, proposed a new plan designed to pay down debt more quickly and secure capital but also to reinstate a principle of you-vote-as-you-pay. The levy on shares would rise from the Bartoli-plan level of 4 scudi for each quarter share to 7.50 and a strict equivalency between shares and votes would be reestablished: a quarter share at 7.50 would yield one vote, a half share at 15 scudi two votes, three-quarters share at 22.50 scudi three votes, a full share at 30 scudi four votes, and so on.[100] The plan was supposed to serve the "Common Body" of the society, save face (*decoro*) by ensuring the society's repayment of loans, and allay doubts about the society's viability, as well as putting the theater into action more quickly so it could start generating income. Supporters had obviously lobbied heavily to overcome natural opposition and got a large attendance at the assembly, where Tini's proposal passed seventy-five to twenty-four.[101]

The Tini plan made the gap between voters greater than ever, and the muscle of money was again writ out in black and white. When at the next general assembly the roster of attendees was made and the record of how many votes each attending individual could cast was duly noted, the numbers ranged all the way from one through eight.[102]

99. "Pro-Memoria. / È stata in verità eccedente la sorpresa degli infrascritti soci, allorchè è giunto a di loro notizia, che nell'adunanza, tenuta sotto il dì . . . [ellipses in original] dello scorso luglio, tumultuariamente, e contro tutti i principi di ragione, e di giustizia si prendesse l'intempestiva, ed inconsiderata risoluzione di dimunuire, e ridurre le voci de gli associati in modo, che non potessero queste per alcun titolo eccedere il numero di due per ciascheduno individuo.

"Si disse contro tutti i principi di ragione, e di giustizia non essendo presumibile, che quelli i quali intervennero ad una tale adunanza, non avessero presenti, e le Costitizioni dell'Accademia, e li diversi piani, a partiti registrati negli atti, e gli Istromenti celebrati all'occasioni, che sono si alli soci caduti in proprietà li Palchi, monumenti tutti, che manifestano essere state le voci mai sempre proporzionate al peso dell'impronto delle somme, e non mai al numero degl'individui. Posto quindi il principio, che con un titolo oneroso alcuni de soci hanno il diritto della pluralità delle voci, chi sarà mai di grazia, che convenir non voglia non poter essere in arbitrio degli altri soci di spogliarsi della di loro facoltà, se contestualmente non gli sgravano eziando di quel di più, che hanno dovuto pagare per godere di un maggior numero di voci" (Memo of protest signed by Vincenzo Tini, Antonio Piazza, Pietro Parriani, and Francesco Maria Rosa; excerpt from I-PEc, *Carteggi*, anno 1780; undated but probably submitted not long before April 6, 1780). The incomplete date of the assembly referred to above is in fact wrong; the decision was actually taken on May 16, 1779.

100. New members admitted at the second general assembly paid 30 scudi (I-PEc, *Verbali*, 26v).

101. I-PEc, *Verbali*, April 6, 1780, 25v–28v.

102. I-PEc, *Verbali*, 30v. For example, as president, Mariotti had four votes while his brother had one. The Piazza brothers, who held two shares jointly between them, had eight votes. Following the April 6 decision, four members, including Bartoli, protested that they wanted only two votes "for their own reasons." Doubtless they preferred going from 15 scudi a year for two votes to 16 scudi a year for four votes, rather than paying 30 scudi regardless of the accompanying increase in voting power. A brief written by Giuseppe Morelli to Tini protested the constant changes in shares and consequent changes in members' rights.

Ironically, the need for capital did create a broader-based and more democratic organization as membership swelled. But it also left the society open to the tyranny of a false majority (or at least a monetary one).[103] In the end, it was only for less than a year that the majority was figured through something close to a calculus of bodies/minds/souls before the monetary majority resumed legislative rule and the relationship between persons and votes was made more unequal than ever. The only corrective to the situation was that a body who was relatively more active than another stood a better chance of having votes count, because motions were voted on only by those who actually showed up at the general assemblies.[104]

TOWARD THE IDEOLOGY OF A BOURGEOISIE

Although Bartoli's proposal was a pragmatic one, it did launch a wider debate on the issues and represented an incipient ideology of individual equality, however hesitant. It was an ideology that also found expression in the Civico's theatrical space. On March 7, 1779, after construction was under way, the original architect, Lorenzini, proposed to revise plans for the proscenium. Ostensibly the goal was to break up the straight lines and symmetries of the original design by edging the proscenium with softer curves, using "more majestic, grand, and beautifully adorned" columns instead of pilasters. But a further goal was to clear sightlines so the stage could be viewed from every box in the theater, and the whole proscenium be exposed with equal vantage point to all spectators, whether in the parterre or the boxes.[105] The revision was forward-

103. Inasmuch as the society's ranks quickly expanded to include lower orders of urban *cittadini* as well as *cittadini* from the countryside outside Perugia proper, its fate paralleled that of other noble bodies in early modern times (e.g., the Casino dei Nobili del Teatro Pavone discussed here).

104. This of course excluded those like the signers of the private petition (cited in n. 99 above). The decisions of 1780 hardly ended matters. On August 29, 1782, a new plan again reduced shares, presumably because payments were in arrears, and throughout the 1780s plans continued to be made to sell more boxes, pay off debts, increase the number of members, rent out dwellings, and so on in order to raise more capital (I-PEc, *Atti*, filza 24).

105. "A quali Signori così congregati fù esposto che si approvò dalla nostra Congregazione tenutasi il di 31 dicembre proposto dell'anno scorso 1778 che si eseguisse il disegno del Signore Alessio Lorenzini per la Fabrica del nostro Teatro in tutto, e per tutto a forma della sua Pianta segnata Let*tera* A, prescindendo del vestibulo, che fù prescelto quello delineato nella Pianta contrasegnata *per* la sua identità colla Lett*era* B. Ma siccome lo stesso Sig*nore* Alessio Lorenzini architetto crede, che sia necessaria una qualche variazione alla Figura della Pianta nel di lei termine prima dell'imboccatura del Teatro, o sia Proscenio, e di dare a questo una più breve intesa simetria ornandolo di Colonne in vece di Pilastri da prima stabiliti, giudicando egli che così il tutto riescirà più vistoso e magnifico, e verrà a togliersi quel Tedio, che certam*ente* pare debba recare quella retta linea, la quale del semicircolo della Platea si stende in non indifferente lunghezza sino al Teatro; perciò ha delineata una nuova Pianta, la quale senza lasciare di essere di Figura di Ferro di Cavallo, come la di già approvata và a finire prossimam*ente* al Proscenio con una dolce voluta, fiancheggiandolo, e lasciandolo libero di modo che il p*rimo*, e l'ultimo Palchetto di ciascuno de i cinque ordini rimane di Facciata al Teatro, e il Proscenio tutto resta esposto in un' medesimo punto di vista si alli spettatori nella Platea,

looking, especially for a provincial theater, for it necessitated pushing those boxes that were closest to the stage back away from the proscenium instead of having them flank it, and thus articulating boundaries, imagined and experienced, between stage and hall. Simultaneously, it introduced a more democratic semiotics of viewing, something the society eventually tried to warrant further by deciding to seek justice against anyone who disturbed the quiet of the spectators.[106]

Did the academists of the Civico really conceive themselves as a new middle class?[107] They were doubtless familiar with French enlightenment waves that had been breaking throughout the peninsula, and sensed that they could assume new symbolic status and provide their class with renewed ammunition against the nobles. How specifically these symbols and ammunition were inhabited with a consciousness that was akin to the French is another matter. The Papal States as a whole were little touched by enlightenment reforms elsewhere in Italy, but the intelligentsia within them had access to many enlightenment books, included censored ones. Even books published in Perugia show that an emergent French politics of class helped shape choices made within the spectrum of Perugian consciousness, one that surely provided Perugians with an ideological and discursive structure that was limited but nevertheless informative and legitimizing. If Perugians were too caught up in ancient factionalist struggles, with very real and immediate histories, to divorce themselves from them, they were also caught up in proving themselves full-fledged, cultivated intellectuals, worthy of the same grandeur, pomp, and power as the nobles. The hints of an incipient bourgeois consciousness are there: in the acceptance of Lorenzini's proposal for more egalitarian sightlines, in Mariotti's infatuation with the Freemasons, in his arguments from natural law and natural right, in the academy's allegiance to ideologies of morality, public faith, and public good, in Bartoli's proposal to make membership broader-based and the counterproposal to give more equitable representation to persons irrespective of buying power, in the academy's avowed opposition to noble privilege, and its emphasis on natural talent and industry.

* * *

In 1999, the opening gambit of the press release for Umbria Jazz defended its use of settecento theaters for jazz shows, perhaps in the face of traditional aficionados who want to hear their jazz in smoky nightclubs:

---

che a tutti quelli ne Palchi e nel tempo stesso maestoso, grandioso, e più vagamente adorno, come possono lor Signori riconoscere dalla stessa nuova Pianta che qui resta esposta" (seventh general assembly, I-PEc, *Verbali*, March 7, 1779, 17r–17v; cf. Guardabassi, *Appunti storici*, 13).

106. Constitution, article 10, print copy in I-PEc, Archivio Morlacchi, Statuti e regolamenti, no. 2, *Costituzioni dell Accademia;* MS copies in I-PEc, *Verbali*, June 30, 1781, 42r–46v, and *Atti*, filza 15.

107. Critical reading here is Maza, "Luxury, Morality, and Social Change," 199–229.

> Theaters are not ideal spaces for jazz. Too "official," too "historical" for a music that lives in the moment and is the height of informality. But sometimes theaters have become just that, ideal containers even for jazz—the gala dedicated to the divine Sarah Vaughn, for example, who sang in the Teatro Pavone, constructed in the eighteenth century for the Perugian aristocracy. Ten years beforehand, at the height of the seventies climate, Sarah had been booed. Or the first concert by Caetano Veloso at the Teatro Morlacchi, the bourgeois theater from the turn of the eighteenth and nineteenth centuries. Or even the two concerts also given by Veloso with Gilberto Gil for the anniversary of Tropicalism and, to stick to Brazil, the recital by Joao Gilberto that kept everyone's breath baited . . . for two hours because he didn't show up at the theater.[108]

The early history of the Civico/Morlacchi suggests that perhaps the writer was onto something he didn't imagine. Theaters may eventually have become official shrines to history, but those like the Civico were built, above all, for a living, breathing audience, aware of itself and its role in creating public consensus. They had a relationship to time and schedules more like the one Leopold Mozart described about the opening night of *Lucio Silla,* when the sovereign arrived three hours late, than a reverential concert of string quartets nowadays. Though anything but a subculture in their self-definition, the *cittadini* built the Civico on the heels of a burgeoning discontent among middle-class intelligentsia in Europe. The paradox is not that a middle-class genre has no place in an eighteenth-century theater, but quite the opposite. The eighteenth-century theater tout court was largely built for a bourgeoisie, many of them middle class. In some of these theaters, nobles were on display as distinct superiors. Not so at the Teatro Civico, where the middle class was not on the periphery but at the center.[109]

108. "I teatri non sono gli spazi ideali per il jazz. Troppo 'ufficiali,' troppo 'storici,' per una musica che vive di cronaca [lives on a daily basis] e che è il massimo dell'informale. Ma qualche volta i teatri lo sono diventati, i contenitori ideali, anche per il jazz. Per esempio il gala dedicato alla divina Sarah Vaughn, che ha cantato nel teatro del Pavone, costruito nel Settecento dall'aristocrazia perugina. Dieci anni prima, in pieno clima da meta' anni '70, Sarah era stata fischiata. Oppure il primo concerto di Caetano Veloso al teatro Morlacchi, il teatro della borghesia a cavallo fra Settecento e Ottocento. O ancora il due dello stesso Veloso con Gilberto Gil per l'anniversario del Tropicalismo, e, per restare in Brasile, il recital di Joao Gilberto, che ha tenuto tutti . . . col fiato sospeso per due ore perché non si presentava in teatro" (from the Web site of the Umbria Jazz festival, www.umbriajazz.com/uj1997/uj97/luoghi/italiano/teatri.html [accessed January 24, 2003]).

109. By the 1790s, political events made *cittadini* involuntarily secure from noble pretensions. On May 23 of year 6 of the Republican Era (1799) the Civico was told that General Valette, comandant of the French militia (then at Gubbio), wanted to see the singers and dancers at Perugia (Guardabassi, *Appunti storici,* 43). *Cittadini* were subsequently exploited to renew enthusiasm for liberty and equality in the souls of citizens, much as at Venice and elsewhere (cf. chap. 9 below). Even Mariotti was coopted into the French revolutionary project (see Fornaini, "Instaurazione del governo repubblicano," 275–83).

APPENDIX: ANNIBALE MARIOTTI'S SPEECH TO THE ACCADEMIA DEL TEATRO CIVICO DEL VERZARO, DECEMBER 31, 1781

Recitato nella gentile adunanza degli Accademici del Verzaro la mattina del dì ultimo dicembre 1781.[110]

Siccome intervenir suole Accademici Riverentissimi che dopo lunga penosa navigazione ai patrii lidi tornando gli stanchi nocchieri, si sentan di bella gioja brillare il cuore nel petto, e i superati pericoli, e fino i sofferti danni con piacer richiamando al pensiero, godano ad uno ad uno narrare agli amici, e disegnar sull'anima que' rischi che giù passarono. Così ora a noi pure addiviene, che avendo al suo termine condotta quella impresa che già vi piacque addossarci, ci sentiam tutti ricolmi il seno d'inusitata allegrezza, e nella ricordanza de' passati travagli un cagion troviamo di sincerissima consolazione. Fin da que' primi giorni, che si pensò allo stabilimento di questa nostra Accademia, e alla costruzione del nostro Teatro i primi avvedutissimi suoi fondatori pare che a tutti noi dir volessero con que' medesimi sentimenti co' quali Enea parlò a suoi seguaci nell'atto di sciogliere le vele per l'onde Terrene.

> Fremano pur venti e procelle intorno:
> Saran glorie i perigli
> e dolce fia di rammentarli un giorno.
> (Metastasio, *Didone* 3.1)

Or finalmente per noi spento questo sospiratissimo giorno; ed oggi è che dolce a noi riesce il rammentare i nostri perigli, con certa speranza ch'essi ancora chiamar si possano nostre glorie giacché per parlar colle frasi del Sofocle Italiano, quando pur trattiam di Teatri

> Fin che un zeffiro soave
> Tien del mar l'ira placata,
> Ogni nave è fortunata,
> È felice ogni nocchier.
>
> È ben prova di coraggio
> Incontrar l'onde funeste
> Navigar fra le tempeste
> E non perdere il sentier.
> (Metastasio, *Ezio,* 1.13)

Furono appena concepiti i primi desideri di uscir finalmente anche noi da quell'infelice terreno ove un ingiusto orgoglio tenea condannati in un duro servaggio tutti i nostri pensieri di onesto comun diletto, e di erudito piacere, che vedemmo subito tra un riso fallace campeggiar lo sdegno di alcuni, i quali con

110. I-PEc, *Atti,* filza 19, December 31, 1781.

picciol legno si credean di dover sempre essi soli signoreggiare sull'immenso pelago che era per ogni legge a tutti aperto, e comune. Affidati però da un Nume maggior di quanti ne vivono in Terra, si cominciò da noi lietamente il lavoro del ben ideato naviglio, e fra i contrasti di piu, e diverse opinioni fu proseguita con mirabile celerità e fu egregiamente compita, e ornata la vostra mole. E nulla piu mancava al compimento de nostri disegni che l'avventurarla all'oceano. Si ebbe perciò ricorso anche in questa occasione al tutelar nostro Nume. Ma per colpa di quei che dovean recar fino al trono i nostri voti si ebbe molto a penare per vederli esauditi. Per le diligenze però di due nostri compagni spediti per tal bisogna più da presso al soglio sovrano, si ottenne da questo il benigno consentimento. Si stabilirono quindi gli ordini piu giusti e piu convenienti pel governo della società raccolta alla impresa; e si desiderò che dalla sovrana autorità ottenesser questi vigor di legge inviolabile. Anche in questo però molti ostacoli si opposero alle nostre brame; e non vi volle meno dell'opera efficace di un altro nostro valoroso compagno, perche i nostri desideri rimanessero soddisfatti.

Parea dopo tutto ciò che fosse assicurato abbastanza l'impegno, e che nulla piu mancasse perche si desser le vele ai venti. Un soffio però nemico, benche mosso dalla piu pura parte del cielo, cercò di opporsi al nostro ideato cammino. Con prudenti mezzi sedato pur fu l'imperversante Aquilone; e finalmente si abbandonò al mare il naviglio non meno carico de' nostri tesori, che delle nostre speranze.

Ahimè però quanti nuovi pericoli gli apparecchiava il nemico destino! Dové pur esso soffrire la infedeltà o la trascuranza in chi era scelto a procurargli in mezzi, onde piu glorioso, e sicuro avanzar nel viaggio. Dové pur esso vedersi nel maggior uopo mancar di fede chi per via de piu venerandi patti promesso avea di servire co' suoi ammirati talenti all'onor suo, alla sua maggiore fortuna. Quando gli convenne fra l'orrore di buja notte errare incerto nel suo viaggio; quando urtare nelle sirte insidiose; quando in balia dell'onde, e agitato da fierissimi venti andar quasi naufrago. Ora una troppo infida calma lo afflisse, or una interna sospetta quiete l'intimorì; ora interne dissensioni il turbarono.

Proseguì, è vero, frattanto il suo difficil viaggio: ma agitato sempre da furiose procelle, e quasi a ogni passo obbligato a contrastar coll'onde, che minacciavan di assorbirlo ne' loro vortici, cogl'erti scogli che minacciavan di frangerlo; co' rabbiosi venti, che l'insultavano, e fiero governo faceva del suo corredo; Ah che pur troppo fu replicate volte costretto per fino a far gettito di quelle richiezze, che con sollecita cura serbar voleva a miglior uso. Quante volte non fu pianto sulla dura necessità di veder dispersa una parte degli affidati tesori per l'imminente pericolo di vedere a mezzo corso arrestato, o sommerso il naviglio!

Getta il nocchier talora
Pur que' tesori all'onde,
Che da remote sponde
Per tanto mar portò.

E giunto al lido amico,
Gli dei ringrazia ancora,
Che ritornò mendico,
Ma salvo ritornò.
(Metastasio, *La clemenza di Tito* 3.11)

Sì: grazie pur sieno agli astri benigni, giunse pur finalmente, al bramato lido il nostro combattivo legno:

E come quei che con lena affannata
Uscita fuor del pelago alla viva
Si volge all'acqua perigliosa, e queta.
(Dante, *Inferno*, canto 1, vv. 22–24)

Così possiamo anche noi in questo sicuro luogo raccolti, dei superati rischi andar lieti e superbi. Potrà bene il pensiero de' sofferti danni turbare in parte il nostro giubilo. Ma siccome le ferite non furon mai di vergogna al guerrier vincitore, così le lacere attenne, le rotte vele al fortunato nocchiero non recaron mai disonore; ma anzi come quello nelle sue cicatrici, così ne' suoi danni il secondo bella cagion ritrova di compiacimento, e di conforto.

Quello solo a che dalla prudenza questo vien consigliato, si è l'attendere con premura a risacire la danneggiata nave, a riordinarne le vele, a ripararlo finalmente in ogni sua parte, per poter quindi a stagion piu propizia, calmata l'ira de' venti, nuovamente commetterla a piu felice navigazione, sotto il governo di piu esperto, e fortunato pilota.

Io mentre a così provvedere caldamente vi esorto, amati Accademici, per quella costante affezione che ad essa serberò fino agli estremi respiri, altro far non posso che accompagnar sempre co' miei caldi voti la veleggiante Nave così.

Spiega, legno onorato, a lieto corso
Piu fortunate a miglior dì le vele.
Assai già fra perigli errando hai scorso
All'ire esposta del destin crudele.
Or porga a danni tuoi pronto soccorso
Di saggi condottier' l'opra fedele,
E sempre per l'instabile elemento
Ti sien gli astri proprizi, e amico il vento.[111]

111. The final ottava rima (anonymous) may well be by Mariotti himself.

CHAPTER 8

Morals and Malcontents

"How to keep interest where persuasion is lacking, where the eye is in a perpetual contradiction with feeling, where passions, which would make the effect, lack sufficient reason to produce it?" ARTEAGA, *Le rivoluzioni del teatro*[1]

DEDICATIONS TO LADIES

When Rust's *Artaserse* was staged, the libretto greeted the women of Perugia with an obsequious dedication. The Pavone had produced many operas with dedications *alle dame* in imitation of its immediate Roman model, the Teatro Alibert o delle Dame, and theaters in many other cities had too. Indeed, Metastasio himself had ratified the practice more than half a century earlier by dedicating his *Semiramide riconosciuta* "to the ladies" in 1728.[2]

Dedications to women were residues of courtly artifice that endured as a curious form of rhetoric exchanged between male opera producers who postured as gallants and collectivities of female operagoers represented as courted ladies. Frankly atavistic, the phenomenon persisted into the nineteenth century, and over time it indexed a variety of shifts: in discursive styles and styles of love, in mores about women's place in public life, between elite ways and populist ways, between values grounded in honor and values vested in the "public good." By now these dedications have become a kind of evidentiary detritus, the unwelcome flotsam that pools up around the century's embarrassing operatic past, but in their own time they inhabited a universe of real social exchange. They are valuable here in broaching broader issues relevant to late-eighteenth-century opera, particularly those that speak to social and specifically gender re-

1. "Come ottener l'interesse dova manca la persuasione, dove l'occhio è in perpetua contradizzione col sentimento, dove la passione, che ne sarebbe l'effetto, manca di ragione sufficiente, che la produca?" (Arteaga, *Le rivoluzioni del teatro* 1:409).

2. Metastasio, *Opere* 1:1411

lations but indivisibly those that connect the changing eighteenth-century self to a larger community. Even though dedications to ladies made public broadcast of female spectators as mistresses of servile males—"you reign supreme among us," they proclaimed, "we are your servants"—they also betrayed ambivalences about women in the public eye. Women might be noble, loyal, resplendent, and forgiving, as the dedications made out, but to laud them in the hackneyed rhetoric of the court could still be the stuff of vanity, falsehood, and depravity. In the eyes of some, fawning dedications were as dissolute as some of their dedicatees. That alone is paradox enough, but female dedicatees also came to be positively implicated in the new emphases on sensibility and even pathos favored by later eighteenth-century reformers, who bundled them loosely together as warrants of truth to nature.

Further on, this chapter explores how qualms about female decadence, expressed in opera and operatic discourse, square with a concurrent fixation on mothers and families, particularly in a milieu in which opera itself was seen by some as violence against morals, as something that tore at the fabric of the new morality, even in Italy. At issue were moral certainty and certain knowledge, as they pertained to oneself and to the wider world. Whether inscripted on your side or mine, women were forces in the battle for a new social regime.

In that respect, dedications *alle dame* mapped court relationships onto urban settings, and not in innocent ways. They were manipulative through and through, ruled by complaint and flattery and tempered by meek apologies for the dedicators' shortcomings and pledges to honor and defend their ladies in exchange for loyalty. These were the tactics of courtly love that sought protection from their "exalted" addressees, unattainable ladies who echo the women of the medieval *tenzone*, the troubadour's lai, the Petrarchan ballata, and a congeries of other chivalric forms. The dedicators—typically *interessati* (investor/patrons), *soci* (members of a theater society), deputies, or impresarios—pretend to woo the ladies in the rhetorical guise of gentlemen/knights, yet pointedly direct their praises to a vague collective: *dame* as "ladies" in a generic sense (women), or *dame* as "ladies of standing," presumably noble ladies?[3]

The trade-off proposed was as clear as its objects were vague: in exchange for an enthusiastic reception, the dedicator(s) offered an opera worthy of the ladies' merit. Thus in 1748 a stock Roman dedication wrote *alle dame:*

> The Fate that this Theater has long enjoyed of being distinguished by the glorious name of Teatro delle Dame, and the Disposition that the Ladies have always shown toward it make us certain that the offering we make you of the present drama will find in your generous spirit the welcome we crave. And since the heroic virtues represented in it can be recognized in your actions, we are persuaded that for your part you will not fail to attend this theater, and that this

3. See "dama," in Battaglia, *Grande dizionario* 4 (1966): 2–4.

drama will be illustrated by your very presence and your frequenting of it. And in hopes from us for both, we declare ourselves most distinctly

Your most obsequious servants, the Interessati.[4]

Here the dedicators feigned subjection, supplicating like chivalric knights, but instead of posing as victims of Eros, they make themselves out as courtly devotees of the ladies' kindness and generosity. All of this belied the largely patriarchal social systems that endured throughout the Italian eighteenth century.[5] Yet the point of pleading abjection, inferiority, and even peril was to index the courtliness proper to a lovelorn medieval *seigneur* and the mode of exchange it presumed. Thus, when the dedicators claimed that their dramas mirrored the ladies' "heroic virtues" and asked for the mercy of good attendance, they implied that the ladies were wont to be merciless, cruel, and distant, like the medieval *bella domna,* but also that by relenting they could relieve the men's fears of a flop and be rewarded with a good opera. Appearing in public, on public display, was a way to do society good, to ensure good entertainment and a superior social life. Disguised in the balance of the exchange was the temporal structure of a feudal love pact. So long as the men supplicated with the women, the women ruled. But a return of favor—a submission—was expected once their faithful vassals had discharged their duties of singing, extolling, lamenting, entreating, defending, protecting.[6]

Some such dedications replaced the courtly trope of the cruel lady with encomia designed to conflate the dedicatees with heroic women of ancient times, particularly in Rome where ancient history functioned unabashedly as founding myth. In 1752 a libretto for the delle Dame set by Girolamo Abos on the theme of Erifile, wife of Amphiaraus, whom she persuaded to take part in the Seven against Thebes raid, was printed with this a dedicatory poem to the "Nobili Dame Romane":

4. "Alle Dame. La sorte, che da gran tempo gode questo Teatro di esser contradistinto colla gloriosa denominazione di Teatro delle Dame, e la propensione, che le medesime hanno sempre dimostrata verso il medesimo ci rende sicuri, che l'offerta, che a voi facciamo del presente dramma, troverà nel vostro animo generoso quel gradimento, che da noi si desidera. E siccome l'eroiche virtù, che in esso si rappresentano, nelle vostre azioni si riconoscono, così siamo persuasi, che non mancarà dal canto vostro di essere e questo Teatro e questo dramma dalla vostro presenza illustrato, e dalla vostra frequenza assistito, e nel tempo, che l'uno, e l'altro da noi si spera, distintamente ci dichiariamo 'Vostri Ossequiosissimi Servi L'Interessati'" (dedication to *Lucio Papirio dittatore,* libretto anonymous, music by Rinaldo di Capua, Teatro delle Dame, Rome, 1748). The exact same dedication was used for the libretto to *Antigona* (Teatro delle Dame, Rome, 1751).

5. Pomata, "Family and Gender," 69–86.

6. Instances of women acting as explicit agents in the realm of theatrical production—the Grimani sisters, who owned the Teatro San Giovanni Grisostomo in eighteenth-century Venice, for example, or the Venetian journalist Elisabetta Caminer Turra (1751–96), translator of many French dramas, who spent one year managing the Teatro San Angelo—were the exception. On Caminer, see Sama, "Verso un teatro moderno," 63–79.

Most Noble Ladies,
lovely, sublime nymphs,
honor of the Tiber,
worthy progeny of heroes,
friend to the gods
whom our century regards with delight
and in whom it enjoys renewing a lively example
of the ancient state and happily applauding
your rare virtuous souls—
you who know how to conjoin
sweetness, love, pity, disdain, and valor
with marvelous art, pure honesty, and singular beauty:
who could possibly sing your praises to the fullest?
Your sweet conversation that inflames our hearts,
the wise thoughts on which every good depends,
those glances through which grace shines
in whose light one learns to manage well,
and the sweet manners that soften
the most savage souls: your mercy arouses
reason when she slumbers, humiliated.
For you the urge for honor is already born in the breast
of so many Excellent and Valorous heroes
that their names are eminent throughout the World.
Sparta remembers them, and so do Athens, Ithaca, and Rome;
so that everyone recognizes a great part
of their former valor through your gift.
Hence I nurture the hope
that this DRAMA having such a lovely name precede it,
will have at once a powerful defense and an honor.
So I present it to you in a humble act:
Illustrious LADIES, do not take it as craven.[7]

7. "Nobilissime Dame. / Leggiadre, eccelse ninfe, / onor del Tebro, / d'Eroi degna progenie, / ai Numi amica [5], / che il secol nostro con diletto ammira, / e un vivo esempio dell'antica etate / gode in voi rinovarsi; e lieto applaude / a tante rare vostre alme virtudi: / Che unir sapete con mirabil arte [10] / Dolcezza, amor, pietà, sdegno, e valore, / Pura onestade, e singolar bellezza: / Chi può ridir le vostre lodi appieno? / Il dolce favellar che i cuori infiamma, / e i pensier saggi onde ogni ben dipende; [15] / quei sguardi, ove del ciel grazia traluce / nel di cui lume a ben oprar s'impara; / e le dolce maniere, che gentili / fan l'alme più selvagge, e mercè vostra / ragion si desta, se avvilita dorme: [20] / per voi desio d'onor già nacque in seno / a tanti eccelsi, e valorosi eroi / Che il nome lor al mondo tutto è chiaro. / Sparta il rammenti, Atene, Itaca e Roma; / ove gran parte del valor primiero [25] / riconosce ciascun per vostro dono. / Quindi rinasce in me speme sì viva / che avendo il dramma un sì bel nome in fronte / possente avrà difesa, e insieme onore. / Ecco a voi, lo presento in atto umile: [30] / Non lo prendete, Illustri Donne, a vile" (libretto to *Erifile* [Teatro delle Dame, Rome, Carnival 1752], [A1v]–[A2v]; libretto anonymous, music by Girolamo Abos; copy in US-Cu, "Roman Opera Libretti," vol. 8, [658]).

Strikingly, the dedication here begins to shed the skin of the court, as the predictable gambit of soliciting the ladies' approval is reduced to a slim "hope" that the opera "will have a powerful defense." If a chivalric language sets the initial tone—with praise of the women's "sweetness, love, pity, disdain, and valor"—the ploy of constructing them within the empire of the ancients overshadows it, and pushes it away completely when the poet pleads shamelessly not to be thought greedy.

Most remarkably, these descendants of ancient heroines are thoroughly modern Millies. It is precisely because they pass demure glances, behave with grace, and above all talk—and talk sweetly—that the "gift" of their approbation will echo throughout the generations, like the wisdom of their ancestors. They are the new women of the public sphere, conversing at the opera publicly in sexually mixed groups and appearing publicly before the gaze of men. Both were inveighed against throughout the eighteenth century more often than they were defended. Yet the lucky women who congregated at the opera were free enough that some visitors to Italy were amazed by the spectacle of them, much as they were amazed by those noted few who found their way into elite, and sometimes public, circles of learning. Of course many Italian women of culture and intellect still remained hidden away in domestic, private, mystical, and oblatory corners of society where they were relatively unpublic and relatively unemancipated.[8] Insofar as women were assimilated at all to an enlightened public culture, they were mostly deemed intellectual inferiors of men in published treatises and were not expected to do much more than dabble in intellectual culture. This, after all, was the century that launched a market of ladies' primers, initiated above all by Algarotti's immensely popular *Newtonianismo per le dame; ovvero Dialoghi sopra la luce e i colori* (Naples, 1738), translated into French as *Newtonianisme pour les dames,* in 1738, into German in 1745, and English in 1765, and followed by many Italian imitations in later decades: an anonymous three-volume *Filosofia per le dame* (Venice, 1777), Pietro Chiari's *Lettere d'un solitario a sua figlia* (Venice, 1777), Giovanni Filiberto's anonymously published *Teologia per le dame,* also in three volumes (Padua, 1792), Giuseppe Compagnoni's *Chimica per le dame* (Venice, 1792), to name a few.[9] Even though these books were simplifying by design, they were also threatening enough to a deep and crusty layer of Italian ideology and social structure to be condemned by many conservatives, who continued to oppose study by the "inferior" sex as pointless and who claimed their forays outside home and church were immoral.[10]

8. See Cavazza, "Between Modesty and Spectacle," and Findlen, "The Scientist's Body," 211–36.

9. For further on these and other such tracts, see Guerci, *La sposa obediente,* 233–51. All of the works cited except the last were dedicated in their titles to particular women (see full titles in the reference list). Chiari was already making compilations for ladies in 1750 and thereafter writing didactic women's digests.

10. A prime example is the *Lettere critiche* of the Venetian nobleman and anti-philosophe Giuseppe Antonio Costantini, first issued in Venice in 1743—a compendium of widely held conservative views of the time. See Guerci, *La discussione sulla donna,* 92–93, 117. On public European debates

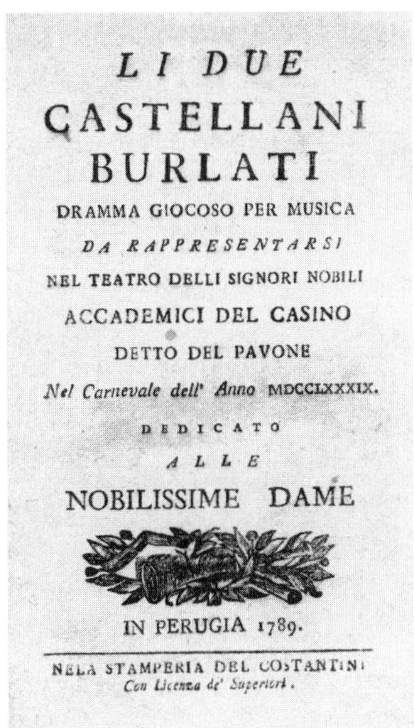

LI DUE
CASTELLANI
BURLATI
DRAMMA GIOCOSO PER MUSICA
DA RAPPRESENTARSI
NEL TEATRO DELLI SIGNORI NOBILI
ACCADEMICI DEL CASINO
DETTO DEL PAVONE
Nel Carnevale dell' Anno MDCCLXXXIX.
DEDICATO
ALLE
NOBILISSIME DAME
IN PERUGIA 1789.
NELLA STAMPERIA DEL COSTANTINI
Con Licenza de' Superiori.

FIG. 8.1. Title page showing a dedication *alle dame* for *Li due castellani burlati*, performed at the Teatro Pavone, Perugia, 1789. Biblioteca Augusta Comunale, Perugia. Reproduced by permission.

In this climate, going to the opera was not an unmarked act. Small wonder then that in the 1770s the Pavone in conservative Perugia was still producing conventional dedications *alle dame* (which may have conciliated theocratic opposers at least a little), and that it was specifically the arrival of Perugia's civic theater in 1781 that changed the tone of Perugian dedicatory address with Rust's *Artaserse*. The opera was dedicated to the city's ladies but only on the title page and with no dedicatory letter. Thereafter even the noble Pavone followed suit with its dedication in 1783 of Filippo Livigni and Domenico Cimarosa's dramma giocoso *Il convito*.[11] When the freighted year of 1789 came along, the dedication of another dramma giocoso, *Li due castellani burlati*, struck a totally new tone that explained the problem (fig. 8.1). Comical, insolent, and as brusque as a Jacobin, the impresario/author conceded that dedicatory letters were out of fashion and that the women were right not to want them. All the same, he promised, if he got their support he would return it by giving his best to the public and would laughingly tell off any rash detractors.

---

about women's capacity for learning, see two studies by Joan Landes, *Women and the Public Sphere* and *Visualizing the Nation*; and Londa Schieberger's *The Mind Has No Sex?*

11. The opera included a send-up of the dramma per musica, with a wicked aria satirizing *Didone* in act 1, "Son Didone abbandonata."

> *Noblest of Women.*
> I know. Dedicatory letters are no longer in use. You have your reasons for no longer wanting them. The most fatuous things, even almanacs, presumed to gain credit with the authoritative name of a protector. To the shame of this modern, solemn proscription against Dedicatory Letters, I nevertheless dare to adorn the first opera to appear on the August Stage of the Teatro dei Nobili del Casino this coming Carnival with your reputable name. In so doing I offer You, among other things, something of yours. I assure you, I am undertaking this out of respect for you. Therefore you must give it your patronage. If you will grace me with your protection, I will draw from it the most valid impetus to oblige myself to satisfy the public's wishes. Nay, honored by it, I will laugh at those few unguarded people who are never gratified by anything. For me it is always a glory to engage myself for You, just as it is an honor for me to be able to declare myself with obsequious respect
> Yours, Noblest of Women.
> *Most Humble, Devoted, Obliged Servant,*
> *The Impresario.*[12]

Who were these "unguarded people" (*indiscreti*)? Those cantankerous critics who groused in public at every chance, and may well have prompted the Roman poet in 1752 to lean on women's mercy to arouse reason when she slumbered? Or progressives bent on unmasking the dedicatory accord, that corrupt vestige of an old-world aristocracy? Whoever they were, they induced our impresario to take up arms and defend his *domne,* even while pleading their pardon and acknowledging their aversion to being courted with dusty plumes and ribbons. Old canons of exchange are exposed, pointed out with unembarrassed irony, but there is also a mocking of the "solemn" pledge to uphold modern egalitarianism, that sanctity of the new antiaristocrats.

The courtly cat is out of the bag. The Perugian impresario has to rebuff his detractors and defend the dedication against the laughter of the moderns while knowing it's time to start luring female operagoers by other means. Like a court

12. "Lo sò, Nobilissime Dame. Non sono più in uso le lettere dedicatorie. Evvi la sua ragione per più non volerle. Le cose più insulse, i lunari medesimi pretendevono d'acquistar credito con l'autorevole nome di un protettore. Ad onta però di questa moderna, solenne proscrizione delle dedicatorie, ardisco fregiare il primo dramma, che comparirà nelle auguste scene del Teatro dei Nobili del Casino nel prossimo Carnovale, con il vostro rispettabile nome. In ciò facendo per altro a voi una cosa vostra tributo. A vostro riguardo, ve ne assicuro, mi sono accinto all'impresa. Dovete dunque patrocinarla. Se della vostra protezione mi grazierete avrò da questa il più valido stimolo per impegnarmi di corrispondere ai desideri del pubblico. Anzi onorato di questa, mi riderò di quei pochi indiscreti, che [di] nulla rimangono mai appagati. Per me è sempre una gloria l'impiegarmi per voi, come mi è d'onore il potermi con ossequioso rispetto dichiarare. Di voi Nobilissime Dame. Perugia 27. Decembre 1788. Umilissimo Devotissimo Obligatissimo Servitore L'Impresario" (*Li due castellani burlati: Dramma giocoso per musica da rappresentarsi nel Teatro delli signori nobili Accademici del Casino detto del Pavone nel carnevale dell'anno 1789*, music by the Neapolitan Vincenzio Fabrizi). The title page was dated 1789, for the Carnival season for which the opera was done, and the dedication dated December 27, 1788. Note the comic servility of the salutation.

jester, he overshoots the claims of conventional midcentury dedications *alle dame* by pretending to cleave to that crustiest of tactics, which designated the dedicatee as true owner of the object of dedication ("I offer You something of yours"). In this he plays on a standard (if quiescent) function within the "economy of dedication" described by Roger Chartier, in which the dedicator effectively renounces his own claims of authorship (or those of credited authors) and virtually ascribes them to the dedicatee.[13] Eventually those dedications that do persist lose most of their courtly character and instead emphasize the apologia pure and simple. This modest dedication to Perugia's "nobil dame" included in the libretto of the dramma giocoso *Carolina e Filandro* refocused the dedicatory point from the heroism of the operagoing ladies to the social standing of their families, whose association with the opera would allegedly improve it.

> *Most Noble Ladies:*
> May this dramma giocoso, which would seem a base thing, a naught before the splendor of your families, become a noble gift on the pleasant illusion of your stage. So much can your attendance and your favor do for it. The former acts as a lure for the latter. Each of them hopes unceasingly, while professing the most profound respect
>
> *For You, Most Noble Ladies*
> *Perugia, 31 July 1808*[14]

Behind the dedications *alle dame* had always stood an "enlightened" set of moral claims. In 1688, when the Accademia dei Nobili of Perugia was first being founded, it produced a *memoriale* that stressed instruction over pleasure, the moral edification of women, and the academy's desire to create a public space where women would not be offended.[15] Pascucci shows that the nobles' agenda was to ensure that the academy be viewed as the *corpo morale* of the Perugian nobility, something the government did eventually recognize in it.[16] Opening in 1723, the Teatro Pavone made one of those last gasps at moralizing the culture of absolutism that was the essence of opera seria from its beginnings. As the upper crust transferred its taste for Carnival jousts to indoor theater, its founders were also forging a feminine symbolic repertory centered on the figure

13. Chartier explains how the archetypal early modern dedication ascribes authorship to its dedicatee much as God is deemed virtual creator of a consecrated church (*Forms and Meanings*, chap. 2).

14. "Nobilissime Dame. / Questo dramma giocoso, che allo splendore delle vostre famiglie vile sembrerebbe e da nulla, possa tra la grata illusione delle vostre scene nobil dono divenire. Tanto può la vostra presenza, ed il vostro favore. Quella porge lusinga di questo. L'una e l'altro sperano incessante, mentre col più profondo rispetto si protestano / di voi Nobilissime Dame / Perugia 31. Luglio 1808" (*Carolina e Filandro dramma giocoso . . . Dedicato al merito sublime delle nobilissimi dame di detta città in Perugia dai Torchi della Società colle dovute licenze*, 3–4). Carolina was played by a woman, as allowed on papal stages by this time.

15. Pascucci, *La nobile accademia del Pavone*, 4–5; and Guardabassi, *Appunti storici*, 5.

16. For Pascucci's nineteenth-century evidence, see *La nobile accademia del Pavone*, 19; see also chap. 7 above.

of Juno—divine protector of women and Perugia's civic deity—shown on the theater's curtain with Turrena admiring her triumph. Juno was also implicated in the theater's main emblem, the beautiful peacock (*pavone*), which had been sacrificed to her by the ancients (and which, according to Serafino Siepi, had had an ancient Perugian temple erected in its honor at a site not far from the theater). Pascucci even makes the plausible proposal that as emblems of rank and glory, peacocks specifically suggested by association with Juno a gallant sacrifice of male vanity to Perugia's women.[17]

The elision of moral rectitude with female patronage was less pointed in the renaming of the Teatro Alibert as the Teatro delle Dame in 1725, yet there too the founding rationale of the new public theater had originally been argued to the pope precisely on moral grounds.[18] Like many other projects across Europe that moralized and institutionalized public meeting places outside the court, both of these created new spaces and instruments for debate and entertainment for publics that were both aristocratic and, increasingly in the second half of the eighteenth century, middle class. Hence the proliferation of moral weeklies and moral tracts, ladies' journals, novels, and bourgeois plays, and in the realm of music, accompanied keyboard sonatas for violin or flute, variation sets, rondòs, accompanied songs, "canzonets," sonatinas, and four-hand pieces, all of which targeted a predominantly middle-class audience. And hence too the spiraling anxieties about a public female presence and female roles at the very time when bourgeois ideals were being set more firmly in place.

CONVERSATIONS AND "SEMIUOMINI"

In 1771, the architect Francesco Milizia visualized the society of the bourgeois theater as inhabiting a vast human well, its high vertical walls lined with crowded cells and undergirded by a rowdy threshing floor.

> Here is a great shaft whose threshing-floor is lined with the people. One of them chitchats, another turns his head around, one reads, another yawns, and there's even one who's asleep. From top to bottom its outline is largely riddled with little cells and ensconced in each one is at least one woman surrounded by a buzzing of men, all armed with telescopes, which serve them like a revolving door to leap from cell to cell, chatting, eating, sipping drinks, and playing games. And the opera, the great opera, where is it?[19]

17. Siepi, *Descrizione topologico-istorica;* Pascucci, *La nobile accademia del Pavone,* 8–9 and 9 n. 1.

18. See de Angelis, *Il Teatro Alibert o delle Dame,* chap. 1, and on the renaming of the theater in 1725 as delle Dame, p. 17. Both the first and second proposals for the theater made by Giacomo Alibert were opposed on moral grounds by Pope Innocent XII (1615–1700), who claimed it would be too near the Piazza di Spagna (cf. the topographical image in tavola 1, near p. 16), where lots of hotels and foreigners were located. Giacomo's son, Antonio, evidently simply opened the theater "cavallerescamente," chivalrously (12).

19. "Ecco un vastissimo pozzo, la cui aia è rigata di gente; chi discorre, chi gira il capo in qua e in là, chi legge, chi sbaviglia, e v'è anche chi dorme. Il contorno è in gran parte da fondo in cima

For Milizia the huge public theaters of Italy promoted an erotic scopophila that was deleterious to social mores and proper relations between the sexes. Most probably it was not the throngs of mistresses and prostitutes that rankled, however—the latter often banned but nevertheless ubiquitous in Italian theaters[20]—but the habits of average society women and their beaus.

Milizia's words presage the growing sense of a disconnect between opera as social event and opera as message that was apparent throughout much of the eighteenth century but was worsening in his time. The lady praised in dedications, product of an old social order, had stepped into a modern world where her presence was loaded with new meanings and, for some, was all too real. Though women represented on the opera seria stage were mostly young and mostly subject to the social and political vicissitudes of male characters, women in the real arena of public life, theatrical and non, were too prominent for the liking of many contemporaries. Most disquieting, and vulnerable to attack, was their participation in *conversazioni*, gatherings in salons and elsewhere that freely mixed the sexes—called *veglie* when held in the evening, and (more commonly) *veglioni* when part of large festivities at the theater. These "conversations" facilitated bonds between males and females who were unrelated by blood or marriage. For their detractors, they were menaces to the social order because they threatened to erode ties between family members and prevent new affinities from developing between properly allied families and, relatedly, because they threatened to loosen boundaries between classes.[21] Even though *conversazioni* were not of the theater in sensu stricto, the whole category of *veglie*, *veglioni*, and *conversazioni* was assimilated to theatrical events; and theater, especially musical theater—though it could enclose and control action, and in this way guard public morals—could be viewed as the most noxious locus of *conversazioni*.

---

tutto bucato di cellette, e in ciascuna è annicchiata almeno una donna circondata da un ronzio d'uomini armati tutti di telescopi, che servono loro come di bussola per saltare da cella in cella, cicalando, mangiando, sorbendo, giuocando. E l'opera, la grand'opera dov'è?" (Milizia, *Trattato completo*, 39–40). The treatise was suppressed by the Roman censors two and a half weeks after its initial publication and republished anonymously as *Il teatro* in 1773. The Baron von Pöllnitz similarly used the metaphor of the chicken coop to describe the Teatro delle Dame: "La Salle en est excessivement grande, ce qui fait que les voix s'y perdent. Il y a sept rangs de Loges qui sont fort basses & petites, ce qui donne un air de Poulailler à la Salle." [The hall is excessively large, which makes the voices get lost. There are seven tiers of boxes, which are very cramped and small and give the hall the feel of a chicken coop (letter from Rome, March 10, 1731; von Pöllnitz, *Lettres*, 241).] De Angelis, *Il Teatro Alibert o delle Dame*, 18, explains why he might have seen seven tiers.

20. Like other "women of ill repute," prostitutes were legally not allowed to attend Roman theaters under pain of the whip, and those who took them there were threatened with the galleys, though by all accounts Roman, like Venetian, theaters were heavily populated by prostitutes and their clients (see chap. 4 above).

21. See Guerci, *La discussione sulla donna*, chap. 3, in particular on Clemente Biondi's *poemetto* of 1778, which talks about how formalities gradually lessen over the course of *conversazioni* as friendships multiply, ties tighten, neglected relatives are replaced with friends, and class divisions break down (91–93). Guerci notes that when the adjective *moderna* was added to the word *conversazione*, it meant a conversation between a lady and her cicisbeo, on which rivers of ink were spilled (95).

* * *

Nobody could have distilled better than Casanova the coded parley that made music and theater touchstones of passions and public encounters between the sexes. In a famous anecdote from about 1756 from *Histoire de ma vie*, volume 3, the author brings to the opera house in Parma his newest mistress, an elegant Frenchwoman named Henriette, who has just shed a male disguise in the course of her mysterious flight from an unwanted marriage. Casanova proposes that they take a box at the theater. She resists, fearing they will be "talked about" if they sit there day after day, but Casanova, never daunted by a challenge, sweet-talks her into it with the suggestive proposal that though he prefers the "conversations" in their private room "to all the music in the universe," they will surely get themselves "talked about" more by not going to the opera than by going.

Only part of Henriette's fear is being seen publicly with her lover. The other part is hearing music together in public, with its risk of exposing their passions to public view. Once there she trains her eyes steadily on the stage and only thus manages to deflect the looks of curious admirers and succeed in hiding her feelings. For that same reason, she begs off an invitation to hear two of the singers deliver their arias in a private drawing room shortly after the season ends. Music is dangerously revealing, as Casanova admits in attempting to change her mind: "If you knew what joy I feel when I see you ravished, as if in ecstasy, when you hear some beautiful piece of music!"[22] Indeed, only the next evening, in that very room among various protagonists from the opera house, she becomes the instrument of their disclosure when suddenly she places a cello between her knees (no less) and gives a performance so rapturous that her lover has to leave to hide his tears.[23]

For the exchange of such currencies, the privacy of the bedchamber is useless. It is precisely in public that Casanova wants to behold her passion—indeed in a context marked by exaggerated courtliness[24]—but also from the public that

22. Casanova, *History of My Life* 3:60. "Si tu savais quelle joie je ressens quand je te vois ravie et comme en extase lorsque tu entends quelque beau morceau de musique!" (*Histoire de ma vie* 3:59). In fact, she has her own copies of arias from the opera for truly private use, commissioned for her by Casanova, who later also buys her a cello.

23. "[W]hat was not my state when I heard her play *a solo*, and when after the first movement the applause almost deafened the orchestra? The transition from fear to a satisfaction as excessive as it was unexpected produced such a paroxysm in me as the most violent fever could not do at its height. The applause had not the slightest effect on Henriette, at least visibly. . . . I vanished to go and weep in the garden, where no one could see me" (Casanova, *History of My Life* 3:62). [Mais que devins-je quand je l'ai entendue jouer l'*a solo*, et lorsque après le premier morceau les claquements des mains avaient fait devenir presque sourd l'orchestre? Le passage de la crainte à une exubérance de contentement inattendu me causa un paroxysme, dont la plus forte fièvre n'aurait pas pu, dans son rédoublement me causer le pareil. Cet applaudissement ne fit à Henriette la moindre sensation du moins en apparence. . . . (J)'ai disparu pour aller pleurer dans le jardin, où personne ne pouvait me voir (*Histoire de ma vie* 3:61).]

24. In the wake of an importunate and unwanted invitation to him and Henriette, he comments, "[S]ince all the guests were seasoned courtiers, the breach of etiquette did not prevent them from

he has to hide. Paradoxically, public spectacle ignites a longed-for transport of emotion, even as it mobilizes a need for privacy that has to be managed against the attractions and hazards of public life. At the center of this ambiguity stands the woman—in this instance a woman who operates deftly in society, with a nimble tongue, elegant manners, and a muscular intellect, capable of colloquial yet trenchant disquisitions on such philosophical themes as the relationship of temporality and happiness—in short, a woman eminently suited to public life but also endangered by it. How poignant, then, that Casanova the libertine, after their brush with an importunate host whose overtures threaten to expose them, never again writes them into a public space except when they are masked; that he has Henriette refuse even the visit of the eminent minister Guillaume du Tillot (whose attentions she believes will mark her as an adventuress); and that he confines them thereafter to increasingly private, sexual scenes until Henriette's family arrives and whisks her away.

Music is perilous, and opera above all. Not only does it promote congress between the sexes, it brings erotic desire to the surface, always threatening to exceed its referent of signification through offers of pure pleasure.

* * *

Characteristically, Casanova's story is part romp and part moral tale, bound up in this instance with the eighteenth-century critique of *conversazioni* and the larger anxiety involving women in theaters and other public spaces. The wider context for this anxiety rested in the gendering of authority in early modern Italy, which had been largely male in the seventeenth century but was at least somewhat less so in the eighteenth. Rulers were still male except by default, and when not (as when two successive duchesses headed regencies in settecento Piedmont) they could face substantial opposition. Oligarchies were always all male and the church city of Rome was the most resolutely patriarchal of all. Yet in various places, patriarchal views of kinship (agnatic) had to yield to views nested in the extended family (cognatic), which had largely originated in the sixteenth century.[25] Where patriarchy presumed a vertical chain of fathers and sons that pulled patrimony and rank though the male line, cognatic modalities operated in horizontal networks of cognates, affines, and specifically women, networks that favored strong familial ties created by marital exchanges of women and wealth. Historians have begun to shown that settecento women staked stronger claims to individual property rights, at least in some city-states, than they had done previously, and that these claims subverted models of male patriliny as women contributed property to their daughters' dowries in gestures of female

paying Henriette all the honors of the gathering" (Casanova, *History of My Life* 3:61). [(C)omme tous les convives avaient le grand usage de la cour ce manque d'étiquette n'empêcha pas qu'on ne fit à Henriette tous les honneurs d'assemblée" (*Histoire de ma vie* 3:60).]

25. Pomata, "Family and Gender"; Kertzer and Saller, *The Family in Italy;* and C. Casanova, *La famiglia italiana.* Cf. Desan, *The Family on Trial,* and Kertzer and Barbagli, *Family Life.*

property devolution. They have also shown how women were gradually able to establish greater senses of selfhood through such acts as personalizing their wills, demanding marital separations, and refusing conventual celibacy.[26] Arguably patterns of the kind even surface (alongside dominant patrilineal ones) in some of Metastasio's characters: Didone, who refuses to be abstracted as a propertied good, declaring her person inalienable from her kingdom; and Cleonice, who, tentatively at least, defines her personhood by struggling with her intense desire for a consort she believes (mistakenly, it turns out) to come from outside the prescriptions of patriarchy.

Elsewhere I have written about how anxieties over women's status accompanied an early modern crisis in marriage, whose public representation in the opera house was effectively rent from its lived reality. Wives and other women moved with relative freedom in theaters and salons, even though in most cases marriages were still arranged by parents whose daughters typically knew little of men, marriage, or future mates. The marriage market had been depressed in Italy from the late sixteenth century through the seventeenth, with too little capital available for marriage, many women becoming nuns, many men not marrying, and many young wives widowed with no chance of remarriage. In the eighteenth century the marriage market was starting to recuperate,[27] but financial expedients still largely dictated choices of husbands, who in turn continued to maintain mistresses at the same time as wives kept up social appearances on promenades, in carriage rides, at the theater, and in daily visits to church, where they still played their role as vessels of virtue by upholding religious practices for aristocratic society as a whole.

The eighteenth century also saw the contradictions of married life exploit a compensatory institution that provided aristocratic wives with surrogate male companions, commonly known as "cicisbei." The precise historical status of cicisbei is ambiguous, though they evidently fulfilled the needs of noble wives for company, intimacy, and above all public partnership, or perhaps more accurately the needs of society to envision them in that role.[28] Married or single and

26. See Chojnacki, *Women and Men in Renaissance Venice;* Ago, "Oltre la dote," 164–82; Cavallo, "What Did Women Transmit?" 38–53; and Chabot and Calvi, *Le richezze delle donne.* In a place such as Florence, dowry and inheritance laws were extremely unfavorable to women (see Calvi, *Il contratto morale*).

27. Schulte van Kessel, "Virgins and Mothers," 132–66, esp. 150.

28. What follows relies preliminarily on late-nineteenth- and early-twentieth-century Italian chroniclers who made very reliable collations of primary sources, though with conclusions that should be read with skepticism: Neri, *Costumanze e sollazzi,* 117–216; Marenduzzo, "I cicisbei," 271–82; Merlato, *Mariti e cavalier serventi;* Salza, "I cicisbei," 184–251; Natali, *Idee, costumi, uomini,* 133–44; and especially Valmaggi, *I cicisbei.* For more recent analyses, see Barbagli, *Sotto lo stesso tetto,* 360–65; Guerci, *La discussione sulla donna,* 89–140; and especially two studies by Bizzocchi, "Cicisbei," 63–90 (translation forthcoming in Findlen et al., *Italy's Eighteenth Century*), and "Parini, Goldoni e i cicisbei," 177–85. Bizzocchi argues provocatively that the practice was not institutionalized in formal contracts, as often suggested, hence is rarely amenable to research in legal archives. A polemical passage by Anastasio Furno says "cicisbeato" usually means a man is "ammogliato"

usually drawn from the noble class, cicisbei appear in some instances to have been chosen by common accord between husband and wife. Whether under contract (as often claimed) or not (probably the usual case), the cicisbeo clearly had an informal pact often involving a long-term and other times an ad hoc or short-term relationship with a single married woman. In the first instance, he took part in numerous activities that presumably had been reserved for a woman's spouse in previous centuries: taking her on outings to public theaters and cafes; attending morning toilet when she was dressed and groomed by her maids and thence to church; and helping to serve her at mealtimes.[29] The fashion for nonspousal escort was so institutionalized that some women complained they were forced to endure the cicisbeo over the company of husbands they preferred. Yet as Charles de Brosses remarked, "it would have been a kind of dishonor had one not been publicly ascribed to her."[30]

Not surprisingly, under the eagle eyes of the painter Pietro Longhi and the playwright Carlo Goldoni (fig. 8.2), cicisbei were parodied as languorous, toadying fops. The practice never met with complete acceptance, even in parts of Italy where it proliferated, though a partial endorsement seems to have had a brief life in moralist literature of the mid-eighteenth century, peaking in a 1741 apologia by the Neapolitan Paolo Mattia Doria and then followed by mounting resistance and renewed invective as the century wore on.[31] Among early touchstones of this evolution were the assertions made by Carlo Maria Maggi in his 1687 "Ritiramenti per le dame" that the practice (then novel) was a sin against God, or at minimum an invitation to sin, and impeded women's religious work, and the less sweeping critique by Giandomenico Barile in his *Moderne conversazioni giudicate nel tribunale della coscienza* (Rome, 1716), which argued that exchanges between women and their cicisbei did not need to be hidden as evil or scandalous when they took place between persons of noble birth or noble habits.[32] Within a short time after Barile, the institution began to be character-

(coupled) with a woman who is not a man's "consorte," or denotes a youth with a lady or married noblewoman, adding that the word shrewdly avoids the vocabulary of love in favor of that of courtship (e.g., "di corteggi, di servitù, di attenzione, di stima") and noting that the men in question all have specious epithets like "serventi, favoriti, galanti, o cicisbei." Costantini adds "zerbini" (see Guerci, *La discussione sulla donna,* 96).

29. Parini, "Il meriggio," vv. 39–49, "Il vespro," vv. 270–83, in parts 2 and 3, respectively, of Caretti, *Il giorno.* Compare the "dichiarazione" series of Pietro Longhi, reproduced in Pignatti, *L'opera completa di Pietro Longhi,* nos. 281–84, and figure 8.2, an engraving by Luigi Ponelato of a cicisbeo bowing to his lady. Longhi, who specialized in private settings, evidently never painted a cicisbeo at an opera house.

30. Barbagli, *Sotto lo stesso tetto,* 363, 364. De Brosses reported having been told by the Venetian ambassador that only about fifty of those he knew of slept with their "wives" (Salza, "I cicisbei," 189), but doubtless he revealed more about what he believed he knew, or wanted people to believe he knew, or what other people wanted to believe or say, than about what actually happened.

31. Valmaggi, *I cicisbei,* 1–44.

32. Maggi, *Trattenimenti,* no. 11, added to *Ritiramenti per le dame* by the French Jesuit François Guilloré, which Maggi translated into Italian and published in 1687 (see Valmaggi, *I cicisbei,* 7–8).

FIG. 8.2. Luigi Ponelato, Cicisbeo bowing to his lady. Engraving from volume 3 of *Commedie buffe in prosa del sig. Carlo Goldoni* (Venice: Antonio Zatta & figli, 1790), volume 13 of *Opere teatrali del sig. avvocato Carlo Goldoni veneziano: Con rami allusive* (Venice: Antonio Zatta & figli, 1788–1795). By permission of the Casa Goldoni, Biblioteca, Venice.

ized as "noble servitude" and the cicisbeo as an honored escort.[33] Doria's *Dialogo* justified the practice by situating the cicisbeo at the endpoint of a quasi-feudal tradition, arguing that courtly manners were preferable to the old feudal modes of so-called honor—the "barbarous and dissolute" way of living previously common in Italy, which valued duels, violence, and abuses of various kinds that Doria wrote were more suited to bandits than men of virtue.[34]

Similar views were expressed by the anonymous author of *Alcune conversazioni* (1711), an extremist in the Madre di Dio order who bristled that the world only pretended the cicisbeo was a "noble servant." For Barile's *Moderne conversazioni*, see Valmaggi, *I cicisbei*, 10–11.

33. See, e.g., Valmaggi, *I cicisbei*, 11, on Costantino Roncaglia's *Moderne conversazioni volgarmente dette dei cicisbei* of 1720.

34. The full title reads *Dialogo nel quale esaminandosi la cagione per la quale le donne danzando non si stancano mai, si fa il ritratto d'un Petit Maître italiano affrettato laudatore delle massime, e dei costumi dei Petits Maîtres oltramontani e cicisbei*, vol. 2, part 1, of *Lettere e ragionamenti vari*, 331ff.

Part of the agenda of Doria and likeminded others was to deny charges linking escorts to sex and to defend the practice by aligning it with models of Platonic love.[35] In this way they played on sentimental nostalgia for the dying tradition of chivalric service linked to an old feudal world, even as they reproposed the cicisbeo on new terrain: not the hilltops and castles of the lord's estate but the salon, church, and theater of the city; and not the firm ground of masculine valor but the precarious one of servility in stockings and lace.[36] But others turned such defenses on their head, like Joseph Baretti, who detailed the cicisbeo's elaborate rituals of servitude at daily churchgoing to show how extravagantly—and laughably—he shadowed and foreshadowed his lady's every move. Arriving for morning services at ten or eleven, Baretti wrote, the cicisbeo ushered his lady through the church portal, preceding her so as to raise the curtain at the entrance door. He bathed his finger in the holy water and came to place it on her, to which she responded with a little bow. If the church had no seats, one of the domestics who followed behind presented them to the woman and her cicisbeo. After mass, she would stay seated for several moments, then genuflect, make the sign of the cross, recite a short prayer, and give the book from which she had read to a domestic or to the cicisbeo. She would then take her fan, rise, make the sign of the cross again, bow to the main altar and exit, preceded by her cicisbeo, who would again present her with holy water, raise the curtain to exit, and extend a hand for the return home.

Though many in fashionable circles considered it important that husbands *not* be seen publicly performing the chivalric tasks of the escort and at the same time essential that women not be seen in public without one[37]—the protagonist of Goldoni's *La dama prudente,* for example, has several male companions so as not to be left stranded when her "cavalier di fiducia" cannot be at her side—these extreme avatars of servitude could not fail to be problematically aligned with the old world of courtly etiquette. What was chivalry for an older age was feminine servitude for the new one.[38] Like the dedication *alle dame,* this contradictory practice became the lockstep of an aristocracy trying keep pace with a modernizing public sphere while still preserving its old ways. Yet cicisbei eventually became assimilated to the sex they served in ways that were discomfiting later in the century, as stigmas became ever more firmly attached to their job of relieving husbands of marital chores. Eventually, the cicisbeo who adorned a woman and subjugated himself to her became a bird in flight, fatuous, vain, so coquettish as to be barely male. By the later part of the century he was a figure

35. Valmaggi, *I cicisbei,* 11–12. Still more progressive was Venetian lawyer Antonio Costantini, who published letters on the subject in 1751–56 (see 12–13).

36. Cited in ibid., 69.

37. See Merlato, *Mariti,* esp. chaps. 2–4, and Valmaggi, *I cicisbei,* 65.

38. The anonymous author of the "Reflessioni filosofiche e politiche sul genio e carattere de' cavalieri detti serventi" portrayed the cicisbeo as "the shade of the body of the woman served, whom he never leaves wherever he goes" (Valmaggi, *I cicisbei,* 45–46 and 46 n. 1).

of sexual instability, uncertain in deed and kind, and thus an easy target of moralists' barbs, and that just when a dimorphic model of sexuality was coming into place.[39]

Most visibly, the cicisbeo flaunted his ambiguity in the spectacle that took place at the theater each evening in his lady's family box. One moralist compared his performance to a "national disease" in which all Italy had become the "stage or theater of a bordello."[40] For his co-conspirators, of course, performances were exactly what was wanted—extravagant displays of honor, feigned spousehood that surpassed the limitations of the real, compensations for absence through an exaggerated show of presence—but for his detractors, he was a corrupt proxy of the good husband, ruinous to the souls of women, a defiler of womanhood, wifedom, and motherhood. Wives under his sway were said to rebel against husbands and even lose their natural love for their own children. The cicisbeo turned into an icon of antiaristocratic discontent, attacked along with the vanities and masks of aristocratic women at a time when the aristocracy was particularly vulnerable.[41] More and more theater, especially opera, was hijacked into condemning the ills of the nobility. The irrepressibly polemical Calzabigi opposed a theater of strong actions and warm passions (which he approved) to one of cold-blooded pronouncements and artificial similes—what he glossed as "chiacchierine cicisbeatorie" (gallant chitchat).[42] Theater in this guise had been ravaged by the falsehoods of aristocratic dissimulation, of which the cicisbeo was a glaring example.

* * *

Shadowing the story of the cicisbeo in the eighteenth-century opera house is that of the castrato, who flourished with the festivity, marvels, and sexual continuities indigenous to the old order and suffered with the emergence of a new order founded in sensibility, moral rectitude, the conjugal family, and the dimorphic sexual regime that came in their wake. When castrati first took the stage in the seventeenth century, they were, as Roger Freitas has shown, seductive figures of idyllic, heroic youth. One seventeenth-century commentator even imagined them paradoxically as empowered by the "semen" of song.[43] During enlightenment times, criticisms of castrati and practices of castration were mounting, but

39. See Herdt, *Third Sex, Third Gender.*

40. Valmaggi, *I cicisbei,* 21.

41. Salza makes recourse to much contemporaneous literature on the vanity of women ("I cicisbei," 235ff.). Moore explains the relationship between masking and cicisbeismo in *A View of Society* 1:240–48.

42. From Calzabigi's outrageous attack on Metastasian opera in his *Risposta . . . di . . . Don Santigliano di Gilblas* of 1790, in Calzabigi, *Scritti teatrali* 2:360–550; cf. Marenduzzo, "I cicisbei," 282.

43. See Freitas, "Sex without Sex," and especially "The Eroticism of Emasculation." It was the Perugian historian Giovanni Andrea Angelini-Bontempi, in his *Historia musica* of 1695, who paradoxically reascribed the generative power of uncastrated men to the vocal powers of the nongenera-

initially at least most Italians still accommodated them easily to the "natural" paradigms of singing—witness Vincenzio Martinelli's blithe explanation to an English count in 1758:

> Around age twelve or thirteen, at the limits of puberty when the tree has become capable of producing fruit, the voices [of boys] become soprano and more often a tolerable if not perfect contralto, especially in Italy; and by means of castration the soprano or contralto is perpetuated into old age, which is the reason castrati were invented. Then comes that perfect puberty, between fifteen and eighteen years of age, when the voice is at its loveliest green, and the lungs are acquiring ever greater force, until age twenty-five when the lungs finish growing and all the organs attain their maturity. And the man has reached his physical perfection and can maintain his vigor thus until his forties.[44]

Martinelli's infatuation, tinged with erotic attraction, was not universally shared. In the same period, when castrati were still in their theatrical heyday, their numbers began to plummet. Where Martinelli saw in them an evolution from beauty and growth to maturity and finally physical perfection, others during the same time, like the Christian moralist Giovanni Antonio Bianchi (alias Lauriso Tragiense, his Arcadian nom de plume), saw only softness, depravity, effeminacy, and—that most loaded of terms—luxury. Bianchi feared that because the castrato was a sexual hybrid, he would drift away from civilized norms. For him the term "musico" ought to have been reserved for real valiant men, not those "semi-male singers with female voices" who were nothing but bad manglers of their art. He did concede that there were good exemplars of them in the church, but in the theater they were all tyrants who made composers serve the singers' vanity and who defied every rational rule of music and words.[45]

---

tive castrati. Apropos, see Finucci, *The Manly Masquerade*, chap. 6, and Feldman, "Strange Births and Surprising Kin."

44. "Verso i dodici o tredici anni su i confini della pubertà, quando l'albero è ridotto capace di produr frutto, specialmente in Italia, le voci vanno al soprano, e le più a un contralto tolerabile se non perfetto, e per mezzo della castrazione si perpetua sino alla vecchiezza il soprano o contralto, che è il fine per cui furono inventati i castrati. Ecco la perfetta pubertà, tra i quindici e i diciott'anni, quando la voce è nel suo più bel verde, quindi vanno i polmoni sempre acquistando maggior forza, fino che venuti i venticinque anni che vale a dire finito di crescere, e condotti tutti gli organi alla loro maturità, l'uomo è giunto alla sua perfezione corporale, e così può mantenersi in vigore sino presso i quaranta" (Martinelli, *Lettere familiari*, 378–79).

45. "[A]vendo adoperato nelle azioni serie una specie di verso lirico, e molle, e tutto lontano dalla gravità che ricerca il verso tragico, ministrarono a poco a poco occasione a quelle strofette anacreontiche di versi corti, le quali si chiamano arie: onde acciocché queste fossero leggiadramente cantate furono introdotte nel palco le cantatrici, e poi i cantori semiuomini di voci femminili, i quali impropriissimamente si dicono musici, non convenendo questo nome se non a quei valenti uomini i quali nell'arte difficilissima della musica, e delle armoniche proporzioni fondate sulle geometriche periti sono. Costoro . . . altro non sono che cattivi esecutori d'un'arte la quale essi storpiano in grazia della loro voce, dei loro sconcertati passaggi, dei loro trilli, dei loro ingorgiamenti, e dei loro voli inconditi sulle corde acutissime. Ne io perciò parlo di tutti i cantori, che sogliono musici chiamarsi:

Even so broad-minded a friend to castrati as Padre Martini expressed pity in 1749 to his friend Girolamo Chiti for the alto castrato Giuseppe Poma because of the abjection of his condition and especially because he had had to play female roles.[46] Martini's comment was not launched against castration as something barbaric that ran counter to nature or produced an artificial man. It conveyed, rather, the uncomfortable sense that the castrato disrupted the proper order of things sought out by enlightened perceptual faculties on behalf of reason and sense and affirmed in a moral realm. The castrato made impossible an accord in the discernment of objects and sensations, and hence made impossible an illusion of socially harmonious parts. Furthermore, his performance forced him to humiliate himself as the objective focus of such disaccord in a way that cut to the core of his subjective being.[47]

REGARDING THE SENSES: CONTINUITY, ACCORDANCE, TRUTH

The objections of Bianchi and Martini were commonplaces in the generations that succeeded them, which ran sensist and moralist objections in a single stream. The castrato satirized by Parini was a grotesque distention of human form, an "elefante canoro" (a singing elephant), and the poet attacked his parents as breeders of bad morals whose son would end up forgetting about them.[48] Sensist reformers who talked a Gluckian line in the 1770s and 1780s, like Antonio Planelli (1772), were de facto against castrati on grounds that they represented a disordering of nature's parts threatening to the moral order.[49] In his myth of the castrato's origins, published in 1777, the raffish Ange Goudar nipped at these moral nodes, personifying the castrato as a charming Neapolitan night-

imperciocché molti e molti sono di questi ben periti nell'arte, e specialmente quelli di Roma destinati alle sacre funzioni, e del Palazzo Apostolico e delle venerande basiliche, i quali . . . modestissimi sono. . . . Ma parlo di una grande parte di quelli che cantano nel teatro, ai quali è necessario che sia soggetto il compositore della musica, acciocché possano far pompa della loro voce, e che stenda le parole dell'aria non in quelle note che sono richieste dal sentimento delle parole, ma in quelle che ad essi piacciono per far spiccare il loro canto ben contrario sovente a quello che il dramma richiede" (Bianchi, *De i vizi*, 93–94). The treatise appeared in an imposing quarto format, some 345 pages long, with an extensive index, numerous footnotes and illustrative plates, and a showy rubricated title page.

46. "Oggi è stato a trovarmi il Signor Poma ritornato ieri sera da Roma, che non ha avuto nemmeno l'attenzione di venire ad usarle un atto di rispetto, siccome io l'avevo pregato; ma bisognarà compatirlo per esser Castrato, e molto più perche egli hà recitato da Donna" (letter to Chiti, March 1, 1749, I-Bc, I.12.65; no. 1443 in Schnoebelen, *Padre Martini's Letters*).

47. One somewhat rare epicure from the time was the Russian prince Belosel'skii-Belozerskii, who in 1778 rehearsed the usual distaste for castration and castrati but said the voice couldn't be matched by women's (*De la musique en Italie*, 38).

48. The quotation is from Parini's "La musica," in *Il giorno*, 331–37. Cf. Rosselli, "The Castrati," 143–79, 174 n. 118.

49. As Degrada points out in his edition of *L'opera in musica*, Planelli was among the first pro-Gluckian voices in Naples but worked in the abstract, without ties to any specific reform movement.

ingale (*rossignol*) who heads a flock of warbling feathered friends, among whom the cuckoo is singled out for causing marital troubles whenever he served as a singing teacher to French ladies.[50] And by revolutionary times, castrati were unambiguously collapsed with the effeminacies and luxuries of the aristocracy. Andrea Chegai notes, for instance, that in 1797 the ban put on "infamous castrati (attori evirati ed infame) by the provisional "democratic" government of Brescia declared that "the corruption of public government" depended "above all on the present system of theater," which was worsened by the "effeminate manners of the vile actors who sing [operas], and all those monstrosities that . . . weaken the common sense of the people and cause them to lose their natural energy (le maniere effeminate dei vili istrioni che li cantano, e per tutte quelle mostruosità che . . . attentano al senso comune del popolo e ne fanno degenerare la naturale energia)."[51]

These various claims differed widely, but all presumed that castrati were immoral because discontinuous with nature, which required accordance of parts for the sake of perceptual and formal unity.[52] One of the most caustic attacks came from the Venetian "filarmonico" Innocenzio della Lena in his 1791 treatise *Dissertazione ragionata sul teatro moderno*.[53] Ostensibly his target was the inverisimilitude of opera seria, but in an Algarottian attempt to smooth all the sensory, bodily, and temporal aspects of opera into a unified field through the domination of poetic truth, the treatise broadsided the whole caste of castrati. "Yes, flee the stage where poetry is not the empress and dominatrix, owing to the ignorance and stupidity of actors who, far from being actors, are insensate machines, or poles, totally devoid of any action or expression adapted to manifest properly its sentiments."[54] Sixty pages thence, the prime example of the "insensate machine" is the castrato Luigi Marchesi (the same singer Perugians

50. Goudar, *Le brigandage*, 8.

51. Chegai, *L'esilio di Metastasio*, 108.

52. Planelli, like Algarotti and Milizia, was concerned with the problem of melodramatic unity because the canons of classicism saw great risk in music turning drama into a centrifugal force, spinning out "like so many rays from a circle" (see Sala di Felice, *Metastasio*, 31). The disputes between Arteaga and Manfredini over the castrato were part of an ongoing vituperative exchange, but nonetheless demonstrate that it was imperative for members of the intelligentsia in the 1770s and 1780s to condemn castration, for reasons we have seen. Arteaga charged Manfredini with having written about the "infame usanza dell'evirazione," simply because he had been attacked by one for his ignorance about singing (namely, Mancini) and so wanted to humiliate them all. Manfredini, whose brother was a castrato, protested on grounds he had never been an enemy of truth, reminding Arteaga that already in his *Regole armoniche* of 1775 he had denounced castration: "[E]sclamai contro l'infame usanza di mutilare gli uomini. Trovo dieci anni dopo, che l'Arteaga fa lo stesso, e si estende assai più di me nel declamare sopra un tale abuso ed oltraggio che si fa alla natura" (Manfredini, *Difesa della musica moderna*, 60).

53. Cf. the comments of Spreti, "Venezia, Carnevale 1791," 198–99.

54. "Si, fuggirsene certamente di là, ove la poesia non è imperante, e dominatrice per ignoranza, e pecoraggine degli attori, che non sono altrimenti attori, ma tante insensate macchine, o stolli, privi affatto d'azione, e d'espressione, adatta a manifestare i giusti sentimenti di quella" (della Lena, *Dissertazione ragionata*, 21).

had tried to hire ten years earlier). Marchesi was known for his good looks, unlike many castrati whose bodily proportions had been distorted as castration deprived them of androgen,[55] but della Lena still managed a graphic caricature that insisted on Marchesi's dissemblance of true nature:

> He is tall rather than short, but not excessively so, nor exactly unbecoming. His head is quite elongated and small in proportion to his chest, or the trunk on which it rests. The whole chest is proportioned enough—that is, the thorax and belly are well-formed and do not at all show that they are those of a mutilated man. The lower extremities, namely the haunches and legs, are quite long in proportion to the trunk; and their forms are well composed, pleasing, and not excessive. That which is otherwise quite rare in this race of people—in whom, owing to a deficiency of a life-sustaining active principle, solids are made inert and yield too much to the impulse of circulating liquids—is made more so, slowed down, and then gives rise to excessive fullness, nourishment, and corpulence, which the cellular tissue, being filled to excess, enlarges, deforming the whole body, especially the belly, haunches, and legs. Perhaps for that reason Marchesi is said to be handsome—not deformed like all the others, in other words, or at least not too deformed. *But nature will not give up her rights, which have extended where they ought not, and where ordinarily she does not in her other creatures.* For the upper extremities, namely the arms, are excessively long and overextended; and if Marchesi had actions and gestures matched to them, then gesture and action, which are the soul and life of every performance, would be only somewhat offended by them. Holding the arms down and raising them . . . makes the deformity stand out clearly to the eyes and makes the excessive length of the arms look just like those orangutans (macaque), or other like animals who form the numerous family of monkeys.[56]

55. The condition was hypogonadism, and the effects ranged from long limbs and excessive height to feminine breasts and bellies. See Melicow, "Castrati Singers," 744–64.

56. "Desso è alto di statura, piuttosto che basso, ma non eccedente, nè punto disdicevole. La testa è alquanto allungata, e picciola in proporzione del busto, o del tronco su cui posa. Tutto il busto è bastantemente proporzionato, cioè il torace ed il ventre, e ben formato, e non mostra al certo che sia d'un mutilo di parti. L'estremità inferiori, cioè le cosce, e le gambe, sono alquanto lunghe in proporzione del tronco; le forme di tali parti, sono ben composte, aggradevoli e nulla eccedenti. Ciò che è altresì ben raro in tal razza di gente, ove per difetto del principio attivo vivificante, i solidi si rendono inerti, e cedono di troppo all'impulso dei liquidi circolanti; s'estendono, si rallentano, e danno adito con ciò, alla soverchia pienezza, e nutrizione, alla pinguedine, che riempiendo ad eccesso il cellular tessuto, ingrandisce, e difforma il corpo tutto, specialmente il ventre, le cosce e le gambe. Perciò s'è forse detto bello Marchesi, cioè, non deforme come tutti gli altri, o almen poco deforme. Ma la natura non perde i suoi diriti, che ha ecceduto dove non doveva, e dove d'ordinario non eccede in altri suoi simili. Poichè l'estremità superiori, cioè le braccia, sono soverchiamente lunghe ed eccedenti, e se Marchesi avesse azione acconcia, e gesto, sarebbe perciò solo alquanto offeso il gesto, e l'azione che è l'anima e vita d'ogni spettacolo: tenendole abbassate, o alzandole, che non si può far di meno, di non alzare, ed abbassar le braccia, dall'avanzarsi tanto all'ingiù della coscia, ed all'insù del vertice, ne spicca agli occhi ben palese la deformità, e nell'eccedente lunghezza rassomigliano certamente le sue braccia, a quelle dell'Orang-Utang, del Maimone, o simiglianti altri animali, che

Notwithstanding the scientistic ploy, della Lena retains a clear debt to humoral theory—which opposed the superior humors of hot, dry males to the less vital humors of cold, wet females—and lamented the lack of vital heat required for motion in the solid matter that made up castrati. What else could one conclude, he sighed, when using comparative science to judge the castrato in a quest for "the truth"?[57] It was this, he claimed, that made them objects of indifference. "These fallen masts of truth and illusion are fatuous fires of sentiment, that, seen once, don't tempt people to see them a second time."[58]

Della Lena's charges all presupposed the usual demands enunciated by reformers from 1755 onward that all parts of an opera accord to form a united, continuous whole. Like many French and English writers, he asserted that motion, which corresponded to feeling, was necessary in order to move the heart.[59] Such a correspondence testified to truth, glossed as fidelity to nature made through proper imitation of the passions but also enhanced through continuities between words, sounds, decor, dance, and other sights, without which the passions could not be moved. Nor were these continuities only synchronic; they were also linear.

> Tragedy in verse, as it is the most sublime product of dramatic poetry and is represented in music, constitutes the lyric poem, that is, the opera par excellence, in which the subject is always grand, extremely moving, and disposed in the simplest manner; where all is action and action tending toward great effects; . . . and all then proceeds with the fullness of its forces to its happy unraveling, without obstacle and without interposing any breaks.[60]

---

formano la numerosa famiglia delle scimmie" (della Lena, *Dissertazione ragionata,* 84–85; emphasis in translation mine).

57. "Io amo, e stimo Marchesi, quant'ogni altro mio simile, ma dovendo fare un paragone d'eccesso di lunghezza nelle braccia, non posso trovarlo che nella natura, e nel confronto di quegli animali, che più eccedono nelle braccia, sebbene abbiano tante parti esteriori di simiglianza coll'uomo. Il confronto dei corpi coi corpi, e delle parti con le parti, è la scienza della verità" (ibid., 85; cf.Laqueur, *Making Sex;* the review of Laqueur by Park and Nye, "Destiny is Anatomy," 53–57; and Schieberger, *The Mind Has No Sex?* chap. 6).

58. "[Q]uesti cadenti appoggi della verità e dell'illusione, sono fuochi fatui del sentimento, che una sola volta veduti non invogliano poi di vederli la seconda. Son necessarie, ed utili le decorazioni, quando servono di abbigliamento, o di pompa alle rappresentazioni per compimento dell'illusione, eccitando però quelle il diletto; e la commozione nell'esatta imitazione degli affetti vari e delle passioni" (della Lena, *Dissertazione ragionata,* 7).

59. See, among other reformist commentary, Arteaga, *Le rivoluzioni* 1:406; Milizia, *Trattato completo,* chap. 8, 58–60 (on the actor); and Calzabigi, *Risposta* (mocking Metastasio's lack of verisimilitude). An important new statement on related French and English views appears in Thomas, *Aesthetics of Opera,* chaps. 6 and 7.

60. "Tragedia espressa in versi, ch' è la più sublime produzione della poesia drammatica, e rappresentata in musica, forma il poema lirico, cioè *l'opera per eccellenza;* dove il soggetto è sempre grande, toccantissimo, e disposto nella più semplice maniera; dove tutto è azione, ed azione tendente a grandi effetti . . . ; e tutto procedendo poi con la pienezza di sue forze al suo felice scioglimento, senza ostacolo, e senza frappore intermissione: e gli scioglimenti avvicendati si fanno poi

Practically all the desiderata of truth, passion, and unity were breached by Marchesi: his action contradicted poetic sentiments, his recitative was all disorder and "disconnection," his gestures more beastly than human. He sang intricate, convoluted ornaments, even at the very start of his arias, as we know from transcriptions by the Czech composer Vaclav Pichi of Marchesi's ornaments for an aria from Zingarelli's *Pirro* (Milan, 1792).[61] Anything but the man of the eighteenth-century enlightenment, he was "extravagant, Gothic, and grotesque"—seicentistic, in short, even medieval.[62] Worst, he was, in all senses, cold.

* * *

Swept away with the carnage of the castrato were a variety of musical and theatrical forms thought to oppose verisimilitude and veracity. Arias governed by what in chapter 2 I called the "frame of once-remove" were doomed to extinction because they broke up continuities by sectionalizing musical time; even through-composed dal segnos and sonata-like arias were guilty of this. Exempt were only two-tempo arias and ensemble pieces, understood to work against both closed and shorter forms such as cavatinas and marches. What ultimately became most viable were forms that could be incorporated into continuous scene complexes, as I discuss further in chapter 9. By a similar token, rectilinear theaters—rectangular, as opposed to horseshoe-shaped—when demolished or lost in fires, were routinely replaced with curvilinear ones that facilitated stageward viewing, and hence more continuous absorption in performances.[63] And ballets were variously refashioned over time to connect them thematically and aesthetically to the operas they interspliced. Opera/ballet links could be forged either through *balli analoghi,* which exploited mutual associations of ambience, plot, or character, or through the *terzo ballo analogo,* which extended the

sempre sotto l'occhio dello spettatore" (della Lena, *Dissertazione ragionata,* 17). The complex issue of how continuity in temporal forms relates to accordance of physical and formal parts and those in turn to truth has been intelligently confronted with respect to the development of operatic form in the late eighteenth and nineteenth centuries by Zoppelli, *L'opera come racconto.*

61. One version of these is given by Crutchfield, "Voices," 303–4.

62. "Niuno ve ne ha fra questi [arbitri e licenze nelle arie], che prenda più sfrenate licenze di Marchesi, e che nelle sue licenze si renda più stravagante, gotico e grottesco di lui, studiandosi di sminuzzolare la voce ove non è richiesto dal sentimento, di saltellar di nota in nota, di far gorgheggi, stravagantissimi cangiamenti, trilli, spezzamenti, rapidi voli, e di mai non rifinirla, e con ciò infiorando, infrascando, sfigurando ogni bellezza, e distruggendo con fatalissima offesa del sentimento la bella semplicità, che può sola imitare la natura. Imperoché è ben certo che i soverchi affinamenti dell'arte sì in musica, sì in canto sebben sorprendendo, mai mai non vanno, nè possono andare al cuore" (della Lena, *Dissertazione ragionata,* 93). Della Lena compares Marchesi to seventeenth-century poets like Achillini, who abused "di *traslati,* di *metafore,* e di *fantasia,* per imporre alla *fantasia,* e non allo spirito ed al cuore" (96) and to artists like Borromini and Tiepolo, charging that Marchesi could not move others because he himself was cold (96–97). To sing well, he insisted, the heart must be transported, agitated, moved. On France, cf. Thomas, *Aesthetics of Opera,* chap 6, "Heart Strings," for related matters.

63. The rebuilding of Perugia's Teatro Pavone was a case in point (see chap. 7 above).

opera's ending in a thematically related visual spectacle, with the added bonus of helping to keep spectators from leaving the theater early. But eventually ballets were made into continuous narratives, or interpolated along with choruses into extended scenic tableaux in the operas themselves.[64] Formally this was a direction already broached in the libretti of Verazi (ca. 1730–94) and his younger colleagues Giovanni de Gamerra (1743–1803), Gaetano Martinelli (flourished 1764–95), and Giovanni Ambrogio Migliavacca (1718–after 1787), who began to move action forward in a way that foreclosed the set number and made it difficult or impossible to applaud after arias. In addition to organizing their scenes in continuous complexes, their libretti challenged cast hierarchies, increased the numbers of ensembles, defied the traditional plot structures and the *lieto fine* of Metastasian opera, and slathered on numerous stage directions that guided staging with a more authorial hand.[65] Stage sets were given a new emotional presence, being pressed to obscure the boundaries of the stage through disappearing backdrops and side wings, which gave the illusion of continuous space and spontaneous irregularities.[66]

* * *

The new formal criteria were deployed to effect new dramaturgical precepts founded in authorial control. Della Lena saw it as imperative to discipline singers by forbidding them to alter in the slightest the composer's score and to en-

64. Notable was Gaetano Sertor and Francesco Bianchi's *La morte di Cesare* (Venice, 1788), and other Venetian operas of the 1790s (see McClymonds's "La morte di Semiramide," 285–92, and her "Alfieri and the Revitalization of Opera Seria," 227–31). On the later developments, see Chegai, *L'esilio di Metastasio*, chap. 4, and for the *terzo ballo analogo*, 167–69 and table 2 on 275. Chegai notes that the *terzo ballo analogo* was performed essentially in the second half century and in particular cities, especially Turin but also Parma and Naples. Rather than giving a *scenario* for the *terzo ballo analogo*, libretti typically give only a short indication of its occurrence, without noting any scene change. Chegai cites the example of *Cook, ossia gl'Inglesi a Othaiti* (Real Teatro del Fondo, Naples, summer 1785; libretto possibly by Calzabigi, music anonymous), which includes internal dances motivated by plot (106, 149, 168). The libretto's dedication to Ferdinando IV declares: "Italy . . . justly vaunts primacy above all other nations and is jealous of this superiority. . . . She hasn't yet wanted to adopt entirely from the French the use of choruses and ballets as part of the drama. Drawing always on the melodic and harmonious style of her national music, she would still have to exempt herself from this exacting practice regarding the sets, choruses, and ballets, which so enliven the plot and which, by varying the spectacle, increase in it the element of pleasurable surprise." [L'Italia . . . vanta a ragione il primato sopra tutte le altre nazioni . . . non ha voluto ancora adottare interamente dai francesi l'uso dei Cori, e dei balletti inerenti al Dramma; e pure dovrebbe, trattenendo sempre lo stile melodico, ed armonioso della musica nazionale, dispensarsi da questa rigorosa osservanza riguardo alle decorazioni, ai cori, ed ai balletti, che avvivano moltissimo l'Azione, e che variando lo spettacolo ne accrescono sempre la piacevole sorpresa.]

65. See McClymonds, "Verazi's Controversial *Drammi in Azioni*," 43–87; Gallarati, *Musica e maschera*, chap. 4; Chegai, *L'esilio di Metastasio*, chap. 2; Gronda, *La carriera di un librettista;* and Goldin, *La vera fenice*.

66. On stage sets see, most authoritatively, Viale Ferrero, "Stage and Set," *La scenografia del '700, Storia del Teatro Regio di Torino,* and *La scenografia della Scala;* and Mancini, *Scenografia italiana*.

sure in turn that the composer subjugate his own will to that of the poet, using natural, simple sentiments so that the music would be imprinted in the memory "and the heart . . . touched . . . in the most lively way."[67] Authors needed to wrest control from singers and deny them their follies of ornamentation and delivery, using a unitary voice to maintain illusion and thus move the spectator. They needed to make sure singers would not step into their former role as actors *in life* but stick to acting *about life*. Were singers to make open spectacle of themselves, they would break the new theatrical pact between doers and viewers, which was predicated on staying in character to sustain the fiction of the fallen wall.

To achieve this new spectatorial goal of continuous absorption—necessary to elicit the desired heightened emotions, ranging from awe to sympathy, sentimentality, and melancholy—a brand-new conception of affect was needed from the one that had ruled the dramma per musica up until about 1760–70. At midcentury even a man of the old regime like Martinelli could routinely criticize excessive ornamentation in arias ("zinfonie" and "cadenze") on grounds that it precluded a properly affective style, turning music into prose and making singers into automatons. His specific quarrel was with certain ostentatious castrati and their "blessed cadenzas in which [they] vomit up in one go the whole essence of their art."[68] Like women's panniers, the size of midcentury arias, often with eight or ten repetitions of a stanza (four or even five in each large A section) with no corresponding expansion of text size, had become so immense that their ability to express word meaning was evacuated. Only once challenges were posed to the very reign of the conventional da capo aria, always now variously modified, did new forms of dramaturgy and spectacle, and new functions for the passions, become truly possible.

Particularly problematic for commentators from Algarotti's time forward was the estrangement of music from words that had accompanied increased aria size.[69] Critics asked moreover how a single text could be subjected, in dif-

67. "L'oggetto principale della musica consiste in imprimere nella memoria più naturale, e più semplice, i sentimenti della poesia, affinché il cuore più vivamente ne sia toccato; ad ottenere sì giusto fine deve il maestro di musica star sempre in tutto senza mai discostarsene sottomesso al poeta e fedelmente seguirlo" (della Lena, *Dissertazione ragionata*, 92–93).

68. "[Quel]le benedette cadenze, nelle quali vomitano i musici talvolta tutto in un colpo l'intero capitale dell'arte loro" (Martinelli, *Lettere familiari*, 373, from a series of letters to the Count of Buckinghamshire, 353–82). Martinelli locates the origin of the problem at the time when the orchestra began "being silent" while the singer was singing, saving its main work for when the singer was quiet. He dates this from a time after the castrato and composer Francesco Antonio Mamiliano Pistocchi (1659–1726) was active and attributes its beginning to Carlo Francesco Pollarolo (1653–1723). Martinelli's position was similar to that of Metastasio and many others at the time.

69. Apropos, Tomlinson posits a Cartesian metaphysic underlying opera seria, which suggests for him an aporia between words and music from the earliest beginnings of opera (*Metaphysical Song*, chap. 3). In eighteenth-century critical discourse, the early Neapolitan layer of opera seria practiced by Leo, Vinci, and Pergolesi never became particularly suspect in this regard, even in the eyes of reformers like Algarotti, though his explicit advocacy was for a return to those text-setting norms

ferent settings by different hands, to a whole medley of different passions. And why a single character should be represented in one opera by five or six separate affects. To many, this state of affairs suggested that imitation of the passions as it had been codified and evolved was too generic. Jommelli, writing on November 14, 1769, on the eve of setting *Ezio* for the third time, despaired in a letter to his librettist, Gaetano Martinelli, at having to carve so many different thoughts out of the same words.[70] He was sick of all the text repetitions in arias and the squared-off metrical phrasing they demanded. In a plea that would have found sympathy with Planelli, he begged for a far more prosodic style—one that under present conditions he could manage musically only by scrambling and fragmenting texts.

> For pity's sake, my friend, for pity's sake. I sing, I sing, and repeat, and ask again: avoid the ordinary in everything, but above all stay away from the usual wearisome, arid rubric or meter of the little aria! Those eternal four lines per section in every aria, and always at the most, seven or eight syllables each, and then still worse, that further repetition of the same words in so small a number of lines, almost as if the poet had to buy them at the market and pay a high price for them (as, for example, in the beautiful arietta, or cavatina of that same Metastasio in *Nitteti*, "Povero cor tu palpiti—Ne a torto in questo dì—Tu palpiti così—Povero core." See what economy of words. The words of the first line make up solely and entirely the third and fourth. Beautiful, very beautiful to read at any rate, but not so suitable for setting to music. If the poet wants to sing this much, very little singing remains to the poor composer—and this always, always, not for just one opera, but for so many, many operas.[71]

---

of early-seventeenth-century court opera that Tomlinson associates with a Ficinian metaphysic of resemblance wherein words and music are bound in a cosmic sympathy.

70. "Oh Dio! Quando penso che ò da scrivere di nuovo quest'Opera, e che l'ò da scrivere di più per un tanto illuminato Sovrano, Conoscitore, che à tutte le altre Musiche mie fatte sull'istesse parole, mi vien la febbre. Io amo, venero, m'inginocchio avanti, adoro Metastasio, e tutte le sue Opere: ma vorrei che anche lui, adattandosi alla moda, ne facesse tante delle nuove, quando è il desiderio di tutto il Mondo di volerle. Poiché, quel dover cavare tanti pensieri diversi, non solo differenti da quelli fatti da se stesso, e più e più volte, ma anche da quelli di tanti, e tanti altri Compositori, sempre, sempre sull'istesse parole; è cosa da far girare la testa anche a chi l'avesse di bronzo" (in McClymonds, *Niccolò Jommelli*, 487–88; original in US-BEu).

71. "Per carità, Amico mio, per carità, canto, canto: e vi replico, e vi ripriego, tiratevi fuora dall'ordinario in tutto; ma sopratutto dalla solita seccaginosa, arida rubrica, o sia misura dell'Ariette. Quegli eterni 4 versetti per parte, in ogni Aria, e sempre per lo più di 7 o 8 piedi l'uno; e peggio poi, quel replicarci di più, in così picciol numero di versi, l'istesse parole, quasi dovesse il Poeta comprarle al Mercato, e pagarle a caro prezzo; /come sarebbe, per esempio, la bella Arietta, o sia Cavatina, dell'istesso Metastasio nella Nitetti, *Povero cor tu palpiti—Ne a torto in questo dì—Tu palpiti così—Povero core*. Vedete che economia di parole. Le sole parole del primo verso, compongono intieramente il 3o ed il 4o. Bella, per altro, bellissima per leggerla; ma non così comoda per metterla in Musica. Se tanto vuol cantare il Poeta; molto poco resta a cantare al povero Musico Compositore. / [E] questo sempre, sempre, non per un' Opera sola, ma per tante, e tante Opere" (McClymonds,

Summarizing objections of this kind in 1788, the "modernist" Vincenzio Manfredini—an almost inanely contentious composer-turned-journalist—complained that in modern Italian operas the same music could serve for a hundred different sentiments.[72] At odds with Arteaga, who thought music should be limited in the range of sentiments and images it imitated, Manfredini wanted to eliminate codified affects in favor of idiosyncratic, changeable ones that would utilize a range of expressions, theoretically without limits.

A crucial corollary of the shift toward prosodic, individualized lyricism was the elevation of the pathetic around 1770. Unlike the "aria d'affetto" or "aria patetica" of earlier decades, the new pathetic in opera was not to be bounded by the system of discrete affects that had dominated the opera seria stage for many decades.[73] Vincenzio Martinelli's "affective style" might refer to one of various possible topoi, each with its own passion, but for the Neapolitan Antonio Planelli writing in 1772, the pathetic was the generalized referent of an ideal operatic expressivity. Planelli meant for the pathetic to become a universal norm, the passion of passions.[74] The pathetic was literally everything that could arouse emotion. It was the contrast and complement of the "aesthetic," which included all the outer qualities that give pleasure through symmetries and proportions among parts, but it surpassed it because the pathetic was the ultimate end of opera and the very grain of its voice. Influenced like many Italians by Vico and especially Diderot, Planelli sought a form of musical tragedy that would please the senses while aiming at human feelings, moving the passions through a dynamic imitation of their most perfect objects. Not literal or pictorial, this kind of imitation was intended to be emotional and sensual—the texture of the voice, the quality of the gesture, the rhetoric of a speaking melody. Where the solution in ballet was Noverre and Angiolini's speaking gesture of pantomime, the solution in Planelli's opera was touching melody, making use of a modicum of notes, a limited ambitus, and a parlante style. To protect the fragile ecology of the pathetic, Planelli also advocated linear progress in opera instead of the abrupt transitions from recitative to aria of traditional opera seria—a progress from the passionate to the sublime, from a "genere sonabile" to a "genere cantabile" (from an instrumental genre to a singing genre), from the aesthetic to the pathetic.[75]

Niccolò Jommelli, 488–49; cf. chap. 7 above on arguments for prosodic verse, and Milizia, *Trattato completo,* 57).

72. Manfredini, *Difesa della musica moderna,* 98. Chegai cites a Roman reviewer of 1784, writing in the *Giornale delle belle arti,* who objects to the same poetic meters being used for different affects (*L'esilio di Metastasio,* 22).

73. Feldman, "Music and the Order of the Passions."

74. Planelli, *L'opera in musica,* part 1, chap. 3, §§iii and vi; part 2, chap. 2; part 3, chap. 1, §3; part 6, chap. 1, §2.

75. According to Degrada, the notion of a move from a "genere sonabile" to a "genere cantabile" was adapted from the Rousseauian Charles de Blainville's 1754 treatise *L'esprit de l'art musical, ou*

At issue was moving the listener, understood always as a moral and political goal that would result from "touching" the heart or from "moving" the passions.[76] Most probably the idea was both metaphorical and literal. Downing Thomas shows that in old-regime France, music was seen as curative precisely because sounds were understood to produce motion in the heart, as the physician Claude-Nicolas Le Cat argued as early as 1740. Eighteen years later, the doctor Joseph-Louis Roger claimed directly that musical sounds could cause motion in fluids and solids—an idea that evidently inflected della Lena's humoral charge against Marchesi—and could thus be used as moral therapy on the mind and nerves of listeners.[77] If these effects could be verified, they could also be instrumentalized. Medical therapies of the kind, centered on effects on the sensations of bodies, were aided in this end by moral philosophy, centered on the sensibility of minds and hearts.

Giorgio Mangini has explored how late in the century moral philosophy was manifest in Italian reform literature, which struggled over the relation of Metastasian models of passion and virtue to new models of pathos and morality.[78] The terms of the debate were set after Arteaga claimed in the mid-1780s that the pathetic mediated between moralism and hedonism, where moralism was a delimitation that protected the operatic stage from degeneracy while hedonism conceded it to public taste. On one side of the issue was the staunch Metastasian moralism of those like Saverio Mattei and on the other side later writers like Manfredini and Matteo Borsa. What bound them together were two elements in particular: the new sway toward the sentimental and the newer Humean views of sympathy as something foundational to social commerce—the latter the result of conjoining bodily and moral theory.[79] Of all musical theatrical forms, none was more powerful than opera for arousing sympathy, but engagement could not be sought in pictorial imitations designed to terrify or amuse specta-

---

Réflexions sur la musique et ses différentes parties (see Planelli, *Dell'opera in musica*, xv–xvi and n. 11 on xxvi).

76. Diderot speaks often of "touching the passions," a metaphor that reached the discourse of Italians like Jommelli, who wrote, "[I]o non so, ne posso farmi un'illusione che mi porti a quel grado di passione che mi è necessaria per fare una Musica espressiva; se l'anima mia da se stessa non n'è tocca, e non la sente." [I do not know how to, nor can I create in myself the illusion that carries me to the level of passion that I need to reach in order to write expressive music if my soul itself is not touched and does not feel it (in McClymonds, *Niccolò Jommelli*, 474–75).] A Florentine journalist of 1779, cited by Chegai, similarly speaks of "i movimenti delle passioni" (*L'esilio di Metastasio*, 20).

77. Thomas, *Aesthetics of Opera*, chap. 6.

78. Mangini, "Le passioni," 114–44. Mangini argues that in Arteaga's effort to balance his encomium of Metastasio with some up-to-date criticisms, he ended up charging Metastasio with having turned love into something "effeminate and soft." The charge keeps pace with efforts to excise the castrato from opera, as if both were too much situated in what Freitas, in "Sex without Sex" and "The Erotics of Emasculation," calls the "intermediate position" between male and female.

79. Mangini, "Le passioni," 128–29; Hume, *A Treatise of Human Nature*, part 2, §359; and esp. part 2, §7, "Of Compassion," 369ff.

tors or "tickle" their ears. Nor could sympathy consist of mere ploys to gain audience favor, least of all in courtly riposte. Sympathy had to be achieved through scrupulous imitation of human passions, effective by virtue of their likeness to those who observed them,[80] indeed, through an approximation that exceeded mere imitation to enter the realm of "expression." It also required that spectators use that most problematic of eighteenth-century faculties, the imagination.

Harnessing the imagination of spectators was a process that paradoxically required a stance less theatrical than antitheatrical. Writing about mid-eighteenth-century illusionistic paintings by Greuze, Michael Fried famously demonstrates that the figures are so absorbed in their own states and the beholder in turn so absorbed by those figures that the very existence of the beholder is fictively negated.[81] In order to sustain this existential fiction and produce sympathy capable of producing identification through the beholder's imagination, it was necessary that the beholder be kept in a state of unfulfilled longing for what was viewed. The "magic picture" scene in *Zémire et Azor* (Paris, 1771)—Marmontel and Grétry's *opéra comique* on the tale of beauty and the beast, staged as a scene within a scene—has been invoked by both Stefano Castelvecchi and Downing Thomas as the paradigmatic theatrical instantiation of this spectatorial distance-cum-sympathy. As Castelvecchi has put it, "The scene displays the link between spectatorial exclusion and emotional involvement." The magic picture of lost loved ones that Zémire beholds has "such a painful effect on Zémire because she cannot reach the figures, be perceived by them, console them. . . . [T]he scene works as a pedagogy of the theatre: the ideal stage-spectator relationship is encapsulated within the play by the relationship between the magic picture and Zémire."[82]

If exclusion of the spectator was essential to the longing that enabled absorption and perpetuated illusion, equally essential was a feint of spontaneity. Everything on stage was to take place in the subjunctive mood, not as if life were acting but as if acting were life[83]—as if it were spontaneous, as if its passions were impetuous, and as if singing were natural. Marchesi's wooden acting and unnatural body would no longer do.

In effect, illusionism served a new bourgeois morality, since far from allow-

80. In his 1769 work, *Observations on the Correspondence between Poetry and Music,* Daniel Webb described how the resonant bodies of listeners could be made to conform to the example of beneficial music. His "principle of assimilation" asserted a homology between musical motions (or movements) and motions of the passions and an ability in music to compel listeners to conform to its example. Webb's is an early physico-aesthetic explanation of the moral phenomenon of sympathetic response. See Thomas, *Aesthetics of Opera,* 196 and, on sympathy and identification, chap. 7.

81. Fried, *Absorption and Theatricality.*

82. Castelvecchi, "From "*Nina* to *Nina,*" 98–99, and Thomas, *Aesthetics of Opera,* 249–62. Important, too, is Heartz, "From Garrick to Gluck," 111–27.

83. See chap. 1 above on Victor Turner. James Johnson's study of changing listening practices at the Opéra in Paris, *Listening in Paris,* traces how the constraint to listen gradually took effect among Parisian audiences over the course of the late eighteenth and nineteenth centuries.

ing viewers more individual control, it made them surrender control to their membership in a group. To this end, the author had to take command of the text and performance. At first the operatic author was mainly the poet, whose predominance was advocated as an article of faith by reformers from Algarotti onward. By late in the century, egged on by the authorial dominance stridently endorsed in Gluck and Calzabigi's preface to *Alceste* and Gluck's approach to his Parisian operas of the 1770s (and epitomized by Mozart's *Idomeneo* of Munich, 1780), the authorial status of composers rose sharply, along with that of various other figures involved in rationalizing and authorizing production.[84] Correlatively, composers' works became less conventionalized, and very gradually their scores began to circulate—though not without difficulty, given that reformist operas could be quite idiosyncratic.[85] Mário Vieira de Carvalho has drawn on Norbert Elias's notions of a "court society" and "civilizing process" to explain how bourgeois culture, while imagining itself as a culture of sincerity (in opposition to the hypocrisy of the court), was actually making obeisance to such forms of authored art. For only through the artist—here the author—could the bourgeois subject experience his own sincerity. "While previously nature was dissimulated (masked in artifice), now artifice should be dissimulated as nature. At both the level of composition and performance the greatest art consisted now in dissimulating art, in presenting it as nature. Thus, what was at stake in the middle-class alternative was not taking off or discarding the mask, but rather making it cling closely and imperceptibly to the face."[86]

* * *

On the Italian peninsula, naturalistic illusion took root by fits and starts. It developed strong advocacy among the intelligentsia, but since Italian places and modes of production were radically decentralized, Italian theaters many and large, and Italians' habits of selective viewing deeply ingrained, opera was always spinning in a kind of cultural centrifuge. The Italian theatrical history of Calzabigi and Gluck's *Orfeo ed Euridice* is exemplary here. After its premiere in

84. This held true for Algarotti, Milizia, Planelli, Arteaga, Manfredini, della Lena, and others. See also documents in Howard, *Gluck*, chaps. 12–21 on Gluck's Paris years, and Mozart, *Briefe* 3:67–92. Cf. Chanan, *From Handel to Hendrix*. On relevant later eighteenth-century libretti, see McClymonds, "Verazi's Controversial *Drammi in Azioni*," 54. Regarding stage direction, see Guccini, "Directing Opera," 142–44. In present times, questions of authorship have received their most signal theoretical definition in Foucault, "What Is an Author?" 101–20. Among important historical treatments, see Rose, "The Author as Proprietor," 51–85. The author begins to find a new place in relations of production, and to make new demands about ownership and compensation for labor (see Quantz, *On Playing the Flute*, 330–31, and Milizia, *Trattato completo*, chap. 8, 51, 58, the last of which repeats the Algarottian line about music being subordinate to poetry).

85. Cf. Jommelli's comments on *Le avventure di Cleomede* and on *Fetonte*, in McClymonds, *Niccolò Jommelli*, 544–45 and 580–82, respectively.

86. Vieira de Carvalho, "From Opera to 'Soap Opera,'" 48; cf. Elias, *The Court Society* and *The Civilizing Process*, and Hobson, *The Object of Art*.

Vienna in 1762, *Orfeo* became a flashpoint within international reform movements, an emblem of their ideals. Stagings of Orfeo operas (and later, following Gluck's 1769 setting, operas on Alceste as well) were carried out in Italy during the 1770s as part of the project of widening the reformist net. Alessandra Martina has shown that the pasticcio version done at Florence in 1771 (deemed a success at the time), though it ventured choruses, ballets, and scenic tableaux, still hewed to the closed number as the apex of particular dramatic events.[87] Like the 1759 *Ippolito ed Aricia* in Parma, it accommodated a reformist program but also featured a beloved virtuoso in the title role, the soprano castrato Giusto Ferdinando Tenducci, who was granted extended fioritura passages in long arias on short texts. Dramatically speaking, the character of Euridice was more autonomous than her Viennese forebear—a prima donna parallel to Orfeo—and the poetics of the whole was much more traditionally four-square and symmetrical (less prose-like, in Jommelli's or Planelli's terms). There were other Italian revivals of *Orfeo*, notably in Naples in 1774.[88] For a while, there was also a rash of other mythological operas, some treating gods and goddesses like Apollo, Cupid, Mars, and Venus, and others treating the encounters with deities of legendary mortals like Iphigenia, Orestes, Helen, and Hercules.[89] But over time, attempts to transplant the Calzabigi/Gluck project into Italian soil largely failed to install Gluckian reform permanently or to erect a dominant mythological tradition. By the 1790s, Italy had largely turned its back on Greek myth as a source of libretti and returned to history.

* * *

Nevertheless, the viaducts that ran between French and Italian conceptions of drama in the later eighteenth century—far more complex than can be indicated here—were critical in the reassessment of fundamental views of truth, gender, and sentiment. Italy fell under the spell of French dramatic theory in the second half of the eighteenth century, at the same time as the drammi giocosi of Italian composers were feeding the French stage. In *Le neveu de Rameau*, Diderot had Rameau's nephew deliver an encomium on the *opéras comiques* of Egidio Duni, who had come to France from Parma in 1757.[90] Like many other members of the

87. Martina, *Orfeo-Orphée*, 95–103; see also Chegai, *L'esilio di Metastasio*, chap. 2, esp. 56–63.

88. Some traditionalists such as Francesco Franceschi, a prime apologist for Metastasio, inveighed against figures like Matteo Borsa who favored *Orfeo*, with its "little" arias and monotonous recitatives, over Metastasian opera. Franceschi's 1786 *Apologia delle opere drammatiche* was a response to (among others) Borsa's work of the preceding year, *Del gusto presente in letteratura italiana*.

89. Important examples include *Le feste d'Apollo* (Parma, 1769), a Habsburg wedding opera redone in Bologna, 1771; the *Oreste* of Luigi Serio and Domenico Cimarosa (Naples, 1783); and Gabriele Boltri and Gaetano Pugnani's *Adone e Venere* (Naples, 1784).

90. "Lui. J'ai eté entendre cette musique de Duni et de nos autres jeunes faiseurs, qui m'a achevé. / Moi. Vous aprouvez donc ce genre. / Lui. Sans doute. / Moi. Et vous trouvez de la beauté

Italian intellectual elite, Alessandro Verri traveled to Paris, where he attended the theater and wrote copiously to his brother Pietro about the encyclopedists he was meeting.[91] Since French was the lingua franca of the European intelligentsia, most French intellectual and scholarly thought was available to a certain stratum of intellectuals, whether they traveled or not. Italian intellectuals had their own spaces of intellectual exchange, cosmopolitan and provincial—Masonic lodges, provincial academies, political clubs, salons, lecture halls, and coffee houses. In Bologna, Giovanni Ristori and Sebastiano Canterzani formed the Società Enciclopedica, dedicated to importing and discussing the *Encyclopédie* and other foreign publications and to printing works by its own members, leading to the journal *Memorie enciclopediche* (Milan, 1781–87).[92] A typical Italian intellectual of the time would have discussed Ben Franklin's theory of electricity in the 1770s, a decade later read Gaetano Filangieri's *Science of Legislation* of 1780–85—in Anna Maria Rao's words, "the authentic manifesto of both the triumph and crisis of the partnership between enlightenment and reform"[93]—and talked heatedly by the late 1780s about the incipient revolution in France. Other conduits gradually made dramatic thought of the French enlightenment accessible to a broader spectrum of literate Italians. Among them were numerous anthologies of French and other writings published in Italian translations particularly from 1760 onward, with a steep increase in numbers in the 1790s,[94] in addition to Italianized French dramas for the middle classes. *Le père de famille* and *Le fils naturel*, Diderot's *drames bourgeois*, were both published by Fantecchi in Michele Bocchini's translations in Livorno as early as 1762, Rousseau's *Pygmalion* in Venice in 1775, and Elisabetta Caminer Turra's many translations of French *drames bourgeois*, published beginning in the early 1770s, were offered with her own strenuously politicized advocacy of the new middle-class drama. Not only were these dramatic texts inherently (if implicitly) incendiary by the measure of the old order, but paradoxically, because of the vast number of the-

---

dans ces nouveaux chants? / Lui. Si j'y en trouve; pardieu, je vous en reponds. Comme cela est declamé! Quelle verité! quelle expression! / Moi. Tout art d'imitation a son modèle dans la nature" (Diderot, *Le neveu de Rameau*, 77). [He: I have been to hear this music by Duni and our other youngsters, and that has finished me off. / I: So you approve of this style of music? / He: Of course. / I: And you find beauty in these modern tunes? / He: Do I find beauty? Good Lord, you bet I do! How well it is suited to the words! what realism! what expressiveness! / I: Every imitative art has its model in nature" (Diderot, *Rameau's Nephew and D'Alembert's Dream*, 97).]

91. Verri and Verri, *Carteggio*, vol. 1, part 1.

92. Dooley, "The Public Sphere and the Organization of Knowledge," 209–28.

93. Rao, "Enlightenment and Reform," 249.

94. These titles included such works as Meloni and Venetici's *Raccolta di opuscoli scientifici* of 1760, with various later editions; *Sulla insensitività ed irritibilità Halleriana* of 1759, a sensist collection with contributions by Le Cat and various other Europeans; and a selection of extracts from the *Encyclopédie* published in 1795–97 as *Dizionario di belle lettere*. Metastasio's writings were published in Neapolitan editions in 1780 and 1785 that included a translation of the article "Poème lyrique" from the *Encyclcopédie*.

aters spread throughout the Italian peninsula, they were accessible to much greater numbers of viewers than they were in France.[95]

THE FAMILY OF OPERA

Where opera seria had been founded in exemplary male types, new representational ideals often led to the staging of distressed and impassioned females. Sympathy for distressed women was driven by the new bourgeois impulse toward sentimentality and sincerity. The history of opera in the later eighteenth century rehearses the frenzies of tearful spectators—many themselves female—who watched with wistful sympathy as Richardson's *Pamela* was reincarnated in Goldoni and Piccinni's *La buona figliuola* (Rome, 1760) and later found a new form in that acme of sentimental opera, Carpani and Paisiello's *Nina* (near Caserta, 1789), both of which were revived innumerable times throughout Italy and elsewhere.[96] Benedetto Croce tells us that Neapolitans were hooked on sentimental plays, even in the 1770s, including French translations.[97] An anonymous reviewer for the *Gazzetta urbana veneta* wrote that the music of Paisiello's *Nina* had "a celestial harmony, an exceptional expressivity, a variety always aptly gauged to the poetic sentiment. It . . . leaves [the mind with] a sweet sensation."[98] And in the later nineteenth century, Francesco Florimo recounted how Neapolitan viewers of *Nina* cried out to the heroine in desperate attempts to console her.[99]

95. Diderot, *Il padre di famiglia;* Rousseau, *Il pimmalione.* On Caminer see Sama, "Verso un teatro moderno," who shows how the outspoken journalist came into opposition with Carlo Gozzi, author of highly successful plays that united old commedia dell'arte traditions with modern elements of exoticism, magic, and fable. Sama also quotes Goldoni (69) on the numbers of theaters and viewers in Italy as opposed to France. In both her writing for the stage and in her ability to penetrate intellectual circles, Caminer had a female predecessor in Luisa Bergalli Gozzi (1703–79), a countess from Venice and the Veneto. Among Bergalli Gozzi's dramatic writings are Italian translations of Terence into blank verse, Italian translations of Molière and Racine, original romance and tragedy for the spoken theater, and two drammi per musica—*Agide, re di Sparta* of 1725 and *L'Elenia* of 1730—but she was not the public polemicist that Caminer was.

96. The opera seria prototype of the passionate female subject is Cleonice, who longs to exist as a person. As a woman she stands in as the ultimate desiring subject among desiring subjects. Mary Hunter argues that in opera buffa (unlike in opera seria), the most heart-rending objects are women, hence distant, powerless, and pleading (*The Culture of Opera Buffa,* 91). "Powerlessness" here is of course a relative term.

97. Croce, *I teatri di Napoli,* 258–61.

98. "La sua musica è di celeste armonia, d'espressione chiarissima, di varietà sempre giustamente proporzionata al sentimento poetico. Apparecchia l'animo degli uditori, lo domina, e penetrato lo lascia di sensazione soave" (*Gazzetta urbana veneta,* vol. 8 [January 21, 1792], no. 6).

99. Florimo, *La scuola musicale di Napoli* 2:268. Castelvecchi, "From *Nina* to *Nina,*" speculates that the production in question must have taken place at a revival at the Teatro dei Fiorentini in 1790, with Celeste Coltellini in the lead. The history of weeping at the theater in France is traced in Vincent-

We are reminded of Casanova's tears. The performance that brings him to his knees is that of a woman, weeping with her cello, the "actor" of her music who loses herself, forgetting her real-life surround and making her lover ache for her even more from a distance than he would from up close, yet compensated by feelings of transporting joy.

It was some time after Casanova's exploit with Henriette that representations and appeals to the family, and especially to women within the family, became central to the shift toward a new kind of theater. *La buona figliuola, Nina,* and countless other drammi giocosi put the bourgeois conjugal family at center stage. Sentimental opera was arguably women's drama about women. The phenomenon itself was dramatized in the later eighteenth century by accounts of women weeping at the opera, as fifties women would cry at "the soaps."

Notions of women's hysteria and their cold, wet nature had already pegged them in earlier times as the sex whose very physiology was designed to set collective feeling in motion. What was new by the 1780s was that sentimental theater coincided with growing pressures on women, public and private, to embody newly formed ideals of naturalness and simplicity, to be better mothers, attentive to new standards of nurturing, health, and hygiene. Women were accommodated to a conception of the natural that wanted to deny them the artificial luxuries of theatergoing and peregrinations outside the domestic sphere, even though, ironically, theater was a prime habitat for internalizing the new mores.

One layer of late-century literature, influenced by Rousseau and by the Genevan Jacques Ballexerd's 1762 treatise *Dissertation sur l'éducation physique des enfans,* dwelt on putting girls in line with nature. The artifices of the aristocracy were seen as injurious to the health of females, who were to be inculcated with the beneficial habits of preventive private hygiene and physical exercise, and outfitted with looser-fitting clothing. A major bone of contention became whalebone, used in the construction of panniers and as stays in corsets. Ballexerd had vociferated against its use in a treatise partly translated as *Doveri annessi allo stato coniugale* (Naples, 1763, and often reprinted thereafter).[100] Whalebone was subjected to a whole treatise in French and decried in Fra Gioachino Trioli da Chiari's *L'educazione delle fanciulle* (Venice, 1765), which wanted a kind of "nature . . . without bodices, without metal stays, without wooden pins, and without strings."[101]

Most important for our purposes, exhortations to women were embedded in an extensive Italian literature on matrimony and child-rearing, partly indebted to French writings. Early on, probably in the mid-1760s or 1770s, an anonymous

Buffault, *A History of Tears,* chap. 4, esp. 75–76 and 237–38. Cf. Morelli, "Opera in Italian National Culture," in Bianconi and Pestelli, *Opera in Theory and Practice,* 386 ff., on women's reading habits.

100. See Guerci, *La sposa obbediente,* 194–95 nn. 82–83.

101. On the French treatise, *Dégradation de l'espèce humaine par l'usage des corps á baleine,* and its precedents, see ibid., 213–15 and n. 133; quote on 214.

Perugian wrote a short pamphlet, *Sul matrimonio e sulle obligazioni del medesimo,* singing the praises of marriage, parenthood, fatherhood (glossed as "the sweet name of father"), and mutual love, and proposing marriage as a nest of warmth and comfort, peace and tenderness, in which spouses devote themselves jointly to their children's education.[102] The pamphlet anticipated more sweeping encomia of marriage made under the spell of Rousseau (whose works were published in Italian translations continually from 1760 through the end of the century), in particular his novel *Émile* (1762), widely read in Italy, which secularized discussions of marriage, locating them in the sensibility of the heart. Along Rousseauian lines, the *illuministo* Melchiorre Delfico, in his *Philosophical Essay on Marriage* of 1774, praised the fullness of conjugal love, its moral pleasures, and even physical pleasures.[103] Marriage as strict duty, unfelt and unwanted—consequently arranged marriage—was transitioning toward new kinds of choices.[104] Delfico went so far as to base his revisionist notions on the recurring motifs of equality and liberty—though, as Guerci points out, equality here pertained to education, age, and feelings rather than to class as determined by either birthright or economic bracket, and certainly not to sex.

Many works, produced as digests for newly married couples, focused on raising children: how to make them physically robust, morally sound, and spiritually content. Duty toward children, state, society, and homeland were run together, as a parent's commitment to a child became the guarantee of commitment to the state and the common good of society. The catchwords of the time were "pubblica felicità," "pubblica prosperità", "comune interesse," "bene pubblico," "pubblica utilità," all familiar from Mariotti's speeches to the Perugian *cittadinanza.* The same phrases also fill the works of Antonio Giuseppe Testa, for whom it was just a short step forward to the idea, bluntly enunciated in his *Riflessioni sullo stato coniugale* (Ferrara, 1788), that procreation belonged not to a couple but to the state and the public sphere. "Most couples [wrongly] judge the business of their own children [*figliuolanza*] as very private to their family, nor do they readily think it something of public importance, the transgression

102. *Sul matrimonio e sulle obbligazioni del medesimo,* esp. 14–19 (I-PEc); Guerci, *La sposa obediente,* 164 n. 19, dates it after 1762. See also Lombardi, *Matrimoni di antico regime;* Menchi and Quaglioni's collection *Matrimoni in dubbio* (which includes Chiara La Rocca's essay on free consent in eighteenth-century Livorno, "Interessi famigliari e libero consenso," 529–50); and Fiume, *Madri.*

103. Delfico's orientation was sensist; see the edition of his "Saggio filosofico sul matrimonio" in Venturi, *Illuministi italiani* 2:1159–1266, as well as Venturi's "The Enlightenment in Southern Italy," in *Italy and the Enlightenment,* 211–12.

104. Working from family archives in Pisa, Roberto Bizzocchi illustrates how such choices evolved as inseparably economic, sentimental, legal, and ideological, and how uneven, though eventually decisive, the evolution toward a modern model of spousal choice was, even as it continually mixed political interests and personal emotions (*In famiglia,* esp. viii–x and chap. 2, "Antonio Maria e Anna: La conversazione; Lussorio: Il matrimonio"). Important in this evolution too were texts that instructed girls destined for marriage in the period around 1790—Venel and Angeli's *Saggio di medica educazione per le fanciulle chiamate a marito* of 1789 and an Italian translation of Fénélon, *Della educazione in genere e specialmente delle fanciulle,* published in 1790.

of which can lead to . . . an abominable infraction of one of the most sacred laws of society."[105]

In such contexts it was inevitable that the mother should be exalted, but also prone to constant charges of lapses and wrongs, since, though she could be aided in the project of motherhood, she could also easily falter. Her first obligation, according to reformists, was to overcome antiquated class prejudices against nursing and suckle her own babies. Following this recommendation by Rousseau and Ballexerd, a greatly influential treatise was published by Marie-Angélique Anel Le Rebours in 1767, translated and expanded in 1780 by a Turinese professor of anatomy and surgery, Giuseppe Maria Reyneri, as *Avvertimenti alle madri che allattar vogliono i loro bambini.* At that time, wet nurses were still a sign of distinction among the upper classes, for whom nursing one's own children remained taboo.[106] Reformists therefore argued that it was incumbent precisely on noblewomen to set an example that would lower infant mortality and improve infants' health. These opinions again looked for support to ideologies of duty to man and state. For statists, building a republic to maximum advantage meant conserving manpower, and for that natural nursing was crucial. Christian moralists invoked a different logic to the same end: resistance to nursing was the consequence of female incontinence, denaturing, bad morals, and bad husbands; acceptance of it was tantamount to embracing a sacred duty to public happiness, state, and society. (One aesthete argued it was even a beauty cure.)[107] This was a transformation of the eighteenth-century myth of virtue, used with new referents while being juxtaposed continually, and awkwardly, with rational thought.[108]

Two major arteries in operatic history, divergent but overlapping, followed alongside the moralization of women and the emergence of the bourgeois conjugal family. One was sentimental opera, as described by Stefano Castelvecchi, which not by accident made heavy weather of wronged, lost, and orphaned girls.[109] The other was opera seria, where afflicted young women like Juliet and Lodoïska came on display. Shakespeare's Juliet was featured in a libretto

105. "La maggior parte di essi giudica l'affare della propria figliuolanza siccome privatissimo della loro famiglia, né pensano facilmente esser esso di così pubblica importanza, che la trasgressione di ciò che può condurre a tanto, sia una abbominevole infrazione di uno dei più santi patti della società" (quoted in Guerci, *La sposa obbediente,* 202). Governments did take initiatives to favor parturients (204 and nn. 105–6).

106. In 1777, Pietro Verri decided to have his daughter Teresa nursed by her mother (see Barbagli, *Sotto lo stesso tetto,* 387–97). More broadly on these issues, see Sussman, *Selling Mother's Milk,* and relevant to French opera in the 1770s, Cole, "'Nature' at the Opéra," chap. 5, who has helped inspire my thinking on the issues in Italy.

107. Guerci summarizes these views as transmitted in Italian sources in *La sposa obbediente,* 221–28.

108. This extended to the public the enlightened "philosopher-king," whose virtue promoted the public happiness (Rao, "Enlightenment and Reform," 231; and see Venturi, *Italy and the Enlightenment,* chaps. 1 and 6).

109. Castelvecchi, "Sentimental Opera."

by Giuseppe Maria Foppa as set by Nicola Zingarelli and staged at Milan on January 30, 1796, with an inversion in the title characters' names to *Giulietta e Romeo,* though in later years the opera was mainly staged and billed as *Romeo e Giulietta* and became one of the most popular of all late-eighteenth-century operas, with a life that extended well into the nineteenth century.[110] Just days before the Milanese opening of the first *Giulietta,* the eponymous *Lodoïska* emerged at La Fenice (January 26, 1796) in a setting by Simone Mayr of Francesco Gonella's libretto, which was destined to become equally popular. Other prominent operatic heroines of the period were married: famously, Domenico Cimarosa's Elfrida and his Penelope, both title characters and both staged for Naples, the first on a libretto by Calzabigi (San Carlo, November 4, 1792) and the second by Giuseppe Maria Diodati (Teatro del Fondo, December 26, 1794). The title character of Gasperini and Zingarelli's *Ines de Castro* (Teatro Carcano, Milan, October 11, 1798) is a secret wife and mother whose children's lives are threatened with death in a renowned prison scene. Occasionally opera in the closing decades of the century also portrayed bad mothers or stepmothers: Semiramide and Phaedra, for instance.

Notable examples of the terrible mother had already appeared in Florence by the mid-1780s, when Metastasio's Semiramide was radically transformed into the notorious virago familiar from Voltaire's play, in which she murders her husband, plots an incestuous marriage, and is stabbed to death by her son. A Milan version of 1784 by Ferdinando Moretti with music by Michele Mortellari was content to have her lover assassinated. But the infamous libretto by Pietro Giovannini (flourished 1779–86), *La vendetta di Nino, ossia La morte di Semiramide,* which was staged at Florence in a dramatic setting by Alessio Prati in 1786, culminated in matricide onstage.[111] Such new preoccupations with blood and horror were strikingly prefigured, paradoxically so, by one of the key books of the Italian enlightenment, a classic read all over Europe, Cesare Beccaria's *Dei delitti e delle pene* (Of Crimes and Punishments) of 1764, where a horror of pain and suffering underlies the case against torture and the death penalty.[112]

Mothers had been virtually absent from Metastasio's canon of opera seria (Dircea is an exception), and wives quite rare (Dircea secretly, and the eponymous Zenobia). There had been no lack of them in Zeno, whose Merope, Griselda, Berenice (of *Lucio vero,* sometimes redone as *Vologeso*), Andromaca (who appears in Astianatte operas), and Zenobia still held the stage in the Metastasian era, as did to a lesser extent Clitennestra (in *Ifigenia*), Giulia Mamma (in *Alessandro severo*), and Pario (in *Nitocri*). Nevertheless, by nearly annihilating mothers and wives from his own operas, Metastasio codified theatrically

110. See De Bei, "Giulietta e Romeo di Nicola Zingarelli," 71–125, and Salvetti, *Aspetti dell'opera italiana fra sette e ottocento.*

111. For an account of the different versions and sources see McClymonds, "La morte di Semiramide."

112. The original Italian, including notes, appears in Venturi, "Cesare Beccaria," in *La cultura illuministica,* ed. Fubini, 120–29.

the patriarchal society of his time, consistent with the settecento described by Italian historians. More mothers were admitted to opera seria in the 1780s and 1790s, but some were killed off and many daughters marooned in the arch-pathos of family calamity, heartbreak, and even horror. Initial shifts in this direction were not very weighty. In Naples's Teatro San Carlo, Phaedra returned to the lyric stage in 1788 in the title role of Paisiello's *Fedra* (libretto adapted by Luigi Salvioni after Carlo Frugoni).[113] She is more a woman of action than the Phaedra of the 1759 Parmesan version—accusing Hippolytus with her own words of trying to seduce her, for instance—but it was largely the musical style rather than the dramatic action or textual characterizations that differed markedly from the version of three decades hence. Yet Fedra's music is not gripping, and in a later version, all of her arias were cut "as though someone decided to downgrade" her with respect to the other characters.[114]

Calzabigi and Paisiello's *Elvira*, a tragedia per musica for the San Carlo done in 1794, stages a monumental Arthurian-styled warrior maiden—less maidenly than monumental.

The two-act *Penelope* that Diodati and Cimarosa brought to the Neapolitan stage in 1794–95 featured the faithful wife of Ulysses, who had been popular around the turn of the previous century on the operatic stages of Venice, Palermo, Milan, Naples, and Rome, especially in settings of Matteo Noris's libretto *Penelope, la casta* staged between 1685 and 1716. Since that time, Penelope had all but disappeared.[115] Amid a host of old feudal themes of honor centered on the opera's male characters and character traits—the magnanimous forgiveness of his enemies by the returning Ulysses, the filial devotion of his son Telemachus, the courage of the Greeks—Diodati's persons and actions rise morally to the top. Penelope herself is a devoted mother and wife who refuses to remarry despite her husband's long and unaccounted absence. She is a true heroine, a veritable headstone of wifedom and motherhood who sacrifices herself for her family: Ulysses, a tenor, played by the great Matteo Babbini; Telemachus, played not by a castrato (as Tenducci had famously done at Florence's Pergola in 1773 and Crescentini again as late as Carnival 1797 at Venice's La Fenice) but by a female soprano, Luisa Negli; and Telemachus's beloved Arsinoe. The role of Penelope was taken by soprano Elena Cantoni, who divided her career between buffa and seria roles, the latter including such leads as Cleopatra, Circe, Marzia (in *Catone in Utica*), Elfrida, Stratonice, and Calphurnia. Already in the introduzione Penelope is plagued by the advances of Evenore, king of Lesbos, who is Other to her by virtue of the thunderous bass-baritone of Antonio Razzani. The voice, still rare in opera seria staged in Italy (especially in major cities), is

113. Score in I-Nc, Rari 2.10.14–15, mostly autograph (excepting the overture and some recitatives), bound with a second version of act 1 (= RISM A/II 850.08.778 and 850.08.779), microfilm copy at US-BEc. See Robinson, *Giovanni Paisiello* 1:408–15.

114. Robinson, *Giovanni Paisiello* 1:415.

115. I consulted the autograph at I-Nc, MS Rari 1.4.20/21, and a copy at F-Pn, MS D.1069–1070.

already heard to great dramatic effect in the trio that makes up the introduzione, which begins with Penelope's "Allegro con spirito."[116] Repulsing Evenore in queenly dotted-note triadic melodies, richly colored by clarinets in A, horns, divided oboes, and bassoons, and supported by vaulting eighth notes in the bass, she declares "Va, non ti temo, o barbaro. / Non curo il tuo favore. / D'una regina il core / timor giamai non ha." (Begone, I fear you not, barbarian. I do not seek your favor. The heart of a queen never feels fear.) Penelope initially alternates between brief passages of excited recitative and passages a tempo, then hurtles forward and nails the tonic in two successive statements, the last of which draws out the final tonic return with repeated stabbing fortepianos. Not about to let her off easily, Evenore steps in on the dominant, but his is a voice of stolid insistence, descending in half-note interpolations—"Dunque lo sdegno mio!" (Then my disdain . . .), "Pensa che Re son io" (Consider that I'm king)—which only succeed in ensuring their battle.[117] When Ulysses later arrives, he is heralded by a majestic march that offsets Penelope's psychological power, but he too is sentimentalized, particularly with his act 1 aria, "Se lungi al tuo nido," which stages him in C major with sotto voce strings bearing a soaringly romantic melody that culminates in a gorgeous curve into E flat at the return of the first stanza.

Relevant to the historical arc of these operas are several aspects of casting. Above all, the castrato is gone. He is neither the returning hero (Ulisse) nor the hero's young son (Telemaco), and most especially he is not any of the female characters. Quite the contrary, several of the singers were well equipped to bring their characters a physical and vocal realism learned from comic opera—not just Cantoni and Razzani but also Negli, who specialized in opera buffa during the mid-1790s; and comic opera, whether Cherubini's opéra comique *Médée* in France (Paris, 1797) or Mozart's *Don Giovanni* in Prague (1787), was of course critical to the evolution from the more stylized neoclassical dramas of the eighteenth century to the melodramatic tragedies of the nineteenth. The configuration of voice and character types in *Penelope* adumbrates the nineteenth-century Italian plot trajectory neatly summed up by George Bernard Shaw: "A tenor and soprano want to make love, but are prevented from doing so by the baritone."

By the 1790s and even beforehand, some opera seria was indeed renamed "tragedia in musica": for example, *Giulietta e Romeo*, Prati's *La morte di Semiramide* as done at Venice's San Benedetto in 1791, and Paisiello's *Elvira* (Naples, 1794). Others were called less tragically "dramma serio"—Moretti and Cima-

116. After 1720, in Venice and elsewhere on the Italian peninsula, basses were hardly used in opera seria until the nineteenth century, or else they were used exceptionally, when an extraordinary voice appeared on the horizon or when an available bass was the best or most prestigious voice available to a small or more provincial theater. By contrast, Handel's operas use them commonly. Razzani is listed in Sartori, *I libretti italiani*, Index, 2:549, as having played the Commendatore in a Don Giovanni opera, the role of Pomponio in *La scuola degli amanti*, and Ulisse in *Pirro* (Rome, 1798) but most of his roles were buffo.

117. Later in 1.5 he sings a rage aria, "Agitato da furore / mille smanie ho intorno al core," marked "Allegro con brio" in D and scored with horns in D, divided oboes, and bassoons (vol. 1, 100r–111v).

rosa's *La morte di Cleopatra* for St. Petersburg, 1789, Zingarelli's *Ines de Castro* as staged at Livorno in 1803, Marchesini and Cimarosa's *Artemisia, regina di Caria* for the San Carlo in summer 1797—and "dramma tragico per musica," a seeming novelty, was used for the libretto *Artemisia* by Cratisto Jamejo (Giovanni Battista Colloredo), partly set by Cimarosa in 1800 before his death and staged posthumously at La Fenice in 1801. Some of these new-styled operas traded in the outright horrific, most notably the whole genre of "morte" operas, which proliferated after Gaetano Sertor and Francesco Bianchi authored *La morte di Cesare* in 1788. But more often they were simply gloomy, unhappy, or long-suffering, and were often remarked by Italians as being inordinately sad. The reviewer of Foppa and Zingarelli's *Giulietta e Romeo* commented, for instance, "The sorrow of the plot, which restricts all its horrors to the third act, is rather heavy for anyone who does not have a soul inclined to melancholy."[118]

By the later 1780s and 1790s, many did seem to have such a soul. When *Giulietta e Romeo* was brought into La Fenice from its recent premiere at La Scala, it was to save the season by replacing Metastasio and Martinelli's *Issipile*, which failed so badly that the theater closed after a few performances.[119] A progressive work, the introduzione of *Giulietta* consists of a tableau of chorus and ballet, scored up with clarinets, divided oboes, horns in F, timpani, and bassoons (the last trading occasional solos with the bass), followed by a Lento aria for Giulietta. All this is a platform for the "gentil donzella," caught in the crossfire of warring choruses of Cappecchi and Montecchi, and worst of all caught in the fury of her father.

La Fenice also mounted two other female operas in 1796. One was a restaging of Calzabigi and Paisiello's darkly medieval tragedia in musica *Elfrida*, whose protagonist, married covertly in defiance of her father and king and then hidden away, kills herself when her husband dies in a duel rather than marry the king.[120] The opera contravened the ideology of old-regime politics, and, like *Penelope*, it tugged on the heart strings of its viewers by bringing each act to climax with the continuous music and action of an extended ensemble. In the other opera of the season, Gonnella and Mayr's *La Lodoïska*, the female protagonist got a happy

118. "La tristezza dell'argomento, che ristrigne tutti i suoi orrori all'atto terzo, riesce un pò pesante a chi non ha l'anima inclinata alla malinconia"; and the passage continues, "e suol dire che va al teatro per divertirsi non per funestarsi. Ma se l'azione lo esige, se la musica risponde alla parola, non si può che lodare la poesia, e chi l'ha vestita di si belle note esprimenti" (*Gazzetta urbana veneta*, no. 96 [Nov. 30, 1796], 765).

119. Copy at US-Wf, MS W.b. 542–43, based on the Milan performance, with added arias for castrato Girolamo Crescentini. Another copy, which I used, is at F-Pn, Mus. MS Ab.o.141 (1) (2) (3).

120. *Elfrida* was originally staged at the San Carlo in Naples, November 1792; the autograph survives at I-Nc, Rari 2.10.8,9: "Originale / Elfrida / Dramma per Musica / Composto / Da Giovanni Paisiello / All'attual servizio delle Loro Maestà / Siciliane / In qualità di Maestro di Cappella, die Camera, e / Compositore / Per la Festività del Glorioso Nome della / Maestà della Regina / Del di quattro Novembre 1792" (microfilm copy at US-BEm). For productions in Bologna (1796) and Parma (1798), the tragic ending was replaced with a happy one. See McClymonds, "Calzabigi and Paisiello's *Elfrida* and *Elvira*," 239–58.

ending but for most of the opera was imprisoned within a harsh Polish landscape, exaggerated with exotic instrumentation and lush harmonies.

* * *

Arrayed before viewers, then, were fidelity, love, marriage, and motherhood, sometimes upheld with disastrous consequences. With them was the start to what Catherine Clément has famously called "the undoing of women."[121] Clément's focus is essentially nineteenth-century, yet from an eighteenth-century perch it would seem that representations of women were never sufficiently done to be "undone." Mothers had been relatively little in evidence on the opera seria stage, probably too reminiscent of grounding in real life to give the kind of mythical support to patriarchy and authority that opera seria was after—especially on a terrain so politically splintered. If power was best served by roving signifiers whose signifieds could best be recruited however the social or political fit was best (father, bishop, king, general), then families that gave true-to-life depictions could only undo the myth.

Even the chivalric addresses of dedications *alle dame* were marked by an invertible asymmetry of courtly exchange that ultimately positioned female operagoers at the mercy of men. In this place, the female was more symbol or instrument than person. Like the Juno of Perugia's Pavone, she was a focus of dedication, veneration, and sacrifice, but could not be assimilated to the ranks of those in charge. In the project of consolidating a bourgeois public, women were caught out, omitted from the revolutionary mission of equality by the Rousseauian program of female duty and subordination, as historians of the French revolution have so often noted. It is not so surprising, then, that in opera the woman does not so much change as usurp interest from opera's "semi-men" at the same time as she becomes more victim, more heroine, more demon.

121. Clément, *Opera, or The Undoing of Women.*

CHAPTER 9

Death of the Sovereign, Venice, 1797: Fourth Case Study

"The city of Venice counts seven theaters. That Republic never obliged itself to create a public theater worthy of its grandeur. Those that are there were casually erected by patrician families." FRANCESCO MILIZIA, *Trattato completo, formale e materiale del teatro*, 1771[1]

By the 1790s, revolutionary ferment was a fledgling political reality in Italy, but geographically the terrain was too scattered for all-out revolution even if a social and political consensus had demanded it—which it definitely did not. On that terrain the Venetian republic had always been a unique case, operatically and politically. For many centuries, it was the beacon throughout Europe of unflinching republicanism, a symbol of balance and justice, goodness and wisdom, notwithstanding critics who found it guilty of all the usual evils of the old order. As the seat of Europe's first public opera house, opened in 1637, it saw itself, and was seen by others, as an axis for opera and a principal site of new operatic waves. Yet the antimonarchical sentiments felt throughout Europe in the 1790s rocked the world of Venetian opera seria, even though the genre still seized more often on the dilemmas of ancient rulers than on those of republics, even in Venice. Distrust of monarchy was tantamount to distrust of the patriciate, and nothing was easier than to transfer that distrust to the meanings of opera.

All the more poignant, then, that late in the century, just as the oligarchy was breathing its last, a group of prominent upper-class Venetians—patricians and wealthy bourgeoisie—opened a new theater devoted exclusively to opera seria. By that time, of course, the whole genre, and its attendant modes of production and social rituals, had been under fire for some time. Yet they remained deeply

1. "La città di Venezia conta sette teatri. Quella Repubblica non s'è mai impegnata a farne uno pubblico degno della sua grandezza. Quelli, che vi sono, furono casualmente eretti da famiglie patrizie" (*Trattato completo*, 78). See chapter 8 above on the history of Milizia's treatise, first published in 1771. Here, as elsewhere, I cite from the 1794 edition.

rooted in the practices of Italian theaters, tied (if elusively so) to the mystifications of absolutist power and the illusions of an august eternal present that such power presupposed.[2]

Conditions in late-eighteenth-century Venice reveal how these ties could be maintained in the midst of an old and crumbling republic. But they also reveal how festivities, which had long been integral to the Venetian political order, could be exploited in an explicitly antiabsolutist project, much as they were in revolutionary France.

The new theater was La Fenice, built to rise like a phoenix from the ashes of fire and discontent. When the nobles' Teatro San Benedetto had burned down in 1774, its society of owners rebuilt it; but since part of its land site was owned by the Venier family, they were forced to sell the rebuilt theater to the Veniers in 1787. The ousted nobles reacted by erecting yet another and still grander theater, Il Nobilissimo Nuovo Teatro La Fenice, in a kind of theatrical potlatch—though not before they secured a waiver of an edict that prohibited the addition of any new theaters.

What follows is the story of how a theatrical institution, created within an absolutist oligarchy, could be remade shortly thereafter under the auspices of a provisional "democracy." I proceed from the opening of La Fenice in 1792—and follow its vicissitudes in the wake of the fall of the Venetian republic five years later.[3]

2. On the long life and afterlife of opera seria (or "neoclassical opera"), see Weiss, "Verdi and the Fusion of Genres," 138–56.

3. La Fenice burned to the ground on January 29, 1996, weeks after I first presented an early version of this chapter at the Annual Meeting of the American Musicological Society (November 1995). See the "The Fire at La Fenice," report on the OperaGlass Web page at Stanford University, http://opera.stanford.edu/misc/fire.html (accessed October 3, 2003). My research on the Fenice archives and later documents was mostly completed at I-Vas and I-Vlevi in 1994–95. The latter housed the Fenice archives at the time, but they have since been moved and the Archivio Storico of the theater (hereafter ASTF) has been digitizing the archive on its official Web site, Teatro La Fenice, Archivio Storico On-Line, www.teatrolafenice.it/archivio/ (accessed July 4, 2006). My sincere thanks to Cristiano Chiarot (curator), Franco Rossi (technical manager), and Marina Dorigo (organizer) for help with the archive over the last decade. For information on La Fenice's rebuilding see the theater's Web site and Gran Teatro La Fenice—La Reconstruzione, www.ricostruzionefenice.it (accessed July 4, 2006). According to the former, the rebuilt edifice, designed by Aldo Rossi with construction directed by Roberto Scibilia, has retained some general architectural features of the theater that burned down in 1996, among them its scale, five tiers, acoustic properties (including those promoted by wooden materials), orchestra pit, stalls, and notably, the royal box added only in the nineteenth century by the Austrians. Of particular relevance is the theater's embeddedness in Venetian urban topography: "The building stands on a narrow plot with irregular borders, laboriously carved out of the complex urban fabric with its spaces skilfully arranged through traverse angles and deviations from the axes of the three main parts of the theatre, a layout from which no subsequent rebuilding work or modifications have been able to diverge" (http://www.ricostruzionefenice.it/english/progetti/bando/2.asp). The theater reopened in 2003.

THE DEATH OF TIME

Not only did the birth of La Fenice essentially converge with the demise of the Venetian oligarchy but also with an era of radical changes in the institution of opera seria. At the node of that convergence, La Fenice rose as a lavish emblem of patrician pride. The society began its efforts by sponsoring an architectural competition for the theater, won by the homegrown Giannantonio Selva in a gale of controversy, and embarking on an elaborate building program. The finished edifice was the third largest in Venice, edged out only by the theaters of San Luca and San Giovanni Grisostomo, and was indisputably the most elegant.[4] Nobles who bought boxes paid dearly to cover singers' fees, opulent productions, and amortization costs of construction, outfitting, and furnishing. In return they spent festive seasons amid sumptuous appointments and stagings that attested their city's supremacy as uniquely independent, a republic still ruled by indigenous nobles for whom the rest of the peninsula was a place swollen with foreign despots.[5]

But the moment was fragile. The republic, once robust and imperial, had long since melted into spectral monumentality, a shadowy relic made of myth and spectacle. When it fell on May 12, 1797, to Napoleonic forces, it was not because the city was overpowered militarily, but because its leaders had no choice but to succumb to ultimatums it was too weak to refuse.[6] The turn of events was not unexpected. Napoleon had been pressing his armies into Lombardy and the Veneto *terraferma* for many months. By mid-April 1797, they occupied Milan, Brescia, Mantua, and Bergamo, among others. At that time Venice was still far from Napoleon's grasp, but two tactical events subsequently took place that quickly spelled the city's doom. Around Easter, French troops in Verona were attacked in repeated popular uprisings, uprisings that the French claimed were goaded by Venetian hostilities and that caused serious losses of French soldiers. Days afterward a French lugger was shot down in the port of Venice. Already provoked—or feigning provocation—Napoleon reacted to the last with demands that the Venetians abdicate their oligarchy or face war, a war Venice was totally unprepared to sustain. Instead the nobles whose ancestors had collectively run the republic for nearly a millennium saved the city and themselves from destruction by handing it over to the French—an act of cowardice by feudal stan-

4. Eighteenth-century plans of the theaters are preserved in I-Vmc, MS Correr 970/25.

5. On La Fenice's early history, see Brusatin and Pavanello, *Il Teatro La Fenice* (with essays by Cesare de Michelis and documents by Susanna Biadene); Mangini, *I teatri di Venezia*, 165–76; and Bauman, "The Society of La Fenice," 332–54.

6. For historical accounts, see Scarabello, "Gli ultimi giorni della repubblica," 487–508; and McClellan, *Venice and Bonaparte*. An important nineteenth-century fictional account is Ippolito Nievo's *Confessioni di un italiano*, vol. 1, chap. 11, ostensibly based on the eyewitness accounts of his grandmother, a Venetian noblewoman.

dards, but one of prudence by the long-established Venetian mores of practical wisdom and reverence for the city.[7]

Since Venice had been the supreme icon of oligarchic independence for longer than any other major state on the Continent, the fall of the republic carried a high symbolic currency in the redistribution of power taking place across Europe, even though its practical implications were negligible. It was a powerful sign of the times, of a new era when time itself would be remapped and reimagined. And it was precisely in this reimagining that La Fenice took center stage. No other new institution so visibly condensed and reiterated the symbols of elite oligarchic power. Yet a terrible paradox lay waiting to be exploited, for in the wake of the fall, the same monument that had served to enshrine patrician status through the pliable media of opera seria were to be easily co-opted once the old older and premises were no longer in place. The new regime quickly appropriated La Fenice to its own ends and transformed opera seria by borrowing but inverting its meanings. Asserting that the republic, which was supposed to have been irreproachable and indestructible, was in fact suspect and vulnerable, the revised offerings rewrote time itself, making a previously timeless past into the burden of a problematic history.

The significance of such views—and the susceptibility of opera seria to transmute at the hands of its co-opters—yield themselves only on close analysis of events that took place between May and October 1797. I use the word pointedly here, for these were "events" in the bona fide sense distinguished by narrative historians—disruptions to the normal flow of activity, which brought frailties in existing forms and ideologies of social life to a visible surface. And yet, as William H. Sewell, Jr., has written, "the uncertainty of structural relations that characterizes events can stimulate bursts of collective cultural creativity" and thus ultimately lead to important cultural transformations.[8] So it was in Venice, where the fall of the republic brought about decisive revisions to numerous institutions, political and cultural, of which theater was but a single, if highly charged and condensed, example. Examining events within this purview exposes fault lines in the premises of eighteenth-century festivity itself, even as the same events affirm the resilience of festive practices. Ultimately, they prompt questions on two fronts: first, how was a monument of the old order suddenly remade in the face of new premises and a new regime in 1797; and second, how could a project devoted to consolidating patrician identity fall prey, at the moment of its ruin, to new fantasies of identity, new narratives of history, and new instruments of power external to its own?

7. Indeed, as Nievo put it in his *Confessioni*, the council that voted itself out of existence maintained agency over its own fate instead of facing bloody defeat in war.

8. Sewell, "Historical Events as Transformations," 845. Sewell takes the storming of the Bastille as a case study to theorize the nature of the "event" and its relationship to historical structure. See also his "A Theory of the Event," 197–224.

* * *

From its inception, La Fenice was intended as a shrine to the elite classes. It was not just the most deluxe of Venice's theaters but the only one that mounted solely opera seria and one of the few such theaters in the genre's history. Its erection took all the membership's considerable clout, financial and political.[9] Among other obstacles, a sumptuary decree of 1756 had prohibited entrepreneurs from building new theaters beyond the seven that already existed, principally because competition among them had reached detrimental levels. Furthermore, creating the theater was going to mean demolishing domestic residences in the area of San Fantin where the theater was to be built, and some of their owners asked exorbitant prices for them. Then, too, all of this came at precisely the moment in the republic's history when the numbers of nobility had suffered a sharp decline, governmental funds were most depleted, noble offices widely unfilled for lack of noble bodies, and trade severely diminished.[10] Still, in 1787 the Society of La Fenice easily succeeded in having the decree in question waived and its petition for an eighth theater approved by the Council of Ten—perhaps helped by the fact that poor finances and neglect had by then driven Venice's other theaters into varying states of dilapidation.[11]

Surviving lists of boxholders, constituted through box ownership, reveal that members of the society came overwhelmingly from the local nobility and (secondarily) the haute bourgeoisie.[12] Of the five tiers of boxes that were ultimately built, the bottom three bore the greatest concentration of nobles, as was customary in Parma and elsewhere (see fig. 9.1 below). The second tier, the *primo ordine,* housed exclusively nobles, save one box. Being elevated, it was the tier that was most analogous to the piano nobile of a palace, the floor inhabited by nobles in their own homes and used for entertaining (as opposed to ground floors, which were typically occupied by servants and, in the lagoon city, were oftentimes very wet and muddy). Twenty-six nobles held boxes in the *pepian* (the bottommost tier), eighteen in the *secondo ordine* (third tier), six in the *terzo ordine* (fourth tier), and two in the *quarto ordine* (fifth tier). In each one of the first three tiers, exactly five of these noble families came not from the ranks of the old nobility—those whose noble status was conferred with the Serrata of 1297, the closing of the patrician ranks—but from families newly added to the *libro d'oro,* mostly in the mid-seventeenth century.[13] A number of bourgeoisie

9. Mocenigo, *Il Teatro La Fenice,* 16.

10. Davis, *The Decline of the Venetian Nobility,* and Venturi, *Settecento riformatore,* vol. 2, chap. 6.

11. Zorzi, "Venezia," 278.

12. What follows builds on my analysis of records in ASTF, Partitario Canoni 2, 1792–1800.

13. Desperate attempts to expand the pool of noble families, and with them the eligible membership for governmental offices and the amount of governmental funds available, were far less successful in the eighteenth century than in the seventeenth. See Davis, *The Decline of the Venetian Nobility,* 119–25.

also bought their way into the lower tiers, although most of them were steered into the slightly less desirable *pepian* (where they owned eight boxes) and the *secondo ordine* (where they owned fourteen).[14] Such a mix had made up La Fenice's central power base from its inception. It was reproduced, for example, in the totality of successive noble and bourgeois "presidents" who ran it at any given time throughout the 1790s.[15] Once the theater got underway, it was intermittently plagued with serious financial difficulties, the most notorious of which led in 1793–94 to the dismissal of the impresario Michele Dall'Agata (who subsequently poisoned himself at the end of the Carnival season).[16] Setbacks, material or otherwise, did not discourage its policies of extravagance, however. Dall'Agata's successor, the choreographer and dancer Onorato Viganò, began his term with a contract that mandated an elaborate annual cycle of operas and ballets.[17] Four opere serie were to be given each year—one in autumn, two at Carnival, and one during Ascension—always along with two ballets inserted between the acts and with all operas being new except possibly that for autumn, which counted as an abbreviated season owing to the nobles' late return from summer sojourns in their country villas (*villeggiature*). Of the two ballets, one was always to be of "carattere serio." The other could be of "mezzo carattere, ma non mai basso, nè indecente" (middling character, but never low nor indecent)—and hence potentially less extravagant—and both were always to be premiered at the same time as the operas with which they were paired. All ballets were to be magnificent, "corrispondente alla Nobiltà, e grandezza del Teatro," with lighting, scenery, and costumes to match and without ever stooping to the "mockable" stage effects of artificial animals and the like. The orchestra, too, was to be choice so as to match the "grandezza del Teatro" and the composer "di conosciuta riputazione" (of wide renown), like the composer of music for the ballets.[18]

The theater's showy image, heralding its aristocratic, old-world conservatism, did not go unremarked by local observers. Reviewers for the *Gazzetta urbana veneta* repeatedly noted the "pompa delle decorazioni" and the "sempre gran gente" who populated the theater.[19] In the years leading up to 1797, pomp and luxury extended to the operatic repertory (see table 9.1), still strongly Metasta-

14. Box ownership began in 1789, when families first had to pay levies on boxes they wished to reserve for the theater's opening. The vast majority of owners retained their boxes through the 1790s, even during and beyond the period of the fall of the republic.

15. Lists of La Fenice presidents compiled by Sandro dalla Libera exist in a typescript preserved at ASTF, "La presidenza del Teatro La Fenice dalle origini al 1968" (Venice, February 18, 1968); and see Girardi and Rossi, *Il Teatro La Fenice*, passim.

16. Mangini, *I teatri di Venezia*, 173.

17. Transcription in Bauman, "The Society of La Fenice," 351–54.

18. Starting in the late 1790s, there were separate ballet *scenari* and often third ballets following the third act of the opera, though usually not of the type called *terzi balli analoghi*.

19. *Gazzetta urbana veneta*, no. 86 (October 28, 1795), and no. 12 (February 11, 1795), respectively.

Table 9.1. Operas performed at Teatro La Fenice, Venice, 1792–1800

Title	*Opening*	*Librettist*	*Composer*	*Selected singers, roles, and notes*
I guochi d'Agrigento (dm), 3	May 16, 1792	Alessandro Pepoli	Giovanni Paisiello	Giacomo David, Gasparo Pacchierotti, Brigida Banti
Alessandro nell'Indie (dm), 3	Nov. 17, 1792	Metastasio	Francesco Bianchi	David, Pacchierotti, Banti; *revival from San Benedetto, 1785*
Tarara, ossia la virtù premiata (dm), 3	Dec. 26, 1792	Gaetano Sertor	Bianchi	David, Pacchierotti, Banti
Ines de Castro (dm), 3	Jan. 28, 1793	C. Giotti	Giuseppe Giordani detto Giordaniello	David, Pacchierotti, Banti
Tito e Berenice (dm), 3	May 8, 1793	Giuseppe Foppa	Sebastiano Nasolini	Girolamo Crescentini, Caterina Lang
Virginia (tm), 3	Dec. 26, 1793	Pepoli	Felice Alessandri	Marianna Vinci, Crescentini, Matteo Babbini
I giuochi d'Agrigento (dm), 3	Jan. 22, 1794	Pepoli	Paisiello	Babbini, Crescentini, Vinci; *revival of 1792 production*
Saffo, ossia I riti d'Apollo Leucadio (dm), 2	Feb. 18, 1794	Simeone Antonio Sografi	Simone Mayr	Vinci, Crescentini, Babbini
Antigono (dm), 3	May 24, 1794	Metastasio	Luigi Caruso	Domenico Mombelli, Teresa Bertinotti, Rosa Mora
Achille in Sciro (dm), 3	Nov. 21, 1794	Metastasio	Marcello Di Capua	Luigi Marchesi (Achille)
Il conte di Saldagna (tm), 3	Dec. 26, 1794	[Ferdinando Moretti]	Nicola Zingarelli	Marchesi (Conte di Saldagna)
Pirro (dm), 3	Feb. 4, 1795	Giovanni de Gamerra	Zingarelli	Marchesi (Pirro)
Artaserse (dm), 3	Nov. 14, 1795	Metastasio	Giuseppe Nicolini	Marchesi (Arbace)
Demofoonte (dm), 3	Nov. 25, 1795	Metastasio	Zingarelli	Marchesi (Timante)
Ifigenia in Aulide (dm), 3	Dec. 26, 1795	Moretti	Zingarelli	Marchesi (Achille)
La Lodoïska (dm), 3	Jan. 26, 1796	Dott. F[rancesco] G[onella] di F[errara]	Mayr	Teresa Maciorletti Blasi (Lodoïska), Marchesi (Lovinski)
Elfrida (tm), 2	May 4, 1796	Ranieri de' Calzabigi	Paisiello	David (Eggardo), Marciorletti Blasi (Elfrida)
Issipile (dm), 2	Nov. 12, 1796	Metastasio	Gaetano Marinelli	Crescentini, Grassini
Giulietta e Romeo (tm), 3	Nov. 25, 1796	[Foppa]	Zingarelli	Giuseppa Grassini (Giulietta), Crescentini (Romeo); *premiered at La Scala, Milan, Jan. 1, 1796*
Gli Orazi e i Curiazi (tm), 3	Dec. 26, 1796	Sografi	Domenico Cimarosa	Crescentini (Curiazio), Babbini (Marco Orazio); *Sografi prominent on title page of libretto*
Telemaco nell'isola di Calipso (dm), 3	Jan. 11, 1797	Sografi	Mayr	Crescentini (Telemaco), Babbini (Mentore)
Gli Orazi e i Curiazi (tm), 3	May 21, 1797	Sografi	Cimarosa	Babbini (Marco Orazio), Antonio Brizzi (Curiazio); *revival*
La morte di Mitridate (tm), 2	May 27, 1797	Sografi	Zingarelli	Babbini (Mitridate); *set by Nasolini for Trieste, autumn 1796*
La morte di Cesare (ds), 2	July 12, 1797	Sertor	Bianchi	Babbini (Bruto), Elisabetta Cafforini (Giulio Cesare), Giovanna Babbi (Calfurnia)

(continued)

Table 9.1. *(continued)*

Title	*Opening*	*Librettist*	*Composer*	*Selected singers, roles, and notes*
Giovanna d'Arco, ossia la pulzella d'Orleans (ds), 4	Aug. 19, 1797	Sografi	Gaetano Andreozzi	Babbi (Giovanna d'Arco), Babbini (Riccardo Talbot)
La Lodoïska (dm), 3	Nov. 15, 1797	Gonella	Mayr	Angelica Catalani (Lodoïska), Marchesi (Lovinski)
Carolina e Mexicow (tm), 3	Dec. 26, 1797	Gaetano Rossi	Zingarelli	Catalani (Carolina), Marchesi (Mexicow)
Il conte di Saldagna (tm), 3	Jan. 10, 1798	Moretti	Zingarelli	Catalani (Cimene), Marchesi (Ramiro)
Lauso e Lidia (dm), 2	Jan. 14, 1798	Foppa	Mayr	Marchesi (Lauso), Catalani (Lidia)
L'Andromaca (dm), 2	May 15, 1798	Antonio Salvi	Paisiello	Catalani (Andromaca), David (Ulisse); *revival of Naples, San Carlo production of Nov. 1797*
Gli Orazi e i Curiazi (tm), 3	Nov. 17, 1798	Sografi	Cimarosa	*Revival*
La morte di Semiramide (dm), 2	Dec. 5, 1798	Sografi	Nasolini	Grassini (Semiramide), Antonio Brizzi (Arsace/Nino)
Alceste (tm), 3	Dec. 26, 1798	Sografi	Marcos António Portugal	Grassini (Alceste)
Zenobia in Palmira (ds), 3	[Jan.], 1799	Sertor	Pasquale Anfossi	Brizzi (Aureliano), Grassini (Zenobia)
Adelaide di Guesclino (dramma di sentimento), 2	May 1, 1799	Rossi	Mayr	Mombelli (Carlo, Duca di Vandomo), Caterina Angiolini (Adelaide)
Le feste d'Iside (dm), 2	Nov. 16, 1799	Rossi	Nasolini	Salvatore de Lorenzi (tenor), Teresa Doliani
Antigono (dm), 2	Dec. 5, 1799	Rossi	Francesco Basile	Doliani, de Lorenzi
Il ratto delle Sabine (dm), 2	Dec. 26, 1799	Rossi	Zingarelli	Doliani (Ersilia), Catalani (Mezio Curzio), de Lorenzi (Romolo)
Gli Orazi e i Curiazi (tm), 3	Jan. 21, 1800	Sografi	Cimarosa	de Lorenzi (Marco Orazio), Doliani (Orazia), Catalani (Curiazio)
Gli Sciti (dm), 2	Feb. 21, 1800	Rossi	Mayr	de Lorenzi (Indatiro), Catalani (Atamaro)
La morte di Cleopatra (tm), 2	May 21, 1800	Sografi and Rossi	Nasolini; 2nd act, subterranean scene, set by Marinelli	Catalani (Cleopatra), Brizzi (Ottaviano Augusto), Antonio Cantù (Marc' Antonio)

Note: Operas are identified by genre and number of acts: dm = dramma per musica; tm = tragedia per musica; ds = dramma serio.

sian, though most of Metastasio's operas were mounted in autumn—*Alessandro nell'Indie* (autumn 1792), *Antigono* (Ascension 1794, the one exception), *Achille in Sciro* (autumn 1794), *Artaserse* and *Demofoonte* (both autumn 1795), and *Issipile* (autumn 1796)—this in a major operatic center during the 1790s. Initially all of the operas were identified as drammi per musica on the title pages of their respective libretti and used the traditional three-act structure. One in the 1793–

94 season, Alessandro Pepoli and Felice Alessandri's *Virginia*, did open with the title "tragedia in musica," and Antonio Sografi and Simone Mayr's *Saffo, ossia I riti d'Apollo Leucadio* used a modern two-act structure, but most of the other operas up through Carnival 1796 had the old genre names and basic dramaturgical structures. Only in the second half of the decade did "tragedie per musica" outnumber "drammi per musica" (or other times the intermediate "dramma serio" appeared), although two acts continued to be less common than three acts. What was new and striking throughout the whole of the 1790s was the ubiquity of choruses, especially in the introduzioni, plus dynamic, action-oriented ensembles and overall dramatic intensity.

Spatially speaking, conservatism at La Fenice, insofar as it did exist, was of a markedly Venetian kind, different, for instance, from that at Perugia and very different from midcentury Naples. Unlike the monarchical San Carlo, La Fenice had no royal box and no equivalent for the doge. Class stratifications were palpable vertically through its hierarchized tiers of boxes, yet the theater's semiotics bespoke dispersal, not centralization.[20] Nor were the most coveted boxes massed together within any given tier. In fact, levies imposed on boxes were evidently based as much on the desirability of the sight lines they provided to the stage as the visibility of their positions from within the hall, since boxes placed in radically differing positions within the curve of the horseshoe could cost identical amounts (see fig. 9.1). In 1797 the proscenium boxes in the *pepian*, for example (numbers 1 through 3 and 27 through 29), together with the single box at dead center (number 15), were levied most heavily at 285.18 lire, followed by the boxes surrounding the centermost one (including numbers 10 through 14, 16, 18 through 20, D, and E) at 238 lire. Within the same tier, there was a steep drop to 190.12 lire for boxes that fell in the curve of the arc (numbers 4 through 9, C, A, B, F, and 21 through 26). Such were the economies of oligarchic republicanism.[21]

* * *

Yet by Day 5, "Year One of Italian Liberty" after the city's fall, oligarchic republicanism was deemed no republicanism at all. On that day, the new provisional municipal government announced its division into various committees, staffed by natives but designed to mimic those of the French revolutionary government and overseen by watchful leaders of the French garrison. Among these, the Committee of Public Instruction, whose Venetian officers included some of the live-

20. On January 18, 1798, the Habsburg Austrians came into Venice to take over occupation from the French, following the Treaty of Campoformio, and in 1866 they added a royal box to La Fenice.

21. ASTF, Partitario Canoni 2, 1792–1800. By designating prime-viewing boxes in locations scattered throughout the theater, rather than in contiguous locations, the Society of La Fenice imitated the demographics of fancy real estate throughout Venice, which traditionally had ensured through various legal mechanisms that noble palaces be built off the Grand Canal (as well as along it) and throughout all six of the city's *sestieri*. This was a distinctive feature of aristocratic demography in Venice in contrast to most other Italian cities.

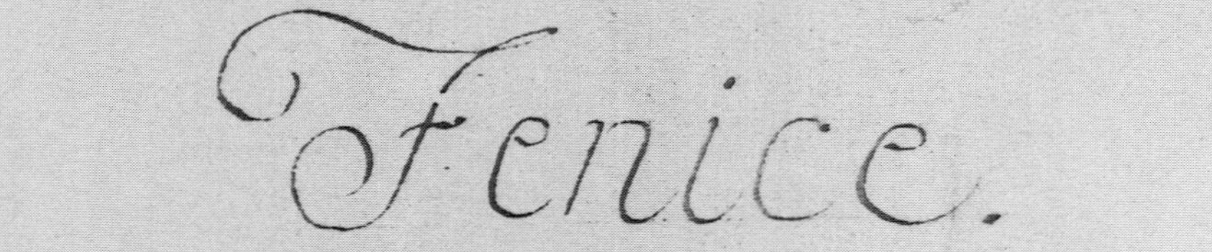

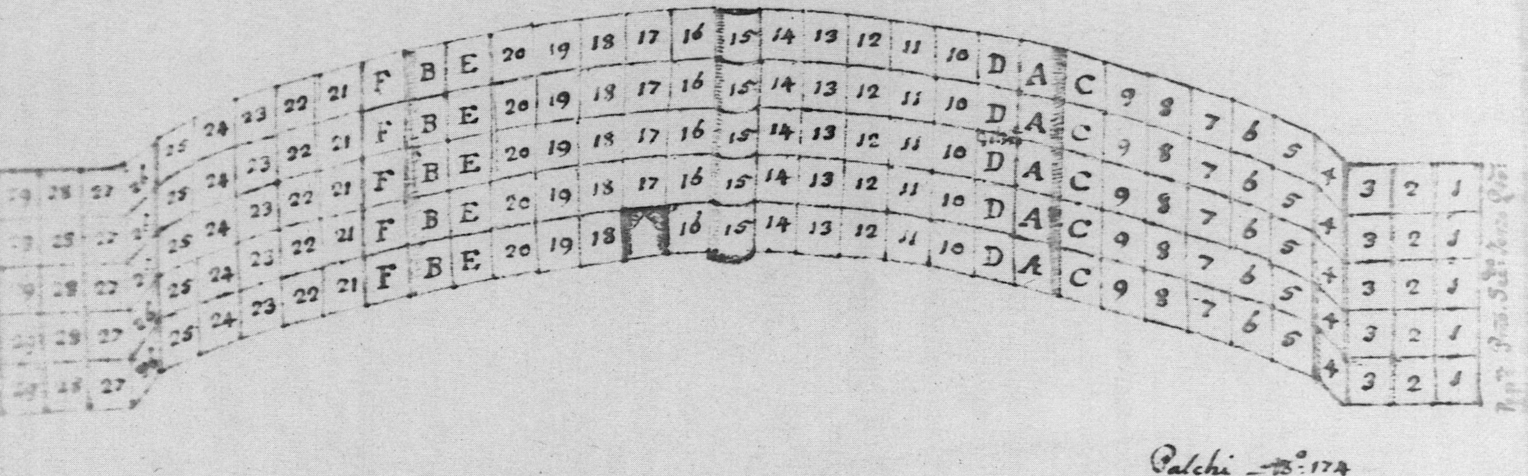

FIG. 9.1. Eighteenth-century plan of boxes at Teatro La Fenice. Museo Civico Correr, Biblioteca, Venice. Reproduced by permission.

liest, and most rabid, sympathizers of the French, was to manage the moral and educational program of the new order. Central to its goals was a zealous educational program designed to inculcate new "democratic" precepts while insisting on a total break with the past. To that end, the committee installed orators in every *campo* to teach the tenets of democracy, extended the hours of the public library, eliminated various forms of aristocratic "vanity" (simplifying public uniforms and the like), supervised the publication in Italian and dialect of tracts by Rousseau, Thomas Paine, and other enlightened "democrats," as well as the publication of various democratic constitutions from abroad, published the minutes of their open sessions (contra Mariotti at Perugia), organized public festivals, and posted endless decrees on matters moral, from prostitution to domestic life, schooling, and church. They also quickly adopted the revolutionary clocks and calendar of the French, which had been authorized in France by the National Convention of the French Revolution three and a half years earlier as a way of rupturing any symbolic, including inseparably Christian, connections to the old Gregorian calendar. In this way, timekeeping under the new system was intended not just to replace the church's real and implicit social controls with the secular controls of government—the new arbiter of nationhood—but to do so through the highly rationalized French decimal system, which counted all weeks, hours, and minutes in tens and emphasized seasonal connections to agriculture in ways intended to make the new calendar seem natural, inevitable, and continuous with a mythical, imaginary past.[22]

These strategies of change did not relinquish festive models of old. Rather, much like the French—indeed prodded by them—the new municipal government appropriated festivity to instruct the masses in the new ideals. A central instrument of their democratic propaganda was theater.[23] Not only did the Committee of Public Instruction field all petitions from theaters regarding rules of management and assume the role of political censor that had previously been the charge of the Inquisitori di Stato; they also involved themselves directly and centrally in the establishment of a theater for the "common people"—a class more or less commensurate with the *popolani*, which did not categorically dissolve with the fall of the oligarchy but hardened into a totem to be worshipped in the more flattering arena of revolutionary drama.[24] Indeed, a statement by the

22. Eviatar Zerubavel gives a basic explanation of the French Republican calendar (which was in effect from November 24, 1793 through January 1, 1806) and its decimal system in *Hidden Rhythms*, 82–96. An astute cultural analysis of transformative meanings of revolutionary time will appear in a forthcoming book by Sanja Perovic, *Untamable Time: Creating the World Anew in Revolutionary France*.

23. Important on Jacobin legislation in Italian theaters is Giovanni Azzaroni, who concludes that Jacobin theater did lead, at least at the time, to the reappropriation of commercial theatrical events by new and wider publics, ending in some instances in a virtual collapse of the boundary between stage and hall through the passions of crowds (*La rivoluzione a teatro*, 371 and passim).

24. On the Teatro Civico, see de Michelis, *Il teatro patriottico*, 9–43 and 44–49, and various texts produced at the theater (including Sografi's *Il matrimonio democratico*). See also Barricelli, "Civic Representations," 153–59. Some attention is given to Jacobin opera in Chegai, *L'esilio di Metastasio*, chap. 3, 107ff.

committee addressed to authors of theatrical works, directors of troupes, and impresarios made explicit its role vis-à-vis a theater of the people:

> One of the principal objects of Public Instruction must be theater. The performances done in it are sometimes more efficacious than laws. To change the spirit of a people abased by long slavery, to inspire a salutary horror of serious crimes, to light the sacred fire of liberty—these must be the principal aims of tragic works; just as enlightening the people, refining the Nation, and correcting it of its habits must be those of comedy, the painter of truth.[25]

OPERA IN A DEMOCRATIC ASCENSION

Since the Committee of Public Instruction constituted the prime organ of theatrical propaganda, it also adjudicated the reopening of La Fenice for the impending Ascension season.[26] Within days after the republic collapsed, the then impresario Alberto Cavos began negotiating with the committee in a series of petitions. The first opera put on was a revival of *Gli Orazi e i Curiazi,* with libretto by the Paduan lawyer Sografi and music by the famed Domenico Cimarosa. This was a shocker in the genre of the tragedia per musica that had premiered to great acclaim during the previous Carnival. As a revival, *Gli Orazi* was easy enough to mount in a time of such chaos, even if its subject matter was somewhat shy of suitable. But the question of which ballets were to be inserted between acts still had to be settled. Time constraints induced the committee to give permission for a ballet called *Il Cesare nelle Gallie,* but it was worried lest people assume that the ballet had passed government inspection. Therefore it ordered the title *Riconciliazione degli Edui* as replacement for the proposed one, so as to avoid any "inappropriate allusion" (though neither title appears in the published libretto).[27]

Similar quandaries beset permissions for the opera itself, since there was no time to order changes in it if the theater was to open on schedule. To circumvent the whole problem the Committee of Public Instruction directed on

25. The text is addressed to "Autori di Teatrali Rappresentazioni," "Capi Comici, ed Impresari di Opere": "Uno tra i principali oggetti della Pubblica Istruzione esser deve il Teatro. Le Rappresentazioni, che in esso si fanno sono talvolta più efficaci delle stesse leggi. Cangiare lo spirito di un Popolo per lunga schiavitù avvilito, ispirare un orror salutare pei gran delitti, accendere il sacro fuoco di libertà esser devono le principali mire di una tragica rappresentazione; siccome illuminare il Popolo, ingentilire la Nazione, correggerne i costumi, quelle esser debbono della pittrice del vero la Commedia" (I-Vas, Democrazia, b. 167, undated, unnumbered).

Helpful in navigating the state archives during the Municipality is Romanelli's "Archivistica giacobina," 325–47.

26. For an old but still-useful classic on Jacobin and anti-Jacobin theater during the Napoleonic occupations in Italy, see Brozzi, *Sul teatro giacobino e antigiacobino.*

27. I-Vas, Democrazia 88.6, May 18, 1797.

May 19 that a note be inserted in the libretto indicating that neither opera nor ballet had been revised owing to lack of time.[28]

The messages projected directly by the works onstage were not the only matters plaguing the reopening of the theater. Running the Ascension season, for which preparations at the Fenice were already underway, had to be accommodated to new procedures of which the management was totally uncertain. Despite the continuities that sustained La Fenice as the theater of an elite, the collapse of the oligarchy had fractured a potentially vast range of cultural mechanisms and to some extent shaken its belief systems, and virtually all modes of finance, management, and power hung in a state of structural uncertainty. Many uncertainties related to theater management, since the practices of running the theater, as elsewhere, were bound up with local ideologies.

On Day 6, "Year One of Italian Liberty," Cavos began forwarding a string of queries and petitions to the Committee of Public Instruction. He petitioned on Day 7 to open the following evening but needed advice on rules: on masking by theatergoers, on when to start the show, on whether ministers of foreign courts were to pay at the door, on how to treat infractions, on how to make financial deposits, and many other matters he could not yet think to name (see, e.g., fig. 9.2).[29]

That same day, an anonymous official of the committee jotted down a checklist of demands made and met, numbering five in all (fig. 9.3). The theater, he noted, had been given permission to open and the libretto and ballet programs cleared.[30] Deposits, previously made to the Council of Ten, were to be redirected to the Committee of Finance. Dedications, now seen as the blight of a feudal patronage system, were forbidden from libretti (recall the absence of a dedication page in the opening opera for the Teatro Civico at Perugia). And a plan was to be instituted for producing patriotic arias. All demands had been met save the last, "non ancora eseguita."

The committee acquiesced in the revival of *Gli Orazi e i Curiazi* as season

28. I-Vas, Democrazia 88.6.4, May 19, 1797, and 88.6.18, May 20, 1797.

29. "Cittadini Municipalisti Provisori. Il Cittadino Alberto Cavos Impressario del Teatro la Fenice, chiede il permesso di poter Sabbato ventuno serà li 20. Maggio corrente aprire con opera seria il Teatro stesso, come pure chiede il metodo, ed il luoco apposito onde poter eseguire il Deposito a cautella certa de' virtuosi, che si presteranno al servizio del Teatro medesimo. Chiede altresì quali metodi si debbano tenere, et osservare per le maschere alla porta, e scena del detto Teatro, chiede pure l'ora precisa da incominciarsi l'opera, non che se debba far pagare alla porta li Ministri delle Corti estere, e il metodo per poter togliere l'abbuso di aprire senza il dovuto biglietto li scagni nel teatro stesso. E finalmente chiede di essere avvertito di tutte quelle discipline, regole, e metodi, che saranno credute opportune da questa provisoria municipalità" (I-Vas, Democrazia 88.6.14, May 20, 1797).

In a meeting of the society on May 19, members expressed similar confusion about whether and how to make deposits for the impresario (ASTF, Processi verbali delle convocazioni sottrati all'incendio 1817 del Palazzo Corner, box 1, fasc. 12).

30. On the role of the Council of Ten (Consiglio dei Dieci) vis-à-vis Venetian theater during the republic, see Wiel, *I teatri musicali veneziani*, lxvii–lxxvi.

Libertà Eguaglianza

Contribuzione de' Possidenti Beni, e Fondi di qualunque sorte in Venezia, imposta col Decreto della Municipalità 30. Pratile (18. Giugno 1797. V. S.)

HA contato nella Cassa Nazionale ~~il Cittadino~~ La Società Teatro Fenice

Effettivi Ducati Duecento uno £7

per la seconda delle cinque Ratte della Contribuzione suddetta ad esso spettante ——— 201 £7

Dono Dieci per Cento 22 £8

Data li 16 annotazione / 6 gmbre. 1797. V. S.

Deputato all' ~~Imposta~~ eccezione

FIG. 9.2. Tax report submitted to the municipal government of Venice by Alberto Cavos, the impresario of La Fenice. A figure of Liberty stamps its heading. Archivio Storico della Fondazione Teatro La Fenice, Venice. Reproduced by permission.

opener not only because it had triumphed in the previous Carnival season and could be staged virtually unchanged with little delay, but because the Fenice was so greatly prized as cultural capital that aborting or further delaying the season was not an amenable alternative.[31] Permission was granted for

31. On the very complex phenomenon of *Gli Orazi e i Curiazi* in relation to opera reform, revolution, the restoration, enlightenment, Venetian mythology (of the phoenix rising from the ashes), and so on—all of which relate to its success but none of which alone can come close to explaining its complexities, contradictions, and evolutions—see the work of Giovanni Morelli and Elvidio Surian, who conclude that the opera's mixing of styles and valences work to fashion an unprecedented (and highly successful) operatic realism. There were 138 different productions of the opera altogether

a May 20 opening, though in the end the opening was put off until the twenty-first.[32]

Gli Orazi offered a fanatical defense of the old patriarchal political order even as it radically and paradoxically demystified, through a particularly bloody ending, the kind of happy outcome that allegories of the old order were supposed to ensure. In Sografi's libretto, the Roman Orazio (Horatio) kills off his Alban foe Curiazio (Curatius), member of an old enemy nation, in a duel designed to settle a war between the nations. But Curiazio is beloved of, and newly husband to, Orazio's sister, Orazia (Horatia). When Orazia in her mad grief denounces Orazio's would-be "valor" before a great crowd of citizens and curses Rome, her brother stabs her and hurls her down a flight of stairs.

The phenomenon of death onstage was still relatively new in Italian theaters, and the murder audiences witnessed here surpassed all precursors not only in intensity but in defying the principle of familial loyalty that bound together settecento stageworks, whose endings had generally reconciled the exigencies of familial ties with principles of loyalty to the state.[33] Even within the opera's own narrative, Orazio's double transgression—forcing fratricide before the delicate eyes of eighteenth-century spectators (onstage and off) and wresting judicial power from the state to mete out punishment—meets with mixed responses. The father of the Orazi and Orazio's wife, Sabina (also sister to Curiazio), react with horror at the monstrosity of Orazio's action, his contempt for family bonds,

---

(Morelli and Surian, "Come nacque e come morì il patriottismo romano nell'opera veneziana," 101–35 and, on the number of productions, n. 2).

32. An ironic commentary was given in anticipation of the occasion in *Il nuovo postiglione*, May 26, 1797, 360: "On Sunday night there will probably be a public festivity given in Teatro La Fenice, where for some evenings the opera from the preceding Carnival, *Gli Orazi e i Curiazi*, has been staged. Oh what a sweet spectacle it was to see many of the most agreeable of our [female] ex-patricians, having set aside the grave character that the prejudice of birth accords them, abandon themselves with their presence and gaiety to that sweet philanthropy that guided their spouses, parents, and relatives! Oh how much more dear they became to their fellow citizens! May the virtuous example of these [ladies], their triumph, their patriotic steadfastness, be followed by all others who inopportune chance has held back until now. Born to govern hearts and not the rights of citizens, they will be ever more the objects of general esteem." [Domenica notte probabilmente si darà un pubblico veglione nel Teatro *la Fenice*, dove si rappresenta da alcune sere le opere dello scorso Carnevale, *Gli Orazi, e [i] Curiazi.* Oh qual soave spettacolo si fù il vedere molte delle amabili nostre ex patrizii, dimesso quel grave carattere che il pregiudizio della nascita le accordava, abbandonarsi colla loro presenza e ilarità a quella dolce filantropia che diresse i loro sposi, i genitori, i parenti. Oh quanto più care esse divennero ai lor concittadini! Possa l'esempio virtuoso di queste, il lor trionfo, la patriotica loro fermezza, esser seguiti da tutte l'altre, che intempestive combinazioni ritennero fino ad ora. Esse nate per dominar su' cuori, e non sui dritti dei Cittadini, formerano sempre più l'oggetti della commune estimazione.]

33. On the Italian reintroduction of onstage death, see most especially McClymonds, "La morte di Semiramide" and her forthcoming book on opera seria in the later eighteenth century. A dissertation currently in progress by Katharina Kost, "Das tragische ende in der italienischen Oper des 18. Jahrhunderts" (University of Heidelberg), looks to treat late-eighteenth-century "morte" operas as a category.

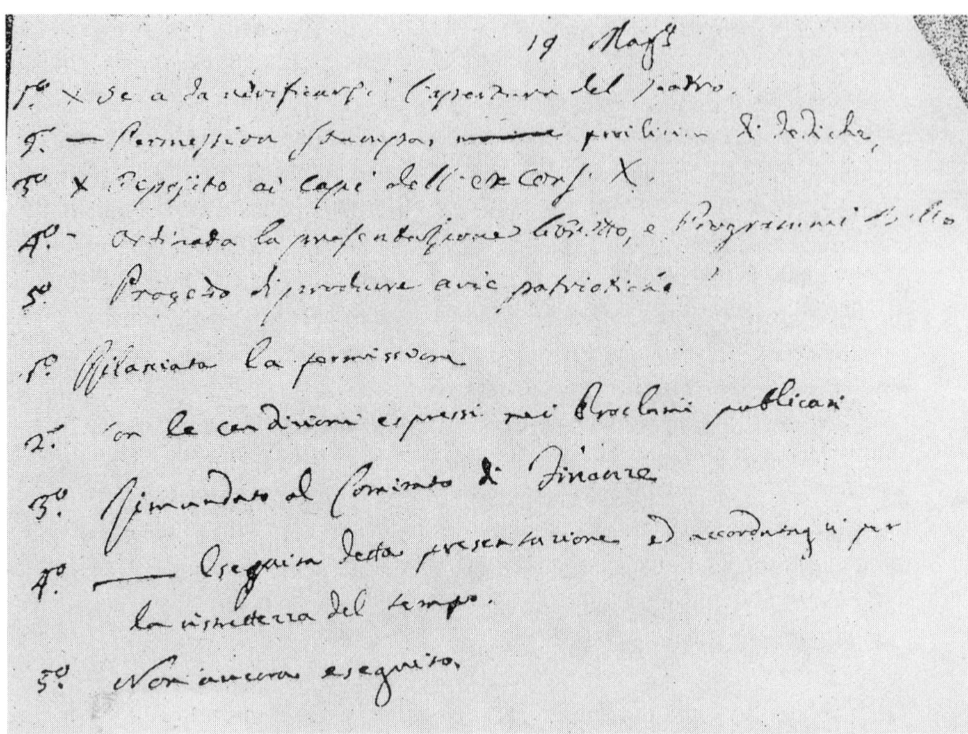

FIG. 9.3. Checklist of an anonymous official of the Committee of Public Instruction, showing demands for changes at La Fenice. Four items are marked as having been done. Municipalità Provvisoria, b. 88, fasc. "Teatri e musica," unnumbered document, May 19, 1797. Archivio di Stato, Venice. Reproduced by permission.

and his defiance of due public process. But they are nearly drowned out in a sea of public praise: the Roman senators and populace cheer Orazio for loyalty to the state, as if the solo voices of Orazio and Sabina were no match for the grand choruses of the vox populi. *Gli Orazi* thus opened a subversive gap in the heroic armature of Metastasian nobility, even as it claimed to perpetuate the trope of Roman valor that had traditionally been purveyed by opera seria and specifically by the civic mythology of Venice perpetuated by its patriciate.

It is unclear how many performances of *Gli Orazi* finally took place in Ascension 1797, but in the eyes of French sympathizers its importance must have paled beside that of the second opera for Ascension, *La morte di Mitridate,* based on a libretto written the previous year for Vicenza and Trieste.[34] Again the librettist—and this time, reviser—was Sografi.

By now Sografi was the leading author of Jacobin stage rhetoric, having

34. On these and other sources of Andreozzi's opera, see Rizzuti, "Music for a *Risorgimento* Myth." Staging two operas for Ascension was unprecedented; the rule had always been one. Most probably *Gli Orazi* was only revived once the republic fell because *Mitridate,* planned as the sole opera of the season, had to be put off while revisions to it were made (see below).

honed a protorevolutionary style in spoken drama, debuted in Venice with a Sappho opera at Carnival in 1794, and come on strong with the tragedia in musica *Gli Orazi,* a genre of which he was the prime practitioner in the 1790s.[35] After Venice fell, he pursued a frenzy of projects toward the installation of a popular "democratic" theater. Among his first tasks was to write what he called an "Azione Teatrale" for the benefit of the "Popolo," based on the Serrata of 1297 and the abortive plot of 1310 to topple the oligarchy, which was to serve as the main fare for a new civic theater. In Sografi's construction, the wicked Serrata that had stood for centuries as the defining event in the formation of the oligarchy had been consolidated shortly after its occurrence by the failed attempt to overthrow it in 1310, a failure that was happily reversed only in 1797 after five hundred years. Replying to the Committee of Public Instruction on May 23, Sografi borrowed the new antiaristocratic rhetoric of clipped propositions to affirm the vitality of a project that sought to discredit the aristocracy on the theatrical stage. The letter addressed itself to fellow "Cittadini," in 1797 a direct translation of the French "Citoyens," now applied to all Venetians with the bludgeoning universality of revolutionary egalitarianism. One salient justification for his project was that theater had been the abiding "pulpit of the great French":

> Can you, intent on the good of the People, with your constant concern, forget that at such a moment? . . . [Within the theater] it is time for the voices of Liberty and Equality to sound again; there it is necessary for the People to obtain knowledge of their rights—usurped, reviled, abused; there[36] . . . but this is not the moment to discuss: it is time to resolve. The undertaking is a difficult one because of time constraints, but liberty has its miracles. Help me: make up your minds. The uniting of the two epochs would be of no little instruction to the people. I speak of the closing of the Maggior Consiglio in 1296 and of the Conspiracy of Baiamonte [Tiepolo] in 1310. These two deeds united would form an Azione Teatrale, Democratic.[37]

35. By 1797 opera seria and tragedia per musica were both embedded in a history of tensions between young librettists of revolutionary bent and the old nobility; see Pepoli's *Due lettere,* cited in Bauman, "The Society of La Fenice," n. 10, and Bauman, "Alessandro Pepoli's Renewal of the *Tragedia per Musica,*" 211–20, as well as Rossini, "L'opera classicista nella Milano napoleonica, 1796–1815," 127–71, and Gronda and Fabbri, *Libretti d'opera italiani,* 357–448, on *Gli Orazi e i Curiazi.* See also McClymonds, "The Venetian Role in the Transformation of Italian Opera Seria," 221–40.

36. The ellipses following are Sografi's.

37. "[On the outside:] 23 Maggio 1797 / Petizione del Cittadino Sograffi per Rappresentazione teatrale. / [On the inside:] Cittadini/ [added: 23 Maggio 1797.] / Petizione del Cittadino Sografi. / Cittadini, Il Pulpito de' bravi Francesi è stato sempre il Teatro. Voi, intenti al bene del Popolo colle vostre assidue cure, potrete dimenticarlo in siffatto momento? Di là è tempo che tuonino ancora le voci di Libertà, di Eguaglianza, di là è necessario che tragga il Popolo la cognizione de' suoi diritti, usurpati, avviliti, abusati: di là . . . ma non è il momento di discorrere; è quello di risolvere. L'impresa è malagevole per la ristrettezza del tempo, ma la libertà ha i suoi miracoli. Assistetemi, decidetevi. L'unire due epoche sarebbe di non poca istruzione al popolo; parlo del chiudersi il fu Maggior Consiglio nel 1296 e della Congiura di Bajamonte nel 1310. Uniti questi due fatti, formerebbesi un

In a follow-up letter on his progress, Sografi claimed to be treating his subject "popolarmente, *ad utilitatem* e non *ad pumpam*," in such a way that his play would show the people that they were regaining what five hundred years ago they had lost and why they had great reason to be happy.[38] As a venue for Sografi's "Teatrale Patriotico" (so-called by the new government), the committee had selected the Teatro San Giovanni Grisostomo owned by Virginia Chigi Grimani, a theater larger but less richly appointed than the Fenice. Grimani was asked to relinquish it throughout the whole summer season in order that it be made into a popular patriotic theater—a site for the so-called Teatro Civico.

It will be useful to review the process by which such a theater was founded, since it was a matter of strenuous concern to the Committee of Public Instruction, which devoted much time in its initial planning sessions to urgent discussions over its location and ethos. Already on May 21 and 22, in reviewing plans for an imminent public *festa* ordered by the president of the Municipalità Provvisoria, Nicolò Corner, the matter of a popular theater had become paramount. Corner's request for the committee's report had stressed that a special *festa* was needed to "animate the people," adding that it was "necessary to do so with public spectacles" and furthermore that "a patriotic meal . . . decreed by law" had in any case already been linked to the occasion.

In settling on a "Festa in Teatro gratis al popolo" as part of the proposed plans, committee members had first recommended La Fenice as the obvious site, only to deem it inappropriate once their discussions turned from the question of a one-time event to a broader proposal for an ongoing popular theater. Everyone agreed that it was useful to promote public spirit through festivity, but one member argued successfully that a comic theater would please the general populace better on a daily basis than would La Fenice (whose repertory had always consisted entirely of opera seria).[39] Ironically, it was these discussions that led to the simultaneous founding of the Teatro Civico within the old Teatro San Giovanni Grisostomo in the delirious (or frightful, depending on your perspective) first weeks after the fall and targeting of La Fenice to be purged symbolically of oligarchic evils in the public *festa* of May 28.[40]

Azione Teatrale, Democratica" (I-Vas, Democrazia 88.6.68). Sografi uses the old Venetian calendar in dating the Serrata to 1296.

38. "Salutate il Gritti, e ditegli che tratterò questo soggetto come siamo rimasti d'accordo, cioè, popolarmente, ad utilitatem e non ad pumpam. Faremo vedere al popolo com'egli oggi acquista ciò che cinquant'anni sono ha perduto e che ha gran motivo di star allegro" (I-Vas, Democrazia 88.6.157 [163], May 28, 1797, from Padua). In fact it was about another hundred years during the Middle Ages before the noble ranks were truly closed, but 1297, when the last large expansion of the Maggior Consiglio took place, was the mythically relevant date.

39. I-Vas, Democrazia 90.67, May 22, 1797.

40. I-Vas, Democrazia 167.73. Grimani answered on May 30 with a list of requests for maintaining the theater in good order throughout the summer (I-Vas, Democrazia 88.6.126). A further petition to Grimani for the opening, now on behalf of a Società Patriotica del Civico Teatro, was submitted on July 6 (I-Vas, Democrazia 88.6), though note, interestingly, that on July 13, Sografi submitted another petition protesting that his work had been "defraudato" ("defrauded" or "cheated," with the sense here of "stolen") and rescinding rights of publication from the committee in ac-

Rejecting La Fenice as the regular theater of the masses and commandeering it instead to fuel fantasies of revolution whose valences could match the theater's social register, the committee succumbed to its mystique as a "nobilissimo teatro." While San Giovanni Grisostomo would be turned into the people's theater, La Fenice was to be the arena of an exultant bourgeoisie, humbled former patricians, new government officials, French officers, and prestigious visitors, its noble character called on to embellish the magnificence of the new regime. To this end, the management had to hand over for regular use by French officials and members of the provisional government six boxes in the lower tiers that had traditionally been reserved for ministers of foreign courts.[41] In summertime, moreover, it became the site of thirty special performances ordered by the French to celebrate the arrival of Bonaparte. For these, the genres remained dramma serio and tragedia per musica in a way that assigned the French a luminous position in the present by allowing them to appropriate the symbolic space of a timeless Venetian—and republican—past.

For May 28, the Fenice's impresario was busy arranging the free public "Festa in Teatro." When the evening arrived, an onstage orchestra played revolutionary songs and hymns to accompany workmen, gondoliers, and other *popolani* who danced on the stage dressed in three-cornered hats.[42] Behind them streamed liberty banners and French flags in red, white, and green, and in the midst of it all stood a liberty pole crowned with the Phrygian cap, ancient symbol of freedom from slavery. The event was commemorated with an engraving (now in the Museo Correr), which shows a stage bedecked with winged Cupids and figures of Liberty bearing celebratory standards (fig. 9.4): "Il Popolo Veneciano è Riconoscente Verso il Suo Liberatore," "La Virtù è il Carattere d'un Popolo Veramente Libero," "Virtù e Indivisibbilità della Reppublica [*sic*] Italica," "Viva il Bravo General Commandante Baragras d'Illiers," "La Uguaglianza [e] la Libertà Formano la Felicità de' Popoli," "Viva la Brava Armata Francese in Italia," "La Democrazia è l'Impero della Ragione."[43] A campaign was in full swing to exalt

---

cordance with ever-growing ideologies that viewed authorial labor as an author's property (I-Vas, Democrazia 88.3).

The San Giovanni Grisostomo, albeit an aristocratic theater, had staged a good deal of comic opera. It had the reputation of being architecturally awkward and of having a public "formed for the most part of footmen and gondoliers," who could enter the theater for free on the first day of the season. The Spanish comic playwright Nicolás Fernández de Moratin observed that in the middle of the parterre there was a stand for selling chestnuts and cooked pears, that during intermissions glasses of wine were passed around, and that there was much noise, simple happiness, clapping and shouting (Mangini, *I teatri di Venezia*, 150).

41. The information comes from the account books of the Fenice, ASTF, Partitario Canoni 2, 1792–1800 (year 1797).

42. I-Vas, Democrazia 167.107. Vittorio Malamani mistakenly gives the date of the occasion as March 28, which is wholly misleading ("Giustina Renier Michiel," 24).

43. The caption on the engraving reads, "Prospetto del Teatro della Fenice in Venezia, per la Festa Pubblica Seguita nella Domenica Sera 28. Mag. 1797. Anno Primo della Libertà Veneta."

On the deployment of revolutionary propaganda in Italian theaters, see Montanile, *I giacobini a teatro*, and Nocciolini, "Teatro musicale e rivolgimenti politici." Various local studies have been

FIG. 9.4. "Festa in Teatro gratis al popolo." Engraving commemorating a festival for the populace held at La Fenice on May 28, 1797. The caption on the engraving reads "View of Teatro La Fenice in Venice, following the public festivity that took place on Sunday, May 28, 1797, Year One of Venetian Liberty." Emblazoned across the flying standards are the phrases "The Venetian People Are Grateful to Their Liberator," "Virtue Is the Character of a People Who Are Truly Free," "Virtue and Indivisibility of the Italian Republic," "Long Live the Great General Commandant Baragras d'Hillers," "Equality and Liberty Form the Happiness of the People," "Long Live the Great French Fleet in Italy," "Democracy Is the Empire of Reason." Museo Civico Correr, Biblioteca, Venice. Reproduced by permission.

the French as redeemers of justice and liberty and to propose festivity in a new light, not as a privilege bestowed by benevolent autocrats but as a fruit of revolution and the basis of collective and individual sovereignty.[44]

---

done: for Milan, see Nocciolini, "Il melodramma nella Milano napoleonica," and Rossini, "L'opera classicista nella Milano napoleonica"; for Florence, see Garlington, "Opera in Florence under French Domination"; for Trieste and Friuli, see Casa, *Influenze ed echi della rivoluzione francese;* for Lucca, see Biagi Ravenni, "The French Occupation of Lucca"; and for Venice, Barricelli, "Civic Representations," "Making a People What It Once Was," and "The Tears and Terror of Foscolo's *Tieste.*" On Zingarelli's *I veri amici repubblicani* (Turin, 1799), see Mattei, "Metastasio con il berretto frigio," and on Sografi's *La morte di Cleopatra,* Nocciolini, "Circolazione di un melodramma."

44. A report was made in *Il nuovo postiglione,* May 26, 1797, 360. Tessitori, *Basta che finissa 'sti cani,* is fascinating on the unsettling combination of new coercions of the public to rejoice in the foreign occupation and the reformist institution of a more systematized police force, radically articulated in Venice in 1797.

In all of this, members of the Committee of Public Instruction proposed themselves as agents, acting upon the realm of cultural production toward the goal of urgent social change. Seemingly forgetful of their puppeteers, they appeared to believe in their power to shape values, symbols, and rules of culture as the French had done, and appealed to their most skilled rhetoricians to furnish the same textual force and "unity" that marked revolution in France. Of course there was not only a mixture of willingness and duress at work, but also a stern template in France, where opera had been drafted into the cause of revolution in the several years preceding.[45]

16 PRATILE / JUNE 4

Originally the festivities of May 28 were to commemorate the change of government as part of a large complex of spectacle encompassing the whole city, solemnly joined together to celebrate its newfound liberty. But the vision of the Committee of Public Instruction, working with and (albeit semi-invisibly) under the French, had grown. In addition, rains had come, and in view of the elaborate preparations planned for the piazza, it was necessary to put off the event by a week.[46] As it turned out, May 28 was a minor preamble to the ambitious festival that finally took place on Pentecost, the following Sunday, June 4—Day 16 of the revolutionary month *pratile* (Prairial).

When the day arrived, San Marco was strung with banners proclaiming peace and liberty through the strong arm of the law. Three slogans were borne aloft: "Liberty Is Preserved by Obeying the Laws," "Dawning Liberty Is Protected by Force of Arms," and "Established Liberty Brings about Universal Peace," and the motto "Regenerated Peace" was ubiquitous.[47] Again, a liberty pole topped with a Phrygian cap stood high in the center of it all. The piazza reverberated with the din of four huge bands and received a vast train of liberated "citizens" who processed twice around the piazza to the sound of the bands' thunder. At the head of the procession were members of the municipality and the commander of the French garrison, Baraguey d'Hilliers. Following them were two children holding lighted candles and a banner with the words "Grow Up, Hope of the Fatherland," succeeded by an engaged couple whose banner read "Democratic Fecundity." Next came an elderly couple, who carried farming tools and "words

45. I borrow the notion of "textual unity" from Hunt, *Politics, Culture, and Class.* On these attempts in Venice, see McClellan, *Venice and Bonaparte.* On French precedents, see, among others, Bartlet, "Patriotism at the Opéra Comique," 839–52, "On the Freedom of the Theater and Censorship," 15–30, and "The New Repertory at the Opéra during the Reign of Terror," 107–56; McClellan, "Battling the Lyric Muse"; and Schneider, "The Administrative History of L'Académie Impériale de Musique in the Age of Napoléon."

46. The initial announcement on May 23 appears in I-Vas, Biblioteca Legislativa 1, no. 40, and the announcement of the postponement on May 31, no. 97. The former is reproduced in *Il codice della libertà italiana,* part 1, p. 240 (I-Vnm 68.c.50).

47. A general description appears in McClellan, *Venice and Bonaparte,* 246–47.

alluding to their advanced age, at which time liberty was instituted,"[48] and last the national guard, foreign consuls, guilds, and civil servants.

The processions culminated in a variety of rituals performed by the new president of the "sovereign People of Venice," Angelo Talier, at the center of the square where the tree of liberty was erected. The central metaphor of the festival was that of regeneration, drawn out in allusions to rebirth, fruitfulness, fertility, and productivity and symbolized by the tree of liberty, with its links to the earth, life, growth, and nature. Extending the metaphor of regeneration, the speech recited by the president at the crux of the ceremony elided nature's progenitors and progeny: wind, sun, and rain; temperance, health, and learning.

> In the replanting that today is solemnly and festively carried out, this prosperous plant, oh Venetian Men (as the Athenian democrats in another age called themselves), brings to my mind the charming images of the poet Catullus: the zephyrs caress it, the sun strengthens it, the rain makes it grow and nourishes it. Tempered social passions are the caressing breezes, exertion adapted to robust people hardens it, just as (conversely) softness and luxury stunt it; finally the rain of manly and healthy education makes it thrive.[49]

Even as Talier invoked tropes of solidarity, fellowship, and harmony, perceptible in the symbols and referents they conjured up were two nearly contradictory rhetorics. Beginning with the more familiar of them, the president retooled long-standing Venetian mythologies of civic virtue by linking the tree to traditional Venetian virtues of goodness, moderation, wisdom, and justice. The tree, he declared, was a native son of Venice, as symbolic genus if not as topographic entity, for Venice had been settled long ago by uncompromising lovers of liberty and equality, who prized those gifts over the more material ones of Ceres:

> Remember that such a precious plant is not something exotic but indigenous and suited to this fortunate soil. Our Venice was born over there in the Rialto. She dispersed herself in these estuaries, shelter and refuge of a few poor people, but lovers of liberty, equality, and goodness, who, animated by the fire of virtue, preferred true equality and liberty to every other comfort and pleasure, subjecting themselves even to the lack of salubrious waters and cultivable earth from which to procure the gifts of Ceres.[50]

48. *Monitore veneto,* June 5, 1797 (Year 1); quoted from McClellan, *Venice and Bonaparte,* 247.

49. "Nel ripiantar che oggi solennemente e festevolmente si fa l'avventurosa pianta, o Uomini Veneziani, come altre volte denominavansi i democratici Ateniesi, mi si affaccian le ridenti immagini del poeta Catullo; gli zeffiri l'accarezzano, il sole la rassoda, la pioggia l'alleva e la nudrisce. Le moderate sociali passioni sono le aure accarezzanti, gli esercizi adattati alle robuste genti ne la rassodano, come per lo contrario mollezza e lusso la intristiscono; finalmente la piova della maschia e sana educazione la fa prosperare" (*Il codice della libertà italiana,* part 2, 15–16). The text of the speech provides a major record of the day's rites.

50. "Sovvengavi, che sì preziosa pianta non è altrimenti esotica, ma indigena e propria di questo fortunato suolo. Nacque Venezia nostra colà in Rialto, si sparse in questi estuari, asilo e rifugio di poche genti povere, ma amanti di libertà, di eguaglianza, e virtuose, le quali animate dal fuoco di

Venetians' insistence on liberty, even at the expense of physical rewards, had made for resistance to invasion: that, so Talier claimed, was Venice's native "plant," its true nature, the fruits of which he called "incessant activity, military courage, industry in trades, growth of commerce, and a navy formidable for those times."[51] The metaphors were saturated with a millennium's worth of aquatic mythology, which sacralized Venice as a Virgin, pure, just, inviolate, and unconquered, a lagoon in a maiden sea.

In the latter half of his speech, the president praised the French while turning to a new rhetoric of sacrifice tinged with violence—one that had grown up in the climate of revolutionary France and found its way into Venetian rhetoric as a mere borrowing.[52] "History," Talier went on, "that portrayer of human actions, bears witness [to the consequences of a passion for liberty]; so that when . . . joining your forces with those of the magnanimous French troops, who honor us here with their hand and sustain us with their counsel, you toppled the already degenerated eastern empire."[53] In the spirit of sacrifice, the empire—glory and honor of Venice in times past—had to be forfeited. Such was the message that had already been disseminated in numerous broadsides and pamphlets, including an attempt of May 23 to herald the forthcoming festivities, which located the city's rebirth in the linguistic domain of the sacred:

> Our regeneration must be celebrated with the *solemn happiness* of a people returned to their rights. The day destined for the erection of the *sacred Tree of liberty* will be a day of joy for all true citizens, who may begin to live the worthy life of man, and it will be a monument of gratitude to our descendants, who will *bless the generosity of France*. The Municipality is setting up a Spectacle *consecrated to Liberty.*[54]

Amid this heady rhetoric of liberty and equality Venice was of course undergoing the trauma of occupation, a trauma that had ruptured for the first time in its history the mythology evoked at the beginning of the president's speech. Be-

---

virtù anteposero ad ogni altro comodo e piacere, vera eguaglianza e libertà, soggiacendo persino a scarseggiar di acqua salubre, e di terra vegetabile, da cui procacciarsi i doni di Cerere" (ibid., 16).

51. See, among numerous other writings, Muir, *Civic Ritual;* Rosand, *Myths of Venice;* and Crouzet-Pavan, *Venice Triumphant*.

52. For an analysis of the link between popular sovereignty and popular violence with respect to the taking of the Bastille, see Sewell, "Historical Events."

53. "Ve ne rende testimonianza la storia pittrice delle umane azioni, allora quando . . . riunendo i vostri sforzi a quelli della magnanima soldatesca francese, la quale qui ci onora, e colla mano e col consiglio ci sostiene, abbatteste il già degenerato orientale impero" (*Il codice della libertà italiana*, part 2, 16–17).

54. Emphases mine. "La nostra rigenerazione dev'essere festeggiata con l'allegrezza solenne del Popolo ritornato ne' suoi diritti. Il giorno destinato all'erezione dell'Albero sacro della Libertà sarà un giorno di gioja per tutti i veri Cittadini, che incominciano a vivere la vita degna dell'Uomo, e sarà un monumento di gratitudine ai nostri Posteri, che benediranno la generosità della Francia. La Municipalità stabilisce uno Spettacolo consacrato alla Libertà" (*Il codice della libertà italiana*, part 1, 119).

cause of this, its myth of origins now had to be summoned up as a victory over homegrown tyranny, as a guarantee against internal affliction and a testimonial of innate redemptive power.[55] A hymn sung in dialect reviled the despotic bonds that had lacerated the people and praised those who had given them a rebirth.[56] All of this naturalized an event that was extraordinary—the demise of Venetian sovereignty—suggesting that the French were merely there to guide the people from their degenerated oligarchic state back to their true natural origins.

Indeed, the president's reference to the French was prelude to a set of culminating rites of particular symbolic weight—a set of what in a proclamation of May 31 were explicitly named "sacrifices," designed to ritualize the final destruction of the oligarchy.[57] The language of violent overthrow was of course merely mimetic, since Venice had barely any military forces at all and had not joined them concretely with those of the French.[58] Yet through such rhetoric, mythologies of freedom and impenetrability to invasion that had sustained Venice for many centuries could be recast as a triumph against Venice's native oppression. The speech climaxed in a sacrifice of particular symbolic weight, the burning of the *libro d'oro*—principal symbol of the aristocratic body and a highly fetishized object—and of the ducal insignia. The significance of the former to the nobility was matched by the significance to the populace of expunging the highly visible doge's crown, an object it would have witnessed at every prior official ritual in the square. As the two were turned to ash, the president made the following appeal:

> May the vain and imposing titles—veils with which ineptitude often wished to cover itself—and other depraved vices of the mind and good morals scatter themselves to the winds. May perfidy and political suspicion stay far from us forever, which, after having imposed on us the hateful and detestable aristocratic yoke, removed our calm of spirit with the fear of hired spies, with the example of insulting ostentation, depraved softness, and their private discords, and made us torpid and nearly paralyzed with the sweet sentiments of brotherly philanthropy.[59]

55. In Barricelli's view, it was precisely this capacity to reinterpret French revolutionary events and symbols in terms of Venetian history and myth that made the trauma of occupation bearable (see "Civic Representations," 141 and passim, and "Making a People What It Once Was," 38–57).

56. Printed as *Ino patriotico per el zorno dell'inalzamento dell'albero della libertà* (I-Vmc, Op. Cicogna XXII [op. 291.11]).

57. I-Vas, Biblioteca Legislativa 2, no. 100; copy in *Il codice della libertà italiana*, part 1, 230.

58. Nor do I mean to invoke the classic associations of sacrifice with violence, now widely derived from René Girard's classic psychological theory of sacrificial violence as collective catharsis (*Violence and the Sacred*). Girard's theory, that violence inheres in sacrifice because sacrifice is an outlet for the violence that is immanent in all human relationships, is too universalizing to fit the Venetian situation, where "revolution" was largely imposed from outside, even though the theory is not incompatible with some of the French revolutionary rhetoric used at Venice.

59. "Spargansi al vento i vani ed imponenti titoli, veli con cui ricoprir volevasi il più della volte la dappocaggine, ed altri vizi depravatori della mente e del buon costume. Lungi stia per sempre da

With the burning of the *libro d'oro*, which listed members of the noble rank and file, along with the ducal insignia, the old Venice of 1297 to 1797 was surrendered, its most exalted members symbolically destroyed to appease and welcome the moral and political forces of the new. From such an offering, a new Venice was to rise, transformed, from the ashes of the old. The feminine "softness" of aristocratic vanity and luxury would be turned into the manly hardness of democratic industry.[60] Signs of despotism condensed in aristocratic symbols were dispersed, scattered by the beneficent winds of nature, which had stood by Venice since its inception and were to be its savior. In this way, Venetians would "come back to their land of origin,"[61] the untamed Venice of times past. The president returned to the naturalistic theme of the sacred tree of liberty, enjoining the populace to sing hymns to the nation of Italy and the heroes of France. Now, however, the tree of liberty was shadowed by the specter of death:

> After having sung hymns of praise and paid adoring tribute to the highest Creator and Governor of all beings, who by unexpected paths wanted to make bloom among us the precious plant of mislaid Liberty and fraternal Equality, and having been pervaded with true jubilation, drunk with internal joy, we all cry out in a full voice: "Long live the first Nation of the universe, Long live the heroes of France, lightenings of war, who without shedding a drop of blood here among us, knew how to break our harsh bonds, who have regenerated us, and who on this day with the mirror of their virtue, plant the most happy vegetation that can take root, to the profit and relief of miserable humanity." People of Venice, sovereign People, vested with a new nature, engrave in your mind and, most piously, in your heart, this golden motto: "Democracy, or death." I have spoken.[62]

Having staged these outdoor festivities, French and municipal authorities proceeded to an exclusive gala performance at La Fenice of Sografi's *La morte di*

---

noi la perfida e suspicosa politica, che dopo averci imposto l'odioso e detestabile aristocratico giogo, ci toglieva la calma dello spirito col timore dei prezzolati delatori, coll'esempio dell'insultante fasto, della depravata mollezza e delle loro private discordie, torpidi ci rendeva, e quasi paralizzati ai dolci sentimenti della fratellevole filantropia" (*Il codice della libertà italiana*, part 2, 17).

60. See n. 49 above.

61. Cf. Mauss, *The Gift*, 15.

62. "Dopo aver cantato inni di laude, e tributato l'adorazione al sommo Creatore e Governatore di tutti gli esseri, che per inaspettati sentieri ha voluto fra di noi far rifiorire la preziosa pianta della smarrita Libertà, e fraterna Eguaglianza, compenetrati da vero giubilo, ebbri d'interna gioja, gridiamo tutti ad alta voce: Viva la prima Nazione dell'universo, vivan gli Eroi di Francia, fulmini di guerra, che senza spargere una stilla di sangue qui tra noi, han saputo rompere le nostre dure ritorte, ci han rigenerati, e collo specchio delle loro virtù in quest'oggi ripiantano la più felice pianta che allignar possa a pro e sollievo della misera umanità. Popolo di Venezia, Popolo sovrano, rivestiti di novella indole, scolpisci nella tua mente, e molto più nel cuore, questo aureo detto: *Democrazia, o morte*. Ho detto" (*Il codice della libertà italiana*, part 2, 17–18). On the phrase "Democracy or death," see David, *Fraternité et la revolution française*. David stresses, however, that the French phrase "fraternité ou mort" did not sound as threatening then as it now does.

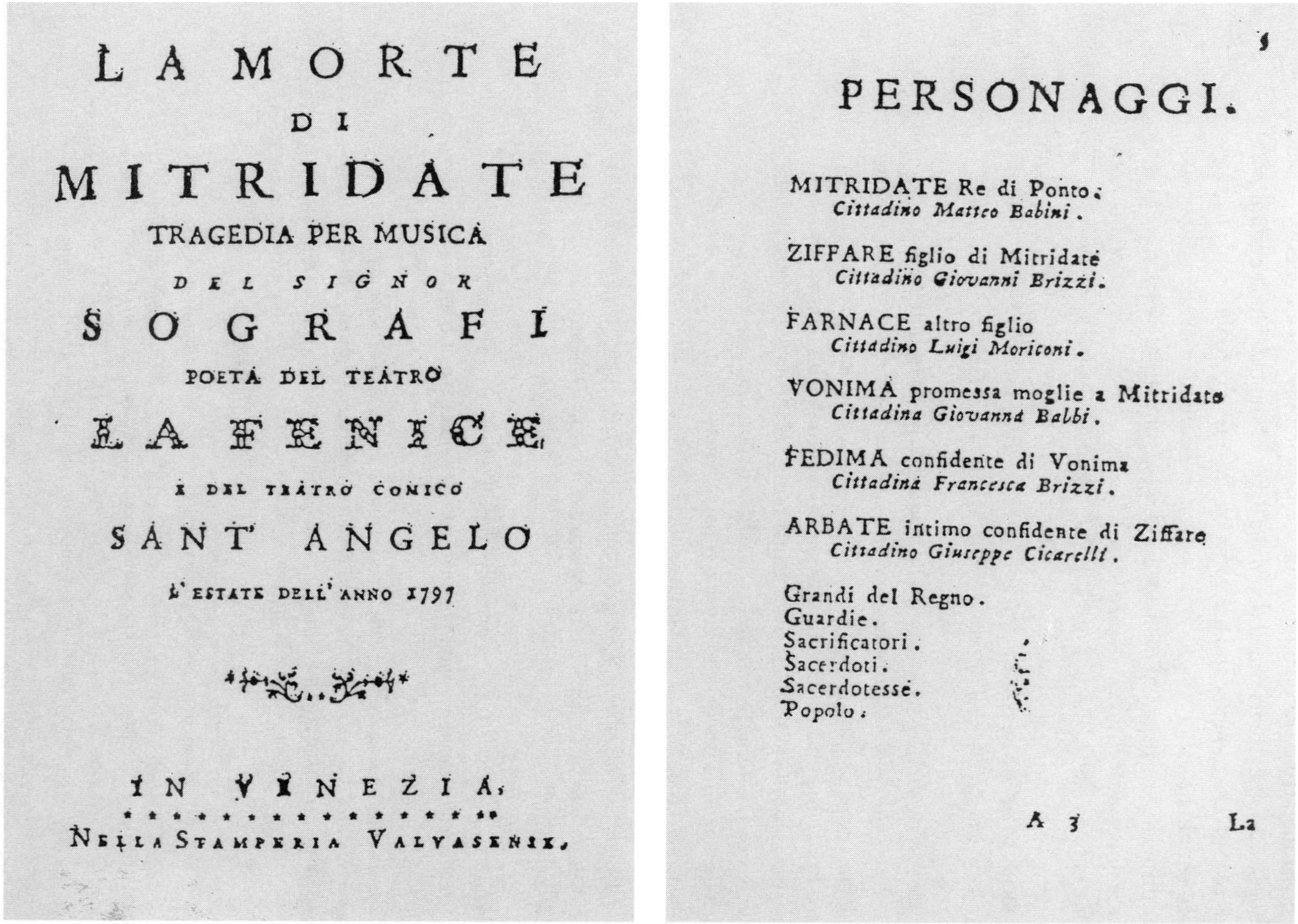

LA MORTE
DI
MITRIDATE
TRAGEDIA PER MUSICA
DEL SIGNOR
SOGRAFI
POETA DEL TEATRO
LA FENICE
E DEL TEATRO COMICO
SANT' ANGELO
L'ESTATE DELL' ANNO 1797

IN VENEZIA,
NELLA STAMPERIA VALVASENSE.

5

PERSONAGGI.

MITRIDATE Re di Ponto.
Cittadino Matteo Babini.

ZIFFARE figlio di Mitridate
Cittadino Giovanni Brizzi.

FARNACE altro figlio
Cittadino Luigi Moriconi.

VONIMA promessa moglie a Mitridate
Cittadina Giovanna Babbi.

FEDIMA confidente di Vonima
Cittadina Francesca Brizzi.

ARBATE intimo confidente di Ziffare
Cittadino Giuseppe Cicarelli.

Grandi del Regno.
Guardie.
Sacrificatori.
Sacerdoti.
Sacerdotesse.
Popolo.

A 3 La

FIG. 9.5. Libretto title page and dramatis personae. From Antonio Simeone Sografi, *La morte di Mitridate* (Venice, 1797). Archivio Storico della Fondazione Teatro La Fenice, Venice. Reproduced by kind permission.

Mitridate, as set by Nicola Zingarelli, the second opera of the "Sensa" season and (unlike *Gli Orazi*), well-honed, at least in crucial parts, to the new ideologies. (Figure 9.5 reproduces the title page and dramatis personae, respectively, from the libretto.)[63] Thus ended the day, marked by an ironic cleavage in vertical class relations that could only have reminded observant commoners of what the previous Sunday had urged them to forget. Yet the two events—popular ceremonies and elitist opera—shared a common set of themes and symbols that illuminate the situation into which La Fenice, as a temple of opera seria, had been enigmatically thrust.

LA MORTE DI MITRIDATE

"Democracy, or death"—this was a duality thematized in numerous, often bizarre, variations throughout the Fenice seasons during which the municipal government reigned. Like the festivities of June 4, the three operas put on for the rest of the spring and summer seasons all tacitly claimed sacrifice as the basis of sovereignty, and not by accident. We might identify two forgers of such a proposition, suggestive and ambiguous though it sometimes was. First was of course the chief librettist of the time, Sografi, whose revolutionary sympathies—like those of a few other librettists—had already capsized the absolutist trope of the *lieto fine* in earlier libretti composed for La Fenice and elsewhere. Under the guidance of the French and the short-lived democratic government, Sografi's texts shattered oligarchic axioms by turning those sympathies to tales of violent release from tyranny. Sografi was on hand to revise *Mitridate* and almost undoubtedly both of the libretti for the following summer season (only one of which was his own). But he would not have done so without direction from the provisional government and its French overseers, who together controlled the Fenice's sudden representations of freedom and rebellion against tyranny.[64]

La morte di Mitridate had first been set by Sebastiano Nasolini in the summer of 1796 for Vicenza, where the French had arrived the previous April, and it was then restaged the following autumn at Trieste, with the famed Matteo Babbini (first encountered in chapter 7 at Perugia) playing the protagonist at both cities.[65] The principal difference between the story told at both Vicenza

63. The dates of performance are given in Girardi and Rossi, *Il Teatro La Fenice,* 24.

64. For spring 1797 through Carnival 1798, the *Indice de' teatrali spettacoli,* part 13, 134, was explicit about the government's role, listing the ballets for *Mitridate* as having been put on "per ordine di quella Municipalità" (facsimile in *Un almanacco drammatico,* ed. Verti, 2:1292). Furthermore, copies of the libretto preserved at I-Vnm and I-Vcg include on the recto preceding the title page the notice "I balli descritti nella presente opera anderà in scena fra' pochi giorni," confirming that the whole production had undergone delays. The copy of the libretto preserved at ASTF can be found online at http://81.75.233.46:8080/fenice/GladReq/libretti.jsp. The digitized archive also includes the libretti for *La morte di Cesare, Giovanna d'Arco,* and others done in the 1790s.

65. Both stagings of *Mitridate* were produced under the impresario Antonio Zardon, who handled the theatrical seasons in the two cities. Like many smaller cities, Vicenza and Trieste seem to have

and Trieste as compared with that at Venice entailed the extent of the choruses and, most important, the nature of the ending.

In two acts, the opera is set in the city of Nymphaeum on the Black Sea in the second century BC, as described in a lengthy stage direction in 1.1. Its central problem involves an attempt by Farnace, son of the tyrannical king of Pontus, Mitridate, to usurp the throne from his brother, Zifare (both tenors), and make the young Vonima his queen. When the opera opens, Mitridate is believed to have died in battle against the Romans, and Vonima, who was betrothed to him, has given her heart to Zifare, prince of Cochlis and hence rightful heir to Pontus. When Mitridate unexpectedly returns triumphant from battle, Vonima and Zifare are forced into an impasse that is resolved only by Mitridate's suicide in act 2.

According to Sografi's directions, the opera opened to reveal upstage, at increasing perspectival depths, a portico leading onto Mitridate's palace, the buildings of Nymphaeum, and behind them the Caucasus Mountains.[66] Closer to the proscenium, the stage was marked by a prophetic partition: on the right, a temple of Venus, readied for wedding festivities, and on the left, a mausoleum for the funeral of Mitridate. As a chorus of subjects urged the populace to celebrate the marriage, Zifare appeared in mourning at the mausoleum, outraged at the insult to Mitridate's honor (though as yet unaware that the would-be bride is his beloved Vonima). Inflecting this scene was a repertory of forms and symbols drawn from imaginary pagan ritual: hence the procession of a wedding party from Mitridate's palace included not just "pompously" dressed guards but the sacrificer of Juno, four priests, and a group of four *donzelle* (girls) dedicated to Venus, followed by Vonima draped in the ancient veil of a virgin.

The spatialized stage served as a kind of primeval dais for the scenic tableaux with which the opera began and by which its development was plotted throughout. The effect must have been at once elegiac, celebratory, and thoroughly monumental. In keeping with this, the final redaction of the musical score rendered scenes as seamlessly as possible, with a minimum of simple recitative, an abundance of dramatic obbligato, and maximum continuity between set numbers, orchestral interludes, recitatives, and choruses, even introducing unconventional interpolations by individual characters or choral groups.[67]

Such a dynamic dramaturgy could serve to release the libretto's mounting emotional charge, particularly once the plot thickened with the appearance of a disheveled Mitridate (Babbini) in 1.3. Mitridate's return made the Freudian dimensions of the family drama loom large, since the first thing he learns on seeing his own mausoleum and the nuptial decorations is that his sons have been vying

---

taken advantage of the availability of superior personnel in "off" seasons. In what follows, I refer to the two jointly as the Vicenza/Trieste version, since the libretti, casts, personnel, management, and (evidently) stagings were all quite similar. Below I cite text from the Trieste libretto (as the later of the two 1796 libretti) and compare with it passages of text that appear in Zingarelli's score.

66. None of Antonio Mauro's scenographic designs for the opera survives.

67. On these directions see, for example, Balthazar, "Mayr, Rossini, and the Development of the Early *Concertato* Finale"; Bartlet, "Grand Opéra"; and Hauk and Winkler, *Werk und Leben: Johann Simon Mayrs* and *Johann Simon Mayr und Venedig*.

for Vonima in his absence.[68] One has forced her hand in a bid to usurp the throne and, with it, his father's power (Farnace), while the other (Zifare) has conquered her heart. But both, in stalking their father's prey, incur his fury, and the remainder of the first act finds Mitridate by turns racked by wrath, grief, and suspicion.[69]

By act 1.5, the evil Farnace is nearly forgotten, however, and Mitridate can subsequently appear as the emoting sovereign, saddened by his sons' desertions and insisting on true love from Vonima in place of her dutiful assent to wedlock (1.8). Here Sografi relied on the old prototype of the feeling tyrant and an amorous superplot, dominated by the love triangle of Mitridate, Vonima, and Zifare. In itself, this prototype did little harm to the new political agenda the opera was destined to project, and it meant that much of Sografi's original act 1 from the 1796 libretto could be left standing.

For the rest it was not just the libretto that had to be revised but the music as well. Zingarelli's autograph, in the Archivio Storico della Casa Ricordi recently transferred to the Biblioteca Nazionale Braidense at Milan, leaves little doubt that the composer had already been at work on the score for a good month or more, setting a version of the libretto close to that of Vicenza/Trieste, when the republic collapsed.[70] His score adds a fascinating component to the picture of cultural transformations precipitated by the changed political situation, since it had to reflect what was fit for the new patriotic stage—or at least accommodate to what would be tolerated.

Evidently neither the management nor the authorities were prepared to have all of Zingarelli's work redone when the republic collapsed. The love intrigues of the somewhat banal first act remained mostly unchanged, easing the task of staging the opera in time for the June 4 celebrations.[71] With the second act, things proceeded differently, since Sografi and the Committee of Public Instruction cared above all how the mechanics of resolution would work upon the sense of an ending. Before the season opened, numerous alterations changed or eliminated those portions of act 2 that most contradicted the new social or-

68. In Racine's version—much closer to the ancient histories—Mitridate amasses mistresses obsessively but has most of them killed off out of jealousy. The function of women as prey is thus plainer and more raw than in the operatic versions of the story.

69. Mitridate exclaims: "Freme Farnace! / Zifare impallidisce! / Vonima piange, e tace! / Potentissimi Dei! / Quel fremito, quel pianto, quel pallore, / quel silenzio fatal mi squarcia il core" (Farnace trembles! Zifare pales! Vonima weeps and is silent! Great powerful gods! What shuddering, what tears, what pallor, what fatal silence tears apart my heart).

70. For more information, see the archival page on the library's Web site: www.braidense.it/ricordi.html (accessed September 21, 2005). This time frame is estimated based on the fact that a full-length opera typically required at least two months to complete; for most composers of the 1790s generation, the estimate is probably too low.

71. In view of the fact that a hastily composed ending was suddenly to valorize Farnace instead of Zifare at the end of the opera, some tinkering did have to be done to act 1. The autograph shows, for instance, that Zingarelli had already set the earlier version of 1.4, "Esitar non poss'io, Farnace è il traditor," as simple recitative (54r). There are also minor interpolations of brief recitatives, simple and string obbligato, by two later hands (20v and 115v–116v by the first, who also did titling on 43r; 93r–93v by the second).

der. In Sografi's Vicenza/Trieste version, Mitridate had represented the same benign and malleable tyrant encountered in act 1, a figure who could realize his true core over narrative time through the indulgence of obsequious subjects. He was a variant of the benevolent despot (familiar from the 1767 libretto of Cigna-Santi, set most famously by Mozart for Milan in 1770), whose ultimately redemptive nature served to pacify potential evil in the imaginings of the absolutist body politic, with Babbini perfectly cast in the title role. (The initial and ultimate stages of Zingarelli's work on act 2 can be compared in the schematic digest given in table 9.2.)

Knotting Mitridate to this type, Zingarelli had evidently already set the same text used in the Vicenza/Trieste 2.3 (or a part of it at least), wherein Vonima maintains her innocence and dedication to Mitridate in the face of his death threats and thereby manages to win his good grace. Unlike its counterpart in the Vicenza/Trieste version, however, Zingarelli's Venice setting of the scene (example 9.1)—again for Babbini—culminates in an enraged aria by a menacing Mitridate with duet-like interjections by Vonima (played by Giovanna Babbi), who sing the following text:

M. Morrai, lo merti. Il voglio.	[M. You will die, you deserve it. I want it.
Ma dell'amante in seno	But [first] I will at least
Vedrò quel core almeno	See that heart of yours
La morte a paventar.	Fear the death of your lover.
Dove si vidde mai	Where has there ever been
Affanno più tiranno?	Such cruel suffering?
Più barbaro dolor?	Such harsh pain?
V. T'amai . . .	V. I loved you . . .
M. Mentisci . . .	M. You're lying . . .
V. Il giuro . . .	V. I swear it . . .
M. Ah! nel mirar quel ciglio	M. Ah! When I look at those eyes,
Sento il primiero affetto	I feel my earlier affection for you.
Si parta! il mio periglio,	Onward! O gods, the risk
Numi, mi fa terror.	I'm taking, terrifies me.
V. Mi va mancando il cor.	V. My heart is failing.
(cade svenuta in braccia alle guardie)	*(she falls, having fainted in the arms of the guards)*
M. Non temer (si finga). *(da sè)*	M. Fear not. (She's pretending.) *(to himself)*
Io t'amo.	I love you.
(si sente suono di bellici strumenti)	*(he hears the sound of warlike instruments)*
M. Sommi Dei, qual suon guerriero!	M. Oh great gods, what a bellicose sound!
Roma cada. Il figlio mora.	Let Rome fall. Let my son die.
Non resisto al mio furor.	I cannot restrain my fury.
Tornerò, ben mio, lo speri	My love, I hope I will return
Là del campo vincitor.	To you as a victor of the field.
(partono)	*(they exit)*]

(Venice, 1797, 2.3)

At a key moment Vonima breaks Mitridate's tirade, swooning to the words "Mi va mancando il cor," marked by drooping, minor-sixth portamenti to a sighing violin accompaniment, to which he responds with energetic if suspicious concern, repeating his avowals of "fear not, I love you." In the eyes of the new censors, Mitridate must have seemed all too concerned. The passage was evidently deleted (example 9.2). Cutting straight to the chase, Mitridate rages until distracted by the sound of "bellicose" trumpets, then promptly abandons Vonima to go off warring with Rome.

Subsequent parts of act 2 were similarly altered to make Mitridate more barbaric. Zingarelli had already set Vonima's aria of supplication midway through act 2 using text from the 1796 versions, where she was depicted in tearful self-reproach while beseeching Mitridate to take pity on Zifare:

Al pianto mio concedi Clemente i giorni suoi; Un sangue reo, se vuoi Tu lo ritrovi in me.	[In exchange for my tears, Let him live out his days mercifully, If you wish, you can find The bad blood in me.
Ah! se sperar mi lice Da te così bel dono, Più lieto, più felice Di questo cor non v'è.	Ah! If I can hope for Such a great gift from you, Then nothing is more happy and content Than this heart.
Lo vedi, Lo comprendi, Lo credi, e già m'intendi . . . La mia speranza è in te. (Vincenza, 1796, 2.10)	You see it, You grasp it, You believe it, and already you understand . . . My hope lies in you.]

In revising the text for a new setting, Sografi intensified Vonima's diction with laments of misery and entreaties to the king to curb his barbarism and instead play the noble part of father:

Per pietà del mio tormento Al tuo sen ricevi il figlio, Che sei padre a te rammento. Frena il barbaro rigor.	[Have pity on my torment, Welcome your son to your breast. I remind you that you are his father. Put an end to your barbarous severity.
Nella calma, e nel contento, Deh, ritorni il genitor. Tu consola, tu 'l difendi Tanto affanno, e questo cor. (Venice, 1797, 2.8)	Ah, let the parent in you return, Calm and content. Console him and defend him From such anguish, and my heart too.]

Similarly, Zingarelli had set her plea in 2.14 to save the king (despite her predicament) using an impassioned obbligato recitative. The text, in which she

Table 9.2. Reconstruction of compositional stages for act 2 of Sografi and Zingarelli's *La morte di Mitridate* (Venice, La Fenice, May 21, 1797)

Preliminary Stages (*portions excluded from eventual performance; some seemingly intended for Venice before May 12, 1797*)			*Final Stage* (*probable version as performed on May 21, 1797*)		
Scene	*Section*	*Folios*	*Scene*	*Section*	*Folios*
(1796 or 1797 libretto)			1	Introduzione: "Amore che l'alme accendi"	89r–91v
			1–2	Simple recit.: Mitridate, Farnace "Basta, gran parte"	92r–v
			2 (end)	Simple recit.: Mitridate "Vonima, s'io t'amai"	93r–v
end 2–3	Simple recit.: Mitridate, Vonima ["-tite e sol Vonima resti" crossed out] → "Vonima, s'io t'amai" [in new hand, marked "scena 3.a"	92v	3	Obblig. recit.: Vonima "I tuoi sospetti"	93v–94v [including inserted leaves]
3	Vomina's fainting music from aria/duet [crossed out]	97v–98r		Aria/duet: Mitridate, (Vonima) "Morrai lo merti" [excluding fols. 97v–98r]	95r–103r
	Coda of Mitridate's aria shortened	99v	4	Simple recit.: Fedima, Farnace "Tutta scorsi la reggia"	107r–v
				Aria: Fedima "Già so che m'intendi"	108r–110r
				Simple recit.: Farnace "Sempre più la vendetta"	110r
			5	Simple recit.: Zifare, Vonima "Vonima, idol mio"	104r
			6	Obblig. recit.: Arbate "Cedi il brando, signor"	104v–105v
				Aria with chorus: Zifare "Per queste amare lagrime"	123r–128v
				Simple recit.: Farnace "Respira il cor al fin"	106r
				Aria: Farnace "Vedrò que' perfidi"	138r–140r
			7	Recit.: Mitridate, Vonima "Vonima a me"	111r–v
8	Simple recit.: Mitridate "Che vuoi da me?"	111v	8	Simple recit. [excerpt]: Mitridate, Vonima ". . . volta io ti possa parlar," → obbligato recit.: "Serba alla gloria . . . versa il mio"	129r–v
				Aria: Vonima "Per pietà del mio tormento"	130r–137r
				Simple recit: Mitridate "E l'ascoltai!"	112r
9 (1796)	Aria: Vonima "Al pianto mio concedi"	118r–122v			
			9–11	"Scena e Duetto": Obblig. recit.: Farnace, etc. "Salvati, genitor"	113r–114v
				Marcia	115r

9–beg. 12	Simple recit.: Farnace, Mitridate, Fedima "Salvati, genitor" (up through "Siam traditi")	112r–112v			
			12	Obblig. recit.: Arbate, Mitridate "Siam traditi"	115v–116r
				Duet: Mitridate and Zifare "Cadrà l'altera Roma ["Notturno" indicated in score, 116v, but no such number is evident]	150r–161r
14 (1796)	Obblig. recit.: Mitridate ". . . ma dove andrò"	116v–117v			
13 (= 15 in 1796)	Simple recit.: Zifare, Vonima [with expansion, fol. 162r, 3rd system ff.]	162r	13	Simple recit.: Zifare, Vonima "Ah! non l'abbandonar" [cut off after words "coll' acciaro in man saprò morire" in keeping with 1797 libretto]	162r
14	Obblig. recit.: Vonima "Fedima, Arbate, tutti, salvate il nostro Re" [crossed out]	141r–141v	14	Obblig. recit.: Mitridate, Vonima "Ombra" scene: "Dove i Romani son? . . ."	141v–143r
14	Obblig. recit. (cont.) [= continuation of 141r–142v in earlier redaction, an expansion of dialogue later cut for the final version, of which 141r–143r = music]	144r–145v			
17 (1796)	Aria: Mitridate "Nume del ciel" "Finale"	145v–146v	15		142r–143r
	Trumpet fanfare	147r			
18 (1796, much altered)	Obblig. recit.: "Che ascolto" [new] → "Pompeo fu vinto il vincitor son io . . . a nuova gloria [il ciel coronerà la tua vittoria]"	147r–149v	15 (mid.–end)	FINALE Chorus w/Mitridate, Zifare "Viva il roman valor . . . Viva la libertà" [Mitridate and Zifare die]; chorus (cont.) with Vonima and Farnace: "Proteggeranno i Dei la nostra libertà" [everything in libretto cut from "Corriamo all'armi" onward except last line, "Viva la libertà"]	163r–168r

Sources: Score: Zingarelli, *La morte di Mitridate* (Venice, 1797), I-Mr, autograph, amended with several other hands. Libretti: Sografi, *La morte di Mitridate* (Trieste, autumn 1796) and *La morte di Mitridate* (Venice, Ascension 1797).

Note: Scene numbers refer to Venice libretto unless Trieste is indicated. Folio numbers refer to the Zingarelli autograph. "Aria/duet" refers to arias with interjections from a second character.

EXAMPLE 9.1. Nicola Zingarelli, aria for Mitridate "Morrai lo merti"

From *La morte di Mitridate* (Teatro La Fenice, Venice, Ascension 1797), 2.3. I-Mr (composer's autograph), 95r. By kind permission of the Proprietà Archivio Storico Ricordi, Milan.

EXAMPLE 9.2. Nicola Zingarelli, "Morrai lo merti," deleted exchange with Vonima

From *La morte di Mitridate* (Teatro La Fenice, Venice, Ascension 1797), 2.3. I-Mr (composer's autograph), 97v. By kind permission of the Proprietà Archivio Storico Ricordi, Milan.

begs the elder confidantes Arbate and Fedima to "guard his days," survived even until the Venice libretto was printed for La Fenice, which must have been done just days before the premiere.

Fedima, Arbate, tutti	[Fedima, Arbate, all of you,
salvate il vostro re. Dei giorni suoi	save your king. Let us protect
cura prendiam. Ver questa parte il vidi	the days of his life. I saw him coming
portar il piè, vacillante . . . io temo . . .	this way, haltingly . . . I'm in terror . . .
(Mitridate comparisce	*(Mitridate appears*
improvvisamente sopra il	*suddenly, half-alive,*
tempio semivivo)	*above the temple)*
Ma s'apre il tempio! . . .	But the temple is opening!
(con sorpresa)	*(with surprise)*
Egli s'appressa . . . oh Dio! . . .	He's approaching . . . oh God! . . .
Come squallido in volto! . . .	How filthy his face is! . . .
(attonita)	*(astonished)*
Vieni, mio prence, a noi? . . .	Are you coming to us, my Prince? . . .]
(Venice, 1797, 2.14)	

But this too is struck from Zingarelli's autograph.

Moments like this, in which the sovereign's inferiors vouchsafe his power, were of course crucial to the earlier narrative paradigm of opera seria, a paradigm wherein the king, supreme among all males, holds an axiomatic claim on women—a claim he forgoes only as an act of benign will—and one wherein the women, in order to maintain the social order, acknowledge his prerogative even when they hope to repel his advances. With the apparent excision of this passage from the performed version, the new regime refused the exemplar of the obsequious subject in tacit favor of the new self-determining citizen. By rejecting the right of the paternal king to seize female quarry, they also implicitly rejected the analogous right of the paterfamilias to dispose of women as he pleased. Even though enlightenment models dating back to Metastasio already saw monarchs and other authority figures checking themselves through self-imposed moral constraints, the absolutist political model of the patriarchal family still viewed the king and his surrogate(s) as seated atop a social hierarchy directly below the universal father figures of God and Christ, from which position they derived their power to settle affinal relations and other matters of alliance. Concomitantly, too, rejection of such a hierarchy meant rejection of the imperative of collective protection from the monarch (or here, the oligarchic body) in favor of the sovereign, even recalcitrant individual. Saving the monarch was no longer the subject's job.

The version produced for the final performance made Mitridate meaner and more barbaric—in short, less worthy of being saved—than he had been on the *terraferma* in 1796, and it failed to save him even spiritually. Consequently, while both versions culminate in the invasion of Mitridate's realm in Asia Minor by Roman armies and in Mitridate's defiant slow suicide to "show how heroes leave

. . . life," only the final Fenice version retaliated for his treatment of Vonima and his antagonism toward mythical Rome. And this it did by visiting on him a truly gruesome death.

Once again, Zingarelli had originally set the death scene from the Vicenza/Trieste version (2.18) using Mitridate's tender solo aria "Nume del ciel," which the tyrant had sung in his death throes following a passage of broken recitative (example 9.3).

[Recitative]	
Contra i Romani andiam!	[Onward, against the Romans!
Coraggio, amici,	Friends, may our courage
quà si soccorra; là si voli. È certa	come to our aid here; let us fly there!
la mia, la vostra gloria:	My glory and yours is certain:
alla pugna, al trionfo, alla vittoria.	to battle, to triumph, to victory.
(Mancando)	*(Losing consciousness)*
Ah, che vacilla . . . ahi lasso!	Ah, what trembling . . . alas!
Tardo . . . tremante il passo . . .	My steps . . . are slow . . . and quaking . . .
in tal momento . . .	at such a moment . . .
Figlio, mi lasci! . . . O dìo!	You are leaving me, my son! . . . Oh god!
morir mi sento.	I feel myself dying.
[Aria]	
Nume del ciel, ridona	God in Heaven, return
A queste braccia il figlio;	My son to these arms:
Con moribondo ciglio	A parent with dying eyes
Tel chiede un genitor.	Asks this of you.
E tu all'ardor perdona *(a Vonima)*	And you, forgive the ardor *(to Vonima)*
Del misero mio cor. *(morendo)*	Of my wretched heart. *(dying)*]
(Vicenza, 1796, 2.18)	

"Nume del ciel" is a classic aria d'affetto. As such, it allowed Mitridate to regain his lyric composure long enough to plead with heaven that he might embrace Zifare one last time before dying and be forgiven his ardor for Vonima. It allowed Zingarelli to project the dying despot with a special dignity and pathos, a gorgeous and stately triple-meter aria cantabile in B flat.

For the sake of "revolutionary" Venice, Sografi ultimately replaced "Nume del ciel" with a new passage of blank verse for Mitridate, "Dove i Romani son?" followed by a revolutionary chorus.

Dove i Romani son? . . .	[Where are the Romans? . . .
Dove Pompeo? . . .	Where is Pompey? . . .
Venga già del velen! . . .	Let the poison run its course!
(mancando)	*(fainting)*
V. Veleno? oh Dei!	V. Poison? Oh, gods!
(da sè)	*(to himself)*

EXAMPLE 9.3. Nicola Zingarelli, death aria for Mitridate, "Nume del ciel, ridona"

From *La morte di Mitridate* (Teatro La Fenice, Venice, Ascension 1797), 2.17 (text from Vicenza/Trieste version, 1796). I-Mr (composer's autograph), 145v. By kind permission of the Proprietà Archivio Storico Ricordi, Milan.

M. Ancora ho il ferro in questa man, io tremo . . . *(cade in braccio alle guardie)* Già di nera caligine si adombra la moribonda luce! . . . Eterna notte . . . mi circonda d'intorno! . . . Un freddo orrore . . . Sento che in sen mi piomba . . . a poco a poco . . . cedasi al fato estremo! . . . Roma trionfa! . . . io vo mancando . . . e fremo . . . *(s'ode gran strepito di trombe, e Coro di Romani vittoriosi. Mitridate resta sorpreso con gran stupore)*	M. I still have this dagger in my hand. I tremble . . . *(falls into the arms of the guards)* Already the dying light is darkening with black, dense fog! Eternal night . . . encircles me all around! . . . A cold horror . . . I feel weighing down my breast . . . little by little . . . let me give in to my final destiny! Rome triumphs! . . . I am collapsing . . . and I am overcome . . . *(A great blast of trumpets and a chorus of victorious Romans is heard. Mitridate is surprised and amazed)*
Coro. Viva il roman valore, *(di dentro)* Viva la Libertà. Viva Pompeo . . . (Venice, 1797, 2.14)	Chorus. Long live Roman valor, *(from inside)* Long live Liberty. Long live Pompey . . .]

With this in hand, Zingarelli could now send Mitridate to hell in a dramatic *scena* of orchestral recitative (2.15), a *scena* he probably sketched shortly before opening night, May 27 (example 9.4). Just before the opera ends, the dying king staggers into the temple with his dagger in hand, gasping out a parlante speech to the accompaniment of shuddering violins and diminished chords ("trema," " . . . eterna notte"), and suffers one final torment as cries of Roman victory begin to sound in the distance.

All these revisions pushed the opera away from the segmented dramaturgy of old opera seria toward a harsher, more grisly stage action, underwritten by an increase in dramatic orchestral recitative, the construction of scenic tableaux that avoided the closure of the set number, and a sharpening of the *parola scenica*, fraught with emotional, broken speech.[72] The new overwrought dialect of the genre could be harnessed to help demonize Mitridate through concerted acts of iconoclasm, acts that turned the tyrant into a figure of absolutist and by extension aristocratic villainy to be symbolically crushed in the very temple in which the aristocracy exalted itself.

The crowning blow was dealt in the final scene, which introduced a sudden chiasmus in the original trajectory toward a quasi-happy ending. Important

72. On these aspects of revolutionary opera, see Pestelli, "Riflessi della rivoluzione francese," 261–78.

EXAMPLE 9.4. Zingarelli, obbligato death *scena* for Mitridate, "Dove i Romani son?"

From *La morte di Mitridate* (Teatro La Fenice, Venice, Ascension 1797), 2:15. I-Mr (composer's autograph), 142r–v. By kind permission of the Proprietà Archivio Storico Ricordi, Milan.

EXAMPLE 9.4. *(continued)*

to note here is that even though the Vicenza/Trieste version had ended with Mitridate's suicide, he had nevertheless died happily, surrounded by grief-struck subjects and visited finally by a triumphant Zifare decked with insignia of the conquered Romans, whom his troops have just pushed into the sea. In Venice, to the contrary, Mitridate was made to die miserably, afflicted by shades of hell to the glee of the populace. The Romans win, Zifare is killed, and the populace rejoices, while Vonima is simply forgotten. Moreover, the final scenes of the Venice version throw Zifare under an evil light at the eleventh hour and make Farnace—the Roman sympathizer and hence traitor in his father's eyes—into the virtuous offspring who suddenly appears in triumph after conquering the evil Eastern empire of "Asia."

Vast amounts of time and space were thus phantasmatically compressed into mere minutes of dramatic time. If this belied geographical and historical truth (not to mention every concern for verisimilitude), it offered a radically transformed narrative for spectators at the Fenice that June. The medium of a merciless death allowed aristocratic claims to be denied and choral lament converted into collective euphoria, as the Venice version resolved in victory choruses.[73]

Sografi's revolutionary enthusiasms probably got the better of him before the final redaction was made, for sixteen lines that appear in the printed libretto, but not the score, have the populace rushing to take up arms with the Roman warriors. The ideology behind Venetian myth made popular violence anathema, nor would it have been sanctioned by French occupying forces, whom Venetian "democrats" repeatedly praised (by whatever instigation) for ridding Venice of tyranny through peaceful intervention.[74] Whatever cathartic power such violence had in France was here displaced onto symbolic and narrative forms to become at most a figurative undercurrent, and one not too real at that. No trumpets call the crowd to battle ("All'armi, all'armi") as in Sografi's text, and the chorus simply resounds with "Viva la libertà!"[75] Thus ended the opening of the Venetian *Mitridate* on June 4, and with it an intelligible ritual sequence that had begun earlier that day in Piazza San Marco.

SUMMER SEASON: CAESAR, BRUTUS, AND JOAN OF ARC

Eight days later, on June 12, the Society of La Fenice was facing orders from on high to stage an unprecedented summer season, with thirty performances

73. See ibid., 270–71, on the reason for tableau-like ensembles in revolutionary opera, as opposed to the action-packed concertato finales otherwise common between 1790 and 1810.

74. Indeed revolution itself was a concept toward which Venice had a longstanding enmity, an enmity that continued into the period of municipal government. See Barricelli, "Civic Representations," 152.

75. Zingarelli's score also suggests that Sografi's final stage direction, calling for the whole cast to arrange itself in military formation to the sound of a march—"*e ponendosi in ordine militare segue gran marcia, e così termine il Dramma*"—was not carried out either, since no march follows the last chorus.

of opere serie to honor the arrival of Bonaparte.[76] Within the next four days, boxholders were required to announce their intention either to retain or give up for the summer the boxes that they alone owned and were accustomed to outfitting, curtaining, and lighting (or renting out at their own will) throughout the festive calendar.[77] The fantasies of revolution that led architects of the revised *Mitridate* to falsify history by making ancient Rome the originary source not of an oligarchic Venice but of a revolutionary one now worked to suppress time in the realm of the everyday by brushing away centuries of cyclic time embedded in the theatrical calendar with a single sweep of the hand.[78] For a summer season in Venice was senseless for its economic elite. It was a concept that contradicted the very foundations of theatergoing, since wealth was largely predicated on real estate and the wealthy traditionally spent summers up to five months long at rural residences in the Veneto. Thus despite the antipathy Venetian landowners must have felt toward such a demand, patrician boxowners, accustomed to their summer *villeggiature*, were for the most part in no mood to change their plans. By June 16, two-thirds of the boxes in the first two ranks—mostly owned by nobles—had been relinquished for the summer, in contrast to less than a quarter in the fourth and fifth ranks, dominated by the bourgeoisie.[79]

It was to be a summer of democratic theater for Venice. While the Teatro Civico staged a succession of patriotic spoken dramas with a regular amateur company of *cittadini*, the Fenice put on two additional operas, Gaetano Sertor and Francesco Bianchi's *La morte di Cesare* and Sografi and Gaetano Andreozzi's *Giovanna d'Arco* (see table 9.1 above).[80] One valorized Brutus's murder of Cae-

76. The document revealing this was first reported by Bauman, "The Society of La Fenice," 350; conserved in ASTF, Processi verbali delle convocazioni sottratti all'incendio 1817 del Palazzo Corner, box 1, fasc. 4. Most of the receipts for the summer season are preserved in ASTF, Fabbrica del Teatro La Fenice, Spese 1789-1794-1798, filza 6, and a few others scattered throughout ASTF, Fabbrica del Teatro La Fenice, Cassa, 1792–97.

77. Boxholders who failed to claim their boxes would lose them for the whole summer. Those given up went back to a special commission.

78. In *Venice and Antiquity*, Patricia Fortini Brown stresses to the contrary the lack of a Roman past as critical to Venetian identity. The standard theater calendar in Venice began with a rather late autumn season, starting in mid-November (for which even at that not all nobles returned in time), followed by the prime season of Carnival beginning on December 26. The last season of the annual Venetian theater calendar was Ascension, which ran during May and June, generally for a month or more. By July of 1797, the old system of theatrical seasons had not only been toppled at La Fenice, but had received a frontal assault of a more general kind in the *Teatro moderno applaudito* 13 (July 1797), which pronounced it "una delle più ridicole ed insieme più tiranniche leggi del passato governo di Venezia" (quoted in Barricelli, "Civic Representations," 157 n. 30).

79. Boxes given up and retained are listed in ASTF, Partitario Canoni 2, 1792–1800, 191r. All told, only seventeen out of seventy owners gave up their boxes in the fourth and fifth ranks. Indeed, only four boxes were given up in the fifth (and top) rank.

80. In 1999, Piero Weiss produced a critical edition of Bianchi's *La morte di Cesare*, with a facsimile of B-Bc, MS 2046 K—a fair copy of the original score from 1789 with alterations made for the 1797 performance—together with editions of Sertor's original libretto and his 1797 version (xli–lxxxviii), the last also available online from ASTF at http://81.75.233.46:8080/fenice/GladReq/libretti.jsp. Also included is Weiss's essay, "*La morte di Cesare:* The Words, the Music," vii–xxxviii. The score

sar, thus rehabilitating once again the greater glory of republican Rome, while the other exalted the courage of the rebel Joan of Arc. Both were retooled from pioneering libretti of 1788–1789,[81] and both claimed liberty over life as their central proposition. Like *Mitridate*, they aimed for realism through the *parola scenica* and an unbroken series of scenic tableaux.

Of the two, the opening dramma serio, *La morte di Cesare*, echoed the Venetian condition most closely, since it glorified Caesar's murder by Brutus (Bruto) in the name of Roman liberty. Like *Mitridate* before it, *La morte di Cesare* aimed for high drama and narrative sweep—so much so that it was performed without ballet intermezzi, the dance being delayed until the opera proper had ended, when a four-act *ballo tragico* was given. Many passages that had been done as simple recitative in Bianchi's 1788–89 setting for the Teatro San Samuele in Venice were cut, raising the dramatic pitch, while added passages of broken obbligato recitative intensified the possibilities of psychological verisimilitude.[82] By dwelling on Brutus's vain attempts to dissuade Caesar from his tyrannical course, the 1797 version could enhance the effect of "realism" and prepare audiences for the shocking end of the opera, when Caesar would be murdered onstage (unlike the 1789 version or the revivals of 1790 and 1791 mounted in Livorno, Reggio, and Milan).[83] The love talk originally given by Sertor to Calphurnia (Calfurnia) shortly before Caesar's death was cut for Venice, in keeping with the more graphic ending, while interruptions to the narrative flow, such as Caesar's three-stanza love aria to Calphurnia in the penultimate scene, were

---

is a parallel case of the claim I make for the autograph of *La morte di Mitridate*. For *Giovanna d'Arco*, only a few musical excerpts survive; see Rizzuti, "Music for a *Risorgimento* Myth," on their state and the continued operatic proliferation and reworking of the Joan of Arc myth in the ottocento.

81. The original libretto for *La morte di Cesare*, conceived for the Teatro San Samuele in Venice and published in 1789, gave the following description and dedication: "Dramma per musica del signor D. Gaetano Sertor da rappresentarsi nel nobilisssimo Teatro di S. Samuele il carnovale dell'anno 1789. Dedicato a . . . Gio. Battista Pignatelli principe di Mariconuovo." *Giovanna d'Arco* was premiered the following summer (also 1789) at Vicenza with this inscription: "Dramma in quattr'atti per musica del Signor A. S. Sografi da rappresentarsi in Vicenza nel nuovo teatro la state dell'anno 1789. Umiliato agli eccellentissimi rettori. In Vicenza per Antonio Giusto con permissioni. Si vende da detto stampatore a S. Michele."

82. As in the inserted 1.9, in which Calphurnia begs Caesar not to leave Rome.

83. In the second act, scene 17 begins with the following description: "Apresi la scena, che dimostra il Senato di Roma con magnifici Sedili d'intorno. Nel mezzo la statua di Pompeo elevata sopra vari gradini, così pure la sedia curule. Veggonsi dei Senatori seduti ma vari posti vuoti. Entra Cesare preceduto da molti littori. Tutti si levano in piedi, e gli vanno incontro, sopra tutto Bruto, Antonio, e vari congiurati, ma Antonio è trattenuto con arte in iscorso vicino ad una delle due porte che introducono da Decimo, e Trebonio. Tutti mostrano una simulata indifferenza, e tutti osservano Cesare." [The set opens to show the Roman Senate surrounded by magnificent chairs. In the middle is the statue of Pompey, elevated by various steps, as well as the curule chair. Some senators can be seen seated, but various places are empty. Caesar enters, preceded by many lictors. All rise to their feet and go to meet him, above all Brutus, Antonius, and various conspirators, but Antonius is artfully detained in conversation by Decimus and Trebonius near one of the two doors that lead in. Everyone displays a feigned indifference and everyone watches Caesar.]

eliminated.[84] Indeed, the ending did more than merely prepare the audience. It facilitated the intended identification of the spectators with the political situation depicted by calling on a popular chorus as co-conspirators. Just before Brutus deals Caesar a mortal blow, the chorus intervenes to urge his death with shouts of liberty, and then cries out, "O morte, o libertà," culminating in the requisite "Viva la libertà!"[85]

Given the enormity of the occasion that prompted the summer season, it is not surprising that both operas were staged on a scale even grander than that of the previous Ascension. The chorus swelled from sixteen members during Ascension to thirty-six strong for the summer, and the numbers of choral groups who figured in the drama increased as well.[86] For instance, to *Cesare*'s original choruses of the 1789 version, consisting of the Popolo Romano (i.e., the magistrates), priests, conspirators, soldiers, and lictors, the 1797 version added choruses of senators, the "Popolo," sacrificers, Roman matrons, and Briton slaves.

84. In the 1789 version, the aria "Rasserena i mesti rai" occurs in 3.7, the scene equivalent to 2.15 in the version of 1797.

85. Ironically Sertor's original version of *La morte di Cesare,* which played at the Teatro San Samuele in Venice during Carnival 1788–89, had ended with a *licenza* in praise of Venetian republicanism comparing Venice favorably against the corrupted image of ancient Rome (see Bianchi, *La morte di Cesare,* and cf. n. 78 above): "Non turbarti, Venezia, oggi al tuo sguardo / la Romana Repubblica fa solo / spettacol de' suoi casi, ma non osa / paragonarsi a te. Conosce /anch'essa, / quanto minor del vero / l'immagine sarebbe, e troppo è chiara / tra voi la differenza. È tutto in lei / violenza, discordia, / tumulto, eccesso, orrore; in te non regna / che virtù, che ragion, che amor del giusto, / che concorde voler. V'ha tra i suoi figli / chi vuol la libertà, le patrie leggi / vederne oppresse; un sol non v'ha tra i tuoi, / che a sostenerle il sangue / non sia pronto a versar. Mille perigli, / mille vicende ella provò; tu illesa, / e intatta ti conservi, qual nascesti; / passaggera ella fù, tu eterna resti. / Serbati, o vivo tempio / D'onor, di sè, di gloria, / E un luminoso esempio / Abbiano i regni in te. / Del tuo felice impero / Quanto soave è il freno. / Ah! non l'intende appieno / Se non chi lo perdè." [Don't be distraught, Venice: today beneath your gaze the Roman Republic makes a spectacle solely of its own events, but it dares not compare itself to you. Even Venice knows how shy of the truth the image would be and the difference between you is all too clear. In Rome all is violence, discord, tumult, excess, and horror; in you nothing reigns but virtue, reason, love of justice, and a harmonious will. There are those among the sons of Rome who want to see freedom and the nation's laws suppressed; there is not one of yours who would not shed his blood to uphold them. Rome has experienced a thousand dangers, a thousand vicissitudes; you are unharmed and maintain yourself intact, as you were born. Rome was fleeting; you remain eternal. Preserve yourself, oh living temple, giver of honor, yourself, and glory, and may kingships have a shining example in you. How sweet is the restraint of your happy empire. Ah, only one who has lost it can completely understands this. (Italian quoted from the copy at I-Rsc, where the *licenza* appears on p. 80; also reprinted in Weiss, *La morte di Cesare,* lxvii).] In 1797 even Caesar acknowledges the liberty-or-death motif, but in the guise of the intrepid ruler. Knowing that his life is in danger he boasts "Morte piuttosto eleggo," to which Brutus rebuts "E morte avrai" (2.16). Brutus kills him as Caesar tries in vain to defend himself, while Cassius proclaims "Roma trionfa" and the chorus sings "O morte, o libertà."

86. The *Indice de' teatrali spettacoli,* part 13, lists "num. 16. Coristi" and "num. 16. Coppie Figuranti" for the Ascension season. For Estate, it lists "num. 36. Coristi" and "num. 32. Ballerini per Corpo di Ballo." Evidently, then, the number of dancers did not change, but the singing chorus more than doubled.

The cast was also expanded, with two new additional Roman senators, Tullio (Tilio) and Casca (Casea), who added weight to the anti-Caesar, hence anti-tyrannical, camp.[87]

MORALIZING THE SPECTATOR

Despite these resonances with events and ideologies in France, however, the "revolution" in which opera participated was vicarious, mimetic, and in the end chimerical. By January of 1798, Venice was occupied by a despotic Habsburg Austria. Moreover, Venetians ultimately cared little for the kind of mythic present created ex novo in revolutionary France, preferring to hearken back to their mythic past.[88] Thus, though time was suddenly calculated *alla francese*, the year 1797 minus the past did not equal "Year One" in Venetian consciousness as it was supposed to for the French. For Venetians, 1797 was always reduced by five hundred to equal 1297, the moment from which Venetian history had rolled forward for aristocrats and oligarchists and before which various Venetian "democrats" hoped to roll the clocks symbolically back. Even Venice's steeliest Jacobins, like Sografi and the poet Ugo Foscolo,[89] focused less on the "Anno primo della libertà italiana" than on recovering for Venice its mythic prehistory before the Serrata when the Venetian empire sat poised to triumph. Venice, they claimed, was born a true republic when Roman sovereigns claimed its muddy waters in their natural, prelapsarian state. Thus, for "revolutionaries" in Venice, democracy was figured not so much through a calculus of total rupture and genesis as one of reinvention, restoration, and regeneration of an ancient past.

Central to regeneration was a renewed morality that would breed communities of patriots by edifying their moral outlooks and animating the spirits of crowds. Ironically, the cultivation of similar loyalties was already presupposed by conditions immanent to opera seria, whose festive nature aimed to reproduce the rites and rules of spectating communities. Yet in revolutionary Venice, serious—now even tragic—opera also aimed to secure the attentions of individuals through new scenographic, poetic, and musical techniques.

* * *

Vast scenes, oblique perspectives, unbroken tableaux in open, syntagmatic forms—all these in the wake of "revolution" could combine with a new raw realism to force the messages of tragedy in the name of collective betterment.[90]

87. Antonio Mauro's sets must have been imposing too, judging from Sografi's descriptions, particularly for the final scene of Caesar's murder (cf. n. 83 above).

88. Cf. Barricelli, "Civic Representations."

89. See Barricelli, "The Tears and Terror of Foscolo's *Tieste*.

90. Such individualist modes fell in line with the intense concerns of Venetians to ensure that citizens take charge of their education, their moral decisions, their judgments—concerns that were

Perhaps it is not so surprising, then, that ultimately the new genre of tragedia per musica deflected its tragic claims through a bloody ending that for some signaled gaiety not gloom, and through revolutionary choruses that affirmed a new kind of *lieto fine*. In this sense, "revolutionary" opera at La Fenice shattered the axioms of the aristocratic body with a tenuous "democratic" populism that only reclaimed ideals of collective celebration in a different form.

Even as an idea, of course, revolutionary festivity at Venice was imposed largely from without and embraced only by a slice of the indigenous population. The spontaneous effervescence that theoretically should have united the collective imagination existed in an impossible tension with the heavy-handed organizational presence that hung behind it, and with the internal resistance to it of many Venetians of all classes. But married to a bureaucratic machine, festivity was nevertheless deployed to colonize Venetians by rupturing assumptions of time and history rather than helping to sustain them, as it had in the past. This arrogation of purpose was a danger Venetians had long avoided, but it was one immanent in the festive practices of which they were among Europe's reigning experts.[91] Even at the oligarchic opera house of La Fenice, festivity was a gift of the nobility to itself and of the nobility to the nonnoble, a display of beneficence, which claimed that the splendors and pleasures of the present were destined for time immemorial.

---

voiced and managed by the bureau in endless sessions and edicts on schools, speeches, sumptuary laws, and the like, and that can also be seen in its anxieties over women's role in theater. On the last, see in particular the criticism of women's presence on the stage of the Teatro Civico penned in 1797 by an anonymous pamphleteer, in *Opinione di un libero cittadino* (I-Vnm 183.c.88, "Scritti sortitti nella Revoluzione di Venezia seguita li 12 Maggio 1797: Tomo Primo," 65–80).

91. Claudio Povolo has argued that Venetian historians in the early nineteenth century would doubtless have glorified the five-hundred-year-old republican era rather unconditionally had it not been for the publication in 1819 of Daru's seven-volume *Histoire de la république de Venise* (see Povolo, "The Creation of Venetian Historiography," 491–519; and Passadore and Rossi, *L'aere è fosco*.

Epilogue

"Enlightenment's program was the disenchantment of the world. It wanted to dispel myths, to overthrow fantasy with knowledge." MAX HORKHEIMER AND THEODOR ADORNO, *Dialectic of Enlightenment*[1]

"The arias that once enchanted our ancestors are to us today tedious and insupportable inanities." PIETRO METASTASIO, Vienna, April 5, 1770[2]

"We no longer have festivities that enlarge and dilate the heart, but cold parlors and horrible dances! This is the opposite of festivity. One feels dried up the day afterward and even more haggard." JULES MICHELET, *Nos fils*, 1869[3]

Opera seria was born under the sign of crisis, as much the expression of a political predicament as a way to contain and regulate it. The crisis was indivisible from absolutist political practice itself, a practice that exploited serious opera by encouraging its proliferation throughout Europe but ended by fighting (and often failing) to keep it in hand. This irony was both representational and real. Even as opera seria asserted the magnanimity of the prince and idealized his subjects, the negation of its claims was always immanent in them. Always opera seria bolstered the hierarchical society for whom old-world sovereignty was beneficial at the same time as it worried it with needles and probes. Always it mimicked the miraculous world of the sovereign's court but thrived amid ever-expanding publics and spaces.

In the end, Italy had no eighteenth-century revolution and did not really kill off opera seria any more than it killed off its monarchs. Nor, practically speaking, could it have done so very easily. Opera was almost literally everywhere on the Italian peninsula. By the end of the century, the institution was lodged in an astonishing number of theaters, large and small, most of them public, and, through interlocking networks of production, patronage, and travel, it was also

1. Horkheimer and Adorno, *Dialectic of Enlightenment*, 1. On the phrase "disenchantment of the world," see Max Weber, *The Essential Weber*, 238 and 408 and chap. 4, n. 111 above.

2. "Le ariette che incantavano un dì gli avi nostri, sono oggi stucchevoli ed insopportabili nenie per noi" (Metastasio, *Opere* 4:816).

3. "Nous n'avons pas de fêtes qui détendent, dilatent le coeur. De froids salons et d'affreux bals! C'est le contraire des fêtes. On est plus sec le lendemain, on est plus contracté encore" (Michelet, *Nos fils*, 417).

spread far abroad. In the absence of any single, totalizing center of power or symbol around which Italian lands could coalesce, opera seria, at home and abroad, was able to give living form, however partial and erratic, to the sovereign ideal of the king who extended himself throughout his kingdom through the body of his people.[4] The institution thus amounted to a vast diffusion, by means of overlapping realms, of a mythical sovereignty. In this respect it was altogether different from France. By 1789 when the Bastille was stormed, the royal genre of *tragédie lyrique* had already fundamentally ended. It had been transformed through the dramatic styles of Italian composers in France, especially Antonio Salieri (notably, his *Les Danaïdes* of 1784) and Antonio Sacchini but also their compatriots Piccinni, Paisiello, Cimarosa, Sarti, and Anfossi, and by 1789 one theater, the Théâtre de Monsieur, later Feydeau, specialized in presenting Italian composers. These developments represented an institutional diversification, one extended in 1791 when laws were enacted that made it possible for anyone to open a theater and stage any genre. The resulting pluralism helped give birth in the works of Cherubini, Méhul, Jadin, and Spontini to operas that combined the dramatic weight of *tragédie lyrique* with the musical variety and naturalism of *opéra comique* and the lyricism of the tragedia per musica, eventually opening the way in the late 1820s to so-called grand opera (*opéra grand*). But the geopolitical stretch of operatic terrain was narrow indeed compared with the riotous Italian landscape, and attempts to widen the French terrain were minor and short-lived.[5]

What opera seria had in spades over French *tragédie lyrique,* both as political propaganda and as political art, and what made it so resilient, because adaptable, was precisely its massive diffusion—a diffusion of theaters, productions, performers, and authors that translated into a diffusion of representations, re-

4. Recall the *licenza* to Metastasio's *L'olimpiade* (1733) quoted above (chap. 6). Reinhard Strohm stresses the durability and flexibility of opera seria on more purely musical grounds: "the *dramma per musica* survived by transforming itself beyond recognition: the tightrope-walk between antinaturalist artificiality and idealist simplicity had been successful. The elasticity of the genre was its lifeline; had it conformed to a rigid formula such as the separation of drama and music (claimed by Freeman), it would have ended with Mozart, of course. But it seems that the *dramma per musica* reached the nineteenth century because it had always been a reform genre striving for an ever-increasing identification of music and drama. Admittedly, its fate was also linked to the social framework of a retrospective court culture, and for that reason opera seria in the narrow sense of the word was, after about 1789, gradually pushed back by bourgeois realities. But opera seria in the wider sense of the word did survive, perhaps even into the age of Hollywood cinema" (Strohm, *Dramma per musica,* 29).

5. On contestation in Parisian opera houses, revolutionary and counterrevolutionary, during the years 1789–1801, see McClellan, "Battling over the Lyric Muse," and "Restraining the Revolution." Approaching the terrain from a different angle, M. Elizabeth C. Bartlet has shown in several articles—"On the Freedom of the Theatre and Censorship," 1:15–30, "Patriotism at the Opéra-Comique during the Revolution," "Grétry and the Revolution," 47–110, and "The New Repertory at the Opéra during the Reign of Terror," 107–56—how emphatically the French turned theater toward the end of moral and patriotic education in the 1790s and how choruses were deployed to that end.

ceptions, sites of power, usurpations. At the same time, opera seria also represented the despoliation of that mythical sovereignty by the occupants of innumerable urban spheres, eager to co-opt and inevitably to cripple it, whether by will or, more often, mere consequence. Yet it was not just the disorderly effects of a large, unmanageable public that transformed the "king's opera," but a relatively new power player and an object of tremendous public infatuation—the singer—whom the public could effectively elect or impeach through mass consensus. To be sure, different forms of what Max Weber called "legitimate" power—the "traditional" kind (as of kings), the "legal" kind (as of states and senators), and the "charismatic" kind (as of persons)[6]—were all complexly located in opera seria. Traditionally, the institution belonged to the monarch or some monarchical surrogate like the oligarchs of Venice (symbolically and often by law). Legally, particularly as eighteenth-century monarchy collaborated increasingly with the state and saw itself increasingly eroded, it was managed and owned by elected or appointed officials, together with legally entitled families, impresarios, individuals, and societies in possession of deeds and contracts. But charismatically, power in opera seria was mobilized above all by the magical spectacle of singing stars, and only gradually, and arguably to a lesser degree, by the power of authors.[7]

In this sense, opera seria expressed sovereignty as a disconcerting shift away from the monarch and toward the socially mobile bourgeois individual, who could succeed (or indeed fail) as a commodity in a world of rapid exchange. In Marxist terms, the singer could become a fetish object, reproducing him- or herself for consumers through manifestations widely dispersed in time and space: public memories, copies of music, engraved portraits, anecdotes that were circulated by word of mouth or in letters, diaries, travel accounts, histories, and singing manuals. In these ways, the successful singer could accrue value through a combination of desirability, mobilized through publicness, publicity, and exchange, and scarcity made inevitable by the impossibility of meeting market demands for performances or manifesting sufficient presence to satisfy public demand.

The significance and irony of these facts can hardly be overstressed. In many city-states of the peninsula, the monarch hangs on tenuously but is swept into insignificance by the chaotic transports of the crowd, the adoring public, whose imaginary allows the stars of the stage to displace the very monarchical figure whose "legitimate power" the singer represents. Over time, as new sovereigns emerge in the later eighteenth and nineteenth centuries, sovereignty also accrues increasingly to operatic authors (as to other authors), especially to the

6. See in Weber, *Economy and Society*, part 1, chap. 3, "The Types of Legitimate Domination," esp. §4, "Charismatic Authority," and §5, "The Routinization of Charisma," 1:241–54, and part 2, chap. 14, "Charisma and Its Transformations," 3:1110–57.

7. There is a whiff of the idea in Richard Taruskin's "Of Kings and Divas," a review article of recordings of *tragédie en musique;* cf. Hunter, "To Play as If from the Soul of the Composer," 357–98.

composer, who will become ever more a site of authority and whose production will become increasingly fetishized. Even the conservative Stendhal suggested as much when he noted how attuned Italian audiences in the early nineteenth century had become to rightful composers of the music they heard, in situations where such rights might barely have been noticed a century before.[8]

If all of this points to the bourgeois individual as a new site of authority, the situation, as we have seen, was not without ambiguities. The supremacy of the author may have demanded a new regime of spectating that catered to a certain self-determination, but it also necessitated collective self-control and even self-repression, as Horkheimer and Adorno argued broadly speaking about "the dialectic of enlightenment." In the eighteenth century, domination by the sovereignty of the author was also redoubled through a new tyranny over the senses. The opera house became a site for governing "common sense," not in the colloquial meaning it has acquired nowadays of down-to-earth reasonableness, but in an earlier meaning that wants the senses to be moved *in common* among people who share a common notion of what is right, rational, and touching.[9]

Changes in late-eighteenth-century opera thus overlap with an overarching shift in the status of sovereignty as a referent of the social and political order. If today we understand "sovereignty" as a condition of states, parliaments, or citizens and increasingly a condition accorded to, proclaimed, or aspired to by "peoples" and "groups," in the early eighteenth century the dominant political order of Europe was still predicated on the sovereignty of exalted persons—kings, emperors, princes, electors, dukes, barons, and members of oligarchies. I have argued here that opera as an institution and the opera house as a place are highly significant sites for understanding this reorientation of sovereignty in affective and ideological terms—especially through opera seria, which was more closely identified with sovereign rulers than any other genre.

Nevertheless, challenged by growing state machines and new forms of action and ideology among its subjects, sovereign persons were already struggling at the beginning of the eighteenth century to hold on to claims of sovereignty and

8. "Si donc le compositeur dont on exécute l'ouvrage a dérobé à un autre un *aria* ou seulement quelques *passages*, quelques *mesures*, dès que le morceau volé commence à se faire entendre, il s'élève de tous côtés des bravos auxquels est joint le nom du véritable propriétaire. Si c'est Piccini qui a pillé Sacchini, on lui criera sans rémission: Bravo, Sacchini! Si l'on reconnaît, pendant son opéra, qu'il ait pris un peu de tout le monde, on criera fort bien: Bravo Galuppi! bravo, Traetta! bravo, Guglielmi!" (Stendhal, *Vies*, 389; from his "Lettre sur l'état actuel de la musique en Italie," Venice, August 29, 1814). [If the composer whose work is being performed has robbed another by stealing an aria, or just some *passaggi* or measures here and there, once the bit stolen starts up, the audience will burst into *bravo!* from every corner, each *bravo!* being accompanied by the name of the true owner. If it's Piccinni who has pillaged from Sacchini, the former will hear unremitting cries of *Bravo, Sacchini!* And if, as his opera proceeds, the audience should realize that he has borrowed a little from everyone they will cry: "Excellent! Bravo Galuppi! bravo, Traetta! bravo, Guglielmi!" (for Coe's translation, see Stendhal, *Lives of Haydn, Mozart, and Metastasio*, 379–80).]

9. See Mangini, "Le passioni," esp. 115; and on the French scene, Thomas, *Aesthetics of Opera*, chap. 9.

their pragmatic benefits.[10] To conceive of an ordinary individual—an upwardly mobile merchant, a *cittadino* (so-called), a singer—as sovereign, in the sense of independent, or beholden only to an autonomous state, meant a weakening of the traditional sovereign, even on a peninsula that never chopped off a ruler's head (though in the early nineteenth century it did shoot Napoleon's puppet king Joachim Murat). Moreover, this weakening took place on the very ground on which a new concept of "nationhood" was founded: that of a standardized literary language. Codified and actively cultivated in Italian-speaking lands earlier than anywhere else in Europe, the literary language and its immense cultural underpinning drove Italian opera such that language and music were inseparable. Language provided a vast arena for Italian speakers to internalize collectively a shared tongue throughout a peninsula that remained riddled with separate dialects and diverse polities, and it spread that tongue throughout Europe and beyond in a standardized musical language and a common set of expressive codes. Italian music and language represented "Italy." In this last sense, opera seria was the means for constructing a distinctly Italian style of absolutist sovereignty but also a means of opposing it on its own turf.

10. Simultaneous with that struggle was a shift (still partial) in the status of sovereign realms, from a broad and slippery notion of territories that could be dominated by the sovereign(s) to the territories governed by state(s) in specific political-legal ways. In Italy these were still basically city-states and, in preunification Italy, they were roughly elided in popular consciousness with concepts of *patria* (homeland), concretely embodied in territories over which the sovereign or state ruled. Where no single sovereign ruled, the image of sovereignty was still largely figured through that of a sovereign person. Hence visitors to Venice often perceived the doge as prince of Venice, even though Venetian law accorded him no such status but gave sovereignty to patricians.

References

Abbate, Carolyn. "Music—Drastic or Gnostic?" *Critical Inquiry* 30 (2004): 505–36.

Acquaro Graziosi, Maria Teresa. "Pietro Metastasio e l'Arcadia." In *Metastasio da Roma all'Europa,* edited by Franco Onorati, 48–61. Rome: Nuova Arti Grafiche Pedanesi, 1998.

Acton, Harold [Mario Mitchell]. *The Bourbons of Naples, 1734–1825.* London: Methuen, 1956.

Adamson, John, ed. *The Princely Courts of Europe: Ritual, Politics, and Culture under the Ancien Régime, 1500–1750.* London: Weidenfeld & Nicolson, 1999.

Ademollo, Alessandro. *La più famosa delle cantanti italiane nella seconda metà del settecento.* Milan: Ricordi, 1890.

———. *I teatri di Roma nel secolo decimosettimo.* Rome: Pasqualucci, 1888.

Agazzi, Nicoletta. "Feste e macchine di fuochi." In *La Parma in festa: Spettacolarità e teatro nel ducato di Parma nel settecento,* edited by Luigi Allegri and Renato di Benedetto, 81–116. Parma: Mucchi, 1987.

Ago, Renata. *Carriere e clientele nella Roma barocca.* Rome: Laterza, 1990.

———. "Ecclesiastical Careers and the Destiny of Cadets." *Continuity and Change* 7 (1992): 271–82.

———. "Oltre la dote: i beni femminili." In *Il lavoro delle donne,* edited by Angela Groppi, 164–82. Rome: Laterza, 1996.

Ajello, Raffaele, Carlo Marinelli [Roscioni], et al., eds. *Il Teatro di San Carlo.* 2 vols. Naples: Guida, 1988.

Albarosa, Nino and Renato di Benedetto, eds. *Musica e spettacolo a Parma nel settecento: Atti del convegno di studi, Parma, 18–20 ottobre 1979.* Parma: Università di Parma, 1984.

Alberti, Annibale and Roberto Cessi, eds. *Verbali delle sedute della Municipalità Provvisoria di Venezia, 1797.* 4 vols. and Appendix. Bologna: Nicola Zanichelli, 1928–40.

Alcune conversazioni e loro difese esaminate coi principi della teologia, dai quali facilmente si può dedurre quando sia illecito l'amore tra la gioventù. Ferrara, 1711.

Algarotti, Francesco. *Essai sur l'opéra.* Translated by François Jean, marquis de Castellux. Pisa, se trouve à Paris chez Rualt, 1773.

———. *An Essay on the Opera* [*Saggio sopra l'opera in musica*]. Anonymous English translation, 1768. Edited by Robin Burgess. Lewiston, NY: Edwin Mellen, 2005.

———. *Newtonianismo per le dame, ovvero dialoghi sopra la luce e i colori.* Naples, 1738.

———. *Opere del conte Algarotti.* 17 vols. Venice: Carlo Palese, 1791–94.

———. *Saggi.* Edited by Giovanni da Pozzo. Bari: Laterza, 1963.

———. *Saggio sopra l'opera in musica: Le edizioni di Venezia (1755) e di Livorno (1763).* Edited by Annalisa Bini. Pisa: Libreria Musicale Italiana, 1989.

Allanbrook, Wye J., Janet M. Levy, and William P. Mahrt, eds. *Convention in Eighteenth- and Nineteenth-Century Music: Essays in Honor of Leonard G. Ratner.* Stuyvesant, NY: Pendragon, 1992.

Allegri, Luigi. "Introduzione allo studio degli apparati a Parma nel settecento." In *La Parma in festa: Spettacolarità e teatro nel Ducato di Parma nel settecento,* edited by Luigi Allegri and Renato di Benedetto, 13–34. Parma: Mucchi, 1987.

———. *Teatro, spazio, società.* Fossalta di Piave: Rebellato, 1982.

Allegri, Luigi, and Renato di Benedetto, eds. *La Parma in festa: Spettacolarità e teatro nel Ducato di Parma nel settecento.* Parma: Mucchi, 1987.

Allocati, Antonio. "La panificazione a Napoli durante la carestia del 1764 in una memoria di Carlo Antonio Broggia." In *Studi in onore di Antonio Genovese nel bicentario della Istituzione della Cattedra di Economia,* edited by Domenico Demarco. Naples: L'Arte Tipografica, 1956.

Allodi, Ivo, ed. *I teatri di Parma "dal Farnese al Regio."* Milan: Nuove Edizioni Milano, 1969.

The Amours and Adventures of Two English Gentlemen in Italy: With a Particular Description of the Diversions of Carnival in Venice: Also the Duels They Fought, the Dangers They Escaped; and Their Safe Arrival in England. Worcester, MA: Printed and sold at the Worcester Bookstore [Isaiah Thomas], 1795.

Anderson, Emily, ed. *The Letters of Mozart and His Family.* 3rd ed. New York: Norton, 1985.

Anderson, Matthew S. "The Italian Reformers." In *Enlightened Absolutism: Reform and Reformers in Later Eighteenth-Century Europe,* edited by H. M. Scott, 55–74. Ann Arbor: University of Michigan Press, 1990.

Anderson, Perry. *Lineages of the Absolutist State.* 1974. Reprint, London: Verso, 1979.

Angelini Bontempi, Giovanni Andrea. *Historia musica. Nella quale si ha piena cognitione della teorica, e della pratica antica della musica harmonica.* Perugia: Costantini, 1695.

Antinori, Giuseppe. "Notizie per la vita del dottor Annibale Mariotti." In *Versi e prose del dottor Annibale Mariotti fra gli Arcadi della Colonia Augusta Orninto Gneosseano.* Vol. 1, *Contenente le sue poesie.* Perugia: Costantini & Santucci, 1809.

Antolini, Bianca Maria. "Rome." §3. From *Grove Music Online,* ed. Laura Macy. http://www.grovemusic.com/ (accessed September 12, 2005).

Antolini, Bianca Maria, and Wolfgang Witzenmann, eds. *Napoli e il teatro musicale in Europa tra sette e ottocento: Studi in onore di Friedrich Lippmann.* Quaderni della Rivista Italiana di Musicologia, Società Italiana di Musicologia, no. 28. Florence: Olschki, 1993.

Apostolidès, Jean-Marie. *Le roi-machine: Spectacle et politique au temps de Louis XIV.* Paris: Minuit, 1981.

Appel, Willa, and Richard Schechner, eds. *By Means of Performance: Intercultural Studies of Theatre and Ritual.* Cambridge: Cambridge University Press, 1990.

Arshagouni, Michael Hrair. "Aria Forms in Opera Seria of the Classical Period: Settings of Metastasio's Artaserse from 1760–1790." Ph.D. diss., University of California at Los Angeles, 1994.

L'Artaserse: Dramma per musica da rappresentarsi nel teatro novellamente eretto . . . nella città di Cremona il carnovale dell'anno MDCCLIX. Brescia, 1749.

Arteaga, Stefano. *Le rivoluzioni del teatro musicale italiano dalla sua origine fino al presente.* Enlarged 2nd ed. 3 vols. Bologna: Carlo Trenti all'Insegna di Sant'Antonio, 1783–88. Bologna: Forni, 1969.

Atlas, Allan W. "The Accademia degli Unisoni: A Music Academy in Renaissance Perugia." In *A Musical Offering: Essays in Honor of Martin Bernstein*, edited by Edward H. Clinkscale and Claire Brook, 5–23. New York: Pendragon, 1977.

Azzaroni, Giovanni. *La rivoluzione a teatro: Antinomie del teatro giacobino in Italia, 1796–1805*. Bologna: CLUEB, 1985.

Babcock, Barbara. "Arrange Me into Disorder." In *Rite, Drama, Festival, Spectacle: Rehearsals toward a Theory of Cultural Performance*, edited by John J. MacAloon, 102–28. Philadelphia: University of Pensylvania Press, 1984.

———. *The Reversible World: Symbolic Inversion in Art and Society*. Ithaca: Cornell University Press, 1978.

Bach, Carl Philipp Emmanuel. *Essay on the Art of Playing Keyboard Instruments*. Translated by William J. Mitchell. New York: Norton, 1949.

———. *Versuch über die wahre Art, das Clavier zu spielen*. 2 vols. in 1. Edited by Lothar Hoffmann-Erbrecht. Berlin, 1753. Leipzig: Breitkopf & Härtel, 1957.

Bach, Johann Christian. *Adriano in Siria: Opera Seria in Three Acts*. Vol. 5 of *The Collected Works of J. C. Bach, 1735–1782*. Edited by Ernest Warburton. New York: Garland, 1985.

Backscheider, Paula R. *Spectacular Politics: Theatrical Power and Mass Culture in Early Modern England*. Baltimore: The Johns Hopkins University Press, 1993.

Baczko, Bronislaw. *Utopian Lights: The Evolution of the Idea of Social Progress*. Translated by Judith L. Greenberg. New York: Paragon, 1989.

Bakhtin, Mikhail. *Rabelais and His World*. Translated by Hélène Iswolsky. Indianapolis: Indiana University Press, 1968.

Balatri, Filippo. *Frutti del mondo: Autobiografia di Filippo Balatri da Pisa, 1676–1756*. Edited by Mark Vossler. Milan: Remo Sandron, 1924.

Ballexerd, Jacques. *Dissertation sur l'éducation physique des enfans, depuis leur naissance jusqu'à l'âge de puberté: Ouvrage qui a remporté le prix le 21 mai, á la Société hollandaise des sciences*. Paris: Vallet–La Chapelle, 1762.

———. *Doveri annessi allo stato conjugale, operetta utile, non solo a chi aspira ad un tale stato, e a chi lo ha di gia intrapreso, ma altresì a parrocchi, e tutti coloro, che hanno la cura fisica, e morale de' figlioli*. Turin, 1778.

Balthazar, Scott L. "Mayr, Rossini, and the Development of the Early *Concertato* Finale." *Journal of the Royal Musical Association* 116 (1991): 236–66.

Barbagli, Marzio. *Sotto lo stesso tetto: Mutamenti della famiglia in Italia dal XV al XX secolo*. Bologna: Mulino, 1984.

Barbier, Patrick. *The World of the Castrati: The History of an Extraordinary Operatic Phenomenon*. Translated by Margaret Crosland. 1989. London: Souvenir, 1996.

Barbieri, Patrizio. "The Acoustics of Italian Opera Houses and Auditoriums, ca. 1450–1900." *Recercare* 10 (1998): 263–328.

Baretti, Giuseppe [Joseph]. *Opere*. Edited by Franco Fido. Milan: Rizzoli, 1967.

Barletta, Laura. *Il carnevale del 1764: Protesta e integrazione in uno spazio urbano*. Naples: Società Editrice Napoletana, 1981.

Barnouw, Jeffrey. "Feeling in Enlightenment Aesthetics." *Eighteenth-Century Culture* 18 (1988): 323–42.

Barricelli, Franca R. "Civic Representations: Theatre, Politics, and Public Life in Venice, 1770–1806." Ph.D. diss., University of Wisconsin at Madison, 1994.

———."'Making a People What It Once Was': Regenerating Civic Identity in the Revolutionary Theatre of Venice." *Eighteenth-Century Life* 23 (1999): 38–57.

———. "The Tears and Terror of Foscolo's *Tieste:* Classicism and Politics in Late Republican Venice." *Prism(s): Essays in Romanticism* 9 (2001): 31–49.

Barrington, Daines. Report in the *Philosophical Transactions of the Royal Society,* 54–64. London, 1771.

Barthes, Roland. *Mythologies.* Translated by Annette Lavers. New York: Noonday Press, 1972.

———. *Mythologies.* Paris: Seuil, 1957.

Bartlet, M. Elizabeth C. *Étienne-Nicolas Méhul and Opera: Source and Archival Studies of Lyric Theatre during the French Revolution, Consulate, and Empire.* 2 vols. Études sur l'opéra français du XIXème siècle, no.4. Heilbronn: Musik-Edition Galland, 1999.

———. "Grand Opéra." From *Grove Music Online,* ed. Laura Macy. http://www.grovemusic.com/

———. "Grétry and the Revolution." In *Grétry et l'Europe de l'opéra-comique,* edited by Philippe Vendrix, 47–110. Liège: Mardaga, 1992.

———. "The New Repertory at the Opéra during the Reign of Terror: Revolutionary Rhetoric and Operatic Consequences." In *Music and the French Revolution,* edited by Malcolm Boyd, 107–56. Cambridge: Cambridge University Press, 1992.

———. "On the Freedom of the Theatre and Censorship: The Adrien Controversy (1792)." In *1789–1989: Musique, histoire, démocratie,* edited by Antoine Hennion, 1:15–30. Paris: Maison des Sciences de l'Homme, 1992.

———. "Patriotism at the Opéra-Comique during the Revolution: Grétry's *Callias, ou Nature et patrie.*" *Atti del XIV congresso della Società Internazionale di Musicologia, Bologna, 1987: Trasmissione e recezione delle forme di cultura musicale,* edited by Angelo Pompilio et al., part 3, 839–52. Turin: EDT, 1990.

Basso, Alberto. *Il teatro della città, dal 1788 al 1936.* In *Storia del Teatro Regio di Torino,* edited by Alberto Basso, vol. 2. Turin: Cassa di Risparmio di Torino, 1976.

Bataille, Georges. *La part maudite: Précédé de "La notion de dépense."* Introduction by Jean Piel. Paris: Minuit, 1967.

———. "La souvraineté." In *Oeuvres complètes* 8:243–395. Paris: Gallimard, 1976.

———. *Sovereignty.* In *The Accursed Share: An Essay on General Economy,* 3 vols. in 2. Translated by Robert Hurley. New York: Zone Books, 1993.

Battaglia, Salvatore, ed. *Grande dizionario della lingua italiana.* Directed by Giorgio Bárberi Squarotti. Turin: UTET, 1961–.

Batten, Charles L. Jr. *Pleasureable Instruction: Form and Convention in Eighteenth-Century Travel Literature.* Berkeley and Los Angeles: University of California Press, 1978.

Batz, Karl, ed. *Beiträge des 1. Internationalen Simon-Mayr-Symposions vom 2.–4. Oktober 1992 in Ingolstadt.* Ingolstadt: Donaukurier, 1995.

Bauman, Richard, ed. *Folklore, Cultural Performances, and Popular Entertainments: A Communications-Centered Handbook.* New York: Oxford University Press, 1992.

Bauman, Thomas. "Alessandro Pepoli's Renewal of the *Tragedia per Musica.*" In *I Vicini di Mozart,* edited by Maria Teresa Muraro, vol. 1, *Il teatro musicale tra sette e ottocento,* 211–20. Florence: Olschki, 1989.

———. "The Eighteenth Century: Serious Opera." In *The Oxford Illustrated History of Opera,* edited by Roger Parker, 47–83. Oxford: Oxford University Press, 1994.

———. "The Society of La Fenice and Its First Impresarios." *JAMS* 39 (1986): 332–54.

Becker, Gerhold K. "The Divinization of Nature in Early Modern Thought." In *The Invention of Nature,* edited by Thomas Bargatzky and Rolf Kuschel, 47–61. Frankfurt: Peter Lang, 1994.

Beckford, Peter. *Familiar Letters from Italy, to a Friend in England.* 2 vols. Salisbury: J. Easton, 1805.

Beckford, William. *The Travel-Diaries of William Beckford of Fonthill.* Edited by G. Chapman. 2 vols. Cambridge: Cambridge University Press, 1928.

Bédarida, Henri. *Parme et la France de 1748 à 1789.* Paris: Librarie Ancienne Honoré Champion, 1928.

Bédarida, Paul, ed. *Feste, fontane, festoni a Parma nel settecento: Progetti e decorazioni, disegni e incisioni dell'architetto E. A. Petitot, 1727–1801.* Rome: Dell'Elefante, 1989.

Beeman, William O. "The Anthropology of Theater and Spectacle." *Annual Review of Anthropology* 22 (1993): 369–93.

Beghin, Tom. "Haydn as Orator: A Rhetorical Analysis of the Keyboard Sonata in D Major, HOB.XVI:42." In *Haydn and His World,* edited by Elaine R. Sisman, 201–54. Princeton: Princeton University Press, 1997.

Bell, Catherine. *Ritual Theory, Ritual Practice.* Oxford: Oxford University Press, 1992.

Belli, Carolina. "Il San Carlo attraverso le fonti documentarie." In *Il teatro del re: Il San Carlo da Napoli all'Europa,* edited by Gaetana Cantone, Franco Carmelo Greco, et al., 173–95. Naples: Edizioni Scientifiche Italiane, 1987.

Bellina, Anna Laura, and Bruno Brizi. "Il melodramma." In *Storia della cultura veneta,* edited by Girolamo Arnaldi and Manlio Pastore Stocchi, vol. 5, part 1, 337–400. *Il settecento.* Vicenza: Neri Pozzi, 1985.

Bellina, Anna Laura, and Carlo Caruso. "Oltre il barocco: La fondazione dell'Arcadia; Zeno e Metastasio, la riforma del melodramma." In *Storia della letteratura italiana,* edited by Enrico Malato, vol. 6, *Il settecento,* 239–312. Rome: Salerno, 1998.

Belosel'skii-Belozerskii, Alexandr. *De la musique en Italie par le prince de Beloselsky.* The Hague, 1778. Institut de Bologne, Bibliotheca Musica Bononiensis, ser. 3, no. 42. Bologna: Forni, 1969.

Benassi, Umberto. "Guglielmo du Tillot, un ministro riformatore del secolo XVIII." Chap. 3, "Il periodo della preparazione." *Archivio storico per le province parmensi,* n.s. 15 (1915): 193–368.

Beniscelli, Alberto. *Felicità sognate: Il teatro di Metastasio.* Genoa: Il Melangolo, 2000.

Bercé, Yves-Marie. *Fête et révolte: Des mentalités populaires du XVIe au XVIIIe siècle, essai.* Paris: Hachette, 1976.

Bercé, Yves-Marie, et al. *L'Italie au XVIIe siècle.* Paris: Sedes, 1989.

Berengo, Marino. *La società veneta alla fine del settecento: ricerche storiche.* Florence: Sansoni, 1956.

Berger, Karol. "The First-Movement Punctuation Form in Mozart's Piano Concertos." In *Mozart's Piano Concertos: Text, Context, Interpretation,* edited by Neal Zaslaw, 239–59. Ann Arbor: University of Michigan Press, 1996.

———. "Musicology according to *Don Giovanni,* or Should We Get Drastic?" *Journal of Musicology* 22 (2005): 490–501.

Bergeret de Grancourt, Pierre Jacques Onésyme. *Journal inédit d'un voyage en Italie, 1773–1774.* Paris: May & Monterroz, 1895.

Bergman, Gösta M. *Lighting in the Theatre.* Translated by N. Stedt. Stockholm: Almkvist & Wiksell, 1977.

Bertelli, Sergio. *The King's Body: Sacred Rituals of Power in Medieval and Early Modern Europe.* Rev. ed. of 2nd Italian ed. Translated by R. Burr Litchfield. University Park: Pennsylvania State University Press, 2001.

Bertezen, Salvatore. *Principi di musica teorico-prattica.* Rome: Stamperia Salomoni, 1780.

Biagi Ravenni, Gabriella. "The French Occupation of Lucca and Its Effects on Music." In *Music and the French Revolution,* edited by Malcolm Boyd, 279–301. Cambridge: Cambridge University Press, 1992.

Bianchi, Francesco. *La morte di Cesare.* Edited by Piero Weiss. Drammaturgia Musicale Veneta 25. Milan: Ricordi, 1999.

Bianchi, Giovanni Antonio [Lauriso Tragiense]. *De i vizi, e de i difetti del moderno teatro e del modo di correggergli e d'emendarli Ragionamenti VI.* Rome: Pallade, 1753.

Bianconi, Lorenzo. "Italy." In *The New Grove Dictionary of Opera,* edited by Stanley Sadie, 2:837–60. London: Macmillan, 1992.

———. "Italy." From *Grove Music Online,* ed. Laura Macy. http://www.grovemusic.com/ (accessed 22 September 2005).

———. "L'opera metastasiana: Prospettive critiche." *Il saggiatore musicale* 4 (1997): 481–85.

———. *Il teatro d'opera in Italia: Geografia, caratteri, storia.* Bologna: Mulino, 1993.

Bianconi, Lorenzo, and Giorgio Pestelli, eds. *Opera in Theory and Practice, Image and Myth.* Translated by Kenneth Chalmers and Mary Whittall. The History of Italian Opera, part 2, Systems, vol. 6. Chicago: University of Chicago Press, 2003.

———. *Opera on Stage.* Translated by Kate Singleton. The History of Italian Opera, part 2, Systems, vol. 2. Chicago: University of Chicago Press, 2002.

———. *Opera Production and Its Resources.* Translated by Lydia G. Cochrane. The History of Italian Opera, part 2, Systems, vol. 4. Chicago: University of Chicago Press, 1998.

Binetti, Domenico. *Tommaso e Filippo Trajetta (Traetta) nella vita e nell'arte.* Palo del Colle: Liantonio, 1972.

Binni, Walter. *L'Arcadia e il Metastasio.* Florence: La Nuova Italia, 1963.

Bizzocchi, Roberto. "Cicisbei: La morale italiano." *Storica* 9 (1997): 63–90.

———. *In famiglia: Storie di interessi e affetti nell'Italia moderna.* Rome: Laterza, 2001.

———. "Parini, Goldoni e i cicisbei." In *L'amabil rito: Società e cultura nella Milano di Parini,* edited by G. Barbarisi et al., 177–85. Milan: Cisalpino, 2000.

Black, C. F. "The Baglioni as Tyrants of Perugia, 1488–1540." *English Historical Review* 85 (1970): 245–81.

———. "Comune and the Papacy in the Government of Perugia." *Annali della Fondazione Italiana per la Storia Amministrativa* 4 (1967): 163–91.

———. "Perugia and Papal Absolutism in the Sixteenth Century." *English Historical Review* 96 (1981): 509–39.

Blackburn, Bonnie, and Leofranc Holford-Strevens. *The Oxford Companion to the Year.* Oxford: Oxford University Press, 1999.

Blainville, Monsieur [Charles] de. *Travels through Holland, Germany, Switzerland, and Other Parts of Europe But Especially Italy . . .* Translated by William Guthrie et al. 3 vols. London: W. Strahan, 1743–45.

Bloch, Maurice. *Ritual, History, and Power: Selected Papers in Anthropology.* London: Athalone, 1989.

Bodin, Jean. *On Sovereignty: Four Chapters from the Six Books of the Commonwealth* [*Les six livres de la république* (Paris, 1576)]. Edited and translated by Julian H. Franklin. Cambridge Texts in the History of Political Thought. Cambridge: Cambridge University Press, 1992.

Boiteux, Martine. "Il carnevale e le feste francesi a Roma nel settecento." In *Il teatro a Roma nel settecento,* edited by Giorgio Petrocchi, 1:321–71. Rome: Istituto della Enciclopedia Italiana, 1989.

Bonaca, Raffaella. "Il Teatro Civico del Verzaro di Perugia: Ricerca storica-documentaria sui lavori di costruzione e di decorazione dell'edificio, 1778–1801." Tesi di laurea, Università degli Studi di Firenze, 1980–81.

Bonazzi, Luigi. *Storia di Perugia dalle origine al 1860.* 2 vols. Perugia: Boncampagni, 1875–79.

Bonds, Mark Evan. *Wordless Rhetoric: Musical Form and the Metaphor of the Oration.* Cambridge: Harvard University Press, 1991.

Bonnaud, Jacques. *Dégradation de l'espèce humaine par l'usage des corps à baleine.* Paris, 1770.

Bonney, Richard. "Absolutism: What's In a Name?" *French History* 1 (1987): 93–117.

Bonora, Ettore, ed. *Letterati memorialisti e viaggiatori del settecento.* Milan: Riccardo Ricciardi, 1951.

———. *Dizionario della letteratura italiana.* 2 vols. Milan: Rizzoli, 1977.

Boorsch, Suzanne. *Fireworks: Four Centuries of Pyrotechnics in Prints and Drawings.* New York: The Metropolitan Museum of Art, 2000.

Borgato, M. "David, Giacomo." In *Dizionario biografico degli italiani* 33:140–42. Rome: Enciclopedico Italiano, 1987.

Borsa, Matteo. *Del gusto presente in letteratura italiana: Dissertazione del sig. dottor Matteo Borsa, regio professore nella universita di Mantova, data in luce e accompagnata da copiose osservazioni relative al medesimo argomento da Stefano Arteaga.* Venice: Antonio Zatta, 1785.

———. *Saggio filosofico sopra la musica imitativa teatrale.* Milan: Marelli, 1781.

Bossa, Renato. "Luigi Vanvitelli, spettatore teatrale a Napoli." *Rivista italiana di musicologia* 11 (1976): 48–70.

Botti, Giovanna. "Il 'Medo' di Pietro Righini: Lo spettacolo fra tradizione bibienesca e scenaquadro." In *Civilità teatrale e settecento emiliano,* edited by Susi Davoli. Bologna: Mulino, 1986.

———. "Pietro Righini, apparatore e scenografo a Parma." In *La Parma in festa: spettacolarità e teatro nel Ducato di Parma nel settecento,* edited by Luigi Allegri and Renato di Benedetto, 139–62. Parma: Mucchi, 1987.

Bouquet, Marie-Thérèse. *Il teatro di corte dalle origini al 1788.* Vol. 1 of *Storia del Teatro Reggio di Torino,* edited by Alberto Basso. Turin: Cassa di Risparmio di Torino, 1976.

Bourdieu, Pierre. *Distinction: A Social Critique of the Judgement of Taste.* Translated by Richard Nice. Cambridge: Harvard University Press, 1984.

———. *The Field of Cultural Production: Essays on Art and Literature.* Edited by Randal Johnson. New York: Columbia University Press, 1993.

Boyd, Malcolm, and Juan José Carreras, eds. *Music in Spain during the Eighteenth Century.* Cambridge: Cambridge University Press, 1998.

Brasil, Hebe Macado. *A musica na cidade do Salvador, 1549–1900.* Salvador: Prefeitura Municipal, 1969.

Brown, A. Peter. "Music, Poetry, and Drama in Mozart's Arias before *Die Entführung aus dem Serail.*" *Studies in Eighteenth-Century Culture* 18 (1988): 263–88.

Brown, Bruce Alan. *Gluck and the French Theatre in Vienna.* Oxford: Oxford University Press, 1991.

Brown, Howard Mayer. "Embellishing Eighteenth-Century Arias: On Cadenzas." In *Opera & Vivaldi,* edited by Michael Collins and Elise K. Kirk, 258–76. Austin: University of Texas Press, 1984.

———, ed. *Italian Opera Librettos, 1640–1770.* 14 vols. New York: Garland, 1983.

Brown, Jennifer Williams. "'Con nuove arie aggiunte': Aria Borrowing in the Venetian Repertory, 1672–1685." Ph.D. diss., Cornell University, 1992.

———. "On the Road with the 'Suitcase Aria': The Transmission of Borrowed Arias in Late Seventeenth-Century Italian Opera." *Journal of Musicological Research* 15 (1995): 4–23.

Brown, John. *Dissertation on the Rise, Union . . . and Corruptions of Poetry and Music.* Dublin: G. Faulkner, 1763.

———. *Letters upon the Poetry and Music of the Italian Opera.* Edinburgh, 1789.

Brown, Judith, and Robert C. Davis, eds. *Gender and Society in Renaissance Italy.* London: Longman, 1998.

Brown, Patricia Fortini. *Venice and Antiquity: The Venetian Sense of a Past.* New Haven: Yale University Press, 1996.

Broyles, Michael. "The Two Instrumental Styles of Classicism." *JAMS* 36 (1983): 210–42.

Brozzi, Antonio Paglicci. *Sul teatro giacobino e antigiacobino in Italia, 1796–1805*. Milan: Luigi di Giacomo Pirola, 1887.

Brumana, Biancamaria. "Il dramma per musica *Artaserse* di Giacomo Rust e l'inaugurazione del Teatro del Verzaro di Perugia nell'autunno del 1781." *Bollettino della Deputazione di Storia Patria per l'Umbria* 99 (2002): 239–78.

Brumana, Biancamaria, and Michelangelo Pascale. "Il teatro musicale a Perugia nel settecento: Una cronologia dai libretti." *Esercizi: Arte, musica, spettacolo* 6 (1983): 71–134.

Brusatin, Manlio, and Giuseppe Pavanello, with Cesare De Michelis. *Il Teatro La Fenice: I progetti, la architettura, le decorazioni*. Venice: Abrizzi, 1987.

Bucciarelli, Melania. *Italian Opera and European Theatre, 1680–1720: Plots, Performers, Dramaturgies*. Turnhout: Brepols, 2000.

Buelow, George J. *The Late Baroque Era: From the 1680's to 1740*. Man & Music. London: Macmillan, 1993.

Burden, Michael. "Twittering and Trilling: Swedish Reaction to Metastasio." *Early Music* 26 (1998): 608–21.

Burgess, Geoffrey. "Cyclic Temporality and Power-Representation in *Tragédies en musique* from Lully to Rameau." *Theory@buffalo*, spring 1997, 68–101.

———. "Ritual in the *Tragédie en Musique* from Lully's *Cadmus et Hermione* (1673) to Rameau's *Zoroastre* (1749)." Ph.D. diss., Cornell University, 1998.

———. "'Le théâtre ne change qu'a la troisième scène': The Hand of the Author and the Unity of Place in Act V of *Hippolyte et Aricie*." *Cambridge Opera Journal* 10 (1998): 275–87.

Burke, Peter. "The Carnival in Venice." In *The Historical Anthropology of Early Modern Italy: Essays on Perception and Communication*. Cambridge: Cambridge University Press, 1987.

———. "Early Modern Venice as a Center of Information and Communication." In *Venice Reconsidered: The History and Civilization of an Italian City State, 1297–1797*, edited by John and Dennis Romano Martin, 389–419. Baltimore: Johns Hopkins University Press, 2000.

———. *The Fabrication of Louis XIV*. New Haven: Yale University Press, 1992.

Burkert, Walter. *Greek Religion*. Translated by John Raffan. 1977. Reprint, Cambridge: Harvard University Press, 1985.

———. *Structure and History in Greek Mythology and Ritual*. Berkeley and Los Angeles: University of California Press, 1979.

Burney, Charles. *Music, Men, and Manners in France and Italy, 1770*. Edited by H. Edmund Poole. London: Eulenburg Books, 1969.

———. *Dr. Burney's Musical Tours in Europe*. Edited by Percy Scholes. Vol. 1, *An eighteenth-century musical tour in France and Italy; being Dr. Charles Burney's account of his musical experiences as it appears in his published volume with which are incorporated his travel experiences according to his original intention*. Vol. 2, *An eighteenth-century musical tour in central Europe and the Netherlands; being Dr. Charles Burney's account of his musical experiences*. London: Oxford University Press, 1959.

———. *The Present State of Music in Germany, the Netherlands and United Provinces; or, A Facsimile of the 1773 London Edition*. New York: Broude, 1969.

———. *The Present State of Music in France and Italy; or, A Facsimile of the 1773 London Edition*. New York: Broude, 1969.

———. *A General History of Music from the Earliest Ages to the Present Period (1789)*. Edited by Frank Mercer. 2 vols. New York: Harcourt, Brace and Company, 1935.

———, ed. *Memoirs of the Life and Writings of the Abate Metastasio in which Are Incorporated, Translations of His Principal Letters*. 3 vols. London: G. G. and J. Robinson, 1796.

Butler, Margaret Ruth. *Operatic Reform at Turin's Teatro Regio: Aspects of Production and Stylistic Change in the 1760s*. Lucca: Libreria Musicale Italiana, 2001.

Cagiano de Azevedo, Letizia Norci. "I viaggiatori francesi: De Brosses spettatore a Roma." In *Le muse galanti: La musica a Roma nel settecento*, edited by Bruno Cagli, 89–99. Rome: Istituto della Enciclopedia Italiana, 1985.

Cagli, Bruno. "Produzione musicale e governo pontificio." In *Le muse galanti: La musica a Roma nel settecento*, edited by Bruno Cagli, 1–21. Rome: Instituto della Enciclopedia Italiana, 1985.

———, ed. *Le muse galanti: La musica a Roma nel settecento*. Rome: Instituto della Enciclopedia Italiana, 1985.

Calabria, Antonio. *The Cost of Empire: Neapolitan Finance during the Period of Spanish Rule*. Cambridge: Cambridge University Press, 1991.

Calasso, Robert. *The Marriage of Cadmus and Harmony*. Translated by Tim Parks. 1988. Reprint, New York: Vintage Books, 1993.

Calvi, Giulia. *Il contratto morale: madri e figli nella Toscana moderna*. Rome: Laterza, 1994.

Calzabigi, Ranieri de'. *Scritti teatrali e letterari*. Edited by Anna Laura Bellina. 2 vols. Rome: Salerno, 1994.

Cametti, Alberto. "Critiche e satire teatrali romane del settecento." *Rivista musicale italiana* 9 (1902): 1–35.

———. *Il Teatro di Tordinona, poi di Apollo*. Tivoli: Arti Grafiche A. Chicca, 1938.

Camporesi, Pietro. "Carnevale, cuccagna e giuochi di villa (analisi e documenti)." *Studi e problemi di critica testuale* 10 (1975): 57–97.

———. *The Land of Hunger*. Translated by Tania Croft-Murray, Claire Foley, and Shayne Mitchell. Cambridge: Polity Press; Oxford: Blackwell, 1996.

———. *Il paese della fame*. Bologna: Mulino, 1978.

Candiani, Rosy. "La fortuna della 'riforma' di Calzabigi e Gluck sulle scene italiane settecentesche." In *Ranieri Calzabigi tra Vienna e Napoli: Atti del Convegno di studi: Livorno, 23–24 settembre 1996*, ed. Federico Marri and Francesco Paolo Russo, 57–84. Lucca: Libreria Musicale Italiana, 1998.

———. *Pietro Metastasio: Da poeta di teatro a "virtuoso di poesia."* Rome: Aracne, 1998.

Cannadine, David, and David Price, eds. *Rituals of Royalty: Power and Ceremonial in Traditional Societies*. Cambridge: Cambridge University Press, 1987.

Cantone, Gaetana, Franco Carmelo Greco, et al. *Il teatro del re: Il San Carlo da Napoli all'Europa*. Naples: Edizioni Scientifiche Italiane, 1987.

Canziani, Roberto. *Il dramma e lo spettacolo: Percorso e congiunzioni teoriche di semiotica teatrale*. Rome: Edizioni dell'Ateneo, 1984.

Capra, Carlo. "Habsburg Italy in the Age of Reform." *Journal of Modern Italian Studies* 10 (2005): 218–33.

Capra, Carlo, Valerio Castronovo, and Giuseppe Ricuperati. *La stampa italiana dal cinquecento all'ottocento*. Bari: Laterza, 1976.

Caraci, Maria, Rosa Cafiero, Angela Romagnoli. *Gli affetti convenienti all'idee: Studi sulla musica vocale italiana*. Naples: Edizioni Scientifiche Italiane, 1993.

Caravale, Mario, and Alberto Caracciolo. *Lo stato pontificio da Martino V a Pio IX*. Vol. 14 of the series Storia d'Italia, edited by Giuseppe Galasso. Turin: UTET, 1978.

Caretti, Lanfranco, ed. *Il giorno, poesie e prose varie*. Florence: Monnier, 1969.

Carlson, Marvin. *Places of Performance: The Semiotics of Theatre Architecture*. Ithaca: Cornell University Press, 1989.

Carolina e Filandro: Dramma giocoso in musica da rappresentarsi nel nobile Teatro del Pavone di Perugia, l'estate del 1808. Perugia: Dai Torchi della Società, 1808.

Carpanelli, Franco. "Architettura dei teatri di Parma." In *I teatri di Parma "dal Farnese al Regio,"* edited by Ivo Allodi, 25–43. Milan: Nuove Edizioni Milano, 1969.

Casa, Gabriella, ed. *Influenze ed echi della Rivoluzione francese a Trieste e nel Friuli (maggio 1789–maggio 1797)*. Trieste: Italo Svevo, 1991.

Casanova, Cesarina. *La famiglia italiana in età moderna: Recherche e modelli*. 1997. Reprint, Rome: Carocci, 2000.

Casanova, de Seingault, Jacques. *Histoire de ma vie*. 12 vols. in 6. Leipzig: F. A. Brockhaus, 1960–62.

———. *History of My Life*. Translated by Willard R. Trask. 12 vols. in 6. Baltimore: Johns Hopkins University Press, 1967.

Castelvecchi, Stefano. "From *Nina* to *Nina:* Psychodrama, Absorption, and Sentiment in the 1780s." *Cambridge Opera Journal* 8 (1996): 91–112.

———. "Sentimental Opera: The Emergence of a Genre, 1760–1790." Ph.D. diss., University of Chicago, 1996.

Cavallo, Sandra. "What Did Women Transmit? Ownership and Control of Household Goods and Personal Items in Early Modern Italy." In *Gender and Material Culture in Historical Perspective*, edited by Moira Donald and Linda Hurcombe, 38–53. London: St. Martin's Press, 2000.

Cavazza, Marta. "Between Modesty and Spectacle: Gender and Science in Eighteenth-Century Italy." In *Italy's Eighteenth Century: Gender and Culture in the Age of the Grand Tour*, edited by Paula Findlen, Wendy Ryworth, and Catherine M. Sama. Stanford: Stanford University Press, forthcoming.

Celani, Enrico. "Musica e musicisti in Roma, 1750–1850." *Rivista musicale italiana* 18 (1911): 1–63; 20 (1913): 33–88; 22 (1915): 1–56, 257–300.

Celletti, Rodolfo. "I cantanti a Roma nel XVIII secolo." In *Le muse galanti: La musica a Roma nel settecento*, edited by Bruno Cagli, 101–7. Rome: Instituto della Enciclopedia Italiana, 1985.

———. *A History of Bel Canto*. Translated by Frederick Fuller. Oxford: Clarendon Press, 1991.

Chabot, Isabelle, and Giulia Calvi, eds. *Le richezze delle donne: Diritti patrimoniali e poteri familiari in Italia, XIII–XIX secc.* Turin: Rosenberg & Sellier, 1998.

Chae, Donald Baird. "Music, Festival, and Power in Louis XIV's France: Court Divertissement and the Musical Construction of Sovereign Authority and Noble Identity, 1661–1674." Ph.D. diss., University of Chicago, 2003.

Chanan, Michael. *From Handel to Hendrix: The Composer in the Public Sphere*. London: Verso, 1999.

Chartier, Roger. *Forms and Meanings: Texts, Performances, and Audience from Codex to Computer*. Philadelphia: University of Pennsylvania Press, 1995.

Chegai, Andrea. *L'esilio di Metastasio: Forme e riforme dello spettacolo d'opera fra Sette e Ottocento*. 2nd ed. Storia dello Spettacolo. 1998. Reprint, Florence: Le Lettere, 2000.

Chiacchella, Rita. *Ricchezza, nobilità e potere in una provincia pontificia: La "Misura Generale del Territorio Perugino" del 1727*. Naples: Edizioni Scientifiche Italiane, 1996.

Chiarelli, Alessandra, and Angelo Pompilio. *Or vaghi, or fieri: Cenni poetici nei libretti veneziani, circa 1640–1740*. With *Il cannocciale per la finta pazza* by Maiolino Bisaccioni, edited by Cesarino Ruini. Bologna: CLUEB, 2004.

Chiari, Pietro. *Lettere d'un solitario a sua figlia per formarle il cuore, e lo spirito nella scuola del mondo: Parte prima*. Venice: Battifoco, 1777.

Chojnacki, Stanley. *Women and Men in Renaissance Venice*. Baltimore: Johns Hopkins University Press, 2000.

Ciatti, Felice. *Delle memorie annali, et istoriche delle cose di Perugia raccolte dal molto R. P. M. Felice Ciatti Perugino francescano*. 2 vols. Perugia: Angelo Bartoli, 1638.

Cimarosa, Domenico. *Gli Orazi e i Curiazi, tragedia per musica in tre atti di Antonio Simeone Sografi*. Edited by Giovanni Morelli and Elvidio Surian. Milan: Edizioni Suvini Zerboni, v1985.

Clark, Caryl. "Reading and Listening: Viennese Frauenzimmer Journals and the Sociocultural Context of Mozart's Opera Buffa." *Musical Quarterly* 87, no. 1 (2004): 140–75.

Clark, Jane. "The Stuart Presence at the Opera in Rome." In *The Stuart Court in Rome: The Legacy of Exile*, edited by Edward Corp, 85–93. Aldershot: Ashgate, 2003.

Clarke, David. *Pierre Corneille: Poetics and Political Drama under Louis XIII.* Cambridge: Cambridge University Press, 1992.

Clément, Catherine. *Opera, or The Undoing of Women.* Translated by Betsy Wing. 1979. Reprint, Minneapolis: University of Minnesota Press, 1988.

Clemente, Pietro. "Idee del carnevale." In *Il linguaggio, il corpo e la festa: Per un ripensamento della tematica di Michail Bachtin.* Milan: Franco Angeli, 1983.

Clementi, Filippo. *Il carnevale romano nelle cronache contemporanee.* Città del Castello: RORE, 1938–39.

Clough, Arthur Hugh, ed. *Plutarch's Lives. The Dryden Translation.* Vol. 1. New York: Random House, 1992.

Cocchiara, Giuseppe. *Il mondo alla rovescia.* Turin: Paolo Boringhieri, 1981.

———. *Il paese di cuccagna e altri studi di folklore.* Turin: Paolo Boringhieri, 1980.

Cochin, Charles-Nicolas. *Lettres sur l'opéra.* Paris, 1781.

———. *Le Voyage d'Italie de Charles-Nicolas Cochin (1758).* A facsimile edition with introduction and notes. Edited by Christian Michel. Rome: École Française de Rome, Palais Farnèse, 1991.

Cochin, Charles-Nicolas, et al. *Projet d'une salle de spectacle pour un théâtre.* 1765. Geneva: Minkoff, 1974.

Cochrane, Eric. *Tradition and Enlightenment in the Tuscan Academies, 1690–1800.* Chicago: University of Chicago Press, 1961.

Il codice della libertà italiana rigenerata nell'anno MDCCXCVII: Conterrà una serie delle carte pubbliche, leggi, proclami ec. di tutte le municipalità d'Italia. Vol. 1, parts 1 and 2.Venice: Antonio Zatta quondam Giacomo, 1797.

Cole, Catherine J. "'Nature' at the Opéra: Sound and Social Change in France, 1750–79." Ph.D. diss., University of Chicago, 2003.

Colesanti, Massimo. "I viaggiatori francesi e il teatro romano nel settecento." In *Orfeo in Arcadia: Studi sul teatro a Roma nel settecento*, edited by Giorgio Petrocchi, 203–15. Rome: Istituto della Enciclopedia Italiana, 1984.

[Collections of Eighteenth-Century Roman Libretti.] The University of Chicago, Joseph Regenstein Library, Special Collections. 9 vols. 1721–83.

Comaroff, Jean, and John Comaroff, eds. *Modernity and Its Malcontents: Ritual and Power in Postcolonial Africa.* Chicago: University of Chicago Press, 1993.

Condillac, Etienne Bonnot de. *Cours d'études pour l'instruction du Prince de Parme.* 16 vols. in 14. Parma: Imprimérie Royale, 1775.

Cone, Edward T. *Musical Form and Musical Performance.* New York: Norton, 1968.

Conti, Francesca Romana. "*Amiti e Ontario* di Ranieri di Calzabigi: L'esotismo 'borghese' di un intelletuale classicista." *Opera & Libretto* 2 (1993): 127–55.

Coote, Jeremy, and Anthony Shelton, eds. *Anthropology, Art, and Aesthetics.* Oxford: Clarendon Press, 1992.

Corio, Giuseppe Gorini. *Politica, diritto e religione.* Milan: F. Agnelli, 1742.

Corri, Domenico. *Domenico Corri's Treatises on Singing:* A Select Collection of the Most Admired Songs, Duetts, &c. *and* The Singer's Preceptor. 4 vols. Edited by Richard Maunder. New York: Garland, 1993–95.

——— *A Select Collection of the Most Admired Songs, Duetts, &c.* London and Edinburgh, 1795.

———. *The Singer's Preceptor.* In *The Porpora Tradition*, edited by Edward Foreman. N.p.: Pro Musica Press, 1968.

Coscia, Fabrizio. "La scena del mito nel teatro di Metastasio." In *Legge, poesia e mito: Giannone, Metastasio e Vico fra "tradizione" e "transgressione" nella Napoli degli anni venti del settecento,* edited by Mario Valente, 323–33. Rome: Aracne, 2001.

Costituzioni dell'Accademia in via del Verzaro di Perugia, ordinate dalla generale adunanza degli Accademici il d 20 febbraio 1781 e confermate dalla Sacra Memoria di Papa Pio VI con sua breve del dì 20 giugno dell'anno suddetto 1781. Perugia: Luigi Calvieri, 1803.

Cotticelli, Francesco, and Paologiovanni Maione. "Funzioni e prestigio del modello metastasiano a Napoli: Saverio Mattei e le proposte di una nuova drammaturgia." In *Legge, poesia e mito: Giannone, Metastasio e Vico fra "tradizione" e "trasgressione" nella Napoli degli anni venti del settecento,* edited by Mario Valente, 281–321. Rome: Aracne, 2001.

Couvreur, Manuel. *Jean-Baptiste Lully: Musique et dramaturgie au service du prince.* Brussels: M. Vokar, 1992.

Covell, Roger. "Voice Register as an Index of Age and Status in Opera Seria." In *Opera & Vivaldi,* edited by Michael Collins and Elise K. Kirk, 193–210. Austin: University of Texas Press, 1984.

Cowart, Georgia, ed. *French Musical Thought, 1600–1800.* Ann Arbor: UMI Press, 1989.

Coyer, Gabriel François. *Voyages d'Italie et de Holande par M. l'Abbé Coyer, des académies de Nancy, de Rome & de Londres.* 2 vols in 1. Paris: Duchesne, 1775.

Cozzi, Gaetano, Michael Knapton, and Giovanni Scarabello. *La repubblica di Venezia nell'età moderna.* Vol. 12 of the series Storia d'Italia, edited by Giuseppe Galasso. Turin: UTET, 1986.

Crafton, Donald. "Audienceship in Early Cinema." *Iris* 11 (1990): 1–12.

Cramer, Carl Friedrich. *Magazin der Musik.* 2 vols. in 4 parts. Hamburg, 1783–87. Hildesheim and New York, 1971.

Crescimbeni, Giovanni Mario. *La bellezza della volgar poesia.* Rome: Buagni, 1700.

Creuzé de Lesser, baron Augustin François. *Voyage en Italie et en Sicile, 1801 et 1802.* Paris: Didot, 1806.

Croce, Benedetto. *Aneddoti e profili settecenteschi.* 2nd ed. Milan: Remo Sandron, 1922.

———. *History of the Kingdom of Naples.* Edited by H. Stuart Hughes, translated by Frances Frenaye. Chicago: University of Chicago Press, 1970.

———. *Storia del regno di Napoli.* 6th ed. 1925. Reprint, Bari: Laterza, 1965.

———. *I teatri di Napoli.* 2 vols. 1891. Naples: Arturo Berisio, 1968.

———. *I teatri di Napoli dal rinascimento alla fine del secolo decimottavo.* 2nd rev. ed. of 1915 with emendations from 3rd ed. (1926) and 4th ed. (1947). Edited by Giuseppe Galasso. Milan: Adelphi, 1992.

Croll, Gerhard, and Irene Brandenberg. "Gabrielli, Caterina." In *New Grove Dictionary of Music and Musicians,* 2nd ed., edited by Stanley Sadie, 9:396–97. London: Macmillan, 2001.

Crosscurrents and the Mainstream of Italian Serious Opera, 1730–1790: A Symposium, February 11–13, 1982. Studies in Music from the University of Western Ontario 7/1 and 2 (1982).

Crouzet-Pavan, Elisabeth. *Venice Triumphant: The Horizons of a Myth.* Translated by Lydia G. Cochrane. 1999. Baltimore: Johns Hopkins University Press, 2002.

Cruciani, Fabrizio. "Problemi per lo studio dello spettacolo settecentesco in Emilia: Introduzione." In *Civiltà teatrale e settecento emiliano,* edited by Susi Davoli, 19–32. Bologna: Mulino, 1986.

Crutchfield, Will. "Voices." In *Performance Practice: Music after 1600,* edited by Howard Mayer Brown and Stanley Sadie, 304–10. New York: Norton, 1990.

Cummings, Graham. "Reminiscence and Recall in Three Early Settings of Metastasio's *Alessandro nell'Indie.*" *Proceedings of the Royal Musical Association* 109 (1982–83): 80–104.

Cusatelli, Giorgio. "Società e teatro: Note di costume." In *I teatri di Parma "dal Farnese al Regio,"* edited by Ivo Allodi, 221–28. Milan: Nuove Edizioni Milano, 1969.

Cyr, Mary. "Declamation and Expressive Singing in the Recitative." In *Opera & Vivaldi*, edited by Michael Collins and Elise K. Kirk, 233–57. Austin: University of Texas Press, 1984.

———. "Rameau e Traetta." *Nuova rivista musicale italiana* 12 (1978): 166–82.

Dahlhaus, Carl. "Das rhetorische Formbegriff H. Chr. Koch und die Theorie der Sonatenform." *Archiv für Musikwissenschaft* 35 (1978): 155–76.

D'Alembert, Jean Le Rond. *De la liberté de la musique*. Amsterdam, 1759. Reprinted in *La querelle des bouffons: Texte des pamphlets avec introduction, commentaires et index*, edited by Denise Launay, 3:2199–2282. Geneva: Minkoff, 1973.

———. *Discours préliminaire de l'Encyclopédie*. 1750. Paris: Librarie Philosophique J. Vrin, 2000.

———. *Oeuvres d'Alembert*. Paris: Belin, 1821.

———. *Preliminary Discourse to the Encyclopedia of Diderot*. Translated by Richard N. Schwab and Walter E. Rex. Chicago: University of Chicago Press, 1995.

D'Ambrosa, Paola."Le opere metastasiane di Giacomo Rust su testi metastasiani, 1780–1783." Tesi di laurea, Università di Pavia, 1992.

Dal Pra, Mario. "Il *Cours d'études* di Condillac: Nuova enciclopedia di sapere." In *Atti di Convegno sul Settecento Parmense nel Secondo Centenario della Morte di C. I. Frugoni*, 25–46. Parma: Deputazione di Storia Patria per le Province Parmensi, 1969.

Dalla Libera, Sandro. "L'archivio del Teatro a Fenice." *Ateneo veneto* 6 (1968): 135–46.

Danilo, Reato. *Storia del carnevale di Venezia*. Venice: Amministrazione della Provincia di Venezia, Assessorato alla Cultura, 1988.

Daru, Pierre Antoine Noël. *Histoire de la république de Venise*. 7 vols. Paris, 1819.

Daston, Lorraine. "Enlightenment Fears, Fears of Enlightenment." In *What's Left of Enlightenment?* edited by Keith Michael Baker and Peter Reill. Stanford: Stanford University Press, 2001.

Daston, Lorraine, and Fernando Vidal, eds. *The Moral Authority of Nature*. Chicago: University of Chicago Press, 2004.

David, Marcel. *Fraternité et la révolution française, 1789–1799*. Paris: Aubier, 1987.

Davies, Drew Edward. "The Italianized Frontier: Music at Durango Cathedral, Español Culture, and the Aesthetics of Devotion in Eighteenth-Century New Spain." Ph.D. diss., University of Chicago, 2006.

Davis, James Cushman. *The Decline of the Venetian Nobility as a Ruling Class*. Baltimore: Johns Hopkins University Press, 1962.

Davis, John A. "The Culture of Enlightenment and Reform in Eighteenth-Century Italy." *Journal of Modern Italian Studies* 10 (2005): 131–32.

Davis, Natalie Zemon. "Reasons of Misrule." In *Society and Culture in Early Modern France*, 97–123. Stanford: Stanford University Press, 1975.

Davoli, Susi, ed. *Civiltà teatrale e settecento emiliano*. Bologna: Mulino, 1986.

De Angelis, Angelo. *Il Teatro Alibert o delle Dame nella Roma papale, 1717–1863*. Tivoli: Arti Grafiche A. Chicca, 1951.

De Bei, Alessandra. "Giulietta e Romeo di Nicola Zingarelli: Fortuna ed eredità di un soggetto shakespeariano." In *Aspetti dell'opera italiana fra sette e ottocento: Mayr e Zingarelli*, edited by Guido Salvetti, 71–125. Lucca: Libreria Musicale Italiana, 1993.

De Biase, Luca. *Amore di stato: Venezia, settecento*. Palermo: Sellerio, 1992.

De Brito, Manuel Carlos. *Opera in Portugal in the Eighteenth Century*. Cambridge: Cambridge University Press, 1989.

De Brosses, Charles. *Lettres familières écrits d'Italie en 1739 et 1740*. 2nd ed. Paris, 1836.

———. *Lettres familières sur l'Italie*. Edited by Yvonne Bézard. Paris, Firmin-Didot & Cie, 1931.

De Domenicis, Giulia. "I teatri di Roma nell'età di Pio VI." *Archivio della Societa Romana di Storia Patria* 46 (1923): 49–243.

De Filippis, F., and R. Arnese. *Cronache del Teatro di S. Carlo.* Vol. 1. Naples: Edizioni Politica Popolare, 1961.

De Grazia, Sebastian. *Of Time, Work, and Leisure.* Garden City, NY: Anchor Books, 1962.

Delfico, Melchiorre. "Saggio filosofico sul matrimonio." 1774. *Illuministi italiani,* ed. Franco Venturi, 2:1159–1266. Naples: Riccardo Ricciardi, 1997–98.

De Luca, Giovanni Battista. *Il dottor volgare, overo Il compendio di tutta la legge civile, canonica, feudale, e municipale, nelle cose più ricevute in pratica.* Rome, 1673.

De Michelis, Cesare, ed. *Il teatro patriotico.* Padua: Marsilio, 1966.

De Renzi, Salvatore. *Napoli nell'anno 1764, ossia Documenti della carestia e della epidemia che desolarono Napoli nel 1764, preceduti dalla storia di quelle sventure.* Naples: G. Nobile, 1868.

De Sade, Marquis. *Voyage d'Italie, ou Dissertations critiques, historiques, politiques et philosophiques sur les villes de Florence, Rome et Naples, 1775–1776.* Edited by Gilbert Lely and George Daumas. Vol. 16 in *Oeuvres complètes.* Paris: Cercle du Livre Précieux, 1967.

De Simone, Roberto, ed. *La cantante e l'impresario e altri metamelodrammi.* Genoa: Costa & Nolan, 1988.

Dean, Winton. "Bordoni, Faustina." From *Grove Music Online,* ed. Laura Macy. http://www.grovemusic.com/ (accessed October 18, 2005).

Degrada, Francesco. "L'opera napoletana." In *Storia dell'Opera,* edited by Alberto Basso, vol. 1, part 1, 237–332. Turin: UTET, 1977.

Del Giudice, Luisa. "Mountains of Cheese and Rivers of Wine: Paesi di Cuccagna and Other Gastronomic Utopias." In *Imagined States: Nationalism, Utopia, and Longing in Oral Cultures,* edited by Luisa Del Giudice and Gerald Porter, 11–63. Logan: Utah State University Press, 2001.

Della celebrazione del Teatro Pavone: Perugia VI Febbraio MCMXXVII. Perugia: Guglielmo Donnini Tipografico della Rivoluzione Fascista, 1927.

Della Lena, Innocenzo. *Dissertazione ragionata sul teatro moderno.* Venice: Giacomo Storti, 1791.

Della Seta, Fabrizio. "Il relator sincero: Cronache teatrali romane, 1739–1756." *Studi musicali* 9 (1980): 73–116.

DellDonna, Anthony Robert. "The Operas of Pietro Alessandro Guglielmi, 1728–1804: The Relationship of His Dialect Operas to His Opere Serie." Ph.D. diss., Catholic University of America, 1977.

DeNora, Tia. *Music in Everyday Life.* Cambridge: Cambridge University Press, 2000.

Dent, Edward J. *Mozart's Operas: A Critical Study.* London: Oxford University Press, 1947.

Desan, Suzanne. *The Family on Trial in Revolutionary France.* Berkeley and Los Angeles: University of California Press, 2004.

Desler, Anne. "From 'Oh virtù che innamora' to 'Son pastorello amante': Farinelli and Metastasio's *Artaserse.*" In *Music Observed: Studies in Memory of William C. Holmes,* edited by Colleen Reardon and Susan Parisi, 117–38. Warren, MI: Harmonie Park Press, 2004.

Detienne, Marcel. "The Powers of Marriage in Ancient Greece." In *Mythologies,* edited by Yves Bonnefoy, vol. 1, part 4, 395–97. Chicago: University of Chicago Press, 1991.

Deutsch, Otto Erich. *Handel: A Documentary Biography.* 1955. Reprint, New York: Da Capo Press, 1974.

Diaz, Furio. "Politici e ideologici." In *Storia della letteratura italiana,* vol. 6, *Il settecento,* ed. Emilio Cecchi and Natalino Sapegno, 105–36, 277–79. Milan: Garzanti, 1968.

Di Benedetto, Renato. "Dal Metastasio a Pergolesi e ritorno: Divagazioni intercontestuali fra l'*Adriano in Siria* e *L'olimpiade.*" *Il saggiatore musicale* 2 (1995): 259–95.

———. "Music and Enlightenment." In *Naples in the Eighteenth Century: The Birth and Death of a Nation State,* edited by Girolamo Imbruglia, 135–53. Cambridge: Cambridge University Press, 2000.

———. "Poetiche e polemiche." In *Storia dell'opera italiana*, edited by Lorenzo Bianconi and Giorgio Pestelli. Turin: EDT, 1987.

——— "Poetics and Polemics." In *Opera in Theory and Practice, Image and Myth*, edited by Lorenzo Bianconi and Giorgio Pestelli, translated by Kenneth Chalmers and Mary Whittall, 35–36. Chicago: University of Chicago Press, 2003.

Diderot, Denis. *Le neveu de Rameau*. Edited by Jean Fabre. Geneva: Droz, 1950.

———. *Il padre di famiglia; commedia in cinque atti in prosa*. Livorno: Gio. Paolo Fantechi, 1762.

———. *Rameau's Nephew and D'Alembert's Dream*. Translated by Leonard Tancock. London: Penguin, 1965.

Diderot, Denis, and Jean le Rond d'Alembert. *Theatre Architecture and Stage Machines: Engravings from the Encyclopédie*. New York: Blom, 1969.

Didone abbandonata: Dramma per musica da rappresentarsi sul Reggio Teatro Danese l'inverno dell'anno 1762. Copenhagen: Lars Nielsen Scare, 1762.

La Didone abbandonata: Dramma per musica da rappresentarsi in Perugia nell'apertura del Nuovo Teatro Civico del Verzaro l'autunno dell'anno MDCCLXXXI. Perugia: Mario Riginaldi, 1781.

Dill, Charles. *Monstrous Opera: Rameau and the Tragic Tradition*. Princeton: Princeton University Press, 1998.

———. "Pellegrin, Opera, and Tragedy." *Cambridge Opera Journal* 10 (1998): 247–57.

———. "Rameau's Imaginary Monsters: Knowledge, Theory, and Chromaticism in *Hippolyte et Aricie*." *JAMS* 55 (2002): 433–76.

Diniz, Jaime Cavalcanti. "A musica na Bahia colonial." *Revista de historia* 60 (1965): 93–116.

Di Robilant, Andrea. *A Venetian Affair*. New York: Knopf, 2003.

Dizionario di belle lettere composto dalli signori D'Alembert, Diderot, Marmontel ed altri letterati di Francia. 3 vols. Rome: Desideri ai Portughesi, 1795–97.

Döhring, Sieghart. "Die Arienformen in Mozarts Opern." *Mozart-Jahrbuch*, 1968/1970, 66–76.

Donati, Claudio. *L'idea di nobiltà in Italia, secoli XIV–XVIII: Collezione storica*. Roma: Laterza, 1988.

Doniger, Wendy. *The Implied Spider: Politics and Theology in Myth*. New York: Columbia University Press, 1998.

Dooley, Brendan. "Political Publishing and Its Critics in Seventeenth-Century Italy." *Memoirs of the American Academy in Rome* (1997): 175–93.

———. "The Public Sphere and the Organization of Knowledge." In *Early Modern Italy, 1550–1796*, edited by John A. Marino, 209–28. Oxford: Oxford University Press, 2002.

———. *Science and the Marketplace in Early Modern Italy*. Lanham, MD: Lexington Books, 2001.

———. *Science, Politics, and Society in Eighteenth-Century Italy: The "Giornale de' letterati d'Italia" and Its World*. New York: Garland, 1991.

———. *The Social History of Skepticism: Experience and Doubt in Early Modern Culture*. Baltimore: Johns Hopkins University Press, 1999.

———, ed. *Italy in the Baroque: Selected Readings*. New York: Garland, 1995.

Dooley, Brendan, and Sabrina A. Baron, eds. *The Politics of Information in Early Modern Europe*. London: Routledge, 2001.

Doria, Paolo Mattia. *Dialogo nel quale esaminandosi la cagione per la quale le donne danzando non si stancano mai, si fa il ritratto d'un Petit Maître italiano affrettato laudatore delle massime, e dei costumi dei Petits Maîtres oltramontani e cicisbei*. Vol. 2, part 1 of *Lettere e ragionamenti vari*. Perugia, 1741.

Dounias, Minos. *Die Violinkonzerte Giuseppe Tartinis als Ausdruck einer Künstlerpersönlichkeit und einer Kulturepoche*. 1935. Reprint, Wolfenbüttel: Möseler, 1966.

Downes, Edward E. D. "*Secco* Recitative in Early Classical Opera Seria, 1720–1780." *JAMS* 14 (1961): 50–69.

Doyle, William. *The Old European Order, 1660–1800*. 2nd ed. 1978. Reprint, Oxford: Oxford University Press, 1992.

Du Boccage, Marie Anne Le Page. *Lettres, contenant ses voyages en France, en Angleterre, en Hollande et en Italie faits pendant les années 1750, 1757 et 1758*. Dresden: G. Walther, 1771.

Dumézil, Georges. *Archaic Roman Religion, with an Appendix on the Religion of the Etruscans*. 2 vols. Translated by Philip Krapp, foreword by Mircea Eliade. 1966. Reprint, Chicago: University of Chicago Press, 1970.

Dunlap, Susanne Emily. "Armida and Rinaldo in Eighteenth-Century Vienna: Context, Content, and Tonal Coding in Viennese Italian Reform Operas." Ph.D. diss., Yale University, 1999.

Dunning, Alfred. "Official Court Music: Means and Symbols of Might." In *La musique et le rite sacre et profane: Proceedings of the 13th Congress of the International Musicological Society Held at Strasbourg 1982*, edited by Marc Honegger and Christian Meyer, 17–21. Strasbourg: University of Strasbourg, 1986.

Durante, Sergio. "The Chronology of Mozart's 'La clemenza di Tito' Reconsidered." *Music & Letters* 80, no. 4 (1999): 560–94.

———. "'La clemenza di Tito" and Other Two-Act Reductions of the Late 18th Century." *Mozart Jahrbuch* 2 (1991): 733–41.

———. "The Opera Singer." In *Opera Production and Its Resources*, edited by Lorenzo Bianconi and Giorgio Pestelli, 345–417. Chicago: University of Chicago Press, 1998.

———. "Strutture mentali e vocabolario di un cantore antico/moderno: Preliminari per una lettura delle fonti didattiche settecentesche." In *Alessandro Scarlatti und seine Zeit*, edited by Max Lütolf, 38–54. Bern: Paul Haupt Verlag, 1995.

———. "Theorie und Praxis der Gesangsschulen zur Zeit Händels: Bermerkungen zu Tosis *Opinioni de' cantori antichi e moderni*." In *Händel auf dem Theater: Bericht über die Symposium der internationalen Händel-Akademie Karlruhe 1986 und 1987*, edited by Hans Joachim Marx, 59–72. Laaber: Laaber-Verlag, 1988.

———. "Two Early Romantic Operas with Iberian Roots: *II conte di Saldagna* and *Ines de Castro*." International Musicological Society CR 15, Madrid 1992. *Revista de musicologia*, 1993, 3089–100.

———. "Vizi privati e virtù pubbliche del polemista teatrale da Muratori a Marcello." In *Benedetto Marcello: La sua opera e il suo tempo*, edited by Claudio Madricardo and Franco Rossi, 415–24. Florence: Olschki, 1988.

Duranti, Alessandro. "The Audience as Co-Author: An Introduction." *Text* 6 (1986): 239–47.

Durkheim, Émile. *The Elementary Forms of Religious Life: A Study in Religious Sociology*. Translated by Joseph Ward Swain. New York: Free Press, 1915.

Duvignaud, Jean. *Spectacle et société*. Paris: Donoël/Gonthier, 1970.

Eco, Umberto. "The Frames of Comic Freedom." In *Carnival!* edited by Thomas A. Sebeok and Marcia E. Erickson, 1–10. Berlin: Mouton, 1984.

Ehrard, Jean. *L'idée de nature en France dans la première moitié du XVIIIe siècle*. 1963. Reprint, Paris: Albin Michel, 1994.

Eisen, Cliff, and Stanley Sadie. "Mozart." §3.2. From *Grove Music Online*, ed. Laura Macy. http://www.grovemusic.com/ (accessed October 5, 2005).

Eliade, Mircea. "Toward a Definition of Myth." In *Mythologies*, edited by Yves Bonnefoy, translation edited by Wendy Doniger, 1:3–5. Chicago: University of Chicago Press, 1991.

Elias, Norbert. *The Civilizing Process: Sociogenetic and Psychogenetic Investigations*. Translated by Edmund Jephcott. Edited by Eric Dunning, Johan Goudsblom, and Stephen Mennell. Oxford: Blackwell, 2000.

———. *The Court Society.* Translated by Edmund Jephcott. 1969. Reprint, Oxford: Blackwell, 1983.

———. *Time: An Essay.* Translated in part by Edmund Jephcott. Oxford: Blackwell, 1992.

Elsaesser, Thomas, ed. *Early Cinema: Space, Frame, Narrative.* London: BFI, 1990.

Engel, Hans. "Hasses Ruggiero and Mozarts Festspiel Ascanio." *Mozart-Jahrbuch,* 1960/1961, 29–42.

Euripides. *Hippolytus.* Edited by John Ferguson. Bristol: Bristol Classical Press, 1984.

Evans-Pritchard, E. E. "The Divine Kingship of the Shilluk of the Nilotic Sudan." In *Social Anthropology and Other Essays.* 1948. Reprint, New York: Free Press, 1962.

Evelyn, John. *The Diary of John Evelyn.* Edited by E. S. de Beer. London: Oxford University Press, 1959.

Eximeno y Pujades, Antonio. *Dell'origine e delle regole della musica.* Rome: M. Barbiellini, 1774.

Fabbri, Mario. "Francesco Zannetti, musicista volterrano 'dall'estro divino.'" In *Musiche italiane rare e vive da Giovanni Gabrieli a Giuseppe Verdi,* edited by Adelmo Damerini and Gino Roncaglia, 161–82. Siena: Accademia Musicale Chigiana, 1962.

Fabbri, Paolo. "Istituti metrici e formali." In *Storia dell'opera italiana,* edited by Lorenzo Bianconi and Paolo Fabbri, 6:163–233. Turin: EDT, 1988.

———. "Metrical and Formal Organization." In *Opera in Theory and Practice, Image and Myth,* edited by Lorenzo Bianconi and Paolo Fabbri, translated by Kenneth Chalmers and Mary Whittall, 151–219. Chicago: University of Chicago Press, 2003.

———. "Saverio Mattei e la 'musica filosofica.'" In *Studien zur italienischen Musikgeschichte 15,* Analecta musicologica, vol. 30. Regensburg: Laaber, 1998.

———. "Vita e funzione di un teatro pubblico e di corte nel settecento." In *Il Teatro di San Carlo, 1737–1987,* edited by Franco Mancini, Bruno Cagli, and Agostino Ziino, 2: 61–76. Naples: Electa Napoli, 1987.

Fagiolo, Marcello, ed. *La festa a Roma.* 2 vols. Turin: Umberto Allemandi, 1997.

Fagiolo dell'Arco, Maurizio, and Silvia Carandini. *L'effimero barocco: Strutture della festa nella Roma del '600.* 2 vols. Rome: Bulzoni, 1978.

Farinelli, Carlo Broschi. *La solitudine amica: Lettere al conte Sicinio Pepoli.* Edited by Carlo Vitali with Francesca Boris. Palermo: Sellerio, 2000.

Feil, Arnold. "Satztechnische Fragen in den Kompositionslehren von F. E. Niedt, J. Riepel, und H. Chr. Koch." Inaugural diss., Ruprecht-Karl Universität, Heidelberg, 1955.

Feldman, Burton, and Robert D. Richardson. *The Rise of Modern Mythology, 1680–1860.* Bloomington: Indiana University Press, 1972.

Feldman, Martha. "The Absent Mother in Opera Seria." In *Siren Songs: Representations of Gender and Sexuality in Opera,* edited by Mary Ann Smart, 29–46 and 254–59. Princeton: Princeton University Press, 2000.

———. *City Culture and the Madrigal at Venice.* Berkeley and Los Angeles: University of California Press, 1995.

———. "Magic Mirrors and the Seria Stage: Thoughts Toward a Ritual View." *JAMS* 48 (1995): 423–84.

———. "Mozart and His Elders: Opera-Seria Arias, 1766–1775." *Mozart-Jahrbuch,* 1991, 2:564–75.

———. "Music and the Order of the Passions." In *Representing the Passions: Visions, Bodies, Texts,* edited by Richard Meyer, 37–67. Los Angeles: Getty Trust, 2003.

———. "L'opera seria e la prospettiva antropologica." *Musica e storia* 5 (1997): 127–51.

———. "Staging the Virtuoso: Ritornello Procedure in Mozart, from Aria to Concerto." In *Mozart's Piano Concertos: Text, Context, Interpretation,* edited by Neal Zaslaw. 149–86. Ann Arbor: University of Michigan Press, 1996.

———. "Strange Births and Surprising Kin: The Castrato's Tale." In *Italy's Eighteenth Cen-*

tury: Gender and Culture in the Age of the Grand Tour, edited by Paula Findlen, Wendy Roworth, and Catherine Sama, afterword by Franco Fido. Stanford: Stanford University Press, forthcoming.

———. "Il virtuoso in scena: Mozart, l'aria, il concerto (K. 135, K. 216 e K. 238)." *Rivista italiana di musicologia* 28 (1993): 255–98.

Felici, Candida. "Dall'oralità alla scrittura dell'ornamentazione durante il XVIII secolo." *Studi musicali* 29 (2001): 369–97.

Fénélon, François de Salignac de La Mothe. *Della educazione in genere e specialmente delle fanciulle.* Florence, 1790.

Ferrara, Paul Albert. "Gregorio Caloprese and the Subjugation of the Body in Metastasio's Drammi per Musica." *Italica* 73, no. 1 (1996): 11–23.

Ferrari, Giuliana. "La compagnia Jean Philippe Delisle alla corte di Parma (1755–58) e la 'riforma teatrale' di Guillaume du Tillot." In *La Parma in Festa: Spettacolarità e teatro nel ducato di Parma nel settecento,* edited by Luigi Allegri and Renato di Benedetto, 163–210. Parma: Mucchi, 1987.

Ferrari, Giuliana, Paola Mecarelli, and Paola Melloni. "L'organizzazione teatrale parmense all'epoca del Du Tillot: I rapporti fra la corte e gli impresari." In *Civiltà teatrale e settecento emiliano,* edited by Susi Davoli, 357–80. Bologna: Mulino, 1986.

Ferrari, Maria Claudia, ed. *1763–1764, Bernardo Tanucci.* Napoli: Società Napoletana di Storia Patria, 1997.

Ferrari, Paolo-Emilio. *Spettacoli drammatico-musicali e coreografici in Parma dal 1628 al 1883.* Parma, 1884. Reprint, Bologna: Forni, 1969.

Ferraro, Joanne. *Family and Public Life in Brescia, 1580–1650.* Cambridge: Cambridge University Press, 1993.

Ferrini, Oreste. "Annibale Mariotti nell'opera sua." In *I professori e gli studenti del Liceo-Ginnasio A. Mariotti di Perugia in memoria di Annibale Mariotti: studi storici e letterari,* 3–118. Perugia: Guerriero Guerra, 1901.

Ferrone, Siro, and Teresa Megale. "Teatro e spettacolo nel settecento: Cerimonie liturgiche e spettacoli di carnevale." In *Storia della letteratura italiana,* edited by Enrico Malato, vol. 6, chap. 14, "Il teatro," part 1, 821–29. Rome: Salerno, 1998.

Ferrone, Vincenzo. *The Intellectual Roots of the Italian Enlightenment: Newtonian Science, Religion, and Politics in the Early Eighteenth Century.* Translated by Sue Brotherton. Atlantic Highlands, NJ: Humanities Press, 1995.

Ferroni, Giulio. "Il Metastasio napoletano tra l' "Istoria civile" e la "Scienza nuova."" ' In *Legge, poesia e mito: Giannone, Metastasio e Vico fra "tradizione" e trasgressione" nella Napoli degli anni venti del settecento,* edited by Mario Valente, 203–22. Rome: Aracne, 2001.

Findlen, Paula. "The Scientist's Body: The Nature of a Woman Philosopher in Enlightenment Italy." In *The Faces of Nature in Enlightenment Europe,* edited by Lorraine Daston and Gianna Pomata, 211–36. Berlin: Berliner Wissenschafts-Verlag, 2003.

Finscher, Ludwig. "Die Opera Seria." *Mozart-Jahrbuch,* 1973/1974, 21–32.

Finucci, Valeria. *The Manly Masquerade: Masculinity, Paternity, and Castration in the Italian Renaissance.* Duke: Duke University Press, 2003.

"The Fire at La Fenice." Report on the OperaGlass Web site, Stanford Universtiy. http://opera.stanford.edu/misc/fire.html (accessed October 3, 2003).

Fischer, Carlos. *Les costumes de l'Opéra.* Paris: Librairie de France, 1931.

Fiume, Giovanna, ed. *Madri: Storia di un ruolo sociale.* Venice: Marsilio, 1995.

Florimo, Francesco. *La scuola musicale di Napoli e i suoi conservatori: Con uno sguardo sulla storia della musica in Italia.* 4 vols. 1881. Bologna: Forni, 1969.

Flothius, Marius. "Bühne und Konzert." *Mozart-Jahrbuch,* 1986, 45–58.

Folkierski, Wladyslaw. *Entre le classicisme et le romanticisme: Étude sur l'esthétique et les esthéticiens du XVIIIe siècle.* Paris: Honoré Champion, 1925.

Forbes, Elizabeth. "Babbini [Babini], Matteo." In *New Grove Dictionary of Music and Musicians,* 2nd ed., edited by Stanley Sadie. London: Macmillan, 2001.

———. "Babbini [Babini], Matteo." From *Grove Music Online,* ed. Laura Macy. http://www.grovemusic.com/ (accessed November 17, 2005).

———. "David, Giacomo." In *New Grove Dictionary of Music and Musicians,* 2nd ed., edited by Stanley Sadie. London: Macmillan, 2001.

———. "Davide [David], Giacomo." From *Grove Music Online,* ed. Laura Macy. http://www.grovemusic.com/ (accessed November 17, 2005).

Foreman, Lewis, and Susan Foreman. *London: A Musical Gazetteer.* New Haven: Yale University Press, 2005.

Forman, Denis. *Mozart's Concerto Form: The First Movements of the Piano Concertos.* London: Hart-Davis, 1971.

Fornaini, Mario. "Instaurazione del governo repubblicano in Perugia." In *I professori e gli studenti del Liceo-Ginnasio A. Mariotti,* 275–83. Perugia: Guerriero Guerra, 1901.

Foucault, Michel. "What Is an Author?" In *The Foucault Reader,* edited by Paul Rabinov, 101–20. New York: Pantheon, 1984.

Franceschi, Francesco. *Apologia delle opere drammatiche di Metastasio.* Lucca: Marescandoli, [1790–99?].

Franchi, Saverio. "Patroni, politica, impresari: Le vicende storico-artistiche dei teatri romani e quelle della giovinezza di Metastasio fino alla partenza per Vienna." In *Metastasio da Roma all'Europa: Incontro di studi, 21 ottobre 1998,* edited by Franco Onorati, 7–48. Rome: Fondazione Marco Besso, 1998.

Frascani, Paolo. "Il dibattito sul lusso nella cultura napoletana del '700." *Critica storica* 11 (1971): 397–424.

Frascarelli, Angelo. "'Elementi teorici-pratici di musica' by Francesco Galeazzi: An Annotated English Translation and Study of Volume 1." Ph.D. diss., University of Rochester, Eastman School of Music, 1968.

Frascarelli, Francesco. *Nobiltà minore e borghesia a Perugia nel sec. XV: Ricerche sui Baglioni della Brigida e sui Narducci.* Perugia: Istituti di Storia della Facoltà di Lettere e Filosofia, 1974.

Frazer, James. *The Golden Bough: A Study in Magic and Religion.* Abridged ed. 1922. Reprint, New York: Macmillan, 1950.

Feeley-Harnik, Gillian. "Issues in Divine Kingship." *Annual Review of Anthropology* 14 (1984): 273–313.

Freeman, Daniel D. "An 18th-Century Singer's Commission of 'Baggage' Arias." *Early Music* 20 (1992): 427–33.

Freeman, Robert S. "Apostolo Zeno's Reform of the Libretto." *JAMS* 21 (1968): 321–41.

———. "Farinello and His Repertory." In *Studies in Renaissance and Baroque Music in Honor of Arthur Mendel,* edited by Robert L. Marshall, 301–30. Kassel: Bärenreiter, 1974.

———. *Opera without Drama: Currents of Change in Italian Opera, 1675–1725.* Ann Arbor: UMI Research Press, 1981.

Freitas, Roger. "The Eroticism of Emasculation: Confronting the Baroque Body of the Castrato." *Journal of Musicology* 20 (2003): 196–249.

———. "Sex without Sex: An Erotic Image of the Castrato Singer." In *Italy's Eighteenth Century: Gender and Culture in the Age of the Grand Tour,* edited by Paula Findlen, Wendy Ryworth, and Catherine M. Sama. Stanford: Stanford University Press, forthcoming.

Fried, Michael. *Absorption and Theatricality: Painting and Beholder in the Age of Diderot.* 1980. Reprint, Chicago: University of Chicago Press, 1988.

Frigo, Daniela, ed. *Politics and Diplomacy in Early Modern Italy: The Structure of Diplomatic Practice, 1450–1800.* Cambridge: Cambridge University Press, 2000.

Frigola, Monserrat Moli. "Fuochi, teatri e macchine spagnole a Roma nel settecento." In *Il teatro a Roma nel settecento,* edited by Giorgio Petrocchi, 1:215–58. Rome: Instituto della Enciclopedia Italiana, 1989.

Frugoni, Abate Carlo. *Ippolito ed Aricia tragedia da rappresentarsi nel Reale Teatro di Parma nella primavera dell'anno MDCCLIX: Nuovamente composta, e adattata alle Scene italiane dal Sig. Abate Frugoni.* Fascimile reprint in *Italian Opera Librettos, 1640–1770,* edited by Howard Mayer Brown, vol. 14. New York: Garland, 1983.

Fubini, Enrico. *Music and Culture in Eighteenth-Century Europe: A Source Book.* Translation edited by Bonnie Blackburn. Chicago: University of Chicago Press, 1994.

———. "L'orecchio del viaggiatore: Miti e realtà della Roma musicale del settecento." In *Le muse galanti: La musica a Roma nel settecento,* 79–87. Rome: Istituto della Enciclopedia Italiana, 1985.

———, ed. *La cultura illuministica in Italia.* Turin: Edizioni Radio Italiana, 1957.

Gaignebet, Claude, with Marie-Claude Florentin. *Le carneval: Essais de mythologie populaire.* Paris: Payot, 1974.

Galasso, Giuseppe. "Metastasio e Napoli." In *Legge, poesia e mito: Giannone, Metastasio e Vico fra "tradizione" e "trasgressione" nella Napoli degli anni venti del settecento,* edited by Mario Valente, liii–lxxvii. Rome: Aracne, 2001.

Galeazzi, Francesco. *Elementi teorico-pratici di musica con un saggio sopra l'arte di suonare il violino analizzata, ed a dimostrabili principi ridotta.* 2 vols. Rome: Pilucchi Cracas, 1791–96. Rev. ed., Rome, 1817.

Galiani, Ferdinando. "Digressione intorno al lusso, considerato generalmente." In *Della moneta, libri cinque.* Naples: G. Raimondi, 1750.

Gallarati, Paolo. *L'Europa del melodramma: Da Calzabigi a Rossini.* Alessandria: dell'Orso, 1999.

———. *Musica e maschera: Il libretto italano del settecento.* Turin: EDT, 1984.

Gallico, Claudio. *Le capitali della musica: Parma.* Cinisello Balsamo: Silvana, 1985.

Gallico, Guido. "Cori a Parma, 1759–1760." *Rivista italiana di musicologia* 32 (1997): 81–97.

Gallini, Giovanni-Andrea. *A Treatise on the Art of Dancing.* London, 1762. New York: Dance Horizons, 1967.

Gamerra, Giovanni de. "Osservazioni su' opera in musica." In *L'Armida, dramma per musica.* [April 4, 1771, Milan]. Milan: Giuseppe Galeazzi, 1771.

Garda, Michela. *Musica sublime: Metamorfosi di un' idea nel settecento musicale.* Milan: Ricordi, 1995.

———. "Sul sublime e il terribile dall'*Alceste* all'*Idomeneo.*" *Il saggiatore musicale* 1 (1994): 335–60.

Garlington, Aubrey S. "Opera in Florence under French Domination: Social and Cultural Considerations." *Opera & Libretto* 1 (1990): 77–100.

Garrick, David. *Letters.* 3 vols. Edited by David Mason Little and George Morrow Kahrl. Cambridge: Belknap Press, 1963.

Gatta, Diego. *Reali dispacci, nelli quali si contengono le sovrane determinazioni de' punti generali o che servono di norma ad altri simili casi nel regno di Napoli.* 3 vols. in 11. Naples: Giuseppe-Maria Severino-Boezio, 1773–77.

Geertz, Clifford. "Centers, Kings, and Charisma: Reflections on the Symbolics of Power." In *Local Knowledge: Further Essays in Interpretive Anthropology,* 121–46. New York: Basic Books, 1983.

———. *Negara: The Theatre State in Nineteenth-Century Bali.* Princeton: Princeton University Press, 1980.

Gell, Alfred. "Technology and Magic." *Anthropology Today* 4 (1988): 6–9.

———. "The Technology of Enchantment and the Enchantment of Technology." In *Anthropology, Art, and Aesthetics*, edited by Jeremy Coote and Anthony Shelton, 40–63. Oxford: Clarendon Press, 1992.

Gerhard, Anselm. "Rollenhierarchie und dramaturgische Hierarchien in der italienischen Oper des 18. Jahrhunderts." In *Opernheld und Opernheldin im 18. Jahrhundert: Aspekte der Librettoforschung—Ein Tagungsbericht*, edited by Klaus Hortschansky, 35–55. Hamburg: Karl Dieter Wagner, 1991.

Giacchè, Piergiorgio. "Antropologia culturale e cultura teatrale: Note per un aggiornamento dell'approccio socio-antropologico al teatro." *Teatro e storia* 3 (1988): 23–50.

Giacomo, Salvatore di. *I quattro antichi conservatorii musicali di Napoli, MDXLIII–MDCCC*. Palermo: R. Sandron, 1924–28.

Gialdroni, Giuliana. "La musica a Napoli alla fine del XVIII secolo nelle lettere di Norbert Hadrava." *Fonti musicali italiane* 1 (1996): 75–143.

Gialdroni, Teresa Maria. "Le 'fatiche dei prologhi,' ovvero la cantata/prologo a Napoli dal 1761 al 1781." *Revista de musicologia* 16 (1993): 2888–2913.

Giannone, Pietro. *Dell' istoria civile del regno di Napoli*. 4 vols. Naples: Niccolò Naso, 1723.

Giarrizzo, Giuseppe. "L'ideologia di Metastasio tra cartesianismo al illuminismo." In *Convegno indetto in occasione del II centenario della morte di Metastasio d'intese con Arcadia*, 43–77. Rome: Accademia Nazionale dei Lincei, 1985.

Giesey, Ralph E. "The King Imagined." In *The Political Culture of the Old Regime*, vol. 1 of *The French Revolution and the Creation of Modern Political Culture*, edited by Keith Michael Baker, 41–59. Oxford: Pergamon Press, 1984.

Ginzburg, Carlo, et al. "Saccheggi rituali: Premesse a una ricerca in corso." *Quaderni storici*, n.s. 65, year 22, fasc. 2 (1987): 615–36.

Gioachino Trioli da Chiari, fra. *L'educazione delle fanciulle: Opera istruttiva d'un filosofo italiano*. Venice: Carlo Palese, 1765.

Girard, René. *Violence and the Sacred*. Translated by Patrick Gregory. Baltimore: Johns Hopkins University Press, 1977.

Girardi, Michele, and Franco Rossi. *Il Teatro La Fenice: Cronologia degli spettacoli, 1792–1936*. Venice: Albrizzi, 1989.

Gleijeses, Vittorio. *Le maschere e il teatro nel tempo*. Naples: Società Editrice Napoletana, 1981.

Glixon, Beth L., and Jonathan E. Glixon. *Inventing the Business of Opera: The Impresario and His World in Seventeenth-Century Venice*. New York: Oxford University Press, 2006.

Goethe, Johann Wolfgang von. *Italian Journey, 1786–1788*. Translated by W. H. Auden and Elizabeth Mayer. San Francisco: North Point Press, 1982.

———. *Italienische Reise*. Part 1. Edited by Christoph Michel and Hans-Georg Dewitz. In *Johann Wolfgang Goethe: Sämtliche Werke; Briefe, Tagebücher und Gesprache*, vol. 4. Frankfurt am Main: Deutscher Klassiker, 1993.

Goffman, Erving. *Frame Analysis: An Essay on the Organization of Experience*. Boston: Northeastern University Press, 1974.

Goldin, Daniela. *La vera Fenice: Librettisti e libretti tra sette e ottocento*. Turin: Einaudi, 1985.

Goldoni, Carlo. *Delle commedie di Carlo Goldoni, avvocato Veneto*. 17 vols. Edited by Giambattista Pasquali. Venice: Pasquali, 1761–[1778].

———. *Mémoires de M. Goldoni, pour servir à l'histoire de sa vie, et à celle de son théâtre*. 3 vols. Paris: Duchesne, 1787. Reprinted in 2 vols., Paris: Ponthieu, 1822.

———. *Memoirs of Carlo Goldoni Written by Himself*. Translated by John Black. Edited by William A. Drake. New York: Knopf, 1926.

———. *Memorie*. Translated by Paolo Bosisio. Milan: Mondadori, 1993.

———. *Tutte le opere di Carlo Goldoni*. Edited by Giuseppe Ortolani. 14 vols. Milan: Mondadori, 1935–56.

Goloubeva, Maria. *The Glorification of Emperor Leopold I in Image, Spectacle, and Text*. Mainz: Von Zabern, 2000.

Goody, Jack. *Technology, Tradition, and the State in Africa*. London: Oxford University Press, 1971.

Gorce, Jérôme de la. *Berain, dessinateur du Roi Soleil*. Paris: Herscher, 1986.

Goudar, Ange. *Le brigandage de la musique italienne*. Geneva: Minkoff, 1972.

Goudar, Sara. *Lettre de Madame Sara Goudar a Monsieur L****. N.p., 1775.

———. *Naples ce qu'il faut faire pour rendre ce Royaume florissant*. Amsterdam, 1771.

———. *Oeuvres mêlée . . . .* With the *Lettre sur les divertissements du Carneval de Naples & de Florence*. 2 vols. in 1. Amsterdam, 1777.

———. *De Venise: Rémarques sur la musique & la danse, ou Lettres de M.r G. . . . a Milord Pembroke*. Venice: Charles Palese, 1773.

———. *Relation historique des divertissements du carnaval de Naples, ou Lettre de Madame Goudar sur ce sujet à monsieur le général Alexis Orlow*. Lucca, 1774.

———. *Supplement au supplement de la musicque et de la danse ou lettres de M.r G. . . . a Milord Pembroke*. [Venice: Charles Palese], 1774.

Grandazzi, Alexandre. *The Foundation of Rome: Myth and History*. Translated by Jane Marie Todd. 1991. Reprint, Ithaca: Cornell University Press, 1997.

Greco, Franco Carmelo, and Gaetana Cantone. *Il teatro del re: Il San Carlo da Napoli all'Europa*. Naples: Edizioni Scientifiche Italiane, 1987.

Grimaldi, Piercarlo. *Tempi grassi, tempi magri: Percorsi etnografici*. Turin: Omega, 1996.

Grimm, Baron Friedrich Melchior von. *Le petit prophète de Boehmischbroda*. Paris, 1753.

Grimm, Frederick Melchior von et al. *Correspondance littéraire, philosophique, et critique par Grimm, Diderot, Raynal, Meister, etc.: Revue sur les textes originaux comprenant outre ce qui a été publié à diverses époques, les fragments supprimés en 1813 par la censure, les parties inédites conservées à la bibliothèque ducale de Gotha et à l'arsenal à Paris*. Paris: Garnier, 1879.

Gronda, Giovanna, et al. *La carriera di un librettista: Pietro Pariati da Reggio di Lombardia*. Bologna: Mulino, 1990.

Gronda, Giovanna, and Paolo Fabbri, eds. *Libretti d'opera italiani dal seicento al novecento*. Milan: Mondadori, 1997.

Grosley, Jean-Pierre. *New Observations on Italy and Its Inhabitants, Written in French by Two Swedish Gentlemen*. 2 vols. Translated by Thomas Nugent. London: L. Davis & C. Reymers, 1769.

———. *Nouveaux mémoires, ou Observations sur l'Italie et sur les Italiens*. 1st ed. 3 vols. London, Jean Nourse, 1764. Naples: Jean Gravier, 1765.

Gross, Hanns. *Rome in the Age of Enlightenment: The Post-Tridentine Syndrome and the Ancien Regime*. Cambridge: Cambridge University Press, 1990.

Grubb, James S. "Elite Citizens." In *Venice Reconsidered: The History and Civilization of an Italian City-State, 1297–1797*, edited by John Martin and Dennis Romano, 339–64. Baltimore: Johns Hopkins University Press, 2000.

Grundman, John P. *The Popolo at Perugia, 1139–1309*. Perugia: Deputazione di Storia Patria per l'Umbria, 1992.

Guardabassi, Francesco. *Appunti storici sull'Accademia Civica del Teatro Morlacchi di Perugia*. Perugia: G. Benucci, 1927.

Guarino, Raimondo. "Il teatro dell'indifferenza: Questioni storiche e storiografiche sullo spettacolo inaugurale del Teatro Argentina." In *Il teatro a Roma nel settecento*, edited by Giorgio Petrocchi, 1:215–58. Rome: Istituto della Enciclopedia Italiana, 1989.

Guazza, Guido. "Italy's Role in the European Problems of the First Half of the Eighteenth

Century." In *Studies in Diplomatic History: Essays in Memory of David Bayne Horn*, edited by Ragnhild M. Hatton and Matthew S. Anderson, 138–54. Harlow: Longmans, 1970.

Guccini, Gerardo. "Directing Opera." In *Opera on Stage*, edited by Lorenzo Bianconi and Giorgio Pestelli, 142–44. Chicago: University of Chicago Press, 2002.

———, ed. *Il teatro italiano nel settecento*. Bologna: Mulino, 1988.

Guerci, Luciano. *La discussione sulla donna nell'Italia del settecento: Aspetti e problemi*. Turin: Tirrenia, 1987.

———. *La sposa obediente: Donna e matrimonio nella discussione dell'Italia del settecento*. Turin: Tirrenia, 1988.

Gullino, Giuseppe. "La congiura del 12 ottobre 1797 e la fine della Municipalità Veneziana." *Critica storica* 16 (1979): 545–622.

Gunning, Tom. "The Cinema of Attractions: Early Film, Its Spectator, and the Avant-Garde." In *Early Cinema: Space, Frame, Narrative*, edited by Thomas Elsaesser, 56–62. London: BFI, 1990.

Habermas, Jürgen. *The Structural Transformation of the Public Sphere: An Inquiry into a Category of Bourgeois Society*. 2nd ed. Translated by Thomas Burger with Frederick Lawrence. 1965. Reprint, Cambridge: MIT Press, 1991.

Haböck, Franz. *Die Gesangskunst der Kastraten, Erster Notenband: A. Die Kunst des Cavaliere Carlo Broschi Farinelli, B. Farinellis berühmte Arien*. Vienna: Universal Edition, 1923.

Hammond, Frederick. *Music and Spectacle in Baroque Rome: Barberini Patronage under Urban VIII*. New Haven: Yale University Press, 1994.

Handelman, Don. *Models and Mirrors: Towards an Anthropology of Public Events*. Cambridge: Cambridge University Press, 1990.

Hanlon, Gregory. *Early Modern Italy, 1550–1800: Three Seasons in European History*. New York: St. Martin's Press, 2000.

———. *The Twilight of a Military Tradition: Italian Aristocrats and European Conflicts, 1560–1800*. London: UCL Press, 1998.

Hansell, Kathleen Kuzmick. "Opera and Ballet at the Regio Ducal Teatro, 1771–1776: A Musical and Social History." 2 vols. Ph.D. diss, University of California at Berkeley, 1980.

———. "Theatrical Ballet and Italian Opera." In *Opera on Stage*, edited by Lorenzo Bianconi and Giorgio Pestelli, 177–308. Chicago: University of Chicago Press, 2002.

Hansell, Sven. "Stage Deportment and Scenographic Design in the Italian Opera Seria of the Settecento." In *Report of the 11th Congress of the International Musicological Society, Copenhagen 1972*, 1:415–24. Copenhagen: Wilhelm Hansen, 1974.

Hansell, Sven and Kay Lipton. "De Mezzo, Pietro." From *Grove Music Online*, ed. Laura Macy. http://www.grovemusic.com/

Hauk, Franz and Iris Winkler, eds. *Werk und Leben: Johann Simon Mayrs im Spiegel der Zeit*. Mayr-Studien 1. Munich: Musikverlag Katzlichler, 1998.

———. *Johann Simon Mayr und Venedig*. Mayr-Studien 2. Munich: Musikverlag Katzlichler, 1999.

Head, Matthew. "'Like Beauty Spots on the Face of a Man': Gender in 18th-Century North-German Discourse on Genre." *Journal of Musicology* 13 (1995): 143–67.

Heartz, Daniel. "Caffarelli's Caprices." In *Music Observed: Studies in Memory of William C. Holmes*, edited by Colleen Reardon and Susan Parisi, chap. 11. Warren, MI: Harmonie Park Press, 2004.

———. *From Garrick to Gluck: Essays on Opera in the Age of Enlightenment*, edited by John A. Rice. Hillsdale, NY: Pendragon, 2004.

———. "From Garrick to Gluck: The Reform of Theatre and Opera in the Mid-Eighteenth Century." *Proceedings of the Royal Musical Association* 94 (1967–68): 111–27.

———. "Hasse at the Crossroads: 'Artaserse' (Venice, 1730), Dresden, and Vienna." *Opera Quarterly* 16 (2000): 24–33.

———. "Hasse, Galuppi, and Metastasio." In *Venezia e il melodramma nel seicento,* edited by Maria Teresa Muraro, 309–39. Florence: Olschki, 1978.

———. *Haydn, Mozart, and the Viennese School, 1740–1780.* New York: Norton, 1995.

———. "Metastasio, 'Maestro dei Maestri di Cappella Drammatici.'" In *Metastasio e il mondo musicale,* edited by Maria Teresa Muraro, 315–38. Florence: Olschki, 1986. Corrected and reprinted in *From Garrick to Gluck: Essays on Opera in the Age of Enlightenment,* edited by John A. Rice (Hillsdale, NY: Pendragon, 2004), 69–83.

———. *Music in European Capitals: The Galant Style, 1720–1780.* New York: Norton, 2003.

———. "Operatic Reform at Parma: *Ippolito ed Aricia.*" In *Atti del Convegno sul Settecento Parmense nel Secondo Centenario della Morte di C. I. Frugoni.* Parma: Deputazione di Storia Patria per le Province Parmensi, 1969. Reprinted as "Traetta in Parma: *Ippolito ed Aricia*" in *From Garrick to Gluck: Essays on Opera in the Age of Enlightenment,* edited by John A. Rice (Hillsdale, NY: Pendragon, 2004), 271–92.

———. "The Poet as Stage Director: Metastasio, Goldoni, and Da Ponte." In *Mozart's Operas,* edited by Thomas Bauman, 89–105. Berkeley and Los Angeles: University of California Press, 1990.

———. "Raaff's Last Aria: A Mozartian Idyll in the Spirit of Hasse." *Musical Quarterly* 60 (1974): 517–43.

———. "Traetta in Vienna: *Armida* and *Iphigenia in Tauride.*" In *From Garrick to Gluck: Essays on Opera in the Age of Enlightenment,* edited by John A. Rice, 293–312. Hillsdale, NY: Pendragon, 2004.

———. *Mozart's Operas.* Edited with contributing essays by Thomas A. Bauman. Berkeley and Los Angeles: University of California Press, 1990.

Heers, Jacques. *Les fêtes des fous et carnavals.* Paris: Fayard, 1983.

Hell, Helmut. *Die neapolitanische Opernsinfonie in der ersten Hälfte des 18. Jahrhunderts: N. Porpora, L. Vinci, G. B. Pergolesi, L. Leo, N. Jommelli.* Tutzing: Schneider, 1971.

Heller, Wendy. "Reforming Achilles: Gender, Opera Seria, and the Rhetoric of the Enlightened Hero." *Early Music* 26 (1998): 562–81.

Henze-Döhring, Sabine. *Opera Seria, Opera Buffa, und Mozarts Don Giovanni: Zur Gattungskonvergenz in der italienischen Oper des 18. Jahrhunderts.* Analecta musicologica, vol. 24. Cologne: Laaber, 1986.

Herdt, Gilbert, ed. *Third Sex, Third Gender: Beyond Sexual Dimorphism in Culture and History.* New York: Zone Books, 1994.

Heriot, Angus. *The Castrati in Opera.* London: Caldar & Boyars, 1956.

Hertz, R. "Contribution à l'étude sur la représentation collective de la mort." *Années sociologiques,* 1907.

Hesse, Carla. "Enlightenment Epistemology and the Laws of Authorship in Revolutionary France, 1777–1793." *Representations* 30 (1990): 109–37.

Heywood, William. *A History of Perugia.* Edited by Robert Langton Douglas. New York: Putnam, 1910.

Hiller, Johann Adam. *Anweisung zum musikalisch-zierlichen Gesange.* 1780. Leipzig: Peters, 1976.

———. *Treatise on Vocal Performance and Ornamentation.* Translated by Suzanne J. Beicken. Cambridge: Cambridge University Press, 2001.

———, ed. *Wöchentliche Nachrichten und Anmerkungen die Musik betreffend.* Leipzig: Zeitungs-Expedition, 1766–70. Hildesheim: Georg Olms, 1970.

Hobbes, Thomas. *Leviathan.* Edited by Edwin Curly. 1651. Indianapolis: Hackett, 1994.

Hobsbawm, Eric, and Terence Ringer, eds. *The Invention of Tradition.* Cambridge: Cambridge University Press, 1983.

Hobson, Marian. *The Object of Art: The Theory of Illusion in Eighteenth-Century France.* Cambridge: Cambridge University Press, 1982.

Holmes, William C. *Opera Observed: Views of a Florentine Impresario in the Early Eighteenth Century.* Chicago: University of Chicago Press, 1993.

Horkheimer, Max, and Theodor W. Adorno. *Dialectic of Enlightenment: Philosophical Fragments.* Edited by Gunzelin Schmid Noerr, translated by Edmund Jephcott. Stanford: Stanford University Press, 2002.

Hortschansky, Klaus, ed. *Opernheld und Opernheldin im 18. Jahrhundert: Aspekte der Librettoforschung.* Hamburg: Karl Dieter Wagner, 1991.

Howard, Patricia. *Gluck: An Eighteenth-Century Portrait in Letters and Documents.* Oxford: Clarendon Press, 1995.

Hubert, Henri, and Marcel Mauss. *Sacrifice: Its Nature and Functions.* Translated by W. D. Halls. Chicago: University of Chicago Press, 1964.

Hume, David. *A Treatise of Human Nature.* 2nd ed. Reprinted from the original edition of 1739. Edited by L. A. Selby-Bigge, revised by P. H. Nidditch. Oxford: Clarendon Press, 1978.

Hunt, Lynn A. *The Family Romance of the French Revolution.* Berkeley and Los Angeles: University of California Press, 1992.

——— *Politics, Culture, and Class in the French Revolution.* Berkeley and Los Angeles: University of California Press, 1984.

Hunter, Mary. *The Culture of Opera Buffa in Mozart's Vienna: A Poetics of Entertainment.* Princeton: Princeton University Press, 1999.

———. "'To Play as If from the Soul of the Composer': The Idea of the Performer in Early Romantic Aesthetics." *JAMS* 58 (2005): 357–98.

Imbruglia, Girolamo, ed. *Naples in the Eighteenth Century: The Birth and Death of a Nation State.* Cambridge: Cambridge University Press, 2000.

Ingarden, Roman. *The Work of Music and the Problem of Its Identity.* Translated by Adam Czerniawski. Edited by Jean G. Harrell. Berkeley and Los Angeles: University of California Press, 1986.

Inno pattriotico da eseguirsi la sera de' 14 settembre nel Teatro La Fenice di Venezia in onore della Guardia Civica dal cittadino Matteo Babini. Venice, 1797.

Iovino, Roberto. *Domenico Cimarosa, operista napoletano.* Milan: Camunia, 1992.

Irace, E. "Il nobilato a Perugia tra cinque e seicento." *Materiale di storia sociali: Quaderni [Università degli Studi di Perugia, Dipartimento di Scienze Sociali]* 1 (1992): 35–40.

Iraci, Alberto. "Cantanti e danzatrici celebri sulle scene del Teatro Civico del Verzaro ora Morlacchi." *Perusia* 9 (1950): 16–19.

———. "Perugia—Accademia Civica del Teatro Morlacchi." In *Accademia e Istituti di Cultura, cenni storici.* Rome: Polombi, 1938.

———. "Il Teatro Morlacchi di Perugia: L'origine dell'Accademia Civica e del Teatro." *Perusia* 13 (1954): 5–13.

Isherwood, Robert M. *Music in the Service of the King: France in the Seventeenth Century.* Ithaca: Cornell University Press, 1973.

Ivanov, V. V. "The Semiotic Theory of Carnival as the Inversion of Bipolar Opposites." Translated by R. Reeder and J. Rostinsky. In *Carnival!* edited by Thomas A. Sebeok with Marcia E. Erickson, 11–35. Berlin: Mouton, 1984.

James, E. O. *Seasonal Feasts and Festivals.* New York: Barnes & Noble, 1961.

Jander, Owen, Lionel Sawkins, J. B. Steane, and Elizabeth Forbes. "Bass." From *Grove Music Online,* ed. Laura Macy. http://www.grovemusic.com/ (accessed November 17, 2005).

Jankélévitch, Vladimir. *Music and the Ineffable*. Translated by Carolyn Abbate. Princeton: Princeton University Press, 2003.

Jarrard, Alice. *Architecture as Performance in Seventeenth-Century Europe: Court Ritual in Modena, Rome, and Paris*. Cambridge: Cambridge University Press, 2003.

Jay, Martin. "Scopic Regimes of Modernity." In *Vision and Visuality*, 3–23.Edited by Hal Foster. Seattle: Bay Press, 1988.

Johnson, James H. *Listening in Paris: A Cultural History*. Berkeley and Los Angeles: University of California Press, 1995.

Joly, Jacques. *Dagli elisi all'inferno: Il melodramma tra Italia e Francia dal 1730 al 1830*. Florence: La Nuova Italia, 1990.

Jommelli, Niccolò. *Armida abbandonata*. Edited by Eric Weimer. Italian Opera, 1640–1770, ser. 2. New York: Garland, 1983.

Kallberg, Jeffrey. *Chopin at the Boundaries: Sex, History, and Musical Genre*. Cambridge: Harvard University Press, 1996.

Kantorowicz, Ernst H. *The King's Two Bodies: A Study in Medieval Political Thought*. Princeton: Princeton University Press, 1957.

Kapferer, Bruce. "Performance and the Structuring of Meaning." In *The Anthropology of Experience*, 188–203. Urbana: University of Illinois Press, 1986.

Kecskeméti, Istvàn. "Opernelemente in den Klavierkonzerten Mozarts." *Mozart-Jahrbuch*, 1968/1970, 111–18.

Kelly, John D., and Martha Kaplan. "History, Structure, and Ritual." *Annual Review of Anthropology* 19 (1990): 1–50.

Kelly, Michael. *Reminiscences*. Edited by Roger Friske. London, 1975.

Kerman, Joseph. "Mozart's Concertos and Their Audience." In *Write All These Down*, 322–34. Berkeley and Los Angeles: University of California Press, 1994.

——— *Opera as Drama*. 2nd ed. New York: Knopf, 1956. 2nd ed., Berkeley and Los Angeles: University of California Press, 1988.

Kintzler, Cathérine. *Jean-Philippe Rameau: Splendeur et naufrage de l'estétique du plaisir à l'âge classique*. Paris: Sycomore, 1983.

———. *Poétique de l'opéra français de Corneille à Rousseau*. Paris: Minerve, 1991.

Klingsporn, Regine. *Jean-Philippe Rameaus Opern im äesthetischen Diskurs ihrer Zeit: Opernkomposition, Musikanschauung und Opernpublikum in Paris, 1733–1753*. Stuttgart: M & P, 1996.

Koch, Heinrich Christoph. *Introductory Essay on Composition: The Mechanical Rules of Melody, Sections 3 and 4*. Translated by Nancy Kovaleff Baker. New Haven: Yale University Press, 1983.

———. *Musikalisches Lexikon*. Frankfurt, 1802. Hildesheim: George Olms, 1964.

———. *Versuch einer Einleitung zur Composition*. 3 vols. Vol. 1, Rudolstadt, 1782. Vols. 2–3, Leipzig: A. F. Böhme, 1787 and 1793.

———. *Versuch einer Einleitung zur Composition: Mit ein vollständigen Register zu allen 3 Bänden*. 3 vols. Reprint edition. Hildesheim: Georg Olms, 1969.

Koenigsberger, Helmut G. "The Italian Parliaments from Their Origins to the End of the Eighteenth Century." *Journal of Italian History* 1, no. 1 (1978): 18–49.

Lalande, Joseph Jérôme Le Français de. *Voyage d'un François en Italie, fait dans les années 1765 et 1766*. 8 vols. Paris and Venice: Desaint, 1769.

Lamberti, Vincenzo. *La regolata costruzion de' teatri di Vincenzo Lamberti ingegnere napoletano dedicata a S. E. D. Andrea Memmo Cavalier della Stola d'Oro, e Procurator di S. Marco nella Repubblica di Venezia*. Naples: Vincenzo Orsini, 1787.

Landes, Joan P. *Visualizing the Nation: Gender, Representation, and Revolution in Eighteenth-Century France*. Ithaca: Cornell University Press, 2001.

———. *Women and the Public Sphere in the Age of the French Revolution.* Ithaca: Cornell University Press, 1988.

Langhans, Edward A., and Robert Benson. "Lighting." From *Grove Music Online,* ed. Laura Macy. http://www.grovemusic.com/ (accessed May 2, 2005).

Laqueur, Thomas Walter. *Making Sex: Body and Gender from the Greeks to Freud.* Cambridge: Harvard University Press, 1990.

La Rocca, Chiara. "Interessi famigliari e libero consenso nella Livorno del settecento." In *Matrimoni in dubbio: Unioni controverse e nozze clandestine in Italia dal XIV al XVIII secolo,* edited by Silvana Seidel Menchi and Diego Quaglioni, 529–50. Bologna: Mulino, 2001.

Larue, Steven C. *Handel and His Singers: The Creation of the Royal Academy Operas, 1720–1728.* Oxford: Clarendon, 1995.

Launay, Denise, ed. *La querelle des bouffons: Text des pamphlets avec introduction, commentaries et index.* 3 vols. Geneva: Minkoff, 1973.

Lautenschläger, Philine. "Phädra-Vertonungen im 18. Jahrhundert von Rameau, Traetta, Paisiello." Diss., Heidelberg University, in progress.

Lavie, Smadar, Kirin Narayan, and Renato Rosaldo. *Creativity/Anthropology.* Ithaca: Cornell University Press, 1993.

Lavin, Irving. "On the Unity of the Arts and the Early Baroque Opera House." In *"All the World's a Stage": Art and Pageantry in the Renaissance and Baroque,* edited by Barbara Wisch and Susan Scott Munshower, part 2, *Theatrical Spectacle and Spectacular Theatre,* 514–79. Papers in Art History from the Pennsylvania State University, vol. 6. University Park: Pennsylvania State University, 1990.

Law, Sin-yan Hedy. "Gestural Rhetoric: In Search of Pantomime in the French Enlightenment, ca. 1750–1785." Ph.D. diss. University of Chicago, in progress.

Leach, Edmund. *Rethinking Anthropology.* London: Athlone, 1961.

Lee, Vernon. *Studies of the Eighteenth Century in Italy.* 2nd ed. London: T. Fisher Unwin, 1907. Reprint, New York: Da Capo Press, 1978.

Leeson, Daniel N., and Robert D. Levin. "On the Authenticity of K. Anh. C 14.01 (297b), a Symphonia Concertante for Four Winds and Orchestra." *Mozart-Jahrbuch,* 1976/1977, 70–96.

Le Goff, Jacques. *Études, au Moyen-Âge: Temps de l'église et temps du marchand.* Paris: Colin, 1960.

Le Guin, Elisabeth. *Boccherini's Body: An Essay in Carnal Musicology.* Berkeley and Los Angeles: University of California Press, 2005.

Lenzi, Deanna, et al., eds. *I Bibbiena: Una famiglia europea.* Bologna: Marsilio, 2000.

Lettre sur le méchanisme de l'opéra italien: Ni Guelfe, ni Gibelin, ni Wigh, ni Thoris. Naples, sold at Paris: Duchesne, 1756.

Levi Pisetzky, Rosita. *Storia del costume in Italia.* 5 vols. Fondazione Giovanni Treccani degli Alfieri. Milan: Istituto Editoriale Italiano, 1967.

Lévi-Strauss, Claude. *The Raw and the Cooked.* Translated by John and Doreen Weightmann. 1964. Reprint, New York: Harper & Row, 1969.

Levin, Robert D. "Das Konzert für Klavier und Violine D-Dur, KV Anh. 56/315^{f} und das Klarinettequintet B-Dur, KV Anh. 91/516^{c}: Ein Ergänzungsversuch." *Mozart Jahrbuch,* 1968/1970, 304–26.

———. *Who Wrote the Mozart Four-Wind Concertante?* Stuyvesant, NY: Pendragon, 1988.

Lewis, Peter. *Fielding's Burlesque Drama: Its Place in the Tradition.* Edinburgh: Edinburgh University Press, 1987.

Leza, J. M. "Metastasio on the Spanish Stage: Operatic Adaptations in the Public Theatres of Madrid in the 1730s." *Early Music* 26 (1998): 623–31.

Libby, Dennis. "Italy: Two Opera Centres." In *The Classical Era from the 1740s to the End of the 18th Century,* edited by Neal Zaslaw, 15–60. Englewood Cliffs, NJ: Prentice-Hall, 1989.

Lincoln, Bruce. *Theorizing Myth: Narrative, Ideology, and Scholarship*. Chicago: University of Chicago Press, 1999.

Lippmann, Friedrich, ed. *Colloquium: "Die stilistische Entwicklung der italienischen Musik zwischen 1770 und 1830 und ihre Beziehungen zum Norden," Rom 1978*. Analecta musicologica, vol. 21. Cologne: Arno Volk–Laaber, 1982.

———. "Il 'Grande Finale' nell'opera buffa e nell'opera seria: Paisiello e Rossini." *Rivista italiana di musicologia* 27 (1992): 225–55.

———. "Tendenzen der italienischen Opera seria am Ende des 18. Jahrhunderts–und Mozart." *Studi musicali* 21 (1992): 307–58.

Litchfield, R. Burr. *Emergence of a Bureaucracy: The Florentine Patricians, 1530–1790*. Princeton: Princeton University Press, 1986.

———. "Franco Venturi's 'Crisis' of the Old Regime." *Journal of Modern Italian Studies* 10 (2005): 234–44.

Lombardi, Daniela. *Matrimoni di antico regime*. Annali dell'Istituto Storico Italo-Germanico in Trento, monografie 35. Bologna: Mulino, 2001.

Lomonaco, Fabrizio. "Tra 'Ragione poetica' e 'Vita civile': Metastasio, discepolo di Gravina e Caloprese." In *Legge, poesia e mito: Giannone, Metastasio e Vico fra "tradizione" e "trasgressione" nella Napoli degli anni venti del settecento*, edited by Mario Valente, 165–202. Rome: Aracne, 2001.

Loomis, George W. "Tommaso Traetta's Operas for Parma." Ph.D. diss., Yale University, 1999.

Lough, John. *Paris Theatre Audiences in the Seventeenth and Eighteenth Centuries*. London: Oxford University Press, 1957.

Lühning, Helga. "Die Rondo-Arie im späten 18. Jahrhundert: Dramatischer Gehalt und musikalischer Bau." *Hamburger Jahrbuch für Musikwissenschaft* 5 (1981): 219–46.

The Lyric Muse Revived in Europe, or A Critical Display of the Opera in All Its Revolutions. London: L. Davis & C. Reymers, 1768.

Mably, Abbé de. *Lettres à Madame la Marquise de P. sur l'Opéra*. 1741. New York: AMS Press, 1978.

MacAloon, John J., ed. *Rite, Drama, Festival, Spectacle: Rehearsals toward a Theory of Cultural Performance*. Philadelphia: University of Pennsylvania Press, 1984.

Maeder, Costantino. *Metastasio,* L'olimpiade *e l'opera del settecento*. Bologna: Mulino, 1993.

Magaldi, Cristina. *Music in Imperial Rio: European Culture in a Tropical Milieu*. Lanham, MD: Scarecrow Press, 2004.

Magrini, Tullia, ed.. *Il maggio drammatico: Una tradizione di teatro in musica*. Bologna: Analisi, 1992.

Maione, Paologiovanni, and Marta Columbro, eds. *Domenico Cimarosa: Un "napoletano" in Europa*. 2 vols. Lucca: Libreria Musicale Italiana, 2004.

Malamani, Vittorio. *I francesi a Venezia e la satira*. Venice: Merlo, 1887.

———. "Giustina Renier Michiel: I suoi amici, il suo tempo." *Archivio veneto*, n.s. 38 (1889): 5–95 (part 1), 279–367 (part 2).

Malinowski, Bronislaw. *Coral Gardens and Their Magic*. Vol. 1, *A Study of the Tilling of the Soil and of Agricultural Rites in the Trobriand Islands*. Vol. 2, *The Language of Magic and Gardening*. 1935. Reprint, New York: Dover, 1978.

———. *Magic, Science, and Religion and Other Essays*. Prospect Heights, IL: Waveland Press, 1992.

Malkiewicz, Michael. "Zur Verkörperung des Kastraten im Musiknotat." In *Verkörperung*, edited by Erika Fischer-Lichte, Christian Horn, and Matthias Warstat, 309–23. Tübingen: Francke, 2001.

Mancini, Franco. "Antonio Joli: La transizione al neoclassico." In *Il Teatro di San Carlo, 1737–*

1787, edited by Franco Mancini, Bruno Cagli, and Agostino Ziino, 2:37–48. Naples: Electa Napoli, 1987.

———. *Feste ed apparati civili e religiosi in Napoli dal viceregno alla capitale*. Naples: Edizioni Scientifiche Italiane, 1968.

———. "Le maschere e i carri di carnevale nel periodo barocco." In *'Nferta napoletana*, edited by Enrico Malato, 51–62. Naples: F. Fiorentino, 1963.

———. *Scenografia italiana dal rinascimento all'età romantica*. Milan: Fratelli Fabbri, 1966.

———. "La storia, le vicende amministrativi: Gli organismi di gestione." In *Il Teatro di San Carlo, 1737–1787*, edited by Franco Mancini, Bruno Cagli, and Agostino Ziino, 1:9–24. Naples: Electa Napoli, 1987.

Mancini, Franco, Bruno Cagli, and Agostino Ziino, eds. *Il Teatro di San Carlo, 1737–1787*. 3 vols. (vols. 1 and 3, ed. Mancini; vol. 2, ed. Cagli and Ziino). Naples: Electa Napoli, 1987.

Mancini, Franco, Maria Teresa Muraro, and Elena Polevedo. *I teatri del Veneto: Verona, Vicenza, Belluno e il loro territorio*. 2 vols. Venice: Corbo & Fiore, 1992.

Mancini, Franco, and Pino Simonelli. "Il rovinismo nella scenografia del settecento." In *Il teatro a Roma nel settecento*, edited by Giorgio Petrocchi, 1:153–60. Rome: Istituto della Enciclopedia Italiana, 1989.

Mancini, Giambattista. *Pensieri, e riflessioni sopra il canto figurato*. Vienna: Ghelen, 1774.

———. *Riflessioni pratiche sul canto figurato*. Rev. 3rd ed. Milan: Giuseppe Galeazzi, 1777.

———. *Practical Reflections on Figured Singing: The Editions of 1774 and 1777 Compared*. Translated by Edward Foreman. Masterworks on Singing, vol. 7. Champaign, IL: Pro Musica Press, 1967.

Mandrou, Robert. *L'Europe "absolutiste": Raison et raison d'Etat, 1649–1775*. Paris: Fayard, 1977.

Manfredini, Vincenzo. *Difesa della musica moderna e de' suoi celebri esecutori*. 1788. Bologna: Forni, 1972.

Mangini, Giorgio. "Le passioni, la virtù e la morale nella concezione tardo-settecentesco dell'opera metastasiana." *Rivista italiana di musicologia* 22 (1987): 114–44.

———. "Sulla fortuna delle azioni sacre di Metastasio al tempo del declino dei drammi seri del poeta." In *I vicini di Mozart: Il teatro musicale tra sette e ottocento*, edited by Maria Teresa Muraro, 19–33. Studi di Musica Veneta 15. Fondazione Giorgio Cini. Florence: Olschki, 1989.

Mangini, Nicola. *I teatri di Venezia*. Milan: Mursia, 1974.

Manning, Frank E., ed. *The Celebration of Society: Perspectives on Cultural Performance*. Bowling Green, OH: Bowling Green University Popular Press, 1983.

Manuel, Frank E. *The Eighteenth Century Confronts the Gods*. Cambridge: Harvard University Press, 1959. Reprint, New York: Atheneum, 1967.

Marcello, Benedetto. *Il teatro alla moda, o sia, Metodo sicuro e facile per ben comporre ed eseguire l'opere italiane in musica all'uso moderno*. Venice: Aldaviva Licante, 1720.

Marchesi, Gustavo. "Il Teatro Ducale." In *I teatri di Parma "dal Farnese al Regio,"* edited by Ivo Allodi, 61–91. Milan: Nuove Edizioni Milano, 1969.

Marenduzzo, Antonio. "I cicisbei nel settecento." *Rivista d'Italia* 8, no. 2 (1905): 271–82.

Marin, Louis. *Portrait of the King*. Translated by Martha Houle, foreword by Tom Conley. Minneapolis: University of Minnesota Press, 1988.

Marinelli, Olga Marcacci. "Lo stemma di Perugia." *Perusia* 9 (1950): 22–27.

Marino, John A. "A Bigger Settecento Italiano: Wider Vistas and Open Terrain." *Journal of Modern Italian Studies* 10 (2005): 131–41.

———, ed. *Early Modern Italy, 1550–1796: Short Oxford History of Italy*. Oxford: Oxford University Press, 2002.

Mariotti, Annibale. *Elogio funebre del sig. Francesco Zannetti celebre maestro di cappella nella chiesa cattedrale di Perugia, detto ne' solenni funerali a lui celebrati dall'Accademia degli Unisoni nell'Oratorio di S. Filippo Neri il dì 15 Marzo 1788.*

———. *Lettere pittoriche perugine o sia Ragguaglio di alcune memorie istoriche risguardanti le arti del disegno in Perugia al Signor Baldassare Orsini pittore e architetto perugino accademico d'onore dell'Accademia Clementina di Bologna ed Etrusco di Cortona.* Perugia: Badueliane, 1788.

———. *Saggio di memorie istoriche civili ed ecclesiastiche della città di Perugia e suo contado.* 3 parts. Perugia: Carlo Baduel, 1806.

———. *Versi e prose del dottor Annibale Mariotti fra gli Arcadi della Colonia Augusta Ornìnto Gneosseano.* Book 1, *Contenente le sue poesie.* Perugia: Costantini, 1809.

Markstrohm, Kurt Sven. "The Operas of Leonardo Vinci, Napoletano." Ph.D. diss., University of Toronto, 1993.

Marmontel, Jean-François. *Élemens de littérature.* In *Oeuvres complettes.* 10 vols. in 6. Paris: Née de la Rochelle, 1787.

———. "Opéra." From *Élemens de littérature,* in *Oeuvres complettes,* 5:47–114. Paris: Née de la Rochelle, 1787.

Marpurg, F. W. *Historisch-kritische Beyträge zur Aufnahme der Musik.* Berlin, 1754.

Marri, Federico, ed. *La figura e l'opera di Ranieri de' Calzabigi: Atti del convegno di studi, Livorno, 14–15 dicembre 1987.* Florence: Olschki, 1989.

Marri, Federico, and Francesco Paolo Russo, eds. *Ranieri Calzabigi tra Vienna e Napoli: Atti del Convegno di studi, Livorno, 23–24 settembre 1996.* Lucca: Libreria Musicale Italiana, 1998.

Martina, Alessandra. *Orfeo-Orphée di Gluck: Storia della trasmissione e della recezione.* Florence: Passigli, 1995.

Martinelli, Vincenzio. *Lettere familiari e critiche.* London: Giovanni Nourse, 1758.

Massaro, Maria Nevilla. "Il ballo pantomimo al Teatro Nuovo di Padova, 1751–1830." *Acta musicologica* 57 (1985): 215–75.

Mattei, Lorenzo. "Metastasio con il berretto frigio: Sui *Veri amici repubblicani* di Niccolò Zingarelli (Torino, 1799)." *Fonti musicali italiane* 8 (2003): 31–52.

Mattei, Saverio. *Memorie per servire alla vita del Metastasio: Ed elogio di N. Jommelli.* Bibliotheca Musica Bononiensis, ser. 3, no. 57, 1785. Bologna: Forni, 1987.

Mattheson, Johann. *Der vollkommene Capellmeister.* Breslau, 1739.

Mauss, Marcel. *A General Theory of Magic.* Translated by Robert Brain. New York: Norton, 1975.

———. *The Gift: The Form and Reason for Exchange in Archaic Societies.* Translated by W. D. Halls. 1950. Reprint, New York: Norton, 1990.

Maza, Sarah. "Luxury, Morality, and Social Change: Why There Was No Middle-Class Consciousness in Prerevolutionary France." *Journal of Modern History* 69 (1997): 199–229.

McClary, Susan. *Conventional Wisdom: The Musical Content of Form.* Berkeley and Los Angeles: University of California Press, 2000.

McClellan, George B. *Venice and Bonaparte.* Princeton: Princeton University Press, 1931.

McClellan, Michael E. "Battling over the Lyric Muse: Expressions of Revolution and Counterrevolution at the Théâtre Feydeau, 1789–1801." Ph.D. diss., University of North Carolina at Chapel Hill, 1994.

———. "Restraining the Revolution: Musical Aesthetics and Cultural Control in France, 1795–1799." *Music Research Forum* 10 (1995): 14–41.

McClymonds, Marita P. "Alfieri and the Revitalization of Opera Seria." In *Music in the Theater, Church, and Villa: Essays in Honor of Robert Lamar Weaver and Norma Wright Weaver,* edited by Susan Parisi, Ernest Harriss II, and Calvin M. Bower, 227–31. Warren, MI: Harmonie Park Press, 2000.

———. "Aria," §4, "18th Century." In *New Grove Dictionary of Music and Musicians,* 2nd ed., edited by Stanley Sadie, 1:890–94. London: Macmillan, 2001.

———. "Calzabigi and Paisiello's *Elfrida* and *Elvira:* Crumbling Conventions within a Rapidly Changing Genre." In *Ranieri Calzabigi tra Vienna e Napoli: Atti del Convegno di Studi, Livorno, 23–24 settembre 1996*, edited by Federico Marri and Francesco Paolo Russo, 239–58. Lucca: Libreria Musicale Italiana, 1998.

———. "*La clemenza di Tito* and the Action Ensemble Finale in Opera Seria before 1791." *Mozart-Jahrbuch,* 1991, 2:766–72.

———. "The Evolution of Jommelli's Operatic Style." *JAMS* 33 (1980): 326–55.

———. "The Great Quartet in *Idomeneo* and the Italian Opera Seria Tradition." In *Wolfgang Amadè Mozart: Essays on His Life and His Music,* edited by Stanley Sadie, 449–76. Oxford: Clarendon, 1996.

———. "Haydn and the Opera Seria Tradition: *Armida.*" In *Napoli e il teatro musicale in Europa tra sette e ottocento: Studi in onore di Friedrich Lippmann,* edited by Bianca Maria Antolini and Wolfgang Witzenmann, 191–206. Florence: Olschki, 1993.

———. "Mannheim, *Idomeneo,* and the Franco-Italian Synthesis in Opera Seria." In *Mozart und Mannheim: Kongressbericht Mannheim 1991,* edited by Ludwig Finscher, Bärbel Pelker, and Jochen Reutter, 187–96. Frankfurt am Main: P. Lang, 1994.

———. "'La morte di Semiramide, ossia La vendetta di Nino' and the Restoration of Death and Tragedy to the Italian Operatic Stage in the 1780s and 90s." In *Atti del XIV congresso della Società Internazionale di Musicologia, Bologna, 1987: Trasmissione e recezione delle forme di cultura musicale,* edited by Angelo Pompilio et al., part 3, 285–92. Turin: EDT, 1990.

———. "Opera seria? Opera buffa? Genre and Style as Sign." *Opera Buffa in Mozart's Vienna,* edited by Mary Hunter and James Webster, 197–231. New York: Cambridge University Press, 1997.

———. *Niccolò Jommelli: The Last Years, 1769–1774.* Ann Arbor: UMI Press, 1980.

———. "The Role of Innovation and Reform in the Florentine Opera Seria Repertory, 1760–1800." In *Music Observed: Studies in Memory of William C. Holmes,* edited by Colleen Reardon and Susan Parisi, 281–300. Warren, MI: Harmonie Park Press, 2004.

———. "Transforming Opera Seria: Verazi's Innovations and Their Impact on Opera in Italy." In *Opera and the Enlightenment,* edited by Thomas Bauman and Marita P. McClymonds, 119–32. Cambridge: Cambridge University Press, 1995.

———. "The Venetian Role in the Transformation of Italian Opera Seria in the 1790s." In *I Vicini di Mozart,* edited by Maria Teresa Muraro, 1:221–40. Florence: Olschki, 1989.

———. "Verazi's Controversial *Drammi in Azioni* as Realized in the Music of Salieri, Anfossi, Alessandri, and Mortellari for the Opening of La Scala, 1778–1779." In *Scritti in Memoria di Claudio Sartori,* edited by Mariangela Donà and François Lesure, 43–87. Lucca: Libreria Musicale Italiana, 1997.

McClymonds, Marita P., and Daniel Heartz. "Opera Seria." From *Grove Music Online,* ed. Laura Macy. http://www.grovemusic.com/ (accessed October 9, 2005).

McGeary, Thomas, and Xavier Cervantes. "From Farinelli to Monticelli: An Opera Satire of 1742 Re-Examined." *Burlington Magazine* 141, no. 1154 (May 1999): 287–89.

Meikle, Robert Burns. "Leonardo Vinci's *Artaserse:* An Edition, with Editorial and Critical Commentary." Ph.D. diss., Cornell University, 1970.

Meldolesi, Claudio. "Ai confini del teatro e della sociologia." *Teatro e storia* 1 (1986): 77–151.

———. "Il teatro dell'arte di piacere: Esperienze italiane nel settecento francese." *Teatro e storia* 3 (1988): 73–97.

Melicow, Meyer M. "Castrati Singers and the Lost 'Cords.'" *Bulletin of the New York Academy of Medicine* 59, no. 8 (1983): 744–64.

Meloni, Antonio, and Giacomo Venetici, eds. *Raccolta di opuscoli scientifici scielti da diversi autori francesi, ed inglesi, nuovamente tr. in italiana favella.* Ferrara: Sansone, 1760.

Menchi, Silvana Seidel, and Diego Quaglioni. *Matrimoni in dubbio: Unioni controverse e nozze clandestine in Italia dal XIV al XVIII secolo.* Bologna: Mulino, 2001.

Mendoza de Arce, Daniel. *Music in Ibero-America to 1850.* Lanham, MD: Scarecrow Press, 2001.

Meredith, Victoria. "The Old World in the New: Metastasio's Verse and Diversity in North America." *Metastasio at Home and Abroad. Studies in Music from the University of Western Ontario* 16 (1997): 155–70.

Merlato, Maria. *Mariti e cavalier serventi nelle commedie del Goldoni.* Florence: G. Carnesecchie, 1906.

Metastasio, Pietro. *Artaserse: Dramma per musica da rappresentarsi nel nobilissimo Teatro della Fenice l'autunno dell'anno 1795.* Venice: nella Stamperia Valvasense, 1795.

———. *La Didone abbandonata: Dramma per musica da rappresentarsi in Perugia nell'apertura del Nuovo Teatro Civico del Verzaro l'autunno dell'anno MDCCLXXXI; Dedicato all'illustris., e Reverendissimo monsignor Gio. Francesco Arrigoni Governatore Vigilantissimo di detta Città, e Preside dell'Umbria & c.* Perugia: Mario Riginaldi, 1781.

———. *Opere.* 12 vols. [Edited by Giuseppe Pezzana.] Paris: Herrissant, 1780–82.

———. *Opere drammatiche.* Rev. 10th ed. 7 vols. in 3. Venice: G. Bettinelli, 1755–57.

———. *Poesie del signor Abate Pietro Metastasio.* 9 vols. [Edited by Ranieri de' Calzabigi.] Paris: vedova Quillau, 1755.

———. *Tutte le opere de Pietro Metastasio.* Edited by Bruno Brunelli. 5 vols. Milan: Mondadori, 1943.

———. *The Works of Metastasio.* Translated by John Hoole. 2 vols. London: T. Davies, 1767.

Meyer, Reinhart, ed. *Bibliographia dramatica et dramaticorum: Kommentierte Bibliographie der im ehemaligen deutschen Reichsgebiet gedruckten und gespielten Dramen des 18. Jahrhunderts nebst deren Bearbeitungen und Übersetzungen und ihrer Rezeption bis in die Gegenwart.* 24 vols. to date. Tübingen: Max Niemeyer, 1986–2005.

———. *Bibliographia dramatica et dramaticorum: Literaturverzeichnis 2001.* Tübingen: Max Niemeyer, 2001.

———. "Die Rezeption der dramen Metastasios im 18. Jahrhundert." In *Legge, poesie e mito: Giannone, Metastasio e Vico fra "tradizione" e "trasgressione" nella Napoli degli anni venti del settecento,* edited by Mario Valente, 417–51. Rome: Aracne, 2001.

Michelet, Jules, with Louis Le Guillou. *Correspondance générale.* Edited by E. Quinet, with Simone Bernard Griffiths and Ceri Crossley. Paris: Honoré Champion, 1994–2001.

———. *Nos fils.* Edited by Françoise Puts. 1869. Paris: Resources and Slatkine, 1980.

Miggiani, Maria Giovanna. "Il Teatro di S. Moisè, 1793–1818: Con cronologia degli spettacoli." *Bolletino del Centro Rossiniano di Studi* 30 (1990): 5–213.

———, ed. *Il canto di Metastasio: Atti di convegno di studi, Venezia, 14–16 dicembre 1999.* Bologna: Forni, 2004.

Milizia, Francesco. *Trattato completo, formale e materiale del teatro.* Bibliotheca Musica Bononiensis, ser. 2, no. 64, 1794. Bologna: Forni, 1969. First published under the title *Il teatro* (Rome, 1771); republished as *Trattato completo, formale e materiale del teatro* (Venice: Giovanni Battista Pasquali, 1794).

Mincuzzi, Rosa, ed. *Lettere di Bernardo Tanucci a Carlo III di Borbone, 1759–1776.* Rome: Istituto per la Storia del Risorgimento Italiano, 1969.

Mocenigo, Mario Nani. *Il Teatro La Fenice: Note storiche e artistiche.* Venice: Giudecca Industrie Poligrafiche Venete, 1926.

Moindrot, Isabelle. *L'opéra seria, ou Le règne des castrats.* Paris: Fayard, 1993.

Momigliano, Arnaldo. *Roma arcaica.* Florence: Sansoni, 1989.

Monaldi, Gino. *I teatri di Roma negli ultimi tre secoli.* Naples: Riccardo Ricciardi, 1928.

Monson, Dale. "Elisi, Filippo." From *Grove Music Online,* ed. Laura Macy. http://www.grovemusic.com/

Montagu, Lady Mary Wortley. *The Letters and Works.* 2 vols. Edited by James Archibald Stuart-Wortley-Mackenzie Wharncliffe. London: Swan Sonnenschein, 1893.

Montanile, Milena. *I giacobini a teatro: Segni e strutture della propaganda rivoluzionaria in Italia.* Naples: Società Editrice Napoletana, 1984.

Montesquieu. *De l'esprit des lois.* Geneva, 1748. In *Oeuvres complètes,* 2 vols., edited by Roger Caillois, 2:225–995. Paris: Gallimard, 1949.

———. *The Spirit of the Laws.* Translated by Anne M. Cohler, Basia Carolyn Miller, and Harold Samuel Stone. Cambridge Texts in the History of Political Thought. Cambridge: Cambridge University Press, 1989.

———. *Voyages.* Edited by Marcel Arland. Paris: Stock, 1943.

Montroni, Giovanni. "The Court, Power Relations, and Forms of Social Life." In *Naples in the Eighteenth Century: The Birth and Death of a Nation State,* edited by Girolamo Imbruglia, 22–43. Cambridge: Cambridge University Press, 2000.

Moore, John. *A View of Society and Manners in Italy: With Anecdotes Relating to Some Eminent Characters.* 4th ed. 2 vols. London: A. Strahan & T. Cadfell, 1787.

Moore, Sally F., and Barbara G. Myerhoff, eds. *Secular Ritual.* Assen: Van Gorcum, 1977.

Morelli, Giovanni. "Castrati, primedonne e Metastasio nel felicissimo giorno del nome di Carlo." In *Il Teatro di San Carlo, 1737–1987,* edited by Franco Mancini, Bruno Cagli, and Agostino Ziino, 2:33–60. Naples: Electa Napoli, 1987.

———. "Maggio e melodramma: La presenza di Metastasio." In *Il maggio drammatico: Una tradizione di teatro in musica,* edited by Tullia Magrini, 167–86. Bologna: Analisi, 1992.

Morelli, Giovanni, and Elvidio Surian. "Come nacque e come morì il patriottismo romano nell'opera veneziana." *Opera & Libretto* 1 (1990): 101–35.

Mozart, Leopold. *A Treatise on the Fundamental Principles of Violin Playing.* Translated by Edith Knocker. Oxford: Oxford University Press, 1985.

———. *Versuch einer gründlichen Violinschule.* Augsburg: J. J. Lotter, 1756.

Mozart, Wolfgang Amadeus. *Ascanio in Alba* [Milan, 1771]. Mod. ed., *Neue Ausgabe sämtlicher Werke* II.5.5. Edited by Ferdinando Tagliavini. Kassel: Bärenreiter, 1956.

———. *Briefe und Aufzeichnungen: Gesamtausgabe.* Edited by Wilhelm A. Bauer and Otto Erich Deutsch. 7 vols. Kassel: Bärenreiter, 1962–75.

———. *Lucio Silla* [Milan, 1772]. Mod. ed., *Neue Ausgabe sämtlicher Werke* II.5.7. Edited by Kathleen Kuzmick Hansell. Kassel: Bärenreiter, 1986.

———. *Mitridate, re di Ponto.* Mod. ed., *Neue Ausgabe sämtlicher Werke* II.5.4. Edited by Ferdinando Tagliavini. Kassel: Bärenreiter, 1966.

———. *Neue Ausgabe sämtlicher Werke.* Internationale Stiftung Mozarteum Salzburg. Kassel: Bärenreiter,1955–91.

Muir, Edward. *Civic Ritual in Renaissance Venice.* Princeton: Princeton University Press, 1981.

———. *Ritual in Early Modern Europe.* Cambridge: Cambridge University Press, 1997.

Muir, Edward, and Guido Ruggiero, ed. *Sex and Gender in Historical Perspective.* Baltimore: Johns Hopkins University Press, 1990.

Mulvey, Laura. "Visual Pleasure and Narrative Cinema." *Screen* 16 (1975): 6–18.

Munn, Nancy D. "The Cultural Anthropology of Time: A Critical Essay." *Annual Review of Anthropology* 21 (1992): 93–123.

———. *The Fame of Gawa: A Symbolic Study of Value Transformation in a Massim (Papua New Guinea) Society.* Cambridge: Cambridge University Press, 1986.

Muraro, Maria Teresa, ed. *Metastasio e il mondo musicale.* Florence: Olschki, 1986.

———, ed. *Venezia e il melodramma nel settecento.* Florence: Olschki, 1978–81.

———, and David Bryant, eds. *I vicini di Mozart: Il teatro musicale tra sette e ottocento.* 2 vols. Studi di Musica Veneta 15. Fondazione Giorgio Cini. Florence: Olschki, 1989.

Muratori, Lodovico Antonio. *Della perfetta poesia italiana.* 1706. Mod. ed., 2 vols., edited by Ada Ruschioni. Milan: Marzorati, 1971.

———. *Della pubblica felicità, oggetto de' buoni principi.* Edited by Cesare Mozzarelli. 1749. Rome: Donzelli, 1996.

Naddeo, Barbara Ann. "Cultural Capitals and Cosmopolitanism in Eighteenth-Century Italy: The Historiography and Italy on the Grand Tour." *Journal of Modern Italian Studies* 10 (2005): 183–99.

———. "Science for the Cosmopolitan: The Culture of Urbanity and the Emergence of Anthropology in the Kingdom of Naples, 1629–1800." Ph.D., University of Chicago, 2001.

———. "Urban Arcadia: Representations of the 'Dialect' of Naples in Linguistic Theory and Comic Theater, 1696–1780." *Eighteenth-Century Studies* 35 (2001): 41–65.

Napoli-Signorelli, Pietro. *Storia critica de' teatri antichi e moderni.* 6 vols. Naples: Vincenzo Orsino, 1787–90.

Nagel, Ivan. *Autonomy and Mercy: Reflections on Mozart's Operas.* Translated by Marion Faber and Ivan Nagel. 1988. Reprint, Cambridge: Harvard University Press, 1991.

Natali, Giulio. *Idee, costumi, uomini del settecento.* Turin: Società Tipografico-Editrice Nazionale, 1916.

Nella celebrazione del Teatro Pavone: Perugia VI Febbraio MCMXXVII. Perugia: Guglielmo Donnini Tipografico della Rivoluzione Fascista, Anno V [1927].

Neri, Achille. *Costumanze e sollazzi: . . . I cicisbei a Genova.* Genoa: R. Istituto Sordo-Muti, 1883.

Neumann, Frederick. *Ornamentation and Improvisation in Mozart.* Princeton: Princeton University Press, 1986.

Neville, Don. "Metastasio and the Image of Majesty in the Austro-Italian Baroque." In *Italian Culture in Northern Europe in the Eighteenth Century,* edited by Shearer West, 140–58. Cambridge: Cambridge University Press, 1999.

———"A Metastasio Database." Eighteenth-Century Studies, University of Western Ontario. http://metastasio.uwo.ca/metastasio (accessed December 1, 2005).

———. "Metastasio, Pietro." In *New Grove Dictionary of Music and Musicians,* 2nd ed., edited by Stanley Sadie, 16:510–20. London: Macmillan, 2001.

———. "Metastasio: Beyond the Stage in Vienna." *Metastasio at Home and Abroad. Studies in Music from the University of Western Ontario* 16 (1997): 87–109.

———. "Moral Philosophy in the Metastasian Dramas." *Crosscurrents and the Mainstream of Italian Serious Opera, 1730–1790. Studies in Music from the University of Western Ontario* 7 (1982): 28–46.

———. "Rondò." In *New Grove Dictionary of Music and Musicians,* 2nd ed., edited by Stanley Sadie, 21:656. London: Macmillan, 2001.

Nicastro, Guido. *Metastasio e il teatro del primo settecento.* Rome: Laterza, 1973.

———. *"Sogni e favole io fingo": Gli inganni e i disinganni del teatro tra settecento e novecento.* Soveria Manelli: Rubbetino, 2004.

Nievo, Ippolito. *Le confessioni di un italiano.* Milan: Rizzoli, 1980.

Nocciolini, Monica. "Circolazione di un melodramma e rivolgimenti politici, 1796–1799: *La morte di Cleopatra.*" *Studi musicali* 23 (1994): 329–65.

———. "Il melodramma nella Milano napoleonica: Teatro musicale e ideologia politica." *Nuova rivista italiana musicale* 29 (1995): 5–30.

———. "Teatro musicale e rivolgimenti politici: Produzione e recezione dello spettacolo operistico in Italia attorno al triennio cisalpino, 1796–1799." Tesi di laurea, Florence, Università degli Studi, 1991–92.

"Non solo jazz." Report on the Web site of La Scuola di Giornalismo Radiotelevisivo, Perugia. http://www.sgrtv.it/ (accessed January 23, 2003).

Norman, Buford. "Remaking a Cultural Icon: *Phèdre* and the Operatic Stage." *Cambridge Opera Journal* 10 (1998): 225–45.

Noverre, Jean Georges. *Lettres sur la danse, et sur les ballets.* 1760. Facsimile reprint, New York: Broude Brothers, 1967.

———. *Observations sur la construction d'une salle d'opéra.* Amsterdam and Paris, 1781. Reprinted in *Lettres sur la danse, sur les ballets et les arts,* vol. 3 of *Oeuvres de Noverre.* 4 vols. St. Petersburg: Jean Charles Schnoor, 1803–04.

Il nuovo postiglione, ossia Compendio de' più accreditati fogli d'Europa. May 26 1797.

Nussdorfer, Laurie. *Civic Politics in the Rome of Urban VIII.* Princeton: Princeton University Press, 1992.

Opinione di un libero cittadino sulla nuova istituzione d'un Teatro Civico. Venice: Francesco Andreola, 1797.

Orbuscan, Marquis d.' *Voyage d'Italie.* Vol. 1 of *Mélanges historiques, critiques.* 1749. Paris, 1768.

Oresko, Robert. "The House of Savoy in Search of a Royal Crown in the Seventeenth Century." In *Royal and Republican Sovereignty in Early Modern Europe,* edited by Robert Oresko et al., 272–350. Cambridge: Cambridge University Press, 1997.

Oresko, Robert, et al., eds. *Royal and Republican Sovereignty in Early Modern Europe.* Cambridge: Cambridge University Press, 1997.

Orsini, Baldassare. *Le scene del Nuovo Teatro del Verzaro di Perugia ragionate dall'autore delle medesime.* Perugia: C. Constantini, 1785.

Ortes, Giammaria. "Reflessioni sopra i drammi per musica." Mod. ed. in Giammaria Ortes, *Calcolo sopra la verità e altri scritti,* edited by Bartolo Anglani, 149–66. Venice, 1957. Genoa: Costa & Nolan, 1984.

Ortkemper, Hubert. *Engel wider Willen: Die Welt der Kastraten.* Berlin: Henschel, 1993.

Ortolani, Giuseppe. "Un romanzo satirico a Venezia sulla metà del settecento." In *Voci e visioni del settecento veneziano,* 97–133. Bologna: Zanichelli, 1926.

Ozouf, Mona. *Festivals of the French Revolution.* Translated by Alan Sheridan. 1976. Reprint, Cambridge: Harvard University Press, 1988.

Pagetti, Carlo. *La fortuna di Swift in Italia.* Bari: Adriatica, 1971.

Palmer, Robert E. A. *The Archaic Community of the Romans.* Cambridge: Cambridge University Press, 1970.

Pancino, Livia, ed. *Johann Adolf Hasse e Giammaria Ortes: lettere, 1760–1783.* Turnhout: Brepols, 1998.

Parenti, Marino. *Un romanzo italiano del settecento: Saggio bibliografico su Zaccaria Seriman.* Florence: Sansoni, 1948.

Parini, Giuseppe. *Poesie e prose.* Edited by Enrico Bianchi. Florence: Salani, 1965.

Park, Katharine, and Robert A. Nye. "Destiny is Anatomy." Review of Thomas Laqueur, *Making Sex: Body and Gender from the Greeks to Freud* (Harvard University Press, 1990). *New Republic,* February 18, 1991, 53–57.

Parker, David. *The Making of French Absolutism.* New York: St. Martin's Press, 1983.

Pascucci, Giuseppe. *La Nobile Accademia del Pavone e il suo teatro.* Perugia, 1927.

Passadore, Francesco, and Franco Rossi. *Il Teatro San Benedetto di Venezia: Cronologia di spettacoli, 1755–1810.* Venice: Fondazione Levi, 2003.

———, eds. *L'aere è fosco, il ciel s'imbruna: Arti e musica a Venezia dall fine della Repubblica al Congresso di Vienna: Atti del Convegno Internazionale di Studi, Venezia, Palazzo Giustilian Lolin, 10–12 aprile 1997.* Venice: Fondazione Levi, 2000.

Pasta, Renato. "The History of the Book and Publishing in Eighteenth-Century Italy." *Journal of Modern Italian Studies* 10 (2005): 200–217.

Pastura Ruggiero, Maria Grazia. "Fonti per la storia del teatro romano nel settecento conservate nell'Archivio di Stato di Roma." In *Il teatro a Roma nel settecento,* edited by Giorgio Petrocchi, 2:505–87. Rome: Istituto della Enciclopedia Italiana, 1989.

———. "Per una storia del teatro pubblico in Roma nel secolo XVIII: I protagonisti." In *Il teatro a Roma nel settecento,* edited by Giorgio Petrocchi, 2:453–86. Rome: Istituto della Enciclopedia Italiana, 1989.

Pavan, Giuseppe. "Il Teatro Capranica: Catalogo cronologico delle opere rappresentate nel secolo XVIII." *Rivista musicale italiana* 29 (1922): 425–44.

Pavan, Giuseppe, and M. Franceschini. "La deputazione dei pubblici spettacoli di Roma e il suo archivio." *Architettura archivi,* 1986, 97–113.

Pejrone, Giulietta. "Il teatro attraverso i periodici romani del settecento." In *Il teatro a Roma nel settecento,* edited by Giorgio Petrocchi. Rome: Istituto della Enciclopedia Italiana, 1989.

Pellini, Pompeo. *Della historia di Perugia.* 2 vols. 1664. Facsimile reprint. 1 vol. Perugia: Arti Grafiche Città di Castello, 1970.

Penzel, Frederick. *Theatre Lighting before Electricity.* Middletown, CT: Wesleyan University Press, 1978.

Pera, Marcello. *The Ambiguous Frog: The Galvani-Volta Controversy over Animal Electricity.* Translated by Jonathan Mandelbaum. Princeton: Princeton University Press, 1992.

Pergolesi, Giovanni Battista. *Adriano in Siria: Dramma per musica.* [1735]. Edited by Dale Monson. New York: Pendragon, 1986.

———. *L'olimpiade.* [1735]. Edited by Howard Mayer Brown. Italian Opera, 1640–1770, no. 34. New York: Garland, 1979.

Pernety, Antoine. *Dictionnaire mytho-hermétique.* Paris: Bauche, 1787.

———. *Les fables égyptiennes et grecques.* 1758. Paris: Bauche, 1786.

Pestelli, Giorgio. "Riflessi della rivoluzione francese nel teatro musicale italiano." In *Eredità dell'ottantanove e l'Italia,* edited by Renzo Zorzi, 261–78. Florence: Olschki, 1992.

Petrobelli, Pierluigi. *Giuseppe Tartini: Le fonti biografiche.* Studi di Musica Veneta 1. N.p.: Universal Edition, 1968.

———. "Un cantante fischiato e le appoggiature di mezza battuta: Cronaca teatrale e prassi esecutiva alla metà del '700." In *Studies in Renaissance and Baroque Music in Honor of Arthur Mendel,* edited by Robert L. Marshall, 363–76. Hackensack, NJ: Boonin, 1974.

———. "Mozart in Italy." *Mozart-Jahrbuch,* 1978/1979, 153–56.

Petrocchi, Giorgio, ed. *Orfeo in Arcadia: Studi sul teatro a Roma nel settecento.* Rome: Istituto della Enciclopedia Italiana fondata da Giovanni Treccani, 1984.

——— , ed. *Il teatro a Roma nel settecento.* 3 vols. Rome: Istituto della Enciclopedia Italiana, 1989.

Petrocchi, Massimo. *Il tramonto della Repubblica di Venezia e l'assolutismo illuminato.* Deputazione di Storia Patria per le Venezie. Miscellanea di Studi e Memorie, vol. 7. Venice: La Deputazione, 1950.

Piazza, Antonio. *Il teatro ovvero fatti di una veneziana che lo fanno conoscere.* 2 vols. Venice: Constantini, 1778.

Piccinni, Niccolò. *Le Cecchina, ossia La buona figliuola.* Facsimile of 1760. Edited by Eric Weimer. Italian Opera, 1640–1770, ser. 2, no. 80. New York: Garland, 1983.

Piergiovanni, Armando. "Il Teatro del Pavone e le sue avventure." *Perusia* 8 (1949): 28.

Pignatti, Terisio, ed. *L'opera completa di Pietro Longhi.* Milan: Rizzoli, 1974.

Pimpinelli, Paola. *I riti nell'Arcadia Perugina.* Perugia: Volumnia, 2000.

Piperno, Franco. "Opera Production to 1780." In *Opera Production and Its Resources,* edited by Lorenzo Bianconi and Giorgio Pestelli, 1–79. Chicago: University of Chicago Press, 1998.

Pirrotta, Nino. "Metastasio and the Demands of His Literary Environment." *Studies in Music from the University of Western Ontario* 7/1 (1982): 10–27.

———. "Metastasio e i teatri romani." In *Le muse galanti: La musica a Roma nel settecento,* edited by Bruno Cagli, 23–34. Rome: Istituto della Enciclopedia Italiana, 1985.

Pisetzky, Rosita Levi. *Storia del costume in Italia.* 5 vols. Milan: Istituto Editoriale Italiano, 1964–67.

Planelli, Antonio. *Dell'opera in musica.* Naples: Campo, 1772. Reprint edited by Francesco Degrada. Fiesole: Discanto, 1981.

Pluche, Noël Antoine. *L'histoire du ciel.* Paris, 1739.

Poizat, Michel. *The Angel's Cry: Beyond the Pleasure Principle in Opera.* Translated by Arthur Denner. Ithaca: Cornell University Press, 1992.

Pöllnitz, Baron Karl-Ludwig von. *Lettres . . . contenant les observations qu'il a faites dans ses voyages et le caractère des personnes qui composent les principales cours de l'Europe.* 4th ed. 3 vols. London: Jean Nourse, 1741.

Polzonetti, Pierpaolo. *Tartini e la musica secondo natura.* Lucca: Libreria Musicale Italiana, 2001.

Pomata, Gianna. "Family and Gender." In *The Family in Italy from Antiquity to the Present,* edited by David I. Kertzer and Richard P. Saller, 69–86. New Haven: Yale University Press, 1991.

Poriss, Hilary. "Artistic License: Aria Interpolation and the Italian Operatic World, 1815–1850." Ph.D. diss., University of Chicago, 2000.

———. "A Madwoman's Choice: Aria Substitution in *Lucia di Lammermoor.*" *Cambridge Opera Journal* 13 (2001): 1–28.

Porter, Roy. *The Enlightenment.* 2nd ed. Houndsmill: Palgrave, 2001.

Povolo, Claudio. "The Creation of Venetian Historiography." In *Venice Reconsidered: The History and Civilization of an Italian City State, 1297–1797,* edited by John Martin and Dennis Romano, 491–519. Baltimore: Johns Hopkins University Press, 2000.

Price, Curtis. "Pasticcio." In *New Grove Dictionary of Music and Musicians,* 2nd ed., edited by Stanley Sadie, 19:213–16. London: Macmillan, 2001.

Price, Curtis, Judith Milhous, and Robert D. Hume. *Italian Opera in Late Eighteenth-Century London.* Vol. 1, *The King's Theatre, Haymarket, 1778–1791.* Oxford: Clarendon Press, 1995.

Prod'homme, J.-G. "Napoleon, Music, and Musicians." Translated by Frederick H. Martens. *Musical Quarterly* 7 (1921): 579–605.

Prodi, Paolo. *The Papal Prince, One Body and Two Souls: The Papal Monarchy in Early Modern Europe.* Translated by Susan Haskins. Cambridge: Cambridge University Press, 1987.

———. *Il sovrano pontefice, un corpo e due anime: La monarchia papale nella prima età moderna.* Bologna: Mulino, 1982.

I professori e gli studenti del Liceo Ginnasio A. Mariotti di Perugia in memoria di Annibale Mariotti: Studi storici e letterari. Perugia: Guerriero Guerra, 1901.

Profeti, Maria Grazia. "Guardare/Fare: Lo spettatore come spettacolo." In *Semiotica della rappresentazione: Atti del Convegno Internazionale di Studi,* edited by Renato Tomasino, 277–84. Palermo: Flaccovio, 1984.

Prota-Giurleo, Ulisse. *La grande orchestra del Teatro S. Carlo nel settecento: Da documenti inediti.* Naples: L'autore, 1927.

Quadrio, Francesco S. *Della storia e della ragione d'ogni poesia.* 4 vols. Bologna: Pisarri, 1739–50.

Quantz, Johann Joachim. *On Playing the Flute.* Translated by Edward R. Reilly. New York: Schirmer, 1966.

———. *Versuch einer Anweisung die Flötetraversiere zu spielen.* Facsimile of 3rd ed. (Breslau, 1789). Edited by Hans-Peter Schmidt. Documenta musicologica 2. Kassel: Bärenreiter, 1953.

Quetin, Laurine. *L'opéra seria de Johann Christian Bach à Mozart.* Geneva: Minkoff, 2003.

Quintilian. *Institutiones oratoriae.* Edited by Giovanni Garuti. Florence: La Nuova Italia, 1977.

Qureshi, Regula Burckhardt. *Master Musicians of India: Hereditary Sarangi Players Speak*. New York: Routledge, 2007.

———. "Mode of Production and Musical Production: Is Hindustani Music Feudal?" In *Music and Marx: Ideas, Practice, Politics,* edited by Regula Burckhardt Qureshi, 81–105. New York: Routledge, 2002.

Raccolta di melodrammi seri scritti nel secolo XVIII. Vol. 2. Milan: Società Tipografica dei Classici Italiani, 1822.

Raccolta di opuscoli scientifici scielti da diversi autori francesi, ed inglesi, nuovamente tr. in italiana favella. 2 parts. Edited by Antonio Meloni and Giacomo Venetici. Ferrara: Sansone, 1760.

Racine. *Phèdre*. Edited by Jacques Morel. Paris: Flammarion, 1995.

Radcliffe-Brown, A. R. *The Andaman Islanders*. New York: Free Press, 1964.

Raguenet, François. *Parallèle des Italiens et Français en ce que regarde la musique et les opéras*. Paris, 1702–5. Geneva: Minkoff, 1976.

Rameau, Jean-Philippe. *Oeuvres complètes*. Edited by Camille Saint-Saëns. Paris: A. Durand, 1900.

———. *Opera omnia*. Edited by Sylvie Bouissou. Kassel: Bärenreiter and Société Jean-Philippe Rameau, forthcoming.

Rao, Anna Maria. Enlightenment and Reform." In *Early Modern Italy, 1550–1796*, edited by John A. Marino, 229–52. Oxford: Oxford University Press, 2002.

———. "Enlightenment and Reform: An Overview of Culture and Politics in Enlightenment Italy." *Journal of Modern Italian Studies* 10 (2005): 142–67.

———. "The Feudal Question, Judicial Systems, and the Enlightenment." In *Naples in the Eighteenth Century: The Birth and Death of a Nation State*, edited by Girolamo Imbruglia, 95–117. Cambridge: Cambridge University Press, 2000.

Rapp, Richard T. *Industry and Economic Decline in Seventeenth-Century Venice*. Cambridge: Harvard University Press, 1976.

Rappaport, Roy A. "Ritual." In *Folklore, Cultural Performances, and Popular Entertainments: A Communications-Centered Handbook,* edited by Richard Bauman, 249–60. New York: Oxford University Press, 1992.

Rava, Arnaldo. *I teatri di Roma*. Rome: Fratelli Palombi, 1953.

Re, Niccolò del. *Monsignor Governatore di Roma*. Rome: Istituto di Studi Romani, 1972.

Reade, Brian. *Victoria and Albert Museum: Ballet Designs and Illustrations, 1581–1940*. London: Her Majesty's Stationery Office, 1967.

Redavid, Gianfranco, ed. *Il teatro e la festa: Lo spettacolo a Roma tra papato e rivoluzione*. Rome: Artemide, 1989.

Restani, Donatella. *Musica per governare: Alessandro, Adriano, Teodorico*. Ravenna: Longo, 2004.

Riccoboni, Luigi. *Réflexions historiques et critiques sur les differens théâtres de l'Europe*. Paris, 1738. English ed., London: Waller & R. Dodsley, 1741.

Rice, John A. *Antonio Salieri and Viennese Opera*. Chicago: University of Chicago Press, 1998.

———. "Sense, Sensibility, and Opera Seria: An Epistolary Debate." *Studi musicali* (15) 1986: 101–38.

———. *W. A. Mozart: La clemenza di Tito*. Cambridge: Cambridge University Press, 1991.

Richard, L'Abbé M. *Description historique et critique de l'Italie, ou Nouveaux mémoires sur l'état actuel de son gouvernement, des sciences, des arts, du commerce, de la population & l'histoire naturelle*. 6 vols. Dijon: Des Ventes, 1766. Rev. ed., Paris: Saillant, Desaint & Coru de la Goibrie, 1769.

Ricoeur, Paul. *Hermeneutics and the Human Sciences: Essays on Language, Action, and Interpretation*. Edited and translated by John B. Thompson. Cambridge: Cambridge University Press, 1981.

———. *Interpretation Theory: Discourse and the Surplus of Meaning.* Fort Worth: Texas Christian University Press, 1976.

Ricuperati, Giuseppe. "The Enlightenment and the Church in the Work of Franco Venturi: The Fertile Legacy of a Civil Religion." *Journal of Modern Italian Studies* 10 (2005): 168–82.

Ricuperati, Giuseppe, and Dino Carpanetto. *Italy in the Age of Reason, 1685–1789.* Translated by Caroline Higgitt. London: Longman, 1987.

Riding, Alan. "Finally, Healing a Wound at the Heart of Venice." *New York Times,* Sunday, December 7, 2003, Arts and Leisure, part 2.

Riedlbauer, Jörg. *Die Opern von Tommaso Trajetta.* Hildesheim: Georg Olms, 1994.

Riesemann, O. von. "Ein Selbstbiographie der Sängerin Gertrud Elisabeth Mara." *Allgemeine musikalische Zeitung* 10 (1875), cols. 609–13.

Riley, Matthew. *Musical Listening in the German Enlightenment: Attention, Wonder, and Astonishment.* Aldershot: Ashgate, 2005.

Rinaldi, Mario. *Due secoli di musica al Teatro Argentina.* 2 vols. Florence: Olschki, 1978.

Rizzuti, Alberto. "Music for a *Risorgimento* Myth: Joan of Arc, 1789–1849." Ph.D. diss., University of Chicago, 2001.

Roberts, John M. "Enlightened Despotisms in Italy." In *Art and Ideas in Eighteenth-Century Italy: Lectures Given at the Italian Institute, 1957–1958,* 25–44. Rome: Edizioni di Arte e Letteratura, 1960.

Robinson, Michael F. "The Ancient and the Modern: A Comparison of Metastasio and Calzabigi." *Studies in Music from the University of Western Ontario* 7/2 (1982): 137–47.

———. "The Aria in Opera Seria, 1725–1780." *Proceedings of the Royal Musical Association* 88 (1961–62): 31–43.

———. "The Da Capo Aria as Symbol of Rationality." In *La musica come linguaggio universale: Genesi e storia di un'idea,* edited by Raffaelle Pozzi, 51–63. Florence: Olschki, 1990.

———. *Giovanni Paisiello: A Thematic Catalogue of His Works.* Vol. 1, *Dramatic Works.* Stuyvesant, NY: Pendragon, 1991.

———. "How to Demonstrate Virtue: The Case of Porpora's Two Settings of *Mitridate.*" *Studies in Music from the University of Western Ontario* 7/1 (1982): 47–64.

———. "A Late Eighteenth-Century Account Book of the San Carlo Theatre, Naples." *Early Music* 18 (1990): 73–81.

———. *Naples and Neapolitan Opera.* Oxford: Clarendon Press, 1972.

Robinson, Michael F., and Renato di Benedetto. "Naples." From *Grove Music Online,* ed. Laura Macy. http://www.grovemusic.com/ (accessed December 1, 2005).

Romagnani, Gian Paolo. *"Sotto la bandiera dell'istoria": Eruditi e uomini di lettere nell'Italia del settecento: Maffei, Muratori, Tartarotti.* Sommacampagna (Verona): Cierre, 1999.

Romanelli, Francesca Cavazzana. "Archivisitica giacobina: La municipalità veneziana e gli archivi." In *Vita religiosa e cultura in Lombardia e nel Veneto nell'età napoleonica,* edited by Gabriele de Rosa and Filiberto Agostini, 325–47. Bari: Laterza, 1990.

Roncaglia, Constantino. *Moderne conversazioni volgarmente dette dei cicisbei.* Lucca: Venturini, 1720. Reprint, 1736.

Rosand, David. *Myths of Venice: The Figuration of a State.* Chapel Hill: University of North Carolina Press, 2001.

Rosand, Ellen. "Italy." §§1–2. From *Grove Music Online,* ed. Laura Macy. http://www.grovemusic.com/ (accessed September 22, 2005).

———. *Opera in Seventeenth-Century Venice: The Creation of a Genre.* Berkeley and Los Angeles: University of California Press, 1991.

Roscioni, Carlo Marinelli, ed. *Il Teatro di San Carlo.* Vol. 2, *La cronologia, 1737–1987.* 2nd ed. Naples: Guida, 1988.

Rose, Mark. "The Author as Proprietor: Donaldson v. Becket and the Genealogy of Modern Authorship." *Representations* 23 (1988): 51–85.

Rosen, Charles. *Sonata Forms*. Rev. ed. New York: Norton, 1988.

Rosselli, John. "The Castrati as a Professional Group and as a Social Phenomenon, 1550–1850." *Acta musicologica* 60 (1988): 143–79.

———. "From Princely Service to the Open Market: Singers of Italian Opera and Their Patrons, 1600–1850." *Cambridge Opera Journal* 1 (1989): 1–32.

———. *The Opera Industry in Italy from Cimarosa to Verdi: The Role of the Impresario*. Cambridge: Cambridge University Press, 1984.

———. "Opera Production, 1780–1880." In *Opera Production and Its Resources*, edited by Lorenzo Bianconi and Giorgio Pestelli, 81–164. Chicago: University of Chicago Press, 1998.

———. *Singers of Italian Opera: The History of a Profession*. Cambridge: Cambridge University Press, 1992.

Rosselli, John, and Richard Macnutt. "Season." In *The New Grove Dictionary of Opera*, edited by Stanley Sadie, 4:281–83. London: Macmillan, 1992.

Rossini, Paolo. "L'opera classicista nella Milano napoleonica, 1796–1815." In *Aspetti dell'opera italiana fra sette e ottocento: Mayr e Zingarelli*, edited by Guido Salvetti, 127–71. Lucca: Libreria Musicale Italiana, 1993.

Rousseau, Jean-Jacques. *Essay on the Origin of Languages and Writings Related to Music*. Translated by John T. Scott. The Collected Writings of Rousseau, vol. 7. Hanover, NH: University Press of New England, 1998.

———. *Il pimmalione: Scena lirica*. Venice: Antonio Graziosi, 1777.

Ruile-Dronke, Jutta. *Ritornell und Solo in Mozarts Klavierkonzerten*. Tutzing: H. Schneider, 1978.

Rushton, Julian. *Classical Music: A Concise History from Gluck to Beethoven*. London: Thames and Hudson, 1986.

Sacchi, Giovenale. *Vita del cavaliere Don Carlo Broschi detto Il Farinello*. Edited by Alessandro Abbate. Naples: Pagano, 1994.

Sadie, Stanley, ed. *The New Grove Dictionary of Music and Musicians*. 20 vols. London: Macmillan, 1980.

———. *The New Grove Dictionary of Opera*. 4 vols. Edited by Stanley Sadie. London: Macmillan, 1992.

Sahlins, Marshall. *Historical Metaphors and Mythical Realities: Structure in the Early History of the Sandwich Islands Kingdom*. Ann Arbor: University of Michigan Press, 1981.

———. *Islands of History*. Chicago: University of Chicago Press, 1985. Italian edition, *Isole di storia: Società e mito nei mari del Sud*, translated by Enrico Basaglia (Turin: Einaudi, 1986).

———. "Poor Man, Rich Man, Big-Man, Chief: Political Types in Melanesia and Polynesia." *Comparative Studies in Society and History* 5 (1963): 285–303. Reprinted in *Culture in Practice: Selected Essays* (New York: Zone Books, 2000), 71–93.

Saint Non, Jean Claude Richard de, with Sébastien-Roch-Nicolas Chamfort. *Voyage pittoresque, ou Description des royaumes de Naples et de Sicile*. 5 parts. Paris: [Clousier], 1781–86.

Sala di Felice, Elena. *Metastasio: Ideologia, drammaturgia, spettacolo*. Milan: Franco Angeli, 1983.

Salatino, Kevin. *Incendiary Art: The Representation of Fireworks in Early Modern Europe*. Los Angeles: Getty Research Institute for the History of Art and the Humanities, 1997.

Salazar, Philippe-Joseph. *Idéologies de l'opéra*. Paris: Presses Universitaires de France, 1980.

Salvetti, Guido, ed. *Aspetti dell'opera italiana fra sette e ottocento: Mayr e Zingarelli*. Lucca: Libreria Musicale Italiana, 1993.

Salza, Abd-el-Kader. "I cicisbei nella vita e nella letteratura del settecento." *Rivista d'Italia* 13, no. 2 (1910): 184–251.

Sama, Catherine M. "Verso un teatro moderno: La polemica tra Elisabetta Caminer e Carlo Gozzi." In *Elisabetta Caminer Turra (1751–1796): Una letterata veneta verso l'Europa*, edited by Rita Unfer Kukoschik, 63–79. Verona: Essedue, 1998.

Sartori, Claudio. *I libretti italiani a stampa dalle origini al 1800*. 7 vols. Cuneo: Bertola & Locatelli, 1990–93.

Saunders, George. *A Treatise on Theatres*. London, 1790.

Saunders, Harris S. Jr. "The Repertoire of a Venetian Opera House, 1678–1714: The Teatro Grimani di San Giovanni Grisostomo." Ph.D. diss., Harvard University, 1985.

Savage, Roger. "Staging an Opera: Letters from the Cesarian Poet." *Early Music* 26 (1998): 583–95.

Savoia, Francesca. *La cantante e l'impresario e altri metamelodrammi*. Genoa: Costa & Nolan, 1988.

Scafoglio, Domenico. *La maschera della cuccagna: Spreco, rivolta e sacrificio nel carnevale napoletano del 1764*. Naples: Guida, 1994.

Scarabello, Giovanni. "Da campoformido al Congresso di Vienna: L'identità veneta sospesa." In *Storia della cultura veneta*, edited by Girolamo Arnaldi and Manlio Pastore Stocchi, vol. 6, *Dall'età napoleonica alla prima guerra mondiale*, 1–20. Vicenza: Neri Pozzi, 1986.

———"Gli ultimi giorni della repubblica." In *Storia della cultura veneta*, edited by Girolamo Arnaldi and Manlio Pastore Stocchi, vol. 5, part 2, *Il settecento*, 487–508. Vicenza: Neri Pozzi, 1986.

Schechner, Richard. *Between Theater and Anthropology*. Foreword by Victor Turner. Philadelphia: University of Pennsylvania Press, 1985.

Scheibe, Johann Adolphe. *Critischer Musikus: Neue vermehrte und unverbesserte Auflage*. Rev. ed. Leipzig: B. C. Breitkopf, 1745. Reprint, Hildesheim: Georg Olms, 1970.

Schieberger, Londa. *The Mind Has No Sex? Women in the Origins of Modern Science*. Cambridge: Harvard University Press, 1989.

Schmitz, Hans-Peter. *Die Kunst der Verzierung im 18. Jahrhundert: Instrumentale und Vokale Musizierpraxis in Beispielen*. 2nd ed. 1955. Reprint, Kassel: Bärenreiter, 1965.

Schneider, Rachel Aleane. "The Administrative History of L'Académie Impériale de Musique in the Age of Napoléon: Opera for Gloire and Indoctrination." Ph.D. diss., University of Akron, 1990.

Schnoebelen, Anne. *Padre Martini's Collection of Letters in the Civio Museo Bibliografico Musicale in Bologna: An Annotated Index*. New York: Pendragon, 1979.

Schulte van Kessel, Elisja. "Virgins and Mothers between Heaven and Earth." In *Renaissance and Enlightenment Parodoxes*, vol. 3 of *A History of Women in the* West, edited by Natalie Zemon Davis and Arlette Farge, 132–66. Cambridge: Belknap Press, 1993.

Scott, H. M., ed. *Enlightened Absolutism: Reform and Reformers in Later Eighteenth-Century Europe*. Ann Arbor: University of Michigan Press, 1990.

Il secolo dei lumi e delle riforme: Storia della società italiana. Milan, 1989.

Serao, Matilde. *Il paese di cuccagna*. 1944. Reprint, Milan: Garzanti, 1981.

Seriman, Zaccaria. *Viaggi di Enrico Wanton*. Edited by Gilberto Pizzamiglio. 2 vols. Milan: Marzorati, 1977.

———. *Viaggi di Enrico Wanton alle terre incognite australi, ed ai regni delle scimie e de cinocefali, nuovamente tradotti da un manoscritto inglese*. 4 vols. [Motto: "Te mecum lectus, non modo Lector etis."] Berna, 1764.

Sertor, Gaetano. *La morte di Cesare: Dramma per musica del signor D. Gaetano Sertor da rappresentarsi nel nobilisssimo Teatro di S. Samuele il carnovale dell'anno 1789; Dedicato a Gio. Battista Pignatelli principe di Mariconuovo*. Venice, 1789.

Sewell, William H. Jr. "Historical Events as Transformations of Structures: Inventing Revolution at the Bastille." In *Logics of History: Social Theory and Social Transformation*, edited by William H. Sewell, Jr., 225–70. Chicago: University of Chicago Press, 2005. Original version published in *Theory and Society* 25 (1996): 841–81.

———. "A Theory of the Event: Marshall Sahlins's 'Possible Theory of History.'" In *Logics of History: Social Theory and Social Transformation*, edited by William H. Sewell, Jr., 197–224. Chicago: University of Chicago Press, 2005.

———. *Logics of History: Social Theory and Social Transformation*. Chicago: University of Chicago Press, 2005.

Sharp, Samuel. *Letters from Italy Describing the Customs and Manners of That Country, in the Years 1765 and 1766*. 3rd ed. London: Henry & Cave at St. John's Gate, [1767].

Shils, Edward. "Charisma, Order, and Status." *American Sociological Review* 30, no. 2 (1965): 199–213.

Shinoda, Hideako. *Re-Examining Sovereignty from Classical Theory to the Global Age*. Houndsmill: Macmillan, 2000; New York: St. Martin's Press, 2000.

Siepi, Serafino. *Descrizione topologico-istorica della citta di Perugia*. Perugia: Garbinesi & Santicci, 1822.

Sisman, Elaine R. *Mozart: The Jupiter Symphony*. Cambridge Music Handbooks. Cambridge: Cambridge University Press, 1993.

———. "Small and Expanded Forms: Koch's Model and Haydn's Music." *Musical Quarterly* 48 (1982): 444–75.

Small, Christopher. *Musicking: The Meanings of Performing and Listening*. Hanover: Dartmouth University Press, 1998.

Smith, Jonathan Z. *To Take Place: Toward Theory in Ritual*. Chicago: University of Chicago Press, 1987.

Smith, William C., and Charles Humphries. *A Bibliography of the Musical Works Published by the Firm of John Walsh during the Years 1721–1766*. London: The Biobliographical Society, 1968.

Sografi, Antonio. *Giovanna d'Arco: Dramma in quattr'atti per musica . . . da rappresentarsi in Vicenza nel nuovo teatro la state dell'anno 1789 . . . . In Vicenza per Antonio Giusto*. Vicenza, 1789.

———. *Giovanna d'Arco, o sia La pulcella d'Orleans: Dramma serio per musica del cittadino Sografi da rappresentarsi nel Teatro La Fenice l'estate dell'anno 1797*. Venice: Stamperia Valvasense.

———. *La morte di Mitridate: Tragedia per musica del Signor Sografi poeta del nobile Teatro la Fenice e del Teatro Comico S. Angelo da rappresentarsi nel Ces. Reg. Teatro di Trieste l'autunno MDCCXCVI*. Trieste, 1796.

———. *La morte di Mitridate: Tragedia per musica del Signor Sografi poeta del teatro La Fenice e del Teatro Comico Sant'Angelo l'estate dell'anno 1797*. Venice: Stamperia Valvasense.

———. *Gli Orazi e i Curiazi: Tragedia per musica del Signor Antonio Sografi poeta del nobilissimo Teatro La Fenice e del comico Sant'Angelo composta per il teatro suddetto per il Carnovale 1797*. Venice: Stamperia Valvasense.

———. *Gli Orazi e i Curiazi: Tragedia per musica del Signor Sografi poeta del Teatro La Fenice e del comico Sant'Angelo composta per il teatro suddetto per il solito tempo dell'Ascensione 1797*. Venice: Stamperia Valvasense.

Solie, John E. "Aria Structure and Ritornello Form in the Music of Albinoni." *Musical Quarterly* 63 (1977): 31–47.

Solie, Ruth A., ed. *Musicology and Difference: Gender and Sexuality in Music Scholarship*. Berkeley and Los Angeles: University of California Press, 1993.

Sommer-Mathis, Andrea. *Tu felix Austria Nube: Hochzeitsfeste der Habsburger im 18. Jahrhundert*. Vienna: Musikwissenschaftlicher Verlag, 1994.

Sonneck, Oscar George Theodore. *Catalogue of Opera Librettos Printed before 1800*. 2 vols. 1914. New York: Johnson Reprint, 1968.

Sonneck, Oscar George Theodore, and Albert Schatz. *Catalogue of Opera Librettos Printed before 1800*. Library of Congress. 2 vols. Washington: Government Printing Office, 1914.

Spinelli, Lorenzo. *La vacanza della sede apostolica dalle origini al Concilio tridentino*. Milan: Giuffre, 1956.

Spitzer, John. "Improvized Ornamentation in a Handel Aria with Obbligato Wind Accompaniment." *Early Music* 16 (1988): 514–22.

Spitzer, John, and Neal Zaslaw. *The Birth of the Orchestra: History of an Institution, 1650–1815*. New York: Oxford University Press, 2004.

———. "Orchestra." Part 5, "18th Century." In *The New Grove Dictionary of Opera*, edited by Stanley Sadie, 3:723–28. London: Macmillan, 1992.

Sprague, Cheryl. "A Comparison of Five Musical Settings of Metastasio's *Artaserse*." Ph.D. diss., University of California at Los Angeles, 1979.

Spreti, Laura. "Venezia, Carnevale 1791." *Rassegna veneta di studi musicali* 9/10 (1993–94): 198–99.

Stallybrass, Peter, and Allon White. *The Politics and Poetics of Transgression*. Ithaca: Cornell University Press, 1986.

Steblein, Rita. "Key Characteristics in the 18th and Early 19th Centuries: A Historical Approach." Ph.D. diss., University of Illinois at Urbana-Champaign, 1980.

Stendhal [Marie-Henri Beyle]. *Lives of Haydn, Mozart, and Metastasio*. Translated and edited by Richard N. Coe from the 1814 edition. London: Caldar & Boyars, 1972.

———. *Vies de Haydn, de Mozart et de Métastase*. In *Oeuvres complètes de Stendhal*, edited by Édouard Champion. Paris: Honoré Champion, 1914.

Stenzl, Jurg. "'Una povera ragazza': Carlo Goldonis *La buona figliuola* in Niccolo Piccinnis Vertonung." In *Zwischen Opera buffa und Melodramma: Italienische Oper im 18. und 19. Jahrhundert*, edited by Jürgen Maehder and Jürg Stenzel, 81–97. Frankfurt am Main: Peter Lang, 1994.

Stevens, Jane R. "Patterns of Recapitulation in the First Movements of Mozart's Piano Concertos." In *Musical Humanism and Its Legacy: Essays in Honor of Claude V. Palisca*, edited by Nancy Kovaleff Baker and Barbara Russano Hanning, 397–418. Stuyvesant, NY: Pendragon, 1992.

———. "The 'Piano Climax' in the Eighteenth-Century Concerto: An Operatic Gesture?" In *C. P. E. Bach Studies*, edited by Stephen L. Clark, 245–76. Oxford: Clarendon Press, 1988.

———. "Theme, Harmony, and Texture in Classic-Romantic Descriptions of Concerto First-Movement Form." *JAMS* 27 (1974): 25–60.

Stieger, Franz. *Opernlexikon*. 4 vols. in 11. Tutzing: Schneider, 1975–83.

Stonehouse, Allison. "*Demofoonte* and Democracy, or The Taming of a French Tyrant." *Metastasio at Home and Abroad. Studies in Music from the University of Western Ontario* 16 (1997): 135–54.

Strohm, Reinhard. "Dramatic Dualities: Metastasio and the Tradition of the Operatic Pair." *Early Music* 26 (1998): 551–61.

———. *Dramma per musica: Italian Opera Seria of the Eighteenth Century*. New Haven: Yale University Press, 1997.

———. "Handel's Pasticci." In *Essays on Handel and Italian Opera*, 164–211. Cambridge: Cambridge University Press, 1985.

———. *Italienische Opernarien des frühen Settecento, 1720–1730*. 2 vols. Cologne: Arno Volk Verlag Hans Gerig, 1976.

———. "Merkmale italienischer Versvertonung in Mozarts Klavierkonzerten." *Analecta musicologica* 18 (1978): 219–36.

———. "Metastasio's *Alessandro nell'Indie* and Its Earliest Settings." In *Essays on Handel and Italian Opera*, 232–48. Cambridge: Cambridge University Press, 1985.

Sul matrimonio e sulle obbligazioni del medesimo . . . ragionamenti di un filosofo. Perugia: Costantini, n.d..

Sulla insensitività ed irritibilità Halleriana. Bologna: Girolamo Corciolani, 1759.

Summers, William John. "Opera Seria in Spanish California: An Introduction to a Newly-identified Manuscript Source." In *Music in Performance and Society: Essays in Honor of Roland Jackson*, edited by Malcolm Cole and John Koegel, 269–90. Warren, MI: Harmonie Park Press, 1997.

Surian, Elvidio. "Metastasio, i nuovi cantanti, il nuovo stile: Verso il classicismo; Osservazioni sull'*Artaserse* (Venezia 1730) di Hasse." In *Venezia e il melodramma nel seicento*, edited by Maria Teresa Muraro, 341–62. Florence: Olschki, 1976.

———"The Opera Composer." In *Opera Production and Its Resources*, edited by Lorenzo Bianconi and Giorgio Pestelli, 291–344. Chicago: University of Chicago Press, 1998.

Sussman, George D. *Selling Mother's Milk: The Wet-Nursing Business in France, 1715–1914.* Urbana: University of Illinois Press, 1982.

Symcox, Geoffrey. "The Political World of the Absolutist State in the Seventeenth and Eighteenth Centuries." In *Early Modern Italy, 1550–1796*, edited by John A. Marino, 104–22. Oxford: Oxford University Press, 2002.

———. *Victor Amadeus II: Absolutism in the Savoyard State, 1675–1730.* Berkeley and Los Angeles: University of California Press, 1983.

Talbot, Michael. "*Ore italiane:* The Reckoning of the Time of Day in Pre-Napoleonic Italy." *Italian Studies* 40 (1985): 51–62.

———. *Tomaso Albinoni: The Venetian Composer and His World.* Oxford: Oxford University Press, 1990.

Tambiah, Stanley J. "A Performative Approach to Ritual." In *Culture, Thought, and Social Action: An Anthropological Perspective.* Cambridge: Harvard University Press, 1985.

———. "A Reformulation of Geertz's Conception of the Theater State." In *Culture,Thought, and Social Action: An Anthropological Perspective*, 316–38. Cambridge: Harvard University Press, 1985.

Tanucci, Bernardo. *Epistolario.* Edizioni di Storia e Letteratura, 13 vols. to date. Rome: Istituto Poligrafico e Zecca della Stato; Naples: Società Napoletana per la Storia Patria, 1980–.

Tanzer, Gerhard. *Spectacle müssen seyn: Der Freiheit in Wien im 18. Jahrhundert.* Vienna: Böhlau, 1992.

Tartini, Giuseppe. *Tratado di musica.* Padua, 1754.

Taruskin, Richard. *A History of Western Music.* 6 vols. Oxford: Oxford University Press, 2005.

———. "Of Kings and Divas: Opera, Politics, and the French Boom." *New Republic*, December 13, 1993.

Tassini, Giuseppe. *Feste, spettacoli, divertimenti e piaceri degli antichi veneziani.* 2nd ed. Venice: Libreria Filippi, 1961.

Taviani, Ferdinando. "Sulla soppravvalutazione della maschera." In *Arte della maschera nella commedia dell'arte.* Edited by Donato Sartori and Bruno Lanata, 105–18. Florence: La Casa Usher, 1983.

Il Teatro di San Carlo. 2nd ed. 2 vols. Edited by Raffaele Ajello et al. (vol. 2, *La cronologia*, ed. Roscioni). Naples: Guida, 1988.

Il Teatro di San Carlo, 1737–1787. 3 vols. Edited by Franco Mancini, Bruno Cagli, and Agostino Ziino (vols. 1 and 3, ed. Mancini; vol. 2, ed. Cagli and Ziino). Naples: Electa Napoli, 1987.

Temple Leader, John. *Libro dei nobili veneti ora per la prima volta messo in luce.* Florence: G. Barbèra, 1884.

Tenenti, Alberto. *Piracy and the Decline of Venice, 1580–1615*. Translated by Janet and Brian Pullan. London: Longmans, 1967.

Tessitori, Paola. *"Basta che finissa 'sti cani": Democrazia e polizia nella Venezia del 1797*. Istituto Veneto di Scienze, Lettere ed Arti, Memorie, vol. 67. Venice: Tipi della Canal & Stamperia Editrice, 1997.

Testa, Giovanni Antonio. *Riflessioni sullo stato coniugale*. Ferrara: Giuseppe Rinaldi, 1788.

Thayer, Alexander Wheelock. *Salieri, Rival of Mozart*. Edited by Theodore Albrecht. Kansas City: The Philharmonia of Greater Kansas City, 1989.

Thomas, Downing A. *Aesthetics of Opera in the Ancien Régime, 1647–1785*. Cambridge: Cambridge University Press, 2002.

Tolkoff, Audrey Lyn. "The Stuttgart Operas of Niccolò Jommelli." Ph.D. diss., Yale University, 1974.

Tomasino, Renato. *Per un'analisi della scena*. Palermo: Flaccovio, 1979.

Tomlinson, Gary. *Metaphysical Song: An Essay on Opera*. Princeton: Princeton University Press, 1999.

Torcellan, Gianfranco. "I viaggi di Enrico Wanton." Review of D. Maxwell White, *Zaccaria Seriman and the "Viaggi di Enrico Wanton."* In *Settecento veneto e altri scritti storici*, 165–9. Turin: Giappichelli, 1969.

Toscani, Claudio. "Soggetti romantici nell'opera italiana del periodo napoleonico, 1796–1815." In *Aspetti dell'opera italiana fra sette e ottocento: Mayr e Zingarelli*, edited by Guido Salvetti, 13–70. Lucca: Libreria Musicale Italiana, 1993.

Toschi, Paolo. *Le origini del teatro italiano*. 1955. Reprint, Turin: Boringhieri, 1976.

Tosi, Pierfrancesco. *Observations on the Florid Song, or Sentiments on the Ancient and Modern Singers*. Translated by Mr. Galliard, edited with additonal notes by Michael Pilkington. London: J. Wilcox, 1743. Reprint, Geneva: Minkoff, 1978.

———. *Opinioni de' cantori antichi, e moderni*. 1723. Monuments of Music and Music Literature in Facsimile, ser. 2, Music Literature, 133. New York: Broude Brothers, 1968.

———. *Opinioni de' cantori antichi e moderni*. Reprint of 1904 Naples edition. Edited by Luigi Leonesi. Bologna: Forni, 1968.

Tosi, Pierfrancesco, and Johann Friedrich Agricola. *Anleitung zur Singkunst*. Berlin, 1757. Edited in facsimile by Kurt Wichmann. Leipzig: VEB Deutscher Verlag für Musik, 1966.

———. *Introduction to the Art of Singing*. Translated by Juliane Baird. Cambridge: Cambridge University Press, 1995.

Touring Club Italiano. *Napoli e d'intorno*. 5th ed. Milan, 1976.

Tovey, Donald Francis. *Concertos*. Vol. 3 of *Essays in Musical Analysis*. London: Oxford University Press, 1936.

Traetta, Tommaso. *Antigone: Tragedia per musica in 3 atti*. Edited by Aldo Rocchi. Florence: Maggio Musicale Fiorentino, 1962.

———. *Ifigenia in Tauride*. Edited by Howard Mayer Brown. Italian Opera, 1640–1770, no. 47. New York: Garland, 1978.

———. *Ippolito ed Aricia*. [Parma, 1759]. Edited by Eric Weimer. Italian Opera, 1640–1770, no. 78. New York: Garland, 1982.

Treitler, Leo, ed. *Strunk's Source Readings in Music History*. Rev. ed. New York: Norton, 1998.

Trevor-Roper, Hugh. "The Highland Tradition of Scotland." In *The Invention of Tradition*, edited by Eric Hobsbawm and Terence Ringer, 15–41. Cambridge: Cambridge University Press, 1983.

Tufano, Lucio. "*Le nozze di Orfeo e Partenope:* Indagini sulla ricezione napoletana della 'riforma' di Gluck." Tesi di laurea, Università degli Studi di Napoli Federico II, 1992–1993.

———. "La via ossianica all'esotica: Primitivismo e intensità delle passioni nella *Comala* di

Calzabigi e Morandi." Paper delivered at the conference "Le arti della scena e l'esotismo in età moderna," Naples, May 6–9, 2004.

Turner, Victor. "Are There Universals of Performance?" In *By Means of Performance: Intercultural Studies of Theatre and Ritual*, edited by Richard Schechner and Willa Appel, 8–18. Cambridge: Cambridge University Press, 1990.

———. *Dramas, Fields, and Metaphors: Symbolic Action in Human Society.* Ithaca: Cornell University Press, 1974.

———. *From Ritual to Theater: The Human Seriousness of Play.* New York: Performing Arts Journal, 1982.

———. "Liminality and the Performative Genres." In *Rite, Drama, Festival, Spectacle: Rehearsals toward a Theory of Cultural Performance*, edited by John J. MacAloon, 19–41. Philadelphia: University of Pennsylvania Press, 1984.

———. *Schism and Continuity in an African Society.* Manchester: Manchester University Press, 1957.

———. "Social Dramas and Stories about Them." In *On Narrative*, edited by W. J. T. Mitchell, 137–64. Chicago: University of Chicago Press, 1981.

Urban, Lina Padoan. "Il carnevale veneziano." In *Storia della cultura veneta*, edited by Girolamo Arnaldi and Manlio Pastore Stocchi, vol. 5, part 1, *Il settecento*, 631–46. Vicenza: Neri Pozzi, 1985.

Vacchelli, A. M. Monterosso. "Babini, Matteo." In *Dizionario biografico degli italiani* 4:789–90. Rome: Enciclopedico Italiano, 1962.

Valente, Mario, ed. *Legge, poesia e mito: Giannone, Metastasio e Vico fra "tradizione" e "trasgressione" nella Napoli degli anni venti del settecento; Atti del Convegno Internazionale di Studi, Palazzo Serra di Cassano, Napoli 3–5 marzo 1998.* Introductory essay by Giuseppe Galasso. Rome: Aracne, 2001.

Valesio, Francesco. *Diario di Roma, 1700–1742.* Edited by Gaetano Scano and Giuseppe Graglia. 6 vols. Milan: Longanesi, 1977–79.

Valmaggi, Luigi. *I cicisbei: Contributo alla storia del costume italiano nel secolo XVIII.* Edited by Luigi Piccioni. Turin: G. Chiantore, 1927.

Van Gennep, Arnold. *The Rites of Passage.* Translated by Monika B. Vizedom and Gabrielle L. Caffee, introduction by Simon T. Kimball. 1908. Reprint, Chicago: University of Chicago Press, 1960.

Van Orden, Kate. *Music, Discipline, and Arms in Early Modern France.* Chicago: University of Chicago Press, 2005.

Vansina, Jan. *L'évolution du royaume Rwanda des origines à 1900.* Brussels: Académie Royale des Sciences d'Outre Mer, Classe des Sciences Morales et Politiques, 1962.

Vanvitelli, Luigi. *Le lettere di Luigi Vanvitelli della Biblioteca Palatina di Caserta.* Edited by Franco Strazzullo. 3 vols. Galatina: Congedo, 1976–1977.

Venel, Jean-André, and Luigi Angeli. *Saggio di medica educazione per le fanciulle chiamate a marito.* Imola: Giovanni dal Monte, 1789.

Ventura, Margherita Maria Rosa, ed. *Teatro Francesco Morlacchi, archivio storico: Inventario.* Perugia: Umbra Cooperativa, 1983.

Venturi, Franco. "Cesare Beccaria e le riforme giuridiche." In *La cultura illuministica in Italia*, edited by Mario Fubini, 120–29. Turin: Edizioni Radio Italiana, 1957.

———. *La chiesa e la repubblica dentro i loro limiti, 1758–1774.* Vol. 2 of *Settecento riformatore.* Turin: Einaudi, 1976.

———. "Church and Reform in Enlightenment Italy: The Sixties of the Eighteenth Century." *Journal of Modern History* 48 (1976): 215–32.

———. "Contributi ad un dizionario storico: Was ist Aufklarung? Sapere aude!" *Rivista storica italiana* 71 (1959): 119–28.

———. "Contributi ad un dizionario storico: Despotismo orientale." *Rivista storica italiana* 62 (1960): 117–26. Translated by Lotte F. Jacoby and Ian M. Taylor in *Journal of the History of Ideas* 24 (1963): 133–42.

———. *Da Muratori a Beccaria.* Vol. 1 of *Settecento riformatore.* Turin: Einaudi, 1969.

———. "Elementi e tentativi di riforme nello Stato Pontificio del settecento." *Rivista storica italiana* 75 (1963): 778–817.

———. *The End of the Old Regime in Europe, 1768–1776: The First Crisis.* Translated by R. Burr Litchfield. Princeton: Princeton University Press, 1989.

———. *The End of the Old Regime in Europe, 1776–1789.* Translated by R. Burr Litchfield. Princeton: Princeton University Press, 1991.

———. "Il movimento riformatore degli illuministi meridionali." *Rivista storica italiana* 74 (1962): 5–26.

———. "Il movimento riformatore degli illuministi napoletani." *Rivista storica italiana* 74 (1962): 198–224.

———. *Italy and the Enlightenment: Studies in a Cosmopolitan Century.* Translated by Susan Corsi. Edited by Stuart J. Woolf. London: Longman, 1972.

———. *Settecento riformatore.* 5 vols. in 7. Turin: Einaudi, 1969–1990.

———. "1764: Napoli nel anno della fame." *Rivista storica italiana* 85 (1973): 394–472.

———. *Utopia and Reform in the Enlightenment, Trevelyan Lectures, 1969.* Cambridge: At the University Press, 1969.

———, ed. *Illuministi italiani.* 3 vols. in 6 (vol. 3, ed. Franco Venturi, Giuseppe Giarrizzo, and Gianfranco Torcellan). Naples: Riccardo Ricciardi, 1997–98.

Vernant, Jean-Pierre. *Mortals and Immortals: Collected Essays.* Edited by Froma I. Zeitlin. Princeton: Princeton University Press, 1991.

Verri, Pietro. "Considerazioni sul lusso." In "*Il caffè,*" *1764–1766,* 2nd ed., ed. Gianni Francioni and Sergio Romagnoli, 1:155–62. Turin: Bollati Boringhieri, 1998.

Verri, Pietro, and Alessandro Verri. *Carteggio di Pietro e Alessandro Verri.* Edited by Emanuele Greppi et al. 12 vols. Milan: Cogliati, 1923–42.

Verti, Roberto. *Un almanacco drammatico:* L'Indice de' teatrali spettacoli, *1764–1823.* 2 vols. Pesaro: Fondazione Rossini, 1996.

Veyne, Paul. *Bread and Circuses: Historical Sociology and Political Pluralism.* Abridged ed. Translated by Brian Pearce. Edited by Oswyn Murray. London: Penguin, 1990.

———. *Le pain et le cirque: Sociologie historique d'un pluralisme politique.* Paris: Seuil, 1976.

Viale Ferrero, Mercedes. *Feste delle Madame Reali di Savoia.* Turin: Istituto Bancario San Paolo, 1965.

———. *Filippo Juvarra, scenografo e archittetto teatrale.* Turin: Edizioni d'Arte Fratelli Pozzo, 1970.

———. *La scenografia del '700 e i fratelli Galliari.* Turin: Fratelli Pozzo, 1963.

———. *La scenografia della Scala nell'età neoclassica.* Milan: Polifilo, 1983.

———. "Stage and Set." In *Opera on Stage,* edited by Lorenzo Bianconi and Giorgio Pestelli, 1–123. Chicago: University of Chicago Press, 2002.

———. *Storia del Teatro Regio di Torino.* Turin: Cassa di Risparmio di Torino, 1981.

———. "Torino e Milano nel tardo settecento: Repertori a confronto." *I vicini di Mozart: Il teatro musicale tra sette e ottocento,* edited by Maria Teresa Muraro, 99–138. Studi di Musica Veneta 15. Fondazione Giorgio Cini. Florence: Olschki, 1989.

Vieira de Carvalho, Mário. "From Opera to 'Soap Opera': On Civilizing Processes, the Dialectic of Enlightenment, and Postmodernity." *Theory, Culture & Society* 12 (1995): 41–61.

Villani, Pasquale. "Una battaglia politica di Bernardo Tanucci: La carestia del 1764 e la questione annonaria a Napoli." In *Studi in memoria di Nino Cortese,* 611–66. Rome: Istituto per la Storia del Risorgimento, 1976.

Vincent-Buffault, Anne. *A History of Tears: Sensibility and Sentimentality in France.* Translated by Teresa Bridgeman. 1986. Reprint, New York: St. Martin's Press, 1991.

Vinci, Leonardo, Johann Adolph Hasse, et al. *Alessandro nell'Indie.* Arranged by Giovanni Ferrandini. Reproduced from a MS score in the Bayerische Staatsbibliothek, Munich (Mus. MS 169). Italian Opera, 1640–1770, no. 72. New York: Garland, 1984.

Vinciguerra, Mario. "La reggenza borbonica nella minorità di Ferdinando IV." In *Archivio storico per le province napoletane.* Naples, 1918.

Volpi, Roberto. "La crisi della nobiltà nelle lettere e negli scritti dei corrispondenti perugini di L. A. Muratori." *Annali della Facoltà di Lettere e Filosofia, Università degli Studi di Perugia* 14 (1978): 361–406.

Voltaire. *Dictionnaire philosophique.* Paris: Garnier, 1954.

———. *Dictionnaire philosophique portatif.* London, 1764.

———. *La raison par alphabet.* Geneva, 1769.

———. *La tragédie de Sémiramis: Précédée d'une dissertation sur la tragédie ancienne & moderne.* Amsterdam: Etienne Ledet, 1750.

Volterra, Angela Paladina. "Il carnevale romano sotto Pio VI." In *Il teatro e la festa: Lo spettacolo a Roma tra papato e rivoluzione,* edited by Gianfranco Redavid, 128–32. Roma: Artemide, 1989.

von Rhein, John. "Fiery Vocalist Captures Magic of Eternal City." Review of Cecilia Bartoli's recordings in the *Chicago Tribune,* October 18, 2005, final edition, Tempo sec., http://www.chicagotribune.com/ (accessed October 20, 2005).

Wahnbaeck, Till. *Luxury and Public Happiness: Political Economy in the Italian Enlightenment.* Oxford: Clarendon Press, 2004.

Webb, Daniel. *Observations on the Correspondence between Poetry and Music.* London: Printed for J. Dodsley, 1769.

Weber, Max. "Charismatic Authority." In Max Weber, *Economy and Society: An Outline of Interpretative Sociology,* ed. Guenther Roth and Claus Wittich, vol. 1, part 4 of chapter 3, "The Types of Legitimate Domination," 241–45. Berkeley and Los Angeles: University of California Press, 1978.

——— *Economy and Society: An Outline of Interpretative Sociology.* 2 vols. Edited by Guenther Roth and Claus Wittich. Berkeley and Los Angeles: University of California Press, 1978.

———. *The Essential Weber: A Reader.* Edited by Sam Whimster. London: Routledge, 2004.

———. *On Charisma and Institution Building: Selected Papers.* Edited by S. N. Eisenstadt. Chicago: University of Chicago Press, 1968.

———. "The Routinization of Charisma." In Max Weber, *Economy and Society: An Outline of Interpretative Sociology,* ed. Guenther Roth and Claus Wittich, vol. 1, part 5 of chapter 3, "The Types of Legitimate Domination," 246–54. Berkeley and Los Angeles: University of California Press, 1978.

Weber, William. "From Integrality to Fragmentation in Musical Institutions and Publics, 1750–1914." In *Musical Life in Europe, 1600–1900: Circulation, Institutions, Representations. European Science Foundation Humanities Programme Newsletter* 4 (May 2002): 22–26.

———. *Music and the Middle Class: The Social Structure of Concert Life in London, Paris, and Vienna between 1830 and 1848.* 2nd ed. Aldershot: Ashgate, 2004.

Weimer, Eric. *Opera Seria and the Evolution of Classical Style, 1755–1772.* Ann Arbor: UMI Research Press, 1984.

Weiss, Piero. "Baroque Opera and the Two Verisimilitudes." In *Music and Civilization: Essays in Honor of Paul Henry Lang,* edited by Edmond Strainchamps, Maria Rika Maniates and Christopher Hatch. New York: Norton, 1984.

———. "Metastasio, Aristotle, and the *Opera Seria.*" *Journal of Musicology* 1 (1982): 385–94.

———. "*La morte di Cesare:* The Words, the Music: 'La morte di Cesare' by Gaetano Sertor and Francesco Bianchi, Venice, 1789/1797." Introduction to Francesco Bianchi's *La morte di Cesare.* Drammaturgia Musicale Veneta 25. Milan: Ricordi, 1999.

———. "Pier Jacopo Martello on Opera (1715): An Annotated Translation." *Musical Quarterly* 56 (1980): 378–403.

———. "Teorie drammatiche e 'infranciosemento': Motivi della 'riforma' melodrammatica nel primo settecento." In *Antonio Vivaldi: Teatro musicale, cultura e società,* edited by Lorenzo Bianconi and Giovanni Morelli, 273–96. Florence: Olschki, 1982.

———. "Opera and Neoclassical Criticism in the Seventeenth Century." In *Studies in the History of Music,* vol. 2: *Music and Drama,* 1–30. New York: Broude Brothers, 1988.

———. "Verdi and the Fusion of Genres." *JAMS* 35 (1982): 138–56.

Weiss, Piero, and Richard Taruskin. *Music in the Western World: A History in Documents.* New York: Schirmer, 1984.

West, Shearer, ed. *Italian Culture in Northern Europe in the Eighteenth Century.* Cambridge: Cambridge University Press, 1999.

Wheelock, Gretchen A. *Haydn's "Ingenious Jesting with Art": Contexts of Musical Wit and Humor.* New York: Schirmer, 1992.

White, Donald Maxwell. *Zaccaria Seriman and the "Viaggi di Enrico Wanton": A Contribution to the Study of the Enlightenment in Italy.* Manchester: Manchester University Press, 1961.

Wiel, Taddeo. *I teatri musicali veneziani del settecento: Catalogo delle opere in musica rappresentate nel secolo XVIII in Venezia, 1701–1800.* 1897. Bologna: Forni, 1978.

Wiener, Margaret J. *Visible and Invisible Realms: Power, Magic, and Colonial Conquest in Bali.* Chicago: University of Chicago Press, 1995.

Wiesend, Reinhard. "Der Held als Rolle: Metastasios Alexander." In *Opernheld und Opernheldin im 18. Jahrhundert: Aspekte der Librettoforschung—Ein Tagungsbericht,* edited by Klaus Hortschansky, 139–52. Hamburg: Karl Dieter Wagner, 1991.

Wiesend, Reinhard. "La rappresentazione dell'eroe come ruolo drammatico: L'Alessandro di Metastasio." *Opera & Libretto* 2 (1993): 67–83.

Wikander, Matthew H. *Princes to Act: Royal Audience and Royal Performance, 1578–1792.* Baltimore: The Johns Hopkins University Press, 1993.

Wilentz, Sean. *Rites of Power: Symbolism, Ritual, and Politics since the Middle Ages.* Philadelphia: University of Pennsylvania Press, 1985.

Wolf, Eugene K. *The Symphonies of Johann Stamitz: A Study in the Formation of the Classic Style.* Utrecht: Bohn, Scheltema & Holkema, 1981.

Woodmansee, Martha. "The Genius and the Copyright: Economic and Legal Conditions of the Emergence of the 'Author.'" *Eighteenth-Century Studies* 17 (1984): 425–48.

Woolf, Stuart J. *A History of Italy, 1700–1860: The Social Constraints of Political Change.* London: Methuen, 1979.

Yorke-Long, Alan. "The Duchy of Parma." In *Music at Court: Four Eighteenth-Century Studies,* 3–40. London: Weidenfeld & Nicolson, 1954.

Zacconi, Ludovico. *Prattica di musica.* 2 vols. Facsimile of the Venice 1592 and 1622 editions. Bibliotheca Musica Bononiensis, ser. 2. Bologna: Forni, 1967.

Zanetti, D. E. *La demografia del patriziato milanese nei secoli XVII, XVIII, XIX.* Pavia, 1972.

Zaslaw, Neal. *The Classical Era, from the 1740's to the End of the 18th Century.* Man & Music. London: Macmillan, 1989.

Zechmeister, Gustav. *Die wiener Theater nächst der Burg und nächst dem Kärntnerthor von 1747 bis 1776.* Vienna: Böhlau, 1971.

Zerubavel, Eviatar. *Hidden Rhythms: Schedules and Calendars in Social Life.* Chicago: University of Chicago Press, 1981.

Žižek, Slavoj, and Mladen Dolar. *Opera's Second Death.* New York: Routledge, 2002.

Zoppelli, Luca. *L'opera come racconto: Modi narrativi nel teatro musicale dell'ottocento.* Venice: Marsilio, 1994.

Zorzi, Lodovico. "Venezia: La repubblica a teatro." In *Il teatro e la città: Saggi sulla scena italiana.* Turin: Einaudi, 1977.

Zorzi, Lodovico, et al. *I teatri pubblici di Venezia, secolo XVII–XVIII.* Venice: Zinchi, 1971.

Zwerin, Mike. "Jazz Alive and Kicking in Perugia." *International Herald Tribune,* August 1, 2001, 10.

Index